The
INTERNATIONAL CRITICAL COMMENTARY
on the Holy Scriptures of the Old and New Testaments

GENERAL EDITORS:

J. A. EMERTON
Fellow of St. John's College
Regius Professor of Hebrew in the University of Cambridge

AND

C. E. B. CRANFIELD
Emeritus Professor of Theology in the University of Durham

FORMERLY UNDER THE EDITORSHIP OF

S. R. DRIVER
A. PLUMMER
C. A. BRIGGS

THE EPISTLE TO THE ROMANS

VOLUME II

THE INTERNATIONAL CRITICAL COMMENTARY

A CRITICAL AND EXEGETICAL COMMENTARY

ON

THE EPISTLE TO THE ROMANS

BY

C. E. B. CRANFIELD

Emeritus Professor of Theology in the University of Durham

IN TWO VOLUMES

VOLUME II

Commentary on Romans IX–XVI and Essays

EDINBURGH

T. & T. CLARK LIMITED, 36 GEORGE STREET

PRINTED IN SCOTLAND BY
MORRISON AND GIBB LIMITED
FOR
T. & T. CLARK LTD., EDINBURGH

0 567 05041 6

First printed 1979
Reprinted 1981 (with corrections)

NOTE

My sincere thanks are due to the Rev. Dr. W. S. Campbell, Head of Religious and Theological Studies in Westhill College, Selly Oak, Birmingham, for most generously helping me with the checking of the proofs of this volume; to all who have shared in my study of Romans here in Durham since the date of the preface to this commentary (they, like their predecessors, have greatly helped me by their friendship and encouragement); and to my wife, who has now added this to all the other help she has given me, that she has carried out the exacting task of compiling all the indices.

In the preparation of this second volume I have had the advantage of being able to consult Heinrich Schlier's commentary (*Der Römerbrief*, Freiburg, Basel, Wien, 1977). The third volume of Otto Kuss's commentary appeared too late for me to be able to use it. I welcome with enthusiasm the impressive first volume (on chapters 1 to 5) of Ulrich Wilckens's *Der Brief an die Römer*, published in 1978.

February, 1979. C. E. B. C.

NOTE ON THE SECOND IMPRESSION

I have taken the opportunity to make a number of corrections, mostly of misprints. There is an additional footnote on p. 861.

C. E. B. C.

CONTENTS OF VOLUME II

THE UNBELIEF OF MEN AND THE
FAITHFULNESS OF GOD
(9.1–11.36)

The difficulties which this division of the epistle presents are
notorious. Gaugler has with good reason likened it to the
precipitous North Wall of the Eiger.[1] One stubborn problem is
that of the relation of these three chapters to the rest of
Romans. Even more daunting are the difficulties presented by
their contents.

A superficial reading of the epistle might easily leave one
with the impression that chapters 9 to 11 are simply an excursus
which Paul has included under the pressure of his own deep
personal involvement in the matter of Israel's destiny but
which is without any real inner relatedness to the main argument of Romans. But a closer study reveals the fact that there
are very many features of chapters 1 to 8 which are not
understood in full depth until they are seen in the light of
chapters 9 to 11—the characterization of the scope of Paul's
apostleship by εἰς ὑπακοὴν πίστεως ἐν πᾶσιν τοῖς ἔθνεσιν in 1.5,
the use of κλητός in 1.6 and 7, the references to God's
promise in chapter 4, the golden chain of 8.29–30, the expression ἐκλεκτοὶ θεοῦ in 8.33, to mention only a few examples.

Furthermore, these chapters may be seen to be an integral
part of the working out of the theme of the epistle. In this
connexion the following points may be noted:
(i) 1.16b–17, in which the theme is stated, contains two
statements concerning the gospel: 'it [i.e. the gospel: it has been
mentioned in v. 16a] is God's saving power . . .'; and 'in it
[i.e. in the gospel] God's righteousness is being revealed . . .'.
But the gospel to which reference is made in these verses must
be understood in the light of its definition in 1.1–4 as God's
gospel 'concerning his Son, who was born of David's seed
according to the flesh, . . . even Jesus Christ'. And the use of
the title 'Christ' and the statement of Jesus Christ's relationship to David mean that the gospel cannot be properly

---

[1] I, p. 327: 'So werden wir uns an die "Eigernordwand" jener steilen
Kapitel von der Liebe Gottes zusammen mühen müssen.'

understood except in relation to Israel, God's special people. Thus the theme of Romans, as set forth in 1.16b–17, requires the inclusion in the epistle of a discussion of the relation of the nation of Israel to the gospel.

(ii) But in 1.1–4 the gospel was also defined as 'God's message of good news, which he [i.e. God] promised beforehand through his prophets in the holy scriptures'. The epistle is concerned, from the statement of its theme onwards, with the question of the true interpretation of the OT. But it is clear that there can be no satisfactory interpretation of the OT, no making sense of it, without taking into account the phenomenon of Israel. If the epistle did not present a serious answer to the question of the Jews, it certainly could not be that key to the true understanding of the OT which Luther claimed that it was.[1] And, had Paul not, in as full and systematic a presentation of the gospel as is included in Romans, come to grips with this question, the seriousness and integrity of his appeals to the OT would have been open to doubt.

(iii) The question of the Jews, raised already by implication in 1.16a by the word 'gospel' understood according to its definition in 1.1–4 as the gospel of Christ and the gospel promised in the OT, becomes explicit in the words 'both for the Jew first and for the Greek' later in the verse (cf. 2.9 and 10). When this question is taken up in 3.1ff, it is dealt with only summarily, and it is clear that a serious discussion of God's πίστις in relation to Israel's ἀπιστία is still outstanding. (Since it is clear that Paul recognizes that the question of the Jews involves the question of God's faithfulness, we can hardly be surprised that he should feel obliged to discuss it at length at some point.)[2]

But why did Paul place these chapters just here, in spite of the obvious connexions of thought which exist between chapters 1 to 8 and 12.1–15.13? To this question the following observations provide, we think, a sufficient reply:

(i) A connexion of thought may be discerned between the subject matter of chapters 9 to 11 and 8.17–39 on life in the Spirit as characterized by hope, and especially vv. 28–39 dealing with the certainty of that hope. In 8.28–30 Paul has referred to God's purpose as the ground of our certainty. But, according to the OT, the nation of Israel had a special place

---

[1] Luther's preface to Romans quoted on p. 57, n. 2.

[2] That in his knowledge of circumstances within the Roman church Paul had a further reason—in addition to the fact that the question of the Jews was inseparably related to his theme—for including in this epistle an extended discussion of this subject is highly likely. For the probability that an incipient Christian anti-semitism was to be seen in the Roman church see on 11.13ff and also on 14.1ff.

within God's purpose. The end of this section was therefore a natural point at which to introduce a discussion of the relation of Israel to the divine purpose. We may, in fact, go further and say that at this point the need for such a discussion has become urgent, since the very reliability of God's purpose as the ground of Christian hope is called in question by the exclusion of the majority of Jews. If the truth is that God's purpose with Israel has been frustrated, then what sort of a basis for Christian hope is God's purpose? And, if God's love for Israel (cf., e.g., Deut 7.7f; Jer 31.3) has ceased, what reliance can be placed on Paul's conviction that nothing can separate us from God's love in Christ (v. 38f)?

(ii) The connexions of thought between chapters 1 to 8 and 12.1–15.13, though close, are not such as to make the insertion of the three chapters between them undesirable; for the ethical consequences of God's deed in Christ have already been indicated in principle in the course of chapters 5 to 8, and what Paul is going to give in 12.1–15.13 is teaching of a different kind, namely, particular and concrete exhortation. Moreover, there is an important positive advantage in the order which has been adopted; for the discussion of God's dealings with Israel makes possible a fuller and profounder understanding of the gospel Paul has already set forth and chapters 1 to 11 are therefore a more satisfactory theological basis for the ensuing ethical exhortation than chapters 1 to 8 could have been.[1]

With regard to the special difficulties which the contents of these chapters present, those features which have struck very many students of the Epistle to the Romans—not surprisingly —as offensive and repugnant, several things may usefully be said at this point.

(i) It is of the utmost importance to take these three chapters

---

[1] W. S. Campbell, 'Some recent literature on Paul's Letter to the Romans', in *BT* 25 (1975), p. 33, has suggested that my description (on p. 434) of 8.31–39 as serving not only as the conclusion to the section beginning with 8.1 but also as a conclusion to the whole course of Paul's foregoing theological exposition may encourage the view that chapters 9 to 11 'are a sort of appendix only loosely attached to what precedes'. I think he was right in seeing a danger of misunderstanding here; and I take this opportunity to say that I certainly did not intend to give any encouragement to such a view. While I do see 8.31–39 as a confident summing up of what has been said in the two main divisions IV and V (and not just of what has been said in V.4) and as marking a really significant stage-point in the argument, I am quite clear in my own mind that 9.1–11.36 and also 12.1–15.13 are—far from being loosely attached appendices—further absolutely necessary stages in the exposition of the theme stated in 1.16b–17.

together as a whole, and not to come to conclusions about Paul's argument before one has heard it to the end; for chapter 9 will certainly be understood in an altogether un-Pauline sense, if it is understood in isolation from its sequel in chapters 10 and 11.

(ii) We shall misunderstand these chapters, if we fail to recognize that their key-word is 'mercy'.[1] Paul is here concerned to show that the problem of Israel's unbelief, which seems to call in question the very reliability of God Himself, is connected with the nature of God's mercy as really mercy and as mercy not just for one people but for all peoples; to show that Israel's disobedience, together with the divine judgment which it merits and procures, is surrounded on all sides by the divine mercy—and at the same time to bring home to the Christian community in Rome the fact that it is by God's mercy alone that it lives.

(iii) It is only where the Church persists in refusing to learn this message, where it secretly—perhaps quite unconsciously! —believes that its own existence is based on human achievement, and so fails to understand God's mercy to itself, that it is unable to believe in God's mercy for still unbelieving Israel, and so entertains the ugly and unscriptural notion that God has cast off His people Israel and simply replaced it by the Christian Church. These three chapters emphatically forbid us to speak of the Church as having once and for all taken the place of the Jewish people.[2]

(iv) Mention must be made here of the magnificent section on God's election of grace in Barth's *CD* II/2, pp. 1–506 (=*KD*

---

[1] Too much weight should not be put on statistics of word-occurrences; but it is hardly accidental that the verb ἐλεεῖν, which only occurs once elsewhere in Romans and five other times in the whole of the Pauline corpus (including the Pastorals), occurs seven times in these chapters, that the noun ἔλεος, which occurs elsewhere in the Pauline corpus only once in Romans, once in Galatians, once in Ephesians and five times in the Pastorals, occurs twice in these chapters, while the verb οἰκτίρειν occurs in the NT only in Rom 9.15.

[2] Cf. Barth, *CD* II/2, p. 290f (=*KD* II/2, p. 319f); Gaugler, 2, pp. 23ff. But the assumption that the Church has simply replaced Israel as the people of God is extremely common. Thus Barrett, for example, writes: 'This fact reminds us that behind Paul's discussion there lies the historical background formed by the ministry of Jesus; his rejection and crucifixion by Israel [but such passages as 1 Th 2.15 and Acts 2.23; 4.10 certainly do not give those of us who are Gentiles any right to ignore the decisive part played by the Romans in the crucifixion of Jesus], which thereby disavowed its own place in God's plan; and the election of a new Israel in Christ to take the place of the old' (p. 191f). And I confess with shame to having also myself used in print on more than one occasion this language of the replacement of Israel by the Church.

II/2, pp. 1–563), which, it may be confidently affirmed, would
have been enough by itself to place its author among the
greatest theologians of the Church, even if he had written
nothing else. It includes a valuable exposition of these chapters
of Romans.[1] The decisive amendment of doctrine which he has
proposed is something which, when once it has been clearly
formulated, seems so entirely obvious that it is almost incredible that it had not been proposed and carried through
long before. It is that 'the doctrine of election must not begin
in abstracto either with the concept of an electing God or with
that of elected man. It must begin concretely with the
acknowledgment of Jesus Christ as both the electing God and
elected man.'[2] Although this insight was present in Reformation theology as a pastoral direction, it was not allowed to
control and illumine the doctrine of election. Instead, the
Church's doctrine of election was isolated from Christology, as
though it had to do with an electing by God from which Christ
was somehow absent. Against this divorce of the doctrine of
election from Christology Barth has protested that 'There is
no such thing as a *decretum absolutum*. There is no such thing
as a will of God apart from the will of Jesus Christ.'[3] And,
because he has recognized in God's election of grace 'the eternal
beginning of all the ways and works of God in Jesus Christ'
and seen that 'In Jesus Christ God in His free grace determines
Himself for sinful man and sinful man for Himself' and 'therefore takes upon Himself the rejection of man with all its
consequences, and elects man for participation in His own
glory',[4] he is able to affirm that the scriptural doctrine of
predestination is 'not a mixed message of joy and terror', but
'is light and not darkness' and 'The election of grace is the sum
of the Gospel'.[5]

For Barth election means first of all and basically God's
election of Jesus Christ, but included in His election Barth
sees both the election of 'the many', i.e. of individual sinful
men, and, in a mediating position between this election of 'the
many' and the election of the One, the election of 'the one
community of God by the existence of which Jesus Christ is to
be attested to the whole world and the whole world summoned
to faith in Jesus Christ'.[6] We thus get a threefold scheme: the

[1] pp. 202–05, 213–33, 240–59, 267–305 (= *KD* II/2, pp. 222–26,
235–56, 264–85, 294–336).
[2] op. cit., p. 76 (= *KD* II/2, p. 81).
[3] op. cit., p. 115 (= *KD* II/2, p. 124).
[4] op. cit., p. 94 (= *KD* II/2, p. 101).
[5] op. cit., p. 13 (= *KD* II/2, p. 12f).
[6] op. cit., p. 195 (= *KD* II/2, p. 215).

election of Jesus Christ, the election of the community, and
the election of the individual. The recognition of these different
elections included in the election of Jesus Christ will save us
from immediately attempting to refer what Paul says to the
ultimate destiny of individuals, on which the traditional
doctrine has tended to concentrate attention almost exclusively. It is, in fact, with the election of the community that
Paul is concerned in Romans 9 to 11, and Barth's account of
the two forms of the one community illumines many of the
difficulties of these chapters. For example, it makes it possible
to see how it is that Paul can speak in 9.6ff of some members of
Israel who in a sense are not members of Israel, and yet in the
sequel speak of Israel as a whole (including these members
who in one sense are not members) as being the people whom
God has elected. For, according to Barth's exposition, the one
community of God exists in history in two forms, on the one
hand, as the Israel within Israel and (continuous with it) the
believing Church made up of both Jews and Gentiles, and, on
the other hand, as that bulk of Israel which is not the inner
Israel and (continuous with it) the unbelieving Jews; and,
while it is only in the one form that its testimony to Jesus
Christ is positive, conscious, voluntary, joyful, even in its
other form it cannot avoid bearing witness to Him and its
testimony is, in its own negative, unconscious, involuntary
and joyless way, most eloquent and effective.[1]

[1] Our indebtedness throughout our treatment of Romans 9 to 11 to
Barth's discussion of election and the suggestive and penetrating
exegesis of these chapters which it incorporates (of which many NT
scholars seem unaware, though it is now three decades since it was
published) will be obvious to all who know Barth, and is most gratefully
acknowledged—though we hope we have never followed him uncritically.
    In addition to Barth's discussion, which contains much valuable
bibliographical information, reference should be made, in connexion
with these three chapters, to the following: K. L. Schmidt, 'Die Verstockung des Menschen durch Gott', in *TZ* 1 (1945), pp. 1–17; J. K. S.
Reid, 'The Office of Christ in Predestination', in *SJT* 1 (1948), pp. 5–19,
166–83; S. Lyonnet, 'De doctrina praedestinationis et reprobationis in
Rom 9', in *VD* 34 (1956), pp. 193–201, 257–71; E. Dinkler, 'The historical
and the eschatological Israel in Rom 9–11: a contribution to the problem
of predestination and individual responsibility', in *Journal of Religion* 36
(Chicago, 1956), pp. 109–27; J. Munck, *Christus und Israel: eine Ausleg-
ung von Röm 9–11*, Copenhagen, 1956 (Eng. tr., Philadelphia, 1967);
J. Gnilka, *Die Verstockung Israels: Isaias 6.9–10 in der Theologie der
Synoptiker*, Munich, 1961; C. Müller, *Gottes Gerechtigkeit und Gottes Volk:
eine Untersuchung zu Röm 9–11*, Göttingen, 1964; F. W. Marquardt, *Die
Entdeckung des Judentums für die christliche Theologie: Israel im Denken
Karl Barths*, Munich, 1967; C. Senft, 'L'élection d'Israel et la justifica-
tion', in *L'Évangile hier et aujourd'hui: mélanges offerts au Prof. F. J.
Leenhardt*, Geneva, 1968, pp. 131–42; M. Zerwick, 'Drama populi Israel

VI. 1. THE SUBJECT OF THIS MAIN DIVISION OF THE EPISTLE IS INTRODUCED (9.1–5)

[1]I speak the truth in Christ, I do not lie—my conscience bears me witness in the Holy Spirit—*when I declare* [2]that I have great grief and continual anguish in my heart. [3]For I would pray that I might myself be accursed *and cut off* from Christ on behalf of my brethren, my kinsfolk according to the flesh, [4]who are Israelites, whose are the adoption and the glory and the covenants and the legislation and the worship and the promises, [5]whose are the fathers, and of whom so far as the flesh is concerned is Christ, who is over all, God blessed for ever, Amen.

With striking emphasis and solemnity Paul declares his own sorrow at his fellow-Jews' unbelief and the strength of his desire for their conversion, thereby introducing the subject with which he will be concerned until the end of chapter 11.

1. Ἀλήθειαν λέγω. Compare 2 Cor 12.6; 1 Tim 2.7.

ἐν Χριστῷ. In view of the order of the words (λέγω being placed between ἀλήθειαν and ἐν Χριστῷ), the absence of the article before ἀλήθειαν, and the content of the rest of the verse (which suggests that what Paul is here concerned to stress is the truth of the statement he is about to make in v. 2), it is unlikely that ἐν Χριστῷ is to be taken closely with ἀλήθειαν (so as to give the sense, 'the truth in Christ', i.e. the truth of the gospel).[1] It must rather be taken with λέγω (cf. ἐν Χριστῷ λαλοῦμεν in 2 Cor 2.17; 12.19).[2] Paul claims that he is speaking in Christ, i.e., in accordance with the standards which obtain for one who is in Christ, with a due sense of his accountability

secundum Rom 9–11', in *VD* 46 (1968), pp. 321–38; U. Luz, *Das Geschichtsverständnis des Paulus*, Munich, 1968; H. L. Ellison, *The Mystery of Israel*, Exeter, 1968; P. Richardson, *Israel in the Apostolic Church*, Cambridge, 1969; G. Maier, *Mensch und freier Wille nach den jüdischen Religionsparteien zwischen ben Sira und Paulus*, Tübingen, 1971; W. S. Campbell, *The Purpose of Paul in the Letter to the Romans with special reference to chapters 9–11*, Edinburgh University Ph.D. thesis, 1972; id., 'The Place of Romans 9–11 within the structure and thought of the letter', to be published in Texte und Untersuchungen (Oxford Congress 1973 papers) in 1978; D. Zeller, *Juden und Heiden in der Mission des Paulus: Studien zum Römerbrief*, Stuttgart, 1973; B. Corley, *The Significance of Rom 9–11: a study in Pauline theology*, Southwestern Baptist Theological Seminary Th.D. thesis, 1975; id., 'The Jews, the future, and God (Rom 9–11)', in *Southwestern Journal of Theology* 19 (1976), pp. 42–56; L. de Lorenzi (ed.), *Die Israelfrage nach Römer 9–11* (Monographische Reihe von *Benedictina*: Biblisch-ökumenische Abteilung, 3), Rome, 1977; W. D. Davies, 'Paul and the people of Israel', in *NTS* 24 (1977–78), pp. 4–39; N. T. Wright, *The Messiah and the People of God*, Oxford University Ph.D. thesis, 1981.

[1] As Barth seems to take it (*Shorter*, p. 113).

[2] In 2 Cor 12.19 ἐν Χριστῷ is omitted by 𝔓⁴⁶ d e.

to Christ. The phrase ἐν Χριστῷ thus strengthens ἀλήθειαν λέγω: one who speaks in a way that is worthy of his union with Christ cannot but speak truth or, at any rate, attempt to do so. The use of the phrase here is thus an implicit appeal to Christ as the ultimate guarantor of the truth of what Paul is about to say.[1]

οὐ ψεύδομαι. Compare Gal 1.20; 2 Cor 11.31. The combination (found also in 1 Tim 2.7) of ἀλήθειαν λέγω and οὐ ψεύδομαι is specially emphatic.

συμμαρτυρούσης μοι τῆς συνειδήσεώς μου ἐν πνεύματι ἁγίῳ is parenthetic, the ὅτι clause in v. 2 depending on 'Αλήθειαν λέγω (not on οὐ ψεύδομαι, which is also parenthetic). To construe v. 2 as dependent on συμμαρτυρούσης, as some do (e.g. Moffatt, Barrett[2]), is unsatisfactory, since it leaves 'Αλήθειαν λέγω ἐν Χριστῷ, οὐ ψεύδομαι in the air without any clear indication of what it is to which it refers. For συμμαρτυρεῖν see the notes on 2.15 and 8.16. Whereas in 8.16 συμμαρτυρεῖν with the dative probably means simply 'testify to', 'assure', it is probable that here it means 'witness along with', 'testify in support of' (the συν- having its force of 'together with'), and that Paul is thinking of the solemn statement which he is about to make (v. 2) as one testimony and of the support of his συνείδησις as a second, corroborative testimony. It is possible that here the biblical law of evidence (Num 35.30; Deut 17.6; 19.15) has influenced Paul's thought. For συνείδησις the reader is again referred to the note on 2.15. Here too it means 'conscience' in the sense which the word has in the English expressions, 'a bad conscience', 'a good conscience', i.e., in the sense of a knowledge shared with oneself which is either painful or not painful. In this case it is a good conscience that is meant. Paul, in asserting that he speaks the truth when he declares that he has great grief and continual anguish in his heart, shares with himself the knowledge that what he asserts is true. But Paul knows that the value of the testimony of a man's good conscience depends on the moral sensitivity of the man. Where the moral sense is dull (cf. the references to the darkening of the καρδία in 1.21 and to the ἀδόκιμος νοῦς in 1.28), the testimony of the συνείδησις is of little or no value. But, where the νοῦς is bound to God's law (cf. 7.23, 25), where it is being

---

[1] The suggestion that ἐν Χριστῷ here actually means 'by Christ' (an oath formula) is (*pace* Bengel, p. 536) unlikely. The use of ἔν τινι with ὀμνύειν (reflecting Hebrew usage) in the LXX and NT (e.g. Judg 21.7; Ps 89.35[LXX: 88.36]; Mt 5.34ff; 23.18ff) is a different matter, since in this case the verb makes clear the sense in which ἐν is used.

[2] p. 174f.

renewed (ἀνακαίνωσις) εἰς τὸ δοκιμάζειν ... τί τὸ θέλημα τοῦ θεοῦ, τὸ ἀγαθὸν καὶ εὐάρεστον καὶ τέλειον (12.2), there the testimony of the συνείδησις is of great worth.[1] So Paul adds the words ἐν[2] πνεύματι ἁγίῳ; for he knows that the testimony which his conscience bears him is the testimony of the conscience of one whose mind is being renewed and illumined by the Holy Spirit (cf. 8.1–16).

2. ὅτι λύπη μοί ἐστιν μεγάλη καὶ ἀδιάλειπτος ὀδύνη τῇ καρδίᾳ μου. It is doubtful whether any clear distinction between λύπη and ὀδύνη (as that λύπη denotes grief of mind, while ὀδύνη 'never quite loses its physical associations',[3] or that ὀδύνη coming after λύπη represents a heightening[4]) can really be sustained in view of the evidence of Greek usage.[5] The general sense of v. 2 is anyway perfectly clear. But the fact that Paul's statement in v. 2 has been introduced with so much emphasis and solemnity[6] calls for explanation. It has sometimes been suggested as an explanation that Paul had been accused of indifference to the fate of his fellow-countrymen and was concerned to rebut such charges and to defend his loyalty to his nation. But this will scarcely do.[7] A more likely explanation,

---

[1] Though it is a mistake to make extravagant claims even for the instructed Christian's συνείδησις; for not even it is the final judge of conduct and character, as 1 Cor 4.4 (οὐδὲν γὰρ ἐμαυτῷ σύνοιδα, ἀλλ᾽ οὐκ ἐν τούτῳ δεδικαίωμαι· ὁ δὲ ἀνακρίνων με κύριός ἐστιν) makes clear.

[2] The conjectural emendation of ἐν to σύν (Pallis, p. 110) is surely to be rejected. Not only is it purely conjectural. It also yields an intrinsically improbable sense—the thought of the Holy Spirit's supporting the witness of a man's clear conscience is understandable, but hardly that of a man's clear conscience's supporting the witness of the Holy Spirit.

[3] Sanday and Headlam, p. 227; cf. Lagrange, p. 225. Lagrange says: '... avec τῇ καρδίᾳ c'est une émotion qui n'est pas sans une angoisse physique.' But, in view of the use of καρδία in the NT, does its association with τῇ καρδίᾳ really support this understanding of ὀδύνη here?

[4] So Godet. It probably is true, however, that ἀδιάλειπτος ὀδύνη represents a heightening of λύπη μεγάλη.

[5] See LSJ, pp. 1065ff and 1199; TWNT 4, pp. 314–25 (R. Bultmann), and 5, p. 118f (F. Hauck); Bauer, col. 952f and col. 1099.

[6] Five successive steps in this solemn emphasis may be distinguished: first the statement about to be made in v. 2 is strengthened by being introduced by 'Αλήθειαν λέγω ..... ὅτι; then 'Αλήθειαν λέγω is further strengthened by the addition of ἐν Χριστῷ; and then by οὐ ψεύδομαι; then the words 'Αλήθειαν λέγω ἐν Χριστῷ, οὐ ψεύδομαι are strengthened by the addition of συμμαρτυρούσης μοι τῆς συνειδήσεώς μου, which is itself strengthened by the addition of ἐν πνεύματι ἁγίῳ. Thus, although Paul does not here formally call God to witness the truth of what he is saying (as he does in 2 Cor 1.23; 11.31; cf. κατέναντι θεοῦ in 2 Cor 2.17; 12.19; and ἐνώπιον τοῦ θεοῦ in Gal 1.20), the statement is made with an extraordinary degree of emphasis and solemnity.

[7] Cf. Gaugler 2, p. 5f.

in view of the contents of the sequel in 9.3–11.36, is that
he recognized that the very integrity and authenticity of his
apostleship to the Gentiles would be called in question, were
he able to give up his fellow-Israelites, were he not to suffer
grief so long as they continued in unbelief; and that he
regarded it as of vital importance that the Christians to whom
he was writing, both Jewish and Gentile, should know of this
grief of his, because for them too such a grief was the only
attitude with regard to the Jews' continuing unbelief that
would be consistent with faith.

3. ηὐχόμην γάρ. The γάρ indicates that this sentence is intended to give some explanation of v. 2—to throw some light
on the character of Paul's grief and anguish.[1] Concerning
ηὐχόμην there are two interrelated problems: (i) that of the
sense in which the verb is used (whether 'pray' or 'wish')[2]; and
(ii) that of the significance of the imperfect indicative. With
regard to (i), the use of εὔχεσθαι in the sense 'wish' goes back
to the fifth century B.C., and the interpretation of ηὐχόμην here
in this sense has been widespread from early times. It is to be
found in the Vulgate (*optabam*), the AV, the RV, Moffatt, the
RSV, and is supported by H. Greeven,[3] Bauer, s.v. εὔχομαι 2
and (among recent commentators) by Lagrange,[4] Gaugler,[5]
Barrett[6]—to mention only a few. But the sense 'pray' is
probably to be preferred (with Weymouth and the NEB). Two
things, in our judgment, point strongly in this direction: first,
the parallel with Moses (in Exod 32.31f, which it is highly likely
that Paul had in mind, we clearly have a prayer), and, secondly,
the evidence of the other occurrences of εὔχεσθαι in the NT.[7]

---

[1] Bengel's suggestion (p. 536) that it is to this sentence rather than to
v. 2 that v. 1 refers (he explains the ὅτι in v. 2 as equivalent to *quia*) on
the ground that what is stated in v. 2 would be readily believed without
such strong asseveration, must surely be rejected.

[2] The meaning 'vow' scarcely comes in question here (*pace* Michel,
who (p. 224) gives as the possible alternatives 'wish' and 'vow' (*wün-
schen, geloben*)), since the term 'vow' is only properly applicable to a
promise (or threat), where the person making the promise (or threat)
can expect to play a determinative part in its fulfilment. While the
substance of this verse could perhaps be reformulated in such a way as to
bring it within the scope of the term, what Paul has written clearly does
not describe a vow.

[3] In *TWNT* 2, p. 776.

[4] p. 225.

[5] 2, pp. 5 and 8.

[6] pp. 174 and 176.

[7] There are only six other occurrences of εὔχεσθαι in the NT (it is
overshadowed by the much more frequent compound προσεύχεσθαι). In
three of them (Acts 26.29; 2 Cor 13.7; Jas 5.16 (?)) the meaning is clearly
'pray', while in a fourth (2 Cor 13.9) it is natural to take it in this sense

With regard to (ii), four possibilities must be mentioned: (a) that ηὐχόμην is an imperfect indicative denoting an action in progress in past time, Paul's meaning being that he used so to pray (or wish), though he no longer does so; (b) that it is a conative imperfect denoting an action attempted but not accomplished, the meaning being that the idea of such a prayer (or wish) entered his mind, but was never actually accepted by him or made his own; (c) that it is an imperfect indicative used to express a present prayer (or wish) that is capable of fulfilment, but to express it with a certain vagueness or diffidence (so equivalent to the classical optative with ἄν); (d) that it is equivalent to the classical imperfect indicative with ἄν, used where the prayer (or wish) is recognized as unattainable or impermissible, the meaning being that Paul would so pray (or wish), were this permissible. Of these four, (b) should probably be set aside as the least likely: it is surely forced.[1] While there is little to be said for (a) in the form in which this interpretation appears in the commentary of Pelagius (he understood Paul to be referring to the time before his conversion),[2] the view that Paul means that he really used to pray (or wish) in this sense has considerable attractiveness; for it seems—at first sight at any rate—to accord very well with the great solemnity of v. 1 and also with the Moses parallel (Exod 32.31f). Thus Michel argues that ηὐχόμην indicates a concrete offer made before God, which sets Paul among the prophets and men of God of the Old Testament, though the imperfect tense shows his awareness of the limit set to his offer by God, the fact that God is free either to accept it or to refuse it.[3] But, in view of the evidence for the use in Hellenistic Greek of the imperfect indicative of verbs of wishing without distinction both for the modest expression of a present attainable wish (cf., for example, Acts 25.22) and also to express an unattainable present wish (cf., for example, Gal 4.20),[4] alternatives (c) and

in view of the proximity of v. 7. Bauer lists 3 Jn 2 under the meaning 'wish' (citing various extra-biblical parallels); but it is at least as likely, in view of the frequency of instances of prayer in the opening verses of NT epistles, that εὐχεσθαι should here also be translated 'pray' (as it is, e.g., in the RV, Weymouth, Moffatt, the NEB). There remains only one occurrence (Acts 27.29), where it is more natural to understand the verb in the sense 'wish' than in the sense 'pray'.

[1] *Pace* Zahn, p. 431.

[2] p. 72: 'Optabam aliquando, cum persequerer Christum, non modo optarem: sciebam enim quod ipsorum essent haec omnia, sed pos[t]quam cognoui ueritatem, dereliqui eos quos taliter diligebam, . . .'

[3] p. 225.

[4] Reference should be made to BDF, §359(2); Moule, *Idiom-Book*, p. 9 (iv); Burton, *MT*, §33; Robertson, *Grammar*, pp. 885f, 918f.

(d) merit serious consideration. (It should be noted that, though there is a clear distinction between these two, explanations of ηὐχόμην here along the lines of (c) sometimes come to approximate closely to (d).) According to (c), Paul's prayer (or wish) is a real present prayer (or wish) for what is thought of as attainable, but expressed in a way which softens it, just as ἐβουλόμην . . . ἀκοῦσαι in Acts 25.22 expresses a real present wish for something attainable, but expresses it (for politeness' sake) less bluntly than βούλομαι ἀκοῦσαι would have done. We may compare the use of 'I should like', 'ich möchte', 'je voudrais', to express with a polite diffidence what is a real present wish for something without any doubt attainable. But both (c) and (a) are open to the very grave objection that it is extremely hard—if not altogether impossible—to understand how Paul the Christian apostle could think (or have thought) of ἀνάθεμα εἶναι, κ.τ.λ. as attainable; or how he could think (or have thought) that its fulfilment could benefit his fellow-Jews;[1] or how he could think (or have thought) that to make such a prayer (or wish) his own could be permissible for him. What is understandable in Exod 32.31f (and it is to be noted that in Exodus Moses' request is rejected) is hardly understandable on the lips or in the thoughts of Paul. And the contrary argument that, standing as it does in the shadow of the solemn asseveration of v. 1, ηὐχόμην cannot be taken to denote something merely hypothetical, is after all not really cogent; for a statement to the effect that he would pray to be accursed and cut off from Christ on behalf of his fellow-Jews, if this were a permissible prayer for him and if its fulfilment could benefit them, is by no means a weak statement on the lips of an apostle, but does very forcefully and vividly indicate the depth of his grief and anguish at their unbelief. We conclude, therefore, that alternative (d) should be accepted,[2] and combined with the acceptance of 'pray', rather than 'wish', as the meaning of εὔχεσθαι here. We may translate: 'For I would pray'—the sense being understood to be: 'For I would pray (were it

---

[1] Michel (p. 225) appeals (referring to his contribution, 'Opferbereitschaft für Israel', in W. Schmauch (ed.), *In memoriam Ernst Lohmeyer*, Stuttgart, 1951, pp. 94–100) to the occurrence of similar 'Sühneformeln' and 'Sühnevorstellungen' in Judaism. But the fact that precedents of a sort were to hand in Judaism does not at all necessarily mean that a Christian would feel free to follow them. But the question whether Paul could or could not have prayed (or wished) such a prayer (or wish) *rightly* has called forth a great deal of discussion down the centuries. For three interesting examples reference may be made to Chrysostom, cols. 547–52; Calvin, p. 192; Martyr, pp. 361–67.

[2] Cf. Lagrange, p. 225.

permissible for me so to pray and if the fulfilment of such a prayer could benefit them) . . .'.[1]

ἀνάθεμα εἶναι. ἀνάθεμα (the Hellenistic form of the Attic ἀνάθημα, which continued to be used alongside it) denotes something delivered over to God—(i) *a consecrated gift* (set up in a temple),[2] though for this sense the LXX always (except for 2 Macc 2.13; Jth 16.19(A)) has the form ἀνάθημα (cf. Lk 21.5[3]); (ii) *something* or *someone delivered over to the divine wrath, devoted to destruction, accursed* (a meaning almost entirely confined, as far as extant evidence goes, to the Bible and dependent literature[4]). In the LXX it renders the Heb. *ḥērem* (e.g. Lev 27.28; Deut 13.17[LXX: 18]; Josh 6.17f; 7.1, 11ff; Zech 14.11).[5] The Pauline use (besides this verse, 1 Cor 12.3; 16.22; Gal 1.8, 9) is to be explained in the light of the LXX. For Paul, 'to be ἀνάθεμα' (when he uses the word, it is always with the verb εἶναι —though in 1 Cor 12.3 the verb is not expressed but has to be understood) is to be delivered over to the divine wrath, accursed. Here in Rom 9.3 ἀνάθεμα εἶναι clearly means 'to forfeit final salvation'. Both the suggestion that the reference is to some such suffering in this present life as that which is reflected in 2 Cor 1.8f; 2.13; 7.5; 12.7[6] and the suggestion that what is referred to is an act of ecclesiastical discipline[7]

---

[1] It is to be noted that there is a widespread tendency to blur the distinction—or rather to fail to distinguish—between our alternatives (c) and (d). Thus even Moule, *Idiom-Book*, p. 9, treats ηὐχόμην here as though it and ἐβουλόμην in Acts 25.22 were examples of the same thing (which seems to imply acceptance of our alternative (c)), and yet suggests for ηὐχόμην the translation: 'I could almost pray', which seems to imply that the prayer is not in fact prayed (in other words, it seems to imply acceptance of our alternative (d)). But the truth is surely rather, as BDF, § 359(2), suggests, that in Hellenistic Greek we have to do with two *distinct* uses of the imperfect indicative of verbs of wishing with a present sense: one to represent what in classical Greek would be expressed by the optative with ἄν (the classical idiom is found once in the NT—in Acts 26.29), and the other to represent what in classical Greek would normally be represented by the imperfect indicative with ἄν.

[2] Theocritus, *Ep.* 13.2; Palatine Anthology 6.162; Philodemus, *Mus.* p. 85K; Plutarch, *Pelop.* 25.5; CIG 2693d.12.

[3] אD *al* have ἀναθέμασιν here.

[4] It occurs in *IG* 3, pars iii, App. xiv b.17 (for reference see LSJ, p. xlii, under *IG*, and p. xliii, under *Tab. Defix.*).

[5] Though *ḥērem* is occasionally represented by other Greek words (e.g. ἀπώλεια, Isa 34.5).

[6] Cf. Zahn, p. 431.

[7] It is, of course, true that *ḥērem* came to be used in Rabbinic Hebrew in connexion with the Synagogue excommunication (see W. Schrage, in *TWNT* 7, p. 845f) and that ἀνάθεμα became a technical term of later ecclesiastical discipline. (The following ἀπὸ τοῦ Χριστοῦ surely rules out the possibility of a reference to something which Paul's non-Christian

must surely be rejected as incompatible with the extreme solemnity of v. 1.[1] Nothing less than final exclusion from that glory which is going to be revealed can be meant.[2]

αὐτὸς ἐγὼ ἀπὸ τοῦ Χριστοῦ. With these words the full horror of ηὐχόμην . . . ἀνάθεμα εἶναι comes to expression. Nothing less than the eschatological sentence of exclusion from Christ's presence (cf. Mt 7.23; 25.41) is involved. In itself αὐτὸς ἐγώ serves to emphasize the intensely personal nature of the self-sacrifice which is contemplated (this self-sacrifice, for which Paul himself is ready—ηὐχόμην . . . εἶναι—concerns him himself, not others,[3] and concerns him in the innermost centre of his own personal being), and, placed thus in immediate juxtaposition to ἀπὸ τοῦ Χριστοῦ,[4] it brings out the poignancy of the separation this self-sacrifice signifies. The use of ἀπό,[5] which here denotes separation,[6] is pregnant (cf. Col 2.20). The pathos of the contrast between αὐτὸς ἐγὼ ἀπὸ τοῦ Χριστοῦ and 8.35–39 was noted by Chrysostom in words which many later commentators have quoted: 'What meanest thou, O Paul? From Christ? From thy Beloved? From Him, from whom neither kingdom nor hell could separate thee, nor things seen, nor things conceived, nor other things so great—dost thou now pray to be accursed and separated from Him?'[7]

ὑπὲρ τῶν ἀδελφῶν μου[8] τῶν συγγενῶν μου κατὰ σάρκα. It is for the sake of, for the benefit of (for ὑπέρ cf., e.g., 5.6, 7, 8; 8.27, 31, 32, 34; 10.1; 14.15; 16.4) his fellow-Jews that Paul is ready to sacrifice his own salvation. He calls them his brethren. That is, he recognizes them still, in spite of their unbelief, as fellow-members of the people of God; for, apart from its primary use to denote a son of the same parents (or parent)

Jewish opponents could inflict on him (see L. Brun, *Segen und Fluch im Urchristentum*, Oslo, 1932).)

[1] Moreover, it is a substantial objection that a sense along the lines of either of these suggestions would be quite inappropriate in 1 Cor 12.3 and Gal 1.8 (with reference to Jesus and an angel, respectively).

[2] See further, on ἀνάθεμα, J. Behm, in *TWNT* 1, p. 356f; Bauer, s.v.

[3] Michel, p. 226, notes the contrast with the ἡμᾶς of 8.39.

[4] Instead of before ἀνάθεμα, which would seem the more obvious position (as in the Vulgate).

[5] The DG variant ὑπό may be due to a desire to soften Paul's statement or to a misunderstanding of the Latin 'a Christo' (Latin 'a' can, of course, mean either 'from' or 'by').

[6] Cf. BDF, § 211.

[7] col. 549.

[8] The absence of τῶν ἀδελφῶν μου in B* could be due to accidental omission or possibly to anti-Jewish feeling. There is no serious doubt about the words' being original. μου alone is omitted by 𝔓⁴⁶ Cypr—a variant probably to be explained as accidental, resulting from the proximity of another μου after συγγενῶν. Clarity here requires the μου.

'brother' is in the Bible nearly always reserved for fellow-members of the elect community (Israel or the Church).[1] The clear implication of this is that for Paul—and this must be stated with emphasis, since it has often been forgotten by Christians—unbelieving Israel is within the elect community, not outside it. But τῶν ἀδελφῶν μου by itself is not specific enough, since the Gentile Christians are also Paul's brethren. So he adds τῶν συγγενῶν μου κατὰ σάρκα. For the use of συγγενής in Hellenistic Greek to denote fellow-countrymen, members of the same nation, compare 16.7, 11, 21; Josephus, *B.J.* 7.262; *A.J.* 12.338. It would be wrong to read into the use of κατὰ σάρκα here any suggestion that the bond of Jewish nationality is *merely* a fleshly matter: in view of vv. 4 and 5 it is clear that Paul cannot have intended any disparagement of the Jews by it.

Chrysostom's comment on this passage raises the question whether it was for love of his fellow-Jews or for love of Christ that Paul was ready for this self-sacrifice. He argues that it was for love of Christ. The contents of vv. 4 and 5 and also of v. 6a show—so he argues—that the real reason for his readiness to sacrifice himself was his desire that Christ should not be blasphemed, that God should not be blasphemed, because those to whom the promises had been made had thus been excluded. (Paul's use of 'for my brethren's sake' rather than 'on account of Christ' he explains as due to his humility: Paul did not want to appear to be boasting or to think he was conferring a favour on Christ.)[2] But Calvin was surely right to refuse to allow himself to be impaled on the horns of this dilemma. Paul did not love his Jewish brethren any less sincerely and deeply because his love for them was grounded in his love for Christ. 'I do not thus accept the opinion of those who think that Paul spoke these words from a regard to God alone and not men. Nor, again, do I agree with others, who say that he had regard only to the love of men without any consideration for God, but I connect the love of men with zeal for the glory of God.'[3]

4f. Paul goes on to list in these two verses the transcendent privileges of the Jews—those privileges which include 'everything on which the faith of the Church is based, from which it draws sustenance'.[4] Their recital serves at the same time to underline the sadness of the Jews' present unbelief, to

[1] Cf. Gaugler 2, p. 10.
[2] col. 549f.
[3] p. 192.
[4] Barth, *CD* II/2, p. 203 (= *KD* II/2, p. 223).

explain the depth of Paul's grief on their behalf, and also to
indicate the continuing fact of their election. The list is
arranged with what appears to be conscious artistry,[1] and
distributed over four relative clauses all of which are dependent
on τῶν συγγενῶν μου κατὰ σάρκα (or, less probably, on τῶν
ἀδελφῶν μου):[2] (i) οἵτινές εἰσιν . . .; (ii) ὧν (εἰσιν understood)
followed by six items arranged in two groups of three, the first
and second items in each group being in the singular and the
third in the plural; (iii) ὧν (εἰσιν understood) . . .; (iv) ἐξ ὧν
(ἐστιν understood) . . .[3]

οἵτινές[4] εἰσιν Ἰσραηλῖται, while it is more naturally taken as
the first item of the list than as standing outside it, is a general
statement of the Jews' special position as the people of God,
and so in a sense embraces the items which follow. Paul asserts
that his συγγενεῖς κατὰ σάρκα are[5] the elect people of God, who,
as such, possess the privileges which he enumerates in the
second, third and fourth relative clauses of v. 4f. In early times
(e.g. Judg 5.2, 7) the name of the sacred confederacy, 'Israel'
was from the first a sacral term, denoting the whole community of those chosen by, and united in the worship of,
Yahweh. From the division of the kingdom until the fall of
Samaria it was limited to the northern kingdom; but from
722 B.C. it was applied to the southern kingdom of Judah (e.g.
Isa 5.7; 8.18; Mic 3.1), though the hope of a restored whole
Israel was still cherished. In later Palestinian Judaism the
name 'Israel' was the regular self-designation of the Jews
expressing their consciousness of being the people of God; the

[1] Cf. Michel, p. 227, n. 2. That the artistry is intentional is highly
probable—though perhaps we should not altogether exclude the
possibility that what we have here is simply the spontaneous shapeliness
of utterance which can be expected of someone who is naturally eloquent,
in a passage where the subject matter is specially elevated.

[2] This is surely a more natural way of taking the Greek than to regard
οἵτινες as the antecedent of the three genitive plural relative pronouns
(in which case Ἰσραηλῖται would be more naturally explained as standing
outside the actual list of privileges as an all-inclusive description).

[3] Michel, ibid., sees here an even more elaborate pattern than that
which we are inclined to recognize. Thus he notices an over-arching
threefold grouping in which he sees a movement 'von der Vielheit über
die Auswahl zur Einheit': Ἰσραηλῖται, πατέρες, ὁ Χριστὸς τὸ κατὰ σάρκα,
and also wonders whether a mutual connexion is intended between
numbers 1 and 4, 2 and 5, 3 and 6, of the items in the second relative
clause.

[4] For οἵτινες see p. 298 (on 6.2).

[5] The presence of the present indicative of εἶναι here (it is of course
often left to be understood in Greek) is to be noted. It gives emphasis
to the fact that the unbelieving Jews, of whom Paul is speaking, are
still (even in their unbelief) Israelites. We might compare the expressed
εἰσιν and ἐσμέν in 8.14 and 16, respectively (see p. 397).

name 'Jew' was used by foreigners and by the Jews themselves in their dealings with foreigners. Thus in Mk 15, while Pilate uses the term 'Jew' (vv. 2, 9, 12, 26: cf. 18), the chief priests and scribes speak of 'the King of Israel' (v. 32). In Hellenistic Judaism 'Israel' was much less frequently used—in fact, only in specifically religious contexts such as prayers and biblical-liturgical formulae and synagogue preaching. In the NT the names 'Israel' and 'Israelite' continue to have a salvation-historical significance (cf., for example, the occurrences in the Fourth Gospel: 1.31, 47, 49; 3.10; 12.13). So here Paul, by saying that his fellow-Jews are Israelites, is asserting that they are the chosen people of God.[1] Compare what is said below on 10.19.

ὧν ἡ υἱοθεσία. For the word υἱοθεσία see p. 397f. The reference here is to God's gracious adoption of the nation as His son (see especially Exod 4.22f; Jer 31.9; Hos 11.1) as the basis and beginning of the long history of His fatherly dealings with it (cf., for example, Deut 1.31; 8.5; Isa 1.2)—fatherly dealings which should have met with the response on Israel's part of reverent love, trust and obedience (cf., for example, Deut 14.1; Isa 1.2; Jer 3.19, 22; Mal 1.6). The use of the word υἱοθεσία underlines the fact, to which the OT consistently bears witness, that Israel's sonship is a matter of grace, a moral relationship, not to be thought of in any naturalistic or mythological way. Though there is a marked reserve in the OT with regard to speaking of God as the Father of the individual Israelite (Deut 14.1 stands out as exceptional; Hos 1.10 [MT: 2.1] refers to the future, not the present; Ps 27.10; 103.13 show the reserve), the thought of God's fatherly relationship to the individual was to some extent implicit all along in the conception of Israel's adoption. For Paul, the Israelites' adoption was a continuing reality (just as their being Israelites was) in spite of their unbelief; but we must naturally distinguish carefully between Paul's use of υἱοθεσία here of what is real objectively by God's grace but not as yet truly grasped or experienced and his use of the same word in 8.15 and (in yet another way) in 8.23.[2]

καὶ ἡ δόξα: that outward sign of God's presence with His

---

[1] See further G. von Rad, K. G. Kuhn and W. Gutbrod, in *TWNT* 3, pp. 356–94.
[2] On the fatherhood of God in the OT and in Judaism see further G. Quell and G. Schrenk, in *TWNT* 5, pp. 969–74 and 977–81; also T. W. Manson, *The Teaching of Jesus* (Cambridge, 2nd ed. 1935), pp. 91–93; J. Jeremias, *The Prayers of Jesus*, London, 1967; *New Testament Theology* 1, London, 1971, pp. 61ff.

people, the 'visible aspect of the invisible God', as T. C. Vriezen calls it,[1] which is often denoted in the OT by 'the glory of the LORD', *keḇôḏ YHWH* (e.g. Exod 16.7, 10; 24.16f; 40.34f; Lev 9.6, 23; Num 14.10, 21; 16.19, 42 [MT: 17.7]; 20.6; 1 Kgs 8.11; 2 Chr 5.14; 7.1–3; Ezek 1.28 and frequently; Hab 2.14), and is also sometimes referred to without *kāḇôḏ* being used (e.g. Exod 13.21f; 14.24; Num 14.14; 1 Sam 4.4 (cf. Heb 9.5); 2 Sam 6.2; 1 Kgs 8.29ff; Neh 9.12, 19; Ps 11.4). Palestinian Judaism sought to underline the truth of the personal presence of God, to which the OT passages cited above bear witness, and at the same time to safeguard the doctrine of the divine transcendence, by introducing the use of the term *šeḵînāh* ('dwelling', 'presence') in this connexion (e.g., 'my glory' in Exod 33.22 is represented by 'the glory of my presence'). It is God's own manifestation of His personal presence with His people, which is always His presence in the sovereign freedom of His gracious condescension, never a presence under their control or at their disposal, which Paul here lists as one of the privileges of his fellow-Jews.[2] The use of 'the glory' absolutely (without any explicit indication that it is God's by means of a pronominal suffix or a following 'of the LORD' or similar expression) is, according to SB 3, p. 262, without parallel in Rabbinic literature.

καὶ αἱ διαθῆκαι. The reading ἡ διαθήκη (𝔓46 B D G *c* vg^el) is, of course, easier—the reference would then clearly be to the covenant at Sinai. But the plural, as the less obvious reading, is to be preferred. It does not present any real difficulty; for both Hellenistic and Rabbinic Judaism referred to covenants in the plural (cf. Wisd 18.22; Ecclus 44.11, 18; 2 Macc 8.15; SB 3, p. 262). Paul probably has in mind the covenants made with Abraham (Gen 15.17ff; 17.1ff: cf. Exod 2.24), with Israel at Mount Sinai (Exod 19.5; 24.1ff), in the plains of Moab (Deut 29.1ff), and at Mounts Ebal and Gerizim (Josh 8.30ff), and possibly also the covenant with David (2 Sam 23.5; Ps 89.3f, 28f; 132.11f).[3]

καὶ ἡ νομοθεσία. Like the English word 'legislation', νομοθεσία can denote both (i) the action of making or giving laws, and

---

[1] *An Outline of Old Testament Theology* (Oxford, 1958), p. 247.

[2] See further G. von Rad and G. Kittel, in *TWNT* 2, pp. 240–50; E. G. Selwyn, *The First Epistle of St. Peter* (London, 1947), pp. 253–8; A. M. Ramsey, *The Glory of God and the Transfiguration of Christ* (London, 1949), pp. 9–28; E. Jacob, *Theology of the Old Testament* (London, 1958), pp. 79–82; Vriezen, op. cit., pp. 150, 246f; C. E. B. Cranfield, *The Service of God* (London, 1965), p. 10.

[3] Possibly also the covenant with Noah (Gen 6.18; 9.8ff)—so Michel, p. 227—though its inclusion does not seem to us very likely.

(ii) the made or given laws considered collectively.[1] Its use
in sense (ii) occurs in Lysias 30.35 (beginning of the fourth
century B.C.) and frequently in later literature (e.g. 2 Macc
6.23; 4 Macc 5.35; 17.16; Aristeas 15; Philo, *Abr.* 5; *Cher.* 87;
Plutarch, *Moralia* 240B). It is more probable that Paul uses
it here in sense (ii) and so as equivalent to ὁ νόμος than that
he means by it the actual giving of the law to Moses[2] (cf.
the preceding αἱ διαθῆκαι, which denotes not the covenant-
makings but the covenants made). The fact that ἡ νομοθεσία is
mentioned among the excellent privileges of Israel is clearly of
the greatest significance for our understanding of Paul's view
of the law.[3] That he is thinking of the law as divinely given
goes without saying.

καὶ ἡ λατρεία. There is no doubt that in referring to ἡ λατρεία
Paul had in mind primarily the sacrificial cultus, the Temple
service of Israel, as the true worship of the true God, in
contrast to all worship devised of men's own hearts (cf. 1 Kgs
12.33) the worship appointed and ordered by God Himself,[4]
that cultus, which (as Paul understood it) had from its
beginning pointed forward to Christ and His redeeming work.
But it does not seem altogether unlikely that, as used by Paul
here, the term embraced also the faithful non-sacrificial
worship of synagogue and pious Jewish home, including such
things as prayer, the reading of the Scriptures, the observation
of the Sabbath, the reciting of the Shema, and, indeed, all that is
meant by the phrase of Mic 6.8, 'to walk humbly with thy God'.[5]

[1] Cf. LSJ, p. 1180.
[2] *Pace* Gaugler 2, p. 14; Michel, p. 227; Käsemann, p. 247; *et al.* But
cf. W. Gutbrod, in *TWNT* 4, p. 1082.
[3] Cf. p. 845f.
[4] Cf. *Ab.* 1.2: 'Simeon the Just . . . used to say: By three things is the
world sustained: by the Law, by the [Temple-]service, and by deeds of
loving-kindness'.
[5] The noun λατρεία occurs only five times in the NT (here and 12.1;
Jn 16.2; Heb 9.1 and 6). In the LXX it is the regular equivalent of
'abōdāh and almost always, when used of the service of God, denotes
cultic worship. According to SB 3, p. 262, it was only after the destruction of the Temple that prayer was also designated 'abōdāh. But Billerbeck himself (SB 3, p. 26) rightly explains Paul's ᾧ λατρεύω ἐν τῷ πνεύματί
μου in 1.9 as referring to his prayers, and equates his phrase with 'service
in the heart', quoting in illustration the passage in *Siphre Deut* which,
in exposition of 'and to serve him with all your heart' (ûle'obedô bekol
lebabekem) in Deut 11.13, states that, in addition to hā'abōdāh in its well-
established sense of the sacrificial worship, prayer too may properly
be called an 'abōdāh. Compare the use of the verb λατρεύειν in Phil 3.3;
also such non-Pauline occurrences of it as those in Lk 2.37; Acts 27.23.
See further on τὴν λογικὴν λατρείαν ὑμῶν in 12.1; and Bauer, s.vv.
λατρεία and λατρεύω; H. Strathmann, in *TWNT* 4, pp. 58–66;
Jastrow, *Dictionary*, p. 1036.

καὶ αἱ ἐπαγγελίαι. The variant ἡ ἐπαγγελία is not so strongly supported as is the parallel variant (ἡ διαθήκη for αἱ διαθῆκαι) earlier in the verse, and the plural should no doubt be accepted here. In view of 4.13–22 and Gal 3.16–29 it is natural to assume that Paul had in mind in the first place the promises made to Abraham (Gen 12.7; 13.14–17; 17.4–8; 22.16–18: also the related promise in 21.12—cf. Rom 9.7f) and repeated to Isaac (Gen 26.3f) and to Jacob (Gen 28.13f); but 2 Cor 1.20 and 7.1 (see also the concluding verses of the previous chapter) suggest the probability that he also had in mind many other OT promises, particularly the eschatological and messianic promises. Such passages as 2 Sam 7.12, 16, 28f; Isa 9.6f; Jer 23.5; 31.31ff; Ezek 34.23f; 37.24ff spring naturally to mind. There are many references in Judaism to God's promises.[1]

ὦν οἱ πατέρες. Compare 11.28. Paul no doubt means specially Abraham (cf., e.g., 4.12, 16; Lk 1.73; 3.8; Jn 8.39, 56), Isaac (cf. 9.10), Jacob (cf. Jn 4.12), and the twelve patriarchs, the sons of Jacob (cf. Acts 7.12, 15)—possibly also other outstanding figures of OT history such as David (cf. Mk 11.10: in Acts 2.29 he is called ὁ πατριάρχης).[2]

καὶ ἐξ ὧν ὁ Χριστὸς τὸ κατὰ σάρκα. Paul completes his list by stating what is the supreme privilege, the supreme dignity, of the Jewish people—the fact that the Messiah Himself is, so far as His human nature, His existence as man, is concerned, of their race.[3] Compare Jn 4.22: . . . ὅτι ἡ σωτηρία ἐκ τῶν Ἰουδαίων ἐστίν. And this honour can never be taken from them: Jesus Christ was—and is—a Jew. The presence of the article τό before κατὰ σάρκα here strongly emphasizes the limitation which it expresses.[4] See on 1.3.

ὁ ὢν ἐπὶ πάντων θεὸς εὐλογητὸς εἰς τοὺς αἰῶνας, ἀμήν has caused a great deal of discussion and argument down the centuries.[5] Broadly speaking, the question is whether the whole

---

[1] For examples see J. Schniewind and G. Friedrich, in TWNT 2, p. 576f.
[2] Though the term was sometimes used more generally, e.g. of the forefathers in Egypt (e.g. Acts 7.19; Aboth 5.4), of the wilderness generation (e.g. 1 Cor 10.1), and of the earlier generations of the Hebrew people quite generally, the forefathers (e.g. Mt 23.30, 32).
[3] The antecedent of ὧν here must, of course, in view of the καί, be τῶν συγγενῶν μου κατὰ σάρκα (or, rather less probably, τῶν ἀδελφῶν μου) in v. 3, not οἱ πατέρες.
[4] Cf. BDF, § 266 (2).
[5] Among more recent discussions outside the commentaries on Romans we may here refer to the following: Cullmann, Christology, pp. 306–14; Whiteley, Theology, pp. 118–20; H. W. Bartsch, 'Röm 9.5 und 1 Clem. 32.4: eine notwendige Konjektur im Römerbrief', in TZ 21 (1965), pp. 401–09; W. L. Lorimer, 'Rom 9.3–5', in NTS 13 (1966–67),

or only part or none of this is to be understood as referring to ὁ Χριστός, but within this threefold framework of possibilities further variations have been suggested. At least the following suggestions have to be considered:

(i) to understand the whole as referring to Christ and connect θεός with ἐπὶ πάντων—'who is God over all, blessed for ever, Amen'.

(ii) to understand the whole as referring to Christ but separate θεός from ἐπὶ πάντων—'who is over all, God blessed for ever, Amen'.

(iii) to understand ὁ ὤν ἐπὶ πάντων as referring to Christ and the rest as an independent doxology—'who is over all. God be blessed for ever, Amen'.

(iv) to understand the whole as an independent doxology having ὁ ὤν ἐπὶ πάντων θεός as its subject—'God who is over all be blessed for ever, Amen'.[1]

(v) to understand the whole as an independent doxology with ὁ ὤν ἐπὶ πάντων as its subject and θεός standing in apposition to the subject—'He who is over all, God, be blessed for ever, Amen'.

(vi) to accept the conjectural emendation of ὁ ὤν to ὧν ὁ, and so to understand the whole as stating the final privilege of the Jews—'whose is the God who is over all, blessed for ever, Amen'.

The conjectural emendation (vi) was mentioned as a possibility more than three hundred years ago by Jonasz Szlichting,[2] though he did not accept it himself. It was accepted

p. 385f; B. M. Metzger, 'The punctuation of Rom 9.5', in B. Lindars and S. S. Smalley (ed.), *Christ and Spirit in the New Testament: studies in honour of C. F. D. Moule*, Cambridge, 1973, pp. 95–112; O. Kuss, 'Zu Römer 9.5', in J. Friedrich, W. Pöhlmann and P. Stuhlmacher (ed.), *Rechtfertigung: Festschrift für Ernst Käsemann zum 70. Geburtstag*, Tübingen and Göttingen, 1976, pp. 291–303.

[1] O. Holtzmann, *Das Neue Testament übersetzt und erklärt* 2, 1926, p. 654, interpreted v. 5b in this way, but regarded it, not as the final sentence of a section 9.1–5, but as the opening sentence of the following section. He explained that Paul began his new discussion in this way with a doxology to God, in order to make it clear from the start that for him God's holiness remained unimpeachable. But in this case it would be hard to account for the δέ at the beginning of v. 6.

[2] Jonae Slichtingii de Bukowiec *Commentaria posthuma in plerosque Novi Testamenti libros*, Amsterdam, 1665?–68, p. 254. Having said that one could think that Paul wrote ὧν ὁ and that 'in Apostoli verba levem et facilem . . . transpositionem irrepsisse' (p. 254), and having explained the sense which ὧν ὁ would give, he goes on (p. 255) to reject this suggestion on two grounds, first, that there is no manuscript support for it, and, secondly, that Scripture nowhere else uses the phrase ὁ ἐπὶ πάντων θεός, and concludes: 'Christo rectius hic titulus convenerit . . .' (though he argues that the word θεός has been wrongly inserted). Szlichting died in 1661 at the age of 69.

enthusiastically by L. M. Artemonius[1] and others in the early eighteenth century, but rejected by Bengel.[2] Accepted in Barth, 1933,[3] it was later rejected by Barth in *CD* II/2 as 'unsatisfactory'[4] and is not mentioned at all in his shorter commentary. It is surely to be rejected;[5] for (a) ὤν (without καί) would be intolerably harsh after the καὶ ἐξ ὧν which is appropriate for the introduction of the last item of the list;[6] (b) though Scripture frequently speaks of God as the God of Israel, it is extremely unlikely that Paul would place the possession of God as a last item in a list of the Jews' privileges in this way; (c) as a purely conjectural emendation it would need specially strong justification.

The one substantial argument[7] which has been adduced in favour of (iii), (iv) or (v) and against (i) and (ii)—and it has been used from early times—is that in the rest of the Pauline corpus there is no clear instance of the use of θεός with

---

[1] (=Samuel Crellius), *Initium Evangelii S. Joannis Apostoli ex antiquitate ecclesiastica restitutum indidemque nova ratione illustratum*, Amsterdam, 1726, pp. 223–38. He says (p. 224): 'Jonas Schlichtingius primus, quod sciam, transpositionem istam animadverterat', and proceeds to quote Szlichting, and then to take him to task for rejecting the emendation himself.
[2] p. 538.
[3] pp. 330f, 339.
[4] p. 205 (=*KD* II/2, p. 226).
[5] *Pace* Lorimer, op. cit.; Bartsch, op. cit.
[6] Cf. Bengel, p. 538.
[7] *Pace* Kuss, who (op. cit., p. 302f) lists seven items which he designates as 'schwerwiegende Argumente' in favour of taking v. 5b as an independent doxology referring to God. On examination, four of these ((c), (e), (f) and (g)) turn out to be merely attempts to minimize the force of particular arguments on the other side. With regard to (d) (that the 'blessed' formula is everywhere else used with reference to God-Yahweh), while it is not identical with the argument we have described in the text above as 'the one substantial argument', it may perhaps not unfairly be considered as bound up with it and answered with it. Arguments (a) and (b) (and this is also true of (c) with its use of the words 'von jüdischen Denkmöglichkeiten her') stand on what we regard as a quite unwarranted assumption, namely, that in chapters 9 to 11 Paul is specially addressing himself 'zumindest mittelbar' to Jews (i.e., apparently non-Christian Jews) and that the argumentation in these chapters rests 'auf jüdischem Grund'. True, Paul appeals—as often enough elsewhere—to the OT, but his appeals are based, not on non-Christian Jewish assumptions about it but on the OT understood as that which attests Christ and to the true understanding of which Christ alone is the key (see for instance 9.30–10.13). It is clear that in these chapters as throughout the epistle Paul is addressing *Christians*; and, while we believe that Paul hoped (among other things) in writing this epistle to be able to clear away some misunderstandings of his teaching among Jewish Christians in Rome, we regard it as likely that in the earlier part of chapters 9 to 11 he was quite as much addressing the

reference to Christ. On the other side, against (iii), (iv) and (v) and in favour of (i) or (ii), the following arguments may be stated:

(a) Pauline doxologies are generally either an integral part of the preceding sentence or else closely connected with it (the doxology referring to a person named in the preceding sentence), and do not stand in complete asyndeton, as, according to (iii), (iv) and (v), this would do. Compare, e.g., 1.25; 11.36; 2 Cor 11.31; Gal. 1.5; 2 Tim 4.18.

(b) Wherever *bārûk* or its Greek equivalent εὐλογητός is used in the Bible in an independent doxology, it is always (apart from one known exception: in the LXX version of Ps 68[LXX: 67].19 where κύριος ὁ θεὸς εὐλογητός—apparently a duplicate translation—has been inserted before εὐλογητὸς κύριος, κ.τ.λ.) the first word of the sentence, and the same rule is regularly applied also in extra-biblical Jewish usage. Compare, e.g., Gen 9.26; 1 Sam 25.32; Ps 28[LXX: 27].6; 31[LXX: 30].21 [MT, LXX: 22]; 41[LXX: 40].13[MT, LXX: 14]; Lk 1.68; 2 Cor 1.3; Eph 1.3; 1 Pet 1.3; 1QM 13.2; 14.4; and in the Eighteen Benedictions. It should be remembered how characteristic of Jewish worship this 'Blessed be . . .' formula is.

(c) The use of τὸ κατὰ σάρκα in v. 5a suggests that an antithesis is going to follow, though it would clearly be wrong to say that it makes an expressed following antithesis necessary. So, while the presence of this expression in v. 5a is a consideration which may well be regarded as probably favouring (i) or (ii), it is certainly not a conclusive argument.

Gentile as the Jewish Christians in Rome: from 11.13 he is, as he himself expressly indicates, particularly addressing the Gentile Christians. While his deep and passionate concern to win Jews to belief in Christ is of course apparent, he is not—so far as we can see—actually trying in writing these chapters to do this, but is rather concerned to enable Christians, both Gentile and Jewish, to get to grips with the theological and pastoral problems presented to the Church by the present unbelief of the majority of Jews.

The argument from the evidence of punctuation in certain early MSS. (which Sanday and Headlam, p. 234, actually call 'the strongest evidence against the reference to Christ') must surely be judged to carry no weight, since the marks of punctuation to be found in the early MSS. are so erratic that the fact that several of them have some evidence of punctuation after σάρκα cannot be taken as proving that the copyists concerned understood v. 5b as an independent doxology. So, for instance, it was unjustifiable to cite A as support for placing a colon after σάρκα, as did Nestle, [22]1956, in view of the fact that A has a similar point and space between Χριστοῦ and ὑπέρ in v. 3 as it has after σάρκα in v. 5, and also has points between σάρκα and οἵτινες (i.e. at the end of v. 3) and between Ἰσραηλῖται and ὤν. On this question of the evidence of punctuation in the ancient MSS. reference should be made to Metzger, op. cit., pp. 97–99, where the matter is treated with considerable thoroughness.

(d) An independent doxology would be rather surprising at this point, since, though a recital of Israel's privileges might well ordinarily be an occasion for such a doxology, in this case they have been mentioned in order to emphasize the grievousness of the Jews' disobedience. (A dependent doxology like that in 1.25 would be a different matter (see p. 124f), and would be perfectly natural.)

(e) The only natural way to take ὁ ὤν in the position it holds in the collocation of words forming vv. 3–5 is as the equivalent of ὅς ἐστιν.

(f) Against (iv) alone—the correct Greek for 'God who is over all' would be ὁ ἐπὶ πάντων θεός, without the ὤν.[1]

(g) Against (iii) alone—had Paul meant to say 'God be blessed for ever', it would have been more natural (though certainly not necessary) for him to have put the definite article before θεός.[2]

With regard to the one really serious argument against (i) and (ii) and in favour of taking either all or part of v. 5b as an independent doxology referring to God, while it may well be true that Paul has nowhere else in the extant epistles explicitly referred to Christ as θεός (much weight cannot be put on the two doubtful instances, 2 Th 1.12 and Tit 2.13), to conclude that he cannot have done so here seems to us quite unjustifiable, in view of the stylistic considerations which strongly suggest that he has done so and also of several features of his letters to be mentioned below. The stylistic arguments, in particular (a) and (b) and (e) are matter of fact and thoroughly objective (we regard (b) as so strong as to be in itself almost conclusive); and, when over against the objection that there is no certain instance of Paul's directly designating Christ as θεός it is possible to set such evidence as the following: (α) Paul's application of LXX passages in which κύριος stands for the Tetragrammaton to Christ (e.g. 10.13); (β) his acceptance of the legitimacy of invoking Christ in prayer (e.g. 10.12–14); (γ) his association of Christ with God in such a way as is to be seen in 1.7b; (δ) his parallel references to Christ and God as in 8.35 and 39; (ε) his reference to Christ in Phil 2.6 as ἐν μορφῇ θεοῦ ὑπάρχων, it seems to us that the superiority of the case for taking v. 5b to refer to Christ is so overwhelming as to warrant the assertion that it is very nearly certain that it ought to be accepted.[3]

[1] Cf. Sanday and Headlam, p. 236.
[2] Cf. BDF, § 254 (1); but note 1 Th 2.5; 2 Cor 5.19.
[3] To insinuate, as some do, that those who conclude that v. 5b refers to Christ must have allowed themselves to be influenced by theological and ecclesiastical preconceptions is, in view of the objectivity of the arguments in favour of so explaining v. 5b, unfair and unworthy.

As between (i) and (ii), (ii) should probably be preferred.[1]
According to this explanation, v. 5b affirms first Christ's
lordship over all things[2] (cf., e.g., 14.9; Phil 2.10) and secondly
His divine nature.[3] To take the three words ἐπὶ πάντων θεός
together is less satisfactory; for a statement that Christ is 'God
over all' would be open to misunderstanding—it could suggest
a meaning which it is absolutely certain that Paul would never
have intended (namely, that Christ is God to the exclusion of,
or in superiority over, the Father). So, putting a comma at the
end of v. 5a, we translate v. 5b: 'who is over all, God blessed
for ever, Amen'.

For εὐλογητὸς εἰς τοὺς αἰῶνας, ἀμήν see on 1.25.

A brief glance at the history of the exegesis of v. 5b must
suffice. As far as patristic commentaries are concerned, the
following definitely take it to refer to Christ: Origen, col. 1140;
Chrysostom, col. 552; Theodore of Mopsuestia, col. 833;
Theodoret, col. 152; Theophylact, col. 461; Ambrosiaster, col.
132; Augustine, col. 2078; Pelagius, p. 73. Diodore of Tarsus is
cited as taking it to refer to God;[4] but the comment given in
Cramer, p. 162, is not absolutely clear. It reads: ἐξ αὐτῶν,
φησίν, ὁ Χριστός. θεὸς δὲ οὐ μόνων αὐτῶν, ἀλλὰ κοινῇ ἐπὶ πάντων
ἐστὶ θεός. It seems perfectly possible to take Christ as the
subject of the second sentence and the first θεός as predicative
(in which case Diodore would be in agreement with the other
commentators just mentioned), and it is interesting to compare
the words used by Diodore's pupil Theodore in the place cited
above (. . . ἐξ αὐτῶν καὶ ὁ Χριστὸς τὸ κατὰ σάρκα, ὅς ἐστι θεὸς
οὐ μόνον αὐτῶν ἀλλὰ κοινῇ πάντων) which perhaps provide the
right clue to Diodore's meaning. Photius (ninth century A.D.)
refers the words to God in his treatise against the Manichaeans
(PG 102, col. 157). Many more Fathers could, of course, be cited
in support of connecting v. 5b with Christ (reference is often
made to the passage in other works besides commentaries).
From the Middle Ages we may mention Abelard (col. 912) and
Aquinas, p. 135 (747), who both clearly take the words as
referring to Christ.

Erasmus mentions four different possibilities in his notes,
and perhaps was inclined personally towards taking the

[1] Cf. Sanday and Headlam, p. 238; Lagrange, p. 227; Leenhardt,
p. 247; Metzger, op. cit., p. 110f.
[2] πάντων is best explained as neuter but an inclusive neuter which
includes persons as well as things (cf. the neuter singular in Jn 6.37, 39;
17.24, and the neuter plural in 1 Cor 1.27f (in the light of 1.26); Col 1.16.
See BDF, §§ 138 (1); 263 (3 and 4).
[3] Note θεός and not ὁ θεός.
[4] Sanday and Headlam, p. 234.

reference to be to God,[1] though in his *Paraphrases* he clearly takes it to be to Christ.[2] Calvin comments forcefully: 'To separate this clause from the rest of the context for the purpose of depriving Christ of this clear witness to his divinity, is an audacious attempt to create darkness where there is full light'.[3] Martyr also, who has a lengthy discussion, understands the words as referring to Christ.[4]

Among recent supporters of the reference to God may be mentioned: Dodd, p. 165; Barth, *CD* II/2, p. 205 (=*KD* II/2, p. 226); Bultmann, *Theology* 1, p. 129; Taylor, *Person of Christ*, pp. 55–57; RSV; NEB; Käsemann, p. 247f; Kuss, op. cit. Among recent supporters of the reference to Christ we may mention: Michel, p. 228f; Cullmann, *Christology*, pp. 306–14; Murray 2, pp. 245–48; Bruce, p. 186f; Best, p. 107; B. M. Metzger, op. cit.;[5] Schlier, p. 288. Barrett, p. 178f, leaves the question open.

VI. 2. THE UNBELIEF AND DISOBEDIENCE OF MEN ARE SHOWN TO BE EMBRACED WITHIN THE WORK OF THE DIVINE MERCY (9.6–29)

[6]But it is not that the word of God has failed. For not all who are of Israel are Israel, [7]nor, because they are Abraham's seed, are they all his children; but 'It is thy descendants through Isaac that shall be called thy seed'. [8]This means that it is not the children of the flesh who are God's children, but the children of the promise are counted as seed. [9]For *a word* of promise is this word: 'At this season will I come and Sarah shall have a son'. [10]But not only this, *there is* also *the case of* Rebecca who conceived *both her sons* at one time by one and the same man, our father Isaac; [11]for, when they were still unborn and had not done anything good or bad, in order that God's electing purpose might stand, [12] being based not on *human* works but on him who calls, it was said to her, 'The elder shall serve the younger', [13]even as it is written, 'Jacob have I loved but Esau have I hated'.

[14]What then shall we say? Is there unrighteousness with God? God forbid! [15]For he says to Moses, 'I will have mercy on him on whom I have mercy and I will have pity on him on whom I have pity'. [16]So then it is not a matter of *man's* willing or running but of God's showing mercy. [17]For the Scripture passage says to Pharaoh: 'For this very purpose have I raised thee up, that I might show in thee my power and that my name might be proclaimed in all the earth'. [18]So then on whom he wills he has mercy and whom he wills he hardens. [19]Thou

---

[1] See Kuss, op. cit., p. 294f.
[2] See Kuss, op. cit., p. 295
[3] p. 196.
[4] pp. 372–74.
[5] I was particularly glad to find in Metzger's essay such weighty confirmation of what I had already drafted on this half-verse.

wilt say to me then, 'Why does he still blame *men*? For who is resisting his will?' [20]Nay, rather, who art thou, O man, who art answering God back? Shall the thing moulded say to him who moulded it, 'Why didst thou make me thus?'? [21]Has not the potter a right over the clay to make from the same lump one part a vessel for honourable service and another a vessel for menial service? [22]But what if God endured vessels of wrath, prepared for destruction, with much longsuffering, because he willed to show forth his wrath and to make known his power, [23]and in order to make known the riches of his glory upon vessels of mercy, which he prepared before-hand for glory, [24]whom he also called, even us, not only from among the Jews but also from among the Gentiles? [25]—as he says in Hosea, 'I will call Not-my-people "My-people" and Unloved "Beloved"; [26]and instead of its being said [to them], "You are not my people", they shall be called the sons of the living God'. [27]But Isaiah cries concerning Israel: 'Though the number of the sons of Israel be as the sand of the sea, *only* a remnant shall be saved; [28]for a sentence complete and decisive will the Lord accomplish upon the earth'. [29]And as Isaiah foretold, 'Had not the Lord of Hosts left us a seed, we should have become as Sodom and been made like Gomorrah'.

The section falls into two parts, the first being vv. 6–13. In support of his categorical statement in v. 6a to the effect that what he has just said about his grief (vv. 1–5) does not imply that the revealed purpose of God, His purpose of election, has failed, Paul goes on to draw a distinction between Ἰσραήλ and οἱ ἐξ Ἰσραήλ, between Abraham's τέκνα and the σπέρμα Ἀβραάμ, and to remind his readers that God's distinguishing within the general area of election (what we have to do with here is the distinction between different levels or forms of election, not between election and non-election) between those who do, and those who do not, stand in a positive relationship to the accomplishment of God's purpose, is a characteristic feature of the biblical history. The fact that at the present time the majority of Jews stand outside the inner circle of election, which is the Israel within Israel, is, since it conforms to the pattern of the working out of God's purpose from the begin-ning, no proof of the failure of that purpose.

But the process of showing that the pattern of God's dealings with contemporary Israel is consistent with the pattern of His dealings with the patriarchs raises the question whether God's ways have not all along been unjust. In vv. 14–29 Paul emphatically rejects as an altogether false inference from what has been said the conclusion that there is unrighteousness with God, and proceeds to argue at some length in support of his rejection of this conclusion. Current interpretations of this paragraph differ very widely. Of crucial importance is v. 15. The interpretation given to it controls the interpretation of the verses which follow. It will be argued below that Paul understood Exod 33.19b as an assertion not of an absolute freedom of an indeterminate will of God distinct from His merciful will but of the freedom of God's *mercy*, and that the double θέλει of v. 18 is to be interpreted as referring not to an unqualified will moving now in one direction, now in another, capriciously, but to the merciful will of God, which, while it is indeed free in the sense of being free to fulfil its own purposes and altogether independent of men's willing and deserving, is also wholly determined in that it is the will of the merciful, righteous God. If we understand him correctly, Paul thinks of both the ἐλεεῖν and the σκληρύνειν, to which he refers in v. 18, as originating in one and the same merciful will. The section as a whole indeed bears witness to the *freedom* of God's mercy, but the freedom to which it bears witness is the freedom of His *mercy*—and no other freedom. And the implication of the argument is that, though the roles they fulfil are so sharply contrasted, Ishmael as well as Isaac, Esau as well as Jacob, Pharaoh as well as Moses, the vessels of wrath as well as the vessels of mercy, that is, the mass of unbelieving Jews (and unbelieving Gentiles too) as well as the believing Church of Jews and Gentiles, stand within—and not without—the embrace of the divine mercy.

6a. Οὐχ οἶον δὲ ὅτι. *Οὐχ οἶον ὅτι*, an unusual expression, is a mixture of two idioms, *οὐχ οἶον* (a Hellenistic idiom) and *οὐχ ὅτι*, both of which mean 'it is not that', 'it is not as if'.[1] (The variant which omits ὅτι and thus gives one of the component idioms by itself, is, of course, readily explicable as an easier reading.) The Vulgate correctly represents it by 'Non . . . quod'. The NEB 'It is impossible that' is a mistranslation (anticipated by Augustine[2]) resulting from confusion with the quite distinct idiom *οὐχ οἶόν τε (ἐστίν)*, or (less frequently) *οὐχ οἶον (ἐστίν)*, followed by the infinitive.[3] The force of the δέ is adversative: Paul wishes to exclude what might seem to be the implication of what he has just said in vv. 1–5. We might paraphrase thus: 'But what I have just said about my grief for my fellow-Jews is not to be understood as meaning that . . .'

ἐκπέπτωκεν ὁ λόγος τοῦ θεοῦ. For *ἐκπίπτειν* used in the sense 'fail', 'come to naught' cf. Ecclus 34.7 ('For dreams have led many astray: And they have failed (ἐξέπεσον) by putting their hope in them'); 1 Cor 13.8 (TR); Plato, *Ep.* 2.314b. It is often used in the LXX of flowers fading and falling (e.g. Job 14.2; 15.30, 33; Isa 40.7[RV: 8]). By ὁ λόγος τοῦ θεοῦ here is meant

---

[1] Cf. BDF, §§ 304 and 480(5); Bauer, s.v. οἶος.
[2] *ad Paulin. ep.* 186.31.
[3] See LSJ, s.v. οἶος III.2.

'the declared purpose of God',[1] and we may compare such OT passages as Num 23.19; Isa 31.2; 55.10f. But it is a mistake to attempt to make a hard distinction between the significance the phrase has here and its significance elsewhere in the NT;[2] for the declared purpose of God, which Paul has in mind, is clearly God's gracious purpose of election which has been declared in the bestowal on Israel of the privileges listed in vv. 4 and 5, and the divine election is indeed, as Barth has rightly stressed, 'the sum of the Gospel'.[3] What Paul has said in vv. 1–5 is certainly not to be understood as implying that the present unbelief of the great majority of Jews has succeeded in making the word of God ineffectual, in frustrating God's declared purpose of grace. This half-verse is the sign under which the whole section 9.6–29 stands—in fact, the sign and theme of the whole of chapters 9–11.

6b–7a. οὐ γὰρ πάντες οἱ ἐξ Ἰσραήλ, οὗτοι Ἰσραήλ· οὐδ᾽ ὅτι εἰσὶν σπέρμα Ἀβραάμ, πάντες τέκνα. In support of v. 6a (hence the γάρ), Paul proceeds, in the first place, to draw a distinction between οἱ ἐξ Ἰσραήλ and Ἰσραήλ, and between the σπέρμα and the τέκνα of Abraham. This really amounts to a distinction between 'Israel' and 'children of Abraham' in a comprehensive sense, on the one hand, and 'Israel' and 'children of Abraham' in a selective or special sense, on the other.[4] (It is important to notice that, while in vv. 6b–7a οἱ ἐξ Ἰσραήλ and σπέρμα Ἀβραάμ are used to express the comprehensive sense, and Ἰσραήλ and τέκνα (Ἀβραάμ) the special or selective, in v. 7b it is σπέρμα which carries the selective sense; and that in v. 8 Abraham's children in the comprehensive sense are indicated by τὰ τέκνα τῆς σαρκός, while in connexion with the children in the selective sense, who are contrasted with them, the terms, τέκνα τοῦ θεοῦ, τέκνα τῆς ἐπαγγελίας, and σπέρμα are used.) The point Paul is making is that not all who are included in the comprehensive Israel are included also in the selective, special Israel. But this does not mean what it has so often been taken to mean—that only part of the Jewish people is the elect people of God. Paul is not contriving to disinherit the majority of his fellow-Jews, to write a charter of Christian anti-semitism. This explanation of his meaning is ruled out by vv. 1–5; for it is clear that the Jews he is referring to in those

[1] Sanday and Headlam, p. 240.
[2] As Sanday and Headlam, ibid., appear to be doing.
[3] *CD* II/2, p. 13f (= *KD* II/2, p. 13).
[4] 'Israel' and 'children of Abraham' are not synonymous, for, even when used comprehensively, the former term includes only Jacob and his descendants, while the latter includes also Ishmael and Esau and their descendants.

verses are the unbelieving ones (for the others he has no need to grieve), and that he recognizes these unbelieving ones as his brethren (τῶν ἀδελφῶν μου) and acknowledges that they are still (εἰσιν), even in their unbelief, Israelites to whom the privileges belong. Paul's meaning is rather that within the elect people itself there has been going on throughout its history a divine operation of distinguishing and separating, whereby 'the Church hidden in Israel'[1] has been differentiated from the rest of the chosen nation. All Jews, πάντες οἱ ἐξ Ἰσραήλ, are members of God's elect people. This is an honour—and it is no small honour—of which no member of this race can be deprived. They are all members of the community, which is the environment of Jesus Christ. They are all necessarily witnesses to God's grace and truth. But not all of them are members of the Israel within Israel, which is the company of those who are willing, obedient, grateful witnesses to that grace and truth. But, if God's purpose of election has, from the very beginning, included a process of distinguishing and separating even within the elected people, then the present unbelief of many Jews is no proof that that purpose has failed, but may be understood rather as part of its working out.

7b. Paul now, going back to the pre-Israel history of the people of God, cites as his first example of this divine distinguishing the case of Isaac and Ishmael. ἀλλ' introduces, instead of a continuation of the sentence in the form in which it began,[2] an exact quotation of the last part of LXX Gen 21.12 (the LXX version is itself an exact translation of the Hebrew): ἐν Ἰσαὰκ κληθήσεταί σοι σπέρμα—literally, 'in Isaac shall seed be called to thee', i.e., 'it is thy descendants by Isaac who shall be recognized as thy seed'.[3] According to Gen 21, when Sarah demanded the expulsion of Hagar and the son she had borne to Abraham, 'the thing was very grievous in Abraham's sight on account of his son'. But God told Abraham not to grieve for his son and his bondwoman, but to do what Sarah asked; and He added as the reason the words which Paul quotes. The point then is this: not Ishmael but Isaac. That is,

[1] Barth, *CD* II/2, p. 214 (= *KD* II/2, p. 236).

[2] For this substitution of a scriptural quotation for the natural grammatical completion of a sentence compare Gal 3.11f.

[3] Paul quite probably saw in the passive (κληθήσεται) a reference to God's action—recognition by God. The suggestion that Paul had in mind the thought of God's calling in the sense of 8.28, 30 (see Michel, p. 232) seems unlikely. Bauer, s.v. καλέω 1.a.δ., suggests that this may be an instance of the use of καλεῖσθαι in a sense approaching 'to be'; but the sense 'be named', so 'be recognized as', is probably more appropriate here.

it is from Abraham's descendants by Isaac, and not from his descendants by Ishmael, that God's special people is to come. But it is to be carefully noted that the Genesis narrative indicates explicitly God's care for Ishmael (cf. Gen 21.13, 17–21: also 16.10–14; 17.20). So we must not read into Paul's argument any suggestion that Ishmael, because he is not chosen to play a positive part in the accomplishment of God's special purpose, is therefore excluded from the embrace of God's mercy.

8 draws out the general truth implicit in the case of Isaac and Ishmael. By οὐ τὰ τέκνα τῆς σαρκὸς ταῦτα τέκνα τοῦ θεοῦ Paul does not mean to imply that the children of God are not also children of the flesh—Isaac was, of course, just as much a child of the flesh, i.e. a child of Abraham by natural birth, as was Ishmael—but to indicate that the mere fact of being physically children of Abraham does not by itself make men children of God.[1] At this point the question arises of the relation of τέκνα τοῦ θεοῦ here to ἡ υἱοθεσία in v. 4. The natural explanation would seem to be that, whereas the adoption referred to in v. 4 is one of the privileges of the Jewish nation as a whole (so that the possibility of a comprehensive use of 'children of God' or 'sons of God' with regard to all Jews is probably implied), the phrase 'children of God' is here used with a selective connotation, of those who are what we have termed 'the Israel within Israel'.

ἀλλὰ τὰ τέκνα τῆς ἐπαγγελίας λογίζεται εἰς σπέρμα. This second half of the verse opposes to the children of the flesh, to whom the first half of the verse referred, 'the children of the promise'. Contrasted with Ishmael is Isaac. Like Ishmael, he was also Abraham's 'child of the flesh'; but the decisive thing about him was not this, but the fact that he was the object of the

---

[1] Leenhardt, p. 248, seeks to elicit the full significance of τέκνα τῆς σαρκός by reference to the details of the circumstances of Ishmael's birth: Ishmael 'owed his birth to the fact that Abraham, by going to Hagar, thought that he might be able to provide for himself, out of his own human resources, the son whom God had promised; but when man attempts to handle the promise on his own initiative he substitutes his own works for those of God, he acts as though he were master of the situation, as though it were a question of his own resources in the realization of God's promises'. But, true though these observations concerning the circumstances of Ishmael's birth may be, it is very doubtful whether Paul was thinking along these lines; for what is germane to his argument is surely simply the fact that Ishmael is only a child of Abraham by natural descent and not also the object of the divine promise, not the special perverseness of Abraham's conduct. Leenhardt's explanation (with its stress on the special carnality of Abraham's conduct) strikes us as akin to the explanation of God's foreknowledge referred to in 8.29 as His foreknowledge of men's future moral fitness (see p. 431, n. 1).

divine promise to Abraham. It was because of the promise, as the child of the promise, that he was Abraham's seed in the special, selective sense, the one who (rather than Ishmael) should be the father of those who should be recognized as Abraham's descendants. The verb λογίζεσθαι is used of God's reckoning in the royal freedom of His grace in 2.26 and ten or eleven times in chapter 4. Here too it is used of God's reckoning.[1]

9. ἐπαγγελίας γὰρ ὁ λόγος οὗτος: 'For *a word* of promise is this word.' Sanday and Headlam rightly recognize that ἐπαγγελίας 'must be the predicate of the sentence thrown forward in order to give emphasis and to show where the point of the argument lies'.[2] The γάρ indicates the connexion with the previous verse: v. 9 supports the statement that τὰ τέκνα τῆς ἐπαγγελίας are reckoned as Abraham's seed by showing that the word which was the efficient cause of Isaac's birth had the character of a promise. Were the Greek intended to be construed as it is by Barrett ('For the promise runs thus')[3] and by NEB, we should expect ἐπαγγελίας to be preceded by the article to match ὁ λόγος,[4] and also a different word-order.

κατὰ τὸν καιρὸν τοῦτον ἐλεύσομαι καὶ ἔσται τῇ Σάρρᾳ υἱός: an abbreviated and slightly free quotation combining LXX Gen 18.10 and 14. The phrase κατὰ τὸν καιρὸν τοῦτον in the LXX must mean 'at this time next year' (though the difficult Hebrew kāʿēṭ ḥayyāh, which it represents, perhaps refers to the nine months' period of pregnancy[5]).

10. οὐ μόνον δέ, ἀλλὰ καί. The case of Isaac and Ishmael might seem less than conclusive as evidence of the truth of the statement in v. 8; for, while it is true that both were children of Abraham's begetting, there was still—apart from the promise quoted in v. 9—a significant difference between them on the human level in the fact that Isaac's mother was Abraham's wife and Ishmael's mother Sarah's handmaid, and this difference (so it might be argued) would explain why Abraham's seed should be reckoned through Isaac and not through Ishmael. So Paul goes on to cite a second and clearer example.

The words **Ῥεβέκκα ἐξ ἑνὸς κοίτην ἔχουσα** indicate that in this case there was for both children the same mother, the same

---

[1] On the use of λογίζεσθαι in Paul's epistles see on 2.3.
[2] p. 242.
[3] pp. 180 and 182.
[4] Cf. Robertson, *Grammar*, p. 780f.
[5] Cf. J. Skinner, *A Critical and Exegetical Commentary on Genesis* (Edinburgh, 1910), p. 301. BDB, p. 312, suggests as its meaning: '*at the time* (when it is) *reviving*, the spring'.

father, and the same moment of conception. The word κοίτη, the primary meaning of which is 'bed', can be used of the act of sexual intercourse (e.g. Wisd 3.13, 16), and also to denote the actual semen (e.g. Num 5.20: cf. κοίτη σπέρματος in Lev 15.16f). It is probably used in this last sense here.[1] This would seem to be implied by the use of the preposition ἐκ. We take it that by ἐξ ἑνὸς κοίτην ἔχουσα Paul means to indicate, not just (as Bauer would have it[2]) that Rebecca had intercourse with only one man, but that from one man (ἑνός, which anticipates the mention of Isaac, emphasizes the fact that Jacob and Esau had the same father as well as the same mother) she received but one emission of semen to become the mother of both her sons.

Ἰσαὰκ τοῦ πατρὸς ἡμῶν. Paul calls Isaac 'our father', associating himself with his 'kinsfolk according to the flesh'.

By the end of this verse Paul has already made it clear that his second example is free from the weakness of his first. But at this point the sentence is interrupted by what seems to have begun as a parenthesis and then been continued so as to complete the thought, though not the grammar, of the original sentence.[3]

11–13. μήπω γὰρ γεννηθέντων μηδὲ πραξάντων τι ἀγαθὸν ἢ φαῦλον.[4] The difficult γάρ is probably to be explained as indicating a connexion with an unexpressed thought in Paul's mind. This thought—it may be assumed to be the recognition that the present example is not only free from the weakness of the first but also exhibits very clearly a characteristic of the divine distinguishing which has not yet been mentioned, namely, its independence of all human merit—would be a kind of unexpressed parenthesis, and the rest of vv. 11–13 is really its explanatory continuation, which takes the place of a grammatical completion of the sentence begun in v. 10. The genitive absolute indicates the circumstances in which the divine distinguishing was revealed (ἐρρέθη αὐτῇ, κ.τ.λ.): it was revealed before the twins were born and therefore before they had had any chance to do either good or ill.

---

[1] *Pace* Käsemann, p. 251. Cf. Lagrange, p. 230; Michel, p. 233.

[2] S.v. 2.b.

[3] We are prevented from explaining vv. 12b–13 (ἐρρέθη, κ.τ.λ.) as the grammatical completion of the sentence begun in v. 10 (taking v. 10 as a nominative absolute) by the fact that vv. 11–12a do not make a satisfactory parenthesis by themselves—what is said in vv. 11–12a needs vv. 12b–13 to complete it.

[4] The variant κακόν (𝔓⁴⁶, ℵ D G 33 *pm*) for φαῦλον is no doubt to be rejected, being explicable as the substitution of an obvious for a much less obvious word. φαῦλος occurs in the NT elsewhere only in Jn 3.20; 5.29; 2 Cor 5.10 (there also there is a variant κακόν); Tit 2.8; Jas 3.16.

ἵνα introduces a final clause dependent on the following
ἐρρέθη. While this clause may be said to indicate the significance of the fact that the intimation, ὁ μείζων δουλεύσει τῷ
ἐλάσσονι was made to Rebecca at the time denoted by the
genitive absolute, it would be unwise to discount the final force
of ἵνα here and not to see a reference to the divine purpose
behind the action; for teleological thinking is characteristic of
Paul and of other NT writers on a much deeper level than that
of a mere mannerism of speech.[1]

ἡ κατ' ἐκλογὴν πρόθεσις τοῦ θεοῦ: 'God's electing purpose', i.e.
'God's purpose which is characterized by election'. It is one
of Paul's definitive expressions for the divine election. Another
is (ἡ) ἐκλογὴ (τῆς) χάριτος. Both phrases denote the same
reality, though they focus attention on different aspects of it.
The substantive ἐκλογή occurs here for the first time in
Romans, though that which it signifies has been the subject of
the preceding verses. Compare 11.5, 28 (in 11.7 it is used for
the concrete, for ἐκλεκτοί). For πρόθεσις see on 8.28.

μένῃ: 'abide' in the sense of standing firm, being accomplished, not failing.[2] As used here, it is the opposite to ἐκπίπτειν
as used in v. 6. God's distinguishing of Jacob from Esau before
ever they were born was a step toward the ultimate triumphant
fulfilment of His saving purpose.

οὐκ ἐξ ἔργων ἀλλ' ἐκ τοῦ καλοῦντος is appended to the final
clause somewhat loosely. It draws out the implication of the
genitive absolute with which v. 11 began. The fact that the
divine distinguishing between Jacob and Esau (v. 12b) preceded their birth excludes altogether the possibility of its being
in any way dependent on the works (the word ἔργον has not
been used since chapter 4: its meaning here is adequately
illustrated by its use in 3.20, 27f; 4.2, 6) of the one who is
preferred. God's purpose of election is wholly dependent on
God Himself who calls.[3] The divine call is that which gives

---

[1] Cf. E. Stauffer, in *TWNT* 3, pp. 324–34.

[2] With this use of μένειν we may compare a number of occurrences of
the word in the LXX: e.g. Ps 33[LXX: 32].11; Prov 19.21; Isa 14.24 (of
God's counsel (βουλή): in the first of these the Hebrew verb used is
'āmaḏ, in the second and third ḳûm); Isa 7.7 (negatively, of a human
βουλή (ḳûm)); Isa 40.8 (of God's word (ḳûm)); also Ps 111[LXX: 110].3;
112[LXX: 111].3, 9; 117[LXX: 116].2. Compare also in the NT the
occurrences in 2 Cor 3.11; 9.9; Heb 7.24; 12.27; 1 Pet 1.23, 25.

[3] That Chrysostom failed to come to terms with what Paul is saying
here is very clear from his comment on v. 11 (col. 557), in the course of
which he says: καὶ δείκνυσιν ὅτι ἡ κατὰ σάρκα εὐγένεια οὐδὲν ὠφελεῖ, ἀλλὰ
ψυχῆς ἀρετὴν δεῖ ζητεῖν, ἣν καὶ πρὸ τῶν ἔργων ὁ Θεὸς οἶδε . . . ., going on a
bit later to draw a parallel with various experts (e.g. the τῶν τιμίων λίθων
κριταί), who choose what the layman would reject. Even Augustine,

effect to the divine election. It is the call to a positive relationship to God's gracious purpose, and so, characteristically, the call to faith and obedience.[1]

ἐρρέθη αὐτῇ. The passive avoids the use of the divine name: Gen 25.23 has 'the LORD said unto her'.

ὁ μείζων δουλεύσει τῷ ἐλάσσονι: an exact quotation of the last part of LXX Gen 25.23.[2] The interest of this Genesis verse as a whole is clearly in Jacob and Esau not just as individuals but also, and particularly, as the ancestors of two nations; for the part quoted is preceded by 'Two nations are in thy womb, And two peoples shall be separated even from thy bowels: And the one people shall be stronger than the other people'. It is important to stress that neither as they occur in Genesis nor as they are used by Paul do these words refer to the eternal destinies either of the two persons or of the individual members of the nations sprung from them; the reference is rather to the mutual relations of the two nations in history. What is here in question is not eschatological salvation or damnation, but the historical functions of those concerned and their relations to the development of the salvation-history.[3]

καθάπερ γέγραπται. The use of καθάπερ, 'a slight literary touch',[4] perhaps gives just a little extra emphasis to the solemnity with which the following scriptural quotation is introduced to conclude this stage of the argument.

τὸν Ἰακὼβ ἠγάπησα, τὸν δὲ Ἠσαῦ ἐμίσησα is quoted from Mal 1.2f, the only variation from the LXX text being in the order of the first three words. There is no doubt that the concern

when he wrote his *Expositio quarumdam propositionum* . . ., could think of God as electing those whom He knew would in the future believe, and could say: 'Nostrum est credere et velle, illius [i.e. Dei] autem dare credentibus et volentibus facultatem bene operandi . . .' (col. 2079), though it is true that he can also say (col. 2081): 'misericordia Dei vocamur ut credamus'.

[1] For Paul's use of καλεῖν in this epistle (in the Pauline epistles it is nearly always used of God's calling) cf. 4.17; 8.30; 9.7, 24–26; cf. also 1.1, 6f; 8.28; 11.29. Of the OT occurrences of ḳārā'/καλεῖν it is enough to mention in this connexion 1 Sam 3.4ff; Isa 41.9; 42.6; 43.1; 49.1; 51.2.

[2] For the use of ὁ μείζων and ὁ ἐλάσσων here in the sense of 'the elder' and 'the younger' cf. the Hebrew use of gāḏōl and ḳāṭān (or ḳāṭōn) or ṣā'îr. This use of μείζων and ἐλάσσων is found elsewhere in the LXX (for μείζων cf., e.g., Gen 10.21; 29.16; for ἐλάσσων cf. Gen 27.6; Josh 6.26 (ἐλάχιστος)). This use is not absolutely without parallel outside the Bible. The positive μέγας is used to distinguish the elder of two persons with the same name in a third century B.C. papyrus (see LSJ, s.v. μέγας A. I. b) and in Polybius, 18.35.9; and μείζων in the sense 'elder' occurs in an ostrakon of the second century A.D. (see LSJ, s.v. μέγας C.1). See also O. Michel, in *TSK* 108 (1937–38), pp. 401ff.

[3] Cf. Gaugler 2, pp. 35–37; Leenhardt, p. 249

[4] Robertson, *Grammar*, p. 967. See on 3.4 (p. 182).

of Mal 1.2–5 is with the nations of Israel and Edom, and it is natural to suppose that by 'Jacob' and 'Esau' Paul also understands not only the twin sons of Isaac but also the peoples descended from them. But what exactly is the connexion in Paul's mind between this quotation and vv. 11 and 12? One view has been that he intended it as a statement of the ground of God's action; the reason why God distinguished between the two brothers was simply that He loved the one and hated the other. According to this view, the Malachi quotation is meant to take us behind the Genesis word and the divine calling of v. 12 to their ultimate ground. But it seems a simpler and more natural understanding of Paul's words, to regard the Malachi quotation as intended, not to explain, but to corroborate what has just been said. Sanday and Headlam, who take the quotation in this way, explain it as an appeal to the evidence of subsequent history (' "God said the elder shall serve the younger, and, as the Prophet has shown, the whole of subsequent history has been an illustration of this. Jacob God has selected for His love; Esau He has hated: He has given his mountains for a desolation and his heritage to the jackals" ').[1] But more probably Paul thought of it as expressing the same truth as the words from Genesis, but expressing it more clearly and pointedly, and therefore suitable as a further and decisive corroboration of what had just been said, and, in particular, of the words of Gen 25.23 ('the elder shall serve the younger').

The word 'hate' should probably not be explained, either in Malachi or in Romans, as an instance of the Semitic use of a direct opposite in order to express a lesser degree of comparison (as, e.g., in Gen 29.31; Deut 21.15): 'love' and 'hate' are rather to be understood as denoting election and rejection respectively. God has chosen Jacob and his descendants to stand in a positive relation to the fulfilment of His gracious purpose: He has left Esau and Edom outside this relationship. But, again, it must be stressed that, as in the case of Ishmael, so also with Esau, the rejected one is still, according to the testimony of Scripture, an object of God's merciful care.[2] That he is, is eloquently hinted by such things as the setting of Gen 27.39f (Isaac's blessing of Esau) in close proximity to Gen 27.27–29 (Isaac's blessing of Jacob), the inclusion of the detailed genealogies of Edom in Genesis 36 and 1 Chronicles 1, the precept of Deut 23.7 ('Thou shalt not abhor an Edomite; for he is thy brother'), and the judgment of Amos 2.1–3, though, not surprisingly, the bitter hatred of Edom often felt

---

[1] p. 247.
[2] Cf. Barth, *CD* II/2, p. 217 (=*KD* II/2, p. 239).

by the Jews has also left its traces in the OT as well as in extra-
canonical Jewish literature.

Here in this section of Romans 9 Paul's special interest in
this quotation from Malachi was focused on its latter half (τὸν
δὲ 'Ησαῦ ἐμίσησα); for his point was that the unbelief of the
great majority of his Jewish contemporaries followed the
pattern of this exclusion of Esau. That he remained all the
time firmly convinced of the positive truth contained in the
first half of the quotation goes without saying.

The argument of vv. 6–13 (as we understand it) may then be
set out as follows: According to Scripture, God distinguished,
in the working out of His purpose, between Isaac and Ishmael
and between Jacob and Esau. But this was a distinguishing
inside the general area of election, since, although they were
not Israelites, offspring of Jacob, Ishmael was a son of
Abraham, 'the friend of God',[1] with whom the covenant had
been established, and Esau was one of the twin sons of Isaac,
that son of Abraham in whom Abraham's seed was to be
reckoned. Therefore the fact that at the present time a large
number of Jews, members of the elect nation, stand outside
the circle of the Israel within Israel, that is, of those who
actually stand in a positive relationship to God's purpose, does
not mean that God's purpose has failed (ἐκπέπτωκεν—v. 6).
On the contrary, it may even be said to confirm it, since it
conforms to the pattern of the working of that purpose right
from the beginning.[2]

14. Τί οὖν ἐροῦμεν; There are seven occurrences of τί ἐροῦμεν
in the Pauline epistles, all of them in Romans. In 4.1 it forms
a single sentence with the rest of the verse, the whole serving
to introduce the example of Abraham. In 8.31 (Τί οὖν ἐροῦμεν
πρὸς ταῦτα;) and 9.30 (Τί οὖν ἐροῦμεν;) it introduces Paul's
own conclusion from what he has been saying. The closest
parallels to the present occurrence are 3.5; 6.1; 7.7, in all of
which it is followed by another question and then by μὴ γένοιτο
(in 3.5 after a brief parenthesis). In 3.5 and here in 9.14 the
form of the following question (μή) expressly indicates that a
negative answer is expected. In 3.5 τί ἐροῦμεν forms one
sentence with the preceding conditional clause: in the other
three instances the conjunction οὖν is used. In these four
parallel cases (3.5; 6.1; 7.7, and here) Paul uses this formula at
a point where he recognizes that a false conclusion could be
drawn, instead of the true one, from what he has just been
saying: in these passages his method is to indicate and reject

---

[1] Jas 2.23: cf. 2 Chr 20.7; Isa 41.8.
[2] Cf. Barth, *CD* II/2, p. 216 (=*KD* II/2, p. 238).

the possible false conclusion before stating his own conclusion. The τί (οὖν) ἐροῦμεν; introduces the indication of the false inference.[1]

μὴ ἀδικία παρὰ τῷ θεῷ; The possible false conclusion is here indicated by means of a question expecting the answer 'No' (μή). It is probably to be explained as being simply the author's own rhetorical question (or we might perhaps here speak of a 'reflective question', meaning by that the sort of question which one asks oneself, when one is trying to think one's way through a difficult matter or, having once thought one's way through it, to retrace the steps of one's own thinking in order to clarify the matter for someone else).[2] Though the possible conclusion here mentioned is being rejected, it is nevertheless recognized by Paul as something to be taken seriously. The process of showing that there is no inconsistency between God's dealings with contemporary Israel and His dealings with Abraham's offspring in the remote past, as attested by Scripture, has indeed raised the question whether God's ways have not been unjust from the very beginning. If His distinguishing between men depends, and has all along depended, οὐκ ἐξ ἔργων ἀλλ' ἐκ τοῦ καλοῦντος, is He not unjust?

μὴ γένοιτο indicates Paul's emphatic rejection of this false conclusion. But it is not a mere dogmatic denial, for—

---

[1] On the view that it is rather Paul's way of introducing an opponent's objection (cf., e.g., Michel, p. 238) see next foot-note.

[2] The words are often regarded as an imaginary opponent's objection. There are several possible ways of so explaining them: (i) the point of 'Is there unrighteousness with God?' is that the conclusion that there is, is (for Christian and Jew alike) a totally unacceptable conclusion, so that what Paul has been saying must be untrue, since (in the objector's judgment) it leads inescapably to this palpably false conclusion; (ii) the question as it stands is not an exact quotation of the objection; but the original question (presumably in the οὐ form, i.e. expecting an affirmative answer) has been incorporated in a Pauline question expecting the answer 'No'; (iii) the question could perhaps just conceivably be explained as being (as it stands) an objector's question, along the lines of the example in Jn 4.29 of a question introduced by μήτι which under its form of incredulity seems to veil the beginnings of a suspicion on the part of the speaker that the true answer would be affirmative. But these explanations should surely all be rejected as needless complication. The imaginary objector is not required here at all (the case with v. 19 is different). It is scarcely necessary to add that the view expressed by a number of patristic commentators (e.g., Origen, col. 1114; Theodore of Mopsuestia, cols. 836–37 (on col. 836 he says with regard to vv. 14–18: Ταῦτα μὲν οὖν ἅπαντα ὡς ἀπὸ τοῦ ἑτέρων ἔφη προσώπου, τάς τε γραφικὰς μαρτυρίας οὕτως εἰπὼν ὡς ἂν ἐκείνων αὐτὰς εἰς σύστασιν τοῦ οἰκείου λόγου προβάλλεσθαι εἰωθότων καὶ τοὺς συλλογισμοὺς ἀκολούθως ἀπὸ τοῦ ἐκείνων ἐπαγαγὼν προσώπου); Chrysostom, col. 558) that the whole of vv. 14–18 plus v. 19 apart from the first three words is to be read as the words of an imaginary objector is certainly to be rejected.

15. τῷ Μωϋσεῖ γὰρ λέγει. Paul goes on to support (γάρ) his μὴ γένοιτο. He does so by appealing to the fact that, according to Exod 33.19, God said to Moses:[1] ἐλεήσω ὃν ἂν ἐλεῶ, καὶ οἰκτιρήσω ὃν ἂν οἰκτίρω. The words are an exact quotation of the LXX, which here follows the Hebrew closely. It is highly likely that Paul (no less than Barth[2]) thought of them as parallel to, and as an explicatory paraphrase of, the *'ehyeh 'ašer 'ehyeh* of Exod 3.14, and therefore as affording a specially significant revelation of the innermost nature of God. The question which has to be asked is: Why did God's use of these words seem to Paul to warrant his emphatic denial that there is unrighteousness in God's distinguishing between Isaac and Ishmael and between Jacob and Esau (and also between those Jews who believe in the Messiah and those who still reject Him), before, and quite independently of, their works? The answer must surely be that he recognized in them an affirmation, not of the freedom of an unqualified will of God, but of the freedom of God's mercy. These words of Exodus clearly do testify to the freedom of God's mercy, to the fact that His mercy is something which man can neither earn nor in any way control. But—and this is most significant, but has often not been recognized—they do not suggest that this freedom of God's mercy is an absolute freedom either to be merciful or to be unmerciful. They give no encouragement at all to the notion that there is behind God's mercy a will of God that is different from His merciful will. Here it is instructive to contrast with Paul's Greek and with the LXX and MT the translation in the Latin Vulgate at Exod 33.19 (in Romans the Vulgate is closer to the original): 'miserebor cui voluero, et clemens ero in quem mihi placuerit', which both obliterates the emphatic double repetition of the idea of mercy and also suggests the existence of a will or pleasure of God that is distinguishable from His merciful will. That the traditional interpretation of this verse of Romans has been along the lines of the meaning given to Exod 33.19 by the Vulgate is clear enough. But this has involved, we believe, a disastrous distortion of Paul's meaning.[3]

---

[1] The word-order τῷ Μωϋσεῖ γάρ draws attention more emphatically than τῷ γὰρ Μωϋσεῖ would have done to the *person* of Moses—Moses the recipient *par excellence* in the OT of God's self-revelation.

[2] *CD* II/2, p. 218 (= *KD* II/2, p. 240). It should be said that a careful comparison of the two passages, Exod 3.1–14 and 33.12–23, is extraordinarily interesting and suggestive.

[3] So, for instance, in the very first sentence of Calvin's comment on this verse a reference to a 'good pleasure' of God as something distinct from His will of mercy slips in ('. . . He favours them with His mercy according to His good pleasure' (p. 204), and Calvin's interpretation of

It is our contention that Paul regarded these words from
Exodus as an appropriate and cogent answer to the suggestion
that there is unrighteousness with God, precisely because he
understood them to be affirming emphatically the *freedom* of
God's mercy (and therefore the fact that God's mercy is not
something to which men can establish a claim whether on the
ground of parentage or of works), and at the same time making
it clear that it is the freedom of God's *mercy*[1] that is being
affirming, and not of some unqualified will of God behind, and
distinct from, His merciful will. And, understanding Paul thus,
we take it that this quotation, set as it is at a keypoint in the
argument, must be allowed to control the interpretation of
what follows (including v. 18!).

16. ἄρα οὖν introduces an inference from the Exodus word
just quoted: compare the use of τοῦτ' ἔστιν in v. 8.

οὐ τοῦ θέλοντος οὐδὲ τοῦ τρέχοντος, ἀλλὰ τοῦ ἐλεῶντος[2] θεοῦ. The
subject has to be supplied, and various possible subjects have
been suggested, such as 'the choice', 'mercy', 'the matter
generally'. It seems most natural to supply 'God's mercy'
from v. 15.[3] The use of the genitive here is rather like that
in Heb 12.11 (πᾶσα ... παιδεία ... οὐ δοκεῖ χαρᾶς εἶναι ἀλλὰ
λύπης, ...). The meaning would seem to be: 'God's mercy is

the passage as a whole follows accordingly. The fact that the last
sentence of his comment on this same verse speaks of the pleasure of
God's mercy and mentions no other pleasure or will of God, interesting
though it is, is clearly only accidental.

In this connexion, Barrett's choice of 'God's Sovereignty' for his title
for vv. 14–29 is, in our view, unfortunate; for, highly reputable though
the phrase, of course, is, its use here can hardly fail to suggest that what
is under consideration is an unqualified freedom of God, even though
Barrett does stress the importance of mercy as 'the key-note of chs.
ix–xi' (p. 185) and speaks of God's purposes being 'governed from first
to last by mercy' (p. 187). Barth is surely right in stressing the importance of the fact that Paul does not at this point 'say that God—by
reason of his sovereignty—has the right in every case and with every
man to do exactly as he pleases, for some reason only known to
him' (*Shorter*, p. 116) and in asserting that 'A bare sovereignty would
indeed not distinguish the electing God from a tyrannical demon'
(ibid.).

[1] It is perhaps necessary to stress here the importance of not allowing
ourselves to be so preoccupied with what may be called the negative
aspect of mercy (the fact that it excludes all ideas of merit on the part
of the object), which is expressed by speaking of the *freedom* of mercy,
that we lose sight of its fundamental positive content—overflowing,
active compassion.

[2] ἐλεῶντος is an instance of an —άω form being shown by an —εῖν verb
(see Robertson, *Grammar*, p. 342; BDF, § 90); a number of MSS. have
the more regular ἐλεοῦντος.

[3] Cf. Sanday and Headlam, p. 254.

not a matter of (or perhaps, 'does not depend on') man's
willing or activity,[1] but God's being merciful'.[2]

17. λέγει γὰρ ἡ γραφή. The γάρ is probably to be explained
as parallel with the γάρ of v. 15,[3] that is, as indicating the
connexion of this verse with v. 14 rather than with v. 16.
Verses 15 and 17 may then be regarded as giving two different
citations in support of Paul's μὴ γένοιτο in v. 14, each of which
is followed by a sentence beginning with ἄρα οὖν drawing out
what is to be inferred from it. It is to be noted that Paul does
not emphasize the contrast between Moses and Pharaoh (as he
could have done by using an adversative conjunction at this
point), but rather sets God's word to Pharaoh alongside His
word to Moses as parallel to it.[4] Michel's suggestion that the
presentation of the Scripture passage, rather than God, as the
subject of λέγει has to do with the fact that Pharaoh is a
heathen[5] can hardly be sustained, in view of Gal 3.8 (προϊδοῦσα
δὲ ἡ γραφὴ ὅτι ἐκ πίστεως δικαιοῖ τὰ ἔθνη ὁ θεός, προευηγγελίσατο
τῷ Ἀβραὰμ ὅτι ἐνευλογηθήσονται ἐν σοὶ πάντα τὰ ἔθνη). No substantial difference would seem to be intended by the use of
λέγει . . . ἡ γραφή here as against λέγει in v. 15—though it is
true that there is, according to Exodus, this difference between
God's word to Moses and His word to Pharaoh, that the former
is represented as spoken directly, whereas the latter is represented as being mediated by Moses.

τῷ Φαραώ. The Pharaoh of the Exodus, the cruel oppressor
of Israel, is here introduced as the type of those who resist God
—as the prefiguration of that disobedient Israel which is now
opposed to the gospel.

For ὅτι *recitativum* introducing a scriptural quotation compare 8.36; 1 Cor 14.21.

**εἰς αὐτὸ τοῦτο ἐξήγειρά σε, ὅπως ἐνδείξωμαι ἐν σοὶ τὴν δύναμίν μου,
καὶ ὅπως διαγγελῇ τὸ ὄνομά μου ἐν πάσῃ τῇ γῇ.** The quotation
of Exod 9.16 differs from the LXX in several respects: (i)
Instead of καὶ ἕνεκεν τούτου Paul has the more forceful εἰς
αὐτὸ τοῦτο, an expression which he uses elsewhere (13.6; 2 Cor
5.5; Eph 6.22; Col 4.8). It represents rather more adequately
the MT *wᵉ'ûlām ba'ᵃḇûr zō't*; and it brings out more emphatically

---

[1] The metaphor is from the arena: cf. 1 Cor 9.24, 26; Gal 2.2; 5.7;
Phil 2.16. Reference may be made to V. C. Pfitzner, *Paul and the Agon
Motif: traditional athletic imagery in the Pauline literature*, Leiden, 1967.
[2] The variant εὐδοκοῦντος in L would seem to reflect the tendency (see
on the previous verse) to think of a will of God distinct from His merciful
will and somehow standing behind it.
[3] Cf. Lagrange, p. 233f.
[4] Cf. Barth, *CD* II/2, p. 220 (=*KD* II/2, p. 242f); *Shorter*, p. 117.
[5] p. 239.

the idea of purpose. (ii) Instead of διετηρήθης Paul has
ἐξήγειρά σε. In the MT the Hiph'il of 'āmaḏ (he'ᵉmaḏtîḵā—RV:
'have I made thee to stand') is probably used in the sense of
keeping alive (i.e., instead of cutting off—cf. v. 15), and this
is clearly the general sense of the LXX διετηρήθης ('thou hast
been preserved'). Paul's ἐξήγειρά σε has sometimes been interpreted along the same lines, and the use of ἐξεγείρειν in 1 Cor
6.14 (of raising from the dead) and the use of the simple verb
in Jas 5.15 (of raising up from sickness, restoring to health)
have been adduced as evidence of the possibility of such a use
of ἐξεγείρειν. But more probably Paul used ἐξεγείρειν here in a
more general sense like that which the word has in the LXX
in Jer 50[LXX: 27].41; Hab 1.6; Zech 11.16.[1] He may have so
understood he'ᵉmaḏtîḵā; for the encroachment of 'āmaḏ on the
domain of ḳûm (the Hiph'il of which lies behind the ἐξεγείρειν
of Hab 1.6; Zech 11.16) had already begun before the end of
the OT period.[2] Or he may have chosen ἐξεγείρειν in order to
'bring out more emphatically the meaning of the passage as he
understood it'.[3] God has raised up Pharaoh, that is, caused
him to appear on the stage of history, for this purpose.[4] (iii)
The ἵνα . . . καὶ ὅπως . . . of the LXX, which reproduces the
distinction between the two final clauses expressed by baʿᵃḇûr
. . . ûlᵉmaʿan . . ., Paul has replaced by ὅπως. . . καὶ ὅπως . . .,
thus making the two clauses formally parallel. The LXX had
already moved in the direction of the assimilation of the former
of the two clauses to the latter by rendering harʾōṯᵉḵā ʾeṯ-kōḥî
by ἐνδείξωμαι ἐν σοὶ τὴν ἰσχύν μου (thus giving the former
clause a sense similar to that of the latter). (iv) The substitution
of δύναμιν for the ἰσχύν of the LXX is quite probably to be
explained as simply the substitution of a word in common use
for one, which, while of frequent occurrence in the LXX, is
relatively rare in Greek usage generally.[5] But the effect of the

---

[1] Cf. the fifth century B.C. comic poet Cantharus, Frag. 1; Josephus,
A J 8.271: also the use of the simple ἐγείρειν in, e.g., LXX Judg 2.16,
18; 3.9, 15; and Mt 11.11; 24.11.
[2] See BDB, pp. 763–5; 877–9; SB 3, p. 268.
[3] Sanday and Headlam, p. 256.
[4] Cf., inter al., Sanday and Headlam, p. 256; Lagrange, p. 234; Michel,
p. 239.
[5] The words δύναμις and ἰσχύς are more or less synonymous. (For an
attempt to discern some distinction between them see W. Grundmann,
in TWNT 2, p. 286, and 3, p. 400.) In the Pauline corpus ἰσχύς occurs
only in Eph 1.19; 6.10; 2 Th 1.9; and in the rest of the NT only seven
times. δύναμις, on the other hand, is, of course, common both in Paul and
in the rest of the NT. Paul may well have made the substitution himself,
whether deliberately or unconsciously: or he may possibly have known
a version of this verse in which δύναμις was used.

change is that a word is used here which has been used already in a highly important verse at the beginning of the epistle (1.16).

Taken together, the variations from the LXX just noted represent a bringing out more sharply of the sovereignty of the divine purpose. Not just Pharaoh's survival, but his role in history as a whole, is seen in relation to God's purpose; and the essential unity of that purpose in relation to Pharaoh is clarified (see (iii) above). The key to the interpretation of the verse, then, lies in the phrases τὴν δύναμίν μου and τὸ ὄνομά μου. What significance did these phrases have for Paul?

God's δύναμις has been mentioned twice in Romans before this point, in 1.16b and 20. In 1.20 τὰ . . . ἀόρατα of God, which ἀπὸ κτίσεως κόσμου τοῖς ποιήμασιν νοούμενα καθορᾶται with the result that men are without excuse, are further defined as ἥ τε ἀΐδιος αὐτοῦ δύναμις καὶ θειότης, but the character of the divine δύναμις is not expressly indicated at this point. But 1.16b does indicate very clearly the nature of the δύναμις of God to which it refers. Here—and it is a sentence of special importance, since it is part of the statement (1.16b–17) of the theme of the epistle—the gospel is defined as δύναμις . . . θεοῦ . . . εἰς σωτηρίαν παντὶ τῷ πιστεύοντι, Ἰουδαίῳ τε πρῶτον καὶ Ἕλληνι.[1] The possibility must therefore be reckoned with that Paul understood the δύναμις of God referred to in Exod 9.16 in the sense in which he had himself used δύναμις θεοῦ in Rom 1.16b, that is, not as unqualified power, but specifically as saving power.[2] And this possibility appears as a strong probability, when other Pauline references to God's δύναμις are taken into account. The following may be mentioned: 1 Cor 1.18, according to which the word of the cross τοῖς . . . σωζομένοις ἡμῖν δύναμις θεοῦ ἐστιν; 1 Cor 1.24, in which θεοῦ δύναμιν καὶ θεοῦ σοφίαν stands in apposition to Χριστόν; 1 Cor 6.14 and 2 Cor 13.4, which speak of God's δύναμις as that by which Christ was raised (now lives) and we shall be raised (shall live); and also 1 Cor 2.5; 4.20; 2 Cor 4.7; 6.7; Eph 1.19; 3.7, 20; 2 Tim 1.8. That Paul should understand the reference to God's power in an evangelical way would not be surprising. Moreover, in so doing he would not have been untrue to what is after all the general sense of the Exodus passage; for there too the thought is not of a mere show of unqualified power, of power for its own sake, but of power directed toward the deliverance of God's people.

---

[1] The phrase Ἰουδαίῳ τε πρῶτον καὶ Ἕλληνι is a significant link between 1.16b and the subject of chapters 9 to 11.

[2] Cf. Barth, CD II/2, p. 220 (= KD II/2, p. 243). Contrast Käsemann, p. 256: 'Hier ist δύναμις die Macht des Schöpfers im Gericht'.

The other phrase, τὸ ὄνομά μου, will no doubt have signified for Paul the character of God revealed in His words and acts, God's self-manifestation and its inherent, overflowing glory. Suggestively Paul has just quoted from Exod 33.19 words which, as we have seen, may be regarded as a drawing out of the meaning of the divine Name already disclosed to Moses (Exod 3.14), words which point to the free, sovereign mercy of God.

But the showing of God's saving power and the publishing abroad of His name, of His self-revelation, of His truth—this is the very purpose of God's election of Israel. The implication of v. 17, then, is that Pharaoh too, 'this dark prototype of all the rejected in Israel', as Barth calls him,[1] serves in his own different way the same gracious purpose of God, to the service of which Moses and the believing in Israel have been appointed. He too is a witness, albeit an unwilling, unbelieving and ungrateful witness, to the saving power and truth of God.

18. ἄρα οὖν (cf. v. 16) introduces an inference from the preceding verse taken in conjunction with v. 15.

ὃν θέλει ἐλεεῖ, ὃν δὲ θέλει σκληρύνει. Two contrasting forms of God's determination of men corresponding to the two different ways in which men may serve the divine purpose are indicated by ἐλεεῖ and σκληρύνει. Some serve it consciously and (more or less) voluntarily, others unconsciously and involuntarily. And men's stances in relation to God's purpose depend ultimately on God. He has mercy on some in the sense that He determines them for a positive role in relation to His purpose, to a conscious and voluntary service: others He hardens in the sense that He determines them for a negative role in relation to His purpose, for an unconscious, involuntary service. But the significance of the double θέλει is controlled by the words quoted in v. 15. We are not free to understand it in the sense in which it has very often been understood, namely, of an altogether unqualified, indeterminate, absolute will, which moves now in one direction, now in another, capriciously; but only to understand it in the light of v. 15, as the merciful will of God, which is indeed free in the sense of being wholly independent of men's deserts and men's contriving, but is wholly determined in that it is the will of the merciful and righteous God. Both the ἐλεεῖ and the σκληρύνει, though so different in their effects, are expressions of the same merciful will (cf. 11.32).

The background of Paul's use of σκληρύνειν is to be seen in Exod 4.21; 7.3; 9.12; 10.20, 27; 11.10; 14.4, 8, 17.[2] That there

---

[1] ibid.
[2] Cf. also Deut 2.30; Isa 63.17.

are difficulties here is not to be denied. It is obvious that for the individual concerned it is a matter of tremendous consequence whether he has been determined for a positive or a negative role in relation to the divine purpose. To miss the inestimable privilege of belonging here in this present life to the company of those who are conscious and (more or less) willing and grateful witnesses to God's grace is far indeed from being a trivial loss. But, while we certainly ought not to attempt to soften away the real difficulties of this verse, it is also important to avoid reading into it what it does not say. Calvin, for example, goes beyond the text when he comments on this verse: 'Paul's purpose is to make us accept the fact that it has seemed good to God to enlighten some in order that they may be saved, and blind others in order that they may be destroyed, . . .'¹ His two final clauses have no warrant in what has so far been said in this chapter. The assumption that Paul is here thinking of the ultimate destiny of the individual, of his final salvation or final ruin, is not justified by the text. The words εἰς ἀπώλειαν are indeed used in v. 22; but we have no right to read them back into v. 18.

19. Ἐρεῖς μοι οὖν introduces two questions which state an obvious and pressing objection to what has just been said. Whereas in v. 14 it was not necessary to think of a real or imaginary opponent, here, at least formally (with the use of the second person singular both in this and in the next verse),² we do have to do with an objector. But to try to identify the objector (e.g. Michel's 'der jüdische Gegner'³) is superfluous, in view of the obviousness of the objection.

τί⁴ ἔτι⁵ μέμφεται; τῷ γὰρ βουλήματι αὐτοῦ τίς ἀνθέστηκεν; The two questions are closely connected, the latter supporting the former. If things are as v. 18 has indicated, why does God find fault with men, holding them responsible (as, according to Scripture, He certainly does)? What grounds has He for reproaching men, since no man actually resists His will? If men's resistance is predetermined by God, it is not really resistance to His will at all, since this predetermination must be assumed to be the expression of His will. Such is the

---

¹ p. 207.
² For the use of the second person singular see on 2.1.
³ p. 241.
⁴ The οὖν which follows τί in 𝔓⁴⁶ B D G is probably an addition—possibly due to a copyist's being accustomed to the frequent occurrence of τί οὖν in Romans (3.1, 9; 4.1; 6.1, 15; 7.7; 8.31; 9.14, 30; 11.7).
⁵ For the use of ἔτι here cf. 3.7; 6.2. Sanday and Headlam comment (p. 258): 'The ἔτι implies that a changed condition has been produced which makes the continuation of the previous results surprising.'

objection. The words τίς ἀνθέστηκεν mean, not 'who can resist' (as Michel,[1] Barrett,[2] RSV, NEB et al. translate), but 'who resists'.[3] The point is not that it is impossible for men to resist, but that no man does, as a matter of fact, resist.[4]

20a. ὦ ἄνθρωπε: not 'my dear sir' (Barrett[5]) or 'sir' (NEB); for, while it is true that in extra-biblical Greek ἄνθρωπος is used in the vocative in this sense (e.g. in lively Platonic dialogue along with such expressions as ὦ θαυμάσιε, ὦ μακάριε, ὦ φίλε, ὦ ἑταῖρε) and also in a contemptuous sense (e.g. in addressing slaves), in the present sentence there is surely a conscious contrast between ὦ ἄνθρωπε and τῷ θεῷ (the first and last words of the sentence), so that the translation 'man' or 'O man' is required.[6] By thus setting man over against God Paul is certainly putting man in his place. But to assume that his intention is to assert the absolute right of an indeterminate divine will over the creature is to ignore the tenor of the argument of chapters 9 to 11, not to mention the evidence of the rest of the epistle. By τῷ θεῷ Paul does not mean a capricious demon but the God revealed in Jesus Christ, the God whose will is wholly determined and has once for all been revealed as mercy. And the address ὦ ἄνθρωπε is to be understood in the light of 5.12–21. It puts man in his place, not by contrasting creaturely weakness with arbitrary almightiness, but by reminding him of what 'man' is according to Holy Scripture—the creature created in the image of God, the sinner for whose sin Christ died and for whose justification He has been raised from the dead. It is because, whether one is Moses or Pharaoh, member of the believing Church or member of still unbelieving Israel, one is this man, the object of God's mercy, that one has no right to answer God back.[7]

μενοῦν γε:[8] 'nay, rather', 'on the contrary'. The expression

---

[1] p. 236: cf. p. 242.

[2] p. 184: cf. p. 187.

[3] So Sanday and Headlam, p. 259, and Lagrange, p. 236, rightly. The perfect ἀνθέστηκεν is best understood as present in sense: so 'resists' rather than 'has resisted'.

[4] Contrast Wisd 12.12 (. . . ἢ τίς ἀντιστήσεται τῷ κρίματί σου; . . .), where the thought is simply of the impossibility of resisting God's judgment.

[5] p. 184: cf. p. 187.

[6] ὦ ἄνθρωπε is also used in 2.1 and 3, but in both cases it is qualified.

[7] Cf. Barth CD II/2, p. 222f (= KD II/2, p. 245f).

[8] Both the TR reading (μενοῦν γε, ὦ ἄνθρωπε) and the reading of 𝔓⁴⁶ D*G (omitting μενοῦν γε) look like attempts to make an easier text. The position of μενοῦν γε after the vocative is certainly rather surprising. But it is probable that Paul adopted the unexpected order for the sake of giving special emphasis to the contrast between ὦ ἄνθρωπε and τῷ θεῷ by making the former the first two, and the latter the last two, words of the sentence.

(used in a reply) introduces in Phil 3.8 a heightening, here and
in 10.18 a correction, of what has just been said. See further
BDF, §450 (4).

σύ is emphatic, and is placed before τίς εἶ for the sake of
greater emphasis.

ὁ ἀνταποκρινόμενος τῷ θεῷ: 'who art answering God back'.
For ἀνταποκρίνεσθαι in the sense 'answer again', 'answer
back', cf. LXX Job 16.8; 32.12; Lk 14.6: and also the use of
ἀνταπόκρισις in LXX Job 34.36 (μὴ δῷς ἔτι ἀνταπόκρισιν ὥσπερ
οἱ ἄφρονες).

20b–21. Paul now makes use of the familiar OT imagery of
the potter (cf. Job 10.9; Ps 2.9; Isa 29.16; 41.25; 45.9; 64.8;
Jer 18.1–12; Wisd 15.7–17; Ecclus 27.5; 33.13; 38.29–30).[1] In
the OT it is used to illustrate different points. The general
warning against trying to apply all the details of such an
illustration indiscriminately, which Chrysostom inserts in his
comment on this passage, is most salutary.[2] If we heed it, we
may be saved from drawing hasty and unfair conclusions from
this passage.

μὴ ἐρεῖ τὸ πλάσμα τῷ πλάσαντι reproduces exactly a part of
LXX Isa 29.16. The words which follow—τί με ἐποίησας οὕτως;
—are in a general way reminiscent of parts of Isa 29.16;
45.9; Wisd 12.12; but cannot properly be called a quotation
from any of these passages. The substance of this question is
determined by the thought which Paul is about to express in
the next verse, which is concerned with the right of the potter
to use his clay for various purposes.

ἢ οὐκ ἔχει ἐξουσίαν ὁ κεραμεὺς τοῦ πηλοῦ ἐκ τοῦ αὐτοῦ φυράματος
ποιῆσαι ὃ μὲν εἰς τιμὴν σκεῦος, ὃ δὲ εἰς ἀτιμίαν; The fact that the
occurrence together of κεραμεύς and πηλός can be paralleled in
some of the LXX potter passages (Isa 29.16; 45.9; Jer 18.6),
and the occurrence together of κεραμεύς and σκεῦος in others
(Ps 2.9; Ecclus 27.5), is hardly surprising. But the contact with
Wisd 15.7 is much more significant, since not only do κεραμεύς,
πηλός and σκεῦος all occur together there, but the thought of
the differences in dignity among the vessels is also expressed.[3]
Paul was no doubt aware that he was using a common biblical

[1] Cf. in the Qumran texts 1QS 11.22; 1QH 1.21; 3.23f; 4.29; 11.3;
12.26, 32; 18.12.

[2] col. 559. The most important sentence is: Καὶ τοῦτο πανταχοῦ δεῖ
παρατηρεῖν, ὅτι τὰ ὑποδείγματα οὐ πάντα καθόλου δεῖ λαμβάνειν, ἀλλὰ τὸ
χρήσιμον αὐτῶν ἐκλεξαμένους, καὶ εἰς ὅπερ παρείληπται, τὸ λοιπὸν ἅπαν ἐᾶν.

[3] The text of Wisd 15.7 is as follows: Καὶ γὰρ κεραμεὺς ἁπαλὴν γῆν
θλίβων ἐπίμοχθον πλάσσει πρὸς ὑπηρεσίαν ἡμῶν ἓν ἕκαστον· ἀλλ᾽ ἐκ τοῦ αὐτοῦ
πηλοῦ ἀνεπλάσατο τά τε τῶν καθαρῶν ἔργων δοῦλα σκεύη τά τε ἐναντία, πάντα
ὁμοίως· τούτων δὲ ἑτέρου τίς ἑκάστου ἐστὶν ἡ χρῆσις, κριτὴς ὁ πηλουργός.

image. It may be that it was actually Wisd 15.7 (a passage which is not metaphorical but literal) which suggested to him the suitability of this image for his present purpose. But the similitude which we have here is Paul's own construction,[1] designed specially with the point he wanted to make in view. The point of the similitude lies in the fact that the potter—as potter—must, in order to fulfil the rational purposes of his craft, be free to make, from the same mass of clay, some vessels for noble, and some for menial, uses. The conclusion to be drawn is that God must be acknowledged to be free—as God, as the One who has ultimate authority—to appoint men to various functions in the on-going course of salvation-history for the sake of the fulfilment of His over-all purpose.[2] And it cannot be emphasized too strongly that there is naturally not the slightest suggestion that the potter's freedom is the freedom of caprice, and that it is, therefore, perverse to suppose that what Paul wanted to assert was a freedom of the Creator to deal with His creatures according to some indeterminate, capricious, absolute will.[3]

22–23a. εἰ δὲ θέλων ὁ θεὸς ἐνδείξασθαι τὴν ὀργὴν καὶ γνωρίσαι τὸ δυνατὸν αὐτοῦ ἤνεγκεν ἐν πολλῇ μακροθυμίᾳ σκεύη ὀργῆς κατηρτισμένα εἰς ἀπώλειαν, καὶ ἵνα γνωρίσῃ τὸν πλοῦτον τῆς δόξης αὐτοῦ ἐπὶ σκεύη ἐλέους constitutes the basic structure of a sentence which extends certainly to the end of v. 23 and probably to the end of v. 24. The sentence is grammatically incomplete, being the protasis of a conditional sentence for which there is no apodosis. Attempts have indeed been made to construe v. 23 or v. 24 or even Τί οὖν ἐροῦμεν; in v. 30 as an apodosis; but these must be rejected, the resulting sentences being much too forced to be acceptable. Such expedients are anyway unnecessary, since ellipsis of the apodosis of a conditional sentence is fairly common in classical Greek[4] and occurs several times in the NT. In Jn 6.62 and Acts 23.9 and also here the construction may be

---

[1] His independence may be seen in his use of τί . . . οὕτως, ἐξουσία, φύραμα, τιμή, and ἀτιμία, none of which occurs in any of the LXX potter passages. φύραμα is used in connexion with the making of concrete in Plutarch, *Moralia* 811 C.

[2] It should be noted that εἰς ἀτιμίαν implies menial use, not reprobation or destruction. The potter does not make ordinary, everyday pots, merely in order to destroy them! Cf. Leenhardt, p. 256, n. *.

[3] The NEB imports alien ideas into the text here. By making the verse into two sentences in the particular way it does so, it translates ἢ οὐκ ἔχει ἐξουσίαν twice over, thus giving these words undue emphasis; and its first sentence ('Surely the potter can do what he likes with the clay') gives a strong suggestion of arbitrary power unwarranted by the Greek.

[4] See LSJ, s.v. εἰ, B. VII. 1 and 2.

reproduced in English by 'what if . . .?', in Lk 19.42 by 'if only . . .!' But in every case the sense has to be understood from the context.[1] Thus in Lk 19.42 something like 'it would have been well' might be supplied, and in Jn 6.62 something like 'what will the effect on you be?' In the present passage we might supply something like 'what wilt thou say?' The point here is that to reckon with the truth (the conditional clause states what Paul believes to be true—it is not hypothetical) expressed in vv. 22–24 will make a big difference to our understanding of God's right to act in the way indicated in v. 18, going beyond what has already been established by vv. 20b–21.

The δέ which connects vv. 22–24 with v. 21 is important. We may compare the δέ in Acts 23.9; but in the present passage it is specially significant, because it makes the connexion between Paul's similitude and what is, in effect, his application of it. His use of δέ, rather than of οὖν or ἄρα, indicates an element of opposition[2] and implies that he regards his illustration as inadequate. What follows does indeed draw out the point of v. 21, but, in doing so, it also brings out the fact that God's ways are not just like the potter's.

There has been much discussion of the question whether the participial clause θέλων . . . ἐνδείξασθαι τὴν ὀργὴν καὶ γνωρίσαι τὸ δυνατὸν αὐτοῦ is to be understood as (i) causal, or (ii) concessive. The choice of (i) involves either (a) coupling together the θέλων clause and the final clause ἵνα γνωρίσῃ τὸν πλοῦτον τῆς δόξης αὐτοῦ ἐπὶ σκεύη ἐλέους, or else (b) taking ἵνα γνωρίσῃ as equivalent to an infinitive after θέλων, and so as parallel to ἐνδείξασθαι and γνωρίσαι[3] (in either case the three purposes expressed by ἐνδείξασθαι, γνωρίσαι, and γνωρίσῃ are brought together). The choice of (ii) involves coupling πολλῇ μακροθυμίᾳ and the ἵνα γνωρίσῃ clause together. Thus, according to (i), the meaning is: 'But what if God endured vessels of wrath, prepared for destruction, with much long-suffering, because he willed to show forth his wrath and to make known his power, and in order to make known the riches of his glory upon vessels of mercy. . . ?' According to (ii), the meaning is: 'What if God, although he willed to show forth his wrath and to make known his power, (nevertheless) endured vessels of wrath, prepared for destruction, with much long-suffering and in order to make

[1] To say that the construction is 'used for "Why should this not be so?"; that is, "This is in fact so, and there is no reason why it should not be so" ' (Barrett, p. 189) is misleading.

[2] *Pace* Lagrange, p. 239; Michel, p. 244, n. 4 (continuation from previous page); Murray 2, p. 33, n. 40; Käsemann, p. 255 (translation).

[3] Cf. Murray 2, p. 35 and ibid., n. 44. But the order makes this rather unnatural.

known the riches of his glory upon vessels of mercy. . . ?'

In support of (ii) it has been argued that it is easy to understand Paul's opposing to each other God's will to show forth His wrath and His enduring vessels of wrath with much long-suffering (as he does, if θέλων is concessive), but difficult to understand how God's will to show forth His wrath could be thought of as being a cause of His enduring such vessels with long-suffering (as it is, if θέλων is causal). The weakness of this argument will appear in the course of our exposition of what we take to be Paul's meaning. In support of (i) the following points may be made: (1) the coupling together of ἐν πολλῇ μακροθυμίᾳ and the final clause (ἵνα γνωρίσῃ, κ.τ.λ.) is very awkward, whereas it is not unnatural to couple the final clause with a causal participial clause;[1] (2) the idea of an as yet unfulfilled will of God to show forth His wrath and to make known His power (involved in (ii)) seems inconsistent with what Paul has said about the revelation of God's wrath in 1.18 and with the implication of 1.16b–17 that God's power is being made known as the gospel is proclaimed; and (3) the parallelism between vv. 17 and 22, apparent in ἐνδείξωμαι — ἐνδείξασθαι, τὴν δύναμίν μου — τὸ δυνατὸν αὐτοῦ and διαγγελῇ — γνωρίσαι, suggests that the explanation of θέλων as causal should probably be preferred on the ground that it yields a better parallel with the structure and general sense of v. 17. Of the two possibilities (i) is surely to be preferred.[2]

But, if the θέλων clause is causal, then two things follow:

(1) the two purposes indicated in it (ἐνδείξασθαι τὴν ὀργήν and γνωρίσαι τὸ δυνατὸν αὐτοῦ) stand in a close positive relation to the statement that God ἤνεγκεν ἐν πολλῇ μακροθυμίᾳ σκεύη ὀργῆς (contrast the adversative relationship which would be indicated, if the clause were concessive);

(2) these two purposes are closely connected with the purpose expressed in the final clause ἵνα γνωρίσῃ τὸν πλοῦτον τῆς δόξης αὐτοῦ ἐπὶ σκεύη ἐλέους, so that together with it they form an integrated whole, a threefold purpose. The truth which Paul is bidding his readers reckon with is that God has endured the vessels of wrath with much long-suffering for the sake of this threefold purpose.

We must now examine more closely both the main part of the sentence and the clauses expressing purpose.

First then the main part of the sentence (we have already seen that the whole sentence is grammatically incomplete)—

---

[1] On the variant which omits καί see below (p. 496, n. 4).

[2] *Pace* Cornely, p. 520; Sanday and Headlam, p. 261; Leenhardt, p. 258, n. *, et al.* The majority of recent commentators seem to prefer (i).

εἰ δὲ . . . ὁ θεὸς . . . ἤνεγκεν ἐν πολλῇ μακροθυμίᾳ σκεύη ὀργῆς κατηρτισμένα εἰς ἀπώλειαν.[1] For the reference to God's enduring[2] with much long-suffering we may compare 2.4 and the first phrase of 3.26 (Nestle's verse-division). It is natural to assume that, unless there is something in this context which clearly precludes such an interpretation, God's μακροθυμία is here, as in 2.4, connected with His kindness and intended to lead those whom He so endures to repentance.[3] The expression σκεύη ὀργῆς,[4] while indicating that those whom it denotes are indeed objects of God's wrath at the time in question, does not imply that they must always remain such. We may compare Eph 2.3, where those who now are believers are spoken of as having been children of wrath (καὶ ἤμεθα τέκνα φύσει ὀργῆς ὡς καὶ οἱ λοιποί).[5] With regard to κατηρτισμένα εἰς ἀπώλειαν, it is perhaps significant that, whereas in v. 23b Paul both uses a προ-compound and uses it in the aorist indicative active (προητοίμασεν), thus emphasizing clearly the divine predetermining, he here uses the verb καταρτίζειν, not προκαταρτίζειν (a word he employs in 2 Cor 9.5), and also uses the perfect passive participle.[6] While it is, of course, true that in the NT a passive often contains the thought of a divine action, it seems probable that Paul wishes here to direct attention simply to

[1] In the Nestle text ἤνεγκεν, σκεύη ὀργῆς, and ἀπώλειαν are printed in bold type, and several passages from the OT and Apocrypha are cited in the margin. The closest verbal parallel is Jer 50[LXX: 27].25 (ἐξήνεγκεν τὰ σκεύη ὀργῆς αὐτοῦ); but this is not a parallel, as far as the thought is concerned, for ἐκφέρειν is used in a quite different sense from that in which φέρειν is used here, and τὰ σκεύη ὀργῆς αὐτοῦ in the Jeremiah passage denotes the instruments or weapons which God uses in expressing His wrath, whereas in Rom 9.22 σκεύη ὀργῆς presumably denotes the vessels (cf. v. 23) which are objects of His wrath.

[2] For φέρειν = 'bear patiently', 'endure', cf., e.g., Heb 13.13; Thucydides, 2.60; Xenophon, An. 3.1.23; Josephus, AJ 7.372; 17.342.

[3] Cf. Mt 18.26, 29; Lk 18.7; 1 Cor 13.4; 2 Pet 3.9; 1 Tim 1.16; 1 Pet 3.20; 2 Pet 3.15. Cf. Chrysostom, col. 560: . . . βουλόμενος αὐτὸν εἰς μετάνοιαν ἀγαγεῖν. Contrast Murray, who says: 'He is reminding his unbelieving kinsmen [But surely Paul's words are addressed to Christians?] that God's long-suffering is not the certificate of God's favour but that, awful though it be, it only ministers in the case of those who are the vessels of wrath to the more manifest exhibition of their ill-desert in the infliction of God's wrath and the making known of his power' (2, p. 35).

[4] Cornely, p. 515, rightly argues that σκεύη ὀργῆς and σκεύη ἐλέους are not to be taken as interpreting the vessels made εἰς τιμήν and εἰς ἀτιμίαν, respectively, of v. 21. Had Paul intended this allegorical interpretation of v. 21, he should have put in definite articles with σκεύη ὀργῆς and σκεύη ἐλέους. σκεῦος is used in vv. 22 and 23 metaphorically (cf. Bauer, s.v. 2) probably—in our view—without any special thought of the literal use of the word in v. 21.

[5] Cf. Leenhardt, p. 258.

[6] Cf. Leenhardt, ibid., n. †; also Bengel, p. 542.

the vessels' condition of readiness, ripeness, for destruction and not to any act, whether of God or of themselves, by which the condition was brought about.[1] That they are worthy of destruction is clearly implied, but not that they will necessarily be destroyed.

We turn now to the three statements of purpose contained in this passage. That the last of these (ἵνα γνωρίσῃ, κ.τ.λ.) is dominant is clear.[2] It alone is introduced by ἵνα; and it is given special emphasis by its position in the sentence, by the fact that it is extended by means of the two relative clauses which follow, and by the fact that vv. 25–29 focus further attention on it. Above all, its content marks it off from the others; for the manifestation of the wealth of the divine glory[3] is nothing less than the ultimate purpose of God.[4] The two other statements of purpose must therefore be explained in relation to it, and not independently of, or in opposition to, it. There is no question of an equilibrium between God's will to show His wrath and God's will to manifest the riches of His glory on the vessels of mercy, as though He sometimes willed the one thing and sometimes the other. The former purpose must be understood as subordinate to the latter. The ἵνα clause indicates the one ultimate gracious purpose of God, for the sake of which He also wills to show His wrath. The relations between the statement ὁ θεὸς ... ἤνεγκεν. . . and the three statements of purpose may therefore be expressed as follows: God has endured . . . for the sake of purpose 3, and also (since the fulfilment of purpose 3 requires the fulfilment of the two other purposes) for the sake of purposes 1 and 2. God has endured a Pharaoh, and He now endures rebellious Israel, with much long-suffering for the sake of the manifestation of the riches of His glory on the vessels of mercy, and also for the sake of the

---

[1] Cf. Sanday and Headlam, p. 261f; Lagrange, p. 240; Huby, p. 352, n.1; Leenhardt, ibid., n. †. Contrast Käsemann, p. 259. The explanation of κατηρτισμένα according to which Paul's meaning is that they have made themselves ready, is to be found, e.g., in Chrysostom, col. 560 (τουτέστι, ἀπηρτισμένον, οἴκοθεν μέντοι καὶ παρ' ἑαυτοῦ); Pelagius, p. 78 ('a semet ipsis ad interitum praeparata').

[2] Pace, e.g., Huby, p. 352, n. 2.

[3] The variant χρηστότητος in P is no doubt due to someone's failure to see the appositeness of δόξης here: χρηστότητος (cf. τοῦ πλούτου τῆς χρηστότητος αὐτοῦ in 2.4) gives a more obvious sense.

[4] The dominance of the purpose expressed in the ἵνα clause would, of course, be still more apparent, were καί omitted (so B 69 pc c vg Or). This statement of purpose would then stand by itself, whereas, if καί is read, it is coupled with the θέλων clause containing the two other expressions of purpose. But the καί should probably be retained, since its omission can easily be explained as due to the desire for a smoother text.

revelation of His wrath (see on 1.18) and of His power (if we were right about τὴν δύναμίν μου in v. 17, His saving power, since, as we have seen, there is a close parallelism between vv. 17 and 22–23a), since this twofold revelation is necessary for the achievement of His ultimate purpose of manifesting the riches of His glory.

A further point must be made before we leave this passage. It is that the relations between God's patient enduring of vessels of wrath, the showing of His wrath, and the manifestation of the wealth of His glory upon vessels of mercy, will be illuminated by 9.30–11.36. We shall see there that the ultimate purpose of that patience of God toward rebellious Israel which is depicted in 10.21 includes the salvation of rebellious Israel itself (chapter 11); but we shall see also how the divine patience must first show up the full seriousness of Israel's sin (9.30–10.21), or, in other words, how God is patient for the sake of showing His wrath, of judging men's sin (His patience shows up the hatefulness of men's sin by showing it to be the rejection of the grace of the God who is thus patient), in order that ultimately He may have mercy. In these chapters it will also become clear that the σκεύη ὀργῆς and the σκεύη ἐλέους are not *numeri clausi*, and that it is God's purpose that the σκεύη ὀργῆς should become σκεύη ἐλέους. It will also become clear that the showing of God's wrath is necessary in order that it may be manifest to the vessels of mercy that what is revealed in their case is indeed the wealth of God's glory, of the glory of His boundless mercy, and not any glory of their own deserving.

23b. ἃ προητοίμασεν εἰς δόξαν. In the case of the vessels of mercy divine predetermining is asserted explicitly and emphatically by the choice of the compound and the use of the third person singular aorist indicative active (contrast what was said above with reference to κατηρτισμένα εἰς ἀπώλειαν). For προητοίμασεν compare Eph 2.10, though there (as also in Mt 20.23 = Mk 10.40; Mt 25.34, 41; 1 Cor 2.9; Heb 11.16; Rev 21.2, passages in which the simple verb is used), while the reference is to God's preparing, the object of the action is not personal, as here. For εἰς δόξαν compare 2.7, 10; 3.23; 5.2; 8.18. For the thought of the clause as a whole, and also of the following verse, 8.28–30 should be compared.

24. οὓς καὶ ἐκάλεσεν ἡμᾶς οὐ μόνον ἐξ Ἰουδαίων ἀλλὰ καὶ ἐξ ἐθνῶν; This has been taken in various ways. It is possible (i) to adopt the alternative punctuation given in the Nestle apparatus (a question mark and a comma at the ends of vv. 23 and 24, respectively) and to take this verse as the beginning of a fresh sentence continued in vv. 25–26; or (ii) to take the whole verse as a relative clause dependent on σκεύη ἐλέους in v. 23; or (iii) to take ἡμᾶς as standing in apposition to σκεύη ἐλέους and the rest of the verse as a relative clause dependent on ἡμᾶς. If either (i) or (ii) is accepted, οὕς must be explained as being masculine *ad sensum*, and ἡμᾶς as standing in apposition to οὕς. Though the use of a relative pronoun, as in Latin, to connect an independent sentence to its predecessor is sometimes found in Greek (it is, in fact, a special feature of the style of Acts[1]), (i) should probably be rejected on the ground that there is a close connexion of sense between vv. 23 and 24.[2] Of (ii) and (iii), the former should probably be preferred as being the simpler and more straightforward explanation.

If it were not for vv. 25–26, one might understand Paul to be making in v. 24 three distinct and equally emphasized points, namely, that God has not only predetermined but also effectually called the vessels of mercy, that Paul and his readers are among them, and that they include Gentiles as well as Jews. But, in view of vv. 25–26 in which καλεῖν is twice used in the affirmation of the acceptance of those who formerly were not accepted, it seems necessary to take ἐκάλεσεν and οὐ μόνον ἐξ Ἰουδαίων ἀλλὰ καὶ ἐξ ἐθνῶν very closely together: God has effectually called[3] the vessels of mercy not only from among the Jews but also from among the Gentiles. It is this that Paul wishes here to assert with emphasis.[4] The presence of Gentiles within the Church is the sign and pledge that the realm of rejection, of Ishmael, Esau, Pharaoh, and of the unbelieving Jews themselves, is not finally shut out from the mercy of God. The ἡμᾶς is slipped in. It has the effect of giving to this statement something of the character of personal confession of faith.

25f does not have the form of an independent sentence, but is loosely attached to vv. 22–24 by ὡς καί. At the same time it is the first element of the catena of confirmatory OT quotations which extends to the end of v. 29. (While grammatical preciseness might favour placing the question mark at

---

[1] Cf. E. Haenchen, *Die Apostelgeschichte* (Göttingen, 3rd ed. 1959), p. 108, n. 5.

[2] Cf., e.g., Lagrange, p. 241.

[3] It seems probable that καλεῖν is used here in its strong sense (cf. 8.30): in vv. 25–26 God's naming is thought of as effecting not a mere change of name but a real change of condition.

[4] The καί before ἐκάλεσεν (hardly to be regarded as merely otiose, as Haenchen, ibid., n. 6, thinks) could be explained as giving emphasis to ἐκάλεσεν (not only predetermined but also effectually called), but is more probably to be taken as giving emphasis to the complete idea expressed in ἐκάλεσεν . . . οὐ μόνον ἐξ Ἰουδαίων ἀλλὰ καὶ ἐξ ἐθνῶν.

the end of v. 26 rather than at the end of v. 24, to do so would have the disadvantage of tending to obscure the close connexion between vv. 25–26 and 27–29.)

ἐν τῷ Ὡσηέ: 'in Hosea', i.e., in the book of Hosea. For this unusual way of giving a reference to a book of the Bible compare Mk 1.2 (ἐν τῷ Ἡσαΐᾳ τῷ προφήτῃ).[1]

λέγει. Understand ὁ θεός.

καλέσω τὸν οὐ λαόν μου λαόν μου καὶ τὴν οὐκ ἠγαπημένην ἠγαπημ-ένην· καὶ ἔσται ἐν τῷ τόπῳ οὗ² ἐρρέθη [αὐτοῖς]·³ οὐ λαός μου ὑμεῖς, ἐκεῖ κληθήσονται υἱοὶ θεοῦ ζῶντος. The rest of vv. 25 and 26 consists of quotations of parts of Hos 2.23[MT and LXX: 25] and 1.10[MT and LXX: 2.1]. The first quotation differs considerably from the LXX text. The two LXX clauses ἐλεήσω τὴν Οὐκ-ἠλεημένην and ἐρῶ τῷ Οὐ-λαῷ-μου Λαός μου εἶ σύ are combined in reverse order⁴ in a single clause, with καλέσω substituted for ἐρῶ, and the construction changed accordingly; and the verb ἀγαπᾶν is used instead of ἐλεεῖν.⁵ Of these variations from the LXX the most significant is the substitution of καλέσω for ἐρῶ, which serves as a link between vv. 24 and 25 and also between vv. 25 and 26. The second quotation agrees exactly with the LXX text of Hos 2.1 (as printed in the Rahlfs edition).⁶ Paul treats the two quotations as a single passage.⁷

The original reference of the Hosea verses was to the northern kingdom of Israel: Paul applies them to the Gentiles (cf. 1 Pet 2.10). The ten tribes were indeed thrust out into the dark

---

[1] SB 2, p. 1, can cite no exact parallel from Rabbinic literature. Such formulae as 'in the prophets', 'in Chronicles', 'in the law of Moses', and 'in the book of Jeremiah', occur, but not 'in Hosea', 'in Jeremiah'. It was probably the unusualness of the formula used by Paul here which suggested the variant reading which omits the ἐν (cf. v. 15: τῷ Μωϋσεῖ . . . λέγει).

[2] The variant ᾧ (𝔓⁴⁶ ℵ*) would appear to be simply a mistake due to assimilation to the preceding dative.

[3] The support for omitting αὐτοῖς (B f syᵖ Aug) is sufficient to cause some doubt, and assimilation to the LXX text is a ready explanation for its insertion; but perhaps this is a case, where to insist on choosing what is certainly the more difficult reading would be unduly doctrinaire. We incline to the view that αὐτοῖς should be read.

[4] As a result of this inversion, the reference to 'not my people', which is particularly suitable to the Gentiles, comes first (cf. Sanday and Headlam, p. 264).

[5] In Hos 2.25 B V have ἀγαπήσω and ἠγαπημένην in place of ἐλεήσω and ἠλεημένην.

[6] Some LXX MSS., however, omit ἐκεῖ before, and add καὶ αὐτοί after, κληθήσονται, while here in Romans there is some textual support for the omission of αὐτοῖς or for the substitution of ἐὰν (ἂν) κληθήσονται for ἐρρέθη αὐτοῖς, and some for the omission of ὑμεῖς.

[7] For a Rabbinic parallel see Num R 2 (138ᶜ) quoted in SB 3, p. 273 (with reference to Rom 9.25).

realm of the heathen, so that there is real justification for regarding them as a type of rejection. But their restoration was promised in Hosea's prophecy, and Paul takes this promise as a proof of God's purpose to include the Gentiles in His salvation. But, in view of the sequel in chapters 10 and 11, it is most unlikely that Paul did not also have in mind the fact that the original reference was to 'that other, *rejected* Israel',[1] the ten lost tribes, and did not see in those lost tribes of Israel not only a type of the Gentiles but also the type of the unbelieving majority of his Jewish contemporaries.

It remains to refer to two details in these verses. First, with regard to καλέσω in v. 25 and κληθήσονται in v. 26, it is true that καλεῖν with a double accusative must mean 'call' in the sense of name, as Sanday and Headlam point out;[2] but the important thing to note is that the thought here is of an effectual naming, a naming which brings about a fundamental change in the condition of the object named, so that this naming corresponds to the effectual calling denoted by ἐκάλεσεν in v. 24.[3] And secondly, with regard to ἐν τῷ τόπῳ οὗ . . . , ἐκεῖ, it has sometimes been argued that Paul must have had in mind that gathering of the nations at Jerusalem to which such passages as Isa 2.2–4; 60.1–22; Mic 4.1–3; Zech 8.20–23 point.[4] It is true that, on the assumption that ἐκεῖ was not in the text of Hosea known to Paul (it is omitted by some LXX MSS.) but was added by him, there is some plausibility in the view that he wished to emphasize the idea of locality. But, in spite of passages like Joel 3.16; Amos 1.2, it is by no means clear that Jerusalem must be the place referred to in Hosea (the passage is after all concerned with the people of the northern kingdom of Israel). It is interesting that there seems to be no support for a reference to Jerusalem in the Rabbinic passages quoted in illustration of Rom 9.26 in SB 3, p. 273f (the Rabbis derived from Hosea's words rather the thought that God is rich in mercy towards His people even in the midst of His wrath against them). Others have taken the reference here in Romans to have been to all those places in which the Gentiles

---

[1] Barth, *CD* II/2, p. 231 (= *KD* II/2, p. 254).

[2] p. 264.

[3] That the action signified by καλέσω is God's is clear. In the case of κληθήσονται the reference might possibly be to their being called by men; but, in view of the fact that ἐρρέθη must refer to a divine action, it is natural to understand κληθήσονται to refer to their being called by God (it is exactly the same Hebrew expression, *yē'āmēr*, which is rendered in one place by ἐρρέθη and in the other by κληθήσονται).

[4] For further references see J. Jeremias, *Jesus' Promise to the Nations*, London, 1958, pp. 58–62.

have resided (and have had to bear the shame of not being God's chosen people). The variant reading ἐὰν (or ἄν) κληθήσονται instead of ἐρρέθη αὐτοῖς might perhaps reflect such an interpretation at an early date. But it is probable that this concentration on geography is uncalled for. It is quite likely that in Hos 1.10 (MT: 2.1) bimᵉḳôm 'ašer yēʼāmēr should be translated 'instead of its being said'[1] and not unlikely that Paul's Greek should be understood similarly.[2] And, even if this explanation is not accepted, it remains exceedingly hazardous to assume that Paul was thinking of any particular place when he used the words ἐν τῷ τόπῳ οὗ . . . ἐκεῖ.

27f. Having provided a scriptural confirmation of the καὶ ἐξ ἐθνῶν of v. 24, Paul now takes up the ἐξ Ἰουδαίων. But all that he has said so far has presupposed the fact that at present the great majority of Jews are unbelieving. Those whom God has so far called ἐξ Ἰουδαίων are but few in number. So in these verses Paul proceeds to show that a situation in which the great majority of Jews suffer exclusion is something which is foretold in Scripture. The burden of the passage quoted is that only a remnant will be saved. That Paul thought of this as a condition through which Israel must pass rather than as God's last word concerning Israel is, however, clear from the sequel in Romans 10 and 11.

Ἡσαΐας δὲ κράζει ὑπὲρ τοῦ Ἰσραήλ. Isaiah's threatening word is contrasted (δέ) with Hosea's word of promise. For the use of κράζειν[3] here compare the frequent use in Rabbinic literature of 'cry' (ṣāwaḥ) with reference to prophetic utterance:[4] in the NT compare Jn 1.15; 7.28, 37; 12.44. For ὑπέρ used instead of περί in the sense 'concerning' compare, for example, 2 Cor 1.8; 8.23. Though common in Attic and in Hellenistic Greek, in the NT it is virtually confined to Paul.[5]

ἐὰν ᾖ ὁ ἀριθμὸς τῶν υἱῶν Ἰσραὴλ ὡς ἡ ἄμμος τῆς θαλάσσης, τὸ ὑπόλειμμα σωθήσεται· λόγον γὰρ συντελῶν καὶ συντέμνων ποιήσει κύριος ἐπὶ τῆς γῆς. The quotation is an abbreviation of Isa 10.22–23. The form of the first part seems to have been assimilated by Paul (ἀριθμὸς τῶν υἱῶν in place of λαός) to the wording of Hos 1.10[MT: 2.1] (the sentence before the one just

---

[1] Cf. BDB, p. 880, s.v. מָקוֹם 7.b.

[2] Cf. Käsemann, p. 262; JB (translation of Rom 9.26, though not of Hos 1.10, which (numbered as 2.1) is placed after 3.5 in this version); Bauer, s.v. τόπος 2. d. There is an example of τόπῳ used in the sense 'instead of' from the third century A.D. in Herodian (the historian) 2.14.5.

[3] It was used in 8.15 in connexion with prayer: see on that verse.

[4] Cf. SB 3, p. 275.

[5] Cf. BDF, § 231 (1).

quoted). It is clear from the context in Isaiah that šᵉ'ār in the
MT and κατάλειμμα in the LXX must be translated 'only a
remnant', and this is no doubt the force of τὸ ὑπόλειμμα here.
Paul, following the LXX, has σωθήσεται, where the MT has
yāšûḇ ('shall return'). In the latter part of the quotation (v. 28)
the words ἐν δικαιοσύνῃ, ὅτι λόγον συντετμημένον, found in the
TR (with Western support) after συντέμνων but absent from
𝔓⁴⁶ ℵ A B, etc., are clearly an assimilation to the text of the
LXX. The Hebrew of Isa 10.23 is difficult, and the LXX
translators were apparently baffled by the details. Nevertheless,
both the LXX rendering and Paul's abbreviation of it, though
differing considerably from the MT, give the general idea of
the original quite correctly. For the thought and language
Isa 28.22 should be compared. The difficult συντελῶν καὶ
συντέμνων[1] here in Romans has been variously understood
(e.g. of God's fulfilling and abridging His promise regarding
Israel, i.e., fulfilling it but in a reduced form; of His fulfilling
His word and reducing Israel to a remnant; of His completing
and abridging His sentence, i.e., accomplishing it completely
and decisively (indicating the thoroughness and dispatch with
which it is executed)). Of these the last, which comes near to
the probable meaning of the Hebrew killāyôn . . . kālāh
wᵉneḥᵉrāṣāh, is the only one which is really probable. We may
translate v. 28, then, in some such way as the following: 'for a
sentence complete and decisive will the Lord accomplish upon
the earth' (literally: 'for a sentence, completing and abridging
it, will the Lord accomplish upon the earth'). It explains how
it will come about that only a remnant of Israel will be saved
(v. 27).

29. καὶ καθὼς προείρηκεν Ἡσαΐας. A second quotation from
Isaiah (1.9) is added in corroboration of the first. This time the
LXX text is reproduced exactly. The idea of a remnant is
present here too (in ἐγκατέλιπεν—the verb ἐγκαταλείπειν is, of
course, cognate with λεῖμμα and ὑπόλειμμα—and in σπέρμα);
but, whereas the point of the previous quotation was that only
a remnant will be preserved, the point of the present quotation
is that the preservation of even a remnant is a miracle of divine
grace—had not God's mercy spared a remnant, Israel would
have been utterly destroyed like Sodom and Gomorrah (Gen
19.24–25). Paul regarded the words of Isaiah's oracle which
referred to what was happening at the time of its utterance as
a foretelling (προείρηκεν) of the circumstances in which, in his
own time, a small number of Jews was included in the Church.

[1] For the use of the two verbs together cf. (in addition to LXX Isa
28.22) Dan 5.27 (LXX) and 9.24 (Theod.).

εἰ μὴ κύριος σαβαὼθ ἐγκατέλιπεν ἡμῖν σπέρμα, ὡς Σόδομα ἂν ἐγενήθημεν καὶ ὡς Γόμορρα ἂν ὡμοιώθημεν. σπέρμα presents something of a puzzle. The MT has *šārîḏ kimeʿaṭ* ('a few survivors', RV: 'a very small remnant'). *šārîḏ* is not Isaiah's characteristic word for 'remnant': he possibly refrained from using *šeʾār* here because he did not regard the survivors of 701 B.C. as the purified remnant of Israel.[1] The LXX translators represented *šārîḏ kimeʿaṭ* by σπέρμα, perhaps under the influence of the development of the idea of the future of God's people as 'the holy seed' (*zeraʿ haḳḳôḏeš*—e.g. Isa 6.13; Ezra 9.2).[2] Paul has already used σπέρμα in this chapter (vv. 7 and 8), and also of course earlier still in 1.3; 4.13, 16, 18 (cf. Gal 3.16, 19, 29); but it is doubtful whether it is really justifiable to assume that he here has consciously in mind the way in which he has used the word elsewhere.[3] It is perhaps rather more likely that he understood σπέρμα in this Isaiah verse simply as a way of expressing the idea of remnant but at the same time focusing attention on the hope for the future attaching to it.[4]

VI. 3. ISRAEL IS WITHOUT EXCUSE, BUT IN THE LIGHT OF SCRIPTURE WE MAY HOPE THAT THE FACT THAT GENTILES BELIEVE WILL PROVOKE ISRAEL TO JEALOUSY: THE OT QUOTATION IN THE LAST VERSE STRIKES A HOPEFUL NOTE IN THAT, WHILE IT INDICATES THE DREADFULNESS OF ISRAEL'S SIN BY SHOWING THE GOODNESS OF HIM AGAINST WHOM THEY HAVE SINNED, IT FOCUSES ATTENTION NOT ON ISRAEL'S SIN BUT ON GOD'S GOODNESS TOWARD ISRAEL (9.30–10.21)

[30]What then shall we say? That Gentiles, who were not pursuing righteousness, have obtained righteousness, but the righteousness of faith; [31]but Israel, which was pursuing the law of righteousness, has not attained to that law. [32]Why? *It was* because *they pursued it* not on

---

[1] Cf. J. Bright, in M. Black and H. H. Rowley (ed.), *Peake's Commentary on the Bible*, London, 1962, p. 490.

[2] Cf. G. Quell, in *TWNT* 7, p. 541. He notes however that *šārîḏ* has also been represented by σπέρμα in Deut 3.3, where this explanation is quite impossible, and mentions the suggestion of F. Wutz, *Die Transkriptionen von der Septuaginta bis Hieronymus*, Stuttgart, 1933, p. 76, that a σαρειδ, of which the last two letters had been lost, might have been read as *zeraʿ*.

[3] *Pace* Barth, *CD* II/2, p. 233 (= *KD* II/2, p. 256); Barrett, p. 191f (cf. p. 181); Murray 2, p. 41.

[4] This is not, of course, to deny that Paul firmly believed that the election of the remnant of Israel rested on Christ alone, but only that this thought was necessarily in Paul's mind in connexion with the use of σπέρμα in this quotation.

the basis of faith but as on the basis of works. They stumbled against the stone of stumbling, [33]even as it is written: 'Behold, I lay in Zion a stone of stumbling and a rock of offence, and he who believes on him shall not be put to shame.' [1]Brethren, as for me, the desire of my heart and my prayer to God for them are that they may be saved. [2]For I bear them witness that they have zeal for God, yet not according to knowledge. [3]For, failing to recognize the righteousness of God, and seeking to establish their own, they did not submit to the righteousness of God. [4]For Christ is the end of the law, so that righteousness is available to every one who believes. [5]For Moses writes that 'the man who does' the righteousness which is of the law 'shall live in' it. [6]But the righteousness which is of faith speaks thus: 'Say not in thine heart, "Who shall ascend into heaven?" ' (that is, to bring Christ down); [7]'nor "Who shall descend into the abyss?" ' (that is, to bring Christ up from the dead). [8]But what does it say? 'The word is near thee, in thy mouth and in thine heart': this means the word of faith which we preach. [9]For, if thou dost confess with thy mouth Jesus as Lord and dost believe in thine heart that God has raised him from the dead, thou shalt be saved. [10]For with the heart one believes unto justification, and with the mouth confession is made unto salvation. [11]For the scripture says: 'Everyone who believes on him shall escape being put to shame.' [12]For there is no distinction between Jew and Gentile. For the same Lord is *Lord* of all, being rich toward all who invoke him: [13]for 'Everyone who invokes the name of the Lord shall be saved'.

[14]How could they invoke one in whom they had not believed? And how could they believe in one they had not heard? And how could they hear without a preacher? [15]And how could people preach unless they had been sent? *Relevant here is the testimony of* the scripture *which* says, 'How beautiful are the feet of those who bring good news of good things!' [16]But not all obeyed the good news. For Isaiah says: 'Lord, who hath believed our message?' [17]It is implied that faith comes of hearing, and hearing comes about through the word of Christ. [18]But I say, did they not hear? They did indeed—'Their voice is gone out into all the earth, And their words to the ends of the inhabited world.' [19]But I say, was Israel without knowledge? First Moses says: 'I will use a nation that is no nation to make you jealous, And a foolish nation to make you angry.' [20]And Isaiah is so bold as to say: 'I let myself be found of those who were not seeking me, I made myself manifest to those who were not inquiring after me.' [21]But concerning Israel he says: 'All the day long I stretched out my hands to a disobedient and gainsaying people.'

In the previous section Paul has spoken of the disobedience of Israel as embraced within the work of the divine mercy and has also referred (in 9.24) to the inclusion of Gentiles in the number of those called by God. But both the nature of Israel's disobedience and the nature of the Gentiles' obedience need to be defined more closely. So now in the first paragraph of the new section, that is, in vv. 30–33, Paul gives this necessary definition in summary form.[1]

[1] On vv. 30–33 reference may be made for a fuller discussion to C. E. B. Cranfield, 'Some notes on Romans 9.30–33', in E. E. Ellis and E. Grässer (ed.), *Jesus und Paulus: Festschrift für Werner Georg Kümmel zum 70. Geburtstag*, Göttingen, 1975, pp. 35–43.

In the rest of the section, that is, in chapter 10, he proceeds to expand, develop and clarify this summary definition, concentrating more particularly on that part of it which deals with Israel (though not exclusively—see, in particular, vv. 11 and 12 and 18–20), and bringing out clearly the fact that Israel is without excuse. Paul acknowledges (v. 2) the reality of Israel's zeal for God, but refers to the disastrous failure of comprehension which distorts and perverts their zeal, their blindness to the righteousness which is God's gift and obstinate determination to establish their own righteousness on the basis of their works, which result in a refusal to accept God's proffered gift humbly as the undeserved gift of His mercy. Verse 4 explains v. 3: what Israel had failed to recognize was that Christ had been all along the goal, the meaning, the substance, of that law which they had been so earnestly pursuing. Verses 5–13 provide explication and substantiation of v. 4: Christ is τέλος . . . νόμου . . . εἰς δικαιοσύνην παντὶ τῷ πιστεύοντι, in that (in accordance with the testimony borne by the law) He has by His perfect obedience earned a status of righteousness both for Himself (with reference to His earthly life) and also for all who will believe in Him (whether Jews or Gentiles), a status which is His by merit,[1] but theirs by faith.

Rom 9.30–10.13 has made the guilt of Israel abundantly clear: it is guilty because it has failed to obey its own law,[2] that very law for which it has been so zealous. It was to faith in Christ that the law was all along leading. But the fact that the law, the inner meaning of which is Jesus Christ, has been committed to Israel does not by itself constitute such a full opportunity to call upon the Lord in the sense of vv. 12 and 13 as would render Israel without excuse. Only if the message that the promises have now been fulfilled has been proclaimed by messengers duly commissioned by God Himself is that fullness of opportunity present. In vv. 14ff Paul is concerned to show that Israel has had that fullness of opportunity and is therefore absolutely without excuse. He first indicates by a chain of related questions (vv. 14–15a) four conditions which must have been fulfilled if they are *truly* to call upon the name of the Lord. The fact that the first and second conditions (the

---

[1] Our intention here is not to deny what Calvin rightly seeks to safeguard in *Institutes* 2.17.6, but simply to bring out the contrast between Christ's righteousness and ours.

[2] Cf. Barth, *CD* II/2, p. 247 (= *KD* II/2, p. 272): 'The Synagogue does not have to choose between the authority to which it knows . . . itself to be responsible and another newly arisen . . . quantity. It has to choose between fulfilment and non-fulfilment in face of the authority recognized by itself.'

fourth and the third in the chain of vv. 14–15a) have been fulfilled is attested by the words of prophecy quoted in v. 15b: God has commissioned messengers and they have proclaimed the message. It is the fourth condition (the first mentioned in v. 14) which is unfulfilled: Israel has not believed in Christ (the fact is stated in v. 16a in the words ἀλλ' οὐ πάντες ὑπήκουσαν τῷ εὐαγγελίῳ). In v. 17 Paul comes back to the third condition (Christ must be heard speaking through the message), which was passed over in v. 16, and indicates by means of another OT quotation (v. 18) that this condition has been fulfilled. The subject of a further condition (or a sub-division of the third) is introduced in v. 19a by the question 'was Israel without knowledge?', and the fact that Israel was not without knowledge is then indicated in vv. 19b and 20 by means of two further quotations from the OT. By this point it is evident that Israel is altogether without excuse for its unbelief.

Finally the quotation of Isa 65.2 in the last verse of the section serves, on the one hand, to gather up all that has already been said concerning Israel's disobedience and, by characterizing it unmistakably as the obstinate rejection of God's patient grace, to bring out as sharply as possible its full seriousness and enormity, and, on the other hand, to point even more emphatically to the unwearying persistence of God's graciousness, and so to bring the section to an end on a note of hope.

30. Τί οὖν ἐροῦμεν; is here used to introduce not a false inference which is going to be rejected, as in v. 14, but Paul's own conclusion from what he has been saying.[1]

ὅτι ἔθνη τὰ μὴ διώκοντα δικαιοσύνην κατέλαβεν δικαιοσύνην. By ἔθνη is meant not 'the Gentiles' (as in AV and RV), nor 'the pagans' (as in JB), but 'Gentiles' without the article;[2] for the reference is not to the Gentiles generally, but just to some Gentiles, namely, those who have believed. To understand δικαιοσύνην here in a different sense from that which it has in its two subsequent occurrences in this same verse, as some do, is surely extremely harsh, and it is clear that in both those other occurrences of the word the reference must be not to moral righteousness but to righteous status in God's sight. So we take Paul's intention to be not to deny that in their former

---

[1] There seems to be no cogent reason (*pace* Michel, p. 249) for thinking that Paul is here concerned with a Jewish opponent's objection. Some have taken vv. 30b–31 as a question (Paul does sometimes follow τί (οὖν) ἐροῦμεν; by a further question); but Michel, p. 250, n. 2 continued from previous page, rightly argues that the parallelism with v. 32 shows that it must be a statement.

[2] Cf. Barrett, p. 192f; RSV; NEB.

pagan life¹ the Gentile Christians had sought after moral
righteousness (some of them no doubt had desired moral
righteousness more or less seriously), but to deny that they had
truly and seriously sought after² righteous status in the sight
of the one and only true God. In spite of the fact that they
were not seeking it, these Gentiles have obtained a status of
righteousness before God. καταλαμβάνειν can mean 'overtake',
and is a natural correlative to διώκειν. The two verbs occur
together also in Phil 3.12.

δικαιοσύνην δὲ τὴν ἐκ πίστεως is added to underline the fact that
the righteous status, which these Gentiles have obtained, is
theirs only by faith, not by their deserving. Compare 1.17;
3.22, etc.

31. Ἰσραὴλ δὲ διώκων νόμον δικαιοσύνης εἰς νόμον οὐκ ἔφθασεν.
What one expects after v. 30 is: Ἰσραὴλ δὲ διώκων δικαιοσύνην
εἰς δικαιοσύνην οὐκ ἔφθασεν. Had Paul written that, his meaning would be clear. But, instead of the expected double
δικαιοσύνην, he has written νόμον δικαιοσύνης and νόμον (with
δικαιοσύνης no doubt to be understood). In such a situation it
is important that we should try to resist both the temptation
to rewrite Paul's sentence for him³ and also the temptation to
treat Greek grammar as though it were a waxen nose that can
be pulled into any shape one pleases. The rendering of JB,
'looking for a righteousness derived from law', for instance,
should surely be rejected as an example of surrender to the
latter temptation.⁴ Had Paul meant this, what reason could
he have had for not using either δικαιοσύνην νόμου or (on the
analogy of δικαιοσύνην . . . τὴν ἐκ πίστεως which he had just
used in v. 30) δικαιοσύνην τὴν ἐκ νόμου (cf. 10.5)? Moreover,
any interpretation which assumes that by νόμον δικαιοσύνης
in v. 31 Paul intended to indicate something which the Jews

---

¹ The present participle has here an imperfect sense. Barrett's
translation ('who do not make righteousness their aim'—p. 192) mis-
represents Paul's meaning: Paul is not likely to have meant to deny that
the Gentile Christians are seeking after a status of righteousness before
God now that they are Christians.

² For διώκειν in the sense it has here ('pursue', 'follow after') cf., e.g.,
12.13; 14.19; 1 Cor 14.1. It suggests an energetic, zealous quest (see note
on 12.13). The metaphor is a familiar OT one (e.g. Deut 16.20; Isa 51.1).
Paul also uses διώκειν in the sense 'persecute' (e.g. 12.14; 1 Cor 4.12; 15.9).

³ So Schmiedel's conjectural emendation of the second νόμον to
δικαιοσύνην should surely be rejected.

⁴ In spite of its highly respectable ancestry, which includes Chrysostom, col. 563; Calvin, p. 217; Bengel, p. 544; RSV. If νόμον δικαιοσύνης
were really an instance of hypallage, surely Paul would either have
repeated the full phrase in the main clause or else have put δικαιοσύνην
there alone rather than νόμον.

were wrong to aim at, falls foul of v. 32; for v. 32 implies that
it was not the object of their pursuit which was wrong but
the way in which they had pursued it (had they pursued it
ἐκ πίστεως instead of ὡς ἐξ ἔργων, they would have been doing
what was required). Why then did Paul introduce the word
νόμος at this point? Surely because he wanted to bring out
the truth that Israel had been given the law to aid it in its
quest for righteousness before God.[1] The law is the law of
righteousness because it was intended and designed to show the
people of Israel how they could be righteous before God, to
show them that the way to this righteousness is—faith.[2] In the
law which they were pursuing so zealously they had that which
was all the time pointing out the way to the possession of a
status of righteousness in God's sight. It was important for
Paul's argument that he should at this point make it as clear
as possible that the disobedient majority of Israel had not just
been seeking in a general way after righteousness before God,
but had actually been pursuing specifically that very thing
which was indeed the way appointed for them to lead them to
that righteousness. The majority of Jews have zealously
pursued the law of God which had been given to them to bring
them to a status of righteousness in God's sight: their tragedy
is that, though they have pursued God's law, and still are
pursuing it, with so much zeal, they have somehow failed
altogether really to come to grips with it, failed altogether to
grasp its real meaning and to render it true obedience.

32a. διὰ τί; ὅτι οὐκ ἐκ πίστεως ἀλλ' ὡς ἐξ ἔργων explains why
Israel εἰς νόμον οὐκ ἔφθασεν. But, before we can draw out the
meaning of v. 32a, several preliminary matters need to be settled.
There is first the matter of punctuation. It is possible (i) to
put a comma after ἔργων and to construe the verse as follows:
'Why? (It was) because, (pursuing it) not on the basis of faith
but as on the basis of works, they stumbled . . .' (according to this
punctuation, from ὅτι right to the end of v. 33 is all the answer
to διὰ τί); or (ii) to put a colon or full stop after ἔργων and to
construe as follows: 'Why? (It was) because (they pursued it)
not on the basis of faith but as on the basis of works. They
stumbled . . .' (according to this punctuation, only ὅτι . . . ἔργων

---

[1] δικαιοσύνης is taken by some to mean 'which requires righteousness'
(e.g. Zahn, p. 471); but it is more probable that it means 'which promises
righteousness (i.e. a status of righteousness before God)' (cf. Käsemann,
p. 465), since in the sentence which balances v. 30 it is much more
natural to take δικαιοσύνη in the sense of righteousness of status than in
the sense of righteousness of life.

[2] Cf. 3.21f; 10.6–13.

is the answer to διὰ τί).[1] Of these, (ii) is to be preferred as being simpler and more natural. Had Paul intended (i), it is unlikely that he would have left the participle to be understood. With regard to two other matters (the verb which has to be supplied and the object which has to be supplied), we have assumed above that διώκοντες or ἐδίωξαν must be supplied, and with it αὐτόν referring to the νόμος δικαιοσύνης mentioned in v. 31. But other views have been maintained. Thus Käsemann supplies a verb which does not occur in the context at all, translating 'Weil es nicht aus Glauben sondern im Wahn aus Werken [lebte]'[2] and Barrett understands δικαιοσύνην as the object of Israel's quest (he translates: 'Because they did not pursue their aim by faith . . .', and comments, 'Paul now means their aim of achieving righteousness').[3] But these suggestions show too little respect for Paul's ability to write competent Greek prose, and strike us as counsels of despair dictated by a preconception with regard to Paul's view of the law. The only verb, surely, which it is at all natural to supply is διώκειν, whether in the indicative or as a participle, and the only object which it is natural to supply for it is the object of διώκων in v. 31, that is, νόμον (δικαιοσύνης). There remains one other preliminary matter, the question of the textual variation. Should νόμου be read after ἔργων? There is little doubt that it should not be read. It is almost certainly due to assimilation (cf. 3.20, 28; Gal 2.16; 3.2, 5, 10).

We may now attempt an explanation of the significance of this half-verse. It gives the reason why Israel εἰς νόμον οὐκ ἔφθασεν. It was because they pursued it not ἐκ πίστεως but ὡς ἐξ ἔργων. It is of the greatest importance to recognize something which is often completely ignored, namely, that there is not the slightest suggestion here that to *pursue* the law was wrong or useless. It is not for its pursuit of the law, not on account of the *fact that* it had pursued, and was still pursuing, the law, that Israel is condemned, but for the *way in which* it had pursued the law. The implication is that Paul thought that, had Israel pursued the law ἐκ πίστεως, it would indeed truly

---

[1] The possibility of understanding the ὅτι clause as dependent on προσέκοψαν ('Because (they pursued it) not on the basis of faith but on the basis of works, they stumbled. . . .') must be ruled out on the ground that ὅτι must introduce the answer to διὰ τί.

[2] p. 264.

[3] p. 193 (cf. Michel, p. 249). In his 'Romans 9.30–10.21: fall and responsibility of Israel', in L. de Lorenzi (ed.), op. cit., pp. 99ff, Barrett has now given a radically different interpretation of this and the next verse (coming very close to the interpretation which we put forward in E. E. Ellis and E. Grässer (ed.), op. cit., pp. 35ff), though what he says about the law on p. 120 seems hardly consistent with it.

have come to grips with it, and that his desire for Israel was
not that it should henceforward not pursue the law, but that
it should cease to pursue it ὡς ἐξ ἔργων and henceforward
pursue it ἐκ πίστεως. The importance of this for a proper
understanding of Paul's attitude to the law is obvious. What
then is this pursuit of the law ἐκ πίστεως? The answer must be,
surely, that it is to respond to the claim to faith which God
makes through the law, and must include accepting, without
evasion or resentment, the law's criticism of one's life, recognizing that one can never so adequately fulfil its righteous
requirements as to put God in one's debt, accepting God's
proffered mercy and forgiveness and in return giving oneself to
Him in love and gratitude and so beginning to be released from
one's self-centredness and turned in the direction of a humble
obedience that is free from self-righteousness; that it is to
allow oneself to be turned again and again by the forgiving
mercy of God in the direction of loving Him with all one's heart
and soul and mind and strength and of loving one's neighbour
as oneself. The tragedy of Israel was that, instead of thus
responding to the law of God with faith and pursuing it on the
basis of faith, they had sought to come to terms with it ἐξ ἔργων,
that is, on the basis of their works, their deserving, cherishing
the illusion that they could so fulfil its demands as to put God
under an obligation to themselves. Such an illusory quest could
only result in failure—in imprisonment in one's own self-
centredness, and so in failure really to get to grips with the law,
failure to comprehend its true meaning. It was probably with
the intention of underlining the illusory character of Israel's
quest that Paul placed a ὡς before ἐξ ἔργων.[1]

32b–33. προσέκοψαν τῷ λίθῳ τοῦ προσκόμματος. The asyndeton
at the beginning of this sentence[2] gives to the whole of vv. 32b–
33 a special solemnity[3] which accords well with the substance
of what is being said. The latter half of v. 32 states the heart
of the matter. This is the inward meaning of Israel's failure to
come to grips with the law; this is the inward meaning of its
obstinate pursuit of the law on the basis of works instead of
on the basis of faith. Israel has failed to recognize Him who
is the meaning and the goal of the law, and has rejected Him.

---

[1] Cf. Bauer,s .v. ὡς III.3; BDF, § 425 (3); Käsemann, p.265f. A different explanation is given by Bengel, p. 544.

[2] According to the punctuation preferred above.

[3] Asyndeton between sentences, while common in hortatory passages
like chapter 12, is rare in the parts of the epistles which contain continuous argument. In such passages a sentence introduced asyndetically
stands out. There is another instance close at hand in 10.1. Reference
may be made to BDF, § 462.

How could it really come to grips with the law, if it was not ready to believe in Him who is the law's innermost meaning? But how could it believe in Him, if it was determined to rely on its own works? So they have stumbled over Christ (cf. 1 Cor 1.23—Ἰουδαίοις μὲν σκάνδαλον. He who was given for their salvation has thus, because of their perverseness, actually proved to be the occasion of their fall. The phraseology anticipates the quotation which is to follow in v. 33.

καθὼς γέγραπται introduces a quotation which is a conflation of two quite separate passages.

ἰδοὺ τίθημι ἐν Σιὼν λίθον προσκόμματος καὶ πέτραν σκανδάλου, καὶ ὁ πιστεύων ἐπ' αὐτῷ οὐ καταισχυνθήσεται. The basis is Isa 28.16, the MT of which is rendered in the RV as follows: 'therefore thus saith the Lord GOD, Behold, I lay in Zion for a foundation a stone, a tried stone, a precious corner *stone* of sure foundation: he that believeth shall not make haste.' The LXX differs from the MT in several respects; but the only differences of consequence in the part of the verse which is reproduced in Romans are that the LXX translators apparently read *yēḇōš* instead of the problematic *yāḥîš*, and so rendered the last two words οὐ μὴ καταισχυνθῇ, and that they added ἐπ' αὐτῷ, where the Hebrew means simply 'he that believeth'. The original meaning of the verse seems to have been that, in contrast with the false security which the rulers of Jerusalem had thought to establish for themselves, God was establishing true and lasting security in Jerusalem for those who trusted in Him. But the passage came to be understood in Judaism messianically. Of this interpretation the LXX addition of ἐπ' αὐτῷ is perhaps the earliest evidence.[1] In the Targum the passage is reproduced as follows: 'Behold, I appoint a king in Zion, a mighty king, an heroic and terrible; I strengthen him and uphold him. The prophet has said: And the righteous, in whom is faith, shall not be shaken, when tribulation comes.'[2] Here in Rom 9.33 the middle part of Isa 28.16 has been replaced by some words from Isa 8.14, and the tenor of the quotation has thereby been radically altered. An element of promise remains in the last part, but a strong note of judgment and threatening has been introduced into the passage.[3] In the words introduced from

[1] Cf. J. Jeremias, in *TWNT* 4, p. 276. The B text of the LXX, however, omits ἐπ' αὐτῷ.

[2] Quoted in SB 3, p. 276. In 1QS 8.7 this Isaiah verse is applied to the Council of the Community. See also the use made of it in 1QH 6.26f.

[3] For the words πρόσκομμα (and προσκόπτειν) and σκάνδαλον (and σκανδαλίζειν) cf. 14.13, 20, 21 and 11.9; 14.13, 21; 16.17, respectively; and reference should be made to G. Stählin, in *TWNT* 6, pp. 745-59, and 7, pp. 338-58, as well as to Bauer, s.vv.

Isa 8.14 the quotation is nearer to the MT (*ûle'eḇen neḡeḟ ûleṣûr mikṣôl*) and to Aquila and Theodotion (εἰς λίθον προσκόμματος καὶ εἰς πέτραν (Aq.: στερεὸν) πτώματος (Aq.: σκανδάλου)) than to the LXX. In Isa 8.14 it is God Himself who will be 'for a stone of stumbling and for a rock of offence to both the houses of Israel' (RV). The fact that the same two Isaiah texts are also combined in 1 Pet 2.6–8 (together with Ps 118.22) and the fact that the form of the text used there shows agreements with that used by Paul over against both the MT and LXX have been seen as supporting the view that a collection of 'stone' testimonies was part of the early tradition of the Church.[1] For Christ as the stone compare Mt 21.42 = Mk 12.10 = Lk 20.17; Mt 21.44 = Lk 20.18; Acts 4.11; 1 Pet 2.4, 6–8.[2] The last part of the quotation (καὶ ὁ πιστεύων, κ.τ.λ.)[3] provides Paul with a statement of the theme of justification ἐκ πίστεως to be worked out in 10.4–13.

What vv. 32b and 33 have done is to add an explicitly Christological dimension to the definition of the disobedience of Israel and of the obedience of some Gentiles which has already been given in vv. 30–32a. That disobedience and that obedience are essentially a matter of relationship to Christ. Israel's pursuit of the law ὡς ἐξ ἔργων was blindness to the law's witness to Christ. Its legalistic misunderstanding and perversion of the law and its rejection of Him were inextricably intertwined. Its determination to establish its own righteousness by its works naturally made it blind to the righteousness which God was making available in Christ as a free gift, while its failure to recognize Christ as the true innermost substance of the law could only drive it deeper into legalistic misunderstanding and perversion of the law. And the faith which is the basis of the righteous status now possessed by some Gentiles according to v. 30 is, of course, faith in Christ—that faith which bears the promise, 'he who believes on him shall not be put to shame'.

1. Ἀδελφοί.[4] See on 1.13.

ἡ μὲν εὐδοκία τῆς ἐμῆς καρδίας. The force of μέν, which here stands by itself without any corresponding δέ, is 'so far as it

---

[1] Cf. J. R. Harris, *Testimonies* 1, Cambridge, 1916, pp. 18f, 26f; C. H. Dodd, *According to the Scriptures*, London, 1952, p. 42f; B. Lindars, *New Testament Apologetic*, London, 1961, pp. 175ff, 241ff.

[2] See further J. Jeremias, in *TWNT* 4, pp. 272–83; Taylor, *Names*, pp. 93–99.

[3] The variant reading which gives πᾶς before ὁ πιστεύων (cf. 10.11) is not likely to be original.

[4] For the asyndeton see on 9.32b.

depends on my desire'.[1] εὐδοκία must here (*pace* Sanday and Headlam[2]) mean 'desire'.[3]

καὶ ἡ δέησις[4] πρὸς τὸν θεόν. Bengel's often quoted observation, 'Non orasset Paulus, si absolute reprobati essent',[5] is worth repeating. The fact that Paul continued to pray for the unbelieving Jews, who had 'stumbled against the stone of stumbling', is clear proof that he did not think of their present rejection as final and closed.

ὑπὲρ αὐτῶν.[6] It makes no substantial difference to the sense of the sentence, whether we take these words as part of the predicate (with the Vulgate and RV) or as part of the subject (with Lagrange, the RSV, Michel).[7]

εἰς σωτηρίαν indicates the aim toward which Paul's desire and prayer are directed, and so is really equivalent to ἵνα σωθῶσιν. In this prayer for Israel's salvation he has set an example for the Church to follow. A church which failed to pray for Israel's salvation would be a church which did not know what it means to be the Church of Jesus Christ.[8]

2. μαρτυρῶ γὰρ αὐτοῖς ὅτι ζῆλον θεοῦ ἔχουσιν.[9] μαρτυρεῖν properly denotes a public, responsible and solemn action. Paul solemnly testifies to his fellow-countrymen's zeal for God. The γάρ indicates the connexion with v. 1. The fact that their zeal for God is such as to call for this testimony is a[10] reason for his desiring and praying for their salvation; and the recipients of the letter will be the better able, because of this testimony, to

---

[1] BDF, § 447 (4). Barrett's attempt (p. 195f)to bring out the force of μέν by inserting into his translation the supplement 'Scripture or no Scripture' is altogether misleading, since it introduces into Paul's sentence a thought which is quite foreign to it and altogether out of harmony with his attitude to Scripture.

[2] p. 282.

[3] Cf. Bauer, s.v. 3; G. Schrenk, in *TWNT* 2, p. 743. The only other occurrences of εὐδοκία in the Pauline corpus are Eph 1.5, 9; Phil 1.15; 2.13; 2 Th 1.11. It is almost confined to Jewish and Christian Greek, appearing first in the LXX (as a translation of rāṣôn). See further *TWNT* 2, pp. 740–48.

[4] The addition of ἡ after δέησις in K L is an obvious grammatical improvement. See BDF, § 272.

[5] p. 544. Cf. Leenhardt, p. 264.

[6] The variants, τοῦ Ἰσραήλ for αὐτῶν, and τοῦ Ἰσραήλ + ἐστιν, are attempts at clarification.

[7] While the question of the right way of construing ὑπὲρ αὐτῶν can hardly be decisively settled, it is perhaps rather more natural to take it, along with πρὸς τὸν θεόν, as qualifying δέησις.

[8] Cf. Gaugler 2, p. 90.

[9] For μαρτυρεῖν with the dative of the person about whom witness is borne and with a following ὅτι, cf. Mt 23.31; Jn 3.28; Gal 4.15; Col 4.13.

[10] We do not have to infer that it was the only reason or even the main reason.

comprehend the earnestness of his desire and prayer. The genitive θεοῦ is objective ('zeal for God'). Compare the use of ḳin'āh, ḳinnē', in the MT and of ζῆλος, ζηλοῦν, in the LXX to denote the zeal of the faithful for God's glory, for the temple, for the law: e.g. Num 25.11, 13 (ἀνθ᾽ ὧν ἐζήλωσεν τῷ θεῷ αὐτοῦ); I Kgs 19.10 and 14 (Ζηλῶν ἐζήλωκα τῷ κυρίῳ παντοκράτορι); 2 Kgs 10.16 (ἰδὲ ἐν τῷ ζηλῶσαί με τῷ κυρίῳ Σαβαωθ); Ps 69.9 [LXX: 68.10] and 119[LXX: 118].139 (ὁ ζῆλος τοῦ οἴκου σου); Jth 9.4 (οἳ καὶ ἐζήλωσαν τὸν ζῆλόν σου); Ecclus 45.23 (ἐν τῷ ζηλῶσαι αὐτὸν ἐν φόβῳ κυρίου); I Macc 2.26 (ἐζήλωσεν τῷ νόμῳ), with which compare 2.27, 50, 58. In the NT compare especially Acts 21.20; 22.3; Gal 1.14. Such zeal for God is the hall-mark of orthodox Judaism in every century. 'Every page of Rabbinic literature', observes Billerbeck,[1] 'reminds one of this word of the apostle.' Both ζῆλον and θεοῦ are emphatic and important here. Their zeal is zeal for God. It is no heathen fanaticism of an empty ideology, but zeal for the true God. Israel is absolutely right in the object of its zeal. And it is undoubtedly zeal—fervent, strenuous, tenacious, concentrated zeal. There is no support here for any patronizing superciliousness on the part of Christians. Indeed, orthodox Judaism puts much that passes for Christianity, and even much true Christianity, to shame both in respect of the seriousness of its zeal and by the fact that its zeal is really zeal for God.

ἀλλ᾽ οὐ κατ᾽ ἐπίγνωσιν. In spite of the earnestness of their zeal, in spite of the fact that it is truly zeal for the true God, there is a disastrous flaw in it—it is not according to knowledge. Paul certainly does not mean to deny that they know God (cf. v. 19). They do indeed know God, and yet they will not know Him as He really is. There is a lack of comprehension at the most vital point. It is a matter of seeing indeed but not perceiving, of hearing indeed but not understanding (cf. Mk 4.12). There is a perverse and obstinate ignorance at the very heart of their knowledge of God, and in the centre of their dedicated and meticulous obedience an obstinate disobedience.

3. ἀγνοοῦντες γὰρ τὴν τοῦ θεοῦ δικαιοσύνην, καὶ τὴν ἰδίαν ζητοῦντες στῆσαι, τῇ δικαιοσύνῃ τοῦ θεοῦ οὐχ ὑπετάγησαν. Paul now provides the explanation (hence γάρ) of οὐ κατ᾽ ἐπίγνωσιν. He does so in a carefully balanced sentence made up of two participial subordinate clauses connected by καί, (a) and (b), and of a main clause (c). It is probably better to understand (a) and (b) as together defining the nature of Israel's ignorance, and (c) as indicating the act of disobedience which resulted from it, than to regard (c) as itself the essential definition of Israel's ignor-

[1] SB 3, p. 276f.

ance. The ignorance of the unbelieving Jews consists in their failure to comprehend and to acknowledge the righteousness of God, that is, God's proffered gift of a status of righteousness in His eyes (see on 1.17), and—what is but the other side, the reverse, of this failure—their stubborn determination to establish their own righteousness, that is, a righteous status of their own earning. It is indeed an ignorance of God's own character, a failure to know Him as He really is, and as He has revealed Himself, as the merciful God. And the act of disobedience resulting from this ignorance is their refusal to submit to God's righteousness, that is, their refusal to humble themselves to accept it as an undeserved gift.[1] It is the refusal to let grace be grace, the refusal to give God alone the glory. But the aorist indicative οὐχ ὑπετάγησαν (like προσέκοψαν in 9.32) was no doubt used because Paul had in mind an historical event, the rejection of the Messiah. And—though Paul does not (in this section) make this absolutely explicit until vv. 4ff[2]—it was in Jesus Christ that God's gift of righteousness was offered, and Israel's ignorance of God's righteousness was identical with its failure to recognize Jesus Christ.

4. τέλος γὰρ νόμου Χριστὸς εἰς δικαιοσύνην παντὶ τῷ πιστεύοντι. The interpretation of this verse has been much debated down the centuries. It has been, and still is, understood in altogether contrary senses. But its importance is not disputed. For not only is it vital for the understanding both of 9.30–10.3 and also of 10.5–13; it is also clearly one of the fundamental theses of Pauline theology as a whole, since, in whatever way it is taken, it is obviously a decisive statement concerning the relation of Christ and the law.

Two less difficult matters may conveniently be referred to before we attempt to decide the meaning of τέλος, the ambiguity of which constitutes the main problem of the verse. The first concerns the structure of the sentence. The natural way to construe it is to take τέλος νόμου as the predicate thrown forward for the sake of emphasis and Χριστός as the subject. Had Paul intended to say that the τέλος of (the) law is Christ, he would surely have used the article with τέλος. The second matter is more controversial: it concerns the reference of νόμου. It has been maintained by a number of commentators (among them Sanday and Headlam,[3] and Zahn[4]) that νόμος here

---

[1] Pelagius's comment on τῇ δικαιοσύνῃ τοῦ θεοῦ οὐχ ὑπετάγησαν is suggestive: '. . . noluerunt se remissioni subicere peccatorum, ne peccatores fuisse uiderentur, . . .' (p. 81).

[2] Jesus Christ is not mentioned by name between 9.5 and 10.4.

[3] p. 284.

[4] p. 475f.

means not 'the law' in the sense of the OT law specifically, but 'law' as a principle, law generally. But the arguments adduced in favour of this interpretation are not at all convincing,[1] and, in view of the whole context (note especially 9.31), the great majority of commentators from patristic times onward are surely right in taking the reference to be to the OT law.

The Greek word τέλος is patient of an extraordinarily wide variety of meanings, including performance, consummation, fulfilment, result, event, power of deciding, supreme power, validity, magistracy, government, decision, task, duty, tax or due, military unit, maturity, completion, end, finish, cessation, achievement, goal, prize, purpose—to mention only some of the meanings indicated in LSJ. By no means all of these, of course, are represented in the NT. In the history of the exegesis of this verse support has generally been distributed between three main possible interpretations of τέλος: (i) fulfilment; (ii) goal; (iii) termination. The Fathers seem generally to have tended toward a combination of (i) and (ii).[2] Mt 5.17 played an

---

[1] Sanday and Headlam (p. 284) rightly recognize that they cannot rely on the absence of the article before νόμου. Their threefold argument is that the interpretation of νόμου in a general sense is necessitated 'by the whole drift of the argument . . ., by the words παντὶ τῷ πιστεύοντι proving that the passage cannot be confined to the Jews, and consequently not to the Mosaic law, and by the correct reading in ver. 5 τὴν ἐκ νόμου'.

[2] Clement of Alexandria, after quoting Rom 10.2–3, comments: 'For they did not know and do what the law willed (τὸ βούλημα τοῦ νόμου), but they thought that the law willed (βούλεσθαι) what they supposed. Nor did they believe the law as prophesying, but only the bare word (λόγῳ δὲ ψιλῷ); and they followed out of fear, and not out of disposition and faith. "For Christ is the end of the law unto righteousness", who was prophesied by the law, "to every one that believeth"' (Strom. 2.9). Cf. 4.21: 'But gnostic perfection in the case of the legal man consists in accepting the gospel, in order that he who is according to the law may become perfect. For so Moses, who was according to the law, foretold that it was necessary to hear, in order that we might receive, according to the apostle, the πλήρωμα of the law, even Christ.' Less clear is 6.11: ' "I must decrease," said the prophet John, and the Word of the Lord alone "increase", εἰς ὃν περαιοῦται ὁ νόμος.' Origen in his commentary on Romans has this comment: 'Finis enim legis Christus: hoc est perfectio legis et justitia Christus' (col. 1160). Eusebius says in his Demonstratio Evangelica (8.2.33): 'This agrees with the saying of the Saviour, "I came not to destroy the law or the prophets, but to fulfil them". "For Christ is the end of the law", and all the prophecies about Him remained unfulfilled and unaccomplished (ἀπλήρωτοι καὶ ἀτελεῖς), until He Himself came and added fulfilment (ἐπιτέθεικεν . . . τέλος) to all the things foretold concerning Him.' John Chrysostom (col. 565) understands τέλος in the sense of goal, and illustrates the meaning of Paul's statement by the proposition that health is the goal of medicine (καὶ γὰρ τέλος ἰατρικῆς ὑγίεια). Pelagius (p. 81) has the comment: 'He who believes in Christ is, on the very day on which he comes to believe, as one who has fulfilled

important part in determining their interpretation of Rom 10.4.
Sanday and Headlam claim Augustine's support for (iii);[1] but,
while it is true that he recognized that Christ had freed us from
the burdens of the law (including of course its condemnation),
he certainly explained 'finis' in this verse in the sense of
'perfectio' and explicitly rejected the meaning 'abolition'.[2]
Aquinas says on this verse that the law 'ordinat homines in
Christum quem promittebat, et praefigurabat. . . . Et hoc est
quod dicit "Christus enim est finis legis", ad quem scilicet tota
lex ordinatur.'[3] Luther, referring to Paul's use of Deut 30 in this
chapter, says: 'It is as if he wanted to give us an impressive
proof of the fact that the whole Scripture, if one contemplates
it inwardly, deals everywhere with Christ, even though in so far
as it is a sign and a shadow, it may outwardly sound differently.
This is why he says: "Christ is the end of the law" (Rom. 10.4);
in other words: every word in the Bible points to Christ.'[4]
Calvin in the course of his longish and interesting comment on
this verse expresses approval of 'completion' or 'perfection'

the whole law.' Theodoret (col. 164) stresses that faith in Christ is not
opposed to, but very much in agreement with, the law. 'For the law has
led us to the Lord Christ. The man who has faith in Christ is, therefore,
the one who fulfils the law's aim (σκοπόν).' Gennadius also speaks of the
law's σκοπός, but says: 'Christ fulfils (τελειοῖ) the aim of the law, by
bestowing righteousness through faith in Him on all those who come to
Him' (in Cramer, p. 370). Cyril of Alexandria expressly denies that
Christians assert that the law has been destroyed. The position is rather
that it was fulfilled (ἐκπεπεράνθαι) when Christ, the truth, shone upon us.
He continues: 'For Christ is the τέλος of the law and the prophets, who is
not to be thought of as lying when He said, "I came not to destroy the
law, but to fulfil it" '; and then, by way of illustration, claims that the
addition of colours to an artist's preliminary drawing does not destroy
the drawing, μεθίστησι δὲ μᾶλλον εἰς ὄψιν ἐναργεστέραν (in Cramer, p. 371).
Euthymius comments: ΄Ὥσπερ τέλος ἰατρικῆς ὑγίεια [cf. Chrysostom
quoted above]· οὕτω τέλος καὶ βούλημα νόμου δίκαιον ποιῆσαι τὸν ἄνθρωπον, ὡς
προείρηται. Ἐπεὶ οὖν ὁ Χριστὸς τοῦτο πεποίηκε, τέλος καὶ βούλημα νόμου ὁ
Χριστός, ὅπερ ὁ νόμος ἐβούλετο ποιήσας. Ὁ τοῦτον νῦν ἔχων τὸν Χριστὸν διὰ τῆς
πίστεως καὶ τέλος τοῦ νόμου ἔχει, λέγω δὴ τὴν δικαιοσύνην· ὁ δὲ τοῦτον μὴ
ἔχων οὐδὲ ἐκεῖνον πάντως ἔχει (p. 118). In contrast with those quoted
above, Irenaeus might perhaps be claimed as lending support to interpretation (iii). He says (Haer. 4.12.4), after quoting Rom 10.3-4, 'And
how is Christ the τέλος of the law, if He is not also its ἀρχή? For he who
has brought in the τέλος has also Himself wrought the ἀρχή.'

[1] p. 285.
[2] 'Finis legis Christus ad justitiam omni credenti: hic enim finis
perfectionem significat, non consumptionem' (In Ps. IV Enarratio 1).
'Dicit enim Apostolus, Finis enim legis Christus ad justitiam omni
credenti. Finis non consumens, sed perficiens; duobus enim modis
dicimus finem: vel quo fit ut non sit quod erat, vel quo fit ut perfectum
sit quod inchoatum erat' (In Ps. XXX Enarratio 2. Sermo 1.1).
[3] p. 152 (819).
[4] p. 288.

(the rendering of Erasmus) as a translation of τέλος, though he is himself content with the word 'end'. He says of the Jews: 'it is evident that they had shamefully mutilated the law of God, for they rejected its soul and snatched at the dead body of the letter', and concludes his comment by saying: 'This remarkable passage declares that the law in all its parts has reference to Christ, and therefore no one will be able to understand it correctly who does not constantly strive to attain this mark.'[1] Bengel also takes τέλος here in a positive sense, explaining it as synonymous with πλήρωμα, and referring to 1 Tim 1.5; Rom 13.10, and Mt 5.17.[2] But in recent times (iii) has been very widely supported—for example, by Sanday and Headlam, Lietzmann,[3] Lagrange, Dodd, Gaugler, Michel, Käsemann,[4] to mention only a few.[5] Others have attempted to combine (iii) with one or other or both of the interpretations (i) and (ii). Leenhardt, for example, makes such statements as 'Jesus brought the law to its culminating point and at the same time suspended it' and 'Thus Christ fulfils the underlying intention of the law and supersedes it';[6] and Barrett, having said that 'the word "end" (τέλος) means not only "termination", but also "purpose", or "intention" ', states: 'He puts an end to the law, not by destroying all that the law stood for but by realizing it'.[7] But, in view of such passages as 7.12, 14a; 8.4; 13.8–10, and of the categorical statement in 3.31, and also of

---

[1] p. 221f. In *Institutio* 3.2.6 he does, it is true, use the verb 'abolere' in this connexion ('Qua etiam ratione alibi (Rom 10.4) dicit, fidei adventu legem abolitam fuisse: hac voce comprehendens novum et insolitum docendi genus, quo patris misericordiam magis illustravit, et de salute nostra certius testatus est Christus, ex quo apparuit magister'), but the following explication softens its significance.

[2] p. 544.

[3] So oblivious of the conceivability of any other interpretation was Lietzmann that in his comment on 13.8 he could write: 'That Paul here, as in 8.4, speaks without trace of embarrassment of "fulfilment of the law" as something worth striving after and seems to have forgotten chapter 7 and 10.4, is characteristic of the unschematic nature of his discourse', p. 113 (my translation).

[4] We may now add to the list H. Schlier, *Der Römerbrief*, Freiburg, Basel, Wien, 1977, p. 311.

[5] It is indicative of the confidence with which this interpretation has been maintained that both NEB and JB have renderings of this verse which allow only for it, in contrast with AV, RV and RSV, which use the ambiguous English substantive 'end' and so allow for both (ii) and (iii). (It might perhaps be maintained that AV left open also the possibility of (i), since as late as 1679 'end' was also used to denote 'completion of an action; accomplishment of a purpose' (*The Shorter Oxford English Dictionary*, Oxford, 1956 (corrected impression of 3rd ed., 1944), s.v. II.5).)

[6] p. 266.   [7] p. 197f.

the fact that Paul again and again appeals to the Pentateuch in support of his arguments (specially suggestive is the fact that he does so in vv. 6–10 of this chapter), we regard (iii) and also all attempted combinations of (iii) with (i) and/or (ii) as altogether improbable. (It is, of course, true that there are a number of passages in the Pauline epistles which are often understood to mean that the law has been abolished by Christ, and if this view of them could be shown to be likely, it would indeed lend support to the choice of interpretation (iii) here; but we are convinced that there is no statement in any of Paul's epistles which, rightly understood, implies that Christ has abolished the law. For a discussion of the passages in question the reader is referred to pp. 852–61.) Between (i) and (ii) it is more difficult to decide, and it is tempting to settle for the view that both meanings were intended. The statement that Christ is the fulfilment of the law and the statement that He is its goal are indeed correlatives: they express the same essential truth but describe it as seen from different angles, and each is necessary for the adequate exposition of the other. But, while the former is quite clearly a statement about Christ, a description of Him in terms of the law, the latter, though it also is formally, and indeed to some extent substantially, a statement about Christ, is in substance primarily a statement about the law, defining it by reference to Christ.[1] And in the present context (9.30–10.13) a statement about the law seems more apposite; for in this passage Paul is concerned to show that Israel has misunderstood the law. At this point a statement that Christ is the goal to which all along the law has been directed, its true intention and meaning, is altogether apposite. Israel has misunderstood the law, because it failed to recognize what it was all about. A statement to the effect that Christ is the fulfilment of the law would be much less apposite. So we conclude that τέλος should be understood in sense (ii): Christ is the goal, the aim, the intention, the real meaning and substance of the law—apart from Him it cannot be properly understood at all.

The words εἰς δικαιοσύνην παντὶ τῷ πιστεύοντι are the corollary of τέλος . . . νόμου Χριστός. The εἰς is consecutive. If Christ is the goal of the law, it follows that a status of righteousness is available to every one who believes.[2]

We conclude that the verse as a whole means: For Christ is

---

[1] This is perhaps what Sanday and Headlam were feeling after in their rather mysterious statement that, if τέλος were taken to mean 'goal', then 'Χριστός would become the predicate' (p. 285).

[2] Some who understand τέλος in the sense of termination have pro-

the goal of the law, and it follows that a status of righteousness is available to every one who believes. The γάρ at the beginning of the verse indicates that it is an explanation of v. 3— particularly of τῇ δικαιοσύνῃ τοῦ θεοῦ οὐχ ὑπετάγησαν. The Jews in their legalistic quest after a righteous status of their own earning have failed to recognize and accept the righteous status which God was seeking to give them; for all along, had they but known it, Christ was the goal and meaning and substance of that law which they were so earnestly pursuing, and the righteousness to which the law was summoning them was all the time nothing other than that righteousness which God offers to men in Christ.

5. Μωϋσῆς γὰρ γράφει ὅτι τὴν δικαιοσύνην τὴν ἐκ νόμου ὁ ποιήσας ἄνθρωπος ζήσεται ἐν αὐτῇ. It will be well to begin by stating three things which can be said about this verse without much fear of contradiction: (i) the γάρ indicates that either v. 5 by itself or the whole of vv. 5–8 is thought of as being in some way explanatory of v. 4; (ii) there is a contrast between v. 5 and vv. 6–8 (hence the δέ in v. 6); (iii) the verse contains a quotation from Lev 18.5.

About the text there is some disagreement. Whereas Nestle and BFBS have the ὅτι immediately after γράφει, Merk and UBS have it after νόμου. The Nestle and BFBS text gives the sense, 'For Moses writes that the man who does the righteousness . . .' (or it could be read as 'For Moses writes, "The man . . ." '); but the text as given by Merk and UBS, which exhibits an instance of a kind of prolepsis, could be rendered: 'For Moses writes concerning (or perhaps 'describes') the righteousness . . ., that the man who does it . . . '. This latter form of the text might seem to favour, though it certainly does not necessitate, acceptance of the interpretation designated (1) below. But there seems to be a close connexion between the reading which puts ὅτι after νόμου and two other readings, which are not adopted by Merk or UBS, namely, the addition of αὐτά after ποιήσας and the substitution of αὐτοῖς for αὐτῇ, both of which are supported by largely the same authorities as place ὅτι after νόμου. To separate these, adopting one of them and rejecting the others, would seem to require very

posed that εἰς δικαιοσύνην should be taken very closely with νόμου, so as to give the meaning, Christ is the end, i.e., termination, of the-law-as-the-way-of-attaining-to-righteousness-before-God (so e.g., Murray 2, p. 50). But, while this would be a way of taking τέλος in the sense of termination and yet avoiding an interpretation which makes nonsense of such Pauline passages as 3.31; 7.12, it seems extremely unlikely in view of the order of the sentence (had Paul meant this, he would surely at least have placed εἰς δικαιοσύνην next to νόμου).

strong justification. And it looks very much as if all three readings should be explained as assimilation to the text of LXX Lev 18.5 (both αὐτά and αὐτοῖς occur in Lev 18.5, and the introduction of αὐτά would necessitate the removal of τὴν δικαιοσύνην τὴν ἐκ νόμου from the ὅτι clause[1]). We conclude that the text as read by Nestle is almost certainly to be preferred.[2] [Nestle[26] has here changed Nestle[25]—in my view, unwisely.]

Two main interpretations of v. 5 have to be considered.
(1) The usual explanation of the verse is that it is intended to indicate the hopeless nature of the quest after a righteous status before God on the basis of works, which is contrasted with the way of justification by faith described in vv. 6–8.[3] According to this interpretation, v. 5 would be related to v. 4 (as we have explained it) in some such way as the following: The fact that Christ is the goal of the law means that a righteous status is available to all who believe in Him (v. 4); for, while justification by works is the hopeless quest that Moses indicates (v. 5), Scripture has all along set forth the glorious possibility of justification by faith (vv. 6–8). Verses 5–8 as a whole would be an explanation of v. 4.
(2) It is possible to understand Paul to be applying the words of Lev 18.5, not to the impossible, hopeless task which men set themselves when they think to earn a righteous status before God by their own works, but to the achievement of the one Man who has done the righteousness which is of the law in His life and, above all, in His death, in the sense of fulfilling the law's requirements perfectly and so earning as His right a righteous status before God.[4] Along these lines we might

---

[1] Since αὐτά would have to be the object of ποιήσας, and there would be no room for a second object.

[2] Nestle mentions three further variants: the addition of τοῦ before νόμου; πίστεως in place of νόμου; and the omission of ἄνθρωπος. Of these, the first is an obvious 'improvement', the second is most likely a slip (ἐκ πίστεως occurs in the next verse), and the last is perhaps assimilation to Gal 3.12. None of these is likely to be original.

[3] e.g., Calvin, p. 223f.

[4] So Barth, *CD*, II/2, p. 245 (= *KD* II/2, p. 270); id., *Shorter*, p. 127. There is a difficulty here, as also in interpretation (1), in the fact that the τὴν δικαιοσύνην τὴν ἐκ νόμου is the object of ποιήσας (unless, of course, we accept the reading which places ὅτι after νόμου *and also* the addition of αὐτά after ποιήσας), which makes it necessary either to understand δικαιοσύνη in a different sense from that in which it is used in 9.30 (probably also 9.31); 10.3, 4, 6 (so Barth, *CD*, II/2, p. 245, explains the phrase as meaning 'the merciful will of God expressed in the law' [but why then ἐκ?]), or else to recognize here a kind of pregnant use of ποιεῖν (with some such sense as 'do the righteous requirement of the law and so earn'). The latter would seem possibly to be the more satisfactory

possibly regard only v. 5 as intended to be explanatory of v. 4 (Christ is the goal of the law, for what Moses declares in Lev 18.5 is Christ's obedience and victory); but it is much more satisfactory to regard the whole of vv. 5–13 as intended to explain v. 4 (not just τέλος . . . νόμου Χριστός, but εἰς δικαιοσύνην παντὶ τῷ πιστεύοντι as well). In accordance with Lev 18.5 Christ has—alone among men—obeyed perfectly and so earned a righteous status and eternal life for Himself,[1] but also (vv. 6–13) for all those who will believe in Him. In either case, the point of the δέ in v. 6 is the contrast between the righteous status which Christ has by His obedience, by His works, and the righteous status which men have through faith in Him.

Of these, (2) has, we are inclined to think, the stronger claim to acceptance; for it yields a more closely knit sequence of thought.[2]

6. ἡ δὲ ἐκ πίστεως δικαιοσύνη οὕτως λέγει. We have already referred to the δέ. The personification of the righteousness of faith is a rhetorical device which could be paralleled from the popular philosophical preaching of Paul's time in which virtues and vices are sometimes represented as speaking.[3] It is a lively and picturesque way of saying that the true nature of righteousness on the basis of faith is set forth in the sentences from the OT which are going to be quoted. What is specially noteworthy here is the fact that it is in the law itself, in Deuteronomy, that Paul hears the message of justification by faith. That a theologically significant contrast between γράφει in v. 5 and λέγει in v. 6 (hinting at the opposition between γράμμα

solution. It is not hard to understand Paul's being led into this grammatical awkwardness here; for, on the one hand, his argument required the use of the expression ἡ δικαιοσύνη ἡ ἐκ νόμου, and, on the other hand, Lev 18.5 presented him with ὁ ποιήσας. (The verb ποιεῖν can, of course, have other meanings besides 'do'—e.g. 'gain', which might on the surface seem appropriate here; but the fact that it has the sense 'do' in Lev 18.5 seems to make a solution, that is simply along this line, difficult.) It could be that this difficulty was actually the cause, or a contributory cause, of the variants, ὅτι after νόμου, the addition of αὐτά, and substitution of αὐτοῖς for αὐτῇ.

[1] But see p. 505, n. 1.

[2] Gal 3.12 might, at first sight, seem to tell against this interpretation. But it is probable that in Gal 3.12 also Paul, in quoting Lev 18.5, has in mind Christ's perfect obedience; for otherwise a step in the argument is missing. Verse 13 goes on to say that Christ has redeemed us from the law's curse by becoming accursed for us; but His becoming accursed (Paul refers this to the Cross) would have no redemptive power, were He not Himself the altogether righteous One, who has fulfilled a perfect obedience.

[3] See Bultmann, *Stil*, p. 87f.

and πνεῦμα) was intended by Paul strikes us as very improbable.[1]

μὴ εἴπῃς ἐν τῇ καρδίᾳ σου reproduces exactly the opening words of two verses of the LXX version of Deuteronomy (8.17 and 9.4). It is significant that both these verses are warnings against a self-complacent, presumptuous boasting in one's own merit. In the former the Israelite is forbidden to say in his heart (i.e., to think to himself), 'My power and the might of mine hand hath gotten me this (LXX adds: 'great') wealth'; in the latter to say, 'For my righteousness (LXX: 'righteousnesses') the LORD hath brought me in to possess this (LXX adds: 'good') land'. Thus the thought of the verses from which these words are quoted is, as Leenhardt who is one of the most helpful of commentators on vv. 6ff has pointed out, 'completely in conformity with the doctrine of "justification by faith"'.[2] But Paul does not go on to quote further from either of the verses from which these words are taken. Instead he quotes (with very considerable freedom) parts of Deut 30.12–14.

τίς ἀναβήσεται εἰς τὸν οὐρανόν; is part of Deut 30.12, which in the LXX reads: οὐκ ἐν τῷ οὐρανῷ ἄνω ἐστὶν λέγων Τίς ἀναβήσεται ἡμῖν εἰς τὸν οὐρανὸν καὶ λήμψεται αὐτὴν ἡμῖν; καὶ ἀκούσαντες αὐτὴν ποιήσομεν. The reference is to the commandment. The previous verse has said: 'For this commandment which I command thee this day, it is not too hard for thee; neither is it far off'. Israel does not have to climb up to heaven[3] to discover God's will; for He has graciously shown them what is good by His law, and that law is simple and clear. They do not have to inquire after the will of a harsh or capricious tyrant. They have received the revelation of the merciful will of the God whose prior grace is the presupposition of all He requires.[4] Essentially what He asks is that they should give Him their hearts in humble gratitude for His goodness to them and in generous loyalty to their fellows.

τοῦτ' ἔστιν Χριστὸν καταγαγεῖν. The expression τοῦτ' ἔστιν is used three times in vv. 6–8 to introduce Paul's interpretation of the OT passage he has just quoted (in the third occurrence the interpretation of a particular word in the quotation). It is a special use, and reflects the exegetical terminology of

---

[1] See Käsemann, p. 274f; H. Schlier, op. cit., p. 311.
[2] p. 268.
[3] For 'climbing up to heaven' as a way of indicating the impossible cf. the Rabbinic material cited in SB 3, p. 281, § 3, and especially the passage quoted in the previous § to which it refers back; also Lietzmann, p. 96.
[4] As, e.g., in the Decalogue (Exod 20.2; Deut 5.6).

Judaism.[1] Thus in 1QS 8.14 Isa 40.3 is quoted, and then line 15
continues (interpreting the words 'way' and 'high way' in the
quotation): 'That is[2] the study of the law,which He commanded
through Moses . . .'; and in 1QpH 12.7f the writer, commenting
on Hab 2.17, says with reference to 'the city' in that verse:
'the city, that is[3] Jerusalem, where the Wicked Priest . . . '.
We may compare the use of *pēšer* (= 'interpretation') which is
specially characteristic of the Qumran biblical commentaries,
occurring most frequently in the formula 'its interpretation
concerns'.[4] This formula is used, like the 'that is' formula, to
introduce an interpretation applying the words of Scripture to
persons and events of the time of the Teacher of Righteousness
and that following his activity. For example, in 1QpH 7.4f the
words from Hab 2.2, 'that he may run that readeth it', are thus
applied: 'its interpretation concerns the Teacher of Righteousness, to whom God made known all the mysteries of the words
of His servants the prophets'. We might then translate Paul's
words: 'Interpreted, this refers to bringing Christ down.'

But what are we to make of Paul's treatment of Deut 30.11ff
as biblical interpretation? Is it merely arbitrary, like much of
the exegesis of Qumran—a matter of forcing upon an OT
passage a meaning essentially foreign to it? So it has certainly
seemed to many. Even as sympathetic a commentator as
Gaugler can speak of it as 'a specially crass example' of the
typological method of interpretation.[5] At first sight it looks
like this; for Deuteronomy is speaking about the law, and Paul
refers what it says to Christ. But, if our understanding of Paul's
view of the law is right, he did not think of Christ and the law
as two altogether unrelated entities; on the contrary, he saw
the closest inner connexion between them. Christ is the goal,
the essential meaning, the real substance of the law. It is
therefore only as one sets one's eyes on Christ, that one can see
both the full significance of that graciousness of the law which
comes to expression in this Deuteronomy passage and also the
full seriousness of its imperatives. On this view of the relation
of Christ and the law there is a real inward justification for
what Paul is doing here. It is not arbitrary typology but true
interpretation in depth. Between the fact that God's law was
addressed directly to the Israelite's heart, requiring faith and
obedience, and was not something esoteric to be first discovered

[1] Cf. Michel, p. 257, n. 2.
[2] *hî'āh*.
[3] *hî'*.
[4] *pišrô 'al* . . .
[5] 2, p. 124.

by human searching, and the fact that the Son of God has now become incarnate, so that there can be no question of man's needing to bring Him down, there is an intimate connexion; for behind both the gift of the law and the incarnation of the Son of God is the same divine grace—that grace, the primary and basic initiative of which was God's election of man in Jesus Christ.

7. τίς καταβήσεται εἰς τὴν ἄβυσσον; (cf. Ps 107[LXX: 106].26) is substituted for the Τίς διαπεράσει ἡμῖν εἰς τὸ πέραν τῆς θαλάσσης . . .; of LXX Deut 30.13, which offered no point of contact with the history of Christ. The word ἄβυσσος occurs in the LXX upwards of thirty times, nearly always representing *teͅhôm*. It usually denotes the depths of waters. So it is used of 'the deep' of Gen 1.2. Elsewhere it is used of the depths of the sea (e.g. Ps 107[LXX: 106].26). Twice in Deuteronomy (8.7 and 33.13) it denotes subterranean waters. But in Ps 71[LXX: 70].20 (. . . καὶ ἐπιστρέψας ἐζωοποίησάς με καὶ ἐκ τῶν ἀβύσσων τῆς γῆς πάλιν ἀνήγαγές με) it is used of the depths of the earth as the place of the dead, i.e. Sheol, and it is clearly in this sense that Paul uses it here.[1]

For τοῦτ᾽ ἔστιν see on v. 6.

Χριστὸν ἐκ νεκρῶν ἀναγαγεῖν. Just as there is no point in wanting to mount up to heaven to bring Christ down, now that the Incarnation has taken place, so neither is there any point in wanting to descend into Sheol to bring Christ up from the dead, since He has already been raised. For the phraseology compare Heb 13.20, the only other place in the NT where ἀνάγειν is used with reference to the Resurrection. For the general thought implied by this verse compare the use of Ps 16.10 in Acts 2.27.

The questions which Deut 30.12–13 sets aside indicate excuses for not responding to the law with the grateful trust in God's mercy and generous loyalty to one's fellow men which it requires. As interpreted in Rom 10.6–7, they describe the attitude of those who, because of their failure properly to comprehend the law, fail also to recognize their Messiah when He has come to them.

8. ἀλλὰ τί λέγει; The variant readings which include ἡ γραφή as the subject of λέγει are easily understandable as secondary amplifications. The subject to be supplied is ἡ ἐκ πίστεως δικαιοσύνη (v. 6).

ἐγγύς σου τὸ ῥῆμά ἐστιν, ἐν τῷ στόματί σου καὶ ἐν τῇ καρδίᾳ σου.

---

[1] Cf. the use of *teͅhôm* in the Mishnah (e.g. *Pes.* 7.7; *Naz.* 9.2) with reference to an unsuspected grave. In the NT ἄβυσσος occurs also in Lk 8.31 and Rev 9.1, 2, 11; 11.7; 17.8; 20.1, 3.

Deut 30.14[1] indicates the essentially gracious character of the
law in which God had stooped down to reveal His will to
Israel and to claim each Israelite for Himself and for his
neighbour: God had drawn near to them in His word which
could be taken on their lips and received in their hearts. But
all along His nearness to Israel by means of His law pointed
forward to His gift of Himself to men in Jesus Christ. The
justification for Paul's application of the verse in the words
which follow is the close relation between the law and Christ.
Many commentators, who have failed to see this close relation
and have insisted on reading into Paul's theology a stark
opposition between Christ and the law, have made unneces-
sarily heavy weather of this passage. More perceptive was the
alternative interpretation offered by Pelagius: 'Sive: Ideo illos
semper iubet legem meditari, ut ibi Christum ualeant inuenire'.[2]

τοῦτ' ἔστιν τὸ ῥῆμα τῆς πίστεως ὃ κηρύσσομεν. The relative
clause indicates that τὸ ῥῆμα τῆς πίστεως denotes not the
confession of faith but the gospel message itself.[3] The justification for Paul's bold identification of 'the word' in Deut
30.14 with the gospel preached by himself and other Christian
preachers is the fact, as Paul sees it, that it is Christ who is the
substance and innermost meaning of the law. The genitive has
been variously explained (e.g., 'which is worthy of being
believed', 'which creates and supports faith', 'the subject of
which is faith'); but the most likely meaning is 'which calls for
(the response of) faith'. Zahn's comparison of νόμος πίστεως in
3.27 is helpful.[4] It is unlikely that πίστις is used in the sense of
fides quae creditur.

9. It is grammatically possible to punctuate with a comma
at the end of v. 8, and to understand ὅτι in the sense 'that' and
v. 9 as indicating the content of the ῥῆμα τῆς πίστεως. But
(pace Barrett[5]) the explanation of τὸ ῥῆμα τῆς πίστεως as
denoting the gospel certainly does not necessitate this interpretation. It is far more natural to take ὅτι in the sense
'because' or 'for', and to understand v. 9 as explaining the
statement, ἐγγύς σου τὸ ῥῆμά ἐστιν, ἐν τῷ στόματί σου καὶ ἐν
τῇ καρδίᾳ σου. The statement of v. 8a is true, because all that one
has to do, in order to be saved, is to confess with one's mouth

---

[1] Paul does not quote the whole of the verse, omitting the la‘aśōṯô
(RV: 'that thou mayest do it'; LXX: αὐτὸ ποιεῖν) as well the LXX's
addition (καὶ ἐν ταῖς χερσίν σου).
[2] p. 82.
[3] Cf. Barrett, p. 200.
[4] p. 481.
[5] p. 200.

Jesus as Lord and to believe—really believe—in one's heart
that God has raised Him from the dead.

ἐὰν ὁμολογήσῃς ἐν τῷ στόματί σου κύριον Ἰησοῦν, καὶ πιστεύσῃς
ἐν τῇ καρδίᾳ σου ὅτι ὁ θεὸς αὐτὸν ἤγειρεν ἐκ νεκρῶν. The order of
the two conditional clauses, at first sight surprising since
confession issues from belief, is no doubt due to the fact that
'in thy mouth' precedes 'in thy heart' in Deut. 30.14: in the
next verse Paul reverses the order. The content of the confession and the content of the belief are differently formulated,
but in Paul's thought they amount to the same thing. He does
not mean to imply that the mouth is to confess anything
other than that which the heart believes.[1] But the two
formulations interpret each other, so that what is to be both
believed and confessed is the more precisely defined.[2]

For the use of ὁμολογεῖν[3] with a double accusative[4] we may
compare Jn 9.22.

With ὁμολογήσῃς . . . κύριον Ἰησοῦν compare 2 Cor 4.5,
where the double accusative construction is used as here; 1 Cor
12.3 and Phil 2.11, in which κύριος Ἰησοῦς (Χριστός) is a
statement; and also 1 Cor 8.6; Col 2.6. In view of the evidence
of this clause, in which the presence of ὁμολογεῖν is suggestive,
and of the other passages just cited, it seems clear that κύριος
Ἰησοῦς was already an established confessional formula.[5] It is
probable that it was used in connexion with baptism (the
present verse—perhaps also the fact that baptism was in, or
into, the name of Jesus[6]—would seem to point in that direction), but also in Christian worship generally.[7] Doubtless the

[1] The inseparability of the confession and the belief was succinctly
stated by Pelagius (p. 82): 'Testimonium cordis est oris confessio'.

[2] The suggestion in Sanday and Headlam, p. 290 (cf. Lagrange, p. 258)
that κύριον Ἰησοῦν is intended specially to correspond to the contents of
v. 6 and ὅτι ὁ θεὸς αὐτὸν ἤγειρεν ἐκ νεκρῶν to the contents of v. 7 does not
seem to us at all likely; for the κύριος-title and the Resurrection are
elsewhere very closely connected together (see, e.g., 4.24), and, as
indicated in the text above, the two formulations in this verse are to be
understood as interpreting each other rather than as focusing attention
on separable facts about Christ in distinction from each other.

[3] On the various uses of ὁμολογεῖν and its cognates in the NT see
Michel, in *TWNT* 5, pp. 199ff.

[4] For the construction see BDF, § 157(2); § 416(3).

[5] The reading of B (supported by sa Cl), which has τὸ ῥῆμα after
ὁμολογήσῃς and ὅτι κύριος Ἰησοῦς instead of κύριον Ἰησοῦν may perhaps
have originated in a desire to make the reference to the actual credal
formula more explicit.

[6] Cf. Acts 2.38; 8.16; 10.48; 19.5; 1 Cor 1.13 (by implication): also
Rom 6.3 (εἰς Χριστὸν Ἰησοῦν). And 1 Cor 6.11 probably refers to baptism.

[7] 1 Cor 12.3 may be relevant here; also 2 Cor 4.5; Phil 2.11.

contrast with the use of κύριος as a title of the Roman emperor[1] will have given to the κύριος Ἰησοῦς formula a special significance, but it is not likely that it originated as a response to κύριος Καῖσαρ. That Christians in the Greek-speaking world were well aware of the fact that κύριος and κυρία were commonly used with reference to the various pagan deities, especially of the oriental-Hellenistic religions, is, of course, unquestionable (Paul himself refers to these κύριοι πολλοί in 1 Cor 8.5). But the contention of Bousset[2] and Bultmann[3] that the title 'Lord' was first applied to Jesus under Hellenistic influence and in a Hellenistic environment must be rejected; for—to mention one obvious objection—the fact that Paul uses the formula μαράνα θά in its original Aramaic form in a Greek letter to Greek-speaking Christians (1 Cor 16.22) points unmistakably to its being a very early liturgical formula (cf. the use of 'Abba' in 8.15 and Gal 4.6), and so to the use of 'Lord' as a title of the exalted Christ in early Aramaic-speaking Christianity. If the Aramaic is rightly divided in Nestle (as it probably is: ἔρχου κύριε Ἰησοῦ in Rev 22.20 may well be confirmation of this, and we may also compare *Didache* 10.6), then the formula is a prayer to the exalted Christ. If the third 'a' is given to the second, rather than to the first, word,[4] the formula would be a confession of faith ('Our Lord has come' (or 'comes')). In either case, it is a natural conclusion that we have to look to the primitive Aramaic-speaking church rather than to a church of the sort envisaged by Bousset as the place where the designation of Jesus as 'Lord' originated.[5]

It is important to remember that in Greek, Hebrew and Aramaic alike the relevant words (κύριος, 'ăḏôn and mār) could be used in non-religious senses like 'lord', 'owner', 'master'; and it is likely that during His ministry Jesus was sometimes addressed by His disciples as mārî ('my lord') or māran(ă') ('our lord') in a sense equivalent to 'Rabbi', 'teacher' or 'revered teacher'. But it would seem that after the Resurrection He was still so addressed, but now no longer with the word bearing the sense of 'Teacher', but as the object of

---

[1] Cf., e.g., Dittenberger, *Syll.* 814.31 (ὁ τοῦ παντὸς κόσμου κύριος used of Nero); *Mart. Pol.* 8.2 (for a later date).

[2] *Kyrios Christos.*

[3] *Theology* I, p. 124.

[4] Unless it is then taken as standing for 'e in Aramaic, in which case the meaning would still be 'Our Lord, come'.

[5] Bousset's embarrassment by the evidence of 1 Cor 16.22 can be seen from the way in which he oscillates between different attempts to explain it in the successive editions of his book.

invocation in prayer, and that He was also referred to in the third person as 'our Lord' or 'the Lord'.

What then did the confession 'Jesus is Lord' mean for Paul? The use of κύριος more than six thousand times in the LXX to represent the Tetragrammaton must surely be regarded as of decisive importance here. In support of this view the following points may be made:

(i) Paul applies to Christ, without—apparently—the least sense of inappropriateness, the κύριος of LXX passages in which it is perfectly clear that the κύριος referred to is God Himself (e.g. 10.13; 1 Th 5.2; 2 Th 2.2).

(ii) In Phil 2.10 he describes the κύριος title as τὸ ὄνομα τὸ ὑπὲρ πᾶν ὄνομα, which can hardly mean anything else than the peculiar name of God Himself.[1]

(iii) He apparently sees nothing objectionable in the invocation of Christ in prayer (the μαράνα θά of 1 Cor 16.22 is, as we have seen, probably to be understood as a prayer; and Paul approves of calling upon the name of the Lord Christ—see 10.12–14 and 1 Cor 1.2—though ἐπικαλεῖσθαι is a technical term for invoking in prayer); but, for a Jew, to pray to anyone other than the one true God was utterly abhorred.

(iv) He associates Christ with God again and again in ways which imply nothing less than a community of nature between them. Thus without any sense of incongruity he can name together 'God our Father' and 'the Lord Jesus Christ' as the source of grace and peace (1.7; 1 Cor 1.3; 2 Cor 1.2) and can speak indifferently of the love of God and the love of Christ (e.g. 8.35 and 39).

We take it that, for Paul, the confession that Jesus is Lord meant the acknowledgment that Jesus shares the name and the nature, the holiness, the authority, power, majesty and eternity of the one and only true God. And, when, as is often the case, there is joined with the title κύριος a personal pronoun in the genitive, there is expressed in addition the sense of His ownership of those who acknowledge Him and of their consciousness of being His property, the sense of personal commitment and allegiance, of trust and confidence.[2]

---

[1] The suggestion that 'the name which is above every name' is the name 'Jesus' (C. F. D. Moule, 'Further reflexions on Philippians 2.5–11', in *Apostolic History*, p. 270, does not convince us.

[2] On the title 'Lord' see further: G. Quell and W. Foerster, in *TWNT* 3, pp. 1038–98; Taylor, *Names*, pp. 38–51; id., *Person of Christ*; Cullmann, *Christology*, pp. 195–237; Whiteley, *Theology*, pp. 99–108; W. Kramer, *Christ, Lord, Son of God* (Eng. tr. of *Christos Kyrios Gottessohn*, 1963), London, 1966; F. Hahn, *The Titles of Jesus in Christology*

For the use of πιστεύειν ὅτι see on 6.8; and for Christ's
resurrection as God's action see on 4.24. The aorist indicative
ἤγειρεν indicates here a unique, once-for-all act. It is significant
that it is the Resurrection which is mentioned—an indication
that for Paul the belief that God raised Jesus from the dead is
the decisive and distinctive belief of Christians, the *articulus
stantis et cadentis ecclesiae* (cf. 1 Cor 15.14: εἰ δὲ Χριστὸς οὐκ
ἐγήγερται, κενὸν ἄρα τὸ κήρυγμα ἡμῶν, κενὴ καὶ ἡ πίστις ὑμῶν,
and v. 17: εἰ δὲ Χριστὸς οὐκ ἐγήγερται, ματαία ἡ πίστις ὑμῶν
[ἐστιν], ἔτι ἐστὲ ἐν ταῖς ἁμαρτίαις ὑμῶν). The formulation of
what is the content (not only) of the confession (but also of the
faith) in terms of Jesus' being Lord has provided a necessary
clarification of the following formulation in terms of the
Resurrection; for it has made it clear that His resurrection was
no mere resuscitation of a corpse only for it to die again, but
God's decisive and irrevocable sealing of Him who was crucified
as the eternal Lord. And now the formulation of what is the
content (not only) of the faith (but also of the confession) in
terms of the Resurrection makes it clear that the Lord with
whom Christians are concerned is no mythological or symbolic
figure like the 'lords many' (1 Cor 8.5) familiar to the pagan
world, but one who has lived a real human life and died a
shameful death under Pontius Pilate, and also (since Christ
raised is the ἀπαρχὴ τῶν κεκοιμημένων (1 Cor 15.20: cf. v. 23))
points to the eschatological significance of His Lordship.

σωθήσῃ. For σῴζειν see on 1.16 (σωτηρία) and on 5.9 and 10.
The reference is to eschatological salvation, the inheriting of
eternal life (cf. 5.9f; Mk 10.17, etc.); but future eschatological
salvation reflects its glory back into the present for those who
confidently hope for it (see on 5.2). The promise of salvation
was often expressed in association with the rite of baptism (see
Mk 16.16; Acts 8.37 (E variant reading): cf. also Acts 11.14 and
16.31 in their contexts).

10. καρδίᾳ γὰρ πιστεύεται εἰς δικαιοσύνην, στόματι δὲ ὁμολογεῖται
εἰς σωτηρίαν supports (γάρ) the previous verse's reference of
'in thy mouth' and 'in thy heart' in Deut 30.14 to confession
and faith, respectively. But here the order of v. 9, which was
determined by that of the Deuteronomy passage, is abandoned
in favour of the natural order, faith being now mentioned
before confession. Whereas in v. 9 σωθήσῃ answered to both
ὁμολογήσῃς and πιστεύσῃς, here σωτηρία is linked only with
ὁμολογεῖται, while πιστεύεται is linked with δικαιοσύνη; but

(Eng. tr. of *Christologische Hoheitstitel: ihre Geschichte im frühen
Christentum*, 1963), London, 1969, pp. 68–135; R. N. Longenecker, *The
Christology of early Jewish Christianity*, London, 1970, pp. 120–47.

it is clear that no substantial distinction is intended between δικαιοσύνη and σωτηρία, both referring to eschatological salvation. With the use of εἰς in this verse (meaning 'with . . . as the result') compare 5.18 (εἰς κατάκριμα and εἰς δικαίωσιν); 10.4 (εἰς δικαιοσύνην παντὶ τῷ πιστεύοντι).

11. λέγει γὰρ ἡ γραφή. γάρ is used because the quotation is being introduced as support for the statement of the previous verse that faith leads to justification (πιστεύεται εἰς δικαιοσύνην). Paul understands οὐ καταισχυνθήσεται as equivalent to δικαιωθήσεται/σωθήσεται.

πᾶς is Paul's addition (in v. 13 the πᾶς is part of the text quoted), which makes explicit, and emphasizes, the universal scope of the general statement of the LXX text—the aspect on which he is going to dwell in vv. 12–13.

On ὁ πιστεύων ἐπ' αὐτῷ οὐ καταισχυνθήσεται (quoted from LXX Isa 28.16) see on 9.33. In 9.33 Paul clearly took αὐτῷ to refer to Christ, and here also this is its natural reference (though it is true that God has been mentioned in v. 9).

12–13 consist of three sentences, each of which explains or supports its predecessor (hence the threefold γάρ). With οὐ γάρ ἐστιν διαστολὴ Ἰουδαίου τε καὶ Ἕλληνος compare 3.22. In 3.22 the point is that, since all are sinners, Gentiles and Jews alike can *only* be justified through faith: here (in view of the content of vv. 11, 12b and 13) the point is rather the *positive* one that the promise pertaining to faith applies equally to Jews and Gentiles. This promise embracing all men without distinction was all along the inner meaning of the law which was placed in the mouths and in the hearts of the Jews. And, though they have to learn the humbling lesson that righteousness with God is not theirs by right of descent or merit, they also stand under the promise that they too may share that righteousness through faith.

ὁ γὰρ αὐτὸς κύριος πάντων is best construed as meaning: 'For the same Lord *is Lord* of all'. In 3.29 the point made was that God is God of the Gentiles as well as of the Jews. Here, in affirming that the same Lord is Lord of all, Paul refers to Jesus, the κύριος of v. 9.[1]

πλουτῶν εἰς. In 11.33 and Phil 4.19 Paul speaks of God's riches absolutely. Elsewhere we read of the riches of God's kindness, longsuffering, glory, etc. (e.g. 2.4; 9.23; Eph 2.7), and of God's being rich in mercy (Eph 2.4). Christ's riches are

---

[1] Cf. Acts 10.36; Rom 9.5; Phil 2.9–11. The explanation of this sentence as referring to God the Father is surely to be rejected, though maintained by some.

referred to in Eph 3.8.[1] The expression πλουτεῖν εἴς τινα occurs in the NT only in Lk 12.21 (οὕτως ὁ θησαυρίζων αὑτῷ καὶ μὴ εἰς θεὸν πλουτῶν) and here. The meaning of the present clause must be that Christ is rich to the advantage of all who call on Him, that is, that He gives liberally of His riches (we may think of His wealth of goodness, kindness, love, glory, etc.) to them.[2]

πάντας. Note the persistent emphasis in vv. 11–13 of the idea of universality: πᾶς — οὐ γάρ ἐστιν διαστολή — πάντων — πάντας — πᾶς. Compare too the παντί of v. 4.

τοὺς ἐπικαλουμένους αὐτόν. The use of ἐπικαλεῖσθαι (middle) of invoking a god in prayer was well established in pagan Greek (it is found in Herodotus, Xenophon, Plato, Polybius, inscriptions and papyri). In the LXX such expressions as ἐπικαλεῖσθαι (τὸν) κύριον, τὸν θεόν, or τὸ ὄνομα (ἐν τῷ ὀνόματι, ἐπὶ τῷ ὀνόματι) κυρίου are used very frequently of invoking God in prayer; and ἐπικαλεῖσθαι can even be used absolutely in the sense 'to pray' (Ps 4.1[LXX: 2]: cf. Acts 7.59). In the NT it is used a few times of the invocation of God the Father; but more often of the invocation of the exalted Christ. In 1 Cor 1.2 οἱ ἐπικαλούμενοι τὸ ὄνομα τοῦ κυρίου ἡμῶν Ἰησοῦ Χριστοῦ is equivalent to 'Christians'. That the word has its technical sense of 'invoke in prayer' here is confirmed by v. 13. The fact that Paul can think of prayer to the exalted Christ without the least repugnance is, in the light of the first and second commandments of the Decalogue, the decisive clarification of the significance which he attached to the title κύριος as applied to Christ (e.g. in this verse and in v. 9).[3]

πᾶς γὰρ ὃς ἂν ἐπικαλέσηται τὸ ὄνομα κυρίου σωθήσεται. The paragraph is concluded with a scriptural quotation from Joel 2.32[MT and LXX: 3.5], Paul applying to the invocation of the exalted Christ what in its OT context was a promise that in the critical period preceding 'the great and terrible day of the LORD' every one who invokes the name of the LORD (i.e. Yahweh) will be saved. The LXX wording is reproduced exactly, with the addition of γάρ, the πᾶς being here part of the quotation in contrast with the πᾶς of v. 11.

---

[1] Cf. 2 Cor 8.9, where πλούσιος ὤν describes the state of our Lord Jesus who for our sakes became poor, and Rev 5.12, where the Lamb is said to be worthy to receive riches.

[2] A close parallel to the use of πλουτεῖν εἰς here is to be found in Philostratus, VA 4.8 (εἰ γὰρ ὁ μὲν ἀπὸ δημαγωγίας θαυμασθήσεται, . . . , ὁ δὲ ἀπὸ τοῦ ἐς τὸ κοινὸν πλουτεῖν, . . .).

[3] On ἐπικαλεῖσθαι see further K. L. Schmidt, in TWNT 3, pp. 498–501.

14–15a. Πῶς οὖν ἐπικαλέσωνται¹ εἰς ὃν οὐκ ἐπίστευσαν; πῶς δὲ πιστεύσωσιν οὗ οὐκ ἤκουσαν; πῶς δὲ ἀκούσωσιν χωρὶς κηρύσσοντος; πῶς δὲ κηρύξωσιν ἐὰν μὴ ἀποσταλῶσιν; We have here four questions which are parallel in structure and together form a logical chain (cf. 5.3b–5; 8.29–30; and also v. 17 of the present chapter, for similar chains).² The third person plural verbs of the first three questions are sometimes understood as indefinite ('How then shall men call . . .');³ but in view of the argument of the section 9.30–10.21 as a whole, it is more natural to assume that the subject of these verbs is the same as that of the third person plural verbs in 9.32; 10.2, 3— namely, the Jews. At this point Paul is concerned to show that the Jews have really had full opportunity to call upon the name of the Lord in the sense of vv. 12 and 13, and are therefore without excuse. That all along the law which was constantly on their lips was pointing to Christ, that all along He had been its innermost meaning, did not by itself constitute this full opportunity. The fullness of opportunity was not present for them until the message that the promises have indeed now been fulfilled had actually been declared to them by messengers truly commissioned for the purpose by God Himself.⁴ Paul makes his point by asking the question whether this fullness of opportunity has really been present for the Jews by means of this chain of related questions, and then answering in the affirmative in v. 15b. The chain of questions does not put the essential question directly but rather indicates the impossibility of the Jews' calling upon Christ unless certain pre-conditions have been fulfilled. Its substance may be summed up in four statements thus: They can only call upon Christ in the sense of vv. 12 and 13, if (iv)⁵ they have already believed on Him; they can only believe on Him, if (iii) they have heard Him (speaking to them through the message about Him); they can only hear Him, if (ii) someone proclaims the

---

¹ The variant, which has the future indicative instead of the aorist subjunctive, probably, in view of the following subjunctives (in the following questions textual support for the future indicative, though existing, is weaker), goes back to a simple mistake. On the use of the subjunctive see BDF, § 366; Burton, *MT*, § 169.

² In this chain the necessary sequence is traced backwards.

³ So, e.g., Calvin, who (pp. 229–32) takes Paul to be justifying the preaching of the gospel to the Gentiles. But the awkwardness of his interpretation is to be seen in the lack of connexion (on his view—see p. 232) between v. 16 and v. 14f.

⁴ See on κλητὸς ἀπόστολος in 1.1.

⁵ We number the pre-conditions thus, because, as in Paul's chain, they are put in the opposite order to that in which they have to be fulfilled.

message; the message can only be proclaimed, if (i) God commissions someone to proclaim it.

With εἰς ὃν ... ἐπίστευσαν compare Gal 2.16 and Phil 1.29, the only occurrences of πιστεύειν εἰς in the Pauline corpus outside the present verse (cf. also πίστις εἰς in Col 2.5). The construction is found once in Matthew, once in 1 Peter, and several times in Acts; but is characteristic of John and 1 John. It is noticeable that it is almost exclusively used of faith in Christ (of faith in God in Jn 14.1: cf. the use of πιστοὺς εἰς θεόν in 1 Pet 1.21, and the fact that πίστιν as well as ἐλπίδα must be connected with εἰς θεόν in the latter part of the same verse). That πιστεύειν εἰς denotes a faith in Christ which includes faith that God has raised Him from the dead and the acceptance of Him as Lord in the sense of v. 9 is not to be doubted.[1]

The same construction is implicit in πῶς δὲ πιστεύσωσιν οὗ οὐκ ἤκουσαν, where εἰς is to be supplied as well as the omitted antecedent of οὗ.

The use of οὗ indicates that in the second and third questions the thought is of their hearing Christ speaking in the message of the preachers. (To explain οὗ οὐκ ἤκουσαν as meaning 'about whom they have not heard' is not really feasible;[2] for the use of ἀκούειν with the simple genitive of the person meaning 'to hear about (someone)' would be very unusual.)

The point of the fourth question is that true Christian preaching, through which Christ Himself speaks, is not something which men can accomplish on their own initiative: it can only take place where men are authorized and commissioned by God. It is illuminating to compare what is said concerning prophetic authority in Jer 14.14; 23.21; 27.15. See further on κλητὸς ἀπόστολος in 1.1. We may understand οἱ κηρύσσοντες from κηρύσσοντος in the previous question as the subject of the verbs κηρύξωσιν and ἀποσταλῶσιν.

15b. καθάπερ[3] γέγραπται· ὡς ὡραῖοι οἱ πόδες[4] τῶν εὐαγγελιζο-

---

[1] We have had πιστεύειν ἐπί with the accusative in 4.5 and 24, both times of faith in God), and with the dative in 9.33 and 10.11 (where the original reference in the OT was to God but Paul is applying the quotation to faith in Christ). The construction πιστεύειν ἐν is not found in Paul's letters, though πίστις ἐν does occur (Gal 3.26; Col 1.4; 1 Tim 3.13; 2 Tim 1.13; 3.15). See further R. Bultmann, in *TWNT* 6, pp. 211–13; BDF, §§ 163, 187 (6), 206 (2), 233 (2), 235 (2); Bauer, s.v. πιστεύω.

[2] *Pace* Bauer, s.v. ἀκούω 3.b.

[3] On the textual question see on καθάπερ in 3.4.

[4] That the additional words τῶν εὐαγγελιζομένων εἰρήνην inserted after πόδες by 'Western' and Byzantine authorities should not be read is clear, in view of the strength of the support for their omission (including

μένων[1] ἀγαθά. The quotation from Isa 52.7,[2] which is closer to the MT than to the LXX, so far from being a mere ornament (as it is sometimes regarded as being), is an essential step in the argument. It serves as a statement of the fact that the first and second conditions (i.e. the last two mentioned in vv. 14–15a) have been fulfilled. Paul does not refer directly to his own apostolic ministry or the preaching of other Christian evangelists, but by appealing to Isa 52.7 he both points to it indirectly and at the same time gives the scriptural attestation of its true significance. If the apostolic preaching is truly the fulfilment of the prophecy, then it is attested as a true κηρύσσειν, and this must mean that the preachers have been duly authorized and commissioned.

16. ἀλλ᾽ οὐ πάντες ὑπήκουσαν τῷ εὐαγγελίῳ. Ἡσαΐας γὰρ λέγει· κύριε, τίς ἐπίστευσεν τῇ ἀκοῇ ἡμῶν;[3] This verse has been interpreted along two quite different lines: (i) that v. 16a is the statement of a possible objection: the fact that not all have submitted to the message is stated because it might seem to indicate that the messengers cannot really have been commissioned by God. Verse 16b is then the answer to this objection: [this fact does not prove that the messengers have not been duly commissioned,] for Isaiah goes on, immediately after his description of the messengers, to describe also the rejection of the message; (ii) that v. 16a continues the thought of v. 15: what has been lacking is submission to the message (i.e. faith) on the part of the hearers. Verse 16b is then a scriptural confirmation of v. 16a: this failure to believe has been foretold by the prophet. Of these, (ii) is to be preferred

𝔓46 ℵ* A B C 1739 Cl Or aeg aeth) and the fact that their insertion can easily be explained as assimilation to the LXX.

[1] Perhaps τά should be read, since it has some important support and its insertion (if not original) is not easily accounted for, as it is not present in the LXX text. Its omission (if original) would of course be quite understandable. Its presence would have the effect of underlining the identification of the message of the εὐαγγελιζόμενοι with the gospel of Christ. Paul may well have wished to underline this identification, in view of the fact that the function of the quotation is not to serve as an ornament nor even to confirm a point already made, but actually to state an indispensable step in his argument.

[2] On the great importance of this verse (with which cf. Nah 1.15 [MT and LXX: 2.1]) in Judaism and for the understanding of the NT use of εὐαγγέλιον and cognates reference may be made to G. Friedrich, in *TWNT* 2, pp. 705ff. In Rabbinic literature Isa 52.7 is almost always interpreted of the messianic age. The feet of the messengers were perhaps mentioned by the prophet because the joyfulness of the tidings would be indicated by the messengers' eager and buoyant walk.

[3] The quotation from Isa 53.1 follows the LXX text exactly. The vocative is not present in the Hebrew.

as being much simpler and more straightforward.[1] Having indicated in v. 15b that the first and second conditions have been fulfilled, Paul now declares that, as far as some of the Jews are concerned, the fourth and final condition (i.e. the one mentioned first in vv. 14–15a) has not been fulfilled. They have not believed in Christ.

Paul's οὐ πάντες is an example of meiosis. We may compare his τινες in 3.3. For the use of ὑπακούειν as equivalent to πιστεύειν compare the phrase ὑπακοὴν πίστεως in 1.5. The obedience which God requires is faith. To obey the gospel is to believe it and to believe in Him who is its content; and to believe the gospel and believe in Christ involves obeying it, obeying Him. The τῷ εὐαγγελίῳ refers back to τῶν εὐαγγελιζο-μένων ἀγαθά (or τὰ ἀγαθά) in the previous verse. In the Isaiah quotation ἀκοή means 'report', 'message'.

17. ἄρα ἡ πίστις ἐξ ἀκοῆς, ἡ δὲ ἀκοὴ διὰ ῥήματος Χριστοῦ. It is not surprising that this verse has troubled commentators. Two questions at once suggest themselves: (i) Would not this verse, marked as it is by the presence of ἄρα as a conclusion from what precedes, more appropriately follow immediately upon vv. 14–15a, the contents of which it appears to summar-ize? (ii) What is the point of including at all what seems to be simply a repetition (in shortened form) of the conditions already listed in vv. 14–15a? Some scholars have suggested a rearrangement of the verses;[2] others, while accepting the order we have as original, have judged that the logic of the paragraph would have been improved, had the order been different;[3] and others have concluded that v. 17 is a gloss.[4] But the apposite-ness of v. 17 here can be defended. Paul's passing over in vv. 15b–16 the third condition (i.e. hearing)[5] may be explained as probably due, on the one hand, to a desire to set directly over against the fulfilment on God's (Christ's) part of the basic first two conditions (namely, the commissioning of the messengers and Christ's speaking through them) the stark fact of Israel's disobedience, which is the problem with which chapters 9 to 11 as a whole are concerned, and, on the other hand, to a feeling that, as he is going to expand his treatment of the matter of the third condition (he is going to introduce

---

[1] The fact that the indication of a possible objection by a statement introduced by ἀλλά is uncharacteristic of Paul is a further reason for preferring (ii).

[2] e.g. F. Müller, in *ZNW* 40 (1941), pp. 249–54.

[3] e.g. Barrett, p. 205.

[4] e.g. Bultmann, 'Glossen', cols. 197–202.

[5] See p. 533.

knowing as a kind of sub-division of hearing), it would be more
conveniently placed last. But he has to come back to the third
condition, and v. 17 effects the transition from the OT quotation in v. 16b to the subject of Israel's hearing. The quotation
speaks of believing a message. But a message's being believed
involves an intermediate occurrence between the message's
being uttered and its being believed, namely, its being heard.
So in v. 17 Paul draws out (ἄρα) what is implied in his quotation, applying it to the matter in hand. Faith results from
hearing the message,[1] and the hearing of the message comes
about through the word of Christ (i.e., through Christ's speaking
the message by the mouths of His messengers).[2] This cor-
roborates what was said in vv. 14–15a, but is not a mere
pointless repetition, since in it hearing becomes the hinge, so
that it leads naturally into v. 18.

18. ἀλλὰ λέγω. In addition to v. 19, compare 11.1 and 11.

μὴ οὐκ ἤκουσαν; An affirmative answer is anticipated, since the
μή introducing a question expecting a negative answer is
followed by a verb which is already negated. Had the Jews
not heard, they would have had an excuse for their not having
believed.

μενοῦν γε. See on 9.20. The colon which follows in Nestle
should perhaps be omitted (as in Merk).

**εἰς πᾶσαν τὴν γῆν ἐξῆλθεν ὁ φθόγγος αὐτῶν,[3] καὶ εἰς τὰ πέρατα τῆς
οἰκουμένης τὰ ῥήματα αὐτῶν.** Instead of stating directly that the
Jews must certainly have heard the gospel preaching, Paul
quotes (though without any explicit indication that he is
quoting) the LXX version of part of Ps 19.4, applying to the
Christian mission what was said of the glorification of God by
the natural order. It is quite unlikely that Paul's use of this
quotation means that he thinks that the preaching to all the
nations (cf. Mk 13.10) has been completed. The fact that he
hopes to undertake a missionary journey to Spain (15.24, 28)
itself disproves this. Probably all that he wants to assert is that
the message has been publicly proclaimed in the world at large
—the significant thing is that it has been quite widely preached
to the Gentiles (cf. v. 19f)—and therefore cannot be supposed

---

[1] In view of v. 18 it seems clear (*pace* RSV; NEB; JB) that ἀκοή is used
in v. 17 in the sense which it normally has in Paul's epistles, namely,
'hearing', in spite of the fact that it has just occurred in the sense of
'message' in the quotation from Isa 53.1.

[2] See on οὖ in v. 14.

[3] The MT has ḳawwām ('their measuring-line'), but this does not fit the
parallelism as well as ὁ φθόγγος αὐτῶν, which may perhaps represent an
original ḳolām or ḳinnām (see Kittel apparatus).

not to have been heard by the generality of Jews. We may compare Col 1.5f, 23.

19–21. A supplementary question (knowing did not figure as a link in the chain in vv. 14–15a) is now raised in parallel form to v. 18a, and the answer is given this time by means of three OT quotations.

ἀλλὰ λέγω, μὴ Ἰσραὴλ οὐκ ἔγνω; For ἀλλὰ λέγω and μὴ . . . οὐκ see on v. 18. At last Israel is mentioned expressly. The natural inference to be drawn from the presence of Ἰσραήλ here is that the subject of ἤκουσαν in v. 18 and of the third person plural verbs in v. 14 must be the Jews.[1] The use of Ἰσραήλ rather than οἱ Ἰουδαῖοι is no doubt rightly explained by Sanday and Headlam (the word itself 'gives an answer to the question, and shows the untenable character of the excuse. Has Israel, Israel with its long line of Prophets, and its religious privileges and its Divine teaching, acted in ignorance? When once "Israel" has been used there can be no doubt of the answer').[2] (See further on Ἰσραηλῖται in 9.4.) It is instructive to notice that throughout chapters 9 to 11 Paul prefers to use Ἰσραήλ (in these three chapters Ἰσραήλ occurs eleven times and Ἰσραηλίτης twice, while Ἰουδαῖος occurs only twice: Ἰσραήλ and Ἰσραηλίτης are used nowhere else in Romans but in these chapters), no doubt because in them he is particularly concerned with the Jewish people as the object of God's election.

This question and the positive answer which it receives must be understood in relation to what was said in 10.2–3.[3] Paul is not withdrawing here what he there said about Israel's ignorance. The truth is that in one sense they know and in another sense they do not know. They have been the recipients of God's special self-revelation, and yet they have been uncomprehending. Compare Mk 4.12 (. . . ἵνα βλέποντες βλέπωσιν καὶ μὴ ἴδωσιν, καὶ ἀκούοντες ἀκούωσιν καὶ μὴ συνιῶσιν, . . .). The ignorance which is blameworthy has been characteristic of them; but the ignorance which would have constituted an excuse they cannot claim.

πρῶτος Μωϋσῆς λέγει. Richard Bentley suggested placing the question mark after, instead of before, πρῶτος, and connecting πρῶτος with Ἰσραήλ; and a number of commentators have followed his suggestion. The meaning would then be, 'Did not Israel know first?' (Was not Israel the first of all the

---

[1] Though some have maintained that Ἰσραήλ here marks a change of subject.

[2] p. 299.

[3] These verses are, in fact, to be understood both as a supplement to v. 18 and also as a clarification of vv. 2 and 3.

nations to get to know the gospel?). But several considerations tell against this punctuation: (i) the parallelism between v. 18a and v. 19a is more exact, if the question mark is placed immediately after ἔγνω; (ii) though the word δεύτερος is not used, the fact that another scriptural witness is introduced in v. 20 makes it natural to take πρῶτος with Μωϋσῆς and to understand it in relation to later testimony; (iii) the quotations in vv. 19–21 seem to fit v. 19a better, if it ends with ἔγνω, than if it includes πρῶτος. The punctuation accepted by Nestle should be preferred. The point of πρῶτος then is that Moses is the first witness to the fact that Israel has indeed known.

ἐγὼ παραζηλώσω ὑμᾶς ἐπ᾽ οὐκ ἔθνει, ἐπ᾽ ἔθνει ἀσυνέτῳ παροργιῶ ὑμᾶς. The quotation follows the LXX text of Deut 32.21b exactly, except that ὑμᾶς is twice substituted for αὐτούς. In their context in the Song of Moses, the words are a warning of God's chastisement of His people Israel for their infidelity: their provoking Him to jealousy and anger by going after no-gods, vanities, He will punish by provoking them to jealousy and anger by means of no-peoples, foolish nations (i.e., the various Gentile nations which God uses as His instruments in the course of history).[1] Paul is of course thinking of the Gentile mission. As Bruce notes,[2] to Paul who was familiar with the Hebrew a connexion between 'no-people' (lō'-'ām) here and 'not my people' (lō'-'ammî) in Hos 1.9f, a passage he has already quoted with reference to the Gentile mission (9.25f), would readily suggest itself. The point of the quotation here is that, if Gentiles who, in relation to the knowledge of God, are, compared with Israel, but no-peoples, foolish nations, have come to know, then it certainly cannot be supposed that Israel has not known. It is a striking feature of the argument here that, instead of appealing directly to the actual course of the Gentile mission in which he himself had played so important a part, Paul keeps steadfastly to the OT. It is a true insight which sees a connexion between the fact—so full of evangelical significance—of Paul's establishment of Israel's guilt in such a way as not to call in question but to confirm its election, and the constancy of his attention to the OT throughout this chapter.[3]

Ἡσαΐας is introduced as a second witness to the fact that Israel has known.

---

[1] On the Jewish exposition of the passage which interpreted the no-people, the foolish nation, variously of the Samaritans (Ecclus 50.25f), the Babylonians (Jerusalem Targum I), etc. see SB 3, p. 284f.
[2] p. 210.
[3] Cf. Barth, CD II/2, p. 258 (=KD II/2, p. 284f).

ἀποτολμᾷ:[1] the only occurrence in the Greek Bible of ἀποτολμᾶν (found in Thucydides, Lysias, Plato, as well as in later writers). Compare the use of the simple verb, e.g. in 15.18, and of the comparative adverb τολμηροτέρως in 15.15. (For the strengthening ἀπο- see on 8.19.) It is more likely that ἀποτολμᾷ is meant to underline the astonishing nature of what is said in Isa 65.1a (as understood by Paul) than that it is meant to indicate the psychological state of the prophet.[2]

εὑρέθην[3] τοῖς ἐμὲ μὴ ζητοῦσιν, ἐμφανὴς ἐγενόμην[3] τοῖς ἐμὲ μὴ ἐπερωτῶσιν. The quotation agrees with the LXX text of Isa 65.1a as given by Rahlfs (the B text has ζητοῦσιν and ἐπερωτῶσιν in the opposite order), except that ἐμφανὴς ἐγενόμην and εὑρέθην have been transposed (probably for the sake of a more satisfactory progression, since that which is manifest does not need to be found, while that which is found is not necessarily manifest).[4] In its context in Isaiah, Isa 65.1ff is probably to be understood (though this is disputed, and the various commentaries on Isaiah should be consulted) as God's answer to His people's prayer in 63.7–64.12, and the sense of vv. 1 and 2 is then that God has graciously and patiently made Himself accessible[5] to His people and continually sought to welcome them into fellowship with Himself, in spite of all their rebelliousness. But Paul (as his explanatory words at the beginning of v. 21 indicate) sees a contrast between vv. 1 and 2, and applies the former to the Gentiles[6] and only the latter to Israel. As used by him, the quotation from Isa 65.1 is parallel

[1] The omission of ἀποτολμᾷ καί by D* G it may be explained as accidental or possibly as due to failure to see the point of ἀποτολμᾷ here.

[2] Cf. Michel, p. 263, n. 5. Contrast Sanday and Headlam, p. 300 ('St. Paul's position in opposing the prejudices of his countrymen made him feel the boldness of Isaiah in standing up against the men of his own time').

[3] The addition of ἐν before both the first and the second τοῖς in some authorities, before the first only in others, is perhaps due to the oddness of a simple dative following the passive of εὑρίσκειν (it is as odd as 'to be found to someone' is in English). Though a dative after ἐμφανής presents no difficulty, it would be natural to add ἐν in the second sentence as well as in the first, for the sake of the parallelism.

[4] Cf. Lagrange, p. 264.

[5] The Hebrew verbs niḍraštî and nimṣēʾṭî in Isa 65.1 have a tolerative sense, and may be rendered in some such way as 'I let myself be inquired of' or 'I made myself accessible to be inquired of', 'I let myself be found' or 'I made myself available to be found', respectively. It is not implied that the people actually inquired or found.

[6] SB 3, p. 285, cites R. Tanchuma (c. 380) as applying Isa 65.1a to Rahab the harlot and Ruth the Moabitess, and expresses the opinion that the LXX translation itself presupposes the reference of the verse to the Gentiles.

to the quotation in v. 19, and serves to confirm that Israel must have known, since God has actually been found[1] by Gentiles who were not seeking Him.

πρὸς δὲ τὸν Ἰσραὴλ λέγει: 'But concerning Israel he says'. ὅλην τὴν ἡμέραν ἐξεπέτασα τὰς χεῖράς μου πρὸς λαὸν ἀπειθοῦντα καὶ ἀντιλέγοντα. The third quotation agrees exactly with the LXX of Isa 65.2, except that ὅλην τὴν ἡμέραν has been placed before, instead of after, ἐξεπέτασα τὰς χεῖράς μου. The phrase ὅλην τὴν ἡμέραν represents the Hebrew kol-hayyôm, which means 'continually'.[2] The spreading out of the hands, in Ps 143.6 a gesture of supplication, is here a gesture of appealing welcome and friendship.[3] The words ἀπειθεῖν and ἀντιλέγειν[4] may not unfairly be regarded as expressing the direct opposites to the obedience of faith (cf. v. 3—ὑποτάσσεσθαι; v. 16— ὑπακούειν; vv. 9–11, 14, 16—πιστεύειν) and to the ὁμολογεῖν of which vv. 9–10 speak, respectively.[5]

The quotations in vv. 19 and 20 have shown not only that Israel has certainly known and that its knowing is foreseen in Scripture, but also that the Gentile mission in which Paul himself is engaged is foretold in Scripture. The quotation in v. 21 confirms incidentally that Israel has known, but its special function is twofold. It (i) looks back to what has already been said concerning Israel's disobedience and gathers it up in one comprehensive statement, which by making it clear that this disobedience is precisely rejection of God's steadfast grace brings out its full enormity; and (ii) looks forward to what is going to be said of hope for Israel, depicting vividly the steadfast patience of that divine grace against which Israel has so continually sinned. But there is no equilibrium between these two things; for in this sentence the statement of Israel's disobedience is strictly incidental (it is confined to the participial phrase dependent on λαόν), but the statement of what God has done with regard to this people is central and decisive. The quotation points firmly to the fact that the last word is not with Israel's disobedience but with God's mercy and

---

[1] As applied to the Gentile mission, the words apparently mean not just that God has on His side made Himself accessible, but also that the Gentiles have actually responded and so found God and received His self-revelation.

[2] Cf., e.g., Deut 28.32; Isa 65.5; Jer 20.7, 8; and see BDB, s.v. יוֹם 7.f.

[3] Cf. E. J. Kissane, The Book of Isaiah 2, Dublin, 1943, p. 301. Chrysostom's comment (col. 575) is interesting: τὸ δὲ ἐκπετάσαι τὰς χεῖρας τὸ καλέσαι καὶ ἐπισπάσασθαι καὶ παρακαλέσαι δηλοῖ.

[4] καὶ ἀντιλέγοντα has no equivalent in the MT. This is probably the reason for its omission here in Romans by G Hil.

[5] Cf. Michel, p. 264.

patience. 'Their guilt could not be defined more clearly and sharply,' comments Barth on this verse, 'and nothing clearer and more comforting could be said about him whom their guilt concerns and who has made them the object of his mercy —who has not abandoned them for what they are, because his mercy is greater than their guilt and than all human guilt'.[1]

VI. 4. GOD HAS NOT CAST OFF HIS PEOPLE (11.1–36)

The theme of the whole section is categorically stated in v. 2a: 'God has not cast off his people whom he foreknew'. That even at the present time the disobedience of Israel is not complete (there exists 'a remnant according to the election of grace', Jews who are believers in Christ) is the burden of the first subsection (vv. 1–10), while the second (vv. 11–24) contributes the assurance that the exclusion of the majority of Jews is not going to last for ever. The third subsection (vv. 25–32) gives an insight into the mystery of the divine plan of mercy concerning both Jews and Gentiles, and finally vv. 33–36 conclude both this section and the whole of main division VI with an expression of adoring wonder and praise.

(i) *The remnant according to the election of grace*
(11.1–10)

[1]I ask then, has God cast off his people? God forbid! for I myself am an Israelite, of the seed of Abraham, of the tribe of Benjamin. [2]God has not cast off his people whom he foreknew. Or do you not know what the scripture says in *the section about* Elijah, how he pleads to God against Israel? [3]'Lord, they have killed thy prophets, they have destroyed thine altars, and I alone am left and they seek my life.' [4]But what does the divine answer say to him? 'I have left myself seven thousand men who have not bent their knees to Baal.' [5]So then in the present time too there has been a remnant according to the election of grace. [6]But if *it is* by grace, then *it is* not on the basis of works; for, if it were, grace would no more be grace. [7]What then? What Israel is seeking it has not obtained, but the elect ones have obtained it. And the rest were hardened, [8]even as it is written: 'God gave them a spirit of torpor, blind eyes and deaf ears, unto this very day.' [9]And David says: 'Let their table become a snare and a trap and a stumbling-block and a retribution to them; [10]let their eyes be darkened so that they cannot see, and do thou bow down their back continually.'

---

[1] So *Shorter*, p. 134. But did Barth perhaps mean by 'als solches' here 'as the object of his mercy' rather than, as the translation seems to suggest, 'for what they are in themselves', i.e., inexcusably unbelieving and disobedient? Cf. *CD* II/2, p. 259 (= *KD* II/2, p. 285).

In support of his emphatic denial of the possibility that God has cast off His people Israel Paul cites the fact of his own Jewishness (God would hardly have chosen a Jew to be His special apostle to the Gentiles, had He cast off His people, the Jews). No, God has certainly not broken His promise not to cast them off, which the OT attests. In vv. 2b–4 he goes on to appeal to the story of Elijah, and to the mysterious 'seven thousand men' of God's reply to him. These seven thousand, of whom the prophet was unaware, were (according to the application in v. 5f) 'a remnant according to the election of grace', and now at the time the apostle is writing the minority of Jews who do believe in Christ is also such a remnant. And the very fact that it is a remnant according to the election of *grace*, and therefore not a remnant standing by its own deserving, makes its existence full of promise for the rest of the nation, a pledge of God's continuing interest in those λοιποί who have indeed been hardened by a divine hardening such as is spoken of in Scripture.

1. **Λέγω οὖν, μὴ ἀπώσατο ὁ θεὸς τὸν λαὸν αὐτοῦ;** For the form of the question compare 10.18 and 19 (ἀλλὰ λέγω, μὴ . . .;) and 11.11 (λέγω οὖν, μὴ . . .;). Common to all these four questions are λέγω and μή, introducing a question expecting a negative answer, and the use of a verb in the aorist tense. This similarity of form underlines the connexion between 11.1 and the preceding verses, a connexion which is indicated by the οὖν. The fact that it has just been confirmed that Israel did hear and did know, and is therefore without any excuse, raises the question whether the conclusion to be drawn from Israel's stubborn disobedience is that God has cast away His people, excluded them from His plan of salvation. But the terms in which the question is expressed presuppose the negative answer it must receive, for they are clearly reminiscent of OT passages which declare categorically that God will not cast off His people: 1 Sam 12.22 (ὅτι οὐκ ἀπώσεται κύριος τὸν λαὸν αὐτοῦ διὰ τὸ ὄνομα αὐτοῦ τὸ μέγα, ὅτι ἐπιεικέως κύριος προσελάβετο ὑμᾶς αὐτῷ εἰς λαόν); Ps 94[LXX: 93].14 (ὅτι οὐκ ἀπώσεται κύριος τὸν λαὸν αὐτοῦ καὶ τὴν κληρονομίαν αὐτοῦ οὐκ ἐγκαταλείψει, . . .).[1]

---

[1] See S.B 3, p. 286 for Jewish comment on these two passages. They are linked together in Midr Ps 94 § 3 (209ᵇ). The reading τὴν κληρονομίαν instead of τὸν λαόν in Rom 11.1 (attested by 𝔓⁴⁶ G Ambst—Merk cites, in addition, Ambrose and Pelagius) is no doubt due to the influence of Ps 94.14b. A further OT passage which may be compared with the two quoted above is Jer 31.37, though RV 'cast off' here represents a different Hebrew verb from that used in 1 Sam 12.22 and Ps 94.14, and the LXX (in the LXX it is 38.37) omits the relevant words. Sanday and

The question is thus tantamount to asking, 'Has God broken His explicit promise not to cast off His people?' So we may say that the first ground of the μὴ γένοιτο which follows is the one which, though unexpressed, is implicit in the language used, namely, that Holy Scripture testifies that God will not cast off His people.

καὶ γὰρ ἐγὼ Ἰσραηλίτης εἰμί, ἐκ σπέρματος Ἀβραάμ, φυλῆς Βενιαμίν is not (*pace* Sanday and Headlam *et al.*) a mere explanation of the vehemence of his deprecation (as though Paul were simply saying that patriotic sentiment would not allow him to entertain such a thought), but the second ground (the first actually stated) of the *denial* expressed by μὴ γένοιτο. Understood as a ground of the denial, it may still be variously interpreted. Very often the point is taken to be simply that Paul's existence as a Jew who is also a Christian proves that the Jewish people as a whole cannot have been rejected. According to Luther the point is that Paul is one who had opposed God with particular fury. If God had cast off His people, then he above all would have been cast off. But God has not cast him off: much less then has He cast off 'the others who did not depart from him as far as I did'.[1] But the most probable explanation is that what Paul has in mind is not just the fact that he, a Jew, is a Christian, nor yet that he who has been so fierce an opponent of the gospel is a Christian, but the fact that he, a Jew (and one who has particularly ferociously opposed the gospel), is God's chosen apostle to the Gentiles.[2] Were God intending only to save a mere handful of Israel, had He really cast off the people of Israel as a whole, would He have chosen an Israelite to be the apostle to the Gentiles and the chief bearer of the gospel message? In his person the missionary vocation of Israel is at last being fulfilled and Israel is actively associated with the work of the risen Christ. This is a more cogent evidence of God's not having cast off His people than is the simple fact that one particular Jew has come to believe.

Headlam refer (p. 309) to Ps 95 [LXX: 94].4; but the words ὅτι οὐκ ἀπώσεται κύριος τὸν λαὸν αὐτοῦ, which are included in that verse by B, are an addition introduced from Ps 94 [LXX: 93].14.

[1] p. 305.

[2] Cf. Chrysostom, col. 576f (Εἶτα ἐπάγων ἀπόδειξιν τοῦ μὴ ἀπῶσθαι τὸν λαόν, φησί· Καὶ γὰρ ἐγὼ Ἰσραηλίτης . . . Προτέρα [κατασκευή] μὲν γάρ ἐστι τὸ δεῖξαι ὅτι αὐτὸς ἐκεῖθεν ἦν· οὐκ ἂν δέ, εἰ ἀπωθεῖσθαι αὐτοὺς ἔμελλεν, ᾧ τὸ κήρυγμα πᾶν καὶ τὰ πράγματα τῆς οἰκουμένης ἐνεπίστευσε, καὶ τὰ μυστήρια πάντα, καὶ τὴν οἰκονομίαν ὅλην, τοῦτον ἂν ἐκεῖθεν ἐξελέξατο. Αὕτη μὲν οὖν μία κατασκευή); Barth, *CD* II/2, p. 268 (= *KD* II/2, p. 295f); *Shorter*, p. 135; Gaugler 2, p. 161f; and also (in one pregnant sentence) Calvin, p. 239.

Paul's purpose in describing himself as ἐκ σπέρματος[1] Ἀβραάμ, φυλῆς Βενιαμίν, in addition to Ἰσραηλίτης, is probably simply 'that he may be regarded as a true Israelite', as Calvin suggests.[2] There is no solid reason for supposing that in mentioning his tribe Paul had specially in mind the fact that it had once been nearly exterminated (Judg 20–21) or that it was the tribe of another Saul, the king whom God had rejected, or that (according to Rabbinic tradition) it had been the first tribe to enter the Red Sea.[3]

2. οὐκ ἀπώσατο ὁ θεὸς τὸν λαὸν αὐτοῦ: a solemn and explicit denial, all the more emphatic for being expressed in the very words which were used in the question.

ὃν προέγνω.[4] The significance of the addition of this relative clause has been disputed. Calvin understood it as having a restrictive sense, limiting the reference of τὸν λαὸν αὐτοῦ to those members of the people of Israel who are the objects of God's secret election.[5] But, in spite of the fact that vv. 4–7 do go on to differentiate between an elect remnant and the rest of the people, this interpretation is most unlikely; for it is hardly to be disputed that in v. 1 (cf. 10.21) τὸν λαὸν αὐτοῦ refers to Israel as a whole, and it is unnatural to give it a different sense in v. 2. We take it then that the relative clause refers to the general election of the people as a whole, and indicates a further ground for denying that God has cast off his people.[6] The fact that God foreknew them (i.e., deliberately joined them to Himself in faithful love) excludes the possibility of His casting them off.

ἢ οὐκ οἴδατε. Compare, for example, 6.3, 16; 7.1; 1 Cor 3.16.

ἐν Ἠλίᾳ: 'in the section about Elijah'. There are many examples in Rabbinic literature of references to sections of

[1] Note that σπέρμα here has its ordinary sense (cf. 9.7a), not the special sense it has in 9.7b, 8.

[2] p. 239.

[3] *Pace* Käsemann, p. 286, we cannot see any justification for the contention that the argumentation and formulation of this verse points to the predominantly Gentile composition of the community which Paul is addressing.

[4] The variant reading which adds these words in v. 1 after αὐτοῦ is clearly an assimilation to this verse. On the verb προγινώσκειν see on 8.29.

[5] p. 239f.

[6] Chrysostom, col. 577, rightly recognized that it was a further ground for this denial; but at the same time he took the reference to be limited to an elect remnant (like Calvin), and also (unlike Calvin) understood the foreknowing as a foreknowing of the character of the people concerned. His words (following immediately on the passage quoted above) are: δευτέρα δὲ μετ' ἐκείνην τὸ εἰπεῖν· Τὸν λαὸν ὃν προέγνω· τουτέστιν, ὃν ᾔδει σαφῶς ἐπιτήδειον ὄντα καὶ τὴν πίστιν δεξόμενον. καὶ γὰρ τρισχίλιοι καὶ πεντακισχίλιοι καὶ μύριοι ἐξ ἐκείνων ἦσαν πιστεύσαντες.

Scripture by means of titles derived from their subject matter. The exact phrase 'in Elijah' occurs in *Midr Ct* 1.6 (88ᵃ).[1] But the usage is not confined to Hebrew. It is found also in Philo, and in the NT (Mk 12.26=Lk 20.37); and the same method was also used by the Greeks in references to Homer. See SB 3, p. 288, and also the full note in Sanday and Headlam, p. 310f. For the placing of ἐν Ἠλίᾳ outside the clause to which it belongs see on 11.31.

ἐντυγχάνει. The verb ἐντυγχάνειν is here used of Elijah's pleading with God against Israel, speaking to God in accusation of Israel. Compare 1 Macc 8.32; 10.61, 63; 11.25; and also the second century B.C. papyrus, P.Giess.1.36.15, cited by LSJ, s.v. ἐντυγχάνω II.3.

The relevance of this appeal to the story of Elijah to what Paul has just said will become clear in vv. 4–6.

3 is constructed out of 1 Kgs 19.10 and 14, the gist of which it reproduces in abridged form. Paul omits the statement that the people have forsaken God's covenant (or, according to the LXX version of v. 10, God Himself), and transposes the statements about the throwing down of the altars and the killing of the prophets. Attempts to discern special motives for these variations from the original are unconvincing. Paul is probably relying on his memory.

4. χρηματισμός: a hapaxlegomenon in the NT. More frequently used in other senses, it occasionally denotes an oracular response (for which χρησμός (derived from χράω) is more usual), so an authoritative divine answer, as here, or a divine warning. For this use compare 2 Macc 2.4;[2] and the use of the cognate verb χρηματίζειν in, for example, Mt 2.12, 22; Lk 2.26; Act 10.22. The verb has a quite different meaning in 7.3.

κατέλιπον ἐμαυτῷ ἑπτακισχιλίους ἄνδρας, οἵτινες οὐκ ἔκαμψαν γόνυ τῇ Βάαλ is based on 1 Kgs 19.18. The MT has *hiš'artî* (RV: 'will I leave'), with which Targum, Peshitta, and Lucianic text agree, but the LXX (both A and B) has καταλείψεις (the second person singular addressed to Elijah). Paul writes the first person, adds ἐμαυτῷ, and uses the aorist tense, referring the words to the divine decision. The number 7,000, occurring, as it does, not in a statement which purports to give matter of fact historical information, but in a solemn and mysterious[3] divine utterance, is hardly to be understood either in 1 Kgs

---

[1] In Hebrew בָּאֵלִיָּהוּ.

[2] Also Clement of Rome 17.5; Artemidorus Daldianus (2nd century A.D.) 1.2; Vettius Valens (2nd century A.D.) 1.7; P.Mag. Par. 1.2206.

[3] Elijah is represented as having no inkling of the existence of these 7,000—no inconsiderable number.

or here as a mere reflection of a traditional estimate of the actual number of those who remained faithful in this time of national apostasy, but is rather to be understood in the light of the special significance attaching to the number seven and to multiples of seven in the Bible and in Judaism,[1] as a symbol of completeness, perfection. God's statement that He is preserving for Himself seven thousand men in Israel amounts to a declaration of His faithfulness to His purpose of salvation for His people, a declaration that that purpose will continue unchanged and unthwarted to its final goal. For the counting of the men only (ἄνδρας) Michel compares Mk 6.44.[2] The explanation of τῇ Βάαλ is that the feminine article was sometimes written with Βάαλ (see, for instance, Jer 2.23; 7.9; 11.13, 17) as an indication that, in reading, the word αἰσχύνη was to be substituted for it (it is actually substituted in the text at 1 Kgs 18.19 and 25, just as bōśeṭ is sometimes substituted for ba'al in the MT (see, for example, Jer 3.24; 2 Sam 2.8 compared with 1 Chr 8.33)).[3]

5–6. οὕτως οὖν καὶ ἐν τῷ νῦν καιρῷ λεῖμμα κατ' ἐκλογὴν χάριτος γέγονεν· εἰ δὲ χάριτι, οὐκέτι[4] ἐξ ἔργων, ἐπεὶ ἡ χάρις οὐκέτι γίνεται χάρις.[5] In these two verses Paul indicates the relevance of the Elijah narrative to the question whether God has cast off His people, drawing out in particular the significance of the divine answer quoted in v. 4. In Elijah's time there was a λεῖμμα, a remnant, but the ground of its existence was the initiative of the divine grace, God's gracious election, and not human merit. By κατ' ἐκλογὴν χάριτος ... οὐκέτι ἐξ ἔργων Paul brings out the significance of κατέλιπον in the previous verse, to which he has already given special emphasis by his addition of ἐμαυτῷ. It was God, by His own decision and for the accomplishment of His own purpose, who made the remnant to stand firm; and for this very reason its existence was full of promise for the rest of the nation. The existence of a remnant, whose faithfulness was their own meritorious achievement, would have had no particularly hopeful significance for the unfaithful majority. But, precisely because this remnant was

---

[1] See further K. H. Rengstorf, in *TWNT* 2, pp. 623–31.

[2] p. 267.

[3] Cf. A. Dillmann, in *Monatsberichte der Akademie der Wissenschaft*, 1881, pp. 601–20; Sanday and Headlam, p. 312.

[4] The variant οὐκ is no doubt to be rejected as a stylistic improvement. The use of οὐκέτι with a logical rather than a temporal force is found several times in Paul's letters (see on 7.17).

[5] The extra words contained in the TR (here supported by B, though with χάρις substituted accidentally for the second ἔργον) are clearly a gloss.

preserved in accordance with the election of grace and not on the basis of works, its existence was a pledge of God's continuing interest in, and care for, the nation, a sign of God's faithfulness to His election of Israel as a whole (though it is to be noted that there is certainly no intention in the Elijah narrative to gloss over the reality of God's punishment of Israel's sin—the biggest part of the divine answer in 1 Kgs 19.15–18 is in fact concerned with it). With this significance of κατέλιπον ἐμαυτῷ, elucidated by κατ' ἐκλογὴν χάριτος and οὐκέτι ἐξ ἔργων, the number seven thousand agrees, for it suggests a remnant which is not a closed but an open number, and so eloquent of promise for the people as a whole (compare Mt 18.22, where the point of ἕως ἑβδομηκοντάκις ἑπτά is that forgiveness of one's brother is to know no limit). The point that Paul is making is that the remnant of the present time,[1] that is, the company of Jews who have believed in Christ, is a similar remnant, the existence of which is also based not on human deserving (he himself had been apprehended by Christ in the midst of his fierce opposition to the gospel), but on God's gracious election, and is therefore also a pledge of the continuing election of Israel as a whole. The words ἐπεὶ ἡ χάρις οὐκέτι γίνεται χάρις (for ἐπεί meaning 'for otherwise' see on 3.6) are added in order to underline οὐκέτι ἐξ ἔργων. Only when this is kept steadily in view is grace taken seriously as grace; for χάριτι and ἐξ ἔργων, standing by grace and standing on the basis of one's own works—these (though not, of course, χάρις and ἔργα as such!) are mutually exclusive.

7. Τί οὖν; introduces a comprehensive conclusion from what has just been said (in vv. 1–6).

ὃ ἐπιζητεῖ Ἰσραήλ, τοῦτο οὐκ ἐπέτυχεν repeats in different words what was said in 9.31. Israel has not obtained that which it is continually seeking after. So much was said in 9.31, but now something else is added—

ἡ δὲ ἐκλογὴ ἐπέτυχεν. The words gather up the positive conclusion of vv. 4–6. The use of the abstract ἐκλογή instead of the concrete ἐκλεκτοί serves to put special emphasis on the action of God as that which is altogether determinative of the existence of the elect. It accords with the decisive features of the last three verses, κατέλιπον ἐμαυτῷ, κατ' ἐκλογὴν χάριτος, and οὐκέτι ἐξ ἔργων.

οἱ δὲ λοιποὶ ἐπωρώθησαν. With ἐπωρώθησαν compare the use of πώρωσις in v. 25. On the words πωροῦν and πώρωσις see K. L. and M. A. Schmidt, in *TWNT* 5, pp. 1024–32. J.

---

[1] For ἐν τῷ νῦν καιρῷ see p. 212 (on 3.26).

Armitage Robinson,[1] while he certainly succeeded in showing
that confusion of πωροῦν, πώρωσις and πηροῦν, πήρωσις was
extremely common among copyists and early translators, that,
in fact, the distinction between them came to be no longer
recognized, never proved that they were not distinguished in
the original texts. We ought therefore to keep some such
translation as 'harden' for πωροῦν, and not to substitute
'blind'. The verb πωροῦν was used with reference to the
formation of a stone in the bladder or of a callus by which the
extremities of fractured bones are reunited, and so came to be
used metaphorically of the hardening of men's hearts. Compare
σκληρύνει in 9.18, and see on that verse. The passive here is
not to be explained away into meaning 'they hardened themselves'—a misinterpretation which can easily lead to a hard
and unbrotherly attitude to the Jews on the part of Christians.[2]
Rather must a divine hardening be recognized; but, as the
context makes abundantly clear, this hardening is not God's
last word with regard to these λοιποί. It is important here to
understand ἡ δὲ ἐκλογὴ ἐπέτυχεν and οἱ δὲ λοιποὶ ἐπωρώθησαν
together, each as qualifying and interpreting the other. For the
former points to the promise which concerns also the λοιποί,
while the latter points to the judgment from which the elect
themselves are by no means exempt. The statement οἱ δὲ λοιποὶ
ἐπωρώθησαν should remind us that the elect, in so far as their
human achievements and deserts are concerned, lie under God's
condemnation, and their ἐπιτυχεῖν is solely by sheer grace.
And the statement ἡ δὲ ἐκλογὴ ἐπέτυχεν should make us aware
of the provisional character of the hardening of those others.
A further point may also be made, namely, that vv. 11ff will
show that the hardening of the others itself belongs to
salvation-history, in that it leads to the salvation of the
Gentiles, which in its turn is to make these others jealous.[3]

8. καθάπερ. See on 3.4.

ἔδωκεν αὐτοῖς ὁ θεὸς πνεῦμα κατανύξεως, ὀφθαλμοὺς τοῦ μὴ βλέπειν
καὶ ὦτα τοῦ μὴ ἀκούειν, ἕως τῆς σήμερον ἡμέρας. The quotation is
basically Deut 29.4[MT and LXX: 3], the most significant
modification being that Paul has considerably strengthened
the statement of Deuteronomy, so as to bring out more clearly
the thought of divine hardening, by replacing the negative
οὐκ ἔδωκεν . . . καρδίαν . . . καὶ ὀφθαλμοὺς . . . καὶ ὦτα . . . (with

[1] St Paul's Epistle to the Ephesians: a revised text and translation, with
exposition and notes, London, ²1904, pp. 264–74.
[2] Cf. Gaugler 2, p. 174f.
[3] Cf. Barth, CD II/2, p. 275 (=KD II/2, p. 303).

its positive infinitival phrases following the three accusatives) by the positive ἔδωκεν . . . πνεῦμα κατανύξεως, ὀφθαλμοὺς . . . καὶ ὦτα . . . (with its negative infinitival phrases following the two accusative plurals). The phrase πνεῦμα κατανύξεως occurs in LXX Isa 29.10, which, along with Isa 6.9f, should also be compared. The text in Deuteronomy has ὑμῖν where Paul has αὐτοῖς, and the words are, of course, addressed to Israel. It is to be noted that the context of this verse in Deuteronomy is a gracious one, speaking of God's goodness to His people, while in Isaiah 29 one does not have to read on for very many verses from the reference to 'the spirit of deep sleep' before one comes to statements strongly suggesting that the divine hardening is not God's last word for His rebellious people. And moreover Paul no doubt means these OT passages to be understood in the light of the OT as a whole.

The expression rûaḥ tardēmāh, a spirit of deep sleep or torpor, is used in Isa 29.10 to denote a state of spiritual insensibility. The Greek κατάνυξις is extremely rare. In LSJ only two occurrences are cited: Ps 60.3[MT: 60.5; LXX: 59.5] and Isa 29.10 (Rom 11.8 is not mentioned); and the suggested meaning is 'stupefaction, bewilderment'. It has been suggested (Sanday and Headlam, Zahn) that the word was connected by a false etymology with νυστάζειν and so understood to mean 'deep sleep' (compare the Hebrew equivalent in Isa 29.10); but, against this, it should be noted that (i) νυστάζειν (LSJ: 'to be half asleep, doze') hardly suggests *deep* sleep; and (ii) in Psalm 60 the Hebrew word rendered by κατάνυξις is not the same as is used in Isa 29.10, but tar'ēlāh ('reeling'). While it is possible that Paul may have recalled the Hebrew word used in Isa 29.10, and so understood κατάνυξις as meaning 'deep sleep', we should probably be wise to explain the word along the lines of the meanings attested for the verb κατανύσσειν: 'stab', 'gouge'; in the passive, 'be sorely pricked', hence 'be bewildered, stunned' (e.g. Isa 6.5; 47.5; Th. Dan 10.15). Some such meaning as 'torpor' would seem most satisfactory. In any case, πνεῦμα κατανύξεως here in Romans, as in Isa 29.10, must denote a state of spiritual insensibility.

The phrase ἕως τῆς σήμερον ἡμέρας (in the LXX of Deut 29.4 it is ἕως τῆς ἡμέρας ταύτης) represents 'aḏ hayyôm hazzeh, which is a common OT phrase to indicate the permanence of a name or situation, or of a result of an event.[1] It is perhaps possible that, in addition to its connotation of permanence up to the present, Paul saw also in it a suggestion of a limit set to this

---

[1] BDB, s.v. יוֹם 7.l.

divine hardening (the idea of 'unto, but not beyond'), which would accord well with the tenor of vv. 11ff.[1]

9–10. Δαυὶδ λέγει. See on 4.6.

The quotation of Ps 69.22–23[MT: 69.23–24; LXX: 68.23–24] differs slightly from the LXX in v. 9,[2] but not at all in v. 10. The psalm is one which was much used in the early Church as a testimony of the ministry, and especially the passion, of Christ.[3] Paul here applies to the unbelieving majority of Israel words which were originally the psalmist's imprecation on his persecutors but which, when the psalm is understood messianically, are naturally referred to the opponents of Christ.

γενηθήτω ἡ τράπεζα αὐτῶν εἰς παγίδα καὶ εἰς θήραν καὶ εἰς σκάνδαλον καὶ εἰς ἀνταπόδομα αὐτοῖς. The general sense of this is no doubt a wish that even the good things which these enemies enjoy may prove to be a cause of disaster to them. The original imagery has been variously explained: for example, with reference to the skin or cloth, spread out on the ground by nomads, upon which the feast was laid, which could entangle the feet of the feasters, if they sprang up suddenly at the approach of danger, or with reference to poisoned viands intended for particular individuals which those who have prepared them are themselves forced to eat. With regard to Paul's use of the words, it is probably wiser to assume that he simply understood them as in a general way suggestive of the divine hardening (it seems likely that it was for the sake of v. 23a[MT and LXX: 24a] that he quoted the passage) than to attribute to him any such interpretation of the details as those suggested by Sanday and Headlam ('So to the Jews that Law and those Scriptures wherein they trusted are to become the very cause of their fall and the snare or hunting-net in which they are caught')[4] or by Barth ('God's table (the sum and substance of all his favours) remains in their midst—even if it causes their downfall . . .')[5] or by Barrett ('Their table is their table-fellowship: the unity and interrelatedness created by the law and so highly valued in Judaism were no more than a

---

[1] Cf. Barth, *CD* II/2, p. 278 (=*KD* II/2, p. 306).

[2] ἐνώπιον αὐτῶν is omitted, καὶ εἰς θήραν added, ἀνταπόδομα substituted for ἀνταπόδοσιν (which itself represents a different reading of the Hebrew consonants from that adopted by the MT—םָמוֹלְשִׁלְו instead of םֶהיֵמוֹלְשִׁלְו), ἀνταπόδομα and σκάνδαλον transposed (probably because σκάνδαλον is more readily associated with παγίς and θήρα than is ἀνταπόδομα, and αὐτοῖς added.

[3] Cf. Mt 27.34, 48; Mk 15.23, 36; Lk 23.36; Jn 2.17; 15.25; 19.29; Acts 1.20; Rom 15.3; Heb 11.26.

[4] p. 315.

[5] *Shorter*, p. 139: cf. *CD* II/2, p. 278 (=*KD* II/2, p. 305).

delusion since they were a union in sin (iii.20), not righteousness')[1] or by Käsemann (that τράπεζα is understood by Paul
in a cultic sense (he appeals to 1 Cor 10.21), his thought being
that the cult as representing Jewish piety causes the blinding
of Israel and its fall, and holds it under the yoke from which it
cannot free itself).[2]

For the use of θήρα in the sense of 'snare' or 'net' see Bauer,
s.v., and LSJ Suppl., p. 71.

σκοτισθήτωσαν οἱ ὀφθαλμοὶ αὐτῶν τοῦ μὴ βλέπειν is no doubt
understood by Paul as expressing the wish that that might
come to pass which the Deuteronomy quotation in v. 8 declares
God has brought about.

καὶ τὸν νῶτον αὐτῶν διὰ παντὸς σύγκαμψον. The LXX differs
here from the MT which has ûmotnēhem . . . ham'ad ('And
make their loins . . . to shake'). It is hardly possible to decide
with certainty (some commentators have been much too dogmatic on the matter) the precise significance of the figure of
the bent back in the LXX version or in Paul's use of it. The
thought could be of, for example, being bowed down under
oppressive slavery, being bent under a heavy burden, cowering
with fear, being bowed down by grief, being too weak to stand
upright, or stooping to grope on the ground because one's sight
is bad or one is blind. Of these, the third or fourth could be held
to correspond best to the Hebrew, while the last would fit the
first half of the verse very neatly; but, if the image is considered
on its own, one of the other suggestions might perhaps be more
natural.

In the second person singular imperative σύγκαμψον it is of
course God who is addressed.

The recent tendency to translate διὰ παντός by 'for ever'
(e.g. Moffatt, Weymouth, RSV, Barclay, Barrett, NEB[1], JB)
is surely mistaken. The meaning is rather 'continually'. The
point here is not that the bowing down of the backs is to go on
for ever, but that, so long as it does go on, it is to be not
intermittent but continuous and sustained. This explanation is
supported by consideration alike of the usage of tāmîd (the RV
correctly renders it 'continually' in the psalm), of the usage of
διὰ παντός both in the Bible and in secular Greek, and of the
context in Romans (vv. 11ff). For a full discussion see C. E. B.
Cranfield, in F. L. Cross (ed.), Studia Evangelica 2, Part i,
Berlin, 1964, pp. 546–50.

[1] p. 211. Cf. Schlier, p. 325.
[2] p. 289.

(ii) *The rejection of the greater part of Israel is not for ever*
(11.11–24)

[11]I ask then, have they stumbled so as to fall *irrevocably*? God
forbid! But by their trespass salvation *has come* to the Gentiles, in
order to make them jealous. [12]But if their trespass means riches for the
world and their defeat riches for the Gentiles, how much more shall
their fullness mean! [13]But it is to you Gentiles that I am speaking.
Contrary to what you may be inclined to think, inasmuch as I am an
apostle of the Gentiles I glorify my ministry [14]in the hope that I may
make my kindred jealous and so save some of them. [15]For if their
rejection means the reconciliation of the world, what shall their
acceptance mean but life from the dead? [16]And if the first-fruit cake is
holy, so also is the *whole* mixture; and if the root is holy, so also are the
branches. [17]But if some of the branches have been broken off and thou,
a wild olive, hast been grafted in among them and made to share the
root, that is the fatness, of the olive-tree, do not triumph over the
branches. [18]But if thou dost triumph over them, *remember that* it is
not thou that bearest the root but the root *that bears* thee. [19]Thou
wilt say then, 'Branches were broken off in order that I might be
grafted in.' [20]True: they were broken off by their unbelief and thou
standest by thy faith. Do not be haughty, but fear. [21]For if God has
not spared the natural branches, neither shall he spare thee. [22]Consider
then the kindness and the severity of God: to those who have fallen
there is severity, but to thee God's kindness, if thou remainest in his
kindness; for otherwise thou too shalt be cut off. [23]But they, if they
do not remain in their unbelief, shall be grafted in; for God is able to
graft them in again. [24]For if thou wast cut off from thy native wild
olive-tree and grafted into the cultivated olive-tree to which thou by
nature didst not belong, how much more shall these that are the
natural branches be grafted into their own olive-tree!

The exclusion of the great majority of Jews is not permanent.
It is the occasion for the coming in of the Gentiles, which, in
its turn, is to have the effect of awakening the unbelieving
Jews to a realization of what they are missing and so to lead
to their repentance. Paul hopes that the very success of his
own mission to the Gentiles may contribute in this way to the
saving of some of his compatriots. And, if the present exclusion
of the majority of Jews means so rich a benefit for the Gentiles,
what glory shall accompany their final restoration? In the
meantime the existence of those Jews who already believe in
Christ serves to sanctify the unbelieving majority. What Paul
says in this subsection and also in the following one is specially
addressed to the Gentiles among the Christians of Rome (cf.
v. 13a). He is clearly concerned to warn them against adopting
an unchristian attitude of superiority toward the unbelieving
Jews. It seems more probable that it is for the sake of directness
and forcefulness that the second person singular is used in
vv. 17–24 (Paul singling out each individual Gentile Christian)
than that the use is collective. The olive-tree imagery of these

verses has caused a good many commentators to make heavy weather; but Paul's meaning is not in doubt. The contemplation of his situation in relation to the unbelieving Jews should lead the Gentile Christian not to haughtiness but to fear for himself; and he ought to realize that God can and will restore the unbelieving Jews.[1]

11. Λέγω οὖν, μὴ ἔπταισαν ἵνα πέσωσιν; μὴ γένοιτο. The form Λέγω οὖν, μὴ . . .; μὴ γένοιτο) is the same as that of v. 1a. The subject of ἔπταισαν is those Jews who have rejected the gospel, i.e., the λοιποί of v. 7. The question μὴ ἔπταισαν ἵνα πέσωσιν; has been variously interpreted. There are two points at issue: (i) the force of ἵνα, and (ii) the significance of πέσωσιν. With regard to (i), it is clear that, if ἵνα has its strict final sense, then the purpose indicated must be God's. But, while the dominance of the thought of the divine purpose in these chapters is not to be doubted, there is cogency in the argument that here, since ἔπταισαν is active (and personal), the purpose indicated by ἵνα, if it were final, would naturally be that of the subject of ἔπταισαν. It is conceivable that Paul has expressed himself carelessly, and that he did mean ἵνα to be understood with reference to the divine purpose,[2] but more probable that ἵνα is to be explained as meaning 'so as to', that is, as expressing what Sanday and Headlam term 'the contemplated result' (compare the Vulgate translation: 'Numquid sic offenderunt ut caderent').[3] With regard to (ii), it is possible to understand πέσωσιν as denoting what has actually happened and to take Paul's meaning to be that (though they have fallen) their falling was not the only (or the main) result (or— if ἵνα is taken as final—not the only (or the main) purpose) of their stumbling.[4] The other possibility is to explain that, while

---

[1] Reference may here be made to M. M. Bourke, *A Study of the Metaphor of the Olive Tree in Romans xi*, Washington, D.C., 1947; K. H. Rengstorf, 'Das Ölbaum-Gleichnis in Röm 11.16ff: Versuch einer weiterführenden Deutung', in E. Bammel, C. K. Barrett, W. D. Davies (ed.), *Donum gentilicium: New Testament Studies in honour of David Daube*, Oxford, 1978, pp. 127–64; W. D. Davies, 'Romans 11.13–24: a suggestion', in *Paganisme, Judaïsme, Christianisme: Mélanges offerts à Marcel Simon*, Paris, 1978, pp. 131–44.

[2] As, e.g., Gaugler 2, p. 180, maintains. Cf. Cornely, p. 590f; Barth, *CD* II/2, p. 278 (= *KD* II/2, p. 306); Käsemann, p. 291.

[3] Cf., e.g., Chrysostom, col. 585 (ἴδωμεν δὲ εἰ τοιοῦτον τὸ πτῶμα ὡς καὶ ἀνίατον εἶναι καὶ μηδεμίαν ἔχειν διόρθωσιν. Ἀλλ' οὐκ ἔστι τοιοῦτον); Sanday and Headlam, p. 321; Lagrange, p. 275.

[4] Cf. Augustine, col. 2083: '. . . non ideo dicit, quia non ceciderunt; sed quia casus ipsorum non fuit inanis, quoniam ad salutem Gentium profecit. Non ergo ita deliquerunt ut caderent, id est, ut tantummodo caderent, quasi ad poenam suam solum; sed ut hoc ipsum quod ceciderunt, prodesset Gentibus ad salutem.' Cf. also Murray 2, p. 75f.

πίπτειν can, of course, be used to denote a falling which is not
final, a fall after which one can pick oneself up again, or be
picked up, this verb is here used to denote that falling which
means irreversible ruin as contrasted with πταίειν which denotes a stumbling from which it is possible to recover.[1] Paul's
μὴ γένοιτο is then denying that the result (or—if ἵνα is taken
as final—the purpose) of the stumbling of the λοιποί is their
irrevocable ruin. While the former interpretation suits the
latter part of the verse very well and also has the advantage of
giving to πεσεῖν the same sort of meaning as it has in v. 22,
the latter interpretation is to be preferred on the ground that it
fits the tenor of the section as a whole much better, and v. 11a
is surely to be understood as the heading of the whole subsection.

ἀλλὰ τῷ αὐτῶν παραπτώματι ἡ σωτηρία τοῖς ἔθνεσιν: 'but by
(dative of cause: cf. ἠλεήθητε τῇ τούτων ἀπειθείᾳ in v. 30)
their παράπτωμα salvation *has come* to the Gentiles'. The
substantive παράπτωμα[2] is frequently used by Paul to denote
'trespass', 'sin' (in the sense of a particular sinful deed), and it
is clear that what is referred to here is the sin committed by the
λοιποί in rejecting the gospel. It is possible that Paul chose to
use this particular word here and in the next verse because of
its literal meaning of 'false step', with the intention of continuing the metaphor in πταίειν; but (*pace* numerous commentators)[3] this is by no means certain, since (i) the metaphorical uses of παράπτωμα were so well established that it
seems doubtful whether the literal sense would spring at all
readily to mind, and (ii) παράπτωμα is, of course, cognate with
πίπτειν,[4] so that it would surely be awkward in a sentence, in
which (if our interpretation of πέσωσιν was correct) πταίειν and
πίπτειν have just been contrasted, to go on to use a cognate of
πίπτειν to denote the idea of πταίειν as opposed to that of
πίπτειν.[5] It seems preferable, therefore, to translate παράπτωμα

[1] Cf. Pelagius, p. 88: '*Ut caderent? absit!* Non penitus et inremedia-
biliter ceciderunt.' So many modern commentators, e.g. Sanday and
Headlam, Lagrange, Michel. For the use of πίπτειν to denote an irrevocable fall LXX Isa 24.20; Ps. Sol. 3.13(10); Heb 4.11 may be compared.
The metaphor of stumbling may have been suggested by σκάνδαλον in
v. 9: cf. 9.32–33 (προσέκοψαν τῷ λίθῳ τοῦ προσκόμματος, κ.τ.λ). On πταίειν
see K. L. Schmidt, in *TWNT* 6, pp. 883–85.

[2] See W. Michaelis, in *TWNT* 6, pp. 170–3.

[3] e.g. Sanday and Headlam, p. 321; Michel, p. 271; Barrett, p. 213.

[4] A direct cognate with πταίειν was available in πταῖσμα, though,
admittedly, it does not seem to have been a very common word.

[5] The use of παράπτωμα might indeed be adduced as support for the
other interpretation of πέσωσιν—though the reason given for preferring
the latter of the two interpretations explained above still seems to us
decisive.

'trespass' rather than to adopt such a rendering as 'false step'. Paul's meaning by the statement as a whole is generally explained by reference to Acts 8.1ff; 13.45–48; 18.6; 28.24–28; and it is indeed likely that Paul did have in mind the fact that it was the rejection of the gospel message by the Jews which compelled the messengers to turn to the Gentiles.[1] But the fact that he goes on to speak in v. 15 of the temporary casting away of the Jews as καταλλαγὴ κόσμου suggests that Barth may be right in thinking that he had something more in mind, namely, that it was the Jews' rejection of Jesus Himself and their delivering Him to the Gentiles (cf. Mk 10.33; 15.1) which led to His death and so to the redemption of the world (of both Gentiles and Jews);[2] for in the only other passage of Romans in which the term 'reconciliation' is used the reference is to reconciliation to God διὰ τοῦ θανάτου τοῦ υἱοῦ αὐτοῦ (5.10).[3]

εἰς τὸ παραζηλῶσαι αὐτούς indicates the divine intention. The coming of salvation to the Gentiles as a result of Israel's rejection of its Messiah is to make Israel jealous in accordance with the words of Deut 32.21 already quoted in 10.19. When Israel, the people whom God has made peculiarly His own, His special possession, see others the recipients of the mercy and goodness of their God, they will begin to understand what they are missing and to desire that salvation which they have rejected. Thus that hardening of which v. 7 spoke has for its ultimate purpose the salvation of those who are hardened.

12. εἰ δὲ τὸ παράπτωμα αὐτῶν πλοῦτος κόσμου καὶ τὸ ἥττημα αὐτῶν πλοῦτος ἐθνῶν, πόσῳ μᾶλλον τὸ πλήρωμα αὐτῶν. Verse 11 could give the impression that the only importance of the salvation of the Gentiles is that by making the unbelieving majority of the Jews jealous it is to lead to their salvation: v. 12 restores the balance by its stress on the greatness of the benefits which result for the Gentiles first from the unbelief of the greater part of Israel and then, much more, from their ultimate conversion.[4] παράπτωμα will have the same sense as it had in v. 11. For πλοῦτος here compare 2 Cor 8.9 (also

---

[1] Lagrange, p. 275, makes the further suggestion that, had the Jews as a whole accepted the gospel at this stage, they might not have allowed the Church to attain that freedom from Jewish national observances without which its appeal to the Gentiles must have been sorely limited; but this takes us into the realm of speculation, and the point is not likely to have been in Paul's mind when he wrote his letter.

[2] *CD* II/2, p. 279 (=*KD* II/2, p. 307): cf. *Shorter*, p. 139.

[3] Though it is to be admitted that in 2 Cor 5.18–20 'reconciliation' is used with reference to the reception of the gospel preaching as well as to the work of Christ.

[4] Cf. Lagrange, p. 276.

1 Cor 1.5; 2 Cor 6.10):[1] the meaning will be substantially the same as is expressed by σωτηρία in the previous verse. κόσμος can denote the world of men generally, and so κόσμου here corresponds to ἐθνῶν. The substantive ἥττημα is known to occur in only two other places, Isa 31.8 and 1 Cor 6.7, in both of which it may be translated 'defeat', which is the sort of meaning one would expect it to have, since it is derived from ἡττᾶσθαι, which can mean 'be less' or 'weaker (than someone)', 'be inferior (to someone)', 'be defeated'[2] (compare ἥττων which means 'inferior', 'weaker', 'less'). And this meaning suits the context here perfectly well. The rejection of the Messiah by the majority of Israel may properly be referred to both as their trespass (παράπτωμα) and also as their defeat—it is, though they do not yet recognize it as such, their defeat, discomfiture, rout, downfall. Both παράπτωμα and ἥττημα describe the action of the majority of Jews from the point of view of the believer; from the present point of view of the majority it is, of course, neither of these things. The habit of explaining ἥττημα as meaning here either 'diminution' or 'fewness', in order to have a neat antithesis to πλήρωμα, goes back a long way and is still widespread among commentators, but should surely be abandoned at last; for (i) neither 'fewness' nor 'diminution' is a likely meaning of the Greek word; (ii) the proper meaning of the Greek word suits the context admirably; and (iii) there is no really cogent reason for expecting here a word antithetical to πλήρωμα: there is just as much reason for expecting a word parallel in meaning to παράπτωμα as for expecting one antithetical in meaning to πλήρωμα. The Vulgate 'diminutio' (some MSS. have 'deminutio' which is more correct: 'diminuo' is of course to be distinguished from 'deminuo', with which the word used here in the Vulgate must be connected) need not mean 'diminution', but can equally well mean 'abasement' or 'dishonouring', and so can come very close to 'defeat' (cf. the comment of Thomas Aquinas on 'diminutio' here: 'qua scilicet decreverunt ab illa celsitudine gloriae quam habebant'[3]).

The general sense of τὸ πλήρωμα αὐτῶν must be what Chrysostom indicated when he explained it as referring to the time when πάντες εἰσιέναι μέλλουσι. What Paul is saying is: If the present unbelief of the majority of Israel actually means the enrichment of the Gentiles, how much more wonderfully

[1] In v. 33 Paul speaks of God's πλοῦτος and in 10.12 the verb πλουτεῖν was used with reference to God.
[2] Not 'defeat', as stated by Barrett, p. 214.
[3] p. 165 (884).

enriching must the situation resulting from the provoking to
jealousy of this majority of Israel be! But to decide what is the
precise significance of τὸ πλήρωμα αὐτῶν is difficult. The word
πλήρωμα here has been variously interpreted. The following suggestions may be mentioned: (i) complete conversion,
complete restoration; (ii) fulfilment, consummation, perfection;
(iii) obedience (fulfilment of God's will—cf. πλήρωμα . . . νόμου
in 13.10); (iv) full and completed number (cf. τὸ πλήρωμα τῶν
ἐθνῶν in v. 25). Of these, (iv) is widely accepted and seems very
much more likely than any of the others. But a further
difficulty has still to be met. It concerns the reference of αὐτῶν.
While, if (i), (ii) or (iii) were adopted, it would be possible (in
the case of (iii) perhaps necessary) to understand αὐτῶν to
refer to the subject of ἔπταισαν, i.e., to the λοιποί of v. 7, the
unbelieving majority of Israel, as does the first αὐτῶν of this
verse and also (unless ἥττημα is taken to mean 'diminution' or
'fewness') the second, if (iv) is adopted, it would seem at first
sight that αὐτῶν must refer to Israel as a whole. So Lagrange,
who was aware of the difficulty, argued that in this verse αὐτῶν
refers either to a part or to the whole of Israel according as the
context demands.[1] But this solution is, though no doubt
possible, surely awkward. It may be suggested that a more
satisfactory explanation is to understand Paul to be thinking,
not of the whole people's being brought up to its full numerical
strength by the restoration of the temporarily lost majority,
but of the unbelieving majority's being brought up to its full
numerical strength (i.e., the full strength of Israel as a whole,
which is the only relevant full strength that a loyal Jew could
properly be concerned with) by being reunited with the believing minority through its own (i.e., the majority's) conversion.
In this way πλήρωμα is taken according to (iv), and αὐτῶν is
also given its natural reference. (If the above suggestion concerning τὸ πλήρωμα αὐτῶν is accepted, a further objection then
lies against taking ἥττημα in the sense of diminution, at any
rate as that interpretation is generally explained; for, if both
the first and the third αὐτῶν in the verse refer to the majority
only, it would be particularly awkward to take the second to
refer to the whole people.)

13. Ὑμῖν δὲ[2] λέγω τοῖς ἔθνεσιν. Ὑμῖν is emphatic and δέ indicates
a slight contrast in thought—'But it is to you Gentiles . . .' .
This is not the beginning of a new paragraph; for the thought

---

[1] p. 276.
[2] There are two variant readings for δέ here: γάρ is read by ℵ D G *pm*
lat, and οὖν by C. But δέ is more strongly attested (𝔅 *al* sy), and should
almost certainly be accepted.

of vv. 11–12 is continued in vv. 15ff. It is rather that Paul recollects at this point that what he has just said in vv. 11–12 ought specially to be pondered by Gentile Christians, and so inserts vv. 13–14 parenthetically and then continues to address himself to the Gentile Christians specifically as far as v. 32. Neither this sentence nor anything else in this section indicates whether Gentile Christians formed the majority or only a minority of the Roman church at this time.[1] All that is clear from this passage is that the Gentile element in the church is here addressed specifically. On the subject of the composition of the Roman church the reader is referred to the discussion in the Introduction (pp. 17–21).

ἐφ' ὅσον μὲν οὖν[2] εἰμι ἐγὼ ἐθνῶν ἀπόστολος. In the Old Latin ἐφ' ὅσον was rendered 'quamdiu'. So Pelagius explains: 'Quam diu fuero in corpore constitutus, . . .' . And this is also the rendering of the Vulgate. But, while ἐφ' ὅσον was occasionally used without χρόνον in this sense (Mt 9.15; 2 Pet 1.13; also in Xenophon and Josephus), Paul would seem to have been in the habit of writing ἐφ' ὅσον χρόνον in full (cf. 7.1; 1 Cor 7.39; Gal 4.1). Moreover, Paul nowhere else speaks of his apostleship as temporary. Here the meaning is 'in so far as' (cf. Mt 25.40, 45). Paul's meaning is that in his very capacity as apostle of the Gentiles—not as some sort of *Nebenarbeit*—he hopes to promote the salvation of his fellow-Jews. As there is no δέ to answer to the μέν, and no δέ clause can be supplied at all plausibly,[3] μὲν οὖν should be understood as a single expression (see on μενοῦν γε in 9.20 and 10.18). Its force here is most probably to indicate Paul's consciousness that what he is about to say is contrary to what the Gentile Christians will probably be inclined to think.[4] We might paraphrase: 'Contrary to what you may be inclined to think'. It would be natural for them to suppose that in turning to the Gentiles Paul was turning his back upon the unbelieving Jews. But quite the contrary is true: his very labours as apostle of the Gentiles have an Israel-ward significance—of good for Israel. For ἐθνῶν ἀπόστολος compare 1.5; 15.16; Gal 1.16; 2.7, 9; 1 Tim 2.7; Acts 9.15; 22.21; 26.17f.

[1] Though it has sometimes been claimed that this section shows conclusively that Paul expected the majority of the church in Rome to be Gentiles.

[2] μὲν οὖν is omitted by D G *al* it, and οὖν by 𝕶 *pm* vg, but both words should no doubt be read (with 𝔓⁴⁶ 𝔥).

[3] *Pace* Cornely, p. 594.

[4] Lagrange's explanation (p. 277) that μὲν οὖν indicates 'simplement une concession: en tant qu'apôtre des gentils, ce que je suis, certes . . .' is much less likely.

τὴν διακονίαν μου: an instance of the general theological-technical use of the διακονεῖν word-group, according to which these words may have a variety of reference. Its reference here is indicated by the context: it clearly denotes Paul's ministry as apostle of the Gentiles. In 15.8 we have another instance of this general theological-technical use, in this case of the substantive διάκονος. See also on 13.4. For the specialized theological-technical use of these words see on 12.7; 15.25, 31; 16.1. For a full discussion see C. E. B. Cranfield, 'Diakonia in the New Testament', in *Service in Christ*, pp. 37ff.

δοξάζω.[1] The meaning of Paul's statement is not, surely, that he esteems his ministry among the Gentiles for the contribution it makes to the conversion of the Jews[2] (15.16 shows his awareness that 'the offering consisting of the Gentiles' is not without significance in itself); nor even that he glorifies his ministry among the Gentiles by achieving the salvation of some Jews by means of it (i.e., that the glory of his apostleship to the Gentiles consists in its converting effect on Israel);[3] nor is δοξάζω to be understood as referring to Paul's prayer of thanksgiving, his blessing of the divine Name.[4] What he actually says in this sentence is surely most naturally explained as meaning that he honours and reverences his ministry to the Gentiles, and so fulfils it with all his might and devotion, in the hope—though we are not to infer that this is the only motive of his labours—that its success may provoke the Jews to jealousy and so bring about the conversion of some of them.[5]

14. εἴ πως : 'if by any means', 'if perhaps', 'in the hope that'.[6]

παραζηλώσω. See on 10.19; 11.11. Here it is the apostle himself who is thought of as provoking to jealousy.

μου τὴν σάρκα: 'my kindred', i.e., Paul's kinsfolk according

---

[1] The variant δοξάσω is probably to be explained as a result of the understanding of ἐφ' ὅσον in the sense of 'so long as'.

[2] So Lietzmann, p. 103.

[3] So Barth, *Shorter*, p. 140; *CD* II/2, p. 280f (= *KD* II/2, p. 309).

[4] So Michel, p. 273 (with reference to G. Harder, *Paulus und das Gebet*, Gütersloh, 1936).

[5] Cf., e.g., Sanday and Headlam, p. 324; Lagrange, p. 277; Barrett, p. 214f.

[6] On the use of εἰ in expressing the expectation accompanying an action see BDF § 375. Here, as in 1.10; Phil 3.11 and Acts 27.12, it is strengthened by πως. It so happens that one cannot tell from the forms whether the two verbs which follow εἴ πως in this verse are future indicative or aorist subjunctive. In 1.10 the future indicative is used; in Phil 3.11 (where again the form is ambiguous) it is perhaps more likely that the verb is aorist subjunctive in view of the use of the aorist subjunctive with the similar εἰ καί in the very next verse; in Acts 27.12 the optative is used.

to the flesh, the Jews as a whole. For this use of σάρξ compare the use of *bāśār* in Hebrew in the sense of 'kindred'[1] and the corresponding use of σάρξ in the LXX (e.g. Gen 37.27; Lev 18.6; 25.49; Judg 9.2; 2 Sam 5.1).

σώσω. σώζειν is here used with the meaning 'convert': compare 1 Cor 9.22.

τινὰς ἐξ αὐτῶν. While Paul may indeed have expected his Gentile mission to disturb the Jewish nation as a whole, he clearly expects it to result in the conversion of only some individuals out of it. Murray comments well: 'But his zeal does not spill over into any excessive claims for the success of his ministry nor does he presume to state how his ministry of provoking to jealousy is related either causally or temporally to the "fulness" of Israel'.[2] It is only if we assume that Paul was possessed by the notion that he himself was going to complete that preaching to the Gentiles which must be accomplished before the Parousia (see further on 13.12; 15.19, 23), that the hope here expressed is at all 'surprisingly limited'.[3] Such conversions of individual Jews, though few in number, are a precious foretoken of the salvation referred to in v. 26.

15. εἰ γὰρ ἡ ἀποβολὴ αὐτῶν καταλλαγὴ κόσμου, τίς ἡ πρόσλημψις εἰ μὴ ζωὴ ἐκ νεκρῶν; To the question whether the connexion, the general nature of which is indicated by the γάρ, is with v. 13f or with v. 12 (v. 13f being regarded as parenthetical) or whether there is a double connexion (so Sanday and Headlam, who maintain that vv. 13–14 are 'to a certain extent parenthetical' and that v. 15 'continues the argument of v. 12, . . . but in such a way as to explain the statement made in vv. 13, 14'[4]), the correct answer would seem to be that it is more probably with vv. 13–14; for, on the one hand, v. 15 clearly does explain how it is that Paul can, not just as a Jewish Christian but precisely in his capacity of apostle of the Gentiles, be specially motivated by the desire to make his own kinsfolk jealous, since it affirms that for all (including the Gentiles) the restoration of Israel is going to

---

[1] See BDB, s.v. בָּשָׂר, 4.

[2] 2, p. 80.

[3] Barrett, p. 215. To suggest, as Käsemann does (p. 293), that Paul's εἴ πως (which is matched by this modest τινὰς ἐξ αὐτῶν) is a matter of diplomatic caution, which avoids laying immediately all one's cards on the table, and that it bears no relation to his real hope, is hardly convincing. It looks to us more like one sign (among a good many others) that the whole idea of the apocalyptic dream of a man, who sought to accomplish in a decade what two thousand years have not achieved, as the driving force of Pauline theology and action (Käsemann, p. 294), must be called in question.

[4] p. 325.

bring ineffable blessing (that is, it clearly does explain the immediately preceding sentence, which is what, all other things being equal, one expects a sentence introduced by γάρ to do), and, on the other hand, while it is true that it repeats the thought of v. 12 in rather more explicit terms, it may be doubted whether this increase of precision is not simply incidental to the fact of repetition rather than deliberately intended as an explanation of the earlier statement.

ἡ ἀποβολὴ αὐτῶν must mean their temporary casting away by God. In view of 5.10–11 (the only other place in Romans in which καταλλαγή is used), it seems better to take καταλλαγὴ κόσμου to refer to the objective reconciliation of the world to God through the death of Christ[1] than to either the subjective reconciliation of conversion (cf. 2 Cor 5.18–20)[2] or the reconciliation of Jews and Gentiles (cf. Eph 2.16).[3] The ἀποβολή of the Jews by God, which (if what we have just said is right) is here thought of as identical with, rather than as consequential on, their rejection of the Messiah, led directly to His death at the hands of the Gentiles and so to the objective reconciliation of the whole world to God. Though the noun πρόσλημψις is a hapaxlegomenon in the NT,[4] its meaning here is clear from the contrast with ἀποβολή and from Paul's use of the cognate verb (14.1, 3; 15.7; Philem 17: cf. Acts 18.26; 28.2). It must mean God's final acceptance of what is now unbelieving Israel, His admittance of them to the community of believers. ζωὴ ἐκ νεκρῶν has been understood in a figurative sense by a good many commentators (including Calvin, Hodge, Godet, Gaugler and Leenhardt), and this view of it has recently been supported with careful and forceful arguments by Murray.[5] But, since ζωὴ ἐκ νεκρῶν must clearly denote something surpassing everything signified by σωτηρία in v. 11, by πλοῦτος κόσμου and πλοῦτος ἐθνῶν in v. 12, and by καταλλαγὴ κόσμου in the present verse, it cannot denote the spiritual blessings already being enjoyed by the believing Gentiles. If it is to be interpreted figuratively, it must mean—so it would seem—a spiritual vivification which Paul expects to come upon the whole world as a result of the conversion of the mass of Israel (as Gaugler[6]

---

[1] See on v. 12.
[2] So, e.g., Sanday and Headlam, p. 325.
[3] So (as one of two suggested alternatives) Barrett, p. 215.
[4] It occurs quite frequently in extra-biblical Greek with various senses corresponding to those of the cognate verb. It is also found in LXX Ecclus 10.21, a verse which is apparently a gloss, and is there contrasted with ἐκβολή.
[5] 2, pp. 82–84.
[6] 2, pp. 186–88.

and Murray explain it with particular clarity). But this interpretation seems inconsistent with v. 25f, according to which
the conversion of τὸ πλήρωμα τῶν ἐθνῶν is apparently to take
place *before* the salvation of the mass of Israel. In view of this
objection which lies against the figurative interpretation in
what would seem its most convincing form, it is difficult to
resist the conclusion that ζωὴ ἐκ νεκρῶν should be taken to
mean the final resurrection itself (an interpretation maintained
by very many from early times to the present day)[1] and that
Paul's meaning is that the πρόσλημψις of the mass of Israel can
signify nothing less than the final consummation of all things.
While the effect of this verse is then, on the one hand, to forbid
all optimistic expectation of this final and complete πρόσλημψις
within the course of the Church's missionary history (and how
much more the folly of looking for it in any secular flowering
of Jewish nationalism!), it is also, on the other hand, to join
together in indissoluble union for all faithful Gentiles the hope
of the final home-coming of the Synagogue and the hope of the
final fulfilment of their own existence in the Church, and to
make the conversion of the individual Jew a particularly
eloquent pointer to that glory of which even the Church has as
yet but a foretaste.

16 provides confirmation[2] of the assertion that unbelieving
Israel too has a future which is implicit in vv. 11–15 (μὴ
ἔπταισαν ἵνα πέσωσιν; μὴ γένοιτο in v. 11a, εἰς τὸ παραζηλῶσαι
αὐτούς in v. 11b, τὸ πλήρωμα αὐτῶν in v. 12, and ἡ πρόσλημψις
in v. 15), and at the same time prepares the way by its use of
the imagery of root and branches for vv. 17–24.

εἰ δὲ ἡ ἀπαρχὴ ἁγία, καὶ τὸ φύραμα. This proverb-like statement, the form of which is reminiscent of Rabbinic maxims,
clearly alludes to the offering of a cake from the first of the
dough enjoined in Num 15.17–21 (Paul's language reflects the
expression ἀπαρχὴ φυράματος in LXX Num 15.20). The OT
nowhere says that this offering hallows the rest of the dough:[3]
its purpose seems rather to have been to free the rest of the
dough for general consumption (cf. Lev 23.14). But a comparison of Lev 19.23–25, according to which the fruits of the
trees are to be regarded as 'uncircumcised' until an offering
has been made to God from them, suggests that it would be

[1] Cf., e.g., Käsemann, p. 294.
[2] The variant γάρ (A Cl Or) is probably due to a recognition of this
function of the verse.
[3] Nor (so Lagrange, p. 279) do Josephus or Philo say that it does this,
though they both refer to it and indicate that the cakes were presented
to the priests (Josephus, *Ant.* 4.71; Philo, *Spec. Leg.* 1.131–144).

quite natural for the Jew to think of the offering of the first-fruit cake as purifying the rest of his dough.[1]

Paul's application of the figure of the first-fruit cake has been variously explained. Three main interpretations have been proposed: (i) that Paul refers to the patriarchs; (ii) that he refers to the Jewish Christians; (iii) that he refers to Jesus Christ. In support of (i), which is favoured by very many commentators,[2] it is urged that ἡ ῥίζα in the latter part of the verse is most naturally taken to refer to the patriarchs (cf. διὰ τοὺς πατέρας in v. 28), and that ἡ ἀπαρχή and ἡ ῥίζα must have the same reference. But, *pace* Sanday and Headlam, Lagrange, Michel, Murray, and many others, there seems to be no sufficient reason for assuming that ἡ ἀπαρχή and ἡ ῥίζα must have the same application,[3] and, once this is allowed, it is natural to see in the former a reference to the Jewish Christians (cf. Paul's use of ἀπαρχή in 16.5 and 1 Cor 16.15 of the first converts from a particular area),[4] and to understand Paul's meaning to be that the existence of Jewish Christians serves to sanctify the unbelieving majority of Israel, as the faith of one partner in a marriage sanctifies both the other partner and the children (1 Cor 7.14). This application of the figure of the ἀπαρχή suits the context well, since Paul has spoken of the λεῖμμα κατ' ἐκλογὴν χάριτος in vv. 1–10. The other interpretation, i.e. (iii), is to be found in some of the Church Fathers (e.g. Clement of Alexandria,[5] Origen,[6] Theodore of Mopsuestia,[7] Gennadius[8]), and receives support in Barth's *Church Dogmatics*[9]. Barrett also, while regarding (ii) as the most likely view, thinks it 'not impossible that behind the Jewish Christians Paul sees the figure of Christ himself, whom he actually describes as the "first-fruit" in 1 Cor xv.20'.[10] That for Paul Jesus Christ Himself is the ground of the holiness alike of the

---

[1] Cf. Lagrange, p. 279.

[2] e.g. Chrysostom, col. 588, who links with the patriarchs the prophets and all the other OT saints; Calvin, p. 249; Sanday and Headlam, p. 326; Lagrange, p. 279; Michel, p. 274; Murray 2, p. 85; Käsemann, p. 294; Schlier, p. 332.

[3] Cf., e.g., Dodd, p. 188; Gaugler 2, p. 191; Leenhardt, p. 286; Bruce, p. 217.

[4] Interpretation (ii) is favoured by Barrett, p. 216, as well as those listed in the previous note.

[5] *Strom.* 6.2.4.

[6] col. 1193.

[7] col. 857.

[8] in Cramer, p. 410.

[9] II/2, p. 285 (= *KD* II/2, p. 314), though he sees both the patriarchs and the Jewish Christians as also included.

[10] p. 216.

Jewish Christians and of the patriarchs is not to be doubted; but it seems improbable that he intended ἡ ἀπαρχή to be taken as referring directly to Christ.

καὶ εἰ[1] ἡ ῥίζα ἁγία, καὶ οἱ κλάδοι. While some take ἡ ῥίζα to refer to Christ,[2] and some take it to refer to the Jewish Christians,[3] there is a very widespread agreement among commentators that it must refer to the patriarchs and that Paul's meaning is that the unbelieving majority of the Jews are hallowed by their relation to the patriarchs. This view is supported by v. 28 (κατὰ δὲ τὴν ἐκλογὴν ἀγαπητοὶ διὰ τοὺς πατέρας). This does not mean that Paul is after all establishing, in spite of what he has said in chapters 2–4, a human claim on God, or that he is now affirming, in spite of what he has said in 9.6b–29, that every Jew must have a positive role in relation to the working out in history of God's purpose, but simply that God is faithful to His own promise (cf. 3.3f). The patriarchs are a holy root, not because of any innate worth or merit of their own, but by virtue of God's election of grace.[4] But the Gentile Christians are to remember that that holiness of the fathers which results from God's gracious election reaches beyond them to all their race.

17 is the beginning of a passage (vv. 17–24) which has often been criticized on the ground that in actual arboricultural practice one grafts slips from cultivated into wild trees, not slips from wild into cultivated trees.[5] According to many, Paul the town-bred man, is here guilty of an elementary blunder. Others have sought to defend him by referring to Columella, *De re rustica* 5.9.16, and Palladius, *De insitione* 53f, which show that the practice of grafting a slip of wild olive into a cultivated tree which was unproductive in order to re-invigorate it was known in ancient times, and also to evidence

[1] The omission of εἰ (𝔓⁴⁶ G P* *al* arm) destroys the parallelism between the two parts of the verse. Is it perhaps to be explained as due to a sense of the difficulty of taking ἡ ἀπαρχή and ἡ ῥίζα to have the same reference, as the parallelism might seem to require?

[2] e.g. some of the Fathers who take ἡ ἀπαρχή to refer to Christ; cf. also Barth.

[3] So Barrett, p. 216.

[4] Cf. Calvin, p. 249 ('. . . the spiritual nobility of their race, which was not peculiar to their nature, but originated from the covenant'); and contrast Sanday and Headlam, p. 327 ('. . . the Patriarchs, for whose faith originally Israel was chosen') and p. 331 (the passage we quoted on p. 41).

[5] e.g., Dodd, p. 189. Origen, col. 1195, notes the contrast with the practice of farmers, but says—sensibly—that Paul 'res magis causis quam causas rebus aptavit'.

of this practice in some countries in modern times.¹ But we still have Paul's reference to the grafting in again of the cut off branches (vv. 23-24), a parallel to which in normal arboricultural practice is hardly likely to be discovered. Others have appealed (probably wrongly)² to the phrase παρὰ φύσιν in v. 24 as an indication that Paul was aware that the procedure he was describing was contrary to ordinary practice. It is more to the point to notice that Paul is here using metaphor neither as an integral part of his argument (he is not appealing to the evidence of arboriculture in the way that Jesus, for example, appeals to the conduct of the owner of sheep in Lk 15.3-7) nor as a literary ornament, but simply as a medium for the expression of his meaning, a meaning which it was not very easy to express clearly and succinctly without any recourse to metaphor. (It is to be noted that he has already referred to 'root' and 'branches' in v. 16, and that in vv. 20-23 there is a free combining of metaphorical and non-metaphorical.) In this use of metaphor—and it is surely a perfectly proper use of it—the verisimilitude of the metaphorical details is not important; the important thing is that the author's meaning should be quite clear.³ And about Paul's meaning here there is no doubt.

Εἰ δέ τινες τῶν κλάδων. For the meiosis compare 3.3 (εἰ ἠπίστησάν τινες).

ἐξεκλάσθησαν. Ramsay notes that 'The cutting away of the old branches was required to admit air and light to the graft, as well as to prevent the vitality of the tree from being too widely diffused';⁴ but Paul's ἐξεκλάσθησαν reflects the course of history and is necessitated by the substance of what he wants to say, not by considerations of verisimilitude in his metaphor.

σὺ δὲ ἀγριέλαιος ὢν ἐνεκεντρίσθης. In v. 13a the second person plural was used, and it is again used in v. 25. In vv. 17-24 we have the second person singular, used for the sake of greater liveliness and here perhaps also personal directness of appeal (compare the other examples in Romans cited on p.

---

¹ Cf. W. M. Ramsay, in *The Expositor*, Sixth series, 11 (1905), pp. 16ff, 152ff, and id., *Pauline and Other Studies* (London, 1906), pp. 217ff; S. Linder, in *Palästinajahrbuch* 26 (1930), pp. 40ff.

² See on v. 24.

³ An interesting parallel to Paul's use of metaphor here is to be found in Marcus Aurelius Antoninus 11.8, in which, as in Romans 11, the grafting back of cut off branches is referred to (ἔξεστι γὰρ πάλιν ἡμῖν συμφῦναι τῷ προσεχεῖ καὶ πάλιν τοῦ ὅλου συμπληρωτικοῖς γένεσθαι. πλεονάκις μέντοι γινόμενον τὸ κατὰ τὴν τοιαύτην διαίρεσιν δυσένωτον καὶ δυσαποκατάστατον [τὸ] ἀποχωροῦν ποιεῖ. ὅλως τε οὐχ ὅμοιος ὁ κλάδος ὁ ἀπ᾽ ἀρχῆς συμβλαστήσας καὶ σύμπνους συμμείνας τῷ μετὰ τὴν ἀποκοπὴν αὖθις ἐγκεντρισθέντι, ὅ τι ποτε λέγουσιν οἱ φυτουργοί).

⁴ *Pauline and Other Studies*, p. 224.

377). ἀγριέλαιος is here possibly an adjective; in v. 24 it is clearly a substantive. The reference is to the true wild olive tree, which is not to be confused with *Elaeagnus angustifolia*. See Bauer, s.v. (bibliography); SB 3, pp. 290–2; *IDB* 3, s.v. 'olive tree'; *BHH* 2, s.v. 'Ölbaum'. Paul's choice of the olive rather than any other tree probably reflects its use in the OT as a figure of Israel (Jer 11.16; Hos 14.6).

ἐν αὐτοῖς: 'among them'—that is, among the remaining branches of the cultivated olive tree, the Jewish Christians. The meaning is imprecisely expressed: αὐτοῖς must be understood to refer to those of the κλάδοι which are not denoted by the preceding τινες τῶν κλάδων.

καὶ συγκοινωνὸς τῆς ῥίζης τῆς πιότητος[1] τῆς ἐλαίας ἐγένου. συγκοινωνός here means 'a sharer together (with the remaining native branches, that is, with the Jewish Christians)'. The word occurs in the NT also in 1 Cor 9.23; Phil 1.7; Rev 1.9. On the κοινων-group of words (represented in Romans also in 12.13; 15.26 and 27) see *TWNT* 3, pp. 789ff (Hauck); *TWB*, pp. 81ff. In τῆς ῥίζης τῆς πιότητος the first genitive (τῆς ῥίζης) is required by συγκοινωνός and denotes the thing shared. The second genitive (τῆς πιότητος)[2] may be explained either as adjectival, qualifying ῥίζης ('in the fat root'), or as a genitive of apposition, defining more precisely what is meant by τῆς ῥίζης (what is actually shared by those that are co-sharers in the root is the fatness which derives from it—'in the root, that is to say, in the fatness (of the root)'). The latter explanation is perhaps slightly preferable as regards sense. For the interpretation of ῥίζα see on v. 16: it is natural to give it the same significance in both verses. If the root signifies the patriarchs, then we may understand its fatness to signify the divine election in which alone their special worth consists.[3]

18. μὴ κατακαυχῶ τῶν κλάδων. The compound κατακαυχᾶσθαι occurs in the NT only in this verse and in Jas 2.13; 3.14. Used with a genitive it means 'to triumph over'. Paul is aware that there is a danger that Gentile Christians will be tempted to despise Jews. Whether by τῶν κλάδων he means only the broken off branches, so just the unbelieving Jews, or the natural branches generally, the remaining ones as well as the

[1] The variants, καί after ῥίζης (A K *pl* vg sy) and omission of τῆς ῥίζης (𝔓⁴⁶ D* G it Ir) would seem to be secondary, reflecting the desire for an easier text.
[2] For the association of fatness with the olive tree cf. Judg 9.9; Test. Levi 8.8.
[3] Substantially the same is Pelagius's succinct comment: 'Radicis patrum; pinguedinis Christi' (p. 89).

broken off, so the Jewish Christians as well as the unbelieving
Jews, is not certain. But in view of the fact that οἱ κλάδοι must
have the inclusive sense in v. 17 (τινες τῶν κλάδων), it seems
more probable that he means the latter. And if he does, it seems
likely that he is reckoning with the possibility (or the actual
existence?) of an anti-Semitic feeling within the Roman church
reflecting the dislike of, and contempt for, the Jews which
were common in the contemporary Roman world.[1] (See the
introduction to 14.1–15.13.) That prejudice belonging to the
Gentile Christians' pagan past would, if it had not yet been
eradicated by the discipline of the gospel, be only too likely to
be revived and aggravated by a sense of spiritual superiority
is evident.

εἰ δὲ κατακαυχᾶσαι,[2] οὐ σὺ τὴν ῥίζαν βαστάζεις ἀλλὰ ἡ ῥίζα σέ.
If the Gentile Christian insists on boasting over those who are
the natural branches, that will never alter the fact that it is
from his incorporation into the stock of Israel, the people of
God's election, to whom the promise was given of the seed in
whom all nations should find blessing, that all his spiritual
privileges derive. No amount of boasting on the part of the
branches which have been grafted in can reverse their relation
to the root. (For the brachylogy compare 1 Cor 11.16. See
BDF, § 483.)

19. ἐρεῖς οὖν· ἐξεκλάσθησαν κλάδοι ἵνα ἐγὼ ἐγκεντρισθῶ exposes the
logic behind such Gentile Christian boasting. 'Branches[3] were
broken off in order that I might be grafted in'—that is how a
self-complacent egotism sees the matter. And to such an egotist
this half-truth seems a conclusive proof of his own superior
importance and a sufficient justification for his contemptuous
attitude.

20. καλῶς admits the truth in the statement just put into
the mouth of the Gentile Christian. It is true so far as it goes;
but, taken in isolation, it is a dangerous half-truth, since ἵνα
ἐγὼ ἐγκεντρισθῶ is not the whole purpose of the breaking off of
the branches. God's[4] purpose includes also that to which εἰς τὸ

---

[1] Reference may be made to M. Stern, *Greek and Roman authors on
Jews and Judaism*, edited with introductions, translations and commentary 1, Jerusalem, 1974; E. M. Smallwood, *The Jews under Roman
rule from Pompey to Diocletian*, Leiden, 1976.

[2] 𝔓46 D* G *pc* read σὺ καυχᾶσαι instead of κατακαυχᾶσαι.

[3] D* *al* insert οἱ before κλάδοι. But this would appear to be a misguided
'improvement'; for there is point in the omission of the article, since not
the branches generally but only some branches are meant (cf. τινες τῶν
κλάδων in v. 17).

[4] The passives, ἐξεκλάσθησαν and ἐγκεντρισθῶ, indicate divine action.

παραζηλῶσαι αὐτούς in v. 11 pointed—which is something Gentile Christians are prone to forget.

τῇ ἀπιστίᾳ ἐξεκλάσθησαν, σὺ δὲ τῇ πίστει ἕστηκας. It was on the ground of[1] their unbelief that the unbelieving Jews were cut off, and it is on the ground of their faith, that is, simply on the basis of God's mercy and not by any merit of their own, that the Gentile Christians stand.[2] And if faith is the decisive factor, then self-complacence and feelings of superiority are out of place.

μὴ ὑψηλὰ φρόνει, ἀλλὰ φοβοῦ. If the Gentile Christians recognize the truth of what was said in v. 20a, they will know that they must not be haughty[3] but must fear God.[4]

21. εἰ γὰρ ὁ θεὸς τῶν κατὰ φύσιν κλάδων οὐκ ἐφείσατο, οὐδὲ σοῦ φείσεται provides support for the injunctions of v. 20b. If God has not spared[5] the unbelieving Jews, natural branches of the olive tree though they were, He will[6] not spare the Gentile Christians, the alien branches which have been grafted in, if they fall from faith.

22. ἴδε οὖν χρηστότητα καὶ ἀποτομίαν θεοῦ. In the grafting in of Gentiles and the breaking off of unbelieving Jews are to be recognized the kindness and the severity of God, both of which

---

[1] The datives τῇ ἀπιστίᾳ and τῇ πίστει are both causal (see BDF, § 196); and it is to be noted that there is no warrant for understanding one differently from the other. Paul does not think of standing as a reward for faith; and there is no good reason for reading into the other dative the idea of 'as a punishment for'. It is rather by the very fact of their unbelief, and by the very fact of their faith, that the ones are cut off and the others stand. Cf. Cornely, p. 604; Lagrange, p. 281; Gaugler 2, p. 194.

[2] For the use of 'stand' cf. 5.2; 1 Cor 7.37; 10.12; 15.1; 2 Cor 1.24; Eph 6.11, 13.

[3] For ὑψηλὰ φρονεῖν cf. 12.16 (τὰ ὑψηλὰ φρονεῖν); 1 Tim 6.17 (ὑψηλοφρονεῖν). Both here and in 1 Tim 6.17 there is variation in the MSS. between ὑψηλὰ φρονεῖν and ὑψηλοφρονεῖν.

[4] That the fear enjoined is the fear of God in the full biblical sense, which of course includes fear of His judgments, seems more likely than that it is merely fear of punishment. Bengel aptly compares Prov 3.7, in which μὴ ἴσθι φρόνιμος παρὰ σεαυτῷ is followed by φοβοῦ δὲ τὸν θεόν. See also on 3.18 and 13.7.

[5] Michel, p. 277, n. 6, notes the special frequency of negative formulations with φείδεσθαι. In seven out of the ten occurrences of the verb in the NT it is negated (twice in this verse, in 8.32, and also in Acts 20.29; 2 Cor 13.2; 2 Pet 2.4 and 5).

[6] The variant which inserts μήπως before οὐδέ (𝔓⁴⁶ ℵ D G pm lat sy Ir), though attested early, is no doubt secondary. It has led to the substitution of the subjunctive φείσηται for the future indicative φείσεται in some MSS. Chrysostom (col. 590) actually makes a point of the fact (as he sees it) that Paul did not say, Οὐδὲ σοῦ φείσεται but Μή πως οὐδὲ σοῦ φείσηται. The effect of the addition of μήπως is, of course, a considerable softening of Paul's categorical statement.

are the expression of God's holy and faithful love. For God's χρηστότης see on 2.4. For the general thought of God's ἀποτομία[1] see on ὀργὴ θεοῦ in 1.18.

ἐπὶ μὲν τοὺς πεσόντας ἀποτομία, ἐπὶ δὲ σὲ χρηστότης θεοῦ. For the use of 'fall' as opposite to 'stand' (used metaphorically)— ἔστηκας was used in v. 20—see on v. 11 (where, however, a special significance probably adheres to πέσωσιν), and compare also 14.4; 1 Cor 10.12. The variants ἀποτομίαν and χρηστότητα for ἀποτομία and χρηστότης are doubtless attempts to improve the grammar which should be rejected. For the use of the nominative compare 2.8–10.

ἐὰν ἐπιμένῃς τῇ χρηστότητι. For the statement of the condition compare Col 1.23; Heb 3.6, 14. The use of τῇ χρηστότητι instead of τῇ πίστει (cf. v. 23a: τῇ ἀπιστίᾳ) brings out the true nature of faith as living from God's kindness, God's grace.

ἐπεὶ καὶ σὺ ἐκκοπήσῃ. As in v. 6; 1 Cor 5.10; Heb 9.26, and quite frequently in classical Greek (e.g. Sophocles, O.T. 390; Xenophon, Mem. 2.7.14), ἐπεί means 'for otherwise'. The clause is a warning against a false and unevangelical sense of security.

23. κἀκεῖνοι δέ,[2] ἐὰν μὴ ἐπιμένωσιν τῇ ἀπιστίᾳ, ἐγκεντρισθήσονται. Not only are the Gentile Christians to beware lest they themselves fall from faith. They are also to recognize that, if the unbelieving Jews desist from their unbelief, they will be restored—grafted back into that holy stock from which they have been broken off. The Gentile Church is not called upon to pass judgment on them, but rather to expect this miracle with eagerness.[3]

δυνατὸς γάρ ἐστιν ὁ θεὸς πάλιν ἐγκεντρίσαι αὐτούς is a solemn affirmation of God's ability to restore them. For the use of δυνατός of God see on 4.21. In view of the argument in v. 24 that the grafting back of the original branches is more understandable than the grafting in of alien branches, we may wonder why Paul felt it necessary specially to stress the power of God here. The best explanation is perhaps that he wanted to guard against an assumption which he felt Gentile Christians would be liable to entertain, when puffed up by the presumptuous confidence he had just condemned in the preceding verses, namely, that Israel, once rejected for its disobedience,

---

[1] The substantive ἀποτομία is used by Diodorus Siculus, Dionysius of Halicarnassus, Plutarch and in papyri, but occurs in the NT only here (the adjective ἀπότομος is used in the sense 'severe' as early as Euripides, and occurs in the LXX in Wisd 5.20; 6.5; 11.10; 12.9; 18.15; and the adverb ἀποτόμως occurs twice in the NT but in neither place does it refer to God).

[2] On καὶ ... δέ see BDF, § 447 (9).

[3] Cf. Gaugler 2, p. 196f.

cannot ever again be established in God's covenant favour and that it has once and for all been replaced by the Church, 'the assumption that to restore Israel is contrary to the implications of their "casting away" (vs. 15) and that consequently grafting in again would violate the divine ordinance. . . . The erroneous assumption Paul meets directly by appeal to God's omnipotence and verse 24 is an additional *argument* to offset the fallacious inferences drawn from the rejection of Israel.'[1] God is the Almighty, and 'Man's disobedience cannot confront God with an everlasting fact. God remains free as regards the disobedient, just as he remains free as regards the obedient.'[2]

24. εἰ γὰρ σὺ ἐκ τῆς κατὰ φύσιν ἐξεκόπης ἀγριελαίου καὶ παρὰ φύσιν ἐνεκεντρίσθης εἰς καλλιέλαιον, πόσῳ μᾶλλον οὗτοι οἱ κατὰ φύσιν ἐγκεντρισθήσονται τῇ ἰδίᾳ ἐλαίᾳ. The phrase κατὰ φύσιν is often understood as referring to the wild olive tree's being a wild olive tree—so AV, RV ('of that which is by nature a wild olive tree'), Moffatt, RSV, Barrett and Käsemann, for example. But there is no point in saying that a wild olive tree is by nature a wild olive tree; for it can hardly be a wild olive tree otherwise than by nature. Paul's point is rather that the wild olive tree is that to which the branch that has been cut out belongs by nature[3] (in other words, the reference of κατὰ φύσιν is not to the tree's being the kind of tree it is but to its relatedness to the branch which is being addressed). The phrase is to be understood in the light of the use of παρὰ φύσιν and οἱ κατὰ φύσιν later in the verse: the Gentile Christian has been cut out of the wild olive tree, which is the tree to which by nature he belongs (ἡ κατὰ φύσιν ἀγριέλαιος), his native tree, and grafted into the cultivated tree to which by nature he does not belong (παρὰ φύσιν), whereas the unbelieving Jews, if they come to believe and are grafted back into the good tree, will be grafted back into their own tree (τῇ ἰδίᾳ ἐλαίᾳ), of which they are natural branches (οἱ κατὰ φύσιν). παρὰ φύσιν is sometimes understood as Paul's indication of his awareness that the procedure which he has described, the grafting of wild branches on to a cultivated tree, is contrary to normal arboricultural practice.[4] But it is much more likely that a contrast is intended between παρὰ φύσιν and οἱ κατὰ φύσιν later in the sentence, and that it is the grafting of a branch on to a tree

[1] Murray 2, p. 89f.

[2] Barth, *Shorter,* p. 143.

[3] So Lagrange, Huby, Michel, NEB, JB. Cf. the Vulgate: 'Nam si tu ex naturali excisus es oleastro . . .'

[4] Cf., e.g., Pelagius's comment: 'Contra naturam est oliuae inserere oleastrum, qui[a] magis ramus solet radicis uim mutare quam radix ramorum in suam ue[r]tere qualitatem' (p. 91).

to which it does not belong by nature which is being characterized as contrary to nature. For καλλιέλαιον see on v. 17. For
πόσῳ μᾶλλον compare 5.9, 10. If the Gentile Christian can
believe that God has actually grafted him into that holy stem
to which he does not naturally belong, how much more readily
ought he to believe that God is able and willing to do what is
less wonderful—to restore to their own native stock the unbelieving Jews, when they repent and believe!

(iii) *The mystery of God's merciful plan*
(11.25–32)

[25]For, so that you may not be wise in your own eyes, I want you to
know this mystery, brethren, that hardening has affected part of
Israel and will last until the fullness of the Gentiles comes in, [26]and
then all Israel shall be saved, as it is written: 'Out of Zion shall come
the Deliverer, he shall turn away iniquities from Jacob. [27]And this is
the covenant I will make with them, when I take away their sins.'
[28]As regards *the progress of* the gospel they are enemies for your sake,
but as regards the election they are beloved for the sake of the fathers;
[29]for the gifts and the call of God are irrevocable. [30]For as you once
were disobedient to God but now have received mercy by their disobedience, [31]so these now have been disobedient in order that they too
may now receive mercy by the mercy shown to you. [32]For God has
imprisoned all men in disobedience, in order that he may have mercy
upon all men.

Paul proceeds to impart a 'mystery', in order that the Gentiles
among the Christians of Rome, whom he is still specially
addressing, may not be wise in their own eyes. Its substance is
in vv. 25b–26a, and has to do with three successive stages of
the fulfilment of the divine plan of salvation: first the unbelief
of the greater part of Israel (the way it is referred to indicates
that this unbelief is not just a matter of human disobedience—
a divine hardening is involved), then the completion of the
coming in of the Gentiles, and finally the salvation of 'all
Israel'. The order of salvation thus described marks significantly an inversion of the order in which the good news is
preached according to 1.16 ('both for the Jew first and for the
Greek'). Verses 26b and 27 provide scriptural confirmation of
'and then all Israel shall be saved': the concentration on the
forgiveness of sins in the composite OT quotation is striking.
The following five verses draw out the implications of vv. 25–
27, and sum them up with evocative succinctness. First with a
few rapid strokes vv. 28 and 29 depict Israel subjected to the
wrath of God for the good of the Gentiles, yet all the time
beloved by God according to election for the patriarchs' sake,
since God is faithful. Then follow the carefully balanced

sentence of v. 30f with its temporal framework and the bold
conclusion which is v. 32. In these human disobedience is
firmly and decisively related to the triumphant, all-embracing
mercy of God. The subsection may be said to gather together
the substance of the whole argument of 9.1–11.24.

25–26a. οὐ γὰρ θέλω ὑμᾶς ἀγνοεῖν, ἀδελφοί. The γάρ indicates
the connexion of vv. 25ff with v. 24b in particular and also
with the argument of vv. 11–24 as a whole. Paul wants the
Gentile Christians in the Roman church to know the mystery
which he is about to state, because it is the solemn confirmation
of what he has just said, which at the same time goes beyond
anything which he has already said. For οὐ . . . θέλω ὑμᾶς
ἀγνοεῖν compare 1.13; 1 Cor 10.1; 12.1; 2 Cor 1.8; 1 Th 4.13.
It is a formula which Paul uses when he wishes to bring home
to his readers with emphasis something which he regards as of
special importance. Each time he uses it he adds the vocative
ἀδελφοί, on which see on 1.13.

τὸ μυστήριον τοῦτο. The word μυστήριον,[1] which occurs in
the Pauline corpus twenty or twenty-one times (in Romans
here and 16.25; also 1 Cor 2.7 (? also in 2.1); 4.1; 13.2; 14.2;
15.51 (which it is particularly interesting to compare); Eph 1.9;
3.3, 4, 9; 5.32; 6.19; Col 1.26, 27; 2.2; 4.3; 2 Th 2.7; 1 Tim 3.9,
16), denotes characteristically in the NT not something which
must not be disclosed to the uninitiated (which is its connotation in extra-biblical Greek, when used in connexion with
the mystery cults), but something which could not be known
by men except by divine revelation, but which, though once
hidden, is now revealed in Christ and is to be proclaimed so
that all who have ears to hear may hear it. The word has strong
apocalyptic associations (cf. LXX Dan 2.18f, 27–30, 47: cf.
also, e.g., 1 Enoch 51.3; 103.2; 104.10; 1QS 4.18; 1QpH 7.5, 8,
14). It is thought by many[2] that Paul is here imparting a new
special revelation which he has himself received, and this is
indeed possible. The word μυστήριον is closely associated with
προφητεία in 1 Cor 13.2, and is used in Eph 3.3 to denote
something which has been made known to the author κατ'
ἀποκάλυψιν. There is no good reason for denying that Paul
received prophetic revelations.[3] On the other hand, he does not

[1] Reference may be made to J. A. Robinson, *St Paul's Epistle to the
Ephesians*, London, ²1904, pp. 234–40; G. Bornkamm, in *TWNT* 4,
pp. 809–34 (p. 829 on its meaning in this verse); C. F. D. Moule, *The
Epistles of Paul the Apostle to the Colossians and to Philemon*, Cambridge,
1957, pp. 80–83; C. E. B. Cranfield, *The Gospel according to Saint Mark*,
⁶(revised)1977, p. 152f; Kuhn, *Konkordanz*, s.v. רז.
[2] e.g., by Gaugler 2, p. 199f; Michel, p. 280; Bruce, p. 221.
[3] *Pace* Zahn, p. 522.

state that what he is imparting is a new revelation or that it has been revealed only to himself; and it can be maintained not unreasonably that the contents of this mystery are to be discerned in the OT seen in the light of the gospel events.[1] In any case, the mystery is something which is knowable only because God has revealed it.

The τοῦτο looks forward: the contents of the mystery are going to be indicated in what follows (ὅτι πώρωσις, κ.τ.λ.).

ἵνα μὴ ἦτε ἐν[2] ἑαυτοῖς φρόνιμοι indicates Paul's motive for desiring that the Gentile Christians in Rome should know this mystery: if they know it, they will be less likely to succumb to the temptation to be wise in their own eyes, to be conceited about their supposed superior wisdom. Compare vv. 17ff, especially v. 18 (μὴ κατακαυχῶ τῶν κλάδων) and v. 20 (μὴ ὑψηλὰ φρόνει).

ὅτι πώρωσις ἀπὸ μέρους τῷ Ἰσραὴλ γέγονεν ἄχρι οὗ τὸ πλήρωμα τῶν ἐθνῶν εἰσέλθῃ, καὶ οὕτως πᾶς Ἰσραὴλ σωθήσεται might conceivably be understood as two statements, of which the latter is the conclusion drawn from the former (καὶ οὕτως meaning 'and consequently'). But it is much more natural to take it as a sentence made up of three members ((a) πώρωσις . . . γέγονεν, (b) ἄχρι οὗ . . . εἰσέλθῃ, (c) καὶ οὕτως . . . σωθήσεται), with καὶ οὕτως having the meaning 'and thus', i.e., when these preconditions have been fulfilled. But, on the assumption that this second alternative is to be accepted, we may still ask where stress falls. That (c) is stressed seems clear from the fact that it is supported by the OT quotation which follows. But with regard to (a) and (b), various possibilities may be considered. The main emphasis could be on πώρωσις (Israel's unbelief is not just a matter of human disobedience, but a divine hardening is involved—and this would be a reason why the Gentile Christians should not give way to feelings of superiority); or on ἀπὸ μέρους (only part of Israel is hardened—compare vv. 5, 7, 17); or on ἄχρι οὗ τὸ πλήρωμα τῶν ἐθνῶν εἰσέλθῃ (Israel's hardening will last until the fullness of the Gentiles comes in, it is in fact for the benefit of the Gentiles—a good reason for their not feeling superior; or, alternatively, Israel's

---

[1] Luther, p. 315, illuminatingly refers to Lk 21.23f; Deut 4.30; Hos 3.4f; 5.14.

[2] ἐν is read by B A, while ℵ C K D pm have παρ', and 𝔓46 Ψ G 1739 pc, supported by latt aeg, have the simple dative. Of these παρ' looks like assimilation to 12.16 and/or LXX Prov 3.7; ἐν has weighty support and is possibly the right reading, but could conceivably be due to Isa 5.21 (οὐαὶ οἱ συνετοὶ ἐν ἑαυτοῖς καὶ ἐνώπιον ἑαυτῶν ἐπιστήμονες). I am inclined to agree with Lagrange (p. 284) that the simple dative is probably to be preferred. (See BDF, § 188 (2) on this dative.)

hardening will *only* last till the fullness of the Gentiles comes in, the point being that Israel's hardening is temporally limited —and therefore the Gentiles must not be puffed up with self-importance by the thought that the Jews are cast off for ever). But it seems more likely that (a), (b), and (c) should be understood as simply indicating three successive stages in the divine plan of salvation, and that it is a mistake to try to give to any particular word or phrase a special emphasis apart from recognizing that it is (c) which is the high-point of the whole.

For πώρωσις see on v. 7 (ἐπωρώθησαν). While Israel's unbelief was something plain for all to see and not needing to be revealed, the fact that a divine hardening was involved was something which could properly come under the heading of μυστήριον. It could not be known by unaided human reason. The phrase ἀπὸ μέρους is adverbial, and modifies γέγονεν:[1] it refers to the fact that not all Jews were hardened (cf. vv. 5, 7, 17). The temporal conjunction ἄχρι οὗ must here mean 'until': though it sometimes means 'while' (e.g. in Heb 3.13), it cannot have that sense here in view of the aorist subjunctive εἰσέλθῃ. Paul's meaning is not that Israel is in part hardened during the time in which the fullness of the Gentiles is coming in, but that the hardening will last until the fullness of the Gentiles comes in. The entry of the fullness of the Gentiles will be the event which will mark the end of Israel's hardening.

The phrase τὸ πλήρωμα τῶν ἐθνῶν is probably to be explained as meaning the full number of the elect from among the Gentiles or the added number needed in order to make up that full total (an alternative which, if we understand εἰσέλθῃ to refer to something to take place in the course of history rather than to an entry taking place after the final judgment, we might perhaps be inclined to prefer, on the ground that the entry in the former sense of those elect Gentiles who are already believers would not naturally be spoken of as in the future), though there seems to be some force in the contention that v. 12 in which also πλήρωμα is used, has a bearing on the significance of the word in the present verse,[2] and, since in v. 12 Paul seems to have in mind a restoration of Israel which goes beyond the completion of the adding together of elect remnants of all generations, it may be wise not to rule out as altogether impossible another explanation, namely, that Paul

---

[1] So Michel, p. 280, rightly: *pace* Barrett, p. 223 ('it may be adjectival (as, apparently, here)'); Käsemann, p. 300. Reference should be made to BDF, § 272. There seems to be no sufficient reason for construing the clause otherwise than in the natural way.

[2] Cf. Murray 2, p. 94f.

means by τὸ πλήρωμα τῶν ἐθνῶν something like 'the Gentile world as a whole' (compare πᾶς 'Ισραήλ in v. 26). The use of εἰσέρχεσθαι is reminiscent of the tradition of the teaching of Jesus, which contains many references to entering into the kingdom of God or into life (e.g. Mk 9.43, 45, 47; 10.15, 23, 24, 25; Mt 5.20; 7.13, 14, 21; 18.3; 19.17; Jn 3.5). The verb is seldom used by Paul, and he uses it in this pregnant sense nowhere but here.

With καὶ οὕτως (see on 5.12) begins the last of the three parts of the statement of the content of the μυστήριον, the part on which the main stress falls (it is the part which is supported by the OT quotation which follows). The word οὕτως is emphatic: it will be in this way, and only in this way, that is, in the circumstances which are indicated by the first two parts of the statement,[1] that πᾶς 'Ισραήλ will be saved. The οὕτως indicates an inversion of the order in which salvation is actually offered to men according to 1.16 ('Ιουδαίῳ τε πρῶτον καὶ "Ελληνι). Barth suggests that the significance of the fact that it is thus and only thus that πᾶς 'Ισραήλ will be saved, is that that salvation will thus be clearly characterized as 'an act of the divine mercy . . . and not the recognition and satisfaction of human claims'.[2]

The meaning of πᾶς 'Ισραήλ has been much disputed down the centuries. Four main interpretations have been proposed:

(i) all the elect, both Jews and Gentiles;[3]

(ii) all the elect of the nation Israel;[4]

(iii) the whole nation Israel, including every individual member;[5]

(iv) the nation Israel as a whole, but not necessarily including every individual member.[6]

Of these (i) must surely be rejected; for it is not feasible to understand 'Ισραήλ in v. 26 in a different sense from that which it has in v. 25, especially in view of the sustained contrast between Israel and the Gentiles throughout vv. 11–32. That πᾶς 'Ισραήλ here does not include Gentiles is virtually certain. Almost as unlikely is (ii); for, on this interpretation, the

---

[1] Cf. Bengel, 550: 'καὶ οὕτω, et sic) Non dicit, et tunc, sed majore vi, et sic, quo ipso τὸ tunc includitur'.

[2] CD II/2, p. 300 (= KD II/2, p. 330).

[3] e.g. Calvin, p. 255, who appeals to the use of 'Ισραήλ in Gal 6.16.

[4] e.g. Bengel, p. 550f.

[5] e.g. Aquinas, p. 170 (916): 'non particulariter sicut modo, sed universaliter omnes'; Kühl, p. 392f; K. L. Schmidt, Die Judenfrage im Lichte der Kap. 9–11 des Römerbriefes, Zollikon-Zurich, ²1947.

[6] e.g. Zahn, p. 524; Lagrange, p. 285; Barrett, p. 223f; Käsemann, p. 300; Schlier, p. 340.

statement πᾶς Ἰσραὴλ σωθήσεται would be so obvious a truth
as to be, at this point, an anticlimax. The references to τὸ
πλήρωμα αὐτῶν in v. 12, to ἡ πρόσλημψις in v. 15, and to the
grafting in again of the broken-off branches in vv. 23 and 24,
point unmistakably to something more than what would
simply amount to the salvation of the elect remnants of Israel
of all the generations. The most likely interpretation is (iv).
We may compare the use of 'all Israel' (LXX: πᾶς Ἰσραηλ) in
1 Sam 7.5; 25.1; 1 Kgs 12.1; 2 Chr 12.1; Dan 9.11. Various
commentators also refer to the Mishnah tractate *Sanhedrin* 10,
in which the statement, 'All Israelites [so Danby, but Hebrew
is 'All Israel'] have a share in the world to come', is followed by
a considerable list of exceptions. On the apparent contradiction
between v. 26a and 9.27 we would refer back to the last
sentence of the first paragraph on 9.27f.

Sanday and Headlam seem to understand σωθήσεται to refer
to a situation to be brought about within the course of history;[1]
but it seems more probable that Paul was thinking of a
restoration of the nation of Israel as a whole to God *at the end,*
an eschatological event in the strict sense.[2] We cannot help
wondering whether this half-verse and Mt 10.23b may not
perhaps have some light to throw upon each other. Could it be
that the meaning of Mt 10.23b (whether its authenticity as a
saying of Jesus is accepted or rejected) is that the conversion
of 'all Israel' will not be accomplished until the Parousia? Some
light on the content of this σωθήσεται in Paul's mind may be
expected from the OT quotation which follows. (For the word
σώζειν see on 1.16b (σωτηρία) and on 5.9f.)

26b–27. καθὼς γέγραπται introduces a composite OT quotation in confirmation of what has just been said, particularly of
v. 26a.

ἥξει ἐκ Σιὼν ὁ ῥυόμενος, ἀποστρέψει ἀσεβείας ἀπὸ Ἰακώβ. καὶ αὕτη
αὐτοῖς ἡ παρ' ἐμοῦ[3] διαθήκη agrees with the LXX version of
Isa 59.20–21a exactly, except that ἐκ is substituted for the
ἕνεκεν of the LXX, perhaps under the influence of Ps 14[LXX:
13].7; 53.6[LXX: 52.7] or 110[109].2, and the καί before

---

[1] p. 336. They say, for example, 'σωθήσεται: "shall attain the σωτηρία
of the Messianic age by being received into the Christian Church"',
and 'Of final salvation Paul is not now thinking', and 'He looks forward
in prophetic vision to a time when the whole earth, including the
kingdoms of the Gentiles (τὸ πλήρωμα τῶν ἐθνῶν) and the people of
Israel (πᾶς Ἰσραήλ), shall be united in the Church of God'.

[2] It is interesting that Chrysostom, col. 585, understands Paul to
mean that the salvation of 'all Israel' is to take place κατὰ τὸν καιρὸν τῆς
παρουσίας τῆς δευτέρας καὶ τῆς συντελείας.

[3] 𝔓⁴⁶ transposes ἡ and παρ' ἐμοῦ.

ἀποστρέψει is omitted. In the MT v. 20 may be understood to refer to God Himself—a promise that God will come as redeemer for Zion. But there is Rabbinic evidence that this was interpreted of the Messiah,[1] and it is likely that Paul so understood it. By this promised coming of the deliverer he probably understood the parousia of Christ (compare I Th I.10: καὶ ἀναμένειν τὸν υἱὸν αὐτοῦ ἐκ τῶν οὐρανῶν, ὃν ἤγειρεν ἐκ τῶν νεκρῶν, Ἰησοῦν τὸν ῥυόμενον ἡμᾶς ἐκ τῆς ὀργῆς τῆς ἐρχομένης). He perhaps understood Σιών as meaning heaven or the heavenly sanctuary (compare Gal 4.26; Heb 12.22; Rev 3.12; 21 passim).[2] If this view of Paul's understanding of the first words of Isa 59.20 is correct, the quotation confirms our explanation of σωθήσεται as denoting a strictly eschatological event. The words ἀποστρέψει ἀσεβείας ἀπὸ Ἰακώβ (here the LXX differs considerably from the MT, which has, as translated in the RV, 'and unto them that turn from transgression in Jacob, saith the LORD') indicate the nature of the deliverance which this deliverer will accomplish; it will consist in turning back ungodlinesses from the nation of Israel. Such a characterization of the work of the Messiah affords a striking contrast to the Jewish expectation of a political messiah (see further on v. 27).

In Isa 59.21 αὕτη looks forward to the latter part of the verse, anticipating the content of the covenant as there set out. But Paul, after quoting the words καὶ αὕτη αὐτοῖς ἡ παρ' ἐμοῦ διαθήκη, instead of continuing with their proper sequel, substitutes a clause (slightly altered) from LXX Isa 27.9: ὅταν ἀφέλωμαι τὰς ἁμαρτίας αὐτῶν. The combination of the two passages, whether originating with Paul or already made in some collection of testimonies, was due no doubt to the fact that they contain similar ideas expressed in similar language and so could easily be connected together in the memory. There is a certain grammatical awkwardness in the composite quotation as it stands in Rom 11.27, since it is difficult to give a satisfying explanation of the ὅταν now that it introduces the

---

[1] So in Sanh. 98ᵃ Rabbi Johanan (about A.D. 250) is reported as saying: 'When thou seest a generation over which many oppressions break like a torrent, then expect him [that is, the Messiah]; for it is said (Isa 59.19), "When the oppressor shall come like a torrent which the tempest of the LORD driveth" [so the Midrash], and thereupon follows (v. 20), "He comes for Zion as redeemer"'. See SB 4, p. 981.

[2] This is surely more likely than that he had in mind the culmination of Christ's earthly ministry in Jerusalem (see Lagrange, p. 286; Leenhardt, p. 294, n. †), or that he was thinking of the work of the exalted Christ through His Church as accomplishing the final deliverance of Israel (see Huby, p. 403).

single clause indicating the content of the covenant;[1] but the general sense is of course clear enough—the substance of the new covenant which God will establish with Israel consists in His gracious forgiveness of their sins (cf. the relation of Jer 31.34c ('for I will forgive . . .') to the rest of Jer 31.31–34).

This composite quotation, then, points unmistakably, by its relentless concentration on God's forgiveness and on Israel's need of it, to the true nature of the deliverance signified by σωθήσεται. It dashes Israel's self-centred hopes of establishing a claim upon God, of putting Him under an obligation by its merits, making it clear that the nation's final salvation will be a matter of the forgiveness of its sins by the sheer mercy of its God. It is also to be noted that there is here no trace of encouragement for any hopes entertained by Paul's Jewish contemporaries for the re-establishment of a national state in independence and political power, nor—incidentally—anything which could feasibly be interpreted as a scriptural endorsement of the modern nation-state of Israel.

28. κατὰ μὲν τὸ εὐαγγέλιον ἐχθροὶ δι' ὑμᾶς, κατὰ δὲ τὴν ἐκλογὴν ἀγαπητοὶ διὰ τοὺς πατέρας. The asyndeton (see BDF, § 463) between vv. 25–27 and 28ff is noticeable. Verses 28ff may be said to draw out, and sum up, the implications of the preceding verses. This verse consists of two contrasted parallel statements. That these are not in equilibrium is clear both from the substance of the latter statement and from the fact that it alone is supported by the following verse: in fact, the addition of the latter statement limits the validity of the former.

In the phrase κατὰ τὸ εὐαγγέλιον the word εὐαγγέλιον must mean, not the gospel message, the content of the gospel, since with regard to that the Jews also are certainly 'beloved', but the progress of the gospel in the world. But the paraphrases offered by Sanday and Headlam ('as regards the Gospel order, the principles by which God sends the Gospel into the world'),[2] Lagrange ('à cause de la disposition convenable à la diffusion

---

[1] The expedient of taking αὕτη as referring backward to the first sentence of the quotation, instead of forward, seems to be impossible, as it does not yield a satisfactory sense. The interpretation suggested by Sanday and Headlam, p. 337 ('and whensoever I forgive their sins then shall my side of the covenant I have made with them be fulfilled'), can scarcely be got out of the Greek. Perhaps the demands of the Greek before us are best satisfied, if we take Paul's thought to be that this, i.e., the time when God at the last takes away His people's sins, will be the final establishment of His covenant with them, in which its true character as the covenant of divine grace (in which no question of human merit arises) will be manifest.

[2] p. 337.

de l'Évangile'),[1] and Barrett ('as far as the immediate results of the preaching of the Gospel go'),[2] would all seem to limit its significance too narrowly. The actual accomplishment in the ministry, passion and resurrection of Jesus of the events which are the basis of the gospel message, the preaching by Jesus Himself, the subsequent preaching by the Church, the acceptance or rejection of the gospel by men, may perhaps all be regarded as included in εὐαγγέλιον here. In relation to all of these unbelieving Israel has been disobedient and has thereby come under the wrath of God. It is surely in this sense of being under the wrath of God that ἐχθροί is to be understood here. The carefully worked out parallelism between the two parts of the verse requires us to take it (in correspondence with ἀγαπητοί) in its passive sense.[3] The point of δι' ὑμᾶς is that Israel's subjection to the divine hostility on account of its disobedience, its temporary rejection by God (cf. v. 15), was, in the divine providence, all along intended to benefit the Gentiles (cf. vv. 11, 12, 15)—so was 'for your sake'.

But all the time that they are ἐχθροί, they are also—and this is the permanent thing, while the other is temporary—with regard to God's election, beloved of God. By 'election' here is meant the election of the people as a whole (cf. v. 2), not that election which distinguishes within Israel (cf. vv. 5 and 7) and which is itself a pointer to the election of the people as a whole.[4] They are beloved of God on account of the patriarchs. Note that διά does not have the same sense in the two parts of the verse, though it may be translated 'for the sake of' in both places. In δι' ὑμᾶς it looks forward, meaning 'for the sake of' in the sense of 'with a view to the advantage of', whereas in διὰ τοὺς πατέρας it looks backward, meaning 'for the sake of' in the sense of 'by reason of'. But διὰ τοὺς πατέρας certainly does not mean by reason of anything which the fathers were in themselves, or did. Though the phrase may call to mind the Rabbinic doctrine of the merits of the fathers,[5] it is certain that

[1] p. 286f.
[2] p. 221.
[3] *Pace* Lagrange, p. 287, who is inclined (following, e.g., Aquinas, p. 170f (922); Zahn, p. 526f; Kühl, p. 394) to take it as active, and also some more recent interpreters, including Schlier, p. 341f.
[4] Cf. Murray 2, p. 101.
[5] For this see, e.g., A. Marmorstein, *The Doctrine of Merits in the Old Rabbinical Literature*, London, 1920; Davies, *P.R.J.*, pp. 268–73. In this connexion reference must now be made to E. P. Sanders, *Paul and Palestinian Judaism: a comparison of patterns of religion*, London, 1977. On Palestinian Judaism Sanders has clearly made a very interesting and important contribution (though even in this field it would be wise not

that doctrine was altogether repugnant to Paul. Paul's meaning in ἀγαπητοὶ διὰ τοὺς πατέρας is rather that Israel is beloved because God is faithful to His own love, which in His sovereign freedom He bestowed upon the fathers on no other ground than His love, which knows no cause outside itself (cf. Deut 7.7f).

29. ἀμεταμέλητα γὰρ τὰ χαρίσματα καὶ ἡ κλῆσις τοῦ θεοῦ. According to Calvin, τὰ χαρίσματα καὶ ἡ κλῆσις is an instance of hendiadys and means 'the benefits of calling';[1] according to Michel, καί is not used here to add ἡ κλῆσις to τὰ χαρίσματα but rather to introduce a particularization (Paul's thought being that among the χαρίσματα of God His κλῆσις is specially important).[2] But, while there is certainly a sense in which God's calling is a gracious gift, there are aspects of the divine calling which do not naturally fall under the description of gift (e.g. the aspects indicated by such words as 'commission', 'function', 'task'), and, in view of this fact, it is perhaps better to take the καί to have its ordinary copulative force. By τὰ χαρίσματα we may understand such privileges of Israel as are listed in 9.4f. (For the word χάρισμα see on 1.11 and 5.15.) By ἡ κλῆσις here we may understand God's calling of Israel to be His special people, to stand in a special relation to Himself, and to fulfil a special function in history. Compare Paul's use of κλητός in connexion with his own call to be an apostle (1.1). The substantive κλῆσις occurs in Romans only here, in the NT also in 1 Cor 1.26; 7.20; Eph 1.18; 4.1, 4; Phil 3.14; 2 Th 1.11; 2 Tim 1.9; Heb 3.1; 2 Pet 1.10. See further on 1.1.[3] Both the χαρίσματα and the κλῆσις of God are here characterized as ἀμεταμέλητα, that is, not liable to be repented of, irrevocable,[4] and ἀμεταμ-

---

to accept his every judgment uncritically): on Paul's thought his contribution is much less substantial and—in our view—not altogether perceptive.

[1] p. 257. Cf. his explanation of χάριν καὶ ἀποστολήν in 1.5 (p. 17).

[2] p. 283. For this use of καί he refers to BDF, § 442 (9).

[3] It may be suggested that the clause οἵτινές εἰσιν Ἰσραηλῖται in 9.4 and ἡ κλῆσις here refer to the same thing, the special position of this particular nation as the people of God; but that, whereas in 9.4 it would seem that the aspect of tremendous privilege is uppermost in Paul's mind, in 11.29 Paul's distinguishing ἡ κλῆσις from τὰ χαρίσματα—if we are right about the copulative force of καί—has the effect of indicating that it is the other aspects of special commission, function, task, service, that he here has specially in mind.

[4] The actual word ἀμεταμέλητος occurs only once more in the NT, in 2 Cor 7.10 where it qualifies μετάνοιαν (or, according to some, σωτηρίαν) as 'bringing no regret'. It is found in extra-biblical Greek (e.g. Plato, Ti. 59d; Lg. 866e; Polybius 21.11.11). The thought of God's not repenting is expressed in the OT quotation in Heb 7.21 (ὤμοσεν κύριος καὶ οὐ μεταμεληθήσεται).

ἐλητα is placed at the beginning of the sentence for the sake of the greatest possible emphasis. For the general sense compare 3.3f; 15.8. The ground of Paul's certainty that the Jews are still beloved of God, though under His wrath because of their unbelief and opposition to the gospel, is the faithfulness of God, that faithfulness, steadfastness, reliability, without which God would not be the righteous God He is.[1]

30f. ὥσπερ γὰρ ὑμεῖς ποτε ἠπειθήσατε τῷ θεῷ, νῦν δὲ ἠλεήθητε τῇ τούτων ἀπειθείᾳ, οὕτως καὶ οὗτοι νῦν ἠπείθησαν τῷ ὑμετέρῳ ἐλέει ἵνα καὶ αὐτοὶ νῦν ἐλεηθῶσιν. Verses 30 and 31 are, respectively, the protasis (introduced by ὥσπερ) and the apodosis (introduced by οὕτως καί) of a very carefully constructed sentence which is connected with what precedes by γάρ (we understand it as explanation, rather than confirmation, of vv. 28–29).[2] The carefully balanced correspondence between the protasis and the apodosis may be set out as follows:

v. 30	v. 31
ὑμεῖς	οὗτοι
ποτε	νῦν (the first νῦν in v. 31)
ἠπειθήσατε τῷ θεῷ	ἠπείθησαν
νῦν (in v. 30)	νῦν (the second νῦν in v. 31)
ἠλεήθητε	ἐλεηθῶσιν
τῇ τούτων ἀπειθείᾳ	τῷ ὑμετέρῳ ἐλέει

With regard to the recognition of these correspondences there

---

[1] With Paul's statement in this verse we may compare Num 23.19; 1 Sam 15.29 (also Ps 110.4; Jer 4.28; 20.16; Zech 8.14), and, of course, very many passages which speak of God's faithfulness and constancy. But Michel (p. 283) is right to note that neither the OT nor the NT propounds a speculative-philosophical doctrine of the immutability of God. And any truly biblical doctrine of the constancy of God must take account of the testimony of such passages as Gen 6.6; 1 Sam 15.11, 35; 2 Sam 24.16; 1 Chr 21.15; Ps 90.13; 106.45; 135.14; Jer 18.8, 10; 26.3, 19; 42.10; Joel 2.13; Amos 7.3, 6; Jon 3.10; 4.2, to the fact that God's constancy is not the same thing as inflexibility. But it must also be noted both that the divine repentance of 2 Sam 24.16; Jer 18.8; Joel 2.13; Jon 3.10; 4.2 is not held in equilibrium by the divine repentance of 1 Sam 15.35; Jer 18.10, and also that all the statements of Scripture about God's repenting (in whichever direction) must be seen as embraced within the fundamental and inclusive truth of God's faithfulness to His gracious purpose and to its declaration in His promises. That God is faithful to His gracious election in Jesus Christ of Israel, and through Israel of all mankind, is the testimony of the whole of Holy Scripture. See further: especially Barth, *CD* II/1, pp. 490–522 (= *KD* II/1, pp. 551–87); also Michel both in his commentary, p. 283, and also in *TWNT* 4, pp. 630–33.

[2] *Pace* Sanday and Headlam, who say: 'The grounds for believing that God does not repent for the gifts that He has given may be gathered from the parallelism between the two cases of the Jews and the Gentiles . . .' (p. 338).

is widespread agreement among recent interpreters.[1] But the question whether τῷ ὑμετέρῳ ἐλέει is to be connected with ἠπείθησαν or with ἐλεηθῶσιν, which involves a significant difference of meaning, has long been, and still is, strongly disputed; and there is also disagreement about the sense of the datives, τῇ τούτων ἀπειθείᾳ and τῷ ὑμετέρῳ ἐλέει. Those who connect τῷ ὑμετέρῳ ἐλέει with ἠπείθησαν—we shall call this interpretation (i)—interpret οὕτως καὶ οὗτοι νῦν ἠπείθησαν τῷ ὑμετέρῳ ἐλέει variously according to the way they understand the dative: e.g. (a) 'so also they have been disobedient because of (i.e., as a result of) the mercy shown to you';[2] (b) 'so also they have been disobedient because of (i.e., for the sake of) the mercy to be shown to you';[3] (c) 'so also they have been disobedient in the interest of (taking the dative as a dative of advantage) the mercy shown to you';[4] (d) 'so now, when you receive mercy, they have proved disobedient';[5] (e) 'so they also now (corresponding to the mercy you have received) have become disobedient'.[6] If, however, τῷ ὑμετέρῳ ἐλέει is connected with ἐλεηθῶσιν—we shall call this interpretation (ii)—we may translate: 'so also they have been disobedient, in order that now they too may receive mercy by the mercy shown to you' (the point of 'by the mercy shown to you' being, probably, either (a) that the Jews are to receive mercy by means of the mercy which has been shown to Gentiles, or (b) that they are to receive mercy by the same sort of mercy as that which the Gentiles have received).

It is sometimes objected to (ii) that to suppose that τῷ ὑμετέρῳ ἐλέει belongs to the ἵνα clause is to attribute to Paul a bizarre (Lagrange's word) construction; but this is surely

[1] It should be noted that the Latin Vulgate, which takes ἀπειθεῖν and ἀπείθεια in these verses to mean 'not believe' and 'unbelief' rather than 'disobey' and 'disobedience' (cf. the Vulgate version of 10.21: but evidence of the use of ἀπειθεῖν and ἀπείθεια as equivalents of ἀπιστεῖν and ἀπιστία as early as the first century A.D. does not seem to be adduced—later there is the evidence of Cyril's comment on these verses (cols. 849 and 852), and LSJ mention the use of the adjective ἀπειθής in the sense 'unbelieving' in Nonnus (? fourth to fifth century A.D.)), treats τῷ ὑμετέρῳ ἐλέει as corresponding, not to τῇ τούτων ἀπειθείᾳ, but to τῷ θεῷ ('Sicut enim aliquando et vos non credidistis Deo, nunc autem misericordiam consecuti estis propter incredulitatem illorum; ita et isti nunc non crediderunt in vestram misericordiam, ut et ipsi misericordiam consequantur', and is followed by the German Bible (Luther's version).
[2] Cf., e.g., Calvin, p. 258; Lagrange, p. 287f.
[3] Cf., e.g., BDF, § 196 ('because God desired to show you mercy'—causal dative).
[4] Cf., e.g., Käsemann, p. 303; Schlier, p. 343.
[5] NEB.
[6] Barrett, p. 221.

quite unfair.[1] We may compare, e.g., Plato, *Chrm*.169d (κἀγὼ ἡμῖν ἵνα ὁ λόγος προΐοι, εἶπον . . .); 2 Cor 2.4 (. . . ἀλλὰ τὴν ἀγάπην ἵνα γνῶτε . . .); Gal 2.10 (μόνον τῶν πτωχῶν ἵνα μνημονεύωμεν . . .); Col 4.16 (. . . καὶ τὴν ἐκ Λαοδικείας ἵνα καὶ ὑμεῖς ἀναγνῶτε); Acts 19.4 (. . . λέγων εἰς τὸν ἐρχόμενον μετ' αὐτὸν ἵνα πιστεύσωσιν . . .); and also examples of the placing of emphatic words before the relative pronoun as in 1 Cor 15.35 (. . . σὺ ὃ σπείρεις . . .); 1 Jn 2.24 (ὑμεῖς ὃ ἠκούσατε . . .), or before the interrogative pronoun as in Rom 11.2 (ἢ οὐκ οἴδατε ἐν Ἠλίᾳ τί λέγει ἡ γραφή . . .), or before ὅτι as in Rom 7.21 (see p. 362). This objection cannot be allowed.

Moreover, there is an important consideration which weighs heavily against (i) and in favour of (ii). It has to do with the parallelism between the verses. The correspondence between six elements of the protasis and six elements of the apodosis is so carefully balanced that it is most unlikely that there is not also a correspondence between the two clauses of the protasis and the two clauses of the apodosis. If τῷ ὑμετέρῳ ἐλέει is taken with ἐλεηθῶσιν there is, in fact, an exact correspondence between them—the corresponding elements being equally distributed between the two clauses in both the protasis and the apodosis in the form 3–3 : 3–3; but, if τῷ ὑμετέρῳ ἐλέει is taken with ἠπείθησαν, the balance is destroyed, and we get an arrangement of 3–3 : 4–2. This consideration is by itself, in our judgment, almost certainly decisive.

A further consideration relates to consonance with the argument of 11.11ff. This and the foregoing consideration taken together are, in our judgment, quite decisive. In view of the statement, τῷ αὐτῶν παραπτώματι ἡ σωτηρία τοῖς ἔθνεσιν, in v. 11, it seems natural to understand τῇ τούτων ἀπειθείᾳ as signifying 'through, or by means of, their disobedience'. But the parallelism between vv. 30 and 31 makes it likely that τῷ ὑμετέρῳ ἐλέει should be understood in a similar sense to that of τῇ τούτων ἀπειθείᾳ (thus 'through, or by means of, the mercy shown to you'). If τῷ ὑμετέρῳ ἐλέει is connected with ἐλεηθῶσιν the final clause is then in close agreement with the last words of v. 11 (εἰς τὸ παραζηλῶσαι αὐτούς)—the mercy shown to the Gentiles is to make the Jews jealous and so lead to their receiving mercy too.[2] But, if τῷ ὑμετέρῳ ἐλέει is taken with

---

[1] See LSJ, s.v. ἵνα B. *init*. ('mostly first word in the clause, but sometimes preceded by an emphatic word').

[2] Lagrange's objection to this explanation that, according to it, Paul adds nothing new but only repeats what he has already sufficiently indicated (p. 288) is not cogent; for in this whole subsection Paul is gathering together his argument in division VI up to 11.24.

ἠπείθησαν, the sense yielded (according to Lagrange, p. 288, Paul's meaning is that the mercy received by the Gentiles has served to aggravate the resistance of the Jews), though in itself capable of being defended, has no support in Romans 9–11— and, in fact, is the opposite of the point Paul does make, namely, that the mercy received by the Gentiles is finally to provoke the Jews to a salutary jealousy.

We conclude that (ii) is to be preferred to (i),[1] and that, between (ii) (a) and (ii) (b), (ii) (a) is to be preferred on the ground of the parallelism with τῇ τούτων ἀπειθείᾳ.[2] In order to clarify what he has said in vv. 28–29, Paul draws a comparison between the cases of the Gentile Christians and the unbelieving Jews, in which he brings out by the phrases, τῇ τούτων ἀπειθείᾳ and τῷ ὑμετέρῳ ἐλέει the fact of their interrelatedness (in explanation of the difficult v. 28a), and affirms with special emphasis—it is the climax of the whole comparison—that the final destiny of the still disobedient Jews is that they too, like those Gentile Christians who were once disobedient, should receive mercy.

The ἵνα of v. 31 must be understood as referring to the divine purpose. Behind the present disobedience of the majority of Jews is to be discerned the merciful purpose and providence of God. Compare v. 32, in which ἵνα follows a verb of which the explicit subject is ὁ θεός.

The second νῦν of v. 31 has caused considerable discussion. Faced with the fact that that to which ἐλεηθῶσιν refers is not yet taking place,[3] some have been inclined to understand this νῦν as the sort of νῦν which indicates a contrast with what might have been under other circumstances (compare LSJ, s.v. I.4; Bauer, s.v. 2 (and also under νυνί 2.a)). But, in view of the correspondence of this νῦν to the νῦν of v. 30,[4] which in turn is contrasted with ποτε earlier in that verse, it seems difficult

---

[1] Cf., e.g., AV; RV; Moffatt; RSV; Bengel, p. 551; Sanday and Headlam, p. 338; Zahn, p. 528 ; Denney, p. 685; Barth, *Shorter*, p. 146f; *CD* II/2, p. 304f (=*KD* II/2, p. 335); Murray 2, p. 102. Contrast Käsemann, p. 303; Schlier, p. 343.

[2] It is true that (ii) (b) would also give a Pauline sense—that the Jews are to be saved by the very same sort of mercy as the Gentiles have received, i.e. sheer mercy (cf. 3.19f, 22f), and would fit v. 32 well. But (ii) (a) fits v. 32 equally well, and has the advantage indicated above.

[3] It was doubtless a sense of this difficulty which caused the omission of this νῦν in 𝔓⁴⁶ A ℵ G *pm* latt, and also the substitution of the less strongly attested variant ὕστερον.

[4] Instead of the νῦν in v. 30 B has νυνί. No difference of meaning is involved. The B reading is probably due to the following δέ and the fact that Paul frequently has νυνὶ δέ. Quite often in the textual tradition there is variation between the two words.

to deny the temporal significance of this νῦν. But to regard it as a proof that Paul was certain that the end of the world would occur within a very short time, as Michel does,[1] is hardly fair.[2] The truth is rather that Paul sees the time which begins with the gospel events and extends to the Parousia as a unity. It is all the eschatological now.

32. συνέκλεισεν γὰρ ὁ θεὸς τοὺς πάντας εἰς ἀπείθειαν ἵνα τοὺς πάντας ἐλεήσῃ. The verse supplies a necessary explanation (hence the γάρ) of vv. 30–31, and at the same time serves finally to draw together and conclude the argument of chapters nine to eleven as a whole. It picks up the two leading themes of vv. 30–31, the themes of human ἀπείθεια and divine ἔλεος (ἠπειθήσατε — ἀπειθείᾳ — ἠπείθησαν and ἠλεήθητε — ἐλέει — ἐλεηθῶσιν) and relates them together in terms of the divine action (συνέκλεισεν . . . ὁ θεός and ἐλεήσῃ). But these two themes have run right through the three chapters;[3] and thematic too in these chapters are the thought reflected here in the use of συγκλείειν,[4] the stress on the sovereign action of God,[5] and also the contrast between the whole and the part[6] presupposed by the twofold τοὺς πάντας here.

The first half of the verse states that God has shut up, imprisoned, τοὺς πάντας in disobedience (or, possibly, has delivered them up to disobedience).[7] There was a tendency among the Greek Fathers to understand this as meaning simply that God has convicted τοὺς πάντας of disobedience. So Chrysostom, for example, explains: τουτέστιν, ἤλεγξεν, ἀπέδειξεν ἀπειθοῦντας.[8] But it is more probable, in view of 1.24, 26, 28, and

---

[1] p. 284.

[2] See further on 13.12.

[3] e.g., (for human disobedience) 9.1–5, 31f; 10.3, 16, 21; 11.3, 7f, 11, 20; and (for divine mercy) 9.15f, 18, 23; 10.21; 11.5f.

[4] Cf., e.g., 9.18 (σκληρύνει); 11.7 (ἐπωρώθησαν), 25 (πώρωσις).

[5] Cf., e.g., 9.11, 16ff, 19ff; 11.4, 8–10.

[6] Cf., e.g., 9.6–8, 27, 29; 10.16; 11.4–7, 12, 14, 16, 17–24, 25f.

[7] The verb συγκλείειν means to shut or coop up, hem in, enclose (e.g. of enclosing fishes in a net, shutting people up in a building), shut (e.g. one's mouth or a door). It occurs frequently in the LXX, where it usually represents the Hebrew verb sāḡar, which also means to shut, shut up, imprison. In 1 Macc 5.5 συγκλείειν means to imprison. But, like sāḡar in the Pi'el and Hiph'il, it can also mean to deliver up (e.g. Ps 78 [LXX: 77].50, 62; Amos 1.6). In the NT it also occurs in Lk 5.6 (of catching fishes in a net) and Gal 3.22 and 23. The fact that in Gal 3.23 it is associated with φρουρεῖσθαι rather suggests that Paul had in mind the idea of imprisoning when he used it, though the possibility that he used it as simply equivalent to παραδιδόναι (cf. 1.24, 26, 28: it is perhaps worth noting that in the last two of these verses εἰς is used, as here) is not to be ruled out.

[8] col. 592; cf. Cyril, col. 852; Theodoret, col. 181.

of Paul's references to God's σκληρύνειν (9.18) and πωροῦν (11.7, 25), that it should be understood as referring to God's providential ordering, which, by allowing men to exercise their freedom and also by that judicial hardening to which such passages as 11.7b point, brings it about that men are imprisoned in their disobedience in such a way that they have no possibility of escape except as God's mercy releases them.[1] 'God does not disdain', says Gaugler, 'even to veil His love by means of the dark and incomprehensible way of His judicial hardening, in order to be able to reveal it altogether in His mercy.'[2]

In view of the fact that this sentence is the climax of the argument and, like vv. 30 and 31, carefully worded and balanced, it is probable that in the clause ἵνα τοὺς πάντας ἐλεήσῃ, which states what was God's purpose in imprisoning all within their disobedience, both τοὺς πάντας and ἐλεήσῃ carry emphasis: that is, that Paul means both 'in order that He might have mercy on *all* (and not just on a few)' and also 'in order that on all alike He might have *mercy* (as opposed both to saving them on the grounds of their merits and also to allowing them to perish)'.[3] The hortatory implications of this verse (which it is likely that Paul had very much in mind) may be stated thus: (i) (a) a specific point—Gentile Christians must not imagine that the at present unbelieving Jews are beyond the reach of God's mercy; (b) a general point, which we may express in Calvin's words—the verse 'shows that there is no reason why those who have some hope of salvation should despair of others. . . . they ought to leave room for that mercy [i.e., God's mercy] to operate among others also'; (ii) salvation is by God's mercy alone—it is sheer mercy; (iii) —and this is the fundamental thing—mysterious though God's ways are and dark and indeed forbidding though they may sometimes now seem to us to be, the end of them is mercy, mercy pure and uncompromised.

How then are we to understand the twofold τοὺς πάντας?[4]

[1] It is interesting that Diodore (though he does also give as an alternative the explanation we have rejected) explains this by reference to 1.26 (he also wrongly cites 2 Cor 4.4, quoting the first words of that verse without τοῦ αἰῶνος τούτου), noting that Paul does not mean that God does evil, but that τοὺς βουληθέντας ἀπειθεῖν εἴασεν ἀπειθεῖν (Cramer, p. 424).

[2] 2, p. 212.

[3] Cf. Calvin, p. 258, who brings out very clearly his view that 'Paul . . . makes two points here'.

[4] The reading τὰ πάντα attested by 𝔓46 D* (G) lat Ir (in G without the article) instead of the first τοὺς πάντας is perhaps (though W. D. Davies, in *NTS* 24, p. 23, is inclined to accept it) an assimilation to Gal 3.22.

We may set aside straight away as quite unlikely the suggestion that it refers only to the unbelieving Jews (the subject of the last verb of v. 31). That it must also include the ὑμεῖς who are addressed in vv. 30–31 is clear enough. But does it mean all men in the sense of every single individual man? Or does it rather mean the different groups which have been mentioned in the preceding verses as wholes, the believing Jews and also Israel as a whole, the believing Gentiles and also the fullness of the Gentiles? The presence of the article might suggest the latter.[1] But, if Paul had been asked whether there were any exceptions to the statement of the first part of the verse, it is highly unlikely that he would have said that there were (cf. 3.9f, 19f). And, if the first τοὺς πάντας does include every individual (though Paul may actually in this context only have meant that God has shut in the various groups he has mentioned as wholes), there is possibly a certain difficulty in maintaining that this interpretation is ruled out for the second τοὺς πάντας.[2] It would seem to be wisdom here *both* to refrain from thinking to establish on the basis of this verse (or of this and other verses like 5.18 and 1 Tim 2.4) a dogma of universalism, *and also* to refrain from treating the solemn and urgent warnings, of which the NT assuredly contains an abundance, as clear warrant for confidently proclaiming the certainty of the final exclusion of some from the embrace of God's mercy.

(iv) *Conclusion to this main division* (11.33–36)

[33]O the depth of God's riches and wisdom and knowledge! How unsearchable are his judgments and incomprehensible his ways! [34]'For who has known the Lord's mind? Or who has been his counsellor? [35]Or who has anticipated him in giving, so as to receive from him a payment earned?' [36]For from him and through him and unto him are all things: to him be the glory for ever. Amen.

---

[1] See BDF, § 275 (7).

[2] A formal difference between this clause and v. 26a should be noted. In v. 26a we have a future indicative statement, whereas here we have an aorist subjunctive following ἵνα. If πᾶς Ἰσραήλ meant every individual Israelite, v. 26a would be a categorical statement that every individual Israelite will be saved. But, even if τοὺς πάντας in v. 32b were understood to mean every individual man, the clause would not be a categorical statement that God will have mercy on every individual man, but a statement that God's purpose in His action indicated by v. 32a was that He might have mercy on every individual man, which is not quite the same thing as a statement that He will do so. (It may also be noted that 'have mercy on' and 'save' are not exact equivalents.)

Verses 33–36 conclude not only section 4 but also main division VI as a whole. They are an eloquent expression of wonder and adoration before the mystery of God's ways, the majesty of His mercy and wisdom. For Paul at any rate the unflinching contemplation of the mystery of divine election cannot lead to gloom or fatalism, but must lead rather to a hymn of wondering praise, because, for him, election is a matter of the freedom and faithfulness of the merciful God. That it is not inappropriate to call these verses a hymn is clear enough. Their poetic character is apparent. That this hymn was composed by Paul as a conclusion to this division of his epistle is far more probable than that he was taking over an already existing hymn; but in composing it he has freely borrowed from several sources, from the OT, perhaps also from extra-biblical apocalyptic, from Hellenistic Judaism, from Stoicism as mediated through Hellenistic Judaism, and from the language of worship. In connexion with these verses reference may be made to Bornkamm, *Gesammelte Aufsätze* I, pp. 70ff; U. Wilckens, in *TWNT* 7, p. 518f; E. Norden, *Agnostos Theos*, Leipzig and Berlin, 1913, pp. 240ff; G. Harder, *Paulus und das Gebet*, Gütersloh, 1936, pp. 51–55; 79ff.

33. Ὦ βάθος πλούτου καὶ σοφίας καὶ γνώσεως θεοῦ. The first of the two exclamations, of which this verse consists, is the only example in the NT of such an exclamation introduced by ὤ, though examples are not uncommon in Hellenistic Greek. For the metaphorical use of βάθος compare 1 Cor 2.10; Rev 2.24: also, outside the Bible, e.g. Sophocles, *Ajax* 130, where, as here, it is used with πλούτου. The thought expressed is of profundity and immensity. It is unlikely that the first καί was intended in the sense 'both', so as to make σοφίας and γνώσεως dependent on πλούτου, or that it should be omitted (so 321 *e* vg) with the same result: the three genitives depend equally on βάθος. For the idea of God's wealth compare 2.4; 9.23; also 10.12. In view of these passages, while it is possible that Paul had in mind here God's infinite resources generally, it is rather more likely that he was thinking specially of the abundance of His mercy and kindness (cf. vv. 31 and 32). σοφία is associated with πλοῦτος in the doxology to the Lamb in Rev 5.12, and σοφία and γνῶσις are natural associates (cf. Col 2.3). By σοφία is perhaps especially meant the wisdom which informs God's purposes and His accomplishment of them (cf. 1 Cor 1.21, 24; Eph 3.10),[1] by γνῶσις perhaps especially God's electing love

---

[1] Reference may be made to Barth's discussion of the wisdom of God in *CD* II/1, pp. 422–39 (=*KD* II/1, pp. 475–95).

and the loving concern and care which it involves (cf. the use
of γινώσκειν[1] in 1 Cor 8.3; Gal 4.9; 2 Tim 2.19 and of
ἐπιγινώσκειν in 1 Cor 13.12 and perhaps 2 Cor 6.9: and, behind
this, the use of the root yd' in the OT in, e.g., 2 Sam 7.20;
Ps 1.6; 31.7[MT: 8]; 37.18; Hos 5.3; 13.5; Amos 3.2).

ὡς ἀνεξερεύνητα τὰ κρίματα αὐτοῦ καὶ ἀνεξιχνίαστοι αἱ ὁδοὶ αὐτοῦ.
The second exclamation, which is introduced by ὡς (cf. 10.15),
directs attention to the mysteriousness (cf. v. 25)[2] of God's
judgments and ways. God's judgments, as the judgments of
the merciful God designed to further His purposes of mercy
(cf. v. 32), do not conform to men's, even believing men's,
preconceptions and defeat our efforts to keep track of them.
The adjectives ἀνεξερεύνητα and ἀνεξιχνίαστοι point to the
truth that God's judgments and ways 'cannot be judged from
a higher vantage point, but are to be discerned as right only
in subjection to them as the affairs and ways of God'.[3] By
κρίμα here is meant 'execution of judgment', which is one of
the senses of the Hebrew mišpāṭ (cf., e.g., Isa 26.8f (MT: the
LXX differs here)). For the association of God's κρίματα and
ὁδοί compare, for example, Ps 10.5[LXX: 9.26]. By God's
'ways' are meant the ways which He takes in the accomplishment of His purposes, so His works or deeds (cf., e.g., Job
26.14; Ps 77.19[LXX: 76.20]; Isa 55.8f; Rev 15.3).[4]

   34. τίς γὰρ ἔγνω νοῦν κυρίου; ἢ τίς σύμβουλος αὐτοῦ ἐγένετο;
agrees almost exactly with the LXX version of Isa 40.13,[5] a
verse which is also quoted in 1 Cor 2.16. The quotation, to-

---

[1] The noun γνῶσις itself is used of God's own knowledge only here in
the NT.
[2] ἀνεξερεύνητος (Hellenistic form: ἀνεξεραύνητος), 'not to be searched
out', occurs in the NT only here and not at all in the LXX. It is found
in Symmachus (Prov 25.3; Jer 17.9); also in Heraclitus and Dio Cassius.
For the thought that the divine counsels are not to be searched out by
men there is an interesting pagan parallel from the fifth century B.C. in
Pindar, Fr. 61 (33), which is a fragment of a dithyramb. The third and
fourth lines are: οὐ γὰρ ἔσθ' ὅπως τὰ θεῶν βουλεύματ' ἐρευνάσει βροτέᾳ φρενί,
θνατᾶς δ' ἀπὸ ματρὸς ἔφυ. The verb ἐξερευνᾶν occurs in 1 Pet 1.10.
ἀνεξιχνίαστος, 'not to be tracked', 'incomprehensible', occurs also in
Eph 3.8 and LXX Job 5.9; 9.10; 34.24.
[3] Barth, CD II/2, p. 302 (=KD II/2, p. 332).
[4] The suggestion that v. 33b is intended to correspond to γνώσεως, v. 34
to σοφίας, and v. 35 to πλούτου (Bornkamm, Gesammelte Aufsätze 1,
pp. 70–73; U. Wilckens, in TWNT 7, p. 518f) is too forced to carry much
conviction.
[5] The γάρ is Paul's addition, the ἤ replaces the καί of the LXX, and
the words σύμβουλος and αὐτοῦ are put in the opposite order to that in
which they occur in the LXX text. The concluding relative clause of the
LXX verse is not quoted here: in 1 Cor 2.16 it is reproduced, while the
second question quoted here is omitted.

gether with that in v. 35, expresses the transcendent wisdom and self-sufficiency of God.

35. ἢ τίς προέδωκεν αὐτῷ, καὶ ἀνταποδοθήσεται αὐτῷ; is not to be found in the LXX (except in the variant reading attested by S* A C at Isa 40.14, where the words are pretty clearly an addition deriving from this passage in Romans), but is quite close to the Hebrew of Job 41.11a[MT: 41.3a] which is a place where the LXX is quite different. Paul is here either quoting according to the Hebrew of Job 41.11 or else from a Greek version other than the LXX.[1] The purpose of the quotation is to underline the impossibility of a man's putting God in his debt.[2]

36. ὅτι ἐξ αὐτοῦ καὶ δι' αὐτοῦ καὶ εἰς αὐτὸν τὰ πάντα (cf. 1 Cor 8.6) probably reflects Hellenistic Jewish borrowing from Stoic sources,[3] which in turn reflect the influence of pre-Socratic philosophers like Xenophanes of Colophon, Heraclitus of Ephesus, and Diogenes of Apollonia.[4] The early Stoic Chrysippus saw an appropriateness in the accusative form of the name Zeus (Δία), because Zeus πάντων ἐστὶν αἴτιος καὶ δι' αὐτὸν πάντα.[5] In the second century A.D. the Stoic Emperor Marcus Aurelius was to write: 'All is in tune with me, O Universe, which is in tune with thee. Nothing is too early or too late for me which is in due time for thee. All that thy seasons bring, O Nature, is fruit for me. All things come from thee, subsist in thee, return to thee (ἐκ σοῦ πάντα, ἐν σοὶ πάντα, εἰς σὲ πάντα).'[6] But the sense of the formula as used by Paul is far from the pantheism of the Stoic use of it. He is affirming that God is the Creator, the Sustainer and Ruler, and the Goal, of all things, and, as Michel rightly notes,[7] is thinking 'grundsätzlich geschichtlich und eschatologisch', not mystically or pantheistically. The affirmation is made here in support and explanation (ὅτι) of what has been said in vv. 33–35. Attempts to refer the three

---

[1] Paul's quotation of Job 5.13 in 1 Cor 3.19 also varies very considerably from the LXX. His reminiscence of Job 1.1, 8; 2.3 in 1 Th 5.22, however, agrees with the LXX.

[2] The verb προδιδόναι here has the sense 'give beforehand', 'give first'. It is used in this sense also in Xenophon, Aristotle, inscriptions, and in a papyrus.

[3] Cf., e.g., Ecclus 43.27; Philo, *Spec. Leg.* 1.208 (. . . ἤτοι ὡς ἐν τὰ πάντα ἢ ὅτι ἐξ ἑνός τε καὶ εἰς ἕν . . .); id. *Cher.* 125f.

[4] See H. Ritter and L. Preller, *Historia Philosophiae Graecae* (10th ed., Gotha, 1934), §§ 103, 36, and 208.

[5] Stobaeus, *Ecl.* 1.1.26, p. 31. Cf. the words ἐκ σοῦ γὰρ γενόμεσθα, . . . οὐδέ τι γίγνεται ἔργον ἐπὶ χθονὶ σοῦ δίχα, δαῖμον from the hymn to Zeus of the still earlier Stoic, Cleanthes.

[6] 4.23.

[7] p. 285.

parts of the formula to the three Persons of the Trinity[1] are clearly inappropriate.

αὐτῷ ἡ δόξα εἰς τοὺς αἰῶνας· ἀμήν. So the discussion of chapters 9–11 comes to its natural and fitting conclusion in a doxology. Paul has certainly not provided neat answers to the baffling questions which arise in connexion with the subject matter of these three chapters. He has certainly not swept away all the difficulties. But, if we have followed him through these chapters with serious and open-minded attentiveness, we may well feel that he has given us enough to enable us to repeat the 'Amen' of his doxology in joyful confidence that the deep mystery which surrounds us is neither a nightmare mystery of meaninglessness nor a dark mystery of arbitrary omnipotence but the mystery which will never turn out to be anything other than the mystery of the altogether good and merciful and faithful God.

VII

THE OBEDIENCE TO WHICH THOSE WHO ARE RIGHTEOUS BY FAITH ARE CALLED
(12.1–15.13)

The first eleven chapters of Romans have already made it clear that the life, which, according to 1.17, is the destiny of the man who is righteous by faith, is a life of obedience to God.[2]

Implied by the moral earnestness which marks the whole of section IV.1 (1.18–3.20), implied specially clearly by 3.8, this becomes explicit in chapter 6. How can those whom God has mercifully decided to see as having died to sin go on living in it

---

[1] They were made by many Church Fathers (see, e.g., Origen, col. 1201f; Ambrosiaster, col. 155).

[2] In this connexion it is interesting to note Chrysostom's observation at the beginning of his homily on 6.5ff. He draws attention to a contrast which has impressed itself on him between Romans and the other Pauline epistles, namely, that Paul's method in the other epistles is to put theology and ethical exhortation into separate divisions but in Romans to mingle them together throughout. His words are: Ὅπερ καὶ ἔμπροσθεν ἔφθην εἰπών, τοῦτο καὶ νῦν ἐρῶ, ὅτι εἰς τὸν ἠθικὸν συνεχῶς ἐκβαίνει λόγον, οὐχ, ὥσπερ ἐν ταῖς ἄλλαις Ἐπιστολαῖς, διαιρῶν αὐτὰς εἰς δύο, τὸ μὲν πρῶτον τοῖς δόγμασιν ἀφορίζει, τὸ δὲ ἕτερον τῇ τῶν ἠθῶν ἐπιμελείᾳ· ἀλλ' οὐκ ἐνταῦθα οὕτως, ἀλλὰ δι' ὅλης αὐτῆς ἀναμὶξ τοῦτο ποιεῖ, ὥστε εὐπαράδεκτον γενέσθαι τὸν λόγον (col. 483.)

contentedly? The only possible conclusion to be drawn from their baptism and what it signifies is that, instead of continuing to allow sin to reign as the undisputed master of their lives, they must—and can—rebel against the usurping tyrant, and henceforth present to God themselves as alive from the dead (ὡσεὶ ἐκ νεκρῶν ζῶντας) and their members to be instruments of righteousness. The latter part of the chapter (6.15–23) makes no fresh point, but rather brings out the significance of vv. 1–14 in a different way. Man's life is always, and inevitably, a serving of a master—a δουλεία. It is either—and these two are mutually absolutely exclusive—a service of God and of righteousness, the end of which is eternal life, or a service of sin, the end of which is death. By the end of chapter 6 the truth that those who by God's mercy have been made partakers in Christ's death and resurrection have thereby been claimed decisively for obedience to God—for sanctification (6.19, 22)—has been made inescapably plain.

And, despite superficial appearances and first impressions, chapter 7 in no way calls in question, but rather underlines, this truth. For, while it indicates that the rebellion against sin's tyranny is no easy matter but something with which the Christian is never done, so long as he is in the flesh, and reveals with relentless frankness the tension, with all its real anguish, in which he is involved and from which he cannot in this life escape, it also makes it clear that there can be no question of his laying down his arms and settling for peace. Standing as it does between chapters 6 and 8, 7.25 ('Thanks be to God through Jesus Christ our Lord! So then I myself serve with my mind the law of God, but with my flesh the law of sin') is totally misunderstood, if it is taken to imply that the Christian may accept his continued sinning with complacence. The ground of Paul's thanksgiving is that, held though he is in this painful tension, he is, through Christ, in it in hope and not in hopelessness. And, while the latter half of the verse honestly acknowledges the fact that the Christian, so long as he remains in the flesh, remains in a real sense the slave of sin (cf. 7.14), its point is that he nevertheless, as one to whom God has given a righteous status in Christ, is altogether bound in his conscience to God's holy law.[1]

In chapter 8 the necessity of obedience is set forth in terms of the gift of the Spirit. To be in Christ is to be indwelt by His

---

[1] τῇ δὲ σαρκὶ νόμῳ ἁμαρτίας is really equivalent to a concessive clause. Cf. 6.17, though there it is the first clause, and not the δέ clause, which has this force.

Spirit, and the Spirit of Christ is the Holy Spirit, who establishes God's law in its true character and function as 'unto
life' (7.10) and 'spiritual' (7.14), and whose pressure on our
lives has set us free from the tyranny of sin and death (8.2).
One cannot have Christ without also having His Spirit (8.9);
the gift of justification through Christ is not to be had in
separation from the Spirit of regeneration and sanctification,
for to separate these 'would be, as it were, to rend Christ
asunder'.[1] Christian obedience, then, is to live under God's
law established in its true nature by the Spirit.[2] And what this
means is summed up in 8.15: 'you have received the Spirit of
adoption, by whose enabling we cry "Abba, Father".' All that
needs to be said about Christian obedience has already been
said in principle in this verse; for to 'cry "Abba, Father" ', to
call the true, holy God 'Father' with full sincerity and seriousness—this is to obey God's law, this is indeed the whole of
Christian obedience. For to address God by the name of Father
sincerely and with full seriousness involves seeking wholeheartedly to be and think and speak and do what is well-
pleasing to Him, and at the same time to avoid all that is
displeasing to Him.

But the obedience required of Christians is not just an
obedience in principle. It is rather an obedience of thought and
attitude, of word and deed, wrought out in the concrete
situations of life—and an obedience, moreover, which has to
be wrought out by Christians who are far from being fully
sincere or fully serious in their calling God 'Father'. Exhortation is therefore necessary—an exhortation which does not
stop at the abstract and general,but is concrete and particular.
It is such exhortation that we find in Romans 12.1–15.13.

It is widely agreed that Paul has in these chapters made
considerable use of traditional material of various sorts, and
from time to time we shall have occasion to notice his probable
sources; but our main concern will be with the significance
which such material has in its context in Romans.[3]

---

[1] Calvin, p. 164.

[2] Cf. Barth, *Shorter*, pp. 88–109.

[3] In connexion with the subject-matter of this main division generally
mention may be made of R. Schnackenburg, *The Moral Teaching of the
New Testament* (Eng. tr. of *Die sittliche Botschaft des Neuen Testamentes*,
[2]1962), New York, 1965; V. P. Furnish, *Theology and Ethics in Paul*,
Nashville and New York, 1968; O. Merk, *Handeln aus Glauben: die
Motivierung der paulinischen Ethik*, Marburg, 1968.

VII. 1. THE THEME OF THIS MAIN DIVISION OF THE EPISTLE IS SET FORTH (12.1–2)

These two verses serve as an introduction to the rest of the main division 12.1–15.13, the theme of which they set forth. As the key to the right understanding of the sections which follow, they require a specially careful and patient study.

> [1]I exhort you, therefore, brethren, by the mercies of God to present yourselves as a sacrifice living, holy and well-pleasing to God, which is your understanding worship. [2]And stop allowing yourselves to be conformed to this age, but continue to let yourselves be transformed by the renewing of your mind, so that you may prove what is the will of God, that which is good and well-pleasing and perfect.

1. Παρακαλῶ οὖν ὑμᾶς, ἀδελφοί, διὰ τῶν οἰκτιρμῶν τοῦ θεοῦ. Supported as it is by the following διὰ τῶν οἰκτιρμῶν τοῦ θεοῦ, which looks back to what Paul has been writing about, οὖν is here better understood not as a mere transition-particle,[1] but as having its full force[2] and indicating that what is going to be said follows from what has already been said. The implication of this 'therefore' is that Christian ethics are theologically motivated or—to put it in a different way—that the Christian's obedience is his response to what God has done for him in Christ, the expression of his gratitude.[3] Given its full force, the οὖν makes clear right from the start the theocentric nature of all truly Christian moral effort; for it indicates that the source from which such effort springs is neither a humanistic desire for the enhancement of the self by the attainment of moral superiority, nor the legalist's illusory hope of putting God under an obligation, but the saving deed of God itself.

But how far back does οὖν look? The words διὰ τῶν οἰκτιρμῶν τοῦ θεοῦ, which (as we have just seen) support οὖν, might seem, in view of the distribution of the verb οἰκτίρειν[4] and the kindred words ἔλεος and ἐλεεῖν in the Pauline epistles (οἰκτίρειν occurs in the NT only in Rom 9.15; ἔλεος occurs twice in Rom 9–11 and only three times elsewhere in Paul apart from the Pastorals; ἐλεεῖν occurs seven times in Rom 9–11 and only four times

---

[1] *Pace* Lietzmann, p. 107; Käsemann, p. 311.

[2] Cf. Barrett, p. 230. For οὖν used with παρακαλῶ (παρακαλοῦμεν) cf. 1 Cor 4.16; 1 Th 4.1; 1 Tim 2.1.

[3] Cf. the title of the third main division of the Heidelberg Catechism, 'Von der Dankbarkeit'—'Thankfulness' (in T. F. Torrance, *The School of Faith: the Catechisms of the Reformed Church*, London, 1959, p. 86); and also Bengel's fine comment (p. 553): 'Christianus . . . ex beneficio Dei miserentis colligit officium suum'.

[4] The noun οἰκτιρμός occurs in Romans only here: it occurs also in four other places in the New Testament, of which three are Pauline.

elsewhere in Paul apart from the Pastorals), to suggest that Paul is thinking only, or, at any rate, specially, of chapters 9 to 11. But, while it is certainly true that chapters 9 to 11 are specially set under the sign of the mercy of God, it is also true that the whole of 1.18–11.36 is concerned with the action of the merciful God. The words οἰκτίρειν, ἔλεος and ἐλεεῖν may indeed be absent from the first eight chapters; but such words as χρηστότης, μακροθυμία, ἀγάπη and χάρις are used, and the reality of the mercy of God is never far from Paul's thought. And, apart from the linguistic consideration, it would seem intrinsically more probable that Paul thought of his exhortation as being based upon the whole of what he had so far written to the Roman Church than as based solely on chapters 9–11. We take it, therefore, that the reference of οὖν is to the whole course of the epistle's argument up to this point.

The words διὰ[1] τῶν οἰκτιρμῶν τοῦ θεοῦ indicate Paul's ground of appeal. (That he intended these words to be taken with παραστῆσαι, his thought being that the mercy of God makes possible the offering, is unlikely: even more unlikely is the suggestion that he intended the words to be taken both with παρακαλῶ and with παραστῆσαι.) If this were not biblical Greek, the use of the plural οἰκτιρμῶν would suggest a number of different manifestations of compassion; but here (as in 2 Cor 1.3; Phil 2.1) it probably reflects the influence of the LXX, which regularly represents the Hebrew plural raḥªmîm by the plural of οἰκτιρμός. The Vulgate represents Paul's meaning accurately by the singular *misericordiam*. What he is appealing to as the basis of his exhortation is the compassion of God revealed in God's dealing with men through Jesus Christ. Calvin's comment is apt. Paul here 'teaches us', he says, 'that men will never worship God with a sincere heart, or be roused to fear and obey Him with sufficient zeal, until they properly understand how much they are indebted to His mercy. . . . Paul, however, in order to bind us to God not by servile fear but by a voluntary and cheerful love of righteousness, attracts us by the sweetness of that grace in which our salvation consists. At the same time he reproaches us with ingratitude if, having had experience of so kind and liberal a father, we do not in return strive to dedicate ourselves wholly to Him.'[2]

---

[1] Cf. 15.30; 1 Cor 1.10; 2 Cor 10.1, in all of which διά followed by the genitive is used in association with παρακαλεῖν. The authority invoked in an urgent entreaty is normally indicated in Greek by means of πρός with the genitive (so, e.g., Sophocles, *Phil.* 468; Euripides, *Hec.* 551). Paul's use of διά is possibly a Latinism—cf. *per deos* (so Michel, p. 291, n. 1, after Zahn, p. 534, n. 6).

[2] p. 263.

Having considered the words which form the link with what Paul has already said in the earlier chapters of Romans, we must now look more carefully at the first word of this section— παρακαλῶ. The verb παρακαλεῖν, is used in the NT in three main senses: (i) beseech, entreat (for our present purpose it is unnecessary to distinguish between those uses where 'beseech' is a natural translation and others where it is more naturally translated 'request', 'invite', etc.)[1]; (ii) exhort (both of exhortation, addressed to the unconverted, to receive the gospel, repent, believe, and also—and this is the characteristic use—as a technical term for Christian exhortation, the earnest appeal, based on the gospel, to those who are already believers to live consistently with the gospel they have received)[2]; and (iii) comfort.[3] It is in the second of these senses that it is used here. When used in this sense it has all the urgency and earnestness that it has when it is used in the sense beseech, but also something more—the note of authority. It denotes the authoritative summons to obedience issued in the name of the gospel. The RV gives a wrong impression by using 'beseech' here. The apostle is not by any means pleading for a favour,[4] he is claiming in Christ's name an obedience which his readers are under obligation to render. Similarly inappropriate is the NEB translation 'implore'. 'Exhort' is surely required here.

Barth is inclined to hear in παρακαλῶ in this verse the sense 'comfort' as well as 'exhort'.[5] But, while it is most certainly true that the exhortation with which we are exhorted in the Church in the name of the gospel is part of the comfort with which God comforts His people, it is surely a questionable exegetical procedure to derive this truth—or support for it— from the linguistic fact that the same Greek verb can mean both 'exhort' and 'comfort'. It seems rather like supporting the statement that playing cricket is an art by an appeal to the fact that one can speak of playing the violin and playing Hamlet as well as of playing cricket. Unless we have some quite solid encouragement to look out for *double entendre* (as we have,

[1] e.g. Mt 8.5; 14.36; Mk 1.40; 5.18, 23; 6.56; 7.32; 8.22; Lk 8.41; 2 Cor 12.8.

[2] e.g. Acts 2.40; 1 Cor 1.10; 4.16; 16.15; 2 Cor 10.1; Eph 4.1; Phil 4.2; 1 Th 4.1; 1 Pet 2.11; 5.1. There are cases where it is not clear whether the word is used in this sense or in sense (i)—e.g. Rom 15.30.

[3] e.g. Mt 2.18; 5.4; 2 Cor 1.4, 6; 7.6, 13; Eph 6.22; Col 2.2; 4.8.

[4] *Pace* Chrysostom, col. 675 (on 16.17): Σκόπει δὲ πῶς καὶ προσηνῶς παραινεῖ, οὐκ ἐν τάξει συμβούλου, ἀλλ' ἐν τάξει ἱκέτου τοῦτο ποιῶν, καὶ μετὰ πολλῆς τῆς τιμῆς · καὶ γὰρ καὶ ἀδελφοὺς ἐκάλεσε, καὶ ἱκετεύει. "Παρακαλῶ γὰρ ὑμᾶς," φησίν, "ἀδελφοί".

[5] *Shorter*, p. 149; cf. Bornkamm, *Early Christian Experience*, p. 82.

for example, in Greek tragedies and in the Fourth Gospel), it seems unadvisable to assume that an ancient Greek writer is any more likely to have in mind other possible senses of the word he is using than we should ourselves be in speaking or writing English.[1]

On the use of the vocative ἀδελφοί see on 1.13. It would be unwise to conclude from the fact that ἀδελφοί quite often occurs at the beginning of a new section that its only function here is to mark the beginning of the new main division.

παραστῆσαι may remind us of 6.13, 16 and 19, in which the verb παριστάναι is used three times, and its collateral παριστάνειν twice; but, if παριστάναι were used here in the sense of 'place (something) at the disposal of (someone)', as it was in those verses of chapter 6,[2] one would expect τῷ θεῷ to be expressed with παραστῆσαι either instead of, or as well as, with εὐάρεστον; for in this sentence, if this were the sense, the dative would surely have to be expressed.[3] It is much more likely that παριστάναι is here used as a technical term of religious ritual with the meaning 'to offer' (i.e. 'to offer (as a sacrifice)'): in this case the omission of τῷ θεῷ is understandable, for it is necessarily implied. Though παριστάναι seems never to be used elsewhere in the Greek Bible of offering a sacrifice, it appears as a technical term for offering sacrifice in extra-biblical Greek.[4]

That which is to be offered to God is **τὰ σώματα ὑμῶν.** σῶμα is not used here in the limited sense which it has, for example, in 1 Cor 6.20; 2 Cor 5.10, but, as in Phil 1.20; Eph 5.28, and, outside the Bible, in Aeschines, 2.58; Xenophon, *Anabasis* 1.9.12, in the sense of 'self'. So τὰ σώματα ὑμῶν means 'your-selves' (cf. Calvin: 'By *bodies* he means not only our skin and

---

[1] On παρακαλεῖν see further O. Schmitz and G. Stählin, in *TWNT* 5, pp. 771–98; C. J. Bjerkelund, *Parakalo*, Oslo, 1967; also J. Barr, *The Semantics of Biblical Language*, Oxford, 1961, pp. 232, 236.

[2] Cf. Mt 26.53.

[3] It is quite a different matter in Acts 23.24.

[4] Cf. Josephus, *BJ* 2.89; *Ant.* 4.113; Polybius 16.25.7; Lucian, *De sacrif.* 13; Dittenberger, *Syll.*, 589.46; 694.49; 736.70; *Or.* 456.20; 764.23, 38. The middle is used in this sense as early as Xenophon (*Anab.* 6.1.22). With regard to the tense of the infinitive, reference may be made to BDF, § 338 (see also §§ 335 and 337); Burton, *MT*, § 113 (also § 35). It is interesting to contrast 16.17. One might perhaps suggest that the choice of the present infinitive was natural there, in view of the essentially continuous character of the action contemplated, and—*very tentatively*—that a sense of the definiteness which characterizes the act of self-surrender (even though it has to be repeated again and again) may have contributed to Paul's choice of the aorist here (cf. Moule's comment (p. 328): 'The Roman Christian' is called here 'to a transaction with the Lord quite definite, whether or no the like has taken place before, or shall be done again').

bones, but the totality of which we are composed. . . . In
bidding us *present* ourselves. . . .').[1] The Christian is to offer to
God himself entire—himself in the whole of his concrete life.

θυσίαν. The noun θυσία, like the English 'sacrifice', can
denote either (i) the act of sacrificing, or (ii) that which is
offered, the material of the sacrifice. The former sense is ruled
out here by the participle ζῶσαν. (Moreover, to understand the
word in this sense here would involve taking θυσίαν ζῶσαν
ἁγίαν τῷ θεῷ εὐάρεστον as in apposition to the whole expression
παραστῆσαι τὰ σώματα ὑμῶν, and this would have the effect of
leaving παραστῆσαι τὰ σώματα ὑμῶν to stand by itself, which,
without either θυσίαν or τῷ θεῷ, it is too vague to do.) So we
take θυσίαν to mean 'as a sacrifice' in the sense of the material
of the sacrifice, the victim.

It is to be noted that the idea of sacrifice is used in the NT
with reference to the Christian life in two distinct ways (the
importance of this for the interpretation of this passage will
appear later): (i) sometimes it is something other than the
Christian's self which is likened to the sacrifice offered—for
example, his praise or his good actions (e.g. Phil 2.17f; Heb
13.15f). This usage has its background in such OT passages as
Ps 141.2; (ii) sometimes, as here, it is the Christian's self which
is thought of as being offered as a sacrifice.[2]

The implication of the words παραστῆσαι τὰ σώματα ὑμῶν
θυσίαν is that those who receive this exhortation are no longer
to be their own, but wholly God's property. For the sacrificial
victim was thought of as passing from the offerer's possession
when it was offered. Henceforth it was holy—that is, it belonged to God. When, in certain sacrifices, the worshippers
consumed the sacrificial flesh, they did not think of themselves
as eating their own provisions, but as sharing the hospitality
of God.[3] Calvin's comment, 'By this he implies that we are no

---

[1] p. 264. Cf. Barth, *Shorter*, p. 149f; Bauer, s.v. σῶμα.

[2] This idea is perhaps present in Mk 9.49 (cf. C. E. B. Cranfield, *The
Gospel according to Saint Mark*, Cambridge, ⁶1977, p. 315f.

[3] Cf., e.g., Philo, *Spec. Leg.* 1.221: '. . . for they [sc. the sacrificial
meals] are now the property not of him by whom but of Him to Whom
the victim has been sacrificed, He the benefactor, the bountiful, Who
has made the convivial company of those who carry out the sacrifices
partners of the altar whose board they share. And He bids them not
think of themselves as the entertainers, for they are the stewards of the
good cheer, not the hosts. The Host is He to Whom the material provided for the feast has come to belong, . . .' (F. H. Colson's translation).
Acknowledgment is due to the Loeb Classical Library (Harvard
University Press: William Heinemann) for permission to quote from
their translation of Philo here and elsewhere in the course of the next
few pages.

longer in our own power, but have passed entirely into the power of God',[1] is thus fully justified. The Christian, already God's by right of creation and by right of redemption, has yet again to become God's by virtue of his own free surrender of himself. And this self-surrender has, of course, to be continually repeated.

In the original Greek the three epithets, ζῶσαν and ἁγίαν and τῷ θεῷ εὐάρεστον all alike follow θυσίαν. But in the AV, RV, RSV, NEB and Moffatt (as also in the translation in Barrett's commentary) ζῶσαν has been separated from the other two epithets and placed before the noun. This introduction of a differentiation between the epithets which is not in the original has not been without its effect on the interpretation of the sentence; for, by giving special emphasis to 'living', it has encouraged English readers to think that Paul's main concern here is to indicate that this sacrifice is not killed like an animal victim, and that the epithets, 'holy' and 'acceptable to God' are added rather as an afterthought, whereas, when all three epithets are seen to be on the same level, it is more natural to look for a meaning for 'living' more akin to that of 'holy' and 'acceptable to God'. If we keep our eyes firmly on the original and recognize that Paul is not connecting ζῶσαν specially closely with θυσίαν and then qualifying the combined θυσίαν ζῶσαν by ἁγίαν and τῷ θεῷ εὐάρεστον, but rather indicating that this sacrifice is (i) ζῶσα, (ii) ἁγία and (iii) τῷ θεῷ εὐάρεστος, we shall probably be inclined to conclude that Paul meant to indicate by ζῶσαν not that this sacrifice does not have to be killed[2] (a rather too obvious point to be worth mentioning?— and it should anyway be remembered that the animal victims were always alive when they were offered), nor even that the Christian is to offer his concrete daily living to God (though this is of course true), but that this sacrifice, the Christian himself freely surrendered to God, is to be 'living' in a deep theological sense—living in that 'newness of life' (καινότης ζωῆς, 6.4), with reference to which the verb ζῆν has already been used a number of times in this epistle (e.g. 1.17; 6.11, 13; 8.13b).[3]

[1] p. 263f.
[2] As, e.g., Chrysostom, col. 595, understands him.
[3] For the recognition that there is a connexion between ζῶσαν here and these other references to life in Romans cf. Pelagius, p. 94 ('alienam ab omni morte peccati'); Luther, p. 323; Calvin, p. 264; Bengel, p. 553 (he says succinctly: '*viventem*) ea vita, de qua cap. 1,17. 6,4ss'); Sanday and Headlam, p. 352; Lagrange, p. 292; Nygren, p. 418. It is illuminating to consider the whole range of occurrences of ζῆν (23 times) and also of ζωή (14 times) in Romans.

The significance of ἁγίαν is not just that, once offered, the Christian's self is no longer his own but God's; the word has also an ethical content.[1] Since God is the sort of God He has revealed Himself to be, to belong to Him involves the obligation to strive to be and to do what is in accordance with His character. The Christian's concrete living is henceforth to be marked by the continuing process of sanctification (ἁγιασμός): it is to be moulded and shaped ever more and more into conformity with God's righteous will.[2] The words τῷ θεῷ εὐάρεστον designate the sacrifice as a true and proper sacrifice, one which is desired by God and which He will accept.[3] The word εὐάρεστος occurs in the next verse also, and in 14.18; 2 Cor 5.9; Eph 5.10; Phil 4.18; Col 3.20; Tit 2.9; Heb 13.21, and the adverb εὐαρέστως in Heb 12.28. Compare the use of εὐπρόσδεκτος in 1 Pet 2.5.

To construe **τὴν λογικὴν λατρείαν ὑμῶν** as in apposition to παραστῆσαι τὰ σώματα ὑμῶν θυσίαν ζῶσαν ἁγίαν τῷ θεῷ εὐάρεστον as a whole (so, e.g. Michel)[4] seems preferable to taking it as in apposition either to τὰ σώματα ὑμῶν or (as Barrett does)[5] to θυσίαν ζῶσαν ἁγίαν τῷ θεῷ εὐάρεστον. In this way it is possible to give to λατρεία its proper significance, namely, worship in the sense of worshipping, i.e., the *action* of worshipping. The continuous offering of our whole selves in all our concrete living is our 'logical' action of worshipping. If, however, one of the other possibilities is preferred, it is then necessary to understand λατρεία to signify the concrete worship offered, the sacrifice in the sense of the victim.[6]

Paul's use here of the word λατρεία (the LXX equivalent of 'abōdāh, which, when used in connexion with God, almost always in the OT denotes cultic service)[7] implies that the true worship which God desires embraces the whole of the Christian's life from day to day. It implies that any cultic worship which is not accompanied by obedience in the ordinary affairs of life must be regarded as false worship, unacceptable to God (cf. the insight of the OT prophets—e.g. Isa 1.10–17; 58.1–11; Amos 5.21–24). But it would be quite unjustifiable to argue that the

---

[1] *Pace* Käsemann, p. 312. We are not suggesting that its meaning is purely ethical, but that an ethical significance is included.

[2] See on ἁγίοις in 1.7, and literature cited there.

[3] The NEB translation 'fit for his acceptance' is unfortunate, as it suggests that the sacrifice in itself deserves to be, is worthy to be, accepted.

[4] p. 292.

[5] p. 231.

[6] So H. Strathmann, in *TWNT* 4, p. 65: he compares Jn 16.2.

[7] See on 9.4.

logical implication of Paul's use of λατρεία here is that no room is left for a Christian cultic worship carried out at particular times and in particular places.[1] Provided that such worship in the narrower sense is always practised as part of the wider worship embracing the whole of the Christian's living and is not thought of as something acceptable to God apart from obedience of life, there is nothing here to deny it its place in the life of the faithful. What Paul is here saying is, in fact, perfectly consonant with the view that such a cultic worship ought to be the focus-point of that whole wider worship which is the continually repeated self-surrender of the Christian in obedience of life.

From the time of Aristotle the adjective λογικός[2] was a favourite expression of Greek philosophy. It was specially popular with the Stoics, for whom man was a ζῷον λογικόν.[3] Epictetus uses it in connexion with the worship of God: 'Were I a nightingale, I would do what is proper to a nightingale, were I a swan, what is proper to a swan. In fact I am λογικός: so I must praise God.'[4] We are here not far from some sort of idea of a λογικὴ λατρεία. The word belongs also to the terminology of ancient mysticism. In the *Hermetica* it is used a number of times with θυσία: e.g., δέξαι λογικὰς θυσίας ἁγνὰς ἀπὸ ψυχῆς καὶ καρδίας πρὸς σὲ ἀνατεταμένης, ἀνεκλάλητε, ἄρρητε, σιωπῇ φωνούμενε (1.31); ὁ σὸς λόγος δι' ἐμοῦ ὑμνεῖ σέ· δι' ἐμοῦ δέξαι τὸ πᾶν λόγῳ λογικὴν θυσίαν (13.18); Τὰτ θεῷ πέμπω λογικὰς θυσίας . . . Εὖ, ὦ τέκνον, ἔπεμψας δεκτὴν θυσίαν τῷ πάντων πατρὶ θεῷ (13.21). It is to be found also in Hellenistic Judaism. It was used apparently in the prayers of the Greek synagogue (see, for example, *Const. Ap.* 7.34.6), and it occurs in Test. Levi (a) 3.6 with reference to the angels, προσφέροντες τῷ κυρίῳ ὀσμὴν εὐωδίας λογικὴν (v.l. λογικῆς) καὶ ἀναίμακτον θυσίαν.[5] Philo uses it in a passage concerned with the true worship of God: '. . . what is precious in the sight of God', he says, 'is not the number of victims immolated but the true purity of a rational spirit (πνεῦμα λογικόν) in him who makes the sacrifice'.[6] He is here saying that the attitude of mind of the person who offers an

[1] As Käsemann seemed rather to be suggesting in *Questions*, p. 191f (= *Versuche*, p. 201); but in his commentary he has expressed himself more carefully.

[2] On λογικός see further G. Kittel, in *TWNT* 4, pp. 145–7, and also J. Behm, in *TWNT* 3, pp. 186–9, to both of whom I am indebted in this and the following paragraph.

[3] e.g., Arrian, *Epict.* 2.9.2; Marcus Aurelius, 2.16.

[4] Arrian, *Epict.* 1.16.20

[5] It is possible, however, that this is a Christian interpolation.

[6] *Spec. Leg.* 1.277.

ordinary sacrifice matters more to God than the number of victims offered. But there are many passages in which he speaks of the inward, mystical sacrifice; and these, though the word λογικός does not occur, are of interest in connexion with Paul's phrase λογικὴ λατρεία: e.g. 'God delights in altars beset by a choir of Virtues, albeit no fire burn on them (βωμοῖς . . . ἀπύροις). He takes no delight in blazing altar fires fed by the unhallowed sacrifices of men to whose hearts sacrifice is unknown';[1] 'For the true oblation (ἱερουργία), what else can it be but the devotion of a soul which is dear to God (ψυχῆς θεοφιλοῦς εὐσέβεια)';[2] 'But it is not possible genuinely to express our gratitude to God by means of buildings and oblations and sacrifices, as is the custom of most people, for even the whole world were not a temple adequate to yield the honour due to Him. Nay, it must be expressed by means of hymns of praise, and these are not such as the audible voice shall sing, but strains raised and re-echoed by the mind (νοῦς) too pure for eye to discern',[3] '. . . unblemished and purged, as perfect virtue purges, it [i.e. mind] is itself the most religious of sacrifices and its whole being is pleasing to God';[4] and (most interesting of all for us, because it combines with the idea of the offering of mental cries, which are audible only to God, the idea of the offering of the self—cf. Paul's παραστῆσαι τὰ σώματα ὑμῶν) 'And indeed though the worshippers bring nothing else, in bringing themselves (αὐτοὺς φέροντες) they offer the best of sacrifices, the full and truly perfect oblation of noble living, as they honour with hymns and thanksgivings their Benefactor and Saviour, God, sometimes with the organs of speech, sometimes without tongue or lips, when within the soul alone their minds recite the tale or utter the cry of praise. These one ear only can apprehend, the ear of God, for human hearing cannot reach to the perfection of such.'[5]

In the LXX the word λογικός is never used; but the OT, of course, makes it clear that the sacrifices of the cultus are unacceptable to God apart from the heart's loyalty and obedience of life (e.g. Isa 1.10ff; Hos 6.6; Amos 5.21ff). It also contains passages which speak of a sacrifice consisting of the worshipper's inward disposition, of prayer and praise (e.g. Ps 51.17; 69.30f; 141.2). And these are echoed in the Apocrypha (e.g. Ecclus 35.1f; Tob 4.11) and among the Rabbis, who declare repentance, the study of the law, the doing of works of mercy,

[1] *Plant.* 108.
[2] *Vit. Mos.* 2.108.
[3] *Plant.* 126.
[4] *Spec. Leg.* 1.201.
[5] *Spec. Leg.* 1.272.

and prayer, to be equivalents of sacrifice.[1] The same insight is found also in sectarian Judaism, from which 1QS 9.3–5 may be quoted: 'When these become members of the Community in Israel according to these rules, they shall establish the spirit of holiness according to everlasting truth. They shall atone for guilty rebellion and for sins of unfaithfulness that they may obtain lovingkindness for the land without the flesh of holocausts and the fat of sacrifice. And prayer rightly offered shall be as an acceptable fragrance of righteousness (kᵉnîhôaḥ ṣedeḳ), and perfection of way as a delectable freewill offering (kᵉnidᵉḇaṭ minḥaṭ rāṣôn)'.[2]

That all this evidence needs to be considered in connexion with Paul's use of the adjective λογικός as a qualification of λατρεία is clear. But it is no simple matter to decide what is the correct conclusion to be drawn with regard to Paul's meaning in the light both of this comparative material and of the context in Romans, and scholars in fact differ widely. Our first inclination, in view of the comparative material, might be to agree with Barrett's statement: 'Paul means, a worship consisting not in outward rites but in the movement of man's inward being. This is better described as "spiritual worship" than as "rational", for Paul is not thinking of what is meant in modern English by "rational" ',[3] and to accept his translation 'spiritual'.[4] But, while it is true that the λογικὴ θυσία of mysticism is an 'ineffable worship consisting of thoughts and feelings',[5] it is difficult to reconcile Paul's use of τὰ σώματα ὑμῶν earlier in the verse with the view that what he wants to indicate by λογικός is the *inwardness* of the true Christian worship. Even if this idea of inward worship might be thought to be present in those NT passages in which the thing sacrificed is something other than the Christian's self, it is surely much more likely that here the contrast in mind is not that between internal and external, immaterial and material, but that between rational and irrational—that the true opposite to λογικός here is in fact ἄλογος. We must beware, however, of understanding 'rational' as though Paul were a Stoic philosopher. For Paul the true worship is rational not in the sense of being consistent with the natural rationality of man (a meaning that is suggested by NEB margin), but in the

---

[1] For examples reference may be made to Behm, in *TWNT* 3, p. 187.
[2] As translated in Vermes, p. 87.
[3] p. 231.
[4] Cf. RV margin; Moffatt; RSV.
[5] Michel, p. 292 (Michel himself is contrasting Paul's conception of λογικὴ λατρεία with that of mysticism).

sense of being consistent with a proper understanding of the truth of God revealed in Jesus Christ.[1] While λογικήν here certainly excludes any external ritual worship in which the heart and mind and will of the worshipper are not involved, it also excludes equally definitely any worship which consists only of interior motions and feelings, however exalted, unaccompanied by outward obedience. There is indeed a genuine inwardness of true worship, but it is inseparable from a no less genuine outwardness. The intelligent understanding worship, that is, the worship which is consonant with the truth of the gospel, is indeed nothing less than the offering of one's whole self in the course of one's concrete living, in one's inward thoughts, feelings and aspirations, but also in one's words and deeds.

2. **καὶ μὴ συσχηματίζεσθε τῷ αἰῶνι τούτῳ, ἀλλὰ μεταμορφοῦσθε.**[2] Very many interpreters[3] have claimed that a significant distinction is to be discerned here between συσχηματίζεσθε and μεταμορφοῦσθε. The former, it is argued, refers to outward form only and so indicates something external and superficial, whereas the latter refers to inward being and so indicates a profound transformation. But there are serious difficulties in the way of accepting this claim:

---

[1] Michel's rendering of λογικήν by 'dem Wort gemässer' (p. 290) seems to be not quite satisfactory; for, while it is true that the worship which Paul is indicating is a worship which is consonant with the truth of the gospel—so with the Word of God, the fact (as it surely is) that the word λογικὴν is here used with reference to λόγος in its sense of 'reason' rather than to λόγος in its sense of 'word', should not be obscured (the situation in 1 Pet 2.2 is different: there a case for seeing in the use of λογικός a reference to the Word of God (cf. the AV translation) may be made on the ground of the context (the use of λόγος in 1.23 and of ῥῆμα in 1.25)).

[2] There is a variation in the textual tradition between imperatives (συσχηματίζεσθε, μεταμορφοῦσθε) and infinitives (συσχηματίζεσθαι, μεταμορφοῦσθαι). The imperatives should undoubtedly be preferred; for they are much more strongly attested, and the variant may be explained as an attempt to make Paul's Greek smoother. Paul makes a similar change to the imperative after παρακαλεῖν in 16.17.

[3] e.g. Chrysostom, col. 597f (Οὐκ εἶπε, Μετασχηματίζου, ἀλλά, Μεταμορφοῦ, δεικνὺς ὅτι τὸ μὲν τοῦ κόσμου, σχῆμα · τὸ δὲ τῆς ἀρετῆς, οὐ σχῆμα, ἀλλὰ μορφή τις ἀληθὴς φυσικὸν ἔχουσα κάλλος, οὐ δεόμενον τῶν ἔξωθεν ἐπιτριμμάτων τε καὶ σχημάτων, τῶν ὁμοῦ τε φαινομένων καὶ ἀπολλυμένων· καὶ γὰρ ἅπαντα ταῦτα, πρὶν ἢ φανῆναι, λύεται. Ἂν τοίνυν τὸ σχῆμα ῥίψῃς, ταχέως ἐπὶ τὴν μορφὴν ἥξεις (an English trans. of this is given by Sanday and Headlam, p. 353)); Theodoret, col. 185; Bengel, p. 553 ('μορφή, forma, penitius et perfectius quiddam notat, quam σχῆμα, habitus. conf. Phil. 2, 6.8. 3, 21. A forma interna non debet abludere habitus sanctorum externus'); J. B. Lightfoot, *Saint Paul's Epistle to the Philippians* (London, 4th ed., reprinted 1908), pp. 127–33; Sanday and Headlam, p. 353; Lagrange, p. 294; Huby, p. 413f; Michel, p. 293.

(i) The explanations of μὴ συσχηματίζεσθε τῷ αἰῶνι τούτῳ to which it leads seem not very convincing. To the most widely-supported interpretation, which may be indicated by quoting Sanday and Headlam's translation, 'Do not adopt the external and fleeting fashion of this world',[1] it may be objected that it seems to presuppose that the primary reference of the σχῆμα implicit in the verb is to the σχῆμα of this αἰών and its qualities, whereas, since the subject of the verb is the Roman Christians, it is surely more natural to take the primary reference to be to their σχῆμα. F. W. Beare's explanation avoids this objection. He refers to the sense of false appearance which σχῆμα may have, and says of this passage: Christian believers 'are exhorted not to be "conformed in fashion to this world" . . .; because the "fashion of this world" would disguise their true nature'.[2] But this is open to another objection, namely, that, when Christians allow themselves to be conformed to this world, what takes place is not just a disguising of their real nature but an inward corruption. Barrett's statement, 'conformity to this age is no superficial matter',[3] is fully justified. (Perhaps, on the assumption (which we do not share) that a special sense of σχῆμα ought to be pressed here, the least unlikely suggestion would be that the idea is neither of impermanence nor of false appearance, but simply of externality and visibility—that Paul is referring in this part of the sentence to their outward and visible life, while in the next he refers to their inward life.)

(ii) While 2 Cor 11.13, 14 and 15, in which μετασχηματίζειν (the actual verb συσχηματίζειν occurs in Paul's epistles only in Rom 12.2) is used, may be adduced in support of the distinction, since μετασχηματίζειν in these verses does have the sense of false appearance, Phil 3.21 weighs heavily on the other side; for here μετασχηματίζειν is used where, had Paul really maintained the distinction he is alleged to have maintained, he must surely have written μεταμορφώσει. Lightfoot's attempt to get over this difficulty ('The meaning however seems to be, "will *change* the *fashion* of the body of our humiliation and *fix* it in the *form* of the body of His glory" . . .' He adds in a footnote: 'Of the two words μετασχηματίζειν would refer to the transient condition *from* which, μεταμορφοῦν to the permanent state *to* which, the change takes place')[4] is scarcely convincing.

[1] p. 353.
[2] *A Commentary on the Epistle to the Philippians*, London, 1959, p. 79: cf. Bengel's comment quoted on p. 605, n. 3.
[3] p. 232f.
[4] *Saint Paul's Epistle to the Philippians*, London, reprinted 1908, p. 131.

(iii) While μεταμορφοῦσθαι is no doubt intended to denote a profound transformation both here and in the only other place in which it occurs in Paul's writings (2 Cor 3.18), the two other occurrences of the word in the NT (Mt 17.2; Mk 9.2) would seem (*pace* Lightfoot),[1] to tell in the opposite direction; for, on the one hand, the Transfiguration was not a transformation of Jesus' inward being, but rather a manifestation of the glory which throughout His earthly life was His though veiled, and, on the other hand, it was clearly a brief and fleeting manifestation.

(iv) In Greek outside the NT, while it is certainly possible to discern differences of meaning between μορφή and its cognates and compounds on the one hand and σχῆμα and its cognates and compounds on the other, there are too many examples of their being apparently treated as simply synonymous[2] for it to be justifiable to assume that a distinction is intended unless the context gives support to the assumption.

In view of what has been said above, it would seem unwise to insist on seeing a distinction in meaning between -σχημα- τίζεσθε and -μορφοῦσθε in this verse.[3] We may accept the AV rendering of the two verbs by 'conform' and 'transform' as adequately representing Paul's meaning.

The use of the passive imperative μεταμορφοῦσθε is consonant with the truth that, while this transformation is not the Christians' own doing but the work of the Holy Spirit, they nevertheless have a real responsibility in the matter—to let themselves be transformed, to respond to the leading and pressure of God's Spirit.[4] We may bring out the force of the tense by translating: 'stop allowing yourselves to be conformed . . . continue to let yourselves be transformed. . . '. The present imperative may be used to indicate that an action already happening is to continue indefinitely, and in a prohibition to indicate that an action which is happening is to stop.[5] So here the συσχηματίζεσθαι which is happening is to stop, the μεταμορφ- οῦσθαι which also is already happening is to go on indefinitely. The transformation is not something which is brought about in an instant; it has to be continually repeated, or, rather, it is a process which has to go on all the time the Christian is in this life.

[1] *op. cit.*, p. 130f.
[2] See *TWNT* 4, p. 751, lines 34–44; Denney, p. 688. We may add the rather interesting use of μετασχηματίζειν in 4 Macc 9.22.
[3] Cf. Denney, p. 688; Barrett, p. 232f; *et al.*
[4] Cf. J. Behm, in *TWNT* 4, p. 766f.
[5] Cf. BDF, §§ 335–7.

Christians still live in this age (ὁ αἰὼν οὗτος).[1] But, if they understand what God has done for them in Christ, they know that they belong, by virtue of God's merciful decision, to His new order, and therefore cannot be content to go on allowing themselves to be continually stamped afresh with the stamp of this age that is passing away. On the basis of the gospel, in the light of 'the mercies of God', there is only one possibility that is properly open to them, and that is to resist this process of being continually moulded and fashioned according to the pattern of this present age with its conventions and its standards of values. The good news, to which the imperative μὴ συσχηματίζεσθε bears witness, is that they are no longer the helpless victims of tyrannizing forces, but are able to resist this pressure which comes both from without and from within, because God's merciful action in Christ has provided the basis of resistance. In the situation in which he is placed by the gospel the Christian may and must, and—by the enabling of the Holy Spirit—can, resist the pressures to conformity with this age.

And this μὴ συσχηματίζεσθε is something which he needs to hear again and again. It must ever be a great part of the content of Christian exhortation, so long as the Church is 'militant here in earth'. For the pressures to conformity are always present, and always strong and insidious—so that the Christian often yields quite unconsciously. And the implication of the present tense (that what is being forbidden is something which is actually happening) is always true. The Christian has always to confess that to a painfully large extent his life is conformed to this age.

Instead of going on contentedly and complacently allowing himself to be stamped afresh and moulded by the fashion of this world, he is now to yield himself to a different pressure, to the direction of the Spirit of God. He is to allow himself to be transformed continually, remoulded, remade, so that his life here and now may more and more clearly exhibit signs and tokens of the coming order of God, that order which has already come—in Christ.

And how is this transformation brought about? Paul indicates that it is τῇ ἀνακαινώσει τοῦ νοός. The substantive νοῦς[2]

---

[1] For ὁ αἰὼν οὗτος, as opposed to ὁ αἰὼν ὁ μέλλων (or ὁ ἐρχόμενος) or ὁ αἰὼν ἐκεῖνος, see Mt 12.32; Lk 16.8; 20.34; 1 Cor 1.20; 2.6, 8; 2 Cor 4.4. The eschatological nature of Paul's thought is, of course, to be remembered in connexion with every part of Romans. See further especially on 13.11–14.

[2] On νοῦς and its cognates see J. Behm and E. Würthwein, in *TWNT* 4, pp. 947–1016.

is used in the NT loosely, 'ohne feste begriffliche Prägung',[1] as in ordinary popular speech, and without reference to its special senses as a philosophical and mystical technical term. The words which follow (εἰς τὸ δοκιμάζειν, κ.τ.λ.) suggest that what Paul has mainly in mind, in addition to the basic moral disposition, is moral sensitiveness and perceptiveness,[2] but it is not necessary to restrict the meaning of νοῦς in this verse. That he does not think of the ἀνακαίνωσις τοῦ νοός as something which his readers can accomplish for themselves is clear enough in the light of Romans 7 and 8. It is the Spirit's work (cf. 7.6 for the connexion between καινότης of life and the Holy Spirit), though, as we saw above, the Christian is not thought of as a merely passive object of the Spirit's action, but as a responsible sharer in it, yielding himself freely to the Spirit's leading.

The noun ἀνακαίνωσις, it should be noted, is first found in Paul's writings, as is also the verb ἀνακαινοῦν. Though the distinction between καινός and νέος[3] was not by any means always observed, there is little doubt that the proper significance of καινός is kept in ἀνακαίνωσις here.

εἰς τὸ δοκιμάζειν ὑμᾶς τί τὸ θέλημα τοῦ θεοῦ, τὸ ἀγαθὸν καὶ εὐάρεστον καὶ τέλειον rounds off the two introductory verses with an indication of purpose. The verb δοκιμάζειν can mean either 'prove', 'test', or 'approve (as a result of testing)'. Here, followed as it is by an indirect question, it is best understood in the former sense, though Paul, of course, implies that the discernment of the will of God will be followed by obedient acceptance of it.[4] This final clause, on the one hand, implies that the νοῦς, so far from being an unfallen element of human nature, needs to be renewed, if it is to be able to recognize and embrace the will of God (it is thus a warning against the illusion that conscience, as such and apart from its renewal by the Spirit and instruction by the discipline of the gospel, is a thoroughly reliable guide to moral conduct); and, on the other hand, it indicates the dignity of the individual Christian called on as he is to exercise a responsible freedom,[5] and is the decisive refutation of every impudent sacerdotalism that would reduce

---

[1] Behm, in TWNT 4, p. 956, line 19.

[2] Cf. Michel, p. 293, n. 1.

[3] See on 6.4.

[4] Cf. Michel, p. 294: 'Er setzt voraus, dass Erkennen, Wollen und Tun miteinander verbunden sind'.

[5] But to read into Paul's use of δοκιμάζειν here the implication that the law is done with (as Michel, p. 294, and Leenhardt, p. 305, seem inclined to do) is unjustified. Such responsible freedom as Paul's words indicate, while indeed incompatible with casuistry and legalism, is in no way incompatible with a proper reverence for the law.

the Christian layman to a kind of second class citizenship in the Church. To know that it is God's intention that the ordinary Christian man should be so transformed by the renewing of his mind as to be able himself responsibly, in the light of the gospel and within the fellowship of the faithful, δοκιμάζειν . . . τί τὸ θέλημα τοῦ θεοῦ, τὸ ἀγαθὸν καὶ εὐάρεστον καὶ τέλειον, is to know that one dare not patronize one's fellow-Christians.

The words τὸ ἀγαθόν, κ.τ.λ. are no doubt better taken as in apposition to τὸ θέλημα τοῦ θεοῦ than as epithets qualifying θέλημα. What may perhaps strike the modern reader as a rather over-anxious concern for defining the will of God may well have been prompted by Paul's knowledge that the Roman church contained those who were inclined to value the more spectacular charismatic gifts more highly than the ethical fruit of the Spirit and those who were impatient of moral restraints and prone to mistake licence for the freedom of the Spirit. For those whose background was Gentile paganism the temptation to think of the Christian religion in terms of an unethical mystical communion must have been strong. ἀγαθός is here more probably used in the quite general sense of morally good (God Himself is good, and His will is that man should also be good) than in the narrower sense of beneficial to men. With εὐάρεστον we must understand τῷ θεῷ[1]; for in every other occurrence of εὐαρεστεῖν, εὐάρεστος, εὐαρέστως, in the NT (with the one exception of Tit 2.9) the reference is clearly to God (or Christ). Dodd's objection that to define the will of God as that which is acceptable to Him 'would be mere tautology' is not really fair; for εὐάρεστον does not stand by itself, but is part of a threefold formula. Perhaps the most likely explanation of Paul's insertion of εὐάρεστον here is that, having, in order to counter any tendencies toward an unethical mysticism, defined the will of God as τὸ ἀγαθόν, he felt it to be necessary also to guard against a possible misunderstanding of τὸ ἀγαθόν. By εὐάρεστον he underlines the fact that the goodness which is in question is no anthropocentric goodness but a goodness determined by the revelation of God's will, a matter of obedience to God's commandments. On the last of the three terms, τέλειον, the best commentary is Mk 12.30f (cf. Mt 22.37, 39; Deut 6.5; Lev 19.18): 'thou shalt love the Lord thy God with all thy heart, and with all thy soul, and with all thy mind, and with all thy strength. . . . Thou shalt love thy neighbour as thyself'. God's will, that which God requires of us, is perfect, complete, absolute; for He claims us *wholly* for Himself and for our

---

[1] *Pace* Dodd, p. 200.

neighbours. Thus the last of the three terms interprets the other two; for it makes it clear that this ἀγαθὸν καὶ εὐάρεστον is not something manageable and achievable, as the rich young ruler foolishly imagined ('Master, all these things have I observed from my youth'[1]), but the absolute demand of God, which Christ alone has fulfilled. It is this absolute demand of God by which He claims us wholly for Himself and for our neighbours, which those who are being transformed by the renewing of their minds recognize and gladly embrace as it meets them in all the concrete circumstances of their lives, and to which they know themselves altogether committed, although in this life they can never perfectly fulfil it.

VII. 2. THE BELIEVER AS A MEMBER OF THE CONGREGATION IN HIS RELATIONS WITH HIS FELLOW-MEMBERS (12.3–8)

This first section of particular ethical exhortation is addressed to the members of the Christian community as recipients of various *charismata*. Each one is to esteem himself soberly in relation to his fellow-believers in the light of the gospel and to give himself wholeheartedly to the particular service to which the God-given *charisma* he has received constitutes his divine vocation.

[3]For by virtue of the grace which has been given me I bid every single one of you not to think of himself more highly than he ought to think, but so to think of himself as to think soberly, each one according to the measure of faith which God has imparted to him. [4]For even as we have in one body many members but all the members do not have the same function, [5]so we, though we are many, are one body in Christ, and severally members of one another. [6]But, having gifts differing according to the grace which has been given us, if *we have the gift of* prophecy, *then let us prophesy* in accordance with the standard of faith, [7]or, if *the gift of* practical service, *let us exercise it* in practical service, or, if one is a teacher, *let him exercise his gift* in teaching, [8]or, if one is an exhorter, *let him exercise his gift* in exhorting; *let him* who distributes *exercise his gift* without ulterior motive, *him* who presides *his* with diligence, *him* who shows mercy *his* with cheerfulness.

3. Λέγω γὰρ διὰ τῆς χάριτος τῆς δοθείσης μοι παντὶ τῷ ὄντι ἐν ὑμῖν. The γάρ at the beginning of v. 3 connects what follows with vv. 1–2. As Paul starts upon particular exhortation, he is conscious that he is drawing out the implications and detailed applications of what he has already set forth in principle in

[1] Mk 10.20.

vv. 1–2. He proceeds to give a solemn command[1] by virtue of[2] the grace, the undeserved favour, which has been shown[3] him by God—he is thinking, no doubt, particularly of the undeserved favour God has shown him in calling him to be an apostle.[4] And this command is addressed παντὶ τῷ ὄντι[5] ἐν ὑμῖν. What is said in v. 3 applies equally to every member of the church. This is expressed most emphatically—παντὶ τῷ ὄντι ἐν ὑμῖν is a good deal stronger than πᾶσιν ὑμῖν.

μὴ ὑπερφρονεῖν παρ᾽ ὃ δεῖ φρονεῖν, ἀλλὰ φρονεῖν εἰς τὸ σωφρονεῖν contains a play on words such as is not infrequently found in Hellenistic literary prose:[6] ὑπερφρονεῖν — φρονεῖν — φρονεῖν — σωφρονεῖν. It is not easy to reproduce it at all neatly in English, and, unfortunately, it is not completely unambiguous. Since φρονεῖν can mean 'be wise', 'think',[7] it is possible to understand Paul to be forbidding the sort of presumptuous, over-confident 'wisdom' which overreaches itself. Calvin, for example, took Paul's meaning to be that we are not to range in our thinking beyond the limits of the amount of faith God has given us. Paul here 'draws us away from the study of those matters which can bring nothing but mental torment without edification' and 'forbids anyone to take upon himself more than his capacity and calling may bear'. By ὑπερφρονεῖν he means—so Calvin explains—'go beyond the bounds of wisdom', which we do 'if we engage in those subjects about which it is improper for us to be anxious'. And a few lines later he says, commenting on the last words of the verse, 'Since there is a varied distribution of graces, each man has determined upon the best manner for becoming wise, while keeping himself within the limits of the grace of faith which is conferred upon him by the Lord.'[8](Another, very much less feasible, interpretation along

[1] In the NT the use of the first person singular of λέγειν is specially characteristic of the speech of Jesus. For λέγειν meaning 'bid' 'command' (followed, as here, by the infinitive in Mt 5.34, 39; Rom 2.22; Rev 10.9; 13.14; more frequently by the imperative of direct speech) see further Bauer, s.v. λέγω, II.1.c; and also Michel, p. 295.

[2] For διά with the genitive meaning 'by virtue of' see BDF, § 223(4).

[3] For χάριν διδόναι here cf. 12.6; 15.15; 1 Cor 1.4; 3.10; Gal 2.9; Eph 3.8; 4.29; 2 Tim 1.9; Jas 4.6 (bis); 1 Pet 5.5, and also the corresponding χάριν λαμβάνειν in 1.5; Jn 1.16. The usage found in Acts 7.10 is different (cf. Gen 43.14; also Exod 3.21; 11.3, etc.).

[4] Cf. 1.5; 15.15f.

[5] Venema's conjecture that τι has fallen out after ὄντι (the meaning of the text as he would emend it would be 'to every one who is specially important among you') is neat; but (pace Moffatt) it would be extremely hard to justify acceptance of it.

[6] Cf. Michel, p. 296. Some parallels are given by Bauer, s.v. ὑπερφρονέω.

[7] Cf. LSJ, s.v. φρονέω I.

[8] p. 266.

the lines of φρονεῖν = 'be wise' is mentioned by Origen, explaining Paul's command in accordance with the doctrine of the 'mean'.)[1] But, in view of the usage of ὑπερφρονεῖν, ὑπερφροσύνη, ὑπέρφρων, and of the common expression μέγα φρονεῖν,[2] the more usual interpretation which takes φρονεῖν here to refer to a man's estimation of himself,[3] is overwhelmingly more probable. We take it then that the RV translation, 'not to think of himself more highly than he ought to think; but so to think as to think soberly', is correct. It is a command not to estimate oneself too highly but to entertain a sober opinion of oneself.

ἑκάστῳ ὡς ὁ θεὸς ἐμέρισεν μέτρον πίστεως. The dative ἑκάστῳ is due to attraction. More correctly expressed the clause would read: ἕκαστος ὡς αὐτῷ ὁ θεός, κ.τ.λ. or—perhaps rather more clearly—ἕκαστος κατὰ τὸ μέτρον τῆς πίστεως, ὃ ἐμέρισεν αὐτῷ ὁ θεός. There are three basic questions which confront us here: (i) In what sense is μέτρον used? (ii) In what sense is πίστις used? and (iii) What kind of genitive is πίστεως? With regard to (i), the noun μέτρον can denote: (a) a means of measurement whether (α) literally, or (β) metaphorically—so a standard or norm; (b) a result of measuring—so (α) a measurement, size, quantity, length; (β) something which has been measured, a measured quantity, length, etc., of anything; (c) due measure, limit, proportion—so (α) full measure, goal, or (β) limit; (d) metre, verse. With regard to (ii), we may note here[4] the following possible meanings of πίστις: (a) 'faithfulness', 'trustworthiness'; (b) 'faith' in the sense of fides qua creditur; (c) 'faith' in the sense of a special charisma possessed not by all, but only by some, Christians; (d) 'faith' in the sense of fides quae creditur, 'the faith', the body of truth believed by Christians; (e) 'trust' in the sense of something entrusted, 'a trust'. With regard to (iii), two possibilities fall to be considered: (a) a partitive genitive; (b) a genitive of apposition. It is obvious that a considerable number of different combinations are at least theoretically possible. We may refer to a fuller discussion in NTS 8 (1961–62), pp. 345–51,[5] and limit ourselves here to indicating the two most generally favoured interpretations and setting out our reasons for rejecting these in favour of another interpretation.

[1] col. 1209f. It is suggested, e.g., that the false teachers referred to in 1 Tim 4.1–3 'plus sapiunt de castitate quam oportet', while the voluptuous and impure man 'minus . . . sapit quam oportet'.
[2] Cf. LSJ, φρονέω, II.2.b.
[3] So, e.g., AV, RV, Moffatt, RSV, N.E.B.
[4] For a discussion of the different senses in which Paul uses πίστις reference should be made to p. 697f.
[5] C. E. B. Cranfield, 'Μέτρον πίστεως in Romans 12.3'.

The two most generally favoured explanations are: (1) the combination of (i) (b) (β), (ii) (c), and (iii) (a), giving the meaning, 'a measure (i.e. a measured quantity) of (special miracle-working) faith';[1] and (2) the combination of (i) (b) (β), (ii) (b), and (iii) (a), giving the meaning, 'a measure (i.e. a measured quantity) of faith (in the sense of *fides qua*, the basic Christian response to God)'.[2] But (1) is open to the objection that Paul is here explicitly addressing *all* the members of the Roman Church (λέγω γὰρ . . . παντὶ τῷ ὄντι ἐν ὑμῖν . . . ἑκάστῳ . . .), whereas he clearly regarded the special miracle-working faith as something possessed not by all, but only by some, Christians (cf. 1 Cor 12.8–11). An even more serious objection lies against both (1) and (2), namely, that, if the usual interpretation of μὴ ὑπερφρονεῖν παρ' ὃ δεῖ φρονεῖν, ἀλλὰ φρονεῖν εἰς τὸ σωφρονεῖν is right, as it surely is, then the implication would be that a Christian is to think of himself more highly than he thinks of his fellow-Christian who has a smaller quantity of faith (according to (1), of the special miracle-working sort; according to (2), of the basic *fides qua* sort). It is surely extremely unlikely that Paul intended to imply this;[3] for such an intention would scarcely be consistent with his apparent purpose in vv. 4ff to encourage the Christians in Rome to conduct themselves in such a way as to maintain their brotherly unity unimpaired. A congregation, the members of which were carefully calculating their relative importance according to the amount of faith (of either sort) which they possessed, would have little chance of being a happy one. (This objection lies equally against such variations of (1) or (2) as are to be found in Origen,[4] Theodoret,[5] Sanday and Headlam,[6] Michel,[7] Gaugler.[8])

---

[1] Favoured by, e.g., Oecumenius, col. 565; Theophylact, col. 501; Lagrange, p. 296; Zahn, p. 542; Huby, p. 415f; Barrett, p. 235.

[2] Favoured by, e.g., Schlatter, p. 336f.

[3] Such calculations of precedence as are encouraged in the Qumran texts, e.g., 'According to whether this [i.e. his understanding and the perfection of his way] is great or little, so shall one man be honoured more than another' (1QSa 1.18—Vermes, p. 119; cf. 1QH 10.27f— Vermes, p. 184: '. . . according to the measure of their knowledge, so shall they be honoured one more than another'; also 14.18f), are alarming enough; but, according to these interpretations of Rom 12.3, Paul would here be enjoining something still more futile—that each Christian should indulge in calculating *his own* precedence.

[4] col. 1211.

[5] col. 188.

[6] p. 355.

[7] p. 296f.

[8] 2, p. 240f.

The combination of (i) (a) (β),[1] (ii) (b), and (iii) (b),[2] giving
the meaning, 'a standard (by which to measure, estimate,
himself), namely, his faith (in the sense of *fides qua*)', is surely
to be preferred. It suits the context well, agreeing with the
words παντὶ τῷ ὄντι ἐν ὑμῖν and ἑκάστῳ (for every Christian has
been given μέτρον πίστεως in this sense) and with μὴ ὑπερφρονεῖν
παρ' ὃ δεῖ φρονεῖν, ἀλλὰ φρονεῖν εἰς τὸ σωφρονεῖν. Every member
of the church, instead of thinking of himself more highly than
he ought, is so to think of himself as to think soberly, measuring
himself by the standard which God has given him in his faith,
that is, by a standard which forces him to concentrate his
attention on those things in which he is on precisely the same
level as his fellow-Christians rather than on those things in
which he may be either superior or inferior to them—for the
standard Paul has in mind consists, we take it, not in the
relative strength or otherwise of the particular Christian's
faith but in the simple fact of its existence, that is, in the fact
of his admission of his dependence on, and commitment to,
Jesus Christ.[3] When Christians measure themselves by themselves (or by their fellow-Christians or their pagan neighbours),
they display their lack of understanding (cf. 2 Cor 10.12), and
are sure to have too high (or else too low) an opinion of themselves; but, when they measure themselves by the standard

---

[1] It is worth noting that 'means of measurement' is actually the
primary meaning of μέτρον, and the word is used in this sense quite often
in the NT (e.g., Mt 7.2; Mk 4.24; Rev 21.15). In the Pauline corpus it
occurs only five times in addition to this occurrence. While in Eph 4.7
it should probably be understood in sense (b) (β), and in Eph 4.13 and
probably also in 16 it is used in sense (c), in 2 Cor 10.13 it probably has
the sense 'means of measurement' or 'standard' in both its occurrences
(cf. H. W. Beyer, in *TWNT* 3, p. 603f: *contra* K. Deissner, in *TWNT* 4,
p. 637). It is interesting that in nine of the ten occurrences of the word
in Aristotle's *Nicomachean Ethics* it has the sense 'means of measurement'. In Greek philosophy, as Deissner points out (*TWNT* 4, p. 635),
the concept of the μέτρον/means of measurement played a significant
part (Protagoras, Plato, Neo-Platonism). From Qumran there is an
interesting example of *middāh* used apparently in the sense of 'standard'
in 1QS 8.4 (*ûlehithallēk 'im kôl bemiddat hā'emet ûbetikkûn hā'ēt*—Vermes
p. 85: 'They shall walk with all men according to the standard of truth
and the rule of the time.').

[2] For the genitive of apposition cf. σημεῖον . . . περιτομῆς in 4.11; see
also on τὴν ἀπαρχὴν τοῦ πνεύματος in 8.23; other references in BDF, § 167.

[3] Whereas, if μέτρον means 'measured quantity' and πίστεως is a
partitive genitive, the last clause of v. 3 directs attention to the *differences* between Christians, if μέτρον is taken in the sense of 'standard'
and πίστεως taken to be a genitive of apposition, the clause directs
attention to that which is common to all Christians. Though some may
have more faith or stronger faith than others, all, if they are Christians
at all, have faith and have it in the same Object.

which God has given them in their faith, they then—and only then—achieve a sober and true estimate of themselves as, equally with their fellows, both sinners revealed in their true colours by the judgment of the Cross and also the objects of God's undeserved and triumphant mercy in Jesus Christ. And, when we look back to vv. 1–2, which set forth the theme of the whole division, 12.1–15.13, what else does the ἀνακαίνωσις τοῦ νοός mean but to be enabled ever more and more consistently to measure oneself and all things by the standard which God has given one in one's faith and so to become ever more and more able δοκιμάζειν . . . τί τὸ θέλημα τοῦ θεοῦ, τὸ ἀγαθὸν καὶ εὐάρεστον καὶ τέλειον? And how well the above interpretation of μέτρον πίστεως fits the following verses will appear in the exegesis which follows. We conclude then that μέτρον πίστεως means 'a standard (by which to measure, estimate, himself), namely, (his) faith'; but at the same time note that this does not mean that Paul is bidding the believer to estimate himself according to his fluctuating subjective feelings and personal opinions but that he is bidding him to estimate himself according to his God-given relation to Christ. True though it most certainly is that Christian faith is the individual's free,personal, response (made in the freedom which is restored by God's gift of His Spirit) to God's action in Christ, it must always be remembered that the most important and, indeed, the controlling, determinative, element in faith is not the believing subject but the believed-in Object; and to estimate oneself according to the standard which consists of one's faith in Christ is really to recognize that Christ Himself in whom God's judgment and mercy are revealed is the One by whom alone one must measure oneself and also one's fellow-men, the One who is, in fact, the true (to borrow the phrase of Protagoras)[1] πάντων χρημάτων μέτρον.[2]

4f. καθάπερ γὰρ ἐν ἑνὶ σώματι πολλὰ μέλη ἔχομεν, τὰ δὲ μέλη πάντα οὐ τὴν αὐτὴν ἔχει πρᾶξιν, οὕτως οἱ πολλοὶ ἓν σῶμά ἐσμεν ἐν Χριστῷ, τὸ δὲ καθ' εἷς ἀλλήλων μέλη is best understood as explaining (notice the γάρ in v. 4) what measuring oneself by

---

[1] Fr. 1 (in H. Diels, *Die Fragmente der Vorsokratiker*, 2).

[2] It is interesting that Barth, 1933, p. 444, allows for an identification of the μέτρον πίστεως with Jesus Christ ('If the crucified Christ is *the measure* of faith which God hath dealt to each man—to each man in his particularity . . .'), though the original German has not *Mass* ('measure') but *Ziel* ('goal'). His *Shorter*, p. 152, has '. . . by thinking "so as to think soberly", which is immediately explained as "starting and completing the course of his Christian faith which God has destined to him" '. But in neither commentary does he anywhere, as far as I can see, make absolutely clear exactly how he understands the phrase μέτρον πίστεως.

this standard means for one's estimation of oneself in relation to one's fellow-Christians. Those who do measure themselves by the standard which God has given them in their faith will not fail to discern the one body; they will recognize that they do not exist for themselves but are ἀλλήλων μέλη and that their fellow-Christians, whether their gifts are more, or less, impressive than their own, are equally with themselves members of the one body. The figure of the body as a unity made up of various members is one that occurs frequently in ancient literature. The best-known example of its use is probably the parable of the belly and the limbs by which in the early days of the Roman Republic Menenius Agrippa is said to have persuaded the plebeian soldiers, who had withdrawn to the Mons Sacrata and threatened to found a new city of their own, to return to Rome.[1] Since Paul had at an earlier date given expression to the idea of Christians' being the body of Christ (1 Cor 12.27; cf. 1 Cor 6.15), it is, of course, quite possible that this idea of the body of Christ was not far from his thoughts, when he dictated this passage. But it is hardly safe to assume this, and much less to assume that the first readers or hearers of the epistle in Rome would have picked up any such reference or that he would himself have expected them to do so, seeing that there has been no reference in this epistle to Christians', or the church's, being the body of Christ (the use of τὸ σῶμα τοῦ Χριστοῦ in 7.4 is quite different). We take it then that what we have here is basically a simile,

---

[1] Livy 2.32; Plutarch, Cor. 6.2–4. There is a very interesting example from an earlier date in Plato, R. 462c–d (cf. 1 Cor 12.26): 'Ἐν ᾗτινι δὴ πόλει πλεῖστοι ἐπὶ τὸ αὐτὸ κατὰ ταὐτὰ τοῦτο λέγουσι τὸ ἐμὸν καὶ τὸ οὐκ ἐμόν, αὕτη ἄριστα διοικεῖται; Πολύ γε. Καὶ ἥτις δὴ ἐγγύτατα ἑνὸς ἀνθρώπου ἔχει; οἷον ὅταν που ἡμῶν δάκτυλός του πληγῇ, πᾶσα ἡ κοινωνία ἡ κατὰ τὸ σῶμα πρὸς τὴν ψυχὴν τεταμένη εἰς μίαν σύνταξιν τὴν τοῦ ἄρχοντος ἐν αὐτῇ ᾔσθετό τε καὶ πᾶσα ἅμα συνήλγησεν μέρους πονήσαντος ὅλη, καὶ οὕτω δὴ λέγομεν ὅτι ὁ ἄνθρωπος τὸν δάκτυλον ἀλγεῖ· καὶ περὶ ἄλλου ὁτουοῦν τῶν τοῦ ἀνθρώπου ὁ αὐτὸς λόγος, περί τε λύπης πονοῦντος μέρους καὶ περὶ ἡδονῆς ῥαΐζοντος; Ὁ αὐτὸς γάρ, ἔφη· καὶ τοῦτο ὃ ἐρωτᾷς, τοῦ τοιούτου ἐγγύτατα ἡ ἄριστα πολιτευομένη πόλις οἰκεῖ. Ἑνὸς δὴ οἶμαι πάσχοντος τῶν πολιτῶν ὁτιοῦν ἢ ἀγαθὸν ἢ κακὸν ἡ τοιαύτη πόλις μάλιστά τε φήσει ἑαυτῆς εἶναι τὸ πάσχον, καὶ ἢ συνησθήσεται ἅπασα ἢ συλλυπήσεται. Ἀνάγκη, ἔφη, τήν γε εὔνομον. In Plutarch, Arat. 24.5, the several Greek states are likened to the parts of a body (ἡγεῖτο γὰρ [the subject of the main verb is Aratus] ἀσθενεῖς ἰδίᾳ τὰς πόλεις ὑπαρχούσας σῴζεσθαι δι' ἀλλήλων ὥσπερ ἐνδεδεμένας τῷ κοινῷ συμφέροντι, καὶ καθάπερ τὰ μέρη τοῦ σώματος ζῶντα καὶ συμπνέοντα διὰ τὴν πρὸς ἄλληλα συμφυΐαν, ὅταν ἀποσπασθῇ καὶ γένηται χωρίς, ἀτροφεῖ καὶ σήπεται, παραπλησίως τὰς πόλεις ἀπόλλυσθαι μὲν ὑπὸ τῶν διασπώντων τὸ κοινόν, αὔξεσθαι δὲ ὑπ' ἀλλήλων, ὅταν ὅλου τινὸς μεγάλου μέρη γενόμεναι κοινῆς προνοίας τυγχάνωσιν). Other references are given, e.g., in H. Lietzmann, An die Korinther I.II, Berlin, ⁴1949 (supplemented by W. G. Kümmel), pp. 62 and 187.

in spite of the form of v. 5, and that the point which Paul is making is simply that Christians, like the various members of a single body, although they differ from one another and have various functions, are all necessary to each other and equally under an obligation to serve one another, because they all belong together in a single whole. There is just one particular which distinguishes Paul's application of the figure of the body and the limbs here in Romans from its use in ancient pagan literature, but that one particular is, of course, all-important. The words ἐν Χριστῷ here in v. 5 indicate that the unity of those whom Paul is addressing, unlike the unity of the various communities which ancient authors liken to a body, is a matter neither of nature nor of human contriving but of the grace of God. Whatever other unity the Christians in Rome may have had, the unity to which Paul is appealing is the unity which they have by virtue of what God has done for them in Christ.[1]

6. ἔχοντες δὲ χαρίσματα. It is possible to punctuate with a comma after μέλη at the end of v. 5 and to take ἔχοντες as dependent on ἐσμεν, thus making vv. 6–8 part of the apodosis, of which v. 4 is the protasis[2]; but it is better (with the majority of commentators) to put a full stop at the end of v. 5 and to supply imperatives, as is done, for example, in the RV, for ἔχοντες δέ (especially coming after τὸ δέ in the previous verse) certainly looks like the beginning of a fresh sentence. Leenhardt gives to ἔχοντες itself an imperative force, translating, 'Sachons avoir' (his point is obscured in the English translation of his commentary by the substitution of the RSV text)[3]; but this is surely forced. It is rather Schlatter, who here, drawing attention to the indicative sense of the participle, makes the apt observation: 'The weight of the sentence rests not on an imperative, but on an indicative: "we have these gifts". Paul speaks not just of what ought to happen, but of what is happening. Out of the received gift arises the function, and therefore also out of the statement which indicates the gift arises the imperative which says how the function is rightly fulfilled.'[4] These verses indicate the unselfconscious, businesslike, sober way in which Christians who do measure themselves by the standard which God has given them in their faith will give themselves to the fulfilment of the tasks apportioned to them by the χαρίσματα they have received, using their par-

---

[1] On ἐν Χριστῷ see Essay II at the end of this volume.
[2] So, e.g., Bengel, p. 553; and especially Denney, p. 689f, who defends this punctuation at length.
[3] p. 309f (Fr., p. 174).
[4] p. 338 (our translation).

ticular χαρίσματα to the full in the service of God and of one another, undistracted by futile calculations of precedence.

The word χάρισμα has already been used several times in Romans (1.11; 5.15, 16; 6.23; 11.29), but not—unless it should be so understood in 1.11 (see note on that verse)—in the sense which it bears here, where it is used of the gifts or endowments which God bestows on believers to be used in His service and in the service of men. Paul's most extensive teaching on these gifts is to be found in 1 Cor 12–14. He connected them closely with the Spirit—so much so, that he occasionally used the neuter plural of the adjective πνευματικός by itself to denote them (e.g. 1 Cor 14.1). It is the Holy Spirit who mediates them. Paul apparently thought that every Christian had a share of such gifts (this is implied here, since the subject of ἔχοντες must be identical with the subject of the previous sentence). Often one person will have had more than one gift. So neither the list which follows nor the list in 1 Cor 12 is to be regarded as in any sense exhaustive.[1]

The gifts are κατὰ τὴν χάριν τὴν δοθεῖσαν ἡμῖν διάφορα. The wide variety of the gifts is grounded in the one grace shown to all; for God's grace, His undeserved love in action, while it is one and the same for all, is free and sovereign, and it is according to this royal freedom of His grace that He bestows different gifts on different persons. The gifts are given for the fulfilment of different functions, and, according to Paul (cf. 1 Cor 12.31: ζηλοῦτε δὲ τὰ χαρίσματα τὰ μείζονα), they differ in value, in importance. But the reception of a greater gift does not carry with it any right to regard oneself, or to be regarded by others, as personally superior to one's fellow-Christian who has only received a lesser gift. While the gifts differ in dignity, the persons of the recipients are—by the measure of faith—of equal dignity, being alike objects of the same judgment and mercy; and the believer, in so far as he is truly a believer, will never forget that his gift is God's free gift, in no way something merited by himself.

εἴτε προφητείαν, κατὰ τὴν ἀναλογίαν τῆς πίστεως. Paul takes as his first example of a χάρισμα prophecy (cf. the list of ministries in 1 Cor 12.28, in which prophets are mentioned directly after

[1] See further H. Conzelmann, in *TWNT* 9, pp. 393–97 (bibliography on p. 393, to which should be added: P. H. Menoud, *L'Église et les Ministères selon le Nouveau Testament*, Neuchâtel and Paris 1949; Chevallier *Esprit*; J. D. G. Dunn, *Jesus and the Spirit*, London, 1975; H. Schürmann, 'Die geistlichen Gnadengaben in den paulinischen Gemeinden', in K. Kertelge (ed.), *Das kirchliche Amt im Neuen Testament*, Darmstadt, 1977, pp. 362–412).

apostles). The high place he assigned to it among the spiritual gifts is indicated by 1 Cor 14.1, 39. While any Christian might from time to time be inspired to prophesy, there were some who were so frequently inspired that they were regarded as *being* prophets and forming a distinct group of persons. Their number included some women (Acts 21.9). The prophet was distinguished from the teacher by the immediacy of his inspiration: his utterance was the result of a particular revelation. It might be a prediction about the future of the community (e.g. Acts 11.27f) or of an individual (e.g. Acts 21.10f), or an announcement of something which God required to be done (e.g. Acts 13.1ff). It was a characteristic of prophecy that it was directed to a particular concrete situation. Though he was dependent on special revelations, the prophet's mind—unlike that of the speaker in tongues—was fully engaged; and his message was addressed to the church's understanding. By it the church was instructed (1 Cor 14.31—ἵνα πάντες μανθάνωσιν), edified (1 Cor 14.3), exhorted (1 Cor 14.3), comforted (1 Cor 14.3), or rebuked. Thus prophecy fulfilled a truly pastoral function.[1]

But Paul recognized the need for prophetic utterances to be received with discrimination. He gives instruction in 1 Cor 14.29 that, while the prophets are prophesying, the rest of the congregation is to 'discern' (καὶ οἱ ἄλλοι διακρινέτωσαν); and in 1 Cor 12.10 the gift of 'discernings of spirits' (διακρίσεις πνευμάτων) is significantly mentioned immediately after the gift of prophecy. For there was the possibility of false prophecy; there was also the possibility of true prophecy's being adulterated by additions derived from some source other than the Holy Spirit's inspiration. Hence the need also to exhort the prophets themselves to prophesy κατὰ τὴν ἀναλογίαν τῆς πίστεως. The close correspondence between this phrase and ἑκάστῳ ὡς ὁ θεὸς ἐμέρισεν μέτρον πίστεως in v. 3 is underlined by the use of the same word in the Peshitta Syriac to translate both μέτρον and ἀναλογία. Once again we have to choose between different possible interpretations. Many commentators understand by ἡ πίστις here a special charismatic faith—in fact, something hardly to be distinguished from prophetic

---

[1] For what Paul has to say about prophecy see especially 1 Cor 12–14; and on NT prophecy see further H. Krämer, in *TNWT* 6, pp. 781–83; G. Friedrich, in *TWNT* 6, pp. 849–57; also H. Greeven, 'Propheten, Lehrer, Vorsteher bei Paulus: zur Frage der "Ämter" im Urchristentum', in *ZNW* 44 (1952–53), pp. 1–43; Chevallier, *Esprit*; Dunn, op. cit., especially pp. 227–36.

inspiration.[1] According to this view, Paul is warning the prophets against the temptation to add something of their own devising,[2] the temptation, when they come to the limit of their inspiration, to go on speaking.[3] According to others,[4] ἡ πίστις is to be understood in the sense of 'the faith', i.e. the body of truth believed, and κατὰ τὴν ἀναλογίαν as meaning 'according to the standard', 'in agreement (with)', 'in accordance (with)': the prophet is to make sure that his message does not in any way contradict the Christian faith. Others take ἡ πίστις in the sense of *fides qua*, as, for example, Denney, who, taking κατὰ τὴν ἀναλογίαν τῆς πίστεως as explication of προφητείαν and not as requiring to be supplemented by an imperative, thinks that the implication is 'that the more faith one has—the more completely Christian he is—the greater the prophetic endowment will be'.[5] It may be suggested that the simplest and most satisfactory interpretation—particularly if our explanation of v. 3 is correct—is 'according to the standard of faith', 'in agreement with faith' (i.e., faith = *fides qua*): the prophets are to prophesy in agreement with the standard which they possess in their apprehension of, and response to, the grace of God in Jesus Christ—they are to be careful not to utter (under the impression that they are inspired) anything which is incompatible with their believing in Christ.

7. **εἴτε διακονίαν,[6] ἐν τῇ διακονίᾳ.** In the NT the verb διακονεῖν and the cognate abstract noun διακονία can have, when used theologically, either a wider or a narrower connotation. Thus they are used, on the one hand, quite generally to denote service rendered to God, to Christ, to the church (e.g. of the ministry of an apostle in 11.13; Acts 20.24; 21.19; 2 Cor 4.1; 5.18); they are used, on the other hand, in a specific sense with

---

[1] So, e.g., Sanday and Headlam, p. 356f; Huby, p. 419; Gaugler 2, p. 243f; Leenhardt, p. 175: cf. G. Kittel, in *TWNT* 1, p. 350f; G. Friedrich, in *TWNT* 2, p. 853.

[2] Cf. Gaugler 2, p. 243: 'dem Geist etwas aus dem eigenen Geist hinzuzufügen, das eingegebene Wort durch religiöse Vitalität zu bereichern'.

[3] Chrysostom, who understands by πίστις the faith which appropriates the χάρισμα of prophecy, gets a different point—viz. that the amount received in inspiration is limited by the capacity of the receiving faith: Εἰ γὰρ καὶ χάρις ἐστίν, ἀλλ᾽ οὐχ ἁπλῶς ἐκχεῖται, ἀλλὰ τὰ μέτρα παρὰ τῶν δεχομένων λαμβάνουσα, τοσοῦτον ἐπιρρεῖ, ὅσον ἂν εὕρῃ σκεῦος πίστεως αὐτῇ προσενεχθέν (col. 602).

[4] e.g. Lagrange, p. 299; Manson, p. 950; R. Bultmann, in *TWNT* 6, p. 214, lines 18–24 (tentatively).

[5] p. 690.

[6] The variant reading ὁ διακονῶν is no doubt assimilation to the following ὁ διδάσκων.

reference to practical service rendered to those who in some
way are specially needy (e.g. Mt 25.44; Acts 6.1, 2; Rom 15.25).
According to some commentators (e.g. Zahn, p. 546; Jülicher;
Lagrange, p. 299; Huby, p. 420), διακονία is used here in its
general sense.[1] In support of this view it is argued: (i) that the
reference cannot be to διακονία in its narrower sense of service
to the needy and suffering, since this is mentioned in v. 8b, and
(ii) that the change of construction from the abstract noun in
the accusative (προφητείαν, διακονίαν) to the nominative
singular masculine participle (ὁ διδάσκων, ὁ παρακαλῶν, ὁ
μεταδιδούς, ὁ προϊστάμενος, ὁ ἐλεῶν) suggests that διακονία is
here used as a general term, some of the particular ministries
covered by it being indicated by the following participles. But
(i) is not decisive. We may leave open for the moment the
question whether the activities indicated in v. 8b should be
explained as subdivisions of διακονία in the narrower sense, or
a distinction made between it and them. In any case, the
classification here should not be regarded as clear-cut or rigid.
With regard to (ii), a more probable explanation of the change
of construction is that εἴτε διδασκαλίαν was avoided because
(ἔχοντες) διδασκαλίαν would not have expressed Paul's meaning
at all clearly.[2] Against taking διακονία in the general sense, it
must further be said that so general a term would hardly be
apposite in such a list as we have here. Moreover, if it were
used in the general sense, it would surely have been placed
before, not after, προφητεία.[3] It seems preferable then to
understand διακονία here in its narrower sense as denoting a
range of activities similar to that which came to be the
province of the deacon.[4]

---

[1] Cf. Chrysostom, col. 602f: Καθολικὸν πρᾶγμα ἐνταῦθα τίθησι. Καὶ γὰρ ἡ
ἀποστολὴ διακονία λέγεται· καὶ πᾶν ἀγαθὸν πνευματικὸν ἔργον, διακονία. Ἔστι μὲν
γὰρ καὶ ἰδικῆς οἰκονομίας ὄνομα τοῦτο· ἐνταῦθα μέντοι καθολικῶς εἴρηται.

[2] Sanday and Headlam, p. 357, state confidently that 'ἔχειν διδασκαλίαν
would mean, not to impart, but to receive instruction'. Certainly it
could mean that. It could also perhaps mean 'to have a (particular piece
of) teaching (to impart)', as διδαχὴν ἔχειν does in 1 Cor 14.26.

[3] It is instructive to compare 1 Pet 4.10f, in which the verb διακονεῖν
occurs twice. In verse 11, contrasted with λαλεῖν, it would seem to be
used in the narrower sense. In verse 10, where it is used quite generally
of the service rendered to one's fellow Christians by making full use of
whatever spiritual gift one has received, it is significantly—as far as
χαρίσματα are concerned—all-embracing.

[4] On the subject of διακονία reference may be made to the following:
H. W. Beyer, in TWNT 2, pp. 81–93; H. Krimm, Das diakonische Amt
der Kirche, Stuttgart, 1953; Barth, CD IV/3, pp. 889–95 (= KD IV/3,
pp. 1020–26); K. Rahner and H. Vorgrimmler, Diaconia in Christo,
Freiburg, 1962; H. Krimm, Quellen zur Geschichte der Diakonie, 2 volumes, Stuttgart, 1963; L. Vischer, 'The Problem of the Diaconate: an

The meaning of ἐν τῇ διακονίᾳ ('let us exercise it in practical service') will be that those who have received this particular gift, the spiritual capacity for practical service, are to give themselves wholeheartedly to the fulfilment of the tasks to which their particular endowment is also their divine vocation. They are to use the spiritual gift they have received to the full, and they are to use it for the purpose for which it was given (a warning against the temptation to undertake services for which one is not divinely equipped would seem to be implicit). This explanation of ἐν τῇ διακονίᾳ applies equally *mutatis mutandis* to ἐν τῇ διδασκαλίᾳ and ἐν τῇ παρακλήσει.

εἴτε ὁ διδάσκων,[1] ἐν τῇ διδασκαλίᾳ. The distinction between διδάσκειν and προφητεύειν is clear enough. Whereas the prophet of the early Church was immediately inspired, the content of his message being a particular and direct revelation, the teacher based his teaching upon the OT scriptures, the tradition of Jesus and the catechetical material current in the Christian community.[2] In 1 Cor 12.28 διδάσκαλοι are mentioned in the third place in the list (after apostles and prophets). In Eph 4.11 they are closely associated with ποιμένες (the two nouns sharing the same article), teachers and pastors apparently being regarded as one group.

8. εἴτε ὁ παρακαλῶν, ἐν τῇ παρακλήσει. The distinction between παρακαλεῖν[3] and διδάσκειν is less easy to determine with exactness than that between διδάσκειν and προφητεύειν. In fact it is clear that in ancient, as in modern times, the activities denoted by these two verbs must have overlapped. But it would not be unfair to say that, while they shared the same ultimate purposes, the edification of the congregation and the glory of God, they had different immediate purposes, and these carried with them certain differences of emphasis and method. While the immediate purpose of teaching was to instruct, to impart information, to explain, the immediate purpose of exhortation was to help Christians to live out their obedience

analysis of Early Christian Sources', in *Encounter* 25, Indianapolis, 1964–65, pp. 23–34; World Council of Churches, World Council studies 2, *The Ministry of Deacons*, Geneva, 1965; C.E.B. Cranfield, *The Service of God*, London, 1965, pp. 23–34; K. F. Nickle, *The Collection: a study in Paul's strategy*, London, 1966; *Service in Christ* (pp. 37–48 are on 'Diakonia in the NT'); C. E. B. Cranfield, 'New church constitutions and diakonia', in *SJT* 20 (1967), pp. 338–41; C. Tatton, 'Some studies of New Testament Diakonia', in *SJT* 25 (1972), pp. 423–34.
[1] The variant reading διδασκαλίαν is no doubt to be explained as assimilation to the preceding προφητείαν and διακονίαν.
[2] Cf. G. Friedrich, in *TWNT* 6, p. 856. See also the article on διδάσκω and cognates by K. H. Rengstorf in *TWNT* 2; Greeven, op. cit.; Chevallier, *Esprit*; Dunn, op. cit.   [3] See on v. 1.

to the gospel. It was the pastoral application of the gospel to a particular congregation, both to the congregation as a whole and also to the members of it severally.[1] So the eyes of the exhorter had to be firmly fixed not only on the gospel but also on the concrete situation of his hearers. Naturally the same person must often have fulfilled both functions in the early Church; in the modern Church the parish minister has normally to fulfil them both.

ὁ μεταδιδοὺς ἐν ἁπλότητι. Sanday and Headlam,[2] Lagrange,[3] and Lyonnet[4] are confident that the use of the verb μεταδιδόναι itself implies that the reference is to the distribution of what is one's own. But, while it is certainly true that μεταδιδόναι often has this meaning (e.g. LXX Job 31.17; Lk 3.11; Eph 4.28), it would seem that it could also be used of distributing what is not one's own; for it is possible to cite a number of examples which may at least be said to lean in this direction (e.g. in LXX Ep Ier 27 [=Bar 6.28] it is used of the wives of the idol-priests who will not distribute 'unto the poor and to the impotent' any of the sacrificial flesh (οὔτε πτωχῷ οὔτε ἀδυνάτῳ μεταδιδόασιν); in Rom 1.11 Paul uses it of his own sharing a χάρισμα πνευματικόν with the Roman Christians; and in Herodotus 4.145 it is used of the Lacedaemonians' assigning allotments of land to the Minyae (δεξάμενοι δὲ τοὺς Μινύας γῆς τε μετέδοσαν καὶ ἐς φυλὰς διεδάσαντο), where it is not a matter of distributing their own personal possessions). So we cannot rule out Calvin's interpretation of ὁ μεταδιδούς as denoting not the person who gives what is his own but the person who is 'charged with the distribution of the public property of the Church',[5] simply on the ground that the word used is μεταδιδόναι. Nevertheless, while Calvin's explanation would seem to be possible, the interpretation, according to which ὁ μεταδιδούς is one who distributes what is his own, is probably to be preferred.[6] On this assumption, Paul presumably thinks of the

[1] Cf. Huby, p. 421: 'Saint Paul ne dit pas que cet office de charité doive nécessairement prendre la forme d'une prédication publique; on conçoit très bien qu'il puisse s'exercer dans les entretiens privés et des visites à domicile.'

[2] p. 357.

[3] p. 300.

[4] In Huby, p. 631.

[5] p. 270.

[6] It is to be found in patristic (e.g. Ambrosiaster, col. 157f; Chrysostom, col. 603), as well as in the majority of modern, commentaries. But, with regard to Chrysostom's interpretation, it should be noted that a comparison with his comments on 1.11 and 15.25ff suggests that, while in this verse he took the reference to be to the Christian's distributing his own property rather than to his distributing the church's alms on

χάρισμα (cf. v. 6) as consisting not in the mere possession of wealth which makes the μεταδιδόναι materially possible but in this person's spiritual capacity, his God-given inclination to give. (If Calvin's explanation were accepted, we could see the χάρισμα in the spiritual capacity which made the particular person suitable for the task of dispensing the church's charity.)

The point of ἐν ἁπλότητι (we have of course to supply μεταδιδότω) is, according to Calvin, that those who are responsible for distributing the church's substance to the needy 'are to administer faithfully what was entrusted to them without fraud or respect of persons';[1] according to Gaugler, whose understanding of 'him who distributes' is similar to Calvin's, it is that they are not to hanker after higher offices in the Church.[2] But, on the assumption that the other interpretation of ὁ μεταδιδούς is to be accepted, the point will be that the person who gives his substance to the poor is to do so without any ulterior motive. We could hardly improve on Althaus's comment: 'Giving requires the simplicity, which without ulterior motives or secondary purposes is wholly directed toward the other person's need and has no other consideration than that of relieving the need'.[3] We may note that, whereas ἐν τῇ διακονίᾳ, ἐν τῇ διδασκαλίᾳ, and ἐν τῇ παρακλήσει indicate the spheres, ἐν ἁπλότητι, ἐν σπουδῇ and ἐν ἱλαρότητι indicate the spirit and manner, in which particular χαρίσματα are to be exercised—the spirit and manner, in which they naturally will be exercised by those whose minds really are being renewed, who really do have faith and know themselves to stand in the light of the death, resurrection and exaltation of Jesus Christ.

Many have seen in ὁ προϊστάμενος the figure of a ruler presiding generally over the life of the congregation. Thus Rufinus's version of Origen uses the expression 'qui praeest

behalf of the church, he was conscious of a reminder in the use of the verb μεταδιδόναι of the important truth that what good things Christians have they hold as gifts from God which they are not free to use merely for their own selfish satisfaction but are in duty bound to use responsibly for the common good. On 1.11 (ἵνα τι μεταδῶ) he says: δεικνὺς ὅτι οὐ τὸ αὐτοῦ αὐτοῖς δίδωσιν, ἀλλ' ἅπερ ἔλαβε μετεδίδου (col. 404), while on 15.27 he says: . . . τὰ δὲ σαρκικὰ οὐ τούτων [i.e. the Gentile Christians'] μόνον, ἀλλὰ κοινὰ πάντων· τὰ γὰρ χρήματα πάντων ἐκέλευσεν εἶναι, οὐχὶ τῶν κεκτημένων μόνον (col. 662).

[1] p. 270.
[2] 2, p. 245.
[3] p. 108f (our translation). Cf. Theodoret, col. 189: Μὴ τὴν τῶν ἄλλων θηρώμενος δόξαν, ἀλλὰ τὴν χρείαν τοῦ δεομένου πληρῶν· μηδὲ λογισμοῖς κεχρημένος, εἴτε ἀπόχρη τὰ ὄντα, εἴτε καὶ μή· ἀλλὰ τῷ Θεῷ θαρρῶν, καὶ φιλοτίμως (i.e. 'zealously') τὴν χορηγίαν ποιούμενος.

ecclesiae',[1] and Calvin comments: 'Paul is properly referring to those to whom the government of the Church was committed. These were the elders (*seniores*), who presided over and ruled the other members and exercised discipline',[2] while Schlatter says boldly: 'Hier erscheint das Episkopat', though qualifying this by adding: 'aber auch hier, ohne dass ihm Paulus durch rechtliche Satzungen eine überall gültige Form gäbe'.[3] It is true that the verb προϊστάναι is used in 1 Th 5.12 and 1 Tim 5.17 of presiding over the church, in 1 Tim 3.4, 5, 12, of ruling one's own household. Others are anxious not to read into Paul's phrase a meaning more definite than he intended. Barrett, for instance, says that προϊστάναι here 'does not describe any office with precision; it rather refers to a function which may have been exercised by several persons, perhaps jointly or in turn. There is no indication whether the "president" presided at a service . . . of preaching and teaching, at the eucharist, or in a church meeting convened for deliberative or disciplinary purposes'.[4] But, since ὁ προϊστάμενος is placed between ὁ μεταδιδούς and ὁ ἐλεῶν (it looks rather as if ὁ διδάσκων and ὁ παρακαλῶν are grouped together, and then ὁ μεταδιδούς, ὁ προϊστάμενος and ὁ ἐλεῶν), the explanation given by Lagrange[5] (following Cornely[6] and Kühl[7]), accepted by Huby[8] and Leenhardt,[9] and regarded as possible and attractive by Gaugler,[10] according to which ὁ προϊστάμενος is the administrator in charge of the charitable work of the congregation, would seem to be more likely. On this view the last three functions referred to in v. 8 are all closely related.[11] Or perhaps we should think, as Michel does, not so much of the administrator of the charitable work as of the person, who by virtue of his social status was in a position to be, on behalf of the church, a friend and protector for those members of the community who were not in a position

[1] col. 1217.
[2] p. 270.
[3] p. 342. Käsemann, p. 327, thinks of 'various organizational functions including the establishment of house-churches and . . . settling of disputes' (our translation).
[4] p. 239.
[5] p. 300.
[6] p. 658.
[7] p. 424f.
[8] p. 422.
[9] p. 312.
[10] 2, p. 246.
[11] Leenhardt (p. 312) envisages a particularly close inter-dependence. According to him, ὁ μεταδιδούς 'provides the church with wealth which ὁ προϊστάμενος 'organises and administers and others [he is thinking of ὁ ἐλεῶν] distribute by concrete acts of charity'.

to defend themselves (e.g. the widows, orphans, slaves, strangers).[1] The verb προϊστάναι can mean 'support', 'succour', 'protect'.[2] The cognate noun προστάτης was used of the patron of resident aliens in Athens, and so was used as a translation of the Latin *patronus*;[3] the feminine form προστάτις is used in 16.2 of Phoebe who in the previous verse is described as διάκονος τῆς ἐκκλησίας τῆς ἐν Κεγχρεαῖς. The injunction ἐν σπουδῇ (προϊστάσθω), i.e., 'with diligence', 'with zeal', is equally appropriate, whichever of the above explanations of ὁ προϊστάμενος we accept.

By ὁ ἐλεῶν is probably meant the person whose special function is, on behalf of the congregation, to tend the sick, relieve the poor, or care for the aged and disabled.[4] The assumption that Paul refers to those who (on behalf of the church) have direct, personal contact with the needy and afflicted is confirmed by the next two words. For ἐν ἱλαρότητι compare LXX Prov 22.8[RV: 9] (ἄνδρα ἱλαρὸν καὶ δότην εὐλογεῖ ὁ θεός), which is echoed in 2 Cor 9.7, and LXX Ecclus 32 [RV: 35].9 (ἐν πάσῃ δόσει ἱλάρωσον τὸ πρόσωπόν σου). Calvin comments: 'As nothing affords more consolation to the sick or to anyone otherwise distressed than the sight of helpers eagerly and readily disposed to afford him help, so if he observes gloominess on the face of those who help him, he will take it as an affront.'[5] A particularly cheerful and agreeable disposition may well be evidence of the special *charisma* that marks a person out for this particular service; but an inward ἱλαρότης in ministering will in any case come naturally to one who knows the secret that in those needy and suffering people whom he is called to tend the Lord is Himself present (cf. Mt 25.31ff), for he will recognize in them Christ's gracious gift to him and to the congregation, in whose name he ministers, of an opportunity to love and thank Him who can never be loved and thanked enough. The fact that a few verses later on we get an injunction to contribute to the necessities of the saints (v. 13) suggests that here in v. 8 Paul is thinking of service which reaches beyond the limits of the Christian fellowship.[6] It need

[1] p. 300. This explanation is to be found already in Bengel, who comments succinctly: '*qui* alios *curat* et in clientela habet' (p. 554).

[2] Cf. LSJ, s.v. προΐστημι B.II.3.

[3] It is interesting that in 1 Clement 61.3 and 64.1, Jesus Christ is referred to as 'the High Priest and Guardian [προστάτης] of our souls' and 'our High Priest and Guardian [προστάτης]', respectively.

[4] Cf., e.g., Calvin, p. 270; Gaugler 2, p. 246; Käsemann, p. 327.

[5] ibid.

[6] Cf. Chrysostom, col. 606 (on v. 13): Ἄνω μὲν γὰρ εἰπών, Ὁ ἐλεῶν, ἐν ἱλαρότητι, πᾶσι τὴν χεῖρα ἀνέῳξεν· ἐνταῦθα μέντοι ὑπὲρ τῶν πιστῶν φησι· διὸ καὶ

hardly be added that the designation of some people specially as those who show mercy in no way implies that the rest of the members of a church are free from the obligation to show mercy personally as they are able; Paul here speaks of those who, having a special aptitude, are appointed by the church to concentrate upon this work in its name.

It is instructive to notice that out of the seven charismata referred to in vv. 6–8 no less than four (εἴτε διακονίαν . . . , ὁ μεταδιδοὺς . . . , ὁ προϊστάμενος . . . , and ὁ ἐλεῶν) most probably have to do with the practical assistance of those who are in one way or another specially in need of help and sympathy. This fact by itself is a clear and eloquent indication of the importance of the place of diakonia in the life of the church as Paul understood it. If this work bulked so large in the thought and activity of the primitive Church in spite of its poverty, it can hardly be right for it to bulk less large in the life of the relatively so affluent churches of the west in the last years of the twentieth century, when more than half the world's population is underfed, inadequately provided with medical services, and in very many other ways underprivileged, and at the same time ease of communications has made the whole world one neighbourhood. At a time when in many churches the need for the renewal of the diaconate is beginning to be felt and recognized, the careful study of these verses is particularly rewarding; for not only do they afford interesting glimpses of the diaconal work of the early Church, they also open up vistas into the future, suggesting varied tasks which a renewed diaconate and a whole Church, reinvigorated in its understanding of its diaconal responsibility by the existence in its midst of such a renewed diaconate, might undertake, and indicating clearly the truly Christian spirit in which they ought to be undertaken.

VII. 3. A SERIES OF LOOSELY CONNECTED ITEMS OF EXHORTATION (12.9–21)

Whereas the different instructions contained in vv. 6–8 were addressed to the recipients of the different χαρίσματα respectively, those which follow apply equally to all the members of the church. The various items of exhortation, though all

ἐπάγει, λέγων, Ταῖς χρείαις τῶν ἁγίων κοινωνοῦντες. Similarly Theophylact, col. 508: *Ἄνω μὲν εἰπών, Ὁ ἐλεῶν ἐν ἱλαρότητι, πᾶσιν ἁπλῶς τὴν χεῖρα ἠνέῳξε· νῦν δὲ περὶ τῆς εἰς τοὺς πιστοὺς ἐλεημοσύνης λέγει· τούτους γὰρ ἁγίους καλεῖ.

deriving from what was said in vv. 1–2, and though they could all more or less easily be brought under some such general heading as 'love in action' or 'the marks of love', are but loosely connected; and it is a mistake to look too anxiously for precise connexions of thought or for a logical sequence in these verses. With v. 14 the construction changes, and this change seems to mark something of a new beginning. In vv. 9–13 Paul has been concerned mainly at any rate with the relations of Christians with their fellow-Christians. In vv. 14–21 he is at any rate mainly concerned with the relations of Christians with those outside the Church. It has been suggested that his use of the verb διώκειν in v. 13 may have brought to his mind the thought of persecution[1] or reminded him of the dominical saying which we have in Mt 5.44,[2] or that the thought of hospitality led him to think of those who were refugees from persecution, and of their persecutors.[3] But, while such an association of ideas is, of course, not to be ruled out, there is no need to assume anything of this sort: the transition from the subject of Christians' relations with their fellow-Christians to that of their relations with non-Christians was in any case a natural one.[4]

[9]Let *your* love be genuine. Abhor what is evil, cleave to what is good. [10]In *your* love for the brethren show one another affectionate kindness. Prefer one another in honour. [11]Be not slack in zeal. Be aglow with the Spirit. Serve the Lord. [12]Rejoice in hope. In affliction endure. Persevere in prayer. [13]Help to relieve the necessities of the saints. Pursue the opportunities you get to be hospitable.

[14]Bless those who persecute you; bless and do not curse. [15]Rejoice with those who rejoice, weep with those who weep. [16]Agree together one with another. Do not be haughty but readily associate with the humble. Do not esteem yourselves wise. [17]Return evil for evil to no one. In the sight of all men take thought for those things which are good. [18]If it is possible, in so far as it depends on you, be at peace with all men. [19]Do not avenge yourselves, beloved, but give place to the wrath *of God*; for it is written, 'Vengeance belongs to me, I will repay, says the Lord'. [20]But, if thine enemy is hungry, feed him; if he is thirsty, give him to drink: for by so doing thou shalt heap coals of fire upon his head. [21]Be thou not overcome by evil, but overcome evil by good.

9. ἡ ἀγάπη. Up to this point in Romans the noun ἀγάπη has been used only with reference to the divine love (5.5, 8; 8.35,

---

[1] So, e.g., Michel, pp. 301, 305; Leenhardt, p. 316; Käsemann, p. 331.
[2] So, as one possibility, Lagrange, p. 305.
[3] Cf. Cornely, p. 665; Lagrange, p. 305 (as another possibility).
[4] On vv. 9–21 reference may be made to C. H. Talbert, 'Tradition and redaction in Rom 12.9–21', in *NTS* 16 (1969–70), pp. 83–93.

39)[1]: it is now used of the love which the Christian owes his fellow-man (cf. 13.8–10). Paul does not give any absolutely clear indication whether, when he uses ἀγάπη here, he is thinking of love of fellow-Christians only or of love which embraces those outside the Church as well; but, in view of v. 10a, it seems more probable that he intends the wider sense, for τῇ φιλαδελφίᾳ εἰς ἀλλήλους φιλόστοργοι will have more point if the ἀγάπη referred to in the previous verse is not just the same thing as φιλαδελφία (the specially intimate affection which is proper between Christians), but an all-embracing love.[2] Something of the meaning of ἀγάπη will become apparent in our study of these verses. Suffice it here to say that God in His love has claimed us wholly for Himself and for our neighbours, and the love, of which Paul speaks here, is the believer's 'yes', in thought and feeling, word and deed, unconditional and without reservation, to that total claim of the loving God, in so far as it relates to the neighbour—a 'yes', which is no human possibility but the gracious work of the Holy Spirit.[3]

Paul exhorts the Roman Christians to let their love be ἀνυπόκριτος.[4] The point of ἀνυπόκριτος is not that love is to be frank and to tell the truth even though it may be unpalatable (an interpretation which the Vulgate translation 'sine simulatione' may possibly have rather encouraged), but that it is to be the real thing, genuine and not counterfeit.[5] The fact that Paul twice uses this word with reference to ἀγάπη (here and in 2 Cor 6.6)[6] suggests that he was aware of the danger in this

---

[1] Ἀγαπᾶν has once been used of man's love to God (8.28): otherwise both ἀγαπᾶν and ἀγαπητός have also only been used so far in Romans with reference to God's love (8.37; 9.13, 25; 1.7; 11.28).

[2] For a reply to H. W. Montefiore's contention that Paul has narrowed down the scope of love of neighbour and made it into love of the fellow-Christian ('Thou shalt love the [sic] neighbour as thyself', in NT 5, pp. 157–70) see C. E. B. Cranfield, 'Diakonia in the New Testament', in Service in Christ, p. 43f.

[3] On ἀγάπη see further on 13.8–10 and the bibliographical details there given.

[4] Ἀνυπόκριτος occurs also in 2 Cor 6.6; 1 Tim 1.5; 2 Tim 1.5; Jas 3.17; 1 Pet 1.22, and in the LXX in Wisd 5.18; 18.16. It is also found in Demetrius, Eloc. 194 (? late first century A.D.), but in the sense of 'undramatic', while the adverb ἀνυποκρίτως occurs in Marcus Aurelius 8.5. See further U. Wilckens in TWNT 8, pp.558–71 (on ὑποκρίνομαι, κ.τ.λ.); also C. E. B. Cranfield, The Gospel according to St. Mark, Cambridge, ⁶1977, pp. 235 and 371.

[5] Cf. the 'non ficta' by which the Vulgate renders it in 2 Cor 6.6. Pelagius, p. 97, in commenting on the present verse, aptly quotes 1 Jn 3.18. Cf. Oecumenius, col. 569: μὴ πλάσμα ἀγάπης, ἀλλὰ ἀγάπη εἰλικρινής.

[6] In 1 Pet 1.22 it is used in connexion with φιλαδελφία..

connexion of deceit and—even more serious—of self-deceit,[1] a danger of which the modern champions of 'Not law but love' seem often to be unaware.

While it would not be untrue to say that all the rest of this chapter is commentary on ἡ ἀγάπη ἀνυπόκριτος, it is, in our opinion, a mistake to connect v. 9b specially closely with v. 9a, taking it as the explanation of, or, at least, the complement of the idea expressed by, ἀνυπόκριτος, as is often done.[2] For when once it is recognized that ἀνυπόκριτος means not 'frank' but 'genuine', 'not counterfeit', this interpretation of v. 9b loses much of its plausibility. Moreover, it is surely unnatural to separate in this way the two participial clauses of v. 9b from the rest of the series of participial clauses extending down to the end of v. 13. So we do not understand ἀποστυγοῦντες τὸ πονηρόν, κολλώμενοι τῷ ἀγαθῷ to have any such special meaning as that Christian love is to abhor the evil in the person loved and only to attach itself to the good in him,[3] but take it to be a quite general exhortation:[4] Christians are to abhor, to hate utterly, that which is evil,[5] and to cleave firmly to that which is good. The fact that this is general does not make it not worth saying.

10. τῇ φιλαδελφίᾳ εἰς ἀλλήλους φιλόστοργοι indicates the tender and intimate affection as between members of the same family which is appropriate within the Church. The use of 'brother' with reference to the adherents of the same religion was, of course, not peculiar to Christians in the ancient world: it was common not only among Jews but also for example in the religious communities of Egypt and among the initiates of Mithras. But its use in the Church had its own special quality derived from the gospel itself. The word φιλαδελφία, used by

---

[1] Cf. Calvin, p. 271: 'It is difficult to express how ingenious almost all men are in counterfeiting a love which they do not really possess. They deceive not only others, but also themselves, while they persuade themselves that they have a true love for those whom they not only treat with neglect, but also in fact reject.' The recognition that the state of the man who believes that he is loving, when he is not, is even worse than that of the man who pretends to be loving, knowing that he is not, is important. Cf. Plato, *R.* 382 b and c (on the lie in the soul).

[2] e.g. by Bengel, p. 554f; Lagrange, p. 301; NEB.

[3] As does, e.g., Lagrange, p. 301.

[4] Though, in denying that this half-verse is specifically intended as explanation of ἀνυπόκριτος, we are not, of course, wishing to deny that it—like all the following injunctions of Rom 12—sets forth distinguishing marks of ἀγάπη ἀνυπόκριτος.

[5] For the intensive force of ἀπο —see on ἀποκαραδοκία in 8.19. What is required is not just a refraining from doing what is evil, but an intense inward rejection of it.

pagan writers in its proper sense of love of natural brothers or sisters, is used in the NT (also 1 Th 4.9; Heb 13.1; 1 Pet 1.22; 2 Pet 1.7 (twice): φιλάδελφος occurs in 1 Pet 3.8) and other early Christian literature metaphorically, of love of fellow-Christians. The word-group, φιλοστοργεῖν, φιλοστοργία, φιλόστοργος, though represented only here in the NT, was in quite frequent use both in earlier and in contemporary Greek, to denote tender affection, particularly family affection.[1] With φιλόστοργοι the participle ὄντες is, of course, to be supplied.

τῇ τιμῇ ἀλλήλους προηγούμενοι can be variously interpreted (i) 'anticipating one another in showing honour' (cf. Vulgate: 'honore invicem praevenientes'. So Oecumenius: . . . ἐὰν ἕκαστος ἀγωνίζηται προλαβεῖν εἰς τὸ τιμῆσαι τὸν πλησίον,[2] and Theophylact: Τοῦτο γάρ ἐστι τὸ προηγεῖσθαι, τὸ προλαμβάνειν ἀλλήλους ἐν τῷ ἀλλήλους τιμᾶν)[3]; (ii) 'surpassing one another in showing honour' (so Chrysostom: Οὕτω γὰρ φιλία καὶ γίνεται, καὶ γινομένη μένει. Καὶ οὐδὲν οὕτω φίλους ποιεῖ, ὡς τὸ σπουδάζειν τῇ τιμῇ νικᾶν τὸν πλησίον)[4]; (iii) 'in honour preferring one another' (so AV, RV). In favour of (i) and (ii) is the fact that προηγεῖσθαι is frequently used in such senses as 'go first and lead the way', 'take the lead of', 'go before', 'precede', and also the fact that the early versions take it this way; but against them is the use of the accusative—one would expect the genitive (cf. LSJ, s.v. προηγέομαι 2). Against (iii) is the difficulty of adducing any other example of προηγεῖσθαι used in the sense 'prefer' (2 Macc 10.12 has been adduced, but it is not absolutely clear that προηγεῖσθαι must be so translated there: the RV in fact translates differently). Nevertheless, it can be said in favour of (iii) that 'prefer' would not be a surprising meaning for προηγεῖσθαι to have (see LSJ, s.v. ἡγέομαι III, and cf. the verb προκρίνειν); and that Phil 2.3 (τῇ ταπεινοφροσύνῃ ἀλλήλους ἡγούμενοι ὑπερέχοντας ἑαυτῶν) provides support for this interpretation.[5] So (with Sanday and Headlam, Denney, Lagrange, Lietzmann, Barrett, et al.: cf. F. Büchsel, in TWNT

---

[1] It is interesting that neither στέργειν nor στοργή is to be found in the NT. In the LXX στέργειν occurs once, στοργή four times, φιλοστοργία three times, φιλόστοργος once, and φιλοστόργως once (all in Maccabees, except the one occurrence of στέργειν which is in Ecclesiasticus). The adjective φιλόστοργος is found in Xenophon, Aristotle, Theocritus, etc. The comparative is used by Cicero in a letter to Atticus. See further C. Spicq, in RB 62 (1955), pp. 497–510.

[2] col. 572.

[3] col. 508.

[4] col. 605.

[5] Phil 2.3 is already quoted in this connexion by Pelagius, p. 97.

2, p. 910f; BDF, § 150) we take the meaning to be 'in honour preferring one another'.

But what exactly does Paul mean by this? We may say at once that he certainly does not mean that one is to pretend that the other Christian is always better or wiser than oneself. What Paul is saying has nothing to do with pretending. It is instructive to compare Lev 19.18 (cf. Rom 13.9; Mk 12.31, etc.). Why does Paul actually go farther and say, not just that one is to honour one's fellow-Christian as oneself, but that one is to honour him above oneself? The only satisfactory explanation (if we remember that we are dealing with theological ethics and that all that Paul says in these chapters must be understood in the light of 12.1–2) would seem to be the one hinted at by Barth.[1] The gospel has disclosed a fact of transcendent importance in connexion with love of the neighbour, namely, that the Son of man Himself is mysteriously present in the other person in his human need (cf. what was said above in connexion with ἐν ἱλαρότητι in v. 8). It is because the other person (Paul is here specially thinking of the other Christian, though it is true of all men) is the representative of Christ to me, or rather the one in whom Christ is mysteriously present for me, that I must honour him, not just as myself, but above myself.

11. τῇ σπουδῇ μὴ ὀκνηροί. The Christians in Rome are not to allow themselves to grow slack in zeal (in the service of God and of their neighbours, in the λογικὴ λατρεία that is required of them). In lives which are truly being transformed by the renewing of the mind there is no room for slackness or sloth, for that attitude which seeks to get by with as little work and inconvenience as possible, which shrinks from dust and heat and resents the necessity for any exertion as a burden and imposition (for ὀκνηρός, an interesting word, cf. Mt 25.26; Prov 6.6, 9; 21.25; 26.13–16; Ecclus 37.11). The mercy of God already experienced (12.1) and the approach of 'the day' (13.12) alike call for an unflagging zeal.

τῷ πνεύματι ζέοντες is significantly paired with τῇ σπουδῇ μὴ ὀκνηροί. Chrysostom thought of it as answering the question, 'How are we to become "not slack in zeal"?'[2] But what exactly does it mean? The same expression is used in Acts 18.25 of Apollos while he was still 'knowing only the baptism of John': there perhaps the reference is to his ardent temperament. But here in Romans it is more natural (*pace* NEB) to

---

[1] *Shorter*, p. 154.
[2] col. 605.

take πνεύματι to refer to the Holy Spirit (as do Origen (probably),[1] Chrysostom,[2] Oecumenius,[3] Theophylact,[4] and also
Calvin and many modern scholars). The Christian is to allow
himself to be set on fire (the verb is usually used of water
boiling, seething, but is also occasionally used of solids, e.g. of
copper, being fiery hot, glowing) by the Holy Spirit.[5] Among
the most illuminating comments are those of Origen ('For he
desires that we, who live under the law of the Spirit, should
have nothing languid, nothing lukewarm in us, but should do
all things with the Spirit's fervour [or 'with fervour of spirit':
Rufinus's Latin is 'cum fervore spiritus'] and the fire of faith')[6]
and Calvin ('It is the fervour of the Spirit alone which corrects
our indolence. Diligence in well-doing, therefore, requires the
zeal which the Spirit of God has kindled in our hearts. Why,
then, someone may say, does Paul exhort us to this fervour?
My answer is that, although this zeal is the gift of God, these
duties are laid upon believers in order that they may shake off
their listlessness and take to themselves the flame which God
has kindled. It usually happens that we stifle or extinguish the
Spirit by our own fault').[7]

The first member of the next pair is τῷ κυρίῳ δουλεύοντες.
The variant reading καιρῷ for κυρίῳ (D* G 5 it Ambst, codd
apud Hier), which is mentioned but rejected by several of the
Fathers, has been favoured by a number of modern scholars.[8]
In favour of καιρῷ it may be said: (i) that it is undoubtedly the
more difficult reading; (ii) that τῷ κυρίῳ δουλεύοντες seems
rather general for this series; (iii) that an eschatological reference is appropriate here in conjunction with the following τῇ
ἐλπίδι χαίροντες (if καιρῷ is accepted, to understand it, in the
light of such passages as 13.11; Col 4.5; Eph 5.16, as denoting
the present time in its eschatological determination[9] is surely
preferable to interpreting it in a general sense of the actual

[1] col. 1219.
[2] col. 605.
[3] col. 572.
[4] col. 508.
[5] It is perhaps relevant to refer in connexion with Paul's use of ζέω
here to his use of the verb σβεννύναι ('extinguish') in 1 Th 5.19 (τὸ πνεῦμα
μὴ σβέννυτε) as implying the comparison of the Spirit to a fire.
[6] col. 1219.
[7] p. 272.
[8] e.g. Schlatter, p. 344f, tentatively; Barth, 1933, p. 450, n. 1 (he does
not deal with the matter in Shorter); Michel, p. 303f; Leenhardt, p. 315;
Käsemann, pp. 327, 330f, with some hesitation. It is marked as a !
variant in Nestle.
[9] Cf. Barth, 1933, p. 457; Michel, ibid.; Leenhardt, ibid.; Lyonnet, in
Huby, p. 631.

situation in which at a particular time one finds oneself, as Schlatter seems inclined to do).

But these arguments are by no means unanswerable. With regard to (ii), it must be said that the force of this argument has been exaggerated. The judgment that the reading τῷ κυρίῳ δουλεύοντες is 'insipid', 'in the context, a quite intolerable generalization', the work of 'some copyist, lacking a sense of humour',[1] depends for its validity upon a particular understanding of the movement of Paul's thought just here. But Paul may well have been conscious that the words he had just used, τῷ πνεύματι ζέοντες, were liable to very serious misunderstanding on the part of those who tended to regard exciting and showy ecstasies as the most precious evidences of the Spirit. If so, it was altogether appropriate to add immediately a sobering reminder of the true nature of this Spirit-given fervour. The real proof of the presence of this fire of the Spirit would be not effervescent religious excitement but renewed energy and determination in the humble and obedient service of the Lord Jesus.

With regard to (iii) it may be said that κυρίῳ is no less appropriate than καιρῷ in relation to the following clause. For the service of the Lord Jesus Christ involves bearing the cross; it means in this present age hardship and suffering. It was very natural for Paul to couple with the injunction to serve the Lord a reference to hope, to that 'glory which is to be revealed in us' with which 'the sufferings of the present time are not worthy to be compared' (8.18) and in which those who now suffer as they serve the Lord may even in this present time rejoice in hope.

With regard to (i), the position would seem to be that καιρῷ is not only lectio difficilior (this it certainly is) but also lectio impossibilis. For the evidence of the occurrences of τῷ καιρῷ δουλεύειν in Plutarch (1st/2nd century A.D.), Arat. 43.2, and (admittedly much later than the New Testament) Anth. Pal. 9.441, and of tempori servire in Cicero, Att. 8.3.6; 10.7.1; Fam. 9.17; Sest. 6.14; Tusc. 3.27.66, supported, as it is, by the emphatic rejection of the reading καιρῷ here by Origen,[2] Athanasius[3] and Jerome,[4] goes a long way toward proving that 'serve the time' was in both Greek and Latin a well-established expression with a quite definite range of meaning which may be indicated by such English expressions as 'opportunism',

[1] Barth, 1933, p. 450, n. 1.
[2] col. 1220.
[3] Ep. ad Dracont. 3.
[4] Ep. 27.3.

'accommodating oneself to the circumstances', 'time-serving'.
If it was, then it is surely extremely unlikely that Paul would
have used it to express anything like what is conveyed by
ἐξαγοράζεσθαι τὸν καιρόν in Eph. 5.16 or of giving oneself wholeheartedly to the fulfilment of the demands of the καιρός
eschatologically understood. Barth regarded the use of it here
in this Christian sense as 'an entirely suitable paradox'[1]; but is
there any other example in the Pauline epistles of quite this
sort of paradox? And, even if the above objection to καιρῷ
could be set aside, there would still remain the objection that
δουλεύειν would be a very unlikely verb for Paul to use of the
relation of the Christian to the present time as eschatologically
determined. A survey of the occurrences of δοῦλος, δουλεύειν
and δουλοῦν in the NT suggests that when these words are used
metaphorically, whether *in bonam*, or *in malam, partem*, they
are used quite carefully and strictly.

The most probable explanation of the variant καιρῷ is that
it originated in a purely accidental error, perhaps due to the
use of abbreviation. What we think is the point of τῷ κυρίῳ
δουλεύοντες (with which compare 14.18; 16.18) in this context
we have already indicated in our answer to (ii) above.

12. The second member of this pair (the verse-division
obscures the pairing)[2] requires little explanation. On its cor-
relation of joy and hope 5.2–5 (cf. 8.16–25) and I Pet 1.3–9
provide the necessary commentary. τῇ ἐλπίδι[3] and χαίροντες
qualify and interpret each other. The Christian is to allow
himself to experience the joy which is his, for the Christian life
is a life of joy (cf. Gal 5.22: ὁ δὲ καρπὸς τοῦ πνεύματός ἐστιν . . .
χαρά . . .); but this joy has its source not in this present age to
which he is not to be conformed, nor in his present circumstances, but in that which is still future, which he grasps by
hope. But this hope is not the sort of hope which disappoints
(cf. 5.5); since that which is hoped for is altogether sure and
certain, this hope means present joy. For 'although believers
are now pilgrims on earth, yet by their confidence they sur-
mount the heavens, so that they cherish their future inheritance
in their bosoms with tranquillity'.[4]

τῇ θλίψει ὑπομένοντες. From ἐλπίς to ὑπομονή is for Paul a

[1] 1933, p. 450, n. 1.
[2] The recognition of six pairs of clauses in verses 9b–13 seems to fit
the contents better than the arrangement implied by the verse-divisions
(of two pairs, followed by two sets of three, and finally one more pair of
clauses).
[3] For the dative see BDF, § 196.
[4] Calvin, p. 105 (on 5.2).

very natural transition (cf. 5.2–4; 8.24f; 1 Cor 13.7; 1 Th 1.3).
Endurance (RV 'patient' is too weak: the RV itself renders this
verb elsewhere by 'endure', e.g. Mk 13.13; Jas 5.11) is necessary,
because an inevitable accompaniment of the Christian's existence in this world is θλῖψις (cf. Jn 16.33; Acts 14.22, etc.). This
θλῖψις, tribulation, affliction (the literal meaning of θλίβειν is to
squeeze, compress, crush), stems from the world's resistance to
Christ. The world hates Him: therefore His followers must
expect to be hated too (cf. Mt 10.22; Mk 13.13 = Lk 21.17;
Jn 15.18f). 'Not all that the world hates is good Christianity;
but it does hate good Christianity and always will.'[1] Like ἐλπίς
and ὑπομονή, θλῖψις has in the NT eschatological associations;
for this hatred is the desperate reaction of 'the night' (13.12),
which is destined to pass away, to all that belong to the
approaching 'day'.[2] In the face of[3] this θλῖψις the Christian is
to endure, to hold out steadfastly, in the knowledge that the
final issue is not uncertain. This he will do not in his own
strength, but in the strength which God supplies; for it is
God who is the source of endurance (cf. 15.5).

Coupled with τῇ θλίψει ὑπομένοντες is τῇ προσευχῇ προσκαρτεροῦντες. Distressed by the pressure from without, by the
θλῖψις of the world's unrelenting hostility, and always in danger
of succumbing to the inward anguish, which is its natural
result, the Christian should indeed have recourse continually
to prayer. Only in his reliance upon the θεὸς τῆς ὑπομονῆς (15.5)
has he hope of holding out to the end. But it is precisely this
thing, which is altogether vital and necessary if he is to endure,
which he is specially tempted whether through sloth or discouragement or self-confidence to give up: hence the special
frequency with which the verb προσκαρτερεῖν is used in the NT
in connexion with prayer (Acts 1.14; 2.42; 6.4; Col 4.2: cf. Eph
6.18, and also Lk 18.1; 1 Th 5.17). It must also be said here,
that, while it is probable that at this point Paul had specially
in mind the connexion between prayer and endurance, it is
also, of course, true, as Aquinas pointed out,[4] that there is an

[1] W. Temple, *Readings in St. John's Gospel* (London, 1945), p. 271f.
[2] On θλῖψις see on 2.9. Reference may be made to the fine section on
'The Christian in Affliction' in K. Barth, CD IV/3, pp. 614–41 (=KD
IV/3, pp. 704–41).
[3] The dative τῇ θλίψει is perhaps to be explained as a temporal dative,
'in tribulation', though BDF, § 196, suggests that it is to be explained as
assimilation to the neighbouring datives—possibly a scribal corruption
(it is noteworthy that Marcion attests τὴν θλῖψιν).
[4] p. 184 (992): 'Per orationem enim in nobis solicitudo excitatur,
fervor accenditur, ad Dei servitium incitamur, gaudium spei in nobis
augetur, et auxilium in tribulatione promeremur'.

intimate connexion between prayer and all the things which are enjoined in these verses.

13. ταῖς χρείαις τῶν ἁγίων κοινωνοῦντες. Instead of χρείαις D* F G read μνείαις, and this reading is supported by some Old Latin manuscripts, and by the Vulgate codex Amiatinus. Both readings are known to Origen, Theodore of Mopsuestia, Jerome, Augustine, and Pelagius. The view of Zahn,[1] Kühl[2] and Barth,[3] that μνείαις is original, being used in the sense of remembrances expressed in concrete and friendly help, the reference being to the collection for the poor saints in Jerusalem, would clearly be attractive, were there any adequate evidence for the possibility of the word's being used in this sense. It would be easy to understand the alteration to the easier χρείαις. But there seems to be no evidence in support of this sense of μνεία. Those early writers who know this reading generally understand it to refer either to the solemn remembrance of the saints (i.e., the 'saints' of the past) in prayer or to the imitation of their lives; but the use of ἅγιος in this sense cannot be attributed to Paul. Nor is it very likely that this sentence was originally intended as an exhortation to intercede for the (living) saints; for the pairing tells against this (the reference to hospitality in the second member makes it more likely that the reference is to practical help), and so does the use of κοινωνεῖν, which, in view of the use of it or its cognates in 15.26f; Gal 6.6; Phil 4.15; 1 Tim 6.18; Heb 13.16, strongly suggests practical assistance. There is very little doubt that χρείαις should be read. The reading μνείαις may have originated in a simple mistake (it is not too difficult to imagine *XP* in a badly written or worn manuscript being mistaken for *MN*), or the reference to prayer in the preceding verse may have suggested the word μνεία to a copyist's mind.[4] The incorrect reading, once in existence, would establish itself quite easily at a time when ἅγιοι tended to mean the 'saints' of the past who were commemorated solemnly (the custom of commemorating the martyrs goes back to the middle of the second century, as *Martyrium Polycarpi* 18 (quoted by Sanday and Headlam) shows).

Once χρείαις is accepted as the original reading, the interpretation of the clause presents no difficulty. The Christian who is being transformed by the renewing of the mind will not doubt his obligation to help in relieving the destitution of his

---

[1] p. 551.
[2] p. 427.
[3] 1933, p. 450, n. 2. Contrast *Shorter*, p. 154.
[4] Cf. Gaugler, 2, p. 256. Μνεία is specially frequent in connexion with intercession (e.g. 1.9; Eph 1.16; Phil 1.3; 1 Th 1.2; Philem 4).

fellow-Christians. Calvin comments: 'He particularly commands us to assist the *saints*. Although our love ought to extend to the whole human race, it should embrace with particular affection those who are of the household of faith, for they are connected to us by a closer bond'.[1] It should, however, be said that, whereas in Paul's (and Calvin's) days a large proportion of the Christian community must have been very poor, at the present time Christians of the west share the affluence of their nations to a great extent, and in the poorer countries the Christians will often be among the less poor members of the community. In view of the different circumstances of the Church, less emphasis would seem to be required today on the special claim of the saints, and more on the claims of human distress generally.

The second member of this last pair is τὴν φιλοξενίαν διώκοντες. In the first century the need for Christian hospitality for individual Christians from other places, though perhaps hardly as great and pressing a problem as it has become in our western European cities with their large numbers of immigrants and foreign workers of various sorts, must have been very considerable,[2] and this would be especially so in Rome. And, in the absence of special church buildings, there was the further need for hospitality to be shown to the church in a particular place as a whole for its meetings for worship and other purposes.[3] There is a hint of the possibilities of disappointment, abuse and exasperation which such hospitality involved in the phrase ἄνευ γογγυσμοῦ in 1 Pet 4.9. The implication of διώκοντες (διώκειν means properly 'pursue', 'chase', as in war or hunting: it is also used in 9.31 of Israel's zealous quest after the νόμος δικαιοσύνης, in 14.19 of the earnest seeking of what makes for peace, and elsewhere in the NT of the Christian's zealous quest for ἀγάπη[4]) that one is not just to wait and take the stranger in, if he actually presents himself at the door, but to go out and

---

[1] p. 273.
[2] Cf. Mt 25.35, 38, 43f; 1 Tim 3.2; Tit 1.8; Heb 13.1f; 1 Clem. 1.2; 10.7; 11.1; 12.1. Paul is here probably thinking at any rate mainly of fellow-Christians, but there is no need to assume that he wished to limit hospitality to them. It is interesting that Theodoret, col. 192, explicitly interprets this injunction as embracing non-Christians as well: 'By "strangers" (ξένους) he means not only the saints but also any who have come from another place and are in need of assistance, and he commands us to care for them'.
[3] Cf. 16.5; 1 Cor 16.19; Philem 2.
[4] 1 Cor 14.1. See also 1 Th 5.15; 1 Tim 6.11; 2 Tim 2.22; Heb 12.14; 1 Pet 3.11.

look for those to whom one can show hospitality, was already brought out by the Fathers.[1]

14. εὐλογεῖτε τοὺς διώκοντας, εὐλογεῖτε καὶ μὴ καταρᾶσθε. Two textual matters call for notice here. One is the omission of the second εὐλογεῖτε by 𝔓[46] Ambr. It is probably to be explained as an accidental omission due to the fact that the word has already occurred in the verse. No substantial difference of meaning is involved. The other matter is the question whether ὑμᾶς should, or should not, be read after διώκοντας. It is read by ℵ A 𝕶 D *pl* lat sy; but omitted by 𝔓[46] B 1739 *pc* Cl. The weight (in spite of their fewness) of the authorities which omit the word, together with the fact that its addition can be explained as due to the influence of Mt 5.44, should probably incline us to omit it. But it is unlikely[2] that any difference of sense is involved. If ὑμᾶς is not read, it is still natural to supply it, and not to understand τοὺς διώκοντας to mean 'all persecutors' in general.[3] It seems probable—we cannot say more—that we have here a free reminiscence of the traditional dominical saying which has come down to us in two different forms in Mt 5.44 and Lk 6.27f, traces of the influence of which are perhaps also to be seen in 1 Cor 4.12, and possibly Jas 3.9–12; 1 Pet 2.23.

Not only to refrain from desiring that harm should come to those who are persecuting us, but to desire good for them and to show that this desire is no mere pretence by actually praying for God's blessing upon them (it should be remembered that blessing and cursing are very serious matters in the NT as well as in the OT)—this is clearly opposed to what is natural to us. As Gaugler points out, 'All these requirements make sense only if they are required of the disciple, of the congregation, which

---

[1] e.g. Origen, col. 1220: 'How finely does he sum up the generosity of the man who pursues hospitality in one word! For by saying that hospitality is to be pursued, he shows that we are not just to receive the stranger when he comes to us, but actually to inquire after, and look carefully for, strangers, to pursue them and search them out everywhere, lest perchance somewhere they may sit in the streets or lie without a roof over their heads. Think of Lot, and you will discover that it was not the strangers who sought him, but he who sought the strangers; and this was to pursue hospitality.' Cf. Chrysostom, col. 606. Some modern commentators (e.g. Lagrange, Gaugler, Michel, Barrett) stress διώκοντες: the NEB translation 'practise' fails to bring out the meaning (it is hardly to be justified by appeal to the use of the Hebrew *rādap* with such objects as *ṣedeḳ* or *šālôm*, since *rādap*, used figuratively, regularly conveys the sense of a quest conducted with eagerness, vigour, diligence, seriousness).

[2] *Pace* T. W. Manson, p. 950 (cf. Bruce, p. 229).

[3] As Manson suggests.

is being transformed by the renewing of the mind, which is ready to renounce the fashion of this world'.[1] What the gospel requires of us—it is what Christ did towards us (5.10)[2]—is the impossible; but the God of the gospel is the God of miracles, with whom 'all things are possible' (Mk 10.27). Calvin adds finely: 'Although there is hardly any one who has made such advance in the law of the Lord that he fulfils this precept, no one can boast that he is the child of God, or glory in the name of a Christian, who has not partially undertaken this course, and does not struggle daily to resist the will to do the opposite'.[3]

15. χαίρειν μετὰ χαιρόντων, κλαίειν μετὰ κλαιόντων is often understood to refer to the relations of Christians with one another;[4] but, while such sympathy is obviously appropriate between Christians, there is nothing in this verse to forbid us to assume that, in view of v. 14, Paul is thinking just as much, or perhaps more particularly, of Christians' relations with those who are outside the Church. There is indeed special point here in such an exhortation with regard to those outside; for truly to bless one's persecutors must surely involve readiness to take one's stand beside them as human beings.[5] Chrysostom makes the point that to rejoice with them that rejoice is harder than to weep with them that weep (he suggests that this is why Paul mentions it first),[6] and various modern commentators have taken up his point.[7] In certain areas and on a certain level this is undoubtedly true (so, for example, to rejoice with the person who has received what one would have liked to have received oneself but has not makes greater demands on unselfishness than to feel real sympathy with someone who has been bereaved); but Gaugler was surely right to raise the question whether to rest content with this sort of point here is not to miss the profundity of what Paul

---

[1] 2, p. 261 (our translation).

[2] Cf. Barth, *Shorter*, p. 155.

[3] p. 274.

[4] So, e.g., Gaugler 2, pp. 258 and 261; Michel, p. 305f. Lagrange, p. 306, while giving it as his opinion that, in view of v. 16, Paul probably has in mind relations between Christians, allows that he has not in any way indicated that Jews or pagans are to be excluded from such sympathy.

[5] Cf. Barth, *Shorter*, p. 155.

[6] col. 610: Καίτοι γε ἐκεῖνο φιλοσοφωτέρας δεῖται ψυχῆς, τὸ χαίρειν μετὰ χαιρόντων, μᾶλλον ἢ τὸ κλαίειν μετὰ κλαιόντων. Τοῦτο μὲν γὰρ καὶ ἡ φύσις αὐτὴ κατορθοῖ, καὶ οὐδεὶς οὕτω λίθινος, ὃς οὐ κλαίει τὸν ἐν συμφοραῖς ὄντα· ἐκεῖνο δὲ γενναίας σφόδρα δεῖται ψυχῆς, ὥστε τῷ εὐδοκιμοῦντι μὴ μόνον μὴ φθονεῖν, ἀλλὰ καὶ συνήδεσθαι. Διὰ τοῦτο καὶ πρότερον αὐτὸ τέθεικεν.

[7] e.g. Sanday and Headlam, p. 363; Lagrange, p. 306; Huby, p. 425f: cf. Denney, p. 693.

wants to say.[1] If Paul means only the sort of thing that Chrysostom understands him to mean, then there is nothing very new in what he is saying, nothing in fact to distinguish it at all radically from the formal parallels to this verse from Judaism and from the Graeco-Roman world which may be cited.[2] It is Origen who has provided us with a more helpful clue; for in drawing attention to a difficulty in what Paul has said he puts us on our guard against accepting the verse lightly and unreflectingly at its face value. The difficulty he sees—a difficulty which modern commentators (an exception here is Michel) generally fail to mention—is that men, both non-Christians and Christians, very often rejoice at things at which they ought not to rejoice, and grieve for reasons for which they ought not to grieve.[3] Origen's own solution of the difficulty, however, is unsatisfactory in two respects: (i) It virtually limits those with whom we are to join in rejoicing or weeping to those who are good, sincere, penitent. But such a limitation of sympathy accords ill with the theological basis of Paul's exhortation: it would be a poor witness to the gospel of the God who 'proves his love for us by the fact that Christ died for us when we were still sinners' (5.8). (ii) It is too narrowly religious—for instance, he excludes explicitly weeping with those who weep because of bereavement. We shall be interpreting this verse in a way more in line with what Paul has himself already said, if we take its meaning to be nothing less than this: that the Christian is to take his stand beside his fellow-man (whoever he may be), to have time and room for him in those experiences in which he is most truly himself,[4] in his real human joy and his real human sorrow, and to strive to be both with him and for him, altogether and without reserve, yet without compromising with his evil or sharing, or even pretending to share, the presuppositions of this age which is passing away, even as God Himself is in Christ both 'with us' (Mt 1.23) and 'for us' (8.31) all.

16. τὸ αὐτὸ εἰς ἀλλήλους φρονοῦντες. The expression τὸ αὐτὸ φρονεῖν occurs also in 15.5; 2 Cor 13.11; Phil 2.2; 4.2. In all these places it surely means 'be of the same mind', 'agree', or (as Barrett translates it here) 'have a common mind'; and there is not much doubt that it has the same meaning here. If any distinction of meaning is intended between εἰς ἀλλήλους here

---

[1] 2, p. 262.
[2] e.g. Ecclus 7.34 and Arrian *Epict.* 2.5.23. Other examples are quoted by Michel, p. 306, n. 2.
[3] cols. 1221–2.
[4] Cf. Gaugler 2, p. 262.

and ἐν ἀλλήλοις in 15.5, it will probably be simply that εἰς ἀλλήλους suggests more strongly the manifestation of the agreement in outward conduct. The explanation of Origen,[1] followed by (among others) Chrysostom,[2] Pelagius,[3] Cornely,[4] Zahn,[5] Huby,[6] and both NEB[1] ('Have equal regard for one another') and NEB[2] ('Care as much about each other as about yourselves'), that τὸ αὐτὸ εἰς ἀλλήλους φρονεῖν denotes having the same esteem of, and the same regard and concern for, your brethren as you have of, and for, yourselves, strikes us as forced, in spite of the very impressive support which it has commanded and the undeniable appropriateness to the context of the sense yielded. That these words refer to relations between Christians is, of course, clear. But it does not follow that Paul's main concern at this point is not really the relations of Christians with those outside the Church; for Christians' relations among themselves are by no means irrelevant to their relations with non-Christians. While it is certainly possible that Paul is here thinking simply of Christians among themselves, it seems more natural, in view of vv. 14 and 17–21, to suppose that, in exhorting the Roman Christians to agree among themselves, he here has in mind specially the effect which their agreement (or disagreement) will have on those outside. We may compare Jn 17.20–23. Agreement among themselves is something which Christians owe to the world. But whenever this is said (and said persistently and emphatically it ought to be), it must also at the same time be remembered that the only agreement in question is agreement in faith in Christ and in loyal obedience to Him. No other agreement is required of us, and no other agreement or unity of Christians is likely to be of benefit to the world.

μὴ τὰ ὑψηλὰ φρονοῦντες is often understood as a warning against ambition; but it is probably preferable to take τὰ ὑψηλὰ φρονεῖν here to have, in spite of the presence of the article, the same meaning as ὑψηλὰ φρονεῖν in 11.20 (cf. 1 Tim 6.17) and to

---

[1] col. 1222.

[2] col. 610: Τί δέ ἐστι, Τὸ αὐτὸ εἰς ἀλλήλους φρονοῦντες; Παρεγένετό σοι ὁ πένης εἰς τὴν οἰκίαν; Γενοῦ κατ᾽ ἐκεῖνον τῷ φρονήματι· μὴ μείζονα λάβῃς ὄγκον διὰ τὸν πλοῦτον· οὐκ ἔστι πλούσιος καὶ πένης ἐν Χριστῷ . . . . μηδέ, ἂν ἴδῃς εὐημεροῦντα, ἐρυθριάσῃς κοινωνῆσαι τῆς ἡδονῆς καὶ συνησθῆναι, ἀλλ᾽ ὃ περὶ σεαυτοῦ φρονεῖς, καὶ περὶ ἐκείνου φρόνησον. . . . Ταπεινὸν καὶ μικρὸν εἶναι ὑποπτεύεις ἐκεῖνον; Οὐκοῦν καὶ περὶ σαυτοῦ τοῦτο ψηφίζου, καὶ πᾶσαν ἀνωμαλίαν ἔκβαλε . . . . Cf. col. 646 (on 15.5), where he comments: Τοῦτο γάρ ἐστιν ἀγάπης, ὃ περὶ ἑαυτοῦ τις φρονεῖ, τοῦτο καὶ περὶ τοῦ ἄλλου.

[3] p. 99: 'ut ita alteri sentias sicut tibi'.

[4] p. 666f.

[5] p. 552.

[6] p. 426.

see here a warning not against ambition, but against haughtiness, as does Origen[1] (cf. RSV and NEB, both of which have 'do not be haughty'). Haughtiness is perhaps specially mentioned at this point as being destructive of the Church's unity and a most effective hindrance to its mission to the world.

ἀλλὰ τοῖς ταπεινοῖς συναπαγόμενοι. Many (including Calvin,[2] Bengel,[3] Michel[4]) take τοῖς ταπεινοῖς to be neuter on the ground that the parallelism with τὰ ὑψηλά demands the neuter. Others (e.g. Chrysostom,[5] Zahn,[6] Lagrange[7]) take it as masculine: in support it is sometimes noted that the neuter τὰ ταπεινά occurs only once elsewhere in the Greek Bible, while the masculine οἱ ταπεινοί occurs frequently. Yet others (e.g. F. Spitta[8]) take it as neuter but referring to persons: in support of this view it is possible to cite 1 Cor 1.27, which Luther[9] mentions in this connexion. But, if our explanation of τὰ ὑψηλὰ φρονοῦντες was correct, τὰ ὑψηλά is virtually part of a compound verb (Paul might have written ὑψηλοφρονοῦντες),[10] and so the argument that τοῖς ταπεινοῖς must be neuter to match τὰ ὑψηλά loses its force. Moreover, 'associate with the humble'[11] contrasts well with 'be haughty'. We take it then that τοῖς ταπεινοῖς is more probably masculine, and that what Paul is enjoining is a friendly and unselfconscious association both with ordinary unimportant people and with the outcasts of society that is free from any suggestion of patronizing or condescension (the AV 'condescend to men of low estate' has come to be a most unfortunate translation because of the bad sense which 'condescend' tends to have today). Such an attitude, so contrary to the nature of the worldly man, comes naturally to those who are being transformed by the renewing of the mind, and it is always a sign of the worldliness of the Church when its 'leaders' no longer associate as readily and freely with humble people both inside and outside the Church as with those who are socially superior, and when such humble people no longer feel free to speak with them as man to man.

[1] col. 1222.
[2] p. 275.
[3] p. 555.
[4] p. 307.
[5] col. 610f.
[6] p. 552, n. 53.
[7] p. 306f.
[8] *Zur Geschichte und Litteratur des Urchristentums* 3, 1, Göttingen, 1901, p. 113.
[9] p. 352.
[10] Cf. 1 Tim 6.17.
[11] i.e., of course, humble in the sense of unimportant, of lowly condition, and not in the sense of humble-spirited.

The last part of v. 16 is reminiscent of Prov 3.7 (cf. Rom 11.25). The presence of a catchword link with the rest of the verse (φρονοῦντες — φρονοῦντες — φρόνιμοι) has been noticed (e.g. by Michel, p. 306), but Paul probably inserted this echo of Proverbs at this point because he recognized in the attitude of the man who is self-sufficient in his confidence in his own wisdom[1] something particularly destructive of the harmony to which he has just referred (τὸ αὐτὸ εἰς ἀλλήλους φρονοῦντες).[2] Michel aptly refers in this connexion to the Corinthian slogan, ἡμεῖς φρόνιμοι, to which Paul alludes in 1 Cor 4.10; 10.15; 2 Cor 11.19.

17. μηδενὶ κακὸν ἀντὶ κακοῦ ἀποδιδόντες. The close similarity between this and 1 Th 5.15 and 1 Pet 3.9 suggests that we have here the fixed formulation of the catechetical tradition. Compare Prov 20.22; 24.29, and, for the general spirit, Exod 23.4f; 2 Chron 28.8–15, and, of course, Mt 5.38f, 44; Lk 6.29, 35. Relevant Rabbinic material is to be found in SB 1, pp. 368–70; 2, p. 299. It is difficult to distinguish between this precept and μὴ ἑαυτοὺς ἐκδικοῦντες in v. 19—except that this is rather more general, whereas 'vengeance' suggests more strongly something particular and positive.

προνοούμενοι καλὰ ἐνώπιον πάντων ἀνθρώπων. It is tempting, for the sake of parallelism, to take ἐνώπιον πάντων ἀνθρώπων[3] in v. 17b as equivalent to a dative, and so to understand the point to be that Christians are to take thought how they may do good to all men.[4] The second part of the verse would be a repetition in positive form of the thought of the first part. But it seems very doubtful whether such an interpretation of ἐνώπιον πάντων ἀνθρώπων can be maintained.[5] We must probably, therefore, translate ἐνώπιον 'before', 'in the sight of'. But what then does Paul mean by his adaptation of LXX Prov 3.4? Hardly that Christians are to concentrate on taking thought[6] for those things which are agreed by all men to be good (e.g. NEB: 'Let your aims be such as all men count

---

[1] The RSV rendering 'never be conceited' is inaccurate, because it gives too general a sense. One can be conceited about many different things: Paul is here concerned only with conceit about one's wisdom.

[2] Cf. Chrysostom's suggestive observation (col. 611): Οὐδὲν γὰρ οὕτως ἀπαίρει καὶ ἀποσχίζει τῶν λοιπῶν ὡς τὸ νομίζειν τινὰ ἀρκεῖν ἑαυτῷ · διὸ καὶ ἐν χρείᾳ ἀλλήλων κατέστησεν ἡμᾶς ὁ Θεός.

[3] The textual variants noted by Nestle for this verse reflect the influence of 2 Cor 8.21 (and Prov 3.4).

[4] Cf. Michel, p. 308.

[5] The examples given by Bauer, s.v. ἐνώπιον 4, are quite different.

[6] Leenhardt, p. 317, n. §, says: 'Προνοέω suggests foresight, providential careful thought; thought which precedes and controls action.'

honourable'); for Paul was well aware of the darkening of men's minds (cf. 1.21) and the need for the human mind to be renewed, if it is to recognize and approve the will of God (cf. 12.2). The meaning is rather that Christians are to take thought for, aim at, seek, in the sight of all men those things which (whether they recognize it or not)[1] are good, the arbiter of what is good being not a moral *communis sensus* of mankind, but the gospel. We should compare Mt 5.16; 1 Cor 10.32; 1 Tim 5.14; 1 Pet 2.12, 15; 3.16, as well as 2 Cor 8.21, which also makes use of the language of LXX Prov 3.4. It can never be a light matter, if Christians, who are called to glorify God and to proclaim the gospel to the world, by their evil deeds bring dishonour on God's name and hinder men from believing.[2]

18. εἰ δυνατόν, τὸ ἐξ ὑμῶν, μετὰ πάντων ἀνθρώπων εἰρηνεύοντες. Compare Mt 5.9. Those who are the ambassadors of God's peace (cf. 2 Cor 5.18–20) must necessarily be peaceably disposed toward all men. Paul is careful, however, to qualify his precept by the words εἰ δυνατόν and τὸ ἐξ ὑμῶν, no doubt with the sort of reservation in mind that Calvin makes explicit: 'We are not to strive to attain the favour of men in such a way that we refuse to incur the hatred of any for the sake of Christ, as often as this may be necessary', and '. . . good nature should not degenerate into compliance, so that for the sake of preserving peace we are complaisant to men's sins'.[3]

19. It was perhaps because he recognized that in μὴ ἑαυτοὺς ἐκδικοῦντες he was enjoining something very hard even for Christians—though the idea that vengeance should be avoided was not altogether strange even to the pagan world[4]—that Paul inserted the affectionate vocative ἀγαπητοί at this point.

ἀλλὰ δότε τόπον τῇ ὀργῇ· γέγραπται γάρ· ἐμοὶ ἐκδίκησις, ἐγὼ ἀνταποδώσω, λέγει κύριος. Instead of avenging themselves they are to give place to, make room for,[5] the wrath of God.[6] In

---

[1] We certainly do not wish to suggest that those outside the Church never do recognize—quite often they see more clearly than those within what is rightly to be expected of Christians.

[2] Reference may be made to W. C. van Unnik, 'Die Rücksicht auf die Reaktion der Nicht-Christen als Motiv in der altchristlichen Paränese', in W. Eltester (ed.), *Judentum Urchristentum Kirche* (Festschrift for J. Jeremias), Berlin, 1960, pp. 221–34.

[3] p. 276f.

[4] e.g. Seneca, *De ira* 2.34: 'Pusilli hominis et miseri est repetere mordentem'; and, at a somewhat later date, Juvenal, *Sat.* 13.190f: 'Semper et infirmi est animi exiguique voluptas ultio' (quoted by Lagrange, p. 308). (Seneca died in A.D. 65, Juvenal *ca* A.D. 130.)

[5] For τόπον διδόναι τινί cf. LXX Ecclus 4.5; 13.22; 19.17; 38.12; Lk 14.9; Eph 4.27. Cf. Hebrew nāṭan māḳôm.

[6] For ἡ ὀργή used absolutely of God's wrath (Bengel calls it 'ellipsis religiosa') cf Rom 5.9; 1 Th 2.16.

confirmation Paul quotes the first part of Deut 32.35 (in a
form nearer to the Aramaic Targum than to either the LXX
or the MT).[1] Already in the OT vengeance is forbidden (e.g.
Lev 19.18a; Prov 20.22; 24.29; 2 Chron 28.8-15: cf. Ecclus
28.1-7); and Judaism gave the same reason for this prohibition
as is given here, namely that vengeance is God's prerogative
(e.g. Test. Gad 6.7: 'And if he be shameless and persist in his
wrong-doing, even so forgive him from the heart, and leave to
God the avenging'; 1QS 10.17f: 'I will pay to no man the reward
of evil; I will pursue him with goodness. For judgment of all
the living is with God and it is He who will render to man his
reward';[2] C.D. 9.2-5: 'And concerning the saying, *You shall not
take vengeance on the children of your people, nor bear any
rancour against them* (Lev 19.18), if any member of the Covenant
accuses his companion without first rebuking him before witnesses; if he denounces him in the heat of his anger or reports
him to his elders to make him look contemptible, he is one that
takes vengeance and bears rancour, although it is expressly
written, *He takes vengeance upon His adversaries and bears
rancour against His enemies* (Nah 1.2)').[3] But, while the influence of the OT and of Judaism is apparent both in the
content and in the form of the last verses of this chapter, Paul's
words must, of course, be understood in the light of all that
has already been said in the epistle. In this context (compare
πάντων ἀνθρώπων in v. 17 and again in v. 18) there is no
question of limitation to one's fellow-members of the religious
community: the prohibition of revenge is freed from the limitations and restrictions which adhered to it in Judaism,[4] and is
universal in its application. τόπον διδόναι τῇ ὀργῇ is to make
way for that wrath 'which alone is righteous, and alone is
worthy of the name of wrath',[5] the wrath of God which was
revealed in its full awfulness in Gethsemane and on Golgotha
as the wrath of the altogether holy and loving God. To make

---

[1] It is quoted in the same form in Heb 10.30.
[2] Vermes, p. 90f.
[3] ibid., p. 110.
[4] Note that in 1QS the passage quoted above is followed by one which
indicates on-going hatred of the enemies of the religious community.
Paul, on the other hand, certainly includes the enemies of the Church
(cf. τοὺς διώκοντας in v. 14) as well as private enemies in his prohibition of
revenge. In this connexion reference may be made to K. Stendahl,
'Hate, non-retaliation, and love: 1QS 10.17-20 and Rom 12.19-21', in
HTR 55 (1962), pp. 343-55, though his understanding of Paul is surely
to be rejected.
[5] Bengel, p. 556 ('τῇ ὀργῇ) *irae* illi, de qua in scripturis tam multa
dicuntur; id est, irae Dei, quae sola justa est, et sola meretur ira dici').

way for this wrath is to recognize that one deserves oneself to be wholly consumed by it, but the Son of God Himself has borne it for one: it is therefore to have the vengeful sword dashed from one's hands.[1] If one is to continue to live by grace, then one cannot do other than make way for this wrath—to do otherwise would be to cease to live by grace.[2] To give place to the wrath is to leave vengeance to God in the knowledge that He is the God who smites in order to heal.[3] When we recall what God has done for us 'when we were enemies' (5.10), we cannot but hope that His mercy will finally embrace those who now are our enemies. 'We *give place* to wrath,' says Calvin, '. . . only when we wait patiently for the proper time for our deliverance, praying in the meantime that those who now trouble us may repent and become our friends.'[4] It certainly does not mean hoping and praying for God to punish our enemies.

20. ἀλλὰ ἐὰν πεινᾷ ὁ ἐχθρός σου, ψώμιζε αὐτόν· ἐὰν διψᾷ, πότιζε αὐτόν. Apart from the initial ἀλλά (which some MSS. omit), v. 20 is an exact quotation of LXX Prov 25.21–22a. The first part of the quotation has the effect of sharpening what has just been said:[5] it is not enough merely to refrain from seeking to inflict injury in return for injury, we are also to do positive good to those who have injured us. For to fail to do to our enemies the good they stand in need of, when it is in our power to do it, is 'a kind of indirect retaliation. . . . By the words *food* and *drink* we are to understand kindness of every sort. According, therefore, to our ability we are to help our enemy in any matter in which he shall stand in need of either our resources, advice or efforts.'[6]

τοῦτο γὰρ ποιῶν ἄνθρακας πυρὸς σωρεύσεις ἐπὶ τὴν κεφαλὴν αὐτοῦ. Chrysostom[7] and a number of other Greek Fathers following his lead (e.g. Theodoret,[8] Oecumenius,[9] Theophylact[10]) see in the ἄνθρακες πυρός of the latter part of the quotation a reference to future divine punishment and understand the thought to be that one's doing good to one's enemy will cause his punish-

---

[1] Cf. 2 Chr 28, especially 10b and 11b.
[2] Cf. Gaugler, 2, p. 266.
[3] Cf. Isa 19.22.
[4] p. 277f.
[5] Cf. BDF, § 448 (6) on ἀλλά 'used to introduce an additional point in an emphatic way'.
[6] Calvin, p. 278.
[7] col. 612.
[8] col. 192f.
[9] cols. 573–6.
[10] col. 512.

ment, in the event of his not repenting, to be the greater (though it is only fair to add—something which those who refer to this interpretation sometimes omit to add—that the same Fathers also say that one is not to do good to one's enemy with this intention[1]). But Origen,[2] Pelagius,[3] and Augustine,[4] as well as the majority of later commentators prefer to take ἄνθρακας πυρός as signifying the burning pangs of shame and contrition. That, as far as Paul's meaning is concerned, this latter interpretation is to be preferred is abundantly clear; for it is congruous with the context in Romans, while the former interpretation is quite incompatible with it. We take the sense of v. 20b, then, to be that by thus ministering to one's enemy's need one will inflict upon him such an inward sense of shame[5] as will either lead him to real contrition and to being no more an enemy but a friend or else, if he refuses to be reconciled, will remain with him as the pain of a bad conscience.[6] (The attempt, while basically accepting the latter interpretation, to see in the 'coals of fire', nevertheless, a secondary reference to the eschatological fire of judgment, as F. Lang (following Schlatter[7]) does ('reagiert der Feind auf deine Wohltat nicht durch Sinnesänderung, das heisst, weicht er jetzt den "Feuerkohlen auf dem Haupt" aus, so wird er doch dem Feuer des kommenden Zorngerichts nicht entgehen'),[8] seems to us artificial, even when one allows fully for the reference to the wrath of God in v. 19.) Perhaps already in Proverbs the meaning was similar. The Targum, at any rate, appears so to have understood Prov 25.21f; for it renders the Hebrew *waYHWH* y^ešallem-lāḵ (RV: 'And the LORD shall reward thee') at the end of v.22: 'and the LORD will deliver him to thee' or 'and the LORD will make him thy friend'.[9]

---

[1] Chrysostom, for example, explains that Paul knew that even if the enemy were a wild beast he would scarcely go on being an enemy after accepting the gift of food, and that the Christian who had been injured would scarcely go on hankering after vengeance after he has given his enemy food and drink; and goes on to say that to give one's enemy food and drink with the intention of increasing his future punishment would be to be overcome of evil.

[2] col. 1224f.

[3] p. 100.

[4] col. 2083.

[5] Not a public putting to shame, for to inflict this was regarded by the Jews as a grievous wrong (cf. Gaugler 2, p. 268).

[6] It would be over-optimistic to assume (as Althaus, p. 111, seems to do) that kindness is *sure* to make the enemy change his attitude.

[7] p. 349.

[8] in *TWNT* 6, p. 944.

[9] See SB 3, p. 301f.

The expression 'coals of fire on the head' occurs also in 2 Esdr 16.53 (cf. Ps 140[LXX: 139].10). A likely suggestion as to its origin is that it goes back to an Egyptian ritual in which a man purged his offence by carrying on his head a dish containing burning charcoal on a bed of ashes.[1]

21. μὴ νικῶ ὑπὸ τοῦ κακοῦ, ἀλλὰ νίκα ἐν τῷ ἀγαθῷ τὸ κακόν. On the first five words of the verse Bengel's terse comment can hardly be bettered. His words are: 'κακοῦ) a malo, hostis tui, et naturae tuae'. To retaliate is to be overcome both by the evil of one's enemy and also by the evil of one's own heart which responds to the other's evil.[2] The enemy has overcome one, in that he has made one like himself.[3] Instead of allowing himself to be overcome of evil, the Christian is to overcome the evil by the good (ἀλλὰ νίκα ἐν τῷ ἀγαθῷ τὸ κακόν). It is, of course, much to be hoped that his victory will include the transformation of the persecutor into a friend, but it will not necessarily do so. He who in the fullest sense has overcome the world (Jn 16.33) has not yet turned the hatred of all His persecutors into love. The Christian's victory over the evil consists in his refusal to become a party to the promotion of evil by returning evil for evil and so becoming himself like the evil man who has injured him, in his accepting injury without resentment, without allowing his love to be turned into hate or even only weakened. Though he may not succeed in making the enemy cease to be an enemy in the sense of one who hates, he can refuse to allow him to be an enemy at all in the sense of one who is hated. By so doing he will be sharing in the victory of the gospel over the world and setting up signs which point to the reality of God's love for sinners; he will be living as one who is being transformed by the renewing of the mind.

Verse 21 may be said to sum up the whole subsection 12.14–21; for the theme of these verses is precisely the victory of the believer, of the man who is held fast by the good of the gospel, over the evil of the world. The victory of the believer, be it emphasized—for the victory with which these verses are con-

[1] Cf. S. Morenz, 'Feurige Kohlen auf dem Haupt', in *TLZ* 78, 1953, cols. 187–92. Reference may also be made to W. Klassen, 'Coals of fire: sign of repentance or revenge?', in *NTS* 9, 1962–63, pp. 337–50; L. Ramaroson, 'Charbons ardents: "sur la tête" ou "pour le feu" (Prov 25.22a—Rom 12.20b)', in *Biblica* 51, 1970, pp. 230–34; S. Bartina, 'Carbones encendidos, ¿ sobre la cabeza o sobre el veneno? (Prov 25. 21–22; Rom 12.20)', in *EB* 31 (1972), pp. 201–203.
[2] That τοῦ κακοῦ is to be understood as neuter can hardly be doubted in view of the following τὸ κακόν.
[3] Cf. Pelagius, p. 101: 'si ergo te fecerit sibi uicem reddere, ille te uicit, sibi similem faciendo . . .'

cerned is something very different (as Origen noted)[1] from any
victory of a self-sufficient human virtue: it is the victory of the
man who has been justified by faith, who is borne up by the
grace of God in Christ, who is indeed confident, but confident
in the knowledge of the victorious power of the gospel, and
not in any sense of his own moral superiority.

VII. 4. THE BELIEVER'S OBLIGATION TO THE STATE (13.1–7)

With regard to the relation of 13.1–7 to its context it has been
said:

(i) That there is a lack of connexion between this section and
its immediate context;

(ii) That it interrupts the continuity between 12.21 and 13.8
(Michel, for example, regards it as certain that 12.21 has its
proper sequel in 13.8: he appeals, in particular, to the repetition
of μηδενί, which both in 12.17 and in 13.8 introduces a paraphrase of the commandment of love to one's neighbour[2]);

(iii) That between this section and its context there are
positive incongruities. Thus it is urged: (a) that the style and
argumentation differ considerably from those of the context,
being reminiscent of 'Jewish-Hellenistic wisdom-teaching';[3]
(b) that the absence of any trace of eschatological reserve with
regard to the state is surprising after 12.2 (μὴ συσχηματίζεσθε
τῷ αἰῶνι τούτῳ and τῇ ἀνακαινώσει τοῦ νοός)[4] and in the same
chapter as 13.11–14; (c) that this section is altogether non-
christological, reference being made only to the ordinance of
God as Creator;[5] (d) that the idea of the state with its use of
force is far removed from that of love which is the theme of
12.9–21 and 13.8–10. Michel goes so far as to say that no
specifically primitive-Christian motif is to be heard in the
section.[6]

It is hardly surprising that Michel regards the section as
'eine selbständige Einlage',[7] a parenthesis independent of its
context which Paul has inserted here.[8] Not surprisingly those

---

[1] col. 1225f.
[2] p. 312.
[3] Michel, p. 289: cf. p. 313f.
[4] Michel, p. 314.
[5] Cf. Michel, p. 313f.
[6] p. 289.
[7] p. 312.
[8] Cf. Käsemann, p. 337 ('ein selbständiger Block, der angesichts
seines singulären Skopus zugespitzt ein Fremdkörper in der paulinischen
Paränese genannt werden kann').

for whom the relation of 13.1–7 to its context is as problematical as this tend to feel particularly strongly the need to postulate some special circumstances in the church in Rome which led Paul to insert such a section here.[1]

With regard to point (i) above, it may be said: that, since in 12.9–21 the different items are only loosely connected, a close logical connexion between 13.1–7 and its context is hardly to be expected; that various connexions of thought, more or less plausible, have been suggested, as, for example, that, having spoken in 12.9–13 (or 16) of the relations of Christians among themselves and in 12.14 (or 17)–21 of their relations with those outside the Church, it was natural for Paul to go on to refer to their obligations toward the civil authorities,[2] or that what has been said in chapter 12 about not rendering evil for evil raised the question of what was to be the attitude of Christians toward institutions concerned with the suppression of evil-doers,[3] and, finally, that a verbal link between 13.1–7 and what follows does exist in ὀφειλάς — ὀφείλετε (13.7 and 8).[4] With regard to (ii) and (iii) (d)—and this is also relevant to (i) —it may be said that, since the state serves the good of men (13.4), to help in maintaining it can be regarded as part of one's debt of love to one's neighbour. With regard to (iii) (a), it should be noted that a number of traces of the influence of Jewish wisdom are to be seen in 12.9–21.

In view of such considerations as these it may be claimed that there is nothing surprising in Paul's referring here to the

---

[1] So Michel thinks of 'einen historischen Anlass . . ., der entweder in jüdischen Unruhen oder in pneumatischer Überheblichkeit liegen kann' (p. 317). Cf. p. 314f: 'Die Abwehr des Enthusiasmus in Röm 12.3–21 legt es nahe, dass Pls auch in Röm 13.1–7 einen falschen Ansatz des Pneumatikertums bekämpfen will. Man denke z.B. an ein zugespitztes Wort des scilitanischen Märtyrers: "ego imperium huius saeculi non cognosco" '. Also Käsemann, p. 335: 'Näher liegt die Vermutung, dass Pls sich gegen eine Haltung wendet, welche den politischen Gewalten im Bewusstsein, Bürger der himmlischen Polis zu sein, indifferent oder sogar verächtlich gegenübersteht'. Others have sought to cut the Gordian knot by simply denying the Pauline authorship of the section (e.g. Pallis, p. 141, and O'Neill, pp. 207–09). This solution is surely rightly rejected by Käsemann, p. 336. The strength of O'Neill's feelings on the matter (he indicates on p. 21 that the section seems to him 'hateful', and states on p. 209 that 'These seven verses have caused more unhappiness and misery in the Christian East and West than any other seven verses in the New Testament') is understandable, since he understands the author to be 'counselling absolute obedience to ruling authority in the State' (p. 210). But see on ὑποτασσέσθω in v. 1.

[2] Cf., e.g., Lagrange, p. 310.

[3] Cf. Leenhardt, p. 322.

[4] Cf. Barrett, p. 249.

question of the Christian's obligation to the state authorities. Indeed one might say that it would have been surprising, if in such a relatively full section of exhortation as 12.1–15.13 he had had nothing to say on a subject which must have been of great importance to Christians of the first century[1] just as it is to Christians today (though those who are individualistic pietists may not realize the fact). A good many commentators are content to leave the matter here. But, if this is as far as we can go, we ought probably to admit that the relation of 13.1–7 to its context remains for us to some extent problematical; for a fully inward, theological connexion can hardly yet be said to have been made out, and it is still difficult to understand why Paul could write *quite* so positively about the authorities.

The crucial question concerns point (iii) (c) above. Is it true to say that this passage is non-christological? It is, of course, true that Christ is not mentioned at all in these seven verses; but this does not necessarily mean that He was absent from Paul's thoughts as he wrote this section or that He would be absent from the thoughts of the Christians in Rome when they read or heard it. Here the distinction made by C. D. Morrison between what an author is *imparting* and the *communication* shared by him and his readers is of very great value.[2] What Paul is imparting here, i.e. the point which he wishes to get across to those whom he is addressing, is that they are to 'be subject' to the civil authorities; but in making this point he presupposes certain convictions which are common to himself and the Christians in Rome. Included in this communication are convictions about God. While it is true that the words Paul uses here could have been used by a Rabbi or a philosopher, it by no means follows that, as used here, they have only the sense which they would have had for a Rabbi or a philosopher. Morrison is surely justified in claiming that Christology was, for Paul, not a self-contained supplement to his theology but 'the central point from which' he 'comprehended the whole of God's revealed plan'[3] and that therefore the view that this section contains nothing distinctively Christian must be challenged; and that, while Paul is not here concerned to impart fresh teaching about God to his readers, we shall fail to share in the communication between him and them, unless 'we

---

[1] *Pace* Käsemann, p. 335, where it is asserted that Christians at this time came into contact with the political authorities 'relativ selten und dann nur passiv'.

[2] *The Powers that Be: earthly rulers and demonic powers in Romans 13.1–7*, London, 1960, pp. 56f, 63–68, 102ff.

[3] op. cit., p. 112.

take into account the significance of Christ in Paul's understanding of God'.[1] The presumption is that Paul, when he used
the word θεός in this passage, used it in a fully Christian sense
and expected his readers so to understand it. The *onus probandi*
rests squarely on the shoulders of anyone who would maintain
anything else. So we take it that the God, of whom these
verses speak, is 'the God and Father of our Lord Jesus Christ'
(15.6), the God whose authority and love are one with the
authority (8.34) and love (8.39) of Jesus Christ. For Paul, to
say that the civil authorities are διάκονοι and λειτουργοί of God
is necessarily to imply that they are in some way linked with
God's holy and merciful purpose in Christ, and in some way
subserve it. Moreover, if we are to enter fully into Paul's
communication here, we must understand these verses in the
light of the central affirmation of Paul's, and the early Church's,
faith, the affirmation κύριος Ἰησοῦς (cf. especially 10.9). It is
clear from the way in which Paul refers to Christ OT passages
in which κύριος represents the Tetragrammaton (e.g. 10.13)
that in calling Christ κύριος he was ascribing to Him the
authority and Lordship of God Himself. But, according to the
Scriptures, that authority included authority over the kingdoms of men (cf., e.g., Isa 10.5ff; 45.1ff; Dan 4.17, 25, 32; 5.21).
A christological understanding of the state (in the sense of an
understanding of it as in some way serving God's purpose in
Christ and lying within the scope of Christ's lordship) is thus
implicit in this passage, quite independently of any acceptance
of the particular explanation of ἐξουσίαις which has come to be
specially associated with the christological interpretation of
the state and which we shall have to consider below. It is also
implicit elsewhere in the NT in the use of the title κύριος with
reference to Christ, in the use made of Ps 110.1 in many places,
and in such passages as Mt 28.18, and Jn 17.2, and explicit in
Rev 1.5; 17.14; 19.16.

We may conveniently refer at this point to the question
whether Paul thought that the civil authorities of this world
were in any way affected by Christ's death, resurrection and
ascension. According to Morrison, '*the governing authorities were
not affected.* Rome was no different the week after the resurrection from what it was the week before it'.[2] Christ had been
Lord over all things from the creation (Col 1.16),[3] and the
confession of Christ as Lord included 'the confident assertion

---

[1] ibid.
[2] op. cit., p. 115.
[3] op. cit., p. 118.

that the Redeemer has presided over the order of history';[1] but the death, resurrection and ascension of Christ have in no way altered Christ's universal Lordship outside the Church. His already accomplished victory is, outside the Church, 'not only unknown but without consequence'.[2] In reply to this it may be suggested that, while the statement, 'When we call the emperor forth to view his new Christological clothes in broad daylight, we find that there are none',[3] contains an important truth, since *outwardly* the civil authorities as such have indeed not been affected, it may nevertheless be true to say that an objective change in their situation has been brought about. The issue by a competent authority of a warrant for a man's arrest effects a radical alteration of his situation, even though he and his associates may at the time know nothing about it and may for a while carry on in just the same way as before. And, though it is true that the governments of this world were, even before the death, resurrection and ascension of Christ, subject to divine control, and that they are now no more submissive than they were before, yet the fact that God's claim over them, as over all other things visible and invisible, has been decisively and finally asserted, means that they fulfil their functions now under the judgment, mercy and promise of God in a way that was not so before.[4]

[1] op. cit., p. 119.
[2] op. cit., p. 122.
[3] op. cit., p. 116.
[4] In connexion with this section reference may be made to the following (in addition to Morrison's book already cited): K. Barth, *Church and State*, London, 1939 (Eng. tr. of *Rechtfertigung und Recht*, Zollikon-Zurich, 1938); W. Bieder, *Ekklesia und Polis im Neuen Testament und in der Alten Kirche*, Zurich, 1941; K. Barth, *CD* II/2, pp. 721–23 (= *KD* II/2, pp. 805–8; id., *Against the Stream: shorter post-war writings 1946–52*, London, 1954, pp. 15–50 (Eng. tr. of *Christengemeinde und Bürgergemeinde*, Zollikon-Zurich, 1946); W. Schweitzer, *Die Herrschaft Christi und der Staat im Neuen Testament*, Zurich, 1948; W. A. Visser 't Hooft, *The Kingship of Christ*, London, 1948; O. Cullmann, *The State in the New Testament*, London, 1957 (Eng. tr. of *Der Staat im Neuen Testament*, Tübingen, 1956); G. Bauer, 'Zur Auslegung und Anwendung von Röm 13.1–7 bei K. Barth', in *Antwort*, pp. 114–23; R. Morgenthaler, 'Roma—Sedes Satanae. Röm 13.1ff im Lichte von Lk 4.5–8', in *TZ* 12 (1956), pp. 289–304; A. Strobel, 'Zum Verständnis von Röm 13', in *ZNW* (1956), pp. 67–93; H. Schlier, 'Der Staat nach dem Neuen Testament', in *Catholica* 13 (1959), pp. 241–59; E. Käsemann, 'Röm 13.1–7 in unserer Generation', in *ZTK* 56 (1959), pp. 316–76; id., 'Principles of the interpretation of Rom 13', in Käsemann, *Questions*, pp. 196–216 (first published in German in 1961); E. Barnikol, 'Römer 13: der nicht-paulinische Ursprung der absoluten Obrigkeitsbejahung von Röm 13.1–7', in *Studien zum Neuen Testament und zur Patristik, E. Klostermann zum 90. Geburtstag dargebracht*, Berlin, 1961, pp. 65–133; W. Böld,

¹Let every person be subject to the governing authorities. For no authority exists as such except by God's appointment, and the authorities which are have been ordained by God. ²So he who refuses to be subject to the authority is opposing God's ordering; and those who oppose that shall bring judgment on themselves. ³For those engaged in government are not a *cause for* fear to the good work but to the evil. Dost thou wish not to fear the authority? Do what is good, and thou shalt receive praise from it; ⁴for it is God's minister to thee for good. But, if thou doest evil, fear; for it is not to no purpose that it is armed with the sword; for it is God's minister, an agent of punishment for wrath to him who does evil. ⁵Wherefore there is a necessity to be subject not just by reason of the wrath but also by reason of conscience. ⁶For it is for this reason that you do actually pay tribute: for, when they busy themselves earnestly with this very matter, they are God's servants. ⁷Render to all that which it is your obligation to render them, to him to whom you owe tribute tribute, to him to whom you owe indirect tax indirect tax, to him to whom you owe fear fear, to him to whom you owe honour honour.

1. Πᾶσα ψυχή: 'every person',¹ that is, in the context of Romans, 'every Christian (in Rome)'.² The phrase is emphatic: no Christian is to imagine himself exempt from the obligation indicated.

ἐξουσίαις. It is, of course, clear and agreed that the civil authorities are referred to. What has been the subject of a considerable amount of dispute is whether there is in ἐξουσίαις a double reference—to the civil authorities and also to angelic powers thought of as standing behind, and acting through, the civil authorities. The suggestion of the double reference goes back (as far as modern times are concerned) to M. Dibelius, *Die Geisterwelt im Glauben des Paulus*, Göttingen, 1909. Though

---

Obrigkeit von Gott? Studien zum staatstheologischen Aspekt des Neuen Testamentes, Hamburg, 1962; F. Neugebauer, 'Zur Auslegung von Röm 13.1-7, in *Kerygma und Dogma* 8 (Göttingen, 1962), pp. 151-72; G. Delling, *Römer 13.1-7 innerhalb der Briefe des Neuen Testaments*, Berlin, 1962; V. Zsifkovits, *Der Staatsgedanke nach Paulus in Röm 13.1-7*, Vienna, 1964; R. Walker, *Studie zu Röm 13.1-7*, Munich, 1966; W. Affeldt, *Die weltliche Gewalt in der Paulus-Exegese: Röm 13.1-7 in den Römerbriefkommentaren der lateinischen Kirche bis zum Ende des 13. Jahrhunderts*, Göttingen, 1969; W. Schrage, *Die Christen und der Staat nach dem Neuen Testament*, Gütersloh, 1971; M. Borg, 'A new context for Rom 13', in *NTS* 19 (1972-73), pp. 205-18; W. C. van Unnik, 'Lob und Strafe durch die Obrigkeit: Hellenistisches zu Röm 13.3-4', in E. E. Ellis and E Grässer (ed.), op. cit., pp. 334-43; J. Friedrich, W. Pöhlmann and P. Stuhlmacher, 'Zur historischen Situation und Intention von Röm 13.1-7', in *ZTK* 73 (1976), pp. 131-66.

¹ The expression is Semitic (*kol nepeš*): Michel compares 2.9; Acts 2.43; 3.23; Rev 16.3. The variant Πάσαις ἐξουσίαις ὑπερεχούσαις ὑποτάσσεσθε (𝔓⁴⁶ D* G it Ir Tert Ambst) is an ancient but worthless reading, due no doubt to the accidental omission of ψυχή.

² *Pace* G. Delling, in *TWNT* 8, p. 45, line 14f.

Dibelius later abandoned it,[1] it was taken up by K. L. Schmidt,[2] G. Dehn,[3] K. Barth,[4] O. Cullmann,[5] and a number of other scholars.[6] It has come to be specially closely associated with Cullmann, and it is he who has borne the brunt of the attacks upon it, in some of which a mood of impatience and irritation has sometimes been noticeable. Such adjectives as 'grotesque', 'eccentric' and 'fantastic' have been used of it, and it has often been very summarily dismissed.

We may summarize the arguments presented by Cullmann in support of the double reference[7] as follows:

(i) In every other place in the Pauline epistles where $\dot{\epsilon}\xi o\upsilon\sigma\dot{\iota}a$ occurs in the plural or the plurally-used singular with $\pi\hat{a}\sigma a$ (apart from Tit 3.1) it clearly signifies invisible angelic powers (1 Cor 15.24; Eph 1.21; 3.10; 6.12; Col 1.16; 2.10, 15; cf. 1 Pet 3.22).

(ii) The conception of the angel powers and of their subjection by Christ is of central importance in Paul's letters and also in the thought of the early Church generally, as is indicated by the fact that these powers are mentioned in most of the primitive confessional formulae, in spite of their brevity.

(iii) The expression $\tau\hat{\omega}\nu\ \dot{a}\rho\chi\dot{o}\nu\tau\omega\nu\ \tauo\hat{\upsilon}\ a\dot{\iota}\hat{\omega}\nuo\varsigma\ \tauo\dot{\upsilon}\tauo\upsilon$ in 1 Cor 2.8, with regard to which there is strong support among exegetes both for a reference to invisible powers and also for a reference to human rulers, is best explained as carrying just such a double reference as is proposed for $\dot{\epsilon}\xi o\upsilon\sigma\dot{\iota}a\iota\varsigma$ in Rom 13.1.

(iv) The mention of angels in 1 Cor 6.3 in connexion with the question of litigation by Christians in the civil courts is best explained by reference to the conception of the civil authorities as the executive agents of angel powers.

(v) Early Christianity shared with late Judaism the belief that invisible powers were at work behind earthly phenomena

[1] 'Rom und die Christen im ersten Jahrhundert', in *SAH* 1941–42, Abhandlung 2 (1942), p. 7, n. 2.

[2] 'Zum theologischen Briefwechsel zwischen Karl Barth und Gerhard Kittel', in *TB* 13 (1934), cols. 328–34, and 'Das Gegenüber von Kirche und Staat in der Gemeinde des Neuen Testaments', in *TB* 16 (1937), cols. 1–16.

[3] 'Engel und Obrigkeit', in E. Wolf (ed.), *Theologische Aufsätze Karl Barth zum 50. Geburtstag*, Munich, 1936, pp. 90–109.

[4] *Church and State.*

[5] *Christ and Time*, London, 1951; *The State in the New Testament.*

[6] For names see Morrison, op. cit., p. 25, n. 2; Affeldt, op. cit., p. 30.

[7] Cf. Cullmann, *The State in the New Testament*, pp. 95ff, and also Morrison, op. cit., pp. 17–39. Barrett's statement that Cullmann 'argues that the word "authorities" ($\dot{\epsilon}\xi o\upsilon\sigma\dot{\iota}a\iota$) refers not to the state itself, but to the "invisible angelic powers that stand behind the State government" ' (p. 244) has been corrected in subsequent impressions by the addition of 'only' after 'not' and 'also' after 'but'.

(Cullmann here adduces the reference to the στοιχεῖα τοῦ κόσμου in Gal 4.3, 9; Col 2.8, 20,[1] to the individual's angel in Mt 18.10; Acts 12.15, and to the angels of the churches in Rev 2 and 3; also 1 Cor 4.9; Eph 6.12, and finally the evidence for the late Jewish belief in the angels of nations[2]).

According to Cullmann, this double reference interpretation of the ἐξουσίαι makes intelligible the relationship between the ascription of a 'thoroughly positive role'[3] to the state in Rom 13, the recognition of 'its provisional, in the last analysis problematical character'[4] in 1 Cor 6, and the representation of the Roman empire as the beast from the abyss in Revelation; for the powers were created in, and for, Christ, and have been subdued by Him, and pressed into His service, and yet they are, so to speak, held on a fairly long tether, and so can 'have the illusion that they are releasing themselves',[5] though they can never actually set themselves free.

A useful account of the negative reaction to this interpretation has been given by Morrison.[6] Among the weightier objections which have been brought against it are the following:

(i) that the reference of ἐξουσία in the plural to spiritual powers or civil authorities depends on its linguistic and substantial context, and the linguistic context of the occurrence in Rom 13.1 differs from that of all the other occurrences in Paul's writings in that here alone it is not accompanied by ἀρχή and does not form part of a list of (at least two) terms, while the substantial context differs in that here alone there is no reference to Christ;

(ii) that Cullmann's interpretation of 1 Cor 2.8 draws too much out of the text;

(iii) that the NT affords no evidence in support of the contention that hostile spiritual powers were re-commissioned, after being subdued, to a positive service of Christ;

(iv) that Paul nowhere else gives any indication that the subjection of the powers to Christ involved their being placed over believers: on the contrary, it is affirmed that in Christ believers are no longer subject to the spiritual powers of the world;

(v) that Paul's teaching in Rom 13.1–7 rests squarely on the

[1] But on these reference should be made to G. Delling, in *TWNT* 7, pp. 684–86.
[2] See especially LXX Deut 32.8; Dan 10.13, 20, 21; 12.1; 1 Enoch 20.5.
[3] *The State in the New Testament*, p. 113.
[4] ibid.
[5] *Christ and Time*, p. 199.
[6] op. cit., pp. 40–54.

OT prophetic, apocalyptic and wisdom tradition of God's appointment and use of human rulers for His own purposes.

Something of a stalemate had been reached in the debate. Morrison made a valiant attempt to break out of this situation and to carry the discussion forward. In chapter 4, the important central chapter, of his book, he provided a wealth of evidence for 'a common Graeco-Roman concept of the State', according to which rulers were 'divinely appointed in relation to a cosmic system of spiritual powers';[1] and, when we were working on this problem in connexion with a study published in 1965,[2] we were inclined to think that he had gone a long way towards proving that this was a conception shared alike by the Graeco-Roman world, Hellenistic Jews, and early Christians, and that his claim that 'All the evidence so favours the wide acceptance of this world view that where Paul, Hellenistic Jews, or early Christians do not openly oppose it we should first of all assume that it was taken for granted until it is found to be incompatible in some particular',[3] might be provisionally admitted. We went so far as to assert: 'In the light of Morrison's contribution we can say that, while the double reference of ἐξουσίαις in Rom 13.1 has not been conclusively proved, it has been shown to be very highly probable'.[4] But, as we have gone over this ground again and again in subsequent years, we have become more and more uneasy about Morrison's confidence that the fact that nowhere in the NT is the relationship between civil rulers and spiritual powers explicitly affirmed is no reason for doubting that it is assumed. While we still think that the double reference interpretation of ἐξουσίαις has often been too cavalierly dismissed, we have now come to regard it as less probable than the interpretation according to which Paul in using ἐξουσίαι here had in mind simply the civil authorities as such.

The rendering of ὑπερεχούσαις by 'supreme'[5] does not commend itself, since for a Roman of Paul's day a single authority, namely, the Emperor himself, stood out as supreme. Here a plurality of authorities is in mind. An English word with a comparative force would convey the meaning more accurately than a superlative. It is possible to explain ὑπερεχούσαις as indicating that the higher grades of authority are intended; but it is more probable that the superiority indicated is super-

---

[1] op. cit., p. 99.
[2] *A Commentary on Romans 12–13.*
[3] op. cit., p. 99.
[4] op. cit., p. 68.
[5] Barrett, p. 243; NEB.

iority over the people who are being addressed, i.e., being in a position of authority over them. In 1 Tim 2.2 οἱ ἐν ὑπεροχῇ ὄντες means 'those in authority' and the same expression occurs in a papyrus of the second century B.C. So Calvin: 'Magistrates, therefore, are so called in relation to those who are subject to them, and not from any comparison between them.'[1]

ὑποτασσέσθω. The verb ὑποτάσσεσθαι (used also in v. 5: note also the presence of the cognate words, τεταγμέναι in this verse and ἀντιτασσόμενος and διαταγῇ in v. 2) is quite clearly a key word in this section. It is often assumed that it means 'to obey'. So, for example, Sanday and Headlam entitle this section 'On Obedience to Rulers', and say in their introductory summary: 'The civil power . . . must be obeyed. Obedience to it is a Christian duty . . .';[2] and, more recently, Barrett uses the phrase 'obedience to magistrates',[3] and UBS has 'Obedience to Rulers' as its section-heading for 13.1–7. If ὑποτάσσεσθαι is equivalent to the English 'obey' in its ordinary modern sense, then we must, of course, assume that Paul's injunction in v. 1a is not meant absolutely, and that he would certainly have agreed that, where there is a conflict between the command of the earthly ruler and the commandment of God, 'We must obey God rather than men' (Acts 5.29: cf. 4.19f).

But is ὑποτάσσεσθαι really represented with proper accuracy by 'obey'? It is true that LSJ gives as one meaning of the passive[4] of ὑποτάσσειν 'to be obedient', but the only references it gives in support of it are, apart from NT passages, Arrian, *Epict.* 3.24.65, and the *Bibloi Cyranides* 15. There is nothing in the article on ὑποτάσσω to suggest that the passive ὑποτάσσεσθαι is an obvious word to use if one means 'obey' in its ordinary sense. There are, of course, three perfectly good Greek verbs meaning 'obey', all of which occur in the NT, namely, πειθαρχεῖν, πείθεσθαι and ὑπακούειν. The LXX evidence confirms the impression given by LSJ. Of the twenty-one occurrences of ὑποτάσσεσθαι listed in HR there seems to be only one (Theod. Dan 6.13) in which the specific idea of obedience is

---

[1] p. 280. Cf. Morrison, op. cit., p. 107, n. 2. The participle ὑπερέχων occurs in the NT also in Phil 2.3; 3.8; 4.7, and 1 Pet 2.13. In 1 Pet 2.13 the RV renders it by 'supreme'; but in this case the translation is suitable as it is the Emperor who is referred to, who is not only 'superior' to the ἡγεμόνες who are mentioned in the next verse but is actually 'superior' to all other civil authorities within the empire.

[2] p. 365.

[3] p. 244.

[4] That what we have to do with here is a passive, and not (*pace* G. Delling, in *TWNT* 8, pp. 40, 41, 43, 44) a middle which is used with a passive aorist, is surely right (cf. Bauer, s.v. ὑποτάσσω 1.b).

clearly prominent. In the NT ὑποτάσσεσθαι occurs thirty times.
Sometimes the specific idea of obedience is clearly prominent
(e.g. Rom 8.7); but in the majority of cases, while it may well
be included, it is not clear that it is the predominant thought.
The word is used to indicate the proper attitude of a Christian
to the leaders of the church (1 Cor 16.16), to the civil authorities
(Tit 3.1;[1] 1 Pet 2.13f and here in Rom 13.1 and 5), to God
(Jas 4.7), of Christian wives to their husbands (Eph 5.22; Col
3.18; 1 Pet 3.1, 5), of Christian slaves to their masters (1 Pet
2.18), of the νεώτεροι to the πρεσβύτεροι (1 Pet 5.5), of the
Church to Christ (Eph 5.24). But it is also used in Eph 5.21
of a reciprocal obligation: ὑποτασσόμενοι ἀλλήλοις ἐν φόβῳ
Χριστοῦ.[2] On the last-mentioned verse J. Armitage Robinson
comments: 'Recognise, says the Apostle, that in the Divine
ordering of human life one is subject to another. We must not
press this to mean that even the highest is in some sense
subject to those who are beneath him. St. Jerome indeed takes
this view, and proceeds to commend the passage to bishops. . . .
But the Apostle is careful in what follows to make his meaning
abundantly clear, and does not stultify his precept by telling
husbands to be subject to their wives . . .', and goes on to speak
of 'the sacred principles of authority and obedience'.[3] In
striking contrast is Calvin's comment on the same verse. 'God
has so bound us', he says, 'to each other, that no man ought to
avoid subjection. And where love reigns, there is a mutual
servitude. I do not except even kings and governors, for they
rule that they may serve. Therefore it is very right that he
should exhort all to be subject to each other'.[4] It is Calvin,
surely, and not Robinson, who here gives us the right clue.
The problem of ὑποτασσόμενοι ἀλλήλοις in Eph 5.21 is to be
solved not by attempting to explain away the idea of recipro-
city, but by recognizing that ὑποτάσσεσθαι here does not mean
'obey'. The real meaning of the phrase becomes clear when we
compare Rom 12.10 (τῇ τιμῇ ἀλλήλους προηγούμενοι) and Phil
2.3f (τῇ ταπεινοφροσύνῃ ἀλλήλους ἡγούμενοι ὑπερέχοντας ἑαυτῶν,
μὴ τὰ ἑαυτῶν ἕκαστοι σκοποῦντες, ἀλλὰ καὶ τὰ ἑτέρων ἕκαστοι).
The three phrases, ὑποτάσσεσθαι ἀλλήλοις and τῇ τιμῇ ἀλλήλους

---

[1] Here it is coupled with πειθαρχεῖν. Are we to infer that the writer
regarded the two verbs as synonymous, or that he added πειθαρχεῖν
because he felt that the idea of obedience was not necessarily included
in ὑποτάσσεσθαι?

[2] Cf. the variant which adds ὑποτασσόμενοι in 1 Pet 5.5b. It is interesting
also to compare 1 Clement 38.1 and its sequel in 38.2.

[3] St Paul's Epistle to the Ephesians, London, ²1904, p. 123.

[4] The Epistles of Paul the Apostle to the Galatians, Ephesians, Philippians and Colossians, tr. by T. H. L. Parker, Edinburgh, 1965, p. 204.

προηγεῖσθαι and ἀλλήλους ἡγεῖσθαι ὑπερέχοντας ἑαυτῶν, would all seem to mean essentially the same thing. In the NT ὑποτάσσεσθαί τινι can denote the recognition that the other person, as Christ's representative to one (cf. Mt 25.40, 45), has an infinitely greater claim upon one than one has upon oneself and the conduct which flows naturally from such a recognition. We can now see how right was Calvin's comment on Eph 5.21—for a king, if he be a Christian, ought to regard his meanest subject as superior to himself in the sense of having a greater claim on him than he has on himself, since his meanest subject is Christ's representative to him.

But what does ὑποτάσσεσθαι mean when it is used, as here, to denote that which the Christian owes to the civil authority as such (which must, of course, be distinguished from what he owes to the magistrate as ·a person)? It means surely recognizing that one is placed below the authority by God,[1] and that, as God's servant and the instrument of Christ's kingly rule, and because, in so far as its existence is for the good of one's neighbour, one's service of it is a part of the debt of love owed to the neighbour in whom Christ Himself is mysteriously present, it has a greater claim on one than one has on oneself, and such responsible conduct in relation to it as results from such a recognition. This will not mean an uncritical, blind obedience to the authority's every command; for the final arbiter of what constitutes ὑποτάσσεσθαι in a particular situation is not the civil authority but God.[2]

Paul has in mind, of course, an authoritarian state, in which the Christian's ὑποτάσσεσθαι to the authorities is limited to respecting them, obeying them so far as such obedience does not conflict with God's laws, and seriously and responsibly disobeying them when it does, paying them direct and indirect taxes willingly, since no government can function without resources, and—a very important element which is not mentioned here but may be supplied from 1 Tim 2—praying persistently for them. In such a state he is bound to do what he can for its maintenance as a just state; but there is no question of the ordinary citizen's having a responsible share in governing.

---

[1] The ὑποτάσσεσθαι which Paul here and elsewhere enjoins is to be understood in terms of God's τάξις or 'order'. It is the responsible acceptance of a relationship in which God has placed one and the resulting honest attempt to fulfil the duties which it imposes on one.

[2] On ὑποτάσσεσθαι reference may further be made to C. E. B. Cranfield, 'Some Observations on Rom 13.1–7', in *NTS* 6 (1959–60), pp. 242–45; G. Delling, in *TWNT* 8, pp. 40–47.

The proper exposition of Paul's words involves for the Christian living in a democracy the translation of them into the terms of a different political order. Such a Christian can, and therefore must, do much more for the maintenance of the state as a just state. His ὑποτάσσεσθαι will include voting in parliamentary elections responsibly, in the fear of Christ and in love to his neighbour, and, since such responsible voting is only possible on the basis of adequate knowledge, making sure that he is as fully and reliably informed as possible about political issues, and striving tirelessly in the ways constitutionally open to him to support just policies and to oppose unjust.[1]

οὐ γὰρ ἔστιν ἐξουσία εἰ μὴ ὑπὸ[2] θεοῦ states a reason for the injunction which has just been given. It expresses a truth already familiar to the Jews (cf., e.g., 2 Sam 12.8; Jer 27.5f; Dan 2.21, 37f; 4.17, 25, 32; 5.21; Wisd 6.3; 1 Enoch 46.5; and see also SB 3, p. 303f), namely, that it is God who sets up (and overthrows) rulers, and that no one actually exercises ruling authority unless God has, at least for the time being, set him up.

αἱ δὲ οὖσαι ὑπὸ θεοῦ τεταγμέναι εἰσίν could be understood as a general statement, the positive equivalent of v. 1b. But it is perhaps more likely that it is a particular statement about the actual authorities with which Paul and the church in Rome had to do, namely, the Roman Emperor and his representatives.[3] Pagan though the imperial government was, it was yet to be acknowledged as a divinely appointed ἐξουσία.

2. ὥστε ὁ ἀντιτασσόμενος τῇ ἐξουσίᾳ τῇ τοῦ θεοῦ διαταγῇ[4] ἀνθέστηκεν· οἱ δὲ ἀνθεστηκότες ἑαυτοῖς κρίμα λήμψονται. Since the civil authority is ordained by God, to fail to render to it the appropriate ὑποτάσσεσθαι and, instead, to set oneself against it (ἀντιτάσσεσθαι) is to be guilty of rebellion against God's

---

[1] I have tried to draw out in some detail the implications for the Christian living in a modern democracy of what the NT says in this connexion in 'The Christian's Political Responsibility according to the New Testament', in *SJT* 15 (1962), pp. 176–92 (reprinted in C. E. B. Cranfield, *The Service of God*, London, 1965, pp. 49–66).

[2] D* G *al* Or read ἀπό here, and G has it also in v. 1c. There was a tendency in Hellenistic Greek for ἀπό to encroach upon ὑπό (see BDF, § 210(2)), and the variant here is perhaps due to it.

[3] Cf., e.g., Denney, p. 696; Leenhardt, p. 327f; Gaugler 2, p. 280; Michel, p. 316.

[4] διαταγή is a rare word in literary Greek (it occurs only once in the LXX, in the NT only here and in Acts 7.53), but common in inscriptions and papyri. The verb διατάσσειν, however, is common both in the NT and in extra-biblical Greek. In διαταγή attention is focused on the action of the subject, whereas in διάταγμα it is focused rather on the result of the action.

ordering; and those who rebel against God's ordering shall
receive to themselves judgment. In view of v. 2a, it is probable
that by κρίμα a divine judgment[1] is meant, and not just the
civil power's reaction. The γάρ in v. 3 is better understood
as introducing a second reason why the Christian must
ὑποτάσσεσθαι (the first was given in vv. 1b and c and 2) than
(pace W. C. van Unnik[2]) as introducing an explanation of
ἑαυτοῖς κρίμα λήμψονται,[3] particularly in view of v. 5, in which,
it may be suggested, διὰ τὴν ὀργήν refers back more particularly
to vv. 1b and c and 2, and διὰ τὴν συνείδησιν to vv. 3 and 4.

3f. οἱ γὰρ ἄρχοντες οὐκ εἰσὶν φόβος τῷ ἀγαθῷ ἔργῳ ἀλλὰ τῷ κακῷ.
θέλεις δὲ μὴ φοβεῖσθαι τὴν ἐξουσίαν; τὸ ἀγαθὸν ποίει, καὶ ἕξεις
ἔπαινον ἐξ αὐτῆς· θεοῦ γὰρ διάκονός ἐστιν σοὶ εἰς τὸ ἀγαθόν. ἐὰν δὲ τὸ
κακὸν ποιῇς, φοβοῦ· οὐ γὰρ εἰκῇ τὴν μάχαιραν φορεῖ· θεοῦ γὰρ
διάκονός ἐστιν ἔκδικος εἰς ὀργὴν τῷ τὸ κακὸν πράσσοντι is puzzling.
The difficulty is that Paul seems to take no account of the
possibility of the government's[4] being unjust and punishing
the good work[5] and praising the evil. There seem to be three
possible explanations: (i) Paul is so taken up with his own good
experiences of the Roman authority that he is oblivious of the
possibility that it might do what is unjust. But Paul himself
had had other experiences (cf. Acts 16.22f, 37; 2 Cor 11.25ff).
And could he ever forget that it was this same authority which
had condemned and executed his Lord? (ii) Paul, though fully
aware of this possibility, is here, as Calvin suggests, speaking
only 'of the true and natural duty of the magistrate', from
which however 'those who hold power often depart'.[6] But it is
hard to see how the giving of such a one-sided picture could be
compatible with a serious pastoral purpose. Moreover, it would

[1] Cf. Michel, p. 318; Delling, Römer 13.1–7, p. 65. But the reference
is not to be limited to the final judgment. We should, in any case, not
allow ourselves to be led by the AV translation 'damnation' into assuming that 'eternal damnation' is meant. For the expression κρίμα λαμβάνειν
cf. Mk 12.40; Lk 20.47; Jas 3.1.
[2] In E. E. Ellis and E. Grässer (ed.), op. cit., p. 335.
[3] Cf. Calvin, p. 281.
[4] A comparison between the first and second sentences of v. 3 suggests
that no distinction of meaning is intended between οἱ ἄρχοντες and
ἡ ἐξουσία.
[5] τῷ ἀγαθῷ ἔργῳ and τὸ ἀγαθόν (in v. 3) are naturally understood as
denoting that which is morally good, that which is according to God's
will for men (cf. 12.2, and what was said above on the latter part of that
verse), pace Käsemann, p. 338, who takes the reference to be to political
behaviour. The variants, both the τῷ ἀγαθοεργῷ of F* aeth and the
genitive plurals (instead of datives) of the Byzantine text, would seem
to be merely attempted improvements.
[6] p. 282. Cf. Martyr, p. 645; Denney, p. 695; Lagrange, p. 312; Michel,
p. 318, et al.

be in striking contrast to the realism of 8.35–39. (iii) Paul means
that consciously or unconsciously, willingly or unwillingly, in
one way or another, the power will praise the good work and
punish the evil. The promise of v. 3 is absolute: the Christian,
in so far as he is obeying the gospel, may be sure that the
power will honour him. It may indeed intend to punish him,
but its intended punishment will then turn out to be praise.
It may take his life, but in so doing it will but confer a crown
of glory. On the other hand, if he does evil, it must needs
punish him—though it may be by shameful honours or a false
security.[1] This third explanation, though admittedly difficult,
seems preferable to the other two.

The two sentences in v. 4 which begin θεοῦ γὰρ διάκονός ἐστιν[2]
indicate the grounds of the promise in v. 3 and the warning in
v. 4. The reason why the ruler cannot help but praise the good
work and punish the evil is that he is (whether he knows it or
not, whether willingly or unwillingly) God's servant (cf. Isa
10.5–15). The purposes to which he ultimately gives effect are,
in spite of all contrary appearances (and we certainly must
not belittle them!), not his own, but God's.

We must now look more closely at the parallel phrases, σοὶ
εἰς τὸ ἀγαθόν and ἔκδικος εἰς ὀργὴν τῷ τὸ κακὸν πράσσοντι, which
indicate the two purposes which this διάκονος serves. Here
several things have to be considered: (i) How are we to understand σοί? Barrett translates the whole phrase σοὶ εἰς τὸ ἀγαθόν
'appointed to promote what is good'.[3] But is Paul's meaning

---

[1] Cf. Barth, *Church and State*, pp. 30 and 54; also Pelagius, p. 102:
'Malus debet timere potestatem, nam bonus non habet quod timeat,
qui si iniuste occiditur, gloriatur' and 'Ipsa laudatio malorum laus est
bonorum'; Augustine, col. 2084: 'Sive enim probet factum tuum bonum,
sive persequatur, *laudem habebis ex illa*; vel cum eam in obsequium Dei
lucratus fueris, vel cum ejus persecutione coronam merueris'; Aquinas,
p. 191 (1030), *et al.* W. C. van Unnik has collected (in his contribution
to the Kümmel *Festschrift*) a fascinating wealth of material illustrative
of the common ancient idea that an important function of the civil
authority is to honour the good citizen and punish the bad; but, while
it is virtually certain that Paul was familiar with this common idea and
quite likely that he was consciously using language reminiscent of the
phraseology in which this common idea tended to be expressed, there
would seem to be nothing in the examples assembled by van Unnik to
match the solemn confidence of these two verses—the passages quoted
by van Unnik, on the one hand, speak of a function of civil authorities
which they ought to fulfil: Paul, on the other hand, is giving what seems
to be an absolute assurance.

[2] Cf. Wisd 6.4: ὑπηρέται ὄντες τῆς αὐτοῦ [i.e. God's] βασιλείας, with
reference to kings and judges; Plutarch, *Moralia* 780D: . . . ἀληθέστερον
δ᾽ ἄν τις εἴποι τοὺς ἄρχοντας ὑπηρετεῖν θεῷ πρὸς ἀνθρώπων ἐπιμέλειαν καὶ σωτηρίαν
. . .

[3] p. 243.

quite so general? Must we not see here, on the one hand, a contrast between σοί and τῷ τὸ κακὸν πράσσοντι, and, on the other hand, a connexion between σοί and the second person singular verbs in v. 3? It is true, of course, that the use of the second person singular in these two verses is a rhetorical device. But, when this device is used in the course of such exhortation as we have here, it is natural to regard it as a singling out, for the purpose of effect, of the individual member of the group addressed. (This use is different from that to be seen, for instance, in 2.1ff.) So we take it that by σοί the *Christian* who is doing 'that which is good' is meant, and that θεοῦ γὰρ διάκονός ἐστιν σοὶ εἰς τὸ ἀγαθόν is an assurance addressed to him. We may compare 8.28: τοῖς ἀγαπῶσιν τὸν θεὸν πάντα συνεργεῖ εἰς ἀγαθόν. (ii) How are we to interpret τὸ ἀγαθόν in v. 4? Not, if we are right concerning σοί, in a merely general sense ('advantage', 'benefit', 'well-being'), but rather in the specific sense which ἀγαθόν has (as the following verses make clear) in 8.28. The ruler helps the Christian toward 'the good' which God has in store for him, toward salvation (we take it that it is salvation to which, mainly at any rate, τὸ ἀγαθόν in this verse refers), if he is a just ruler, by providing him with encouragement to do good and discouragement from doing evil (which even the Christian needs in so far as he is still also an unbeliever), and by curbing the worst excesses of other men's sinfulness and providing them with selfish reasons for acting justly; while, if he is unjust, he still, by God's over-ruling and in spite of his own intentions, must needs help (for the troubles which he will contrive for the faithful Christian will be among those 'troubles of this life' of which Calvin says in his comment on 8.28, that 'so far from hindering our salvation . . . they rather assist it').[1] (iii) The civil authority is also God's servant inasmuch as it is ἔκδικος εἰς ὀργὴν τῷ τὸ κακὸν πράσσοντι. Through the state there takes place a partial, anticipatory, provisional manifestation of God's wrath against sin. But (to judge from other NT passages, e.g., I Tim 2.1-4) σοὶ εἰς τὸ ἀγαθόν and ἔκδικος εἰς ὀργὴν τῷ τὸ κακὸν πράσσοντι are not two evenly balanced purposes; the former is primary and pre-eminent.

To refer to the *jus gladii* in explanation of οὐ γὰρ εἰκῇ τὴν μάχαιραν φορεῖ as some commentators do (e.g. Michel,[2] Barrett[3])

---

[1] p. 179. A different interpretation of σοὶ εἰς τὸ ἀγαθόν is given by Pallis (p. 141); Lietzmann (p. 112); Leenhardt (p. 331, n. *); Michel (p. 312); Delling (*Röm. 13, 1-7*, p. 59)—as meaning 'to help you to do what is good'; but it is more difficult to get this out of the Greek.
[2] p. 318.
[3] p. 247.

is confusing; for it seems clear that in Paul's time (and, in fact, for the first two centuries of the Empire) the phrase *jus gladii* denoted the power given to provincial governors having Roman citizen troops under their command to enable them to maintain military discipline unhampered by the provisions of the laws of *provocatio*: it was the right to condemn to death a Roman citizen serving in the forces under one's own command.[1] Since neither Paul nor the vast majority, at any rate, of the Christians in Rome were soldiers, it is highly unlikely that he is here referring to the *jus gladii* (in the contemporary sense of the term). Is he then perhaps referring to the full powers of life and death over citizens as well as others possessed by the Emperor? Or to the power of an ordinary governor to condemn to death non-citizen provincials (a passage from a later date distinguishes the proconsul of the province as δικαστὴς ξίφος ἔχων from those who could only inflict less serious penalties)[2]? At first sight the context (vv. 3–4) seems to support the assumption that the reference must be to the power of capital punishment. But a reminder that the government is possessed of military power and so is in a position to quell resistance would surely be equally appropriate. Perhaps the fact that Paul uses φορεῖν here (rather than ἔχειν or φέρειν) rather suggests that the expression τὴν μάχαιραν φορεῖ should be understood either as a quite general statement concerning the authority's possession of military power ('wears the sword', i.e. is armed, is able to employ force), or else—less probably—as a particular reference to the dagger worn by the Emperor as *Imperator*.[3] In the latter case, the thought might be of the Emperor's possession of military power and/or of his powers of life and death.[4]

5. διὸ ἀνάγκη ὑποτάσσεσθαι, οὐ μόνον διὰ τὴν ὀργὴν ἀλλὰ καὶ διὰ τὴν συνείδησιν. It follows from what has been said in vv. 1b–4 (διό) that the Christian must be subject not only for fear of wrath (cf. the last part of v. 4) but also διὰ τὴν συνείδησιν.

---

[1] Cf. A. N. Sherwin-White, *Roman Society and Roman Law in the New Testament*, Oxford, 1963, pp. 8–11. See also *OCD*, s.v. 'provocatio'.

[2] Philostratus, *V.S.* 1.25.2.

[3] For information on the subject of the wearing of the *pugio* (sometimes referred to as a *gladius*) the reader is referred to T. Mommsen, *Römisches Staatsrecht* (Leipzig, 3rd ed. 1887) 1, pp. 433–5. Elsewhere in the same work (2, p. 806) he sums up: 'Der Degen, in der Republik das Abzeichen des Offiziers und vom Magistrat nur geführt, insofern er als Offizier fungirt, kommt dem Kaiser, da er nothwendig *imperator* ist, durchaus und von Rechts wegen zu'.

[4] In Tacitus, *Hist.* 3.68 the 'jus necis vitaeque civium' is singled out for mention as signified by the *pugio*, presumably as being that aspect of the Emperor's *imperium* which concerned all specially personally: it is not implied that it is the only thing signified by it.

According to C. A. Pierce, Paul means by ἀνάγκη ὑποτάσσεσθαι
. . . διὰ τὴν συνείδησιν that one must be subject because, if one
were not, one would incur that painful sharing of knowledge
with oneself which is a guilty conscience.[1] But perhaps it is
better to understand συνείδησις here in the sense of 'knowledge'
(cf. p. 159, lines 36–38, and p. 160, lines 19–21) or—rather less
probably—to give συν- its sense of 'together with' but to
understand the reference to be not to the knowledge's being
shared with oneself but to its being shared with one's fellow-
Christians.[2] In either case, the knowledge is the knowledge that
the ruler is, whether consciously or unconsciously, willingly or
unwillingly, God's minister. Whereas the pagan fulfils his
obligation to the state (if he does) for fear of punishment and
perhaps also because he realizes that the state is, on the whole,
beneficial to society, the Christian has a further, and all-
important, reason for fulfilling his obligation to it, namely, his
knowledge of the secret of the relation in which it stands to
God and to Christ.

6. **διὰ τοῦτο γὰρ καὶ φόρους τελεῖτε.** The διὰ τοῦτο refers backward (as, e.g., in 1.26), not forward (as, e.g., in 4.16). It can
be taken as parallel to διό in the previous verse,[3] and so referring back to what has been said in vv. 1b–4, or—perhaps rather
more probably—as referring back to διὰ τὴν συνείδησιν. If
συνείδησις is to be understood as we have suggested, no substantial difference of meaning is involved. The Christians of
Rome do, as a matter of fact, pay taxes (τελεῖτε is to be understood as indicative: if it were imperative, the γάρ would be
inexplicable), and the real ground of their doing so is their
knowledge of the place of civil authority in the divine purpose.
Paul appeals to their actual practice, reminding them of its true
significance. The distinction between φόρος and τέλος (as used
in the next verse) is that between direct and indirect taxes.

λειτουργοὶ γὰρ θεοῦ εἰσιν εἰς αὐτὸ τοῦτο προσκαρτεροῦντες. The
word λειτουργός in the latter part of the verse carries rather more
suggestion of solemnity and dignity than διάκονος used in v. 4;
but the suggestion (Cornely,[4] Kühl) that it should be translated
'priest' is surely to be rejected; for it is only rarely that it is
used in this sense in the LXX, while in Rom 15.16 the sacral
sense is supported by the context. The comparison of the
collection of taxes with the collection of sacrificial gifts is
artificial. While it is true that λειτουργία sometimes in extra-

[1] *Conscience in the New Testament*, London, 1955, p. 71.
[2] Cf. Pierce, op. cit., pp. 105ff, on 1 Pet 2.19.
[3] Cf. Lietzmann, p. 113.
[4] p. 679.

biblical Greek denotes the public service of the gods (e.g. Aristotle, *Pol.* 1360ᵃ 13), it means characteristically a public service or work in the ordinary secular sense (specially a public service carried out by a private citizen at his own expense); and λειτουργός denotes the person who fulfils a λειτουργία, and so, quite generally, a public servant, an official.

It is possible to take αὐτὸ τοῦτο[1] in various ways—thus: (i) as referring to the idea conveyed by λειτουργοὶ θεοῦ (so, e.g., W. Grundmann, in *TWNT* 3, p. 620f (=Eng. tr., p. 618, lines 23–26); 'die Regierenden sind Gottes Diener und sind in ihrer ganzen Arbeit und Forderung, z.B. auch in der Steuerforderung —an die Verpflichtung, Steuer zu zahlen, schliesst unser Satz an—bedacht auf die Erfüllung dieses Dienstes: sie sind Gottes Diener und verharren beständig dabei'); (ii) as referring to what has been said in vv. 3 and 4 (so, e.g., Barrett: 'attending upon the purpose I have described (that is, of promoting good, and of restraining evil)')[2]; or (iii) as referring to the receiving of taxes. It is hard to choose between these; but possibly the third interpretation should be preferred. The meaning will then be probably that it is as God's servants (and therefore as those whose claim must not be rejected or evaded) that they busy themselves earnestly with this very thing, namely the matter of taxes. Paul is not, of course, addressing the authorities; but his words do carry with them the implication that, if the authorities are to be respected as God's 'officials' even when they are claiming taxes and dues, then they *ought* to behave in a way worthy of God's 'officials' and (in Calvin's words) 'to remember that all that they receive from the people is public property, and not a means of satisfying private lust and luxury'.[3]

7. ἀπόδοτε πᾶσιν τὰς ὀφειλάς, τῷ τὸν φόρον τὸν φόρον, τῷ τὸ τέλος τὸ τέλος, τῷ τὸν φόβον τὸν φόβον, τῷ τὴν τιμὴν τὴν τιμήν sums up the section. That there is some connexion between this version and the logion given in Mk 12.17 (=Mt 22.21=Lk 20.25) seems extremely likely (note, in addition to the common reference to the subject of paying taxes, the use of ἀπόδοτε in both, and the similarity of idea between τὰς ὀφειλάς and τὰ τοῦ . . .). It seems quite probable—though it is of course not certain—that Paul is consciously echoing a dominical saying known to him

---

[1] εἰς with the accusative is here used instead of the usual dative with προσκαρτερεῖν. This is probably to be preferred to Sanday and Headlam's explanation (p. 368) that προσκαρτερεῖν is here used absolutely (as in Xenophon, *H.G.* 7. 5.14), and that εἰς αὐτὸ τοῦτο means 'for this purpose', 'with this end in view'.

[2] p. 247.

[3] p. 284.

from tradition.[1] The compound verb ἀποδιδόναι means 'give back' or 'pay something which one owes as a debt'. The idea of obligation is further emphasized by ὀφειλάς. For the *concisa locutio* of τῷ τὸν φόρον ('to him to whom you owe tribute'), etc., Bengel aptly compares 2 Cor 8.15.[2]

It is generally taken for granted that φόβος in this verse denotes a greater, and τιμή a lesser, degree of respect, and that by τῷ τὸν φόβον is meant the magistrate who is entitled to the greater degree of respect (so, for instance, Bengel defines φόβος here as 'major honoris gradus',[3] while Gaugler says: ' "Fear" is the attitude which is owed to the highest official, the one who is preceded by the lictor, since he can decide between life and death. "Honour" is the attitude, which is proper toward officials generally'[4]). While it is possible—perhaps indeed we ought to say 'probable'—that this interpretation is right, there are certain difficulties about it, which ought not to be simply ignored.

(i) Paul has just said in v. 3f: 'For those engaged in government are not a *cause for* fear (φόβος) to the good work but to the evil. Dost thou wish not to fear (μὴ φοβεῖσθαι) the authority? Do what is good . . . But, if thou doest evil, fear (φοβοῦ) . . .' Is there not at least a certain awkwardness or harshness in Paul's using φόβος in the sense of 'respect' in a general positive exhortation to the Christians in Rome concerning their duty with regard to the authorities three verses after this very emphatic use of φόβος and φοβεῖσθαι with reference to the fear of the authorities from which they are to be free?

(ii) If there is a real possibility of a connexion between this verse and the logion which we have in Mk 12.17, then it would seem natural at least to raise the question whether perhaps (as in the logion) there is in this verse a reference to the debt which is owed to God. Could it be that Paul intended by τῷ τὸν φόβον not the human authority but God?

(iii) A comparison with 1 Pet 2.17, which is probably also connected with the logion to which we have just referred, is

---

[1] We agree with Käsemann, p. 336, that this is unprovable; but differ from him in thinking that it is quite probable. It is of some interest in this connexion that the logion occurs in a Marcan pericope, of which Bultmann writes: 'There is no reason, in my view, for supposing that this is a community product' (*The History of the Synoptic Tradition*, Eng. tr. by J. Marsh, Oxford, 1963, p. 26).

[2] p. 557.

[3] ibid.

[4] 2, p. 286 (our translation).

very suggestive. Here, as in the logion, the debt to God is mentioned distinctly as well as the debt to the Emperor: 'Fear God. Honour the king.' But these two commands are preceded by two others: 'Honour all men. Love the brotherhood', so that the whole verse contains four commands which may be compared with the four commands, 'to him to whom you owe tribute tribute, to him to whom you owe indirect tax indirect tax, to him to whom you owe fear fear, to him to whom you owe honour honour' in the present verse. If the suggestion about τῷ τὸν φόβον is right, then both here and in 1 Pet 2.17 the debt to God is mentioned in the third place and the debt to the civil ruler in the fourth (though, whereas the first two commands in 1 Pet 2.17 indicate the general debt to all men and the special debt to one's fellow-Christians respectively, here the first two commands are subsidiary to the fourth, and indicate one's debt to the various public officers subordinate to the Emperor).

(iv) Furthermore, it is noteworthy that in 1 Pet 2.17 the wording of Prov 24.21 has been significantly altered. In Proverbs we have: 'My son, fear thou the LORD and the king'; but in 1 Peter two different verbs have been used, presumably in order to avoid using the same verb to denote what is owed to the Emperor and what is owed to God.[1] God is to be feared (φοβεῖσθε) and the Emperor honoured (τιμᾶτε). Whether this alteration was original in 1 Peter or whether it had already been made in the primitive catechetical material of the Church, it suggests that there was in the early Church a feeling that φόβος was particularly due to God and that τιμή rather than φόβος was what was due to the Emperor.[2]

(v) A survey of the occurrences of φοβεῖσθαι and φόβος in the NT confirms the suspicion derived from 1 Pet 2.17 that φόβος is not characteristically used of what is due to an earthly ruler. A great many of the occurrences of the verb φοβεῖσθαι are not relevant to our purpose (for example, instances of φοβεῖσθαι followed by the infinitive or by μή). As for those that are, it is noteworthy that God is often the object (for example, Lk 1.50;

---

[1] This seems a more probable explanation than the one suggested by E. G. Selwyn, *The First Epistle of St. Peter*, London, 1947, p. 175, namely, that the modification was made 'for reasons of style'.

[2] This may be seen at a later date in the *Acts of the Scillitan Saints* (martyred in A.D. 180): 'Cittinus said: "We have none other to fear save the Lord our God who is in heaven." Donata said: "Give honour to Caesar as unto Caesar, but fear to God [*honorem Caesari quasi Caesari, timorem autem Deo*]" ' (as translated in E. C. E. Owen, *Some Authentic Acts of the Early Martyrs*, London, 1927, p. 72.

18.2; 23.40; Acts 10.2, 22, 35; 13.16, 26; Rev 19.5), and that in every instance of a positive command to fear with a personal object expressed, apart from Eph 5.33 (ἡ δὲ γυνὴ ἵνα φοβῆται τὸν ἄνδρα), God or Christ is the object (Mt 10.28 = Lk 12.4f; Col 3.22; 1 Pet 2.17; Rev 14.7). In Rom 13.4 'the authority' is no doubt the object to be supplied; but in this case we have a command addressed to the wrongdoer, not a general command. Nowhere in the NT is there a general exhortation to fear (φοβεῖσθαι) the civil authority. When we turn to the noun φόβος, which occurs in all forty-seven times in the NT, we find five instances of φόβος θεοῦ, τοῦ κυρίου, Χριστοῦ, a large number of instances of φόβος used to denote the reaction occasioned by Jesus' miracles, the appearance of angels, the apostles' witness to Jesus, and also a number of instances of φόβος used to denote a fear that is regarded as blameworthy. There are four passages where it might plausibly be maintained that fear of masters, husbands, etc. is being commended (Eph 6.5; 1 Pet 2.18; 3.2, 16); but, in view of the fact that in Eph 5.21 we have ὑποτασσόμενοι ἀλλήλοις ἐν φόβῳ Χριστοῦ and that in 1 Peter there are verses which forbid the fear of men (3.6 and 14, which may be taken to control 3.2 and 16), while in 2.17 the Proverbs quotation has been altered in the way indicated above, it seems reasonable to prefer to take φόβος in these doubtful passages to mean rather the fear of God or of Christ. Apart from v. 3 and possibly the verse which is under discussion, it is not used in connexion with rulers.

It may further be said that, in view of the explicit references to God in vv. 1, 2, 4, and 6, and the implicit reference in v. 5, there would hardly be anything surprising in the inclusion of a reference to what is owed to God in the verse which sums up the section.

Could Paul then have meant by τῷ τὸν φόβον not the higher magistrate, but God? Two objections immediately present themselves: (a) there is a certain awkwardness about πᾶσιν on this view, in that it includes God along with the functionaries of government; (b) there is the difficulty of understanding why, if Paul meant this, he did not make his meaning clearer. Perhaps neither difficulty is insuperable. With regard to (b) it may be argued that, if the association of 'fear' with God was already strongly established in the Church (as the evidence indicated above rather suggests that it was), then this objection has much less force that at first appears.

It may perhaps be judged that the advantage is still with the generally accepted interpretation of v. 7. But, in view of the difficulties which beset it, which seem to have been ignored by most commentators,[1] the alternative interpretation suggested above should not, in our opinion, be cavalierly dismissed.

VII. 5. THE DEBT OF LOVE (13.8–10)

Having dealt in 13.1–7 with the Christian's fulfilment of his political responsibility, which, as Calvin puts it, 'constitutes not the least part of love',[2] Paul now goes on to sum up his particular ethical exhortation in the all-embracing commandment of love.[3]

[8] Leave no debt outstanding to anyone, except the debt of love to one another; for he who loves the other has fulfilled the law. [9] For 'Thou shalt not commit adultery', 'Thou shalt not kill', 'Thou shalt not steal', 'Thou shalt not covet', and whatever other commandment there is, it is all summed up in this word, 'Thou shalt love thy neighbour as thyself'. [10] Love does not do the neighbour wrong: love is therefore the fulfilling of the law.

8. Μηδενὶ μηδὲν ὀφείλετε[4] repeats in negative form the positive injunction of v. 7, ἀπόδοτε πᾶσιν τὰς ὀφειλάς, and so forms a neat transition from the preceding paragraph. Christians are to leave no debts, no obligations to their fellow-men, undischarged.

[1] It is interesting that some of the patristic commentaries do show awareness of the difficulties. Chrysostom, col. 618, for example, notices the apparent contradiction between τῷ τὸν φόβον τὸν φόβον and v. 3, but explains τὸν φόβον thus: Τὴν ἐπιτεταμένην λέγων τιμήν, οὐ τὸν ἐκ τοῦ πονηροῦ συνειδότος φόβον, ὃν ἀνωτέρω ᾐνίξατο. And Pelagius, p. 103, comments: 'Cui timorem, timorem. Quo modo ergo scriptum est alibi: "praeter dominum neminem esse timendum"? sed sic, inquit, age ut neminem timeas: timor enim dei timorem expellit humanum. sed quoniam causas adhuc timoris habetis, necesse est ut timeatis.' Origen, col. 1230, actually goes one better than the suggestion made above; for he refers not only 'fear' but 'honour' too to God! 'Timorem vero et honorem ad illum potius referre debemus qui dicit per prophetam: Nonne et Dominum, et Patrem vocatis me? Et si Dominus sum ego, ubi est timor meus? et si Pater sum ego, ubi est honor meus?' See now also Schrage, op. cit., p. 61.

[2] p. 285.

[3] See further J. Moffatt, Love in the New Testament, London, 1929; G. Quell and E. Stauffer, in TWNT 1, pp. 20–55; A. Nygren, Agape and Eros, Part 1, revised Eng. tr., London, 1953 (original Swedish, 1930); Barth, CD I/2, pp. 381–454; IV/2, pp. 727–840 (= KD I/2, pp. 408–504; IV/2, pp. 825–953); C. Spicq, Agapé dans le Nouveau Testament 1 and 2, Paris, 1958–59; V. P. Furnish, The Love Command in the New Testament, Nashville and New York, 1972.

[4] Both ὀφείλητε (ℵ³) and ὀφείλοντες (ℵ* pc Or) would seem to be secondary variants.

εἰ μὴ τὸ ἀλλήλους ἀγαπᾶν. Two questions require to be decided here: the former concerns the meaning of εἰ μή, and the latter the implication of ἀλλήλους. With regard to the former, it has been maintained by some that εἰ μή should here be translated 'but' (it occasionally has this meaning: e.g., 14.14; Mt 12.4; 1 Cor 7.17), and that the whole of v. 8a means 'Owe no man anything, but you ought to love one another'.[1] But this involves supplying in the second half of a sentence a verb used in the first half, and supplying it not just in a different sense but also in a different mood; and, while the supplying of the same verb in a different sense would be a quite feasible word-play (cf. 14.13, where the same verb is used in different senses in the two parts of the verse), the combination of change of sense and change of mood, where the verb is not repeated, is surely so harsh as to be extremely improbable. Moreover, the presence of τό is a further difficulty in the way of this interpretation.[2] If then we take εἰ μή in its ordinary sense of 'except', the meaning will be 'Leave no debt outstanding to anyone, except the debt of love to one another'; and the point of the latter part of the sentence will be that the debt of love, unlike those debts which we can pay up fully and be done with, is an unlimited debt which we can never be done with discharging. This interpretation is, as Sanday and Headlam say, 'more forcible' than the other:[3] it is also the only one which is a natural interpretation of the Greek. It goes back to patristic commentators. Thus Origen comments: 'So Paul desires that our debt of love should remain and never cease to be owed; for it is expedient that we should both pay this debt daily and always owe it'.[4] With regard to the other question, ἀλλήλους has sometimes been understood as implying that the love

[1] So, e.g., Barrett, p. 250. ὀφείλειν can, of course, mean 'owe', and be used with a dative of the person to whom the debt is owed and an accusative of the thing owed; and it can also be used with an infinitive in the sense 'be obliged', 'have an obligation' to do something. Reference may be made to A. Fridrichsen, 'Exegetisches zu den Paulusbriefen', in *TSK* 102 (1930), pp. 294–7; Michel, p. 324.

[2] If ὀφείλετε is to be understood in the indicative after εἰ μή, then the τό cannot very well be explained as anaphoric (BDF, § 399), and there is no following μή (as there is, e.g., in 14.13b)—see BDF, ibid. (3).

[3] p. 373.

[4] Cf. Chrysostom, col. 618: 'he speaks of it [i.e. love] as a debt, not indeed a debt like the amount of tribute or custom due, but a perpetual debt. For he will not have it discharged and done with, but rather discharged continually and yet never completed but always owed. For such is this debt that one must both pay it and for ever owe it'; Pelagius, p. 103: 'This alone is always to remain, which can never be fully discharged'.

referred to is limited to fellow-Christians.[1] But it is much more
likely that, having just said Μηδενὶ μηδὲν ὀφείλετε, Paul meant
τὸ ἀλλήλους ἀγαπᾶν in an all-embracing sense. The universal
negative, with which the sentence begins, is naturally understood to control the reference of the following words.[2] 'There
is . . . nobody that is not included in "one another".'[3] The
'debitum immortale',[4] the debt which we can never be finished
with discharging, is a debt which is owed to every man without
exception.

ὁ γὰρ ἀγαπῶν τὸν ἕτερον νόμον πεπλήρωκεν. Before we can discuss
the connexion between this sentence and the half-verse we
have been considering, it is necessary to decide whether τὸν
ἕτερον is to be taken with ἀγαπῶν or with νόμον. It has been
argued recently by W. Marxsen[5] (and his view is accepted by
Leenhardt[6]) that it is to be taken with νόμον, and that by 'the
other law' Paul means the Mosaic law as opposed to the civil
law of Rome which is suggested, he thinks, by Μηδενὶ μηδὲν
ὀφείλετε, when understood in close connexion with vv. 1–7.
Others who have construed τὸν ἕτερον in this way have understood τὸν ἕτερον νόμον in the sense of 'the rest of the law', or
taken it to mean the double commandment of love (perhaps
identical with the 'law of Christ' of Gal 6.2) contrasted with
the OT law, or the commandment of love to neighbour contrasted with that of love to God.[7] But against all attempts to
construe τὸν ἕτερον with νόμον (including Marxsen's) the objection that there has been no clear reference to any law in the
preceding sentences—the word νόμος itself has not been used
since 10.5—is surely decisive. In addition, the fact that Paul
nowhere else uses ἀγαπᾶν absolutely—though certainly not a

---

[1] By, e.g., Chrysostom, col. 618 (apparently, since he goes on in his
comment on v. 8b to say: 'for you owe love to your brother on account
of spiritual kinship' (col. 618)); Lietzmann, p. 113; Barth, *Shorter*, p. 160
(he explains that this sentence would be intolerable, were it not for the
fact that 12.9–13 has already made it clear that the love within the
Church is 'significant and beneficial' not just for the members of the
Church but for the whole world. This love within the Church is necessary,
if the Church is truly to be the Church; and it is this that the Church
owes the world, that it should in all circumstances go on being the
Church); H. W. Montefiore, 'Thou shalt love the [*sic*] neighbour as
thyself', in *NT* 5 (1962), p. 161.
[2] Cf. Lagrange, p. 315.
[3] Manson, p. 950.
[4] Bengel, p. 557; cf. Chrysostom (col. 618): ὀφείλημα . . . διηνεκές.
[5] 'Der ἕτερος νόμος Röm. 13, 8', in *TZ* 11 (1955), pp. 230–37.
[6] p. 337f (the fact that in the Eng. tr. the RSV has been substituted
for the author's own version has made matters rather obscure).
[7] See, in addition to Marxsen's article cited above, W. Gutbrod, in
TWNT 4, pp. 1063, 1069, and Bruce, p. 240.

decisive objection—may also be mentioned. There is very little doubt that we should (along with the great majority of interpreters from the earliest times until the present day) take τὸν ἕτερον as the object of ἀγαπῶν. It means not just 'another' (AV) or 'someone other than himself' (Barrett), but 'the other', that is, the one who at a particular moment confronts him as his neighbour in the NT sense—and so *all* those who from time to time present to him God's claim to his service. A man has not fulfilled the law by the mere fact that he loves *an*other, some*one* other than himself[1] (most men surely do this, though more or less inadequately, at least at some time in their lives). The definite article before 'other' is important—it has a generalizing effect. Fulfilment of the law involves not just loving someone other than oneself, but loving *each* man whom God presents to one as one's neighbour by the circumstance of his being someone whom one *is in a position to* affect for good or ill. The 'neighbour' in the NT sense is not someone arbitrarily chosen by us: he is given to us by God.

The γάρ indicates that what is said in v. 8b is in some way a reason for, or an explanation of, what is said in v. 8a. Two possible interpretations present themselves: (i) v. 8b may be understood as stating a reason for loving one another: to do so is to fulfil the law.[2] Paul would hardly mean to imply that some people do as a matter of fact fulfil the law in the sense of obeying it fully (for that would be inconsistent with what he says elsewhere in Romans (e.g. 3.20)), but simply that love is the way of obedience to the law. (ii) v. 8b may be understood as explaining why the debt of love can never be fully discharged: it stands to reason that it cannot be fully discharged, because, if there were people who were in the fullest sense loving their neighbours, they would have done what we have seen to be impossible for fallen men—they would have perfectly fulfilled the law. Of these interpretations (ii) would seem to be preferable.[3] It fits what seems to be the movement of Paul's thought better, and, if it is accepted, the use of the perfect πεπλήρωκεν presents no difficulty.

9. τὸ γὰρ οὐ μοιχεύσεις, οὐ φονεύσεις, οὐ κλέψεις, οὐκ ἐπιθυμήσεις, καὶ εἴ τις ἑτέρα ἐντολή, ἐν τῷ λόγῳ τούτῳ ἀνακεφαλαιοῦται, [ἐν τῷ·

---

[1] Not even when Barrett's very necessary warning that 'Love for the *neighbour* can too easily be misinterpreted as "love for the like-minded man who is congenial to me"; love is not Christian love if it cannot include love for the man who differs from me in every way' (p. 250) is taken to heart.

[2] The perfect πεπλήρωκεν could be explained as indicating the general validity of the statement (cf. Michel, p. 325, n. 2; BDF, § 344).

[3] Cf. Lagrange, p. 316.

ἀγαπήσεις τὸν πλησίον σου ὡς σεαυτόν. In confirmation of v. 8b Paul goes on to indicate that the particular commandments of the 'second table' of the Decalogue are all summed up[1] in the commandment to love one's neighbour as oneself (Lev 19.18). He specifies only four,[2] indicating by καὶ εἴ τις ἐτέρα ἐντολή that he is only giving some instances. Lev 19.18[3] is also quoted in Mt 5.43 (the first four words only); 19.19; Mk 12.31 = Mt 22.39; Mk 12.33 (loosely—τὸ ἀγαπᾶν . . . ὡς ἑαυτόν); Lk 10.27; Gal 5.14; Jas 2.8. While in Lev 19.18 the neighbour is clearly the fellow-Israelite, as the first part of the verse indicates, for Jesus the term had a universal range, as is shown by Lk 10.25–37. *Pace* Montefiore,[4] there is no adequate ground for thinking that its scope was less wide for Paul than for Jesus. It has sometimes been argued that the commandment to love one's neighbour as oneself legitimizes, and indeed actually requires, self-love.[5] The significance of ὡς σεαυτόν is rather that God addresses His command to us as the men that we actually are, the sinners who do, as a matter of fact, love ourselves, and claims us as such for love to our neighbours.[6] And this form of the commandment indicates that the love for our neighbour which is required of us is a love which is altogether real and sincere—as real and sincere as our sinful self-love, about the reality and sincerity of which there is no shadow of doubt.[7]

---

[1] On ἀνακεφαλαιοῦσθαι ('sum up') see H. Schlier, in *TWNT* 3, p. 681f; also G. Delling, in *TWNT* 6, p. 303; SB 1, pp. 356ff; 3, p. 306.

[2] οὐ ψευδομαρτυρήσεις, read after οὐ κλέψεις by some authorities, is clearly a later addition. The order in which Paul gives these commandments differs from that of the MT of Exodus 20 and Deuteronomy 5, but is that in which they are given in the B text of LXX Deuteronomy 5, in the Nash Papyrus, in Lk 18.20, in Jas 2.11, and also in Philo, *De Decalogo*.

[3] The ἐν τῷ before the quotation is omitted by 𝔓⁴⁶ vid B G latt, and is probably not original: it is possibly assimilation to Gal 5.14. In connexion with the variant ἑαυτόν (G L P 69 *pm*) see Bauer, s.v. ἑαυτοῦ 2.

[4] op. cit., pp. 161ff. See further on 12.9.

[5] e.g. by Augustine, *De civ. Dei* 19.14; *De doct. christ.* 1.22f; Aquinas, *Summa theol.* II². qu.25, art.4c; and even by S. Kierkegaard, *Leben und Walten der Liebe*, 1847, p. 24f. See the discussion in Barth, *CD* I/2, p. 387f (=*KD* I/2, p. 426f).

[6] Cf. Barth, *CD* I/2, p. 450f (=*KD* I/2, p. 499f).

[7] In this connexion Luther's words in his comment on 15.2 are also worth quoting. In the course of an extended discussion he says: 'I believe, therefore, that by this commandment "as yourself" man is not commanded to love himself but he is shown the wicked love with which in fact he loves himself; in other words, it says to him: You are wholly bent in on yourself and versed in self-love, and you will not be straightened out and made upright unless you cease entirely to love yourself and, forgetting yourself, love only your neighbour' (p. 407f). And in his comment on the verse with which we are now concerned he makes the

10. ἡ ἀγάπη τῷ πλησίον κακὸν οὐκ ἐργάζεται. The negative formulation is due to the negative form of the commandments to which Paul has just referred. But, as in the commandments themselves, so here a positive content is also implied, as Pelagius rightly recognized. 'Indeed, to omit to do good is an actual wrong-doing', he says; 'for, if a man sees his neighbour in danger of dying of starvation, is he not himself guilty of murdering him, if, having abundance, he does not give him food . . .? For whoever is able to succour someone who is in danger of dying of want (whatever sort of want it may be), if he does not relieve him, murders him'.[1]

But it is a mistake of the sentimental to despise the negative formulation as though it were something altogether inferior and unworthy of serious consideration; for the negative formulation will always be necessary (in addition to the positive) as a touchstone of the reality of love. How often is Christian love brought into disrepute, because those who are loud in their praise of love and confident that they themselves are loving, persist in injuring their neighbours![2]

πλήρωμα οὖν νόμου ἡ ἀγάπη forms a chiasmus with v. 10a, ἡ ἀγάπη both beginning and ending the whole verse. πλήρωμα is best understood (with RV, Sanday and Headlam,[3] Lietzmann,[4] et al.) as being used in the sense of πλήρωσις, 'fulfilling', in view of the sense in which the cognate verb πληροῦν is used in v. 8. This is better than taking πλήρωμα to mean 'fullness' (as, e.g., Vulgate plenitudo, Lagrange,[5] Dodd[6]), for it fits the argument more closely, and the οὖν suggests that this sentence is stating a conclusion to be drawn from what has just been said. (It would, of course, anyway be more correct to speak of the commandment to love one's neighbour as oneself as the fullness or sum total of the law, and of love as the fullness or

point that 'by the phrase "as yourself" every kind of simulated love is ruled out' and all love of others merely for what we can get out of them, for a man loves himself even 'if he is poor, dull, and a complete nonentity' (p. 367).

[1] p. 104.
[2] Cf. Chrysostom, col. 465: 'For this I grieve, that, living among brethren, we need to be on our guard against injury . . .' and a few lines later he speaks of 'truceless war' among brethren, and goes on to say: 'For this reason one may find many who trust pagans sooner than Christians' (Διὰ τοῦτο πενθῶ, ὅτι μεταξὺ ζῶντες ἀδελφῶν, φυλακῆς δεόμεθα πρὸς τὸ μὴ ἀδικηθῆναι . . . πόλεμος ἄσπονδος. Διά τοι τοῦτο πολλοὺς εὕροι τις ἂν Ἕλλησι θαρροῦντας μᾶλλον ἢ Χριστιανοῖς).
[3] p. 374.
[4] p. 113.
[5] p. 317.
[6] p. 213.

sum total of what the law requires.) The suggestion that Paul, while meaning by πλήρωμα primarily 'fulfilling', intended also to suggest the idea of 'fullness'[1] is perhaps just conceivable, hardly more. The suggestion of Leenhardt[2] that by νόμου Paul here means both the law of God and the civil law of Rome is surely, in the absence of any clear reference in the context to any other law but the scriptural, most improbable.

To draw the conclusion from Paul's statement that love is the fulfilling of the law that we can therefore afford to forget the Ten Commandments and all the rest of the law and just make do with the general commandment to love (or, as those who are inclined to draw this conclusion, would probably prefer to call it, the principle of love) would be altogether mistaken. For, while we most certainly need the summary to save us from missing the wood for the trees and from under-standing the particular commandments in a rigid, literalistic, unimaginative, pedantic, or loveless way, we are equally in need of the particular commandments, into which the law breaks down the general obligation of love, to save us from resting content with vague, and often hypocritical, sentiments, which—in ourselves and quite often even in others—we all are prone to mistake for Christian love.

VII. 6. THE ESCHATOLOGICAL MOTIVATION OF CHRISTIAN OBEDIENCE (13.11–14)

Paul has already referred to the eschatological context of Christian obedience in 12.2 (μὴ συσχηματίζεσθε τῷ αἰῶνι τούτῳ, ἀλλὰ μεταμορφοῦσθε τῇ ἀνακαινώσει τοῦ νοός). Throughout chapters 12 and 13 it is assumed. Now at the end of the more general part of his ethical exhortation Paul takes up again the reference of 12.2, and makes explicit the eschatological motiva-tion of Christian obedience.

[11]And this, knowing the time, that now it is high time for you to awake out of sleep; for now salvation is nearer to us than when we became believers. [12]The night is far advanced, and the day is close at hand. Let us then lay aside the works of darkness, and let us put on the armour of light. [13]Let us walk honourably as in the day, not in revels and bouts of drunkenness, not in repeated promiscuity and debauchery, not in strife and jealousy. [14]But put on the Lord Jesus Christ, and cease to make provision for the flesh for the satisfaction of its lusts.

[1] Michel, p. 327.
[2] p. 338.

11. Καὶ τοῦτο εἰδότες τὸν καιρόν. As used here καὶ τοῦτο (in classical Greek καὶ ταῦτα) is an idiom serving to introduce an additional circumstance heightening the force of what has been said (cf. 1 Cor 6.6, 8; Eph 2.8; Heb 11.12).[1] The things which Paul has been exhorting his readers to do (probably we should think not just of 13.8–10, but of chapters 12 and 13 as a whole) they must—and they will—strive all the more earnestly to do, because they know the significance of the time. For this appeal to eschatology as an incentive to moral earnestness we may compare, for example, Phil 4.4–7; 1 Th 5.1–11, 23; Heb 10.24f; Jas 5.7–11; 1 Pet 4.7–11, and also such passages in the Gospels as Mt 25.31–46; Mk 13.33–37. Paul's readers know the significance of (εἰδότες) the time, because, as believers in Christ, they see the present time in the light both of what He has done and of what He is going to do. The word καιρός, which the RV translates by 'season', has already been used a number of times in Romans (3.26; 5.6; 8.18; 9.9; 11.5). See especially pp. 212f and 409 on 3.26 and 8.18, where the expression ὁ νῦν καιρός is used. The omission of νῦν here is understandable in view of the fact that Paul is going on to say ὅτι ὥρα ἤδη and the rest of what follows in vv. 11–12a.

ὅτι ὥρα ἤδη ὑμᾶς[2] ἐξ ὕπνου ἐγερθῆναι indicates something of the significance of the present time: to know the significance of the present time certainly includes the knowledge that now it is time to awake out of sleep. Barrett says of ὥρα: 'Like "time", "hour" is an eschatological term';[3] but, while it is true that ὥρα is used more often in Daniel than in any other OT book (e.g. Dan 8.17, 19; 11.35, 40, 45) and that in the NT it sometimes has an eschatological reference, it is much more often used in the NT in quite ordinary and non-eschatological senses, and here it is unnatural to see anything more than an ordinary instance of a quite common Greek idiom— ὥρα (ἐστίν) followed by the infinitive, or by the accusative (as here) or dative and infinitive, meaning 'it is time (to do something)'.[4]

---

[1] Cf. LSJ, s.v. οὗτος C.VIII.2; Bauer, s.v. οὗτος 1.b.γ; BDF, §§ 290 (5); 442 (9). In English 'and that', in Latin 'idque', and in German 'und zwar' are used similarly.

[2] The variant ἡμᾶς, though strongly supported, should be rejected. It may be explained as assimilation to the ἡμῶν of the next sentence. Rapid changes of person are, of course, a notable characteristic of Paul's style: compare, for example, how in this same paragraph, after changing to the first person plural for vv. 11b, 12b and 13, he returns in v. 14 to the second person plural.

[3] p. 252; cf. Michel, p. 328; Käsemann, p. 346.

[4] Cf. LSJ, s.v. ὥρα (C), B.3. For a biblical example of the idiom see LXX Gen 29.7: Καὶ εἶπεν Ιακωβ, Ἔτι ἐστὶν ἡμέρα πολλή, οὔπω ὥρα συναχθῆναι τὰ κτήνη. . . .

Of course, ὥρα ἤδη ὑμᾶς ἐξ ὕπνου ἐγερθῆναι is in this context a thoroughly eschatological statement, but its eschatological significance derives from the context in Romans rather than from any associations of the word ὥρα. It is more natural (*pace* Sanday and Headlam[1]) to connect ἤδη with ὥρα ('that now it is high time . . .') than with ἐγερθῆναι ('. . . to awake forthwith'). For the metaphor ἐξ ὕπνου ἐγερθῆναι compare Eph 5.14; 1 Th 5.6–8. Sleep is a vivid image for that state which is altogether opposed to that of readiness for the imminent crisis.

νῦν γὰρ ἐγγύτερον ἡμῶν ἡ σωτηρία ἤ ὅτε ἐπιστεύσαμεν supports the statement that 'now it is high time for you to awake out of sleep'. It is probable that ἡμῶν should be taken with ἐγγύτερον rather than with σωτηρία. For, as Lagrange argues,[2] it would be pointless here to indicate that the salvation in question is the salvation of the faithful; the important thing is the nearness to the faithful of this salvation. But it is to be noted that from early times the words were sometimes construed the other way, as, for instance, in the Vulgate Latin, which has 'Nunc enim propior est nostra salus'; and, lest it should be inferred from Barrett's comment ('Paul is not thinking of salvation in a pietistic way as something that happens to *us* in *our* experience, but as a universal eschatological event')[3] that Paul would have objected on principle to attaching a personal pronoun in the genitive to σωτηρία, mention may be made of 2 Cor 1.6; Phil 2.12 (cf. Eph 1.13). These words certainly imply that Paul was looking forward realistically to a divine event to happen at a particular time, that his future tenses were no mere 'accommodation of language',[4] that his eschatology was no eschatology of 'the timeless fact'.[5] They imply that he regarded the amount of time which had passed between his own, and his readers', conversion[6] and the moment of writing as of real significance in relation to the Parousia—it was that much nearer than it had been. But do they also imply that he was certain that this amount of time would necessarily prove to be an appreciable fraction of the whole interval

---

[1] p. 378.
[2] p. 318.
[3] p. 253.
[4] C. H. Dodd, *The Parables of the Kingdom*, London, reprint of 1948, p. 108.
[5] ibid.
[6] The aorist ἐπιστεύσαμεν is ingressive (cf. BDF, § 331; Moule, *Idiom-Book*, p. 10f)—'we came to believe', 'we became believers'. Michel, p. 329, n. 3, compares 1 Cor 3.5; 15.2, 11; Gal 2.16; and also Mk 16.16; Acts 19.2.

between the Ascension and the Parousia? Do they, in fact, imply that he was certain that the Parousia would necessarily occur within, at the most, a few decades? It is sometimes assumed that they do. But there is nothing in this verse by itself—for the moment we confine ourselves to this verse—to compel us to accept such an assumption. It is clear that, if the Parousia is really going to happen at a particular time, each hour that we live must bring us an hour nearer to it, however far off it may be. Moreover, the point of this sentence was to underline the urgency of the need to awake: the time of opportunity for faith and obedience was for Paul and his readers the shorter by this lapse of time. And, with this point in mind, it was surely natural for him not just to think of this lapse of time as a fraction of the interval before the Parousia but also to think of it in relation to the ordinary span of human life. It may further be said that the very transcendent importance of the expected Event itself lends significance to each passing moment and period of time.

12. ἡ νὺξ προέκοψεν, ἡ δὲ ἡμέρα ἤγγικεν. ἀποθώμεθα οὖν τὰ ἔργα τοῦ σκότους, ἐνδυσώμεθα δὲ τὰ ὅπλα τοῦ φωτός. The whole verse is characterized by the metaphorical use of 'night', 'day', 'darkness', 'light', for which the reference in the previous verse to awaking from sleep has prepared the way. This imagery occurs again and again in the Bible (e.g. Ps 43.3; Isa 2.5; 9.2; 42.6; 60.1ff; Lk 16.8; Jn 1.4ff; 3.19ff; 8.12; Acts 26.18; 2 Cor 6.14; Eph 5.8; 1 Th 5.4f), and is also characteristic of the Qumran texts (e.g. 1QS 1.9f; 2.16; 3.13, 19ff; 1QM 1.1, 3, 7, 9f; 3.6, 9; 13.16). Here 'the night' clearly denotes the present age (cf. 12.2), and 'the day' the coming age of God's new order. The verb προκόπτειν means 'to advance'. The aorist may here be translated 'is far advanced' or (with the RV) 'is far spent'. We have argued elsewhere[1] that in Mk 1.15 the verb ἐγγίζειν should be given its local sense, and that the meaning of ἤγγικεν ἡ βασιλεία τοῦ θεοῦ is that the kingdom of God has come close to men (and is now actually confronting them) in the person of Jesus—an interpretation which finds support in Mk 12.34. But in Rom 13.12 a strictly local significance for ἤγγικεν is excluded by the fact that the subject is a temporal term, ἡ ἡμέρα. The meaning here must be that the day is imminent. We might paraphrase v. 12a: 'The night is almost over, the day is almost come.'

We have then in the first half of the verse an instance of the NT insistence on the nearness of the End. We may compare

---

[1] *The Gospel according to Saint Mark*, Cambridge, ⁶1977, p. 67f.

16.20 (ἐν τάχει); Mk 13.29 = Mt 24.33; Lk 18.8a (as understood apparently by Luke: cf. the latter part of the verse);[1] Jn 16.16ff (if, as is probable, the author intended a double reference to be recognized in πάλιν μικρὸν καὶ ὄψεσθέ με—both to the Resurrection and to the Parousia); 1 Cor 7.29; Phil 4.5; Heb 10.25; Jas 5.8f; 1 Pet 4.7; 1 Jn 2.18; Rev 22.20. What is the meaning of this *Naherwartung* (i.e., 'near-expectation')? It is well known that very many scholars regard it as an assured result that the primitive Church was convinced that the End would certainly occur within, at the most, a few decades, and that its conviction has been refuted by the indisputable fact of nineteen hundred years of subsequent history. The true explanation, we believe, is rather that the primitive Church was convinced that the ministry of Jesus had ushered in the last days, the End-time. History's supreme events had taken place in the ministry, death, resurrection and ascension of the Messiah. There was now no question of another chapter's being added which could in any way effectively go back upon what had been written in that final chapter. All that subsequent history could add, whether it should last for few years or for many, must be of the nature of an epilogue.[2] The completeness, the decisiveness, the finality, of what had already been wrought had stamped it indelibly with this status of something added after the conclusion of the final chapter. As the interval provided by God's patience in order to give men time to hear the gospel and to make the decision of faith, its continuance depending entirely upon God's patience, it could hardly be properly characterized otherwise than as 'short time'. However long it should continue, it could never be more than this; and this present age, which Paul refers to as 'the night', could never again have a higher status than that of something 'far spent'. Henceforward 'the day' would always be imminent, until it should finally break.

Such a *Naherwartung* is not the same thing as a certainty that the End would *necessarily* occur within, at the most, a few decades. Some Christians apparently did misunderstand it in this sense (cf. Jn 21.23; 2 Pet 3.3ff); but there is—so far as we can see—no compelling reason why we should believe that the *Naherwartung* of the Church as a whole was of this sort or accept what E. Thurneysen has called 'the dull doctrine concerning the postponed coming of the kingdom in which the

---

[1] Cf. *SJT* 16, p. 297ff.
[2] For this use of the word 'epilogue' cf. M. Wight, 'The Church, Russia and the West', in *The Ecumenical Review* 1(1948–9), p. 38f.

renunciation of hope has found its expression today'.[1] To say this is not, of course, to deny that the primitive Church reckoned absolutely seriously with the *possibility* that the Parousia might occur very soon. Nor is it to deny that there is this significant difference between the *Naherwartung* of the apostle Paul and that of Christians today: we—unlike him—*know* that the Parousia has *not* occurred within nineteen centuries. Whereas, with the passage of years, it becomes more and more natural to regard the possibility of a long interval still outstanding as quite probable, in the first decades the natural tendency may perhaps have been to reckon more readily with a short, than with a long, interval.

The true significance of the statement, ἡ νὺξ προέκοψεν, ἡ δὲ ἡμέρα ἤγγικεν, is well expressed by Calvin's words in his comment on 1 Pet 4.7: 'Besides, we must remember this principle, that from the time when Christ once appeared there is nothing left for the faithful except always to look forward to His second coming with minds alert'.[2] It is this that is the meaning of the 'short time' to which the NT witnesses so persistently point, that the time which is left is time in which watching for Christ's second coming 'suspensis animis'—with proper eagerness and a proper sense of urgency, and with all the active and resolute engagement in the tasks of faith and obedience and love which these involve—is indeed the whole duty of Christians. Truly to apprehend this shortness of the time is to be turned in the direction of obedience to the exhortation of 12.1–13.10—that, surely, is why Paul wrote in 13.11: Καὶ τοῦτο εἰδότες τὸν καιρόν . . .[3]

---

[1] K. Barth and E. Thurneysen, *Revolutionary Theology in the Making*, London, 1964, p. 15f.

[2] *The Epistle of Paul the Apostle to the Hebrews and the First and Second Epistles of St Peter*, tr. by W. B. Johnston, Edinburgh, 1963, p. 303 (I have inserted the word 'always', to represent Calvin's *semper*). Calvin's Latin is as follows: 'Praeterea tenendum est illud principium, ex quo semel apparuit Christus, nihil fidelibus relictum esse, nisi ut suspensis animis semper ad secundum eius adventum intenti essent.'

[3] I have tried to expound this view of the primitive *Naherwartung* in various places: in 'St. Mark 13', in *SJT* 7 (1954), pp. 284–99; 'The Witness of the New Testament to Christ', in T. H. L. Parker (ed.), *Essays in Christology for Karl Barth*, London, 1956, pp. 87–91; *I & II Peter and Jude*, London, 1960, pp. 110–13 187–90; *The Gospel according to Saint Mark*, Cambridge, 61977, especially p. 285–8, 405–12, and 484f; 'Mark, Gospel of', in *IDB* 3, p. 274f; 'The Parable of the Unjust Judge and the Eschatology of Luke-Acts', in *SJT* 16 (1963), pp. 297–301. For a fuller treatment of the whole subject reference should be made to A. L. Moore, *The Parousia in the New Testament*, Leiden, 1966. Reference may also be made to G. E. Ladd, *Jesus and the Kingdom: the eschatology of biblical realism*, London, 1966, pp. 303–24; id., *A*

The frequency with which ἀποτίθεσθαι and ἐνδύεσθαι occur in passages of moral teaching in the NT suggests the possibility that their use was a feature of primitive catechetical material;[1] the metaphor is, however, as Barrett notes, 'a very simple one, which might easily have occurred independently to many different minds'.[2] Moreover, if the variant reading ἀποβαλώμεθα is accepted as original, as it seems very probable that it should be,[3] the case for seeing here the influence of a common catechetical code becomes still weaker. Though the metaphor in ἀποθώμεθα (or ἀποβαλώμεθα) and ἐνδυσώμεθα is that of taking off and laying or casting aside clothes and putting on other clothes, it is not likely that Paul had in mind the change from night-clothes to day-clothes, as has sometimes been suggested; for it does not seem to have been normal practice in the first century to have special garments for wearing at night.[4]

The readers are exhorted[5] to cast off τὰ ἔργα τοῦ σκότους, that is, those works which belong to, and are characteristic of, the night of this present age (cf. what was said above on the metaphorical use of 'night' and 'day', 'darkness' and 'light', in this

Theology of the New Testament, Guildford and London, 1975, pp. 206–10. For a recent treatment of these verses from a different point of view reference may be made to A. Vögtle, 'Röm 13.11–14 und die "Nah"-Erwartung', in J. Friedrich, W. Pöhlmann and P. Stuhlmacher (ed.), op. cit., pp. 557–73. See also T. F. Torrance, _Space, Time and Resurrection_, Edinburgh, dated 1976 though not published until 1977, pp. 143-58.

[1] Cf. P. Carrington, _The Primitive Christian Catechism_, Cambridge, 1940; E. G. Selwyn, _The First Epistle of St. Peter_, London, ²1947, pp. 393–400.

[2] p. 253.

[3] The reading ἀποβαλώμεθα cannot be dismissed as a Western error due to the Latin translation 'abiciamus'; for, in view of the fact that in the three other places in the Pauline corpus in which ἀποτίθεσθαι occurs it was represented in the Old Latin by 'deponere', it is highly likely that the Greek text behind the Old Latin had here not ἀποθώμεθα but ἀποβαλώμεθα, the reading attested by D* F G. Moreover, this reading, since it now has the support of 𝔓⁴⁶, can no longer be regarded as a specifically Western reading. It affords a perfectly suitable meaning in this context; and its replacement by ἀποθώμεθα can be satisfactorily explained as the replacement of a Pauline _hapax legomenon_ by a verb which occurs in similar contexts in the Pauline corpus (Eph 4.22, 25; Col 3.8) and also in Heb 12.1; Jas 1.21; 1 Pet 2.1. The difference of meaning involved is, of course, very slight. The verb ἀποβάλλειν occurs elsewhere in the NT (only in the active) in two places, Mk 10.50 (where it is used of casting aside one's cloak), and in Heb 10.35. Cf. Zuntz, p. 94.

[4] Cf. Michel, p. 330; J. Carcopino, _Daily Life in Ancient Rome_, London, 1941.

[5] On the use of the first person plural in the next verse Chrysostom comments: Καὶ οὐκ εἶπε Περιπατεῖτε, ἀλλὰ Περιπατήσωμεν, ὥστε ἀνεπαχθῆ ποιῆσαι τὴν παραίνεσιν καὶ κούφην τὴν ἐπίπληξιν (col. 623); his comment is equally applicable to the use of the first person plural here.

verse)—though there is possibly another thought also present in Paul's mind, the thought that the things he is going to mention (in the latter part of v. 13) are the sort of things which were frequently indulged in during the night in a pagan city, but which many would be ashamed to do in broad daylight. Jn 3.20f should be compared.

Paul does not repeat τὰ ἔργα in the second clause, but substitutes τὰ ὅπλα instead[1]—no doubt 'because we are to fight in the service of the Lord', as Calvin says.[2] In 6.13 the word was used in the sense of 'instruments': here it must mean 'armour', and will include both defensive and offensive armour (cf. 2 Cor 6.7; 10.4; Eph 6.11ff; 1 Th 5.8). τὰ ὅπλα τοῦ φωτός may be explained (with Denney) as '(on the analogy of τὰ ἔργα τοῦ σκότους) such armour as one can wear when the great day dawns, as we would appear on the Lord's side in the fight'[3] or (with Gaugler) as the armour which is to be obtained 'from the arsenal of the light',[4] i.e., that armour which God provides, which is the strength that derives from the coming Day. These two explanations are not mutually exclusive. They are, in fact, combined in Althaus's comment: '. . . Waffen, wie sie das Licht fordert und schenkt'.[5] The meaning of 'the armour of light' will be clarified by v. 14, just as that of 'the works of darkness' is clarified by the list in v. 13.

13. ὡς ἐν ἡμέρᾳ εὐσχημόνως περιπατήσωμεν. The first three words are puzzling. They can be understood in various ways, thus: (i) with reference to the relative respectability of what men do in broad daylight, as opposed to the revelries and debaucheries of the night-time; (ii) with reference to the Coming Age and with an 'if' understood ('as if in the day', 'as if the day were already here'[6]), the day being thought of as not yet come; (iii) with reference to the Coming Age, the day being thought of as in some sense at any rate already here for Christians; (iv) 'day' being used, quite independently of its use in the previous verse, as a metaphor for the state of enlightenment and regeneration in which the Christian is at present, contrasted with the condition of paganism. The fact that they involve taking 'day' in a quite different sense from that in which it is used in the previous verse would seem to tell against both (i)

---

[1] The variant ἔργα (A D pc) is clearly to be rejected. ἐνδυσώμεθα δέ is surely to be preferred to the variants καὶ ἐνδυσώμεθα, ἐνδυσώμεθα οὖν, and ἐνδυσώμεθα by itself.
[2] p. 287.
[3] p. 699.
[4] 2, p. 309.
[5] p. 116.
[6] Barrett, p. 254.

and (iv), though (iv) is widely supported. While (ii) fits the context (ἡ δὲ ἡμέρα ἤγγικεν) more smoothly, (iii) is probably to be preferred, on the ground that it is more forceful and more in line with Paul's manner of exhortation generally. The element of unreality involved in (ii) tells against it. It is not Paul's custom to appeal to Christians to behave as they would if something were true, which in fact is not true. When in 6.11 he exhorts: οὕτως καὶ ὑμεῖς λογίζεσθε ἑαυτοὺς εἶναι νεκροὺς μὲν τῇ ἁμαρτίᾳ ζῶντας δὲ τῷ θεῷ ἐν Χριστῷ Ἰησοῦ, he means, not that his readers are to pretend that they are 'dead to sin, but alive to God in Christ Jesus', but that they are to recognize this as the *truth* which the gospel reveals.[1] We take it then that Paul's meaning here probably is that he and his readers are to walk[2] honourably as those who in Christ belong already to God's new order, whose lives are already illumined by the brightness of the coming day. For εὐσχημόνως compare 1 Cor 14.40; 1 Th 4.12. The adjective εὐσχήμων occurs in Mk 15.43; Acts 13.50; 17.12; 1 Cor 7.35; 12.24. Together with the noun εὐσχημοσύνη, they occur quite frequently in classical Greek. Originally referring to elegance of bearing, outward gracefulness (εὐ + σχῆμα), they came to be used frequently in pagan Greek in a metaphorical sense with reference to conduct. The adverb εὐσχημόνως, which Paul uses here, is not found at all, and εὐσχήμων and εὐσχημοσύνη are each found only once, in the LXX.

μὴ κώμοις καὶ μέθαις, μὴ κοίταις καὶ ἀσελγείαις, μὴ ἔριδι καὶ ζήλῳ[3] provides examples of the works of darkness which are to be shunned. The relation between the two nouns in each pair is very close: each pair may, in fact, be understood as suggesting one composite idea (e.g. drunken revelries) rather than two distinct ideas. The plurals in the first and second pairs suggest frequent repetition. Jealous strife and brawling often resulted from the drunken revels and the debauchery to which they led. Lagrange aptly illustrates by a quotation from Suetonius' life of Nero, chapter 26: 'No sooner was twilight over than he would catch up a cap or a wig and go to the taverns or range about the streets playing pranks, which however were very far from harmless. . . . In the strife which resulted he often ran the risk of losing his eyes or even his life, for he was beaten almost to death by a man of the senatorial

---

[1] Cf. H. W. Heidland, in *TWNT* 4, p. 290f.

[2] For περιπατεῖν used with reference to moral conduct see on 6.4.

[3] The reading ἔρισι καὶ ζήλοις (B sa (Cl) Ambr) looks like assimilation to the preceding plurals.

order, whose wife he had maltreated'.[1] With regard to the connexion between μέθη and the other things mentioned in this list, Chrysostom comments (and his words recall poignant memories to one who for some months during the Second World War shared pastoral responsibility for a large concentration of venereal disease patients): 'For nothing so kindles lust and sets wrath ablaze as drunkenness and tippling',[2] returning later to the subject with the appeal, 'Wherefore, I exhort you, flee from fornication and the mother thereof, drunkenness'.[3]

14. As μὴ κώμοις καὶ μέθαις, μὴ κοίταις καὶ ἀσελγείαις, μὴ ἔριδι καὶ ζήλῳ interprets ἀποθώμεθα . . . τὰ ἔργα τοῦ σκότους, so ἀλλὰ ἐνδύσασθε τὸν κύριον Ἰησοῦν Χριστόν interprets ἐνδυσώμεθα τὰ ὅπλα τοῦ φωτός, as Origen pointed out.[4] To put on the armour (in the sense intended by Paul) is not to cultivate various virtues thought of independently, but to put on the Lord Jesus Christ. Paul has used the expression Χριστὸν ἐνδύσασθαι in connexion with baptism in Gal 3.27, and a comparison of Gal 3.27 with Rom 6.2ff makes it clear that, as we have to reckon with several different senses in which the believer may be spoken of as dying with Christ and being raised with Christ,[5] so too we must distinguish different senses in which the believer may be said to put on Christ. He has already put on Christ in his submission to baptism and his reception through the sacrament of God's pledge that—in what is the fundamental sense—he has already been clothed in Christ by virtue of that divine decision to which the προέθετο of 3.25 refers (cf. 5.6, 8, among other passages). So in Gal 3.27 Paul uses the indicative. But here in the present verse he uses the imperative, since putting on Christ has here its moral sense (answering to sense (iii) of our dying and being raised with Him in our note on 6.2). To put on the Lord Jesus Christ means here to embrace again and again, in faith and confidence, in grateful loyalty and obedience, Him to whom we already belong, and (in Chrysostom's words) 'never to be forsaken of Him, and His always being seen in us through our holiness, through our gentleness'.[6] It means to follow Him in the way of discipleship and to strive to let our lives be moulded according to the

---

[1] Quoted from J. C. Rolfe's trans. in Loeb ed., London, 1920, 2, p. 129.
[2] col. 623.
[3] col. 626.
[4] col. 1234: 'Quod vero dixit: *Induamus arma lucis*, quomodo debeat fieri nunc exponit: *Sed induite*, inquit, *Dominum Jesum Christum*, . . .'
[5] See pp. 296–300.
[6] col. 627.

pattern of the humility of His earthly life.[1] It means so trusting in Him and relying wholly upon the status of righteousness before God which is ours in Him, that we cannot help but live to please Him. It means being 'defended on every side by the power of His Spirit, and thus rendered fit to discharge all the duties of holiness'.[2]

In order to explain the use of the expression Χριστὸν ἐνδύσασθαι here and in Gal 3.27, recourse is sometimes had to the mythology of the Primal Man or Urmensch; but, while it would be rash indeed to deny the possibility that Paul's thinking about the relation of believers to Christ could in some way have been indirectly influenced by the Urmensch myth, there is no need to look to such influence to explain his references to putting on Christ, in view of the rich and varied metaphorical use of ἐνδύειν in the LXX,[3] in the NT,[4] and in extra-biblical Greek,[5] and of induere in Latin.[6] The expression 'to put on Christ' is hardly as 'peculiar' (eigentümlich) or 'grotesque' (grotesk) as Gaugler supposes.[7] It was, in fact, a quite easy step from such metaphors as putting on one's strength (Isa 52.1), incorruption, immortality (1 Cor 15.53f), the breastplate of righteousness (Eph 6.14), to that of putting on Christ, seeing that Paul could already speak of Christ's being for us wisdom, righteousness, sanctification, and redemption (1 Cor 1.30).[8]

After 'put on the Lord Jesus Christ' Paul adds its negative counterpart: καὶ τῆς σαρκὸς πρόνοιαν μὴ ποιεῖσθε εἰς ἐπιθυμίας. For the meaning of σάρξ, which has not been used before in these two chapters, 7.18, 25; 8.3–9, 12f should be compared. It signifies the whole of our human nature in its fallenness, organized as it is in rebellion against God. The list of 'the works of the flesh' in Gal 5.19ff makes it quite clear that it is

[1] Cf. Chrysostom, ibid.
[2] Calvin, p. 288.
[3] e.g. 2 Chr 6.41; Job 8.22; Ps 35 [LXX: 34].26; Isa 52.1; 1 Macc 1.28.
[4] Lk 24.49; 1 Cor 15.53f; Eph 4.24; 6.11, 14; Col 3.10, 12; 1 Th 5.8.
[5] LSJ, s.v. ἐνδύω, quotes Aristophanes, Ec. 288: ἐνδυόμενοι τόλμημα, and Dionysius of Halicarnassus, Ant. Rom. 11.5: τὸν Ταρκύνιον ἐνδύεσθαι. From Chrysostom, col. 627, we learn that ἐνδύσασθαί τινα was used in his time in a sense similar to that of the English idiom, 'to be wrapped up in someone'. His words are: Οὕτω καὶ ἐπὶ φίλων λέγομεν, Ὁ δεῖνα τὸν δεῖνα ἐνεδύσατο, τὴν πολλὴν ἀγάπην λέγοντες καὶ τὴν ἀδιάλειπτον συνουσίαν.
[6] e.g. Cicero, Tusc. 1.38.92: 'somnum imaginem mortis . . . quotidie induis'; id., Off. 3.10.43: 'ponit enim personam amici, cum induit judicis'; Tacitus Ann. 11.7: 'magnum animum induisse'; 1.69: 'femina ingens animi munia ducis per eos dies induit'; 16.28: 'nisi . . . proditorem palam et hostem Thrasea induisset'.
[7] 2, p. 312f.
[8] Cf. Col 3.4 (ὁ Χριστὸς . . . ἡ ζωὴ ἡμῶν).

a much wider term than 'flesh' as it tends to be used in much Christian piety. Paul's readers are exhorted not to make provision for, to care for, the flesh with a view to the satisfaction of its desires. That those who now walk not according to the flesh but according to the Spirit (8.4) should make provision for the satisfaction of the flesh's desires would plainly be ridiculous. The interpretation which sees here a qualified approval of care for the natural life of the body (e.g. the Luther Bible: 'wartet des Leibes, doch also, dass er nicht geil werde') cannot be defended as an interpretation of the Greek text. Here 'flesh' is clearly used in its bad sense and not in a neutral sense, and the negative μή governs not just εἰς ἐπιθυμίας but the whole sentence. That Paul approved of a proper care of the body is no doubt true, but he is not thinking about this here.

VII. 7. THE 'STRONG' AND THE 'WEAK' (14.1–15.13)

Some recent commentators have exhibited great confidence in their approach to the interpretation of this section. This we find surprising; for it seems to us to be extremely difficult to decide with certainty what exactly the problem is with which Paul is concerned in this section. Though some interpreters of the epistle seem to take it for granted that the nature of the problem is obvious, various suggestions regarding it have, as a matter of fact, been put forward; and there would seem to be at any rate six suggestions which must be considered.[1]

(i) It is often assumed that the people referred to in this section as 'weak in faith' or simply 'weak' are people who are legalists in the sense that they think to earn a status of righteousness before God by their own works and imagine that their abstention from meat and wine and observance of special days constitute a claim on God, people who have not yet learned to accept justification as God's free gift. Thus Barrett holds that the weakness to which this passage refers 'attests a failure to grasp the fundamental principle, which page after page of this epistle emphasizes, that men are justified and

---

[1] It should be noted that the six suggestions which are set out here are not to be understood as each necessarily representing the whole explanation offered by a particular interpreter or group of interpreters. Some would combine two or even more of these suggestions. So, for example, Barrett, to whom we refer as supporting (i), also incorporates (v) in his explanation. We have tried to separate out what seem to be the main suggestions which have to be considered; but the reader must reckon with the fact that different variations and combinations of them have also been suggested.

reconciled to God . . . by faith alone—or, better, by God's own free electing grace'.[1] But what is surely a conclusive objection to this view of the matter has quite often been stated, namely, that to seek to be justified on the ground of one's works would have been, for Paul, a matter of having ceased to have, or of never having had, true faith, and, had the people referred to really failed to grasp the truth that justification is by faith alone, Paul would not have regarded them as genuine believers.[2] Though he might perhaps have been less vehement than he was in Galatians, since, unlike the Judaizers with whom he was concerned in Galatians, these people were clearly not very aggressive,[3] he would surely have taken a quite different line with regard to them from that which he has taken in Rom 14.1–15.13.

(ii) It has been suggested that the disagreement between the weak and the strong of this passage is about the question of 'things sacrificed to idols', with which Paul is concerned in 1 Corinthians 8 and 10. It is clear at once that there are an impressive number of contacts between the present section and those two chapters:

(a) compare the use of ἀσθενεῖν in 14.1, 2,[4] and of ἀσθένημα in 15.1 (cf. also the use of ἀδύνατος in the same verse) with the use of ἀσθενεῖν in 1 Cor 8.11, 12, and of ἀσθενής in 1 Cor 8.7, 9, 10;

(b) compare 14.13, 20, 21, with 1 Cor 8.9, 13; 10.32 (on the need to avoid putting a πρόσκομμα or σκάνδαλον in the way of the weak brother);

(c) compare the use of λυπεῖν in 14.15 with the use of τύπτειν in 1 Cor 8.12;

(d) compare μὴ . . . ἐκεῖνον [i.e. the weak brother] ἀπόλλυε, ὑπὲρ οὗ Χριστὸς ἀπέθανεν in 14.15 with ἀπόλλυται γὰρ ὁ ἀσθενῶν . . . ὁ ἀδελφὸς δι' ὃν Χριστὸς ἀπέθανεν in 1 Cor 8.11;

(e) compare the use of ἀρέσκειν in 15.1 and 2 with its use in 1 Cor 10.33;

---

[1] p. 256.

[2] See, e.g., Denney, p. 700; Barth, *Shorter*, p. 164f.

[3] It is evident that, as well as being weak in faith, they were also weak in character, people who, though prone to indulge in censoriousness with regard to their fellow-Christians, were fundamentally timid. They were liable to yield to social pressure, succumbing to contempt and ridicule and falling in with the practices of their fellow-Christians, in spite of their scruples and misgivings. Their integrity as persons was at risk. The choice of the verb ἐξουθενεῖν to describe the attitude which the strong were liable to adopt towards them (14.3, 10) and the references to their being made to stumble (14.13, 20, 21), to their being grieved (14.15) and to their doubting (14.23), all point to this fact of their weakness of character.

[4] The use of ἀσθενεῖν in the variant reading at 14.21 is rather different.

(f) compare the references to edification in 14.19 and 15.2 with those in 1 Cor 8.1 (the use of οἰκοδομεῖν in v. 10 is different) and 10.23;

(g) compare 14.17 with 1 Cor 8.8 (both verses make the point that to have to abstain from food by which one's brother could be offended is no great hardship, since it does not make one any worse off with regard to what really matters);

(h) compare the use of πίστις in 14.22 with that of ἐξουσία in 1 Cor 8.9 and of ἐλευθερία in 1 Cor 10.29;

(i) compare 14.6 with 1 Cor 10.30 (on the significance of the thanksgiving in connexion with the food taken);

(j) compare 14.14 and 20b with 1 Cor 8.4-7; 10.19f, 25f, 28 (on the fact that things which are not unclean in themselves are unclean for the man who thinks them unclean);

(k) compare 14.21 with 1 Cor 8.13 (it is good to abstain altogether from that which can be enjoyed only at the risk of making one's brother to stumble).

Moreover, it is not difficult to understand how some Christians, knowing that the meat to be purchased in the butchers' shops of a pagan city would normally have been involved in sacrifice to a pagan deity,[1] would decide to become vegetarian as the only way of being sure that they were not being accomplices in idolatry. The abstention from wine (14.21) is also explicable along these lines, since libations were offered from the first-fruits of the wine.[2] But the explanation of this section as being mainly concerned with the problem of 'things sacrificed to idols' should also, we think, be rejected; for, first, it is scarcely credible, in view of its prominence in 1 Corinthians 8 and 10, that Paul should never once have used the word εἰδωλόθυτος in this passage, had he had this problem in mind (and there are, moreover, other indications in 1 Corinthians 8 and 10 of the nature of the question at issue besides the use of εἰδωλόθυτος); secondly, the mention of the observance of days can hardly be brought within the framework of this explanation; and, thirdly, there is no indication in this section that Paul saw any harm at all in the practice of the strong in itself, apart from its effect on the weak, but in 1 Cor 10.20-22 there is a warning against a danger to which the Corinthian φρόνιμοι were exposed, the reality of which was quite independent of the presence of weak brethren with their scruples. While it is clear that Paul saw the tension between the strong and the weak with which he was concerned in Rom 14.1-15.13 as involving the same issues of

---

[1] Cf. H. Lietzmann, *An die Korinther I.II*, Tübingen, ⁴1949, p. 51f.

[2] Cf. Augustine, col. 2085: 'de primitiis vini libabant Gentes simulacris suis, et quaedam in ipsis torcularibus sacrificia faciebant'.

the respect due to one's fellow-Christian's conscience and the absolute obligation to refrain from insisting on exercising the liberty allowed one by one's own faith at the risk of wrecking a fellow-Christian's faith, which were raised by the question of 'things sacrificed to idols' (hence the very close similarities between this section and 1 Corinthians 8 and 10), it seems unlikely that it was the problem of the εἰδωλόθυτα that Paul had specially in mind here.[1]

(iii) It has been suggested that this abstention from meat and wine was a fast of sorrow for the continued unbelief of the great majority of Jews,[2] a fast to which Jewish Christians would naturally be more inclined than Gentile Christians (that the division between the weak and the strong tended to be one between Jewish and Gentile Christians is suggested by 15.7–13), a fast comparable with that of some Pharisees who neither ate flesh nor drank wine after the destruction of the Temple.[3] But there is no positive support for this suggestion in Rom 14.1–15.13, and it does not seem very likely.

(iv) Another suggestion is that the abstinence referred to was a fasting from things regarded as in themselves good and desirable, aimed at the disciplining of the body and at bringing it under control;[4] but the use of κοινός in 14.14 and of καθαρός in 14.20, suggesting as it does that the weak felt that that from which they made a practice of abstaining was in some way or other unclean, tells against this suggestion, and it is difficult to understand how, if the abstinence had been of this sort, the refusal of a fellow-Christian to share it could possibly have had such a disastrous effect on the Christian who practised it— however seriously he took his abstinence—as is envisaged in 14.15.

(v) A fifth suggestion sees this twofold abstinence as a manifestation within primitive Christianity of ideas and practices which were characteristic of various religious-philosophical movements in antiquity and which persisted with remarkable vitality down the centuries.[5] If such were the

---

[1] Though the view that the weak of this section were abstaining from meat and wine for fear of becoming unwitting accomplices in idol-sacrifices was maintained by, e.g., Augustine, col. 2085, and Cornely, p. 693.

[2] Cf. Schlatter, p. 367.

[3] Cf. *TSot.* 15.11–15 and other passages cited in SB 3, p. 307f.

[4] Cf. Schlatter, ibid.

[5] The adherents of Orphism, a religious movement which is known to have been present in Athens as early as the sixth century B.C. while its origins are much earlier, refused to kill animals and eat their flesh, probably because of a belief in metempsychosis. Plato refers (*Lg.* 6.782c)

provenance of the vegetarianism of the weak, the use of the words κοινός in 14.14 and καθαρός in 14.20 would be understandable, since the adherents of these movements regarded the killing of living creatures for food as unnatural and defiling.[1] Abstention from wine on the ground that it was inimical to the higher and more refined uses of human reason and to the reception of divine communications was less widespread than the abstention from flesh, but not uncommon.[2] There is wide support for this suggestion in one or another of its possible variations.[3] A disadvantage of it is that a plausible explanation of the third feature, the observing of special days (14.5f) is not to be had along these lines, but has to be sought elsewhere.[4]

(vi) A sixth possibility is that the weakness of the weak consisted in a continuing concern with literal obedience of the ceremonial part of the OT law, though one that was very different from that of the Judaizers of Galatians. The Judaizers of Galatians were legalists who imagined that they could put God under an obligation by their obedience and insisted on the

to certain ancients who lived 'what is called an Orphic life', abstaining altogether from animate things (. . . ἀλλὰ Ὀρφικοί τινες λεγόμενοι βίοι ἐγίγνοντο ἡμῶν τοῖς τότε, ἀψύχων μὲν ἐχόμενοι πάντων, ἐμψύχων δὲ τοὐναντίον πάντων ἀπεχόμενοι); and the fourth century comic poet Aristopho speaks of someone who is 'a veritable caterpillar for eating vegetables' (10.3f, in T.Koch (ed.), *Comicorum Atticorum Fragmenta* 2, p. 280). Abstinence from meat was characteristic of the Pythagoreans, a religious society founded by Pythagoras (sixth to fifth centuries), revived in the first century B.C. (Neopythagoreanism) and persisting in its new form until it merged with Neoplatonism. Philostratus (*V.A.* 1.8) tells how Apollonius of Tyana renounced on becoming a disciple of Pythagoras (τὰς μὲν ἐμψύχους βρώσεις ὡς οὔτε καθαρὰς καὶ τὸν νοῦν παχυνούσας παρῃτήσατο). Among the Jews the Therapeutai of Egypt seem to have been vegetarian (cf. Philo, *Vit. Contempl.* 37). And in the Jewish Christian community James, the Lord's brother, abstained from flesh (according to Hegesippus, *ap.* Eusebius, *H.E.* 2.23.5), as did also the Ebionites (according to Epiphanius, *Haer.* 30.15).

[1] Cf. Plato, *Lg.* 6.782c: . . . σαρκῶν δ' ἀπείχοντο ὡς οὐχ ὅσιον ὂν ἐσθίειν οὐδὲ τοὺς τῶν θεῶν βωμοὺς αἵματι μιαίνειν . . . (cf. the words ὡς οὔτε καθαράς in the quotation from Philostratus in the previous note).

[2] Cf., e.g., Aristopho 10.3 (the words immediately preceding those to which reference was made in the last note but one are: ὕδωρ δὲ πίνειν βάτραχος—'a veritable frog for drinking water'); Philo, *Vit. Contempl.* 37; Philostratus, *V.A.* 1.8 (. . . καὶ τὸν οἶνον καθαρὸν μὲν ἔφασκεν εἶναι πῶμα ἐκ φυτοῦ οὕτως ἡμέρου τοῖς ἀνθρώποις ἥκοντα, ἐναντιοῦσθαι δὲ τῇ τοῦ νοῦ συστάσει διαθολοῦντα τὸν ἐν τῇ ψυχῇ αἰθέρα);Eusebius, *H.E.* 2.23.5 (James, the Lord's brother, οἶνον καὶ σίκερα οὐκ ἔπιεν). Cf. also Dan 10.3ff.

[3] See, e.g., Lagrange, pp. 335–40; Käsemann, p. 350ff.

[4] Presumably in Judaism. Had this observance of days been derived from pagan ideas about lucky and unlucky days, it would scarcely have been treated so sympathetically by Paul. (For the penetration of pagan notions about lucky and unlucky days into Judaism reference may be made to SB 3, p. 308f).

literal fulfilment of the ceremonial part of the law as necessary for salvation. With such legalism Paul could not compromise. But the possibility which we have in mind here is that the weak, while neither thinking they were putting God in their debt by their obedience nor yet deliberately trying to force all other Christians to conform to their pattern, felt that, as far as they themselves were concerned, they could not with a clear conscience give up the observance of such requirements of the law as the distinction between clean and unclean foods, the avoidance of blood, the keeping of the Sabbath and other special days.

In our opinion it is not possible to decide with absolute certainty between (v) and (vi); but we incline to the view that (vi) is the more probable of them. In support of it a number of things may be said:

(a) It agrees well with 15.7–13 which strongly suggests that the division between the weak and the strong was also, to a large extent at any rate, a division between Jewish and Gentile Christians.

(b) It agrees well with the use of κοινός in 14.14 and of καθαρός in 14.20 (on the use of κοινός in the sense of ṭāmē' and of καθαρός in the sense of ṭāhôr see on 14.14 and 14.20, respectively). Specially suggestive is a comparison of Mk 7.19, which would seem to imply that the question whether Christians ought to observe the distinction between clean and unclean foods was still, or had been quite recently, a live issue in the church for which Mark was writing. That Christians in a pagan city, wishing to be sure of avoiding meat which was in one way or another unclean according to the OT ritual law, should decide simply to abstain altogether from meat would scarcely be surprising. There was a notable biblical precedent for such a course in Dan 1.8, 12, 16; and Barrett's statement that, in view of the fact that there was a large Jewish colony in Rome, 'it must be regarded as certain that suitable meat could be obtained by anyone who wished to do so'[1] does not take account of the possibility that Jewish Christians may not have been able to rely on the willingness of their unbelieving fellow-Jews to accommodate them (moreover, the pressing problem may well have been the meat which their strong fellow-Christians were liable to offer them).

(c) It agrees well with the mention of observance of days in 14.5f.

(d) It accords with the implication of the whole section that

[1] p. 256.

the weak in faith are also characterized by a certain weakness of character, a liability to yield to social pressure and allow themselves to be blown off the course which their own faith has set them. The attachment to the ceremonial requirements of the law which suggestion (vi) presupposes in the weak is not the stubborn self-righteous legalism of the Galatians Judaizers but a feeling, which, while it goes very deep, is ill-defined and difficult to defend by argument.

(e) It accords too with what is said about the grief, the spiritual ruin, to which the weak can easily be brought; for to have a deeply-felt conviction but be unable to marshal clear-cut arguments in its defence is to be in very serious danger of losing one's personal integrity.

(f) It also accords well with the sympathetic gentleness of Paul's attitude to the weak in this section. The fact that the main thrust of his exhortation here is directed, not to the weak, but (*pace* Chrysostom)[1] to the strong, to persuade them to go out of their way to 'please' the weak and to refrain from doing anything likely to 'grieve' them, is strong support for the view that the weak were not abstaining from meat and observing days with the intention of earning thereby a status of righteousness before God (being ignorant of the fact that it is only by grace through faith that we can be justified), but because they felt sincerely, albeit mistakenly, that it was only along this particular path that they could obediently express their response of faith to God's grace in Christ.

The mention of abstinence from wine (14.21) is not so easily accommodated in the framework provided by suggestion (vi) as are the references to not eating meat and to observing days. The OT law nowhere forbids the drinking of wine, except to priests on duty (Lev 10.9) and to Nazirites (Num 6.2f). And the interesting fact that Daniel and the other Jewish youths refuse the king's wine as well as the king's meat in Dan 1.8, 12, 16, will hardly explain the abstinence from wine on the part of the weak which is generally taken to be implied by what Paul says in 14.21. But perhaps (as is argued in the comment on 14.21) the reference to abstinence from wine should be understood as hypothetical rather than as indicating an actual characteristic of the weak.

In our view, then, the most probable explanation of the nature of the disagreement between the weak and the strong,

---

[1] See cols. 627ff, where he maintains that what Paul says to the strong about the weak is intended as a tactfully indirect rebuke to the weak designed to bring home to them the wrongness of their position.

to which this section refers, is that, whereas the strong had recognized that, now that He who is the goal and substance and innermost meaning of the OT law has come, the ceremonial part of it no longer requires to be literally obeyed, the weak felt strongly that a continuing concern with the literal obedience of the ceremonial law was an integral element of their response of faith to Jesus Christ, though their attitude was fundamentally different from that of the Judaizers of Galatians in that they did not think to put God under an obligation by their attempted obedience but only to express their faith.

One further matter can be more conveniently discussed here than in the course of the following verse by verse commentary —the problem presented by the use of πίστις and πιστεύειν in this section. In view of the way in which the verb is used in 14.2 and of the difficulties presented by 14.22f, we might wonder whether it would not be better to render πίστις in this section by some such word as 'assurance' or 'confidence' than by the word 'faith'. We might perhaps translate 14.2a: 'One man has confidence to eat all things' (cf. Demosthenes 30.7: προέσθαι δὲ τὴν προῖκ' οὐκ ἐπίστευσεν—'but he was not confident enough to abandon her marriage-portion').[1] In 14.22f to render πίστις by 'confidence' or 'assurance' would have the advantage of making it clear that Paul does not mean that one is to keep one's faith a secret between oneself and God or that every action which does not spring from faith (so every action of a non-Christian) is simply sin. But, while it is certainly possible in this way to bring out something of the sense and also to prevent some misunderstandings, it is probably preferable to keep to 'faith' and at the same time to underline the fact that in the Pauline epistles 'faith'[2] can have several distinct, though not completely unconnected, meanings, namely: (i) faith in the sense of *fides qua creditur*, the basic Pauline sense; (ii) miracle-working faith, a χάρισμα which only some believers receive; (iii) the assurance that one is permitted by one's faith (in the sense of *fides qua*) to do some particular thing; and, just possibly (this is a matter of dispute), also (iv) faith in the sense of *fides quae*,

[1] Other examples of πιστεύειν with the infinitive are cited by commentators in connexion with 14.2, as, e.g., Acts 15.11 (with which the use of the noun in Acts 14.9 should be compared); LXX Job 15.22; but they do not seem to be precisely parallel. Lietzmann cites 4 Macc 5.25 (reading καθιστάναι) which is nearer (but Rahlfs reads here καθεστάναι). The meaning given for πιστεύειν with the infinitive in LSJ, s.v., I.3, '*believe that, feel confident that* a thing is, will be, has been', seems unsuitable for Demosthenes 30.7, and is certainly unsuitable in Rom 14.2. We may also compare the use of θαρρεῖν with the infinitive (e.g. 2 Cor 5.8; Arrian, *Epict.* 3.22.96).

[2] The Greek can have a further sense, 'faithfulness'.

the faith', the body of doctrine believed.[1] In 14.2a πιστεύει
φαγεῖν means 'believes (or 'has the faith') to eat' in the sense
of 'has the assurance that his faith [i.e. his faith in the basic
sense] permits him to eat'. Similarly in 14.1 πίστις is 'faith' in
sense (iii). It is very likely that the strong tended to assume
that, because they were strong in faith in the sense listed above
as (iii), they must also be strong in faith in the basic Christian
sense of the word (sense (i)), and that their brethren who were
weak in faith in sense (iii) must also be weak in faith in sense (i).
But such easy assumptions would not have been justified.
While it is true that weakness in faith in sense (iii) will often—
perhaps always—have been an indication of a certain element
of weakness in faith in sense (i), it was no proof of a general
weakness in faith in sense (i); and it is quite clear from the
urgency of Paul's exhortation that many of those who were
strong in faith in sense (iii) were actually exceedingly weak in
basic Christian faith—so weak in it that they were prepared to
risk the spiritual ruin of a brother for whom Christ had died
for the sake of a mere plate of meat (14.15, 20).[2]

   [1]Him who is weak in faith receive, *but* not in order to pass judgments
on his scruples. [2]One man has the faith to eat any food, but he who is
weak eats *only* vegetables. [3]Let not him who eats despise him who
does not eat, and let not him who does not eat pass judgment on him
who eats, for God has received him. [4]Who art thou that passest
judgment on Another's house-slave? It is his own Lord whose concern
it is whether he stands or falls; and he shall stand, for his Lord has
the power to make him stand. [5]One man esteems one day more than
another, another man esteems every day *alike*. Let each be settled
in his own mind. [6]He who observes the day observes it to the Lord.
And he who eats eats to the Lord, for he gives thanks to God; while
he who abstains from eating abstains to the Lord, and gives thanks to
God *for his meatless meal*. [7]For none of us lives to himself, and none
dies to himself; [8]for, if we live, it is to the Lord that we live, and, if we
die, it is to the Lord that we die. Whether we live, then, or die, it is to
the Lord that we belong. [9]For it was for this purpose that Christ died
and lived *again*, namely, that he might become Lord both of the dead
and of the living. [10]But thou—why dost thou pass judgment on thy
brother? Or thou on the other side—why dost thou despise thy

[1] See Bauer, s.v. πίστις 3; R. Bultmann, in *TWNT* 6, p. 214.
[2] My grateful thanks are due to the Rev. Dr. Luděk Brož, the editor
of *Communio Viatorum,* for allowing me to incorporate in the above
introduction to section VII.7 material published in *CV* 17 (1974),
pp. 193ff ('Some observations on the interpretation of Rom 14.1–15.13').
On this section reference may be made to O. E. Evans, 'What God
requires of man—Rom 14.14', in *ET* 69 (1957–58), pp. 199–202;
J. Dupont, 'Appel aux faibles et aux forts dans la communauté romaine
(Rom 14.1–15.13)', in *Studiorum Paulinorum Congressus . . . Internationalis Catholicus* (1961) 1, Rome, 1963, pp. 357–66; P. S. Minear, *The
Obedience of Faith*, London, 1971.

brother? For we shall all of us stand before the judgment-seat of God. [11]For it is written: 'As I live, saith the Lord, to me shall every knee bend, And every tongue shall acclaim God'. [12]So [then] each one of us shall give account of himself [to God].

[13]So let us pass judgment on one another no more; but decide rather not to put a stumbling-block or an occasion of falling in your brother's way. [14]I know and am persuaded in the Lord Jesus that nothing is ritually unclean objectively; but if a man reckons something to be unclean, for him it is unclean. [15]For, if thy brother is grieved on account of *thy* food, thou walkest no longer in accordance with love. Do not by thy food destroy him for whom Christ died. [16]So let not thy good thing be reviled. [17]For the kingdom of God is not eating and drinking, but righteousness and peace and joy in the Holy Spirit; [18]for he who therein serves Christ is well-pleasing to God and deserves men's approval. [19]So then let us pursue what makes for peace and what makes for mutual edification. [20]Do not for the sake of *a particular* food destroy God's work. All things are indeed clean, but for the man who eats in such a way as results in the presence of a stumbling-block, it *(that is, his eating)* is evil. [21]It is a good thing to abstain from eating meat or drinking wine or *doing* anything else by which thy brother stumbles. [22]The faith which thou hast keep to thyself before God. Blessed is the man who does not condemn himself over what he approves. [23]But he who is troubled by doubts is condemned if he eats, because *he does* not *do so* from faith: and whatever is not from faith is sin.

[1]But we who are strong have an obligation to carry the infirmities of the weak and not to please ourselves. [2]Let each one of us please his neighbour for his good with a view to his edification. [3]For even Christ did not please himself; but, as scripture says, 'The reproaches of them that reproached thee fell upon me'. [4]For whatsoever things were written of old *in the scriptures* were written for our instruction, in order that with patient endurance and *strengthened* by the comfort which the scriptures give we might hold hope fast. [5]May the God *who is the source* of patient endurance and of comfort grant you to agree together among yourselves according to Christ Jesus, [6]in order that you may glorify the God and Father of our Lord Jesus Christ with one heart and one mouth.

[7]Wherefore receive one another, even as Christ also received us, to the glory of God. [8]For I declare that Christ has become the minister of the circumcision for the sake of God's faithfulness, in order to establish the promises made to the fathers, [9]but the Gentiles glorify God for his mercy, even as it is written in scripture, 'Wherefore I will praise thee among the Gentiles and sing hymns to thy name'; [10]and again it says, 'Rejoice, you Gentiles, together with his people'; [11]and again, 'Praise the Lord, all you Gentiles, and let all the peoples praise him'. [12]And again Isaiah says, 'There shall be the scion of Jesse, and he who rises to rule the Gentiles: on him shall the Gentiles hope'.

[13]May the God of hope fill you with all joy and peace in believing, so that you may abound in hope in the power of the Holy Spirit.

1. Τὸν δὲ ἀσθενοῦντα τῇ πίστει. The δέ marks the transition to a new section within the main division 12.1–15.13. Verbally τὸν ... ἀσθενοῦντα[1] τῇ πίστει recalls ἀσθενήσας τῇ πίστει in 4.19

---

[1] The singular is generic (cf. BDF, § 139), the reference being to any individual distinguished by the weakness in question.

(cf. διεκρίθη τῇ ἀπιστίᾳ in 4.20, with which ἐνεδυναμώθη τῇ πίστει, which bears a verbal similarity to the use of δυνατός in 15.1, stands in contrast); but what ἀσθενεῖν τῇ πίστει denoted in 4.19 is something very different from what it denotes here. In 4.19 the reference was to a weakening of faith in God, a failure to trust His promise in the face of adverse circumstances, but here in 14.1 the reference is to something less radical and less far-reaching in its effects. With τὸν . . . ἀσθενοῦντα τῇ πίστει here (also ὁ . . . ἀσθενῶν in v. 2 and τὰ ἀσθενήματα τῶν ἀδυνάτων in 15.1) compare the occurrences of ἀσθενής in 1 Cor 8.7, 9, 10; 9.22, and of ἀσθενεῖν in 1 Cor 8.11 and 12. The weakness in faith to which this chapter refers is not weakness in basic Christian faith but weakness in assurance that one's faith permits one to do certain things (cf. what was said about πίστις in the introduction to this section). That the use of the term 'weak' to be seen here and in 1 Corinthians 8 originated with those who disagreed with the persons so described is virtually certain. The weak will hardly have referred to themselves as 'the weak (in faith)'. Paul shares the assurance of the strong (so in 15.1—ἡμεῖς οἱ δυνατοί—he numbers himself among them), and so accepts, and makes use of, their application of the terms 'strong' and 'weak', as having at least a limited validity, while he disapproves of their unbrotherly insistence on expressing their inward freedom outwardly to the full, quite regardless of the effects on others.

προσλαμβάνεσθε is the fundamental imperative of this passage. It is the church as a whole which is addressed (no particularizing vocative is inserted), the implication being that the Christian community in Rome as a whole is strong and that the weak are a minority—most probably a fairly small minority. They are to accept the weak in faith, to receive them into their fellowship, recognizing them frankly and unreservedly as brothers in Christ. This προσλαμβάνεσθε[1] must surely include both the official recognition by the community, of which Michel thinks,[2] and also the brotherly acceptance in everyday intercourse suggested by Käsemann.[3]

μὴ εἰς διακρίσεις διαλογισμῶν introduces a qualification. The

---

[1] προσλαμβάνεσθαι is also used in v. 3, in 15.7 (twice) and in Philem 17: in addition to its five occurrences in the Pauline corpus, it occurs seven times in the rest of the NT (Mt 16.22; Mk 8.32; Acts 17.5; 18.26; 27.33, 36; 28.2). In the LXX it is used of God's gracious acceptance of men (1 Sam 12.22; Ps 18.16[LXX: 17.17]; 27[LXX: 26].10; 65[LXX: 64].4; 73[LXX: 72].24), and also twice with a human subject (2 Macc 8.1; 10.15) and once with πονηρία as its subject (Wisd 17.11[LXX: 10])).

[2] p. 335f.

[3] p. 351.

words are patient of a very wide variety of interpretations,[1] since both substantives can have several different meanings (διάκρισις can mean 'distinguishing', 'judging', 'decision', 'dispute'; διαλογισμός can mean 'reasoning', 'thought', 'opinion', 'doubt', 'scruple') and the genitive might be either objective or (as is presupposed by the text of the AV and RV) adjectival. But the context would seem to tell in favour of taking διάκρισις in the sense 'judging', 'passing judgment on', and this would necessitate understanding the genitive as objective. In the context the most likely meaning for διαλογισμός would seem to be 'scruple'. They are not to stultify their brotherly acceptance of the man who is weak in faith by proceeding to pass judgment on his scruples.[2]

2. ὃς μὲν πιστεύει φαγεῖν πάντα, ὁ δὲ ἀσθενῶν λάχανα ἐσθίει.[3] For the change of construction (ὁ δὲ ἀσθενῶν is no doubt to be understood as 'but he who is weak' and not as 'another, being weak')[4] Sanday and Headlam compare 1 Cor 12.8–10; Mk 4.4; Lk 8.5. On πιστεύει and also on the substance of this verse, which describes the strong and the weak with whose relations to each other Paul is concerned in this section, see above (pp. 690–98). With λάχανα (cf. Gen 9.3; 1 Kgs 21[LXX: 20].2; Ps 37[LXX: 36].2; Prov 15.17) understand μόνον.

3. ὁ ἐσθίων τὸν μὴ ἐσθίοντα μὴ ἐξουθενείτω, ὁ δὲ[5] **μὴ ἐσθίων τὸν ἐσθίοντα μὴ κρινέτω.** The choice of the verbs ἐξουθενεῖν and

---

[1] e.g. 'but (RV: 'yet') not to doubtful disputations' (AV and RV text); 'but not to judge his doubtful thoughts' (AV margin); 'yet not for decisions of doubts' (RV margin); 'but not to pass judgments on their thoughts' (Sanday and Headlam, p. 384); 'but not for the purpose of passing judgment on his scruples' (Moffatt); 'but not for disputes over opinions' (RSV); 'and do not take him in simply for discussions of his scruples' (Barrett, p. 255); 'without attempting to settle doubtful points' (NEB); 'without starting an argument' (JB).

[2] It is surely rather more natural (*pace* Käsemann, p. 351, *et al.*) to take διακρίσεις as used with reference to actions of which only the people to whom the imperative προσλαμβάνεσθε is addressed (i.e. the strong majority) would be the subjects than to suppose that it is used with reference to actions which would be the actions of both the strong and the weak alike.

[3] The variant ἐσθιέτω (𝔓46 D* G lat Ephr) is perhaps to be explained as assimilation to ἐξουθενείτω and κρινέτω in the next verse, or else as a modification reflecting the antipathy felt in some church circles towards those who were understood to be the group to whom Paul was referring. That ἐσθίει must be read is not to be doubted.

[4] *Pace* Käsemann, p. 349 ('Der andere isst als Schwacher . . .').

[5] The reading ὁ δέ should probably be preferred both as having strong support in 𝔓46 ℵ D* Cl and also as the more difficult reading—the variant καὶ ὁ (K pl) would be a very obvious improvement. That the reading ὁ δέ is an accidental assimilation to the ὁ δέ of v. 2 would seem less likely.

κρίνειν is significant; for in the situation which Paul envisages, in which the eaters (i.e., those who eat all things) are the great majority, the non-eaters (i.e., those who abstain from meat) a small minority, the eaters would be liable to despise the non-eaters as not worth taking seriously, while the non-eaters would be prone to adopt a censorious attitude to the eaters.[1]

ὁ θεὸς γὰρ αὐτὸν προσελάβετο states the all-important reason why the non-eater must not pass judgment on the eater: God Himself has received the eater into His fellowship. For a believer to presume to pass judgment on one whom God has thus received clearly cannot be right. While it is certainly true that Paul believed that God had also received the non-eater in the same way (cf. 15.7, where the ἡμᾶς, which is the object of Χριστὸς προσελάβετο, includes strong and weak alike), to state, as Käsemann does,[2] that the last clause of v. 3 refers in principle to both groups (those who eat and those who abstain) is to take an unjustifiable liberty with the text; for αὐτόν can properly be taken to refer only to the eater (τὸν ἐσθίοντα). At this particular point (as also in v. 4) Paul directs his exhortation to the weak: he will presently bring the full weight of his exhortation to bear on the strong.

4. σὺ τίς εἶ ὁ κρίνων ἀλλότριον οἰκέτην; For the use of the second person singular see on 2.1 (ἀναπολόγητος εἶ, κ.τ.λ.) and for the general form of the question compare 9.20a. In view of the link with ὁ δὲ μὴ ἐσθίων τὸν ἐσθίοντα μὴ κρινέτω in v. 3 constituted by the use here of κρίνειν, it is natural to assume that it is the representative of those who abstain from eating meat who is here being addressed. The abstainer, who is passing judgment on his fellow-Christian who does not abstain, is challenged to consider who he himself is who thus presumes to pass judgment on someone who, like himself, is a household-slave of Christ (or of God)[3] and therefore only answerable to

---

[1] Cf. Pelagius, p. 107: 'illi istos quasi carnales iudicabant, et isti illos tamquam stultos inridebant et superstitiosos putabant'.

[2] p. 353.

[3] It is not easy to decide whether Paul had Christ or God in mind here. The last clause of v. 3 may be adduced in support of the view that he was thinking of God: on the other hand, v. 9 makes it necessary to understand the repeated τῷ κυρίῳ of v. 8 to refer to Christ. But anyway Paul is inclined in this passage to oscillate between references to God and to Christ (this is to be seen, at any rate, in vv. 6–10, where we have τῷ θεῷ—Χριστός—τοῦ θεοῦ), though the textual tradition shows traces of a tendency to try to tidy matters up (thus in v. 4 there is a variant θεός for κύριος, and in v. 10 a variant Χριστοῦ for θεοῦ. The view that the master indicated by the use of ἀλλότριον is just a human master (the question being an appeal to ordinary practice) seems less likely.

Him (according to ordinary human law governing slavery the
household-slave was answerable solely to his master). The point
made by ἀλλότριον is not, of course, that the strong Christian
belongs to a master other than the one to whom the weak
Christian belongs, but that he belongs to a master other than
the weak Christian—he is not the weak Christian's slave, but
Another's, i.e., Christ's (or God's), and therefore not answerable
to the weak Christian.

τῷ ἰδίῳ κυρίῳ στήκει ἢ πίπτει. The first three words of this
sentence are often understood to mean 'by his own Master's
decision', and the last three to refer to God's judgment (whether
present or eschatological). Thus Calvin, for example, comments: 'This means that the Lord properly has the power either
to disapprove or to accept the action of His servant. Those who
attempt to seize this power to themselves are offending against
Him';[1] and similarly Barrett ('his master, not his fellow-
Christian, determines the acceptability of his service')[2] and
W. Grundmann ('das heisst, dass der Herr über Stehen oder
Fallen seines Verwalters die letzte Entscheidung hat, nicht aber
Menschen').[3] But it is very doubtful whether the dative can
bear the sense which these interpreters put on it. The explanation of it as an example of the dative of advantage and disadvantage is much more likely to be right.[4] On this view the
meaning of the sentence is that it is his own Master whose
interest is involved, who is concerned, in his standing or falling.
The metaphor of standing or falling could still perhaps just
conceivably be explained as referring to the divine judgment,[5]
but is much more naturally understood as denoting persever-
ance in, or falling away from, faith and obedience.[6] Christ (or
God) Himself is concerned, His interest is at stake, in the
question whether the strong Christian continues in faith or falls
away from it.

σταθήσεται δέ: 'and he shall stand'.[7] To take the verb to
mean 'he shall be made to stand' (i.e., made to continue standing) yields a less satisfactory progression of thought from
στήκει ἢ πίπτει to δυνατεῖ γάρ, κ.τ.λ., there being much less

[1] p. 291.
[2] p. 258.
[3] in *TWNT* 7, p. 637.
[4] Cf. BDF, § 188 (2); also, e.g., Denney, p. 701; Lagrange, p. 324;
Michel, p. 337.
[5] For the metaphorical use of 'stand' to denote acceptance in the
divine judgment we may refer to Ps 130 [LXX: 129].3; Mal 3.2; Rev 6.17.
[6] Cf. 11.20, 22; 1 Cor 10.12; 16.13; Gal 5.1; Phil 1.27; 4.1; 1 Th 3.8;
2 Th 2.15.
[7] Cf. Bauer, s.v. ἵστημι, II.1.d.

point to the last clause of the verse if the thought of the divine action denoted by στῆσαι is already present in σταθήσεται. The other translation which has been suggested, namely, 'he shall be raised up' (i.e., raised up again after having fallen),[1] is surely even less likely to be right; for it involves reading into the text the thought that the strong brother actually does fall, which cannot at all plausibly be said to be implicit in it. According to the translation accepted above, σταθήσεται δέ is a confident affirmation made on the basis of the preceding statement of the divine concern.

δυνατεῖ γὰρ[2] ὁ κύριος[3] στῆσαι αὐτόν is added in confirmation of the promise just made: the certainty of the promise rests not on the strong Christian's ability to stand but on the Lord's ability to make him stand.

5. ὃς μὲν [γὰρ] κρίνει ἡμέραν παρ' ἡμέραν, ὃς δὲ κρίνει πᾶσαν ἡμέραν. Zahn defends the appropriateness of γάρ here, while admitting that it may perhaps be a gloss, on the ground that vv. 5 and 6 cite another example of lack of uniformity in Christian practice, one recognized as permissible, and so afford support for the view that the lack of uniformity indicated in v. 2 is allowable.[4] But Zahn's explanation of the connexion of thought between v. 5f and what precedes it is scarcely convincing. It seems better to assume that Paul is simply introducing another example of the controversy between the strong and the weak. We should probably decide that γάρ is not original. While it does have quite strong support in 𝕭 al lat, there is rather stronger support for its omission (𝔓46 B 𝕶 D G pm sy). It could perhaps have been added by mistake because of the γάρ following δυνατεῖ in the previous verse, or it could just conceivably be a gloss originating with someone who understood a connexion of thought along some such lines as Zahn suggested. The words κρίνει ἡμέραν παρ' ἡμέραν must mean 'prefers one day to another', 'esteems one day more than another'.[5] Being contrasted with κρίνει ἡμέραν παρ' ἡμέραν, the

---

[1] So Kühl, p. 449, who connects this statement specially closely with the preceding πίπτει. On this view στῆσαι in the following sentence will of course mean 'raise up'.

[2] The variants δυνατὸς γάρ and δυνατὸς γάρ ἐστιν are understandable as examples of the substitution of a familiar expression for an unfamiliar. On δυνατεῖν, which occurs in the Greek Bible only here and in 2 Cor 9.8; 13.3 (LSJ also cites an occurrence in the first century B.C. writer Philodemus) see BDF, § 108 (2).

[3] The variant θεός is assimilation to v. 3.

[4] p. 573. He was followed by Barth, 1933, p. 510.

[5] For κρίνειν meaning 'choose', 'prefer', cf. Plato, R.399e (. . . κρίνοντες τὸν Ἀπόλλω καὶ τὰ τοῦ Ἀπόλλωνος ὄργανα πρὸ Μαρσύου τε καὶ τῶν ἐκείνου ὀργάνων); Phlb.57e (. . . εἴ τινα πρὸ αὐτῆς ἄλλην κρίναιμεν); and for παρά

words κρίνει πᾶσαν ἡμέραν can only mean 'esteems every day alike', 'makes no difference between days'.

As to the nature of this disagreement about days to which Paul refers various suggestions have been made: that it was closely connected with the disagreement about foods referred to in v. 2 and related to the observance of particular days as days of abstinence (this was the view generally taken by ancient interpreters, and it has been maintained in modern times by, for example, Weiss, Lagrange, Gaugler, Leenhardt); that it had to do with the observance of the special days of the OT ceremonial law (possibly also with the change from Sabbath to Lord's Day); that it had to do with the distinguishing of lucky and unlucky days. Of these suggestions the last is surely to be rejected,[1] on the ground that, had this been the reference, Paul would have shown his own attitude unambiguously (there can be no shadow of doubt as to what his attitude must have been to such superstition).[2] We have already indicated (in the introduction to this section) our preference for the second suggestion.

ἕκαστος ἐν τῷ ἰδίῳ νοῖ πληροφορείσθω is a rule applying equally to every member of the church. In this area of disagreement between the strong and the weak, in which equally sincere Christians may feel constrained by their faith to take, and follow out in practice, opposite decisions, each[3] is to seek to be as settled as possible in his own mind, using his own powers of reasoning which have at least begun to be renewed by the gospel[4] to form his own judgment as to what course of action obedience to the gospel requires of him, in responsible independence, neither ignoring, nor yet showing undue deference to, the opinions of his fellows. This is not an injunction to cultivate a closed mind, which refuses all further discussion, but an injunction to resist the temptation (to which those whom Paul calls 'weak' were no doubt particularly liable) to luxuriate in indecision and vacillation and to allow himself to be so preoccupied with balancing again and again the opposing arguments in what are anyway not the essential issues, that he is quite incapacitated for resolute and courageous action. It is a reminder to each member that, whether his faith leads him to

meaning 'more than' compare 1.25; 12.3; Lk 13.2, 4; and see further BDF, § 236 (3).
[1] *pace* Käsemann, p. 354.
[2] Cf. Michel, p. 338.
[3] Cf. v. 12; also 2.6; 12.3; 15.2. It is noticeable that the word ἕκαστος is specially frequent in 1 Corinthians (twenty-two times).
[4] Cf. 12.2.

adopt the practice of the strong or the practice of the weak, it can, and must be allowed to, set him free for an obedience which (according to his own particular way of faith) is firm, decisive, resolute, courageous, joyful.[1]

6. ὁ φρονῶν τὴν ἡμέραν κυρίῳ φρονεῖ. The Christian who is concerned about, pays regard to, observes, the day (cf. ὃς ... κρίνει ἡμέραν παρ᾽ ἡμέραν in v. 5) observes it 'to the Lord', that is, with the intention and desire of serving the Lord by so doing. This dative, like that in v. 4, is best explained as a dative of advantage.[2] The variant which adds καὶ ὁ μὴ φρονῶν τὴν ἡμέραν κυρίῳ οὐ φρονεῖ after φρονεῖ (𝕮 33 *pl* sy) is no doubt due to a natural feeling that a pair of sentences referring to the question of special days is required to balance the pair of sentences concerned with eating and not eating; but the person responsible for the addition did not properly grasp Paul's thought, for the two positive sentences (ὁ φρονῶν, κ.τ.λ. and ὁ ἐσθίων, κ.τ.λ.) do not correspond, since the former refers to a weak Christian, while the latter refers to a strong one.

καὶ[3] ὁ ἐσθίων κυρίῳ ἐσθίει, εὐχαριστεῖ γὰρ τῷ θεῷ. With his previous statement about the weak Christian who observes days Paul couples this statement concerning the strong Christian who eats all things, in order to make the point that both alike do what they do with the intention of serving the Lord. That the strong Christian does so is shown by the fact that he renders thanks to God for what he eats. The point Paul wishes to make here has now been made; but it seems that he felt that in what he had just said he had given the strong an advantage over the weak, since it had been only with regard to the former that he had mentioned the giving of thanks to God, and so added **καὶ ὁ μὴ ἐσθίων κυρίῳ οὐκ ἐσθίει, καὶ εὐχαριστεῖ τῷ θεῷ** in order to restore the balance.[4] It is also with the intention of serving the Lord that the Christian who abstains from meat abstains, as is demonstrated[5] by the fact that he

---

[1] On πληροφορεῖν see further on 4.21; also G. Delling, in *TWNT* 6, p. 307f.

[2] This is better than explaining it as equivalent to Hebrew *lipnê*.

[3] The omission of καί (𝕻⁴⁶ *pc*) would appear to be a tidying up after the addition of ὁ μὴ φρονῶν, κ.τ.λ., which makes it superfluous. The fact that many MSS. which have the additional sentence also have the superfluous καί is a strong indication that the additional sentence is not original.

[4] Cf. Lagrange, p. 325.

[5] The change from εὐχαριστεῖ γάρ in the previous sentence to καὶ εὐχαριστεῖ here is surely just a stylistic variation. The suggestion that καί should be understood to have an adversative force ('and yet') is unlikely.

gives thanks to God for his meatless meal[1] just as truly as his fellow-Christian does for the meat he enjoys.

7–9. οὐδεὶς γὰρ ἡμῶν ἑαυτῷ ζῇ, καὶ οὐδεὶς ἑαυτῷ ἀποθνῄσκει· ἐάν τε γὰρ ζῶμεν, τῷ κυρίῳ ζῶμεν, ἐάν τε ἀποθνῄσκωμεν, τῷ κυρίῳ ἀποθνῄσκομεν.[2] The first γάρ indicates that the purpose of vv. 7–9 (for these three verses are to be taken closely together) is to support what has been said in v. 6. That both weak and strong alike do what they do, as they follow their different ways, as service of the Lord, is necessarily true, since no Christian at all (ἡμῶν must mean 'of us Christians', not 'of us men') lives or dies 'to himself', that is, with no other object in view than his own gratification,[3] for, in fact,[4] all Christians live 'to the Lord', that is, they live with the object of pleasing Christ, they seek to use their lives in His service, and, when it comes to dying, they glorify Him by committing themselves to His keeping.[5]

ἐάν τε οὖν ζῶμεν ἐάν τε ἀποθνῄσκωμεν, τοῦ κυρίου ἐσμέν states in a summary form the underlying theological truth. This is why we live and die τῷ κυρίῳ—because we belong to Him both in life and in death. This theological statement is then supported by v. 9.

[1] The comment of F. A. Philippi ('But the thanks are given neither for *what* he eats not, which were absurd, nor *that* he eats not, which were Pharisaic (Luke xviii.1), but for what he eats, namely vegetable food'), quoted by Murray 2, p. 179, is of course true.

[2] The variant ἀποθνῄσκωμεν (ℵ C L *pm*), which involves taking the second ζῶμεν as subjunctive as well, reflects (cf. Käsemann, p. 356) someone's desire for a touch of edifying exhortation at this point.

[3] The expression 'live to oneself' is used both in Greek and in Latin of living selfishly, caring only for one's own interest and comfort: e.g. Terence, *Ad.* 863–65 ('ille suam egit semper vitam in otio, in conviviis, . . . sibi vixit, sibi sumptum fecit'); Plutarch, *Cleom.* 31 (αἰσχρὸν γὰρ ζῆν μόνοις ἑαυτοῖς καὶ ἀποθνῄσκειν). Paul's use of ἑαυτῷ ζῆν and ἑαυτῷ ἀποθνῄσκειν resembles Plutarch's. The interpretation which is often put on v. 7, which sees it as a statement of a general principle applying to all men, namely, the principle of—to use Barclay's phrase—'the impossibility of isolation' (e.g. Barclay, p. 202: 'Here Paul lays down the great fact that it is impossible in the nature of things to live an isolated life. There is no such thing in this world as a completely detached individual. . . . No man can disentangle himself either from his fellow men or from God') is to be rejected. It ignores the function of this verse and its immediate sequel in Paul's argument. That 'no man is an island' (profound truth though it is) is no proof of the point Paul has made in v. 6.

[4] The probable explanation of the γάρ at the beginning of v. 8 (where an adversative conjunction might perhaps seem rather more natural) is that the positive statement in v. 8a is felt to be an elucidation of the negative statement in v. 7.

[5] For the general line of interpretation followed in this sentence cf. Lagrange, p. 325f.

εἰς τοῦτο γὰρ Χριστὸς ἀπέθανεν καὶ ἔζησεν,[1] ἵνα καὶ νεκρῶν καὶ ζώντων κυριεύσῃ. It was for this very purpose that Christ died and rose again (ἔζησεν, coming after ἀπέθανεν, must refer to the resurrection, not the earthly life, of Christ: the aorist is to be explained as ingressive[2]—'came to life'), namely, that He might become Lord[3] of both the dead and the living.[4] Barrett rightly rejects the proposal that v. 9 should be analysed into two parallel statements (that Christ died in order that He might become Lord of the dead, and that He came to life in order that He might become Lord of the living).[5] Christ's death and resurrection are not to be separated in this way. They are essentially one complex event; and both Christ's being Lord of the dead and His being Lord of the living equally depend on both His death and His resurrection. With regard to the question of whose purpose it is that is denoted by the ἵνα-clause, Denney, on the one hand, has stated quite definitely that it is 'God's purpose in subjecting His Son to this experience',[6] and Murray, on the other hand, speaks of 'the purpose Christ had in

---

[1] There is considerably more variation in the textual tradition here than the Nestle apparatus shows. Reference should be made to the fuller apparatus for v. 9 in UBS. The καί placed immediately after Χριστός (𝕂 al) looks like an attempted improvement (cf. the καί = 'both' before νεκρῶν later in the verse), and need not detain us. There is little doubt that ἀπέθανεν καὶ ἔζησεν (𝕭 pc arm) is original (the use of ἀποθνῄσκειν and ζῆν here is probably intentionally reminiscent of the repeated use of these two verbs in vv. 7 and 8). The substitution of ἀνέστη (cf. ἀπέθανεν καὶ ἀνέστη in 1 Th 4.14) for the rather difficult ἔζησεν (G lat Or) would be a very obvious clarifying improvement. The emergence of a three-verb form of the text is easily explicable as due to the conflation of the original ἔζησεν and the variant ἀνέστη. But the textual tradition presents us not just with one three-verb form but with several, the problematic ἔζησεν appearing as a floating member placed in various positions, apparently according to the way in which it was understood. Thus, understood in connexion with the Resurrection, it is found before ἀνέστη (1962) and after it (𝕂 pm)—sometimes improved into the compound ἀνέζησεν. It also appears as the first of the three verbs (D* c d* e Ir^lat), the addition of ἀνέστη which could cover the Resurrection making it possible to take ἔζησεν to refer to the earthly life of Christ.

[2] Cf. BDF, § 331.

[3] The aorist subjunctive κυριεύσῃ is best understood as having an ingressive sense.

[4] The unexpected order of καὶ νεκρῶν καὶ ζώντων may be due either to the influence of the preceding ἀπέθανεν καὶ ἔζησεν (which had to be in that order) or to a desire for a chiasmus with ἐάν τε ... ζῶμεν ἐάν τε ἀποθνῄσκωμεν in the previous sentence. The suggestion (Leenhardt, p. 359) that it is to be explained by 2 Cor 5.14f and Rom 6.11 is not very likely, for in the present verse 'dead' and 'living' surely have their ordinary meanings.

[5] p. 260.

[6] p. 703.

view in dying and rising again'.[1] We shall probably best do justice to Paul's thought, if we refuse to be forced into making an exclusive choice between these alternatives.[2] As to the meaning of κυριεύειν as used in this verse, it will be enough here to refer to the notes on 1.4 (τοῦ κυρίου ἡμῶν) and 10.9 and to pp. 838–39, adding merely that what Paul is here particularly interested in is the relational aspect of Christ's lordship, His securing and exercising lordship over men.

10. σὺ δὲ τί κρίνεις τὸν ἀδελφόν σου; ἢ καὶ σὺ τί ἐξουθενεῖς τὸν ἀδελφόν σου; With these reproachful questions Paul takes up again the thought of v. 3, addressing first the individual weak Christian and then the individual strong Christian (the order is the opposite of that in v. 3).[3] In the light of the fact (affirmed in v. 6 and supported by the weighty argument of vv. 7–9) that the strong and the weak alike follow their differing ways with the intention of serving Christ, how can the weak Christian presume to set himself up to judge his strong brother, or the strong Christian dare to despise his weak brother? It is to be noted that Paul strengthens his appeal by using in both questions the word ἀδελφός, which he has not used since 12.1: it is yet one more reminder that the member of the other group, in spite of his different ideas and different practice, is in the fullest sense a fellow-believer, one who belongs altogether to the same Lord.

πάντες γὰρ παραστησόμεθα τῷ βήματι τοῦ θεοῦ[4] is added in support of the reproaches of the former part of the verse. The remembrance that all Christians will have to stand[5] before the judgment-seat of God is a powerful dissuasive from all sitting in judgment on one's fellows.

---

[1] 2, p. 182.

[2] Paul can certainly speak of both the death and the resurrection of Christ as God's action (see, e.g., 4.25, where the passive is used of the death as well as of the resurrection; and cf. 8.32 with reference to the death, and 4.24 with reference to the resurrection); and, in so far as he thought of Christ's death and resurrection as God's act, he will naturally have thought of the purpose they were to achieve as God's purpose. But he can also speak of Christ's death as Christ's own deliberate act (e.g. Gal 1.4; 2.20b). Can we exclude the possibility that he thought of a purpose of Christ Himself not only in relation to His death (cf. Gal 1.4 —ὅπως ἐξέληται, κ.τ.λ.) but in relation to the whole complex event of His death and its sequel?

[3] For the use of the second person singular cf. v. 4.

[4] The variant Χριστοῦ (𝔎 pl vg^cl sy Polyc Mcion) may well be assimilation to 2 Cor 5.10. Origen, col. 1243, notes that Paul speaks here of the 'tribunal Dei', but in writing to the Corinthians, refers to the 'tribunal Christi'.

[5] On the use of παριστάναι as a forensic technical term see Bauer, s.v. παρίστημι 1.e and 2.a.α.

11. γέγραπται γάρ· ζῶ ἐγώ, λέγει κύριος, ὅτι ἐμοὶ κάμψει πᾶν γόνυ, καὶ πᾶσα γλῶσσα ἐξομολογήσεται τῷ θεῷ adds a scriptural quotation in support of the last sentence of v. 10. From ὅτι onwards the quotation follows exactly the latter part of the LXX text of Isa 45.23 as printed by Rahlfs[1] apart from the transposition of ἐξομολογήσεται and πᾶσα γλῶσσα. But Paul has placed before these words a formula which occurs in Isa 49.18 (and in a number of other places, e.g. Num 14.28; Jer 22.24; Ezek 5.11) and not the κατ' ἐμαυτοῦ ὀμνύω with which Isa 45.23 begins. According to Black, Paul has done this 'with the clear intention of identifying "the Lord" in the quotation with the Lord Christ who "lived again" (verse 9 . . .), and is the Lord both of the dead and of the living (verse 9). It is to the Risen and Living Lord that every knee shall bow'.[2] But it is by no means clear that this was Paul's intention; for v. 11 is naturally understood as meant to support not v. 9 but the last sentence of v. 10, and, since this speaks of standing before *God's* judgment-throne (Black himself[3] apparently accepts the reading θεοῦ in v. 10), it is surely much more likely that Paul was thinking of ἐμοί in his quotation, and therefore also ἐγώ and κύριος, as referring to God than that he was identifying the κύριος of the quotation with Christ. It is anyway difficult to separate ἐμοί and κύριος from the τῷ θεῷ at the end of the quotation. (It is true, of course, that Isa 45.23 is quoted with reference to Christ in Phil 2.10f; but it is significant that in Phil 2.11 there is no τῷ θεῷ with ἐξομολογήσηται.) In spite of the verbal link between ζῶ ἐγώ, in v. 11 and ἔζησεν in v. 9, to which Black appeals, the most probable explanation of Paul's substitution of ζῶ ἐγώ, λέγει κύριος for κατ' ἐμαυτοῦ ὀμνύω is that, quoting from memory, he inadvertently replaced one OT divine asseverative formula by another perhaps slightly more familiar. We conclude that Paul understood the words of the quotation as a solemn affirmation that at the last every individual man shall do homage to God as Sovereign and Judge of all, and every human tongue acclaim Him;[4] and, so understood, the quotation is support for v. 10c.

[1] M. Black, 'The Christological Use of the Old Testament in the New Testament', in *NTS* 18 (1971–72), p. 8, may well be right in thinking that in Isa 45.23 ὀμεῖται and τὸν θεόν should be read in place of ἐξομολογήσεται and τῷ θεῷ.

[2] p. 167: cf. the article cited in the previous note, p. 8.

[3] p. 167f.

[4] In the echo of Isa 45.23 in Phil 2.11 ἐξομολογεῖσθαι is used without an accompanying dative but with a following ὅτι and has the sense 'confess', 'acknowledge'. Here in Rom 14.11 some (e.g. Michel, in *TWNT* 5, p. 215; Manson, p. 951) understand it to mean 'confess' in the sense of

12. ἄρα [οὖν]¹ ἕκαστος ἡμῶν περὶ ἑαυτοῦ λόγον δώσει² [τῷ θεῷ]³ is
a hortatory conclusion drawn from the foregoing OT quotation:
it reiterates the thought of v. 10c. Denney was probably right
to insist that ἕκαστος, περὶ ἑαυτοῦ, λόγον δώσει and τῷ θεῷ
are all emphatic.⁴ Each one of us (that is, each individual
Christian) will indeed have to give account: none will be
exempted. He will have to give account of himself (his fellow-
Christian, who may be very ready now to interfere with him
where he has no right to interfere, will not be able to answer
in his stead then). And it will be to God, not to men, that he
will have to give his account of himself.

13. Μηκέτι οὖν ἀλλήλους κρίνωμεν sums up succinctly the
exhortation of the preceding paragraph. It may also be seen as
the conclusion to be drawn from what has been said in vv. 10c–
12. It is best understood as addressed to both strong and weak
alike.⁵

ἀλλὰ τοῦτο κρίνατε μᾶλλον, τὸ μὴ τιθέναι πρόσκομμα τῷ ἀδελφῷ
ἢ σκάνδαλον is directed to the strong.⁶ The RV preserves the

confessing sins. But, while v. 12 might seem to afford support for this
interpretation (and Lagrange's objection that the idea of confession of
sins 'ne s'appliquerait qu'aux pécheurs' (p. 327) need not discourage us,
for Paul surely believed all men to be sinners), it is much more likely
that the word has, as in 15.9, the meaning 'praise' or 'acclaim', which is
its characteristic LXX meaning.

¹ οὖν, attested by ℵ 𝔎 pl, is omitted by B D* G 1739. The question
whether it should be read or not can hardly be answered with confidence.
The omission could perhaps be accidental in origin. Pauline usage will
not decide the matter, since Paul, while he often uses ἄρα οὖν, uses also
simple ἄρα, sometimes placing it as the second word of the sentence (in
accordance with classical usage), as in 7.21, and sometimes putting it
as the first word (contrary to classical usage), as in 10.17. See BDF, § 451
(2).

² The reading ἀποδώσει is very probably an attempted improvement of
an original δώσει.

³ τῷ θεῷ, attested by ℵ 𝔎 D pl lat, but omitted by B G 1739 it, must
be at any rate slightly in doubt; but its originality is highly probable.
The reading which omits τῷ θεῷ is undoubtedly the more difficult; but
we are inclined to think that this is a case where we should pay more
heed to the argument from intrinsic probability than to the principle
of difficilior lectio potior (here intrinsic probability is surely strongly in
favour of accepting the longer reading, for, without τῷ θεῷ, the sentence
is most unsatisfactory as the conclusion to the paragraph, although
there can be no doubt about Paul's meaning).

⁴ p. 704.

⁵ In vv. 3, 4, 10 κρίνειν was specially used to denote the censorious
attitude of the weak; but, in view of the content of v. 13b and of
vv. 14 and 15, Paul can hardly mean his exhortation in v. 13a for the
weak alone. On the other hand, it does not seem likely (pace Murray 2,
p. 187) that v. 13a is addressed only to the strong.

⁶ Whether or not we allow (with Murray 2, p. 187) the possibility of
the weak brother's being in a position to place a stumbling-block in the

word-play (κρίνωμεν — κρίνατε) by rendering κρίνατε 'judge ye';
but this hardly brings out the sense which κρίνειν has here,
which is 'decide', 'determine' (cf. 1 Cor 2.2; 7.37; 2 Cor 2.1;
and see Bauer, s.v. κρίνω 3). μᾶλλον has an adversative force
here—'instead'. On πρόσκομμα[1] and σκάνδαλον see on 9.32 and
33. In this second part of the verse Paul turns to a fresh
aspect of the subject under discussion, namely, the effect one's
conduct may have on one's brother, in particular, the effect
which the exercise by the strong of the liberty he himself
possesses may have on the weak. The possibility that here
and also in v. 20f Paul may be indebted to the tradition of
Jesus' teaching (cf. Mt 18.6–7; Mk 9.42; Lk 17.1–2) should be
recognized.

14. οἶδα καὶ πέπεισμαι ἐν κυρίῳ Ἰησοῦ is strikingly emphatic.
The first person (singular in the first two cases and plural in
the third) of the strong perfect active of πείθειν is used in
combination with ἐν κυρίῳ and with a following ὅτι-clause in
Gal 5.10 (with εἰς ὑμᾶς), in Phil 2.24 and in 2 Th 3.4 (with
ἐφ' ὑμᾶς); but here in Rom 14.14 the first person singular of
the perfect passive of the same verb is employed,[2] and it is
strengthened by being preceded by οἶδα καί, and Ἰησοῦ is
added to the following ἐν κυρίῳ. That great weight is being
given to the content of the ὅτι-clause is not to be doubted.[3] By
the words ἐν κυρίῳ Ἰησοῦ Paul may perhaps have meant simply
that what he was about to say was an insight derived from his
fellowship with the risen and exalted Christ or—more generally
—that it was consonant with God's self-revelation in Jesus
Christ as a whole, that is, with the gospel, or that his certainty
of its truth rested on the authority of the risen and exalted
Christ; but we certainly cannot rule out the possibility that
he had in mind some specific teaching of the historic Jesus (the
use here of the personal name Ἰησοῦς could be, as has been

way of the strong, it is quite clear that vv. 14 and 15 are so closely
related to v. 13b that the reference of v. 13b must be to what the strong
are certainly in a position to do to the weak.

[1] B syp Ephr omit πρόσκομμα and ἤ; but the longer reading is here
more likely to be original. It is πρόσκομμα that is picked up later in the
paragraph (διὰ προσκόμματος in v. 20 and προσκόπτει in v. 21).

[2] For πέπεισμαι cf. 8.38; 15.14; 2 Tim 1.5, 12.

[3] The possibility of placing a comma instead of a colon after ἑαυτοῦ
and taking the whole of the latter part of v. 14 as dependent on the ὅτι
should perhaps be mentioned; but it is not at all probable, for, while it
is certainly true that the authority of Christ could be claimed for
Paul's insistence in the rest of this chapter on the limitations which love
imposes on the Christian's right to exercise his freedom, Paul's concern
just at this point is surely to make quite clear his own full acceptance
of the principle that οὐδὲν κοινὸν δι' ἑαυτοῦ.

suggested,[1] a pointer to the presence of such a reference), and
the evidence of Mk 7.15–23 and Mt 15.10–11, 15–20, has, of
course, to be considered.[2]

ὅτι οὐδὲν κοινὸν δι' ἑαυτοῦ is the truth, his acceptance of which
Paul has stated so emphatically. The words need to be ex-
amined closely. δι' ἑαυτοῦ must here mean 'in itself'—so we
may render it 'objectively'.[3] But Paul certainly did not mean
that he was convinced that nothing is objectively unclean (the
sense of the verse as a whole is not that 'there is nothing either
good or bad' morally, 'but thinking makes it so').[4] Pelagius's
use of *creatura* in his comment on v. 20 ('Repetit quod prius
dixerat, ne creaturam damnare uideatur')[5] provides a useful
clue to Paul's intention. He is not thinking of men's actions,
attitudes, desires, thoughts, etc., but only of the resources of
the created world which are available for men's use. Thus
οὐδέν is used in a restricted sense. The word κοινός too has a
special significance. It is not used here in its ordinary sense,
but as equivalent to the Hebrew *ṭāmē* (cf. 1 Macc 1.47, 62;
Mark 7.2; Acts 10.14, 28; 11.8): its meaning here is 'ritually
unclean'.[6] The point Paul is making in the first half of this
verse is essentially the same as that made in Mk 7.15a.[7] He is
indicating his own agreement with the basic position of the
strong, namely, that the fact that Christ's work has now been
accomplished has radically transformed the situation with
regard to the ceremonial part of the OT law: now it is no longer
obligatory to obey it literally—one obeys it by believing in
Him to whom it bears witness.

εἰ μὴ[8] τῷ λογιζομένῳ τι κοινὸν εἶναι, ἐκείνῳ κοινόν. While for the
believer who has grasped the truth that, since it was given
in order to point to Christ, the ceremonial law does not have

[1] Cf., e.g., Lagrange, p. 329.
[2] In fact, it seems highly likely that (i) the οὐδὲν κοινὸν δι' ἑαυτοῦ of this
verse and the πάντα . . . καθαρά of v. 20 are slogans of the strong; (ii) the
strong appealed to the tradition of the teaching of Jesus in support of
their position; and (iii) Paul is here accepting that these slogans of the
strong are indeed true to the teaching of Jesus.
[3] ἑαυτοῦ is surely to be preferred to the variant αὐτοῦ (A C 𝔎 D G *pm*),
which has been understood as referring to Christ.
[4] The words quoted refer, as they are used by Hamlet to Rosencrantz
in *Hamlet* 2.2.259, not, of course, to what is morally good or morally
bad, but to what is pleasing or unpleasing.
[5] p. 111.
[6] On κοινός see further Bauer, s.vv. κοινός and κοινόω; F. Hauck, in
TWNT 3, pp. 789–98, 810; C. E. B. Cranfield, *The Gospel according to
Saint Mark*, Cambridge, ⁶1977, pp. 232 and 239.
[7] Cf. Cranfield, op. cit., p. 244f.
[8] The sense of εἰ μή here is 'but'. Cf. 1 Cor 7.17; and see BDF, § 448(8)
note.

to be obeyed literally any more now that He has fulfilled His ministry, the foods which the law had pronounced unclean are no longer unclean, there are other believers who have not yet clearly understood this, and for them, not yet having been given this inward liberty, to neglect the literal obedience of the ritual law is wrong. The meats, which had been forbidden, though no longer ritually unclean in themselves objectively, are still for them, subjectively, unclean.

15. εἰ γὰρ διὰ βρῶμα ὁ ἀδελφός σου λυπεῖται, οὐκέτι κατὰ ἀγάπην περιπατεῖς. The γάρ[1] connects the sentence, not with v. 14 (which is a parenthesis inserted asyndetically, introduced for the purpose of making clear both Paul's own acceptance of the basic assumption of the strong and at the same time the fact that there is an important qualification of that assumption which must not be forgotten), but with v. 13b.[2] The weak in faith will be grievously hurt, he will have the integrity of his faith (i.e., faith in its deepest sense of *fides qua*) and obedience destroyed, and his salvation put at risk,[3] if he is led by his strong fellow-Christian's insistence on exercising the liberty, which he (the strong Christian) truly has, into doing something for which he as yet does not possess the inward liberty. The strong will therefore not be acting in accordance with Christian love, if his weak brother is thus seriously hurt[4] on account of

[1] The variant δέ (see Merk's apparatus, and compare the AV 'But') is no doubt to be rejected as an attempt to give a smoother text on the assumption that v. 15a is to be connected with v. 14.

[2] Sanday and Headlam, p. 391, explain the γάρ by assuming a 'suppressed link in the argument' (' "You must have respect therefore for his scruples, although you may not share them, for if," &c.'), while Lagrange, p. 330, prefers the explanation that the fact that the food is unclean for the weak presupposes his fall, so that γάρ in the attenuated sense of 'en effet' is justified; but neither of these explanations, surely, is as straightforward as the one accepted above.

[3] The NEB rendering of λυπεῖται by 'is outraged' should probably be regarded as unsatisfactory: it is quite certainly unsatisfactory, if it is intended to indicate merely 'the grief and pain caused by outraged feelings' (Black, p. 168). For what Paul has in mind (as the sequel makes clear) is not merely the weak brother's distressed feelings (a serious thing though they are), but something much worse, the actual destruction of his integrity as a Christian by his being led by example or social pressure into a deliberate violation of what he believes to be the will of God. The specially strong sense of 'grieve' which attaches to λυπεῖν as used here by Paul is to be understood from the whole context (cf. πρόσκομμα and σκάνδαλον in v. 13, ἐκείνῳ κοινόν in v. 14, ἀπόλλυε in the latter part of the present verse, διὰ προσκόμματος in v. 20, προσκόπτει in v. 21, and κατακέκριται in v. 23). Elsewhere, of course, Paul uses both λυπεῖν and λύπη less weightily.

[4] Luther, p. 397, seems to be making the rather interesting suggestion that by using the passive rather than saying λυπεῖς Paul is effectively

the food which he (the strong Christian) eats. It is to be noted that once again Paul drives home the earnestness of his exhortation by changing to the use of the second person singular in this verse and also in vv. 20–22.[1]

μὴ τῷ βρώματί σου ἐκεῖνον ἀπόλλυε, ὑπὲρ οὗ Χριστὸς ἀπέθανεν. To bring about the spiritual ruin[2] of one's brother by insisting on exercising outwardly[3] one's own inner freedom with regard to the ritual law was to trample on the sacrifice of Jesus Christ. Luther comments with vigour: 'you are also a cruel murderer, because you ruin your brother. . . . Furthermore, and this likewise surpasses every kind of cruelty as well as of ingratitude, you despise, in your brother, the death of Christ, for he died certainly also for him'.[4] Compare 1 Cor 8.11.

16. μὴ βλασφημείσθω οὖν[5] ὑμῶν τὸ ἀγαθόν. With regard to this verse three main questions require to be answered, and they are very closely interrelated. They are:

(i) Is this verse addressed only to the strong, or is it addressed to both strong and weak?

(ii) What is meant by ὑμῶν τὸ ἀγαθόν?

(iii) Whom does Paul have in mind as being likely to do the reviling or speaking evil to which he refers?

Of these (ii) has been continuously debated since patristic times, and opinion is still divided about it. On the one hand, the answer is often given that liberty from the ceremonial observances is meant.[6] On the other hand, various suggestions

---

abolishing an excuse which the strong might be inclined to make, namely, that he has done nothing unloving since he has had no intention of grieving his brother—it's the brother's fault for being grieved.

[1] For the use of περιπατεῖν see on 6.4. In Eph 5.2 we have περιπατεῖτε ἐν ἀγάπῃ.

[2] The verb ἀπολλύναι is here used to denote the bringing about of someone's ultimate (eschatological) ruin, his loss of his share in eternal life. Cf. the former use of ἀπολέσει in Mk 8.35 and ζημιωθῆναι τὴν ψυχὴν αὐτοῦ in the following verse. Michel, p. 345, n. 2, cites the use of 'ibbēḏ in Sanh. 4.5 ('Therefore but a single man was created in the world, to teach that if any man has caused a single soul to perish from Israel Scripture imputes it to him as though he had caused a whole world to perish . . .' —Danby, p. 388; the paragraph deals with the admonishing of witnesses in capital cases).

[3] Bauer, s.v. βρῶμα 1, would seem to be right in taking βρῶμα here in its ordinary sense of 'food', as against those who explain that it is here used in the sense of βρῶσις—an unnecessary complication.

[4] p. 398.

[5] οὖν is omitted by G, but should surely be read.

[6] e.g. by Pelagius, p. 110 ('Libertas [nostra], quam habemus in domino, ut omnia nobis munda sint'); Calvin, p. 298; Sanday and Headlam, p. 391; Lagrange, p. 330; Gaugler 2, p. 349; Barrett, p. 264 ('probably "your Christian freedom" '); Murray 2, p. 193; Käsemann, p. 360f.

of a more comprehensive reference have often been made, such as Christ's doctrine generally,[1] 'the kingdom of God',[2] 'salvation',[3] 'faith'.[4] If to (i) the answer 'to both the strong and the weak' is given, then (ii) is settled at the same time, and very probably (iii) also; for, if the verse is addressed to both the strong and the weak, ὑμῶν τὸ ἀγαθόν clearly cannot refer to the inner freedom enjoyed only by the strong but must refer to something common to both parties, and it is almost, if not quite, certain that the people Paul has in mind as liable to turn to reviling or speaking evil must be people outside the church. If, however, the answer 'to the strong alone' is given to question (i), questions (ii) and (iii) remain open to discussion. As an argument in favour of understanding the verse as addressed to both groups the change from the second person singular in v. 15 to the second person plural[5] in this verse is sometimes adduced. But this will bear no weight; for the second person plural is naturally understood as addressed to the group, of which—for the sake of greater vividness and emphasis— each individual member has just been addressed in the second person singular in v. 15. In view of the thrust of the exhortation in this whole passage it is much more likely that Paul is here addressing the strong alone.

---

[1] So, e.g., Ambrosiaster, col. 169, explains: 'Hoc est, doctrina Dominica, cum sit bona et salutaris, non debet per rem frivolam blasphemari'; and Lagrange, p. 330, sums up the interpretations of various ancient and modern commentators as taking 'the good thing' to be the treasure of doctrine and spiritual life comprised by Christianity.

[2] e.g. Barth, *Shorter*, p. 169.

[3] Michel, p. 345, though himself regarding it as more likely that Paul is addressing only the strong, says that, if both groups were being addressed, ὑμῶν τὸ ἀγαθόν would be a periphrasis for 'salvation' and compares ἀγαθά in 10.15.

[4] i.e., 'faith' in the sense of *fides qua*; 'faith' in the sense of *fides quae* would be a much less probable suggestion, while 'faith' in the special sense it has in 14.22 would simply be equivalent to the 'freedom' of the alternative answer. Luther in his very interesting comment (p. 398) includes 'your faith' in his exposition of the meaning of 'your good', but his explanation embraces much more ('For your good, i.e., what you are in God and what you have from God, will impress the heathen in such a way that they flee from it rather than desire to obtain it. . . . What the apostle here calls "good" is everything we are through Christ. What he means to say, then, is this: Be careful that the heathen do not berate your faith, your religion, and all your Christianity, for its good reputation should attract them and its actual goodness should edify them— through you').

[5] The variant ἡμῶν (Ψ D G lat syᵖ sa Cl) is hardly to be accepted (*pace* Zahn, p. 581). It could well be an attempted clarification by someone who was convinced that Paul meant by τὸ ἀγαθόν something common to all Christians.

With regard to (ii), it is often assumed that, if the answer to (i) is 'only to the strong', then ὑμῶν τὸ ἀγαθόν must denote the freedom enjoyed by the strong. But, though the possibility of the interpretation, according to which Paul is here warning the strong not to bring reproach upon the ἀγαθόν which consists of their inner freedom by selfishly insisting on exercising it outwardly at the cost of hurting their weak brothers, is not to be denied, we are inclined to think that it is more probable that Paul is in this verse warning the strong against an even more serious danger, namely, the danger that they may by a selfish insistence on the exercise of their freedom bring reproach upon an ἀγαθόν which is even more precious than their freedom, that ἀγαθόν, which is both theirs (ὑμῶν) and also at the same time the ἀγαθόν of their weak fellow-Christians, the gospel itself, the message of what God has done, is doing, and will do, for man's salvation.[1] The extreme seriousness of the hurt to the weak envisaged in v. 15 (note particularly the use of ἀπολλύναι) may, we think, be justifiably regarded as a strong point in favour of this understanding of ὑμῶν τὸ ἀγαθόν; for the presence among Christians of such selfishness as would willingly risk causing a weak brother's spiritual ruin for the sake of a plate of meat would surely bring into disrepute not just the liberty of the strong but also the very gospel itself.

With regard to (iii), if the verse is addressed to both strong and weak, or if (as has been argued above) it is addressed only to the strong but ὑμῶν τὸ ἀγαθόν refers to the gospel, we may be quite confident that the people whom Paul has in mind as possible revilers are those outside the church. If, however, the view that the verse is addressed to the strong alone and ὑμῶν τὸ ἀγαθόν refers to their liberty were accepted, that would probably entail deciding that Paul might have in mind weak Christians, outsiders, or both, as being liable to revile.

17. οὐ γάρ ἐστιν ἡ βασιλεία τοῦ θεοῦ βρῶσις καὶ πόσις, ἀλλὰ δικαιοσύνη καὶ εἰρήνη καὶ χαρὰ ἐν πνεύματι ἁγίῳ. The point of the γάρ is that this verse provides support for vv. 15b and 16: it appeals to the nature of the kingdom of God as proof of the terrible absurdity of the strong Christian's readiness to bring about his weak brother's spiritual ruin for the sake of such a triviality as the use of a particular food and thereby to cause the gospel to be reviled by unbelievers. The kingdom of God (Paul is here thinking of it in its present reality)[2] is not a matter

---

[1] The thought of the gospel may be said to be present in the last four words of v. 15. Cf. what is said in v v. 4, 7–9.

[2] References to the kingdom of God as such are infrequent in the Pauline corpus. This is the only reference in Romans. Cf. 1 Cor 4.20;

of eating and drinking.[1] It is not one's insistence on expressing
one's freedom to eat a particular food which attests the presence
of God's kingdom (nor is one in the slightest degree worse off
in relation to it for having foregone the expression of one's
freedom for one's brother's sake):[2] its presence is attested
rather by the presence of δικαιοσύνη καὶ εἰρήνη καὶ χαρὰ ἐν
πνεύματι ἁγίῳ. It is possible (with Käsemann)[3] to connect ἐν
πνεύματι ἁγίῳ with all three preceding nouns (both χαρά and
εἰρήνη are specifically included in the καρπὸς τοῦ πνεύματος in
Gal 5.22, and there is no doubt that in Paul's view it is by the
work of the Spirit that Christians are, in some measure, morally
δίκαιοι); but it seems on the whole preferable to connect it only
with χαρά (cf. 1 Th 1.6) and assume that Paul was conscious
of a special need to define 'joy' because of possible misunderstanding.[4] The joy, which is a sign of the presence of God's
kingdom, is specifically the joy given by God's Spirit,[5] and it is
to be carefully distinguished from any joy which is merely the
temporary result of the satisfaction of one's own selfish desires.
By δικαιοσύνη Paul probably means the status of righteousness
before God which is God's gift, by εἰρήνη the state of having
been reconciled with God, by χαρά the joy which is the Spirit's
work in the believer; for so to understand these three terms
here is surely, in view of the fact that they are combined as a
definition of the kingdom of God, much more natural than to
explain them as denoting, respectively, righteousness as a

6.9, 10; 15.50; Gal 5.21; Eph 5.5; Col 4.11; 1 Th 2.12; 2 Th 1.5; also
1 Cor 15.24. When Paul does refer to it, it is nearly always as future;
but here and in 1 Cor 4.20 he is thinking of it as present. In both these
places, as Käsemann, p. 361, has noted, the kingdom is defined pole-
mically (in 1 Cor 4.20 as being not ἐν λόγῳ but ἐν δυνάμει, here as being
not βρῶσις καὶ πόσις but δικαιοσύνη, κ.τ.λ.). Käsemann, ibid., rightly
insists that the presence of the kingdom of God, which Paul refers to
here, is to be understood christologically: it is in the presence and
activity of the Lord Jesus Christ, and only so, that the kingdom of God
is experienced in the present.

[1] The οὐ . . . βρῶσις is, of course, to be expected here in view of what
has already been said in chapter 14. With regard to καὶ πόσις, the
question arises whether Paul added it because of actual controversy in
the church about drinking wine or simply because it was suggested by
association, the word βρῶσις having once been used. With reference to
this see further on v. 21. (That Paul's οὐ . . . βρῶσις καὶ πόσις was in any
way intended as a protest against the use of banquet imagery in connexion with the final consummation is most unlikely.)

[2] Cf. 1 Cor 8.8.

[3] p. 361.

[4] Cf. Michel, p. 346.

[5] The ἐν is probably best explained as causal (see Bauer, s.v., III;
BDF, § 219 (2)).

moral quality or 'righteous action',[1] 'a peaceful state of mind'[2] or 'the peace promoted and preserved by believers',[3] and joy thought of mainly as a subjective human feeling.[4] Where the things signified by δικαιοσύνη, εἰρήνη and χαρά in this verse (if the view preferred above is correct) are really present and understood in the life of the church, there the wickedness and the absurdity of destroying a brother for the sake of eating a particular food will be clearly recognized.

18. ὁ γὰρ ἐν τούτῳ δουλεύων τῷ Χριστῷ εὐάρεστος τῷ θεῷ καὶ δόκιμος τοῖς ἀνθρώποις. Käsemann[5] is surely right (as against Michel,[6] who, taking vv. 18 and 19 together, says of them both that they draw out paraenetically the consequence of v. 17) in taking this verse (with its γάρ) closely with v. 17 as an underlining of what is said there. The most puzzling thing in the sentence is ἐν τούτῳ. This has received very various explanations: for example,

(i) that it means 'in the Holy Spirit';[7]

(ii) that τούτῳ refers to δικαιοσύνη καὶ εἰρήνη καὶ χαρὰ ἐν πνεύματι ἁγίῳ, the singular being used rather than the plural because the three items are viewed together as forming a single whole;[8]

(iii) that ἐν τούτῳ means 'thus', 'in this way', in the sense of recognizing the truth expressed by v. 17 as a whole;[9]

(iv) that it means 'in this matter';[10]

(v) that Paul uses the singular because he has in mind only the will to promote peace (the concentration of the following verse on peace-making is urged as support for this view).[11]

Of these, (iv) strikes us as very weak, (v) as forced, and (i) and (iii) seem less natural and satisfactory in relation to the context

---

[1] Barrett, p. 265; Murray 2, p. 194.

[2] Barrett, ibid.

[3] Murray, ibid.

[4] So Murray, ibid.: cf. Barrett, ibid. It is interesting to compare this triad with 5.1–2. As far as δικαιοσύνη and εἰρήνη are concerned, the correspondence of δικαιωθέντες and εἰρήνην ἔχομεν is obvious. As corresponding to χαρά we may see either (with Michel, p. 346, n. 3) the reference to ἐλπίς (cf. possibly τῇ ἐλπίδι χαίροντες in 12.12) or (with Lagrange, p. 331)—perhaps more satisfactorily—the verb καυχώμεθα.

[5] p. 361.

[6] p. 347. The ἄρα οὖν at the beginning of v. 19 tells against Michel's explanation.

[7] So, e.g., Origen, col. 1251.

[8] So, e.g., Sanday and Headlam, p. 392; Murray 2, p. 194; Käsemann, p. 361; Black, p. 169.

[9] So, e.g., Barrett, p. 265.

[10] Michel, p. 347, lists 'in diesem Stück' and 'auf diesem Gebiet' among possible meanings.

[11] So, e.g., Gaugler 2, p. 351; cf. Michel, p. 347, n. 2.

than (ii). We conclude that (ii) should be accepted as the most probable explanation. It receives a measure of support from the variant reading τούτοις, which is clearly a clarification from the point of view of someone who understood the reference to be to the three things, δικαιοσύνη καὶ εἰρήνη καὶ χαρὰ ἐν πνεύματι ἁγίῳ. The man who serves Christ in the knowledge that he has been justified by God, that he is reconciled with God, that he has received the Holy Spirit's gift of joy, the man whose service of Christ has its source in, and is determined by, these facts of what God has done for him, is well-pleasing to God. The words καὶ δόκιμος[1] τοῖς ἀνθρώποις are probably rightly seen as intended to stand in contrast to βλασφημείσθω in v. 16. The Christian who serves Christ in the way indicated will not bring shame on the gospel by deserving the disapproval of men (whether his fellow-Christians or unbelievers), but will deserve (though, of course, he may not always receive)[2] their approval.

19. ἄρα οὖν τὰ τῆς εἰρήνης διώκωμεν καὶ τὰ τῆς οἰκοδομῆς τῆς εἰς ἀλλήλους. For ἄρα οὖν see on 5.18; also on 7.25b and 8.12. If διώκωμεν is the correct reading, then what we have here is a hortatory first person plural subjunctive (that is a milder form of exhortation than a second person plural imperative would have been) as the practical conclusion drawn from what has just been said. But, if the correct reading is διώκομεν, what we have is probably to be regarded as Paul's statement of what he sees as the natural response of sincere Christians either to the situation envisaged in this section or to the truth to which vv. 17 and 18 have given expression. The indicative, which is both strongly attested (ℌ G L *pm*) and also the more difficult reading, is preferred by many,[3] and is said to be more forceful. But the reading διώκωμεν (C ℵ D *al* latt sy) is not just to be dismissed as 'une correction banale'.[4] The fact that in the ancient MSS. it is more common for an original ω to be altered into an ο than for the opposite change to be made

---

[1] The adjective δόκιμος occurs in Romans only here and in 16.10, and in the rest of the NT only in 1 Cor 11.19; 2 Cor 10.18; 13.7; 2 Tim 2.15; Jas 1.12. See also on 1.28 (ἐδοκίμασαν and ἀδόκιμον) and on 5.4 (δοκιμήν): further W. Grundmann, in *TWNT* 2, pp. 258–64 (on this verse in particular: p. 263, n. 20).

[2] Paul certainly realized that in the world which hated Christ Himself His followers must expect to have to endure hatred (cf., e.g., 8.35f; 12.12b, 14, 17–21). It is unlikely that he was forgetting that here. The variant δοκίμοις (B G* (also, in different word-order, 131)) looks as if it may be a clumsy attempt to take account of the fact that not all men will actually approve of those of whom they ought to approve.

[3] e.g., Sanday and Headlam, p. 392; Lagrange, p. 331f; Michel, p. 347f; Käsemann, p. 362.

[4] Lagrange, p. 331.

ought to be taken into account; and it would seem that in this particular textual problem the *difficilior lectio potior* principle may well be inapplicable, and that we should rather give precedence to considerations of intrinsic probability. διώκωμεν surely gives a much better transition from vv. 17 and 18 to vv. 20–23. An exhortation seems to be required at this point, and, if the indicative is read, the introduction of the second person singular prohibition in v. 20a seems awkwardly abrupt. We conclude, therefore, that διώκωμεν should be preferred.[1] The expression εἰρήνην διώκειν is found in LXX Ps 33[MT: 34].15 (as equivalent to *šālôm rādap*) and also in the NT in Heb 12.14; 1 Pet 3.11 (quotation of Ps 34).[2] The effect of the combination of the neuter plural article with the genitive here may be brought out by some such translation as 'what makes for peace'. Whereas in v. 17 it most probably denoted peace with God, εἰρήνη here denotes peace with one's fellow-Christians (in 12.18 εἰρηνεύειν was used of the believer's relations with his fellow-men generally, but the narrower reference is more likely in the present verse, in spite of the last three words of v. 18). With τὰ τῆς εἰρήνης Paul couples together[3] τὰ τῆς οἰκοδομῆς τῆς εἰς ἀλλήλους. To insist on understanding these two objects of the verb διώκωμεν as denoting two quite distinct sets of things would probably be to misunderstand Paul's meaning. The addition of καὶ τὰ τῆς οἰκοδομῆς, κ.τ.λ. should probably be understood as serving more to fill out and clarify the significance which τὰ τῆς εἰρήνης has in this context than to introduce a reference to any further things. What is required is an altogether earnest seeking to promote among brethren such a true peace (based on the fundamental peace with God which God Himself has established in Christ) as must manifest itself in mutual upbuilding. Paul's use of οἰκοδομή[4] is to be seen in the light of the rich and varied use of the language of building in the OT, in extra-biblical Jewish writings, and also in the rest of the NT.[5] In the OT God is spoken of as building (*bānāh*—

---

[1] Cf. Zahn, p. 583; W. Foerster, in *TWNT* 2, p. 414; Gaugler 2, p. 352; Barrett, pp. 262 and 265 (without discussion).

[2] For relevant Rabbinic material reference may be made to SB 1, pp. 215–18; 3, pp. 748, 765. See also on 12.18.

[3] For φυλάξωμεν after ἀλλήλους (D G* latt) is surely secondary.

[4] In Romans it occurs only here and in 15.2, and the cognate verb only in 15.20. The bulk of the occurrences of both words in the Pauline corpus are to be found in 1 and 2 Corinthians. On these two words and their cognates, see O. Michel, in *TWNT* 5, pp. 139–51; and also P. Bonnard's brief but illuminating article in *VB*, pp. 43–45.

[5] An indication of the extraordinarily intricate pattern of ideas and images which intertwine in the NT with the uses of οἰκοδομεῖν and οἰκοδομή

οἰκοδομεῖν) not just such things as Jerusalem (Ps 147.2), Zion (Ps 102.16), the throne of David (Ps 89.4), but also His people Israel itself (Jer. 31.4), and even—if in the light of the contrast in the following verse the passive may be understood as conveying a reference to God's action—as building up Gentiles in the midst of His people (Jer 12.16), that is, incorporating them into the community of His own people: we also hear of the prophet's divinely-given authority 'over the nations and over the kingdoms' to build as well as to destroy and overthrow (Jer. 1.10). The substantive οἰκοδομή, is used in 1 Cor 3.9 and Eph 2.21 and (with a different reference) in 2 Cor 5.1 of the result of building, the structure built, but in its other occurrences in the Pauline corpus it denotes the act of building or building up, the object of the act (sometimes explicit, sometimes only implicit) being either the Church as such or its individual members. While it is no doubt true that there has quite often been a tendency in some quarters to understand 'edification' individualistically as meaning simply the spiritual advancement of the individual independently of his relation to the Christian community and that this tendency ought to be guarded against, it would seem to be going rather too far in the opposite direction to state, as Barrett does,[1] that ' "Edification" is for Paul . . . corporate . . ., and "building up" means the building up of the Church', and to draw the conclusion that τὸ ἔργον τοῦ θεοῦ in the next verse must mean 'not the individual Christian . . ., but the Church, the outcome of God's work in Jesus Christ'. Paul's thought seems to be that God Himself, His apostles and other ministers, and also all the members of the Church, are engaged both in the building of the Church as such and also in the building up, in faith and obedience, of each several member. It is true that the building up of the Church and the building up of the individual members are two aspects of the same process, but the process will hardly be understood in its true wholeness, if either aspect has attention concentrated on it in such a way that the other is lost sight of. That, in so far as the building up is a human activity, it is not just intended to be in one direction but to be mutual, is brought out by the τῆς εἰς ἀλλήλους in this verse (cf. 1 Th 5.11).[2]

is the fact that οἶκος, ναός, θεμέλιος, πέτρα, λίθος, σῶμα, μέλος, κεφαλή, αὐξάνειν and φυτεύειν are only a selection of the key-words which feature in it.

[1] p. 265.

[2] It should be noted that Paul can also use the verb οἰκοδομεῖν in a bad sense of emboldening someone to do what he should not do (1 Cor 8.10).

20. μὴ ἕνεκεν βρώματος κατάλυε τὸ ἔργον τοῦ θεοῦ. Paul takes up again the more forceful second person singular (last used in v. 15, the general sense of which is here repeated with certain variations). καταλύειν[1] is the natural opposite to the οἰκοδομεῖν suggested by the noun οἰκοδομή which he has just used (cf., e.g., Mt 5.17; 24.2; 26.61; 27.40; 2 Cor 5.1; Gal 2.18: see also LSJ and Bauer, s.v. καταλύω). τὸ ἔργον τοῦ θεοῦ is understood by some[2] as referring to the Church which God is building up (cf. 1 Cor 3.9); by Michel[3] as referring to the salvation event itself (cf. the mention of the death of Christ in v. 15); but, in view of the context, it is more probable that Paul has in mind God's work in the weak brother, the new man He has begun to create.[4]

πάντα μὲν καθαρά.[5] What appears to be a slogan of the strong (see on v. 14, and compare Mk 7.19, especially the last four words; Lk 11.41; Tit 1.15) is first conceded (μέν) by Paul, but then qualified by the sentence he adds.[6] As with the οὐδὲν κοινὸν δι’ ἑαυτοῦ of v. 14, we have to understand this statement as intended in a restricted sense, the reference being not to such things as men's thoughts, desires and actions, but only to the resources of the created world which are available and appropriate for human consumption. For the use of καθαρός in the sense of ṭāhôr compare, for example, LXX Gen 7.3, 8; Lev 11.47; 14.4.

ἀλλὰ κακὸν τῷ ἀνθρώπῳ τῷ διὰ προσκόμματος ἐσθίοντι is Paul's necessary qualification—but a qualification which the strong are very liable to fail to take into account. The man who eats διὰ[7] προσκόμματος has very often been understood to be the weak brother who eats with hurt to himself. So Chrysostom, for example, explains the words as referring to the weak Christian who, under pressure from his strong fellow-Christians who do not share his scruples, eats 'with a bad conscience'.[8] This interpretation, which receives a measure of support from

---

[1] The variant ἀπόλλυε is doubtless an assimilation to v. 15.
[2] e.g., Barrett, p. 265; Käsemann, p. 362. (Reference may also be made to E. Peterson, 'ἔργον in der Bedeutung "Bau" bei Paulus', in *Biblica* 22 (1941), pp. 439–41.)
[3] p. 348.
[4] Cf., e.g., Lagrange, p. 332; Gaugler 2, p. 353.
[5] The variant reading which has τοῖς καθαροῖς after καθαρά would appear to be an assimilation to Tit 1.15. It is quite clearly not original here.
[6] Cf. 1 Cor 10.23.
[7] διά here is to be explained as 'διά of attendant circumstances' (see on 2.27 and on 4.11b, and BDF, §223(3)).
[8] col. 639 (μετὰ συνειδότος πονηροῦ). Cf. Ambrosiaster, col. 170f.

v. 14b and its relation to v. 14a, is still favoured by a good many commentators.[1] Others[2] take the reference to be to the strong Christian who by insisting on eating his meat causes his weak brother to stumble; and this view should probably be preferred, since it suits the context, in which Paul's exhortation is directed mainly toward the strong, rather better, and, in particular, gives a better connexion with what follows.[3] With regard to the grammar of the sentence, the simplest solution would seem to be to supply ἐσθίειν from ἐσθίοντι as the subject of κακόν (ἐστιν):[4] for the man who eats in the way indicated his eating is morally evil.

21. καλὸν τὸ μὴ φαγεῖν κρέα μηδὲ πιεῖν οἶνον μηδὲ ἐν ᾧ ὁ ἀδελφός σου προσκόπτει. The verse, which, like both the two preceding, and also the two following, sentences (vv. 20a and b, and 22a and b), is introduced asyndetically, is an authoritative pronouncement, commending as definitely good,[5] in contrast with the evil (κακόν in v. 20) of insisting upon the outward expression of one's inner freedom to one's brother's hurt,[6] the unselfish course of action which is open to the strong. That Paul should put here τὸ μὴ φαγεῖν[7] κρέα is not at all surprising in view

---

[1] e.g., Cornely, p. 720f; Lagrange, p. 332; Murray 2, p. 195; Käsemann, p. 358 (but see also p. 362).

[2] So, e.g., Origen, col. 1252f; Pelagius, p. 111; Aquinas, p. 211 (1133); Calvin, p. 300; Sanday and Headlam, p. 393; Barrett, p. 266 (though see next foot-note); Black, p. 169.

[3] But the difficulty of deciding between the two ways of taking τῷ διὰ προσκόμματος ἐσθίοντι is notorious. Barrett, while apparently inclined to take the view we have attributed to him in the previous foot-note, actually goes on to suggest that Paul may himself have had both possibilities in mind and so expressed himself in such a way as to allow for both (p. 266). While we regard the interpretation we have supported above as very probable, we doubt whether an absolutely firm decision can be reached on this question.

[4] Cf. Lagrange, p. 332, though his understanding of the reference of τῷ ... ἐσθίοντι is the opposite of ours. To take κακόν as a substantive ('there is evil ...') or to understand from the preceding πάντα some such subject as τὸ βρῶμα αὐτοῦ or to suggest, as Barrett does (p. 265), 'that "all things" continues to form (in thought, if not grammatically) the subject. "All things are clean, but *they cause* evil to the man who ..."' is surely very much less natural.

[5] For the use of καλόν here cf. 1 Cor 7.1, 8, 26; Heb 13.9. Denney, p. 706, compares also Mk 14.6.

[6] It is here assumed that ἐσθίοντι in v. 20 refers to the strong. See the note on the verse.

[7] It is possible that aorist infinitives were used in this verse because Paul was thinking of the specific occasions when eating or drinking might cause a brother to stumble rather than of continuous abstention (cf. BDF, § 338 (1)); but we should not care to put this more strongly. On this sort of matter careful study of Burton, *MT*, is instructive.

of v. 2 and what has been said since v. 2. The strong Christian who 'has the faith to eat any food' has more room in which to manoeuvre than the weak Christian who 'eats *only* vegetables'. He has the inner freedom not only to eat flesh but also equally to refrain from eating it. So for him to refrain for his weak brother's sake is assuredly good. Paul's continuing with the words μηδὲ πιεῖν οἶνον is less easy to understand. It is usually taken as definite evidence that the weak, or at any rate some of them, abstained from wine. But it is to be observed that, whereas both abstinence from meat and observance of days are mentioned near the beginning of the section and in a way which makes it quite clear that these are actual practices of the weak, abstinence from wine is not mentioned until the end of chapter 14 and the reference is then to abstinence on the part of the strong, not—except indirectly—to abstinence on the part of the weak. Moreover, μηδὲ πιεῖν οἶνον is the second term of a series of three, the third term of which is quite indefinite and general. In view of these facts, the possibility that not drinking wine is mentioned simply as an hypothetical example cannot be ruled out. We are indeed inclined to think that this is the most probable explanation of these words. The choice of abstinence from wine as an example could perhaps have been suggested by the use in v. 17 of the stereotyped phrase βρῶσις καὶ πόσις. The third term of the series, μηδὲ ἐν ᾧ ὁ ἀδελφός σου προσκόπτει,[1] serves both to indicate the comprehensiveness of the pronouncement's scope and also at the same time to under-line the requirement of Christian love, already formulated in vv. 13 and 15, that one should be ready to forego the outward expression of the inner freedom one has received with regard to the sort of matters which Paul has in mind in this section, whenever, by insisting on expressing it outwardly, one would be running the risk of causing the spiritual ruin of a fellow-

---

[1] These words, which are the last seven words of the verse as printed in Nestle, should probably be accepted as giving the correct form of the text. Neither Hofmann's reading of εν as ἕν rather than ἐν (though it is true that it gives us a simple dative with the verb προσκόπτειν as in 9.32) nor Mangey's conjectural addition of ἕν before ἐν is really convincing. A verb would still need to be supplied; and μηδὲ ἐν ᾧ, κ.τ.λ., (with which something like ἄλλο τι ποιῆσαι would have to be supplied), harsh though it is, strikes us as much more credible than either of these attempted improvements. Of the variant readings attested by ℵ* P (the addition of λυπεῖται after σου) and by B ℵ D G *pl* lat sy^h sa (the addition of ἢ σκανδαλίζεται ἢ ἀσθενεῖ after προσκόπτει), the former is probably to be explained as due to the influence of v. 15 and the latter (*pace* Lagrange, p. 333; Michel, p. 349) as due to the influence of 1 Cor 8.11–13 (cf. Käsemann, p. 362).

Christian, by leading him to do something for which he has not received the necessary inner freedom and so cannot do without violating his personal integrity as a believer.[1]

22. σὺ πίστιν ἣν ἔχεις κατὰ σεαυτὸν ἔχε ἐνώπιον τοῦ θεοῦ. If ἥν is omitted (with 𝔎 D G *pl* lat sy), a question mark or another mark of punctuation must be placed after ἔχεις; but it is better to read ἥν, since it is strongly attested and its omission is easily explicable as an attempted stylistic improvement. That πίστις is used in its special sense of confidence that one's faith allows one to do a particular thing (see on vv. 1 and 2) is clear —Paul would not be likely to exhort Christians to make a secret[2] of their faith in the basic sense of *fides qua*. To be free from the sort of scruples which trouble the weak is in itself a precious gift. The inward freedom does not have to be expressed outwardly in order to be enjoyed: one may enjoy it in one's own inner life—a secret known only to oneself and God.[3] And, if a weak brother is going to be hurt by one's giving outward expression to one's freedom, then one should be content with the inward experience of it, of which God is the only witness.

μακάριος ὁ μὴ κρίνων ἑαυτὸν ἐν ᾧ δοκιμάζει is difficult and has been variously explained. One obvious possibility—it makes a good connexion with what precedes—is to take the sentence to be a declaration of the blessedness of the strong Christian who, heedful of the truths which vv. 21 and 22a set forth, avoids judging or condemning himself (in the sense of bringing

---

[1] The passage from *Siphre Deut* 14.21 quoted in SB 3, p. 313, with reference to this verse (it runs as follows: 'For thou art an holy people unto the LORD thy God (Deut 14.21). Sanctify thyself in that which is permitted thee: if things are allowed, but others treat them as forbidden, then thou art not entitled to treat them as permitted before their eyes') is interesting in that, at first sight, it appears to be a close parallel to Paul's pronouncement; but, as the accompanying comment in SB makes clear, it is not a real parallel, the thought being not that the person (the reference was understood to be to the Samaritans) who sees the Jew doing something which is permitted to him may be encouraged to do the same thing against his own (weaker) conscience, but that he may take the liberty to excessive and altogether impermissible lengths.

[2] For κατὰ σεαυτὸν ἔχε cf. Heliodorus (3rd century A.D.) 7.16.1 (κατὰ σαυτὸν ἔχε καὶ μηδενὶ φράζε). Bauer, s.v. κατά II.1.c, cites also Josephus, *Ant.* 2.255; but the use of καθ' αὑτόν in conjunction with ἔχειν there is a less clear parallel.

[3] The variant (𝔎* *pc*) which omits ἐνώπιον τοῦ θεοῦ should doubtless be rejected. For the thought of the last six words of v. 22a Denney (p. 706) compares 1 Cor 14.28.

God's judgment upon himself)[1] by[2] what he approves (that is, by allowing himself to insist on the outward exercise of his liberty, to the ruin of his weak fellow-Christian). But it would seem that justice is more fully done both to the word-play ὁ μὴ κρίνων ἑαυτόν — ὁ . . . διακρινόμενος — κατακέκριται and also to the presence of δέ in v. 23a (the five sentences which make up vv. 20–22 have all been introduced asyndetically), if we take ὁ μὴ κρίνων ἑαυτὸν ἐν ᾧ δοκιμάζει as descriptive of the strong Christian as being truly possessed of the inner freedom to do those things which he approves and therefore untroubled by the scruples which afflict the weak Christian. That the scope of this statement (that is, of v. 22b) is limited to the sort of matter which is at issue between the weak and the strong referred to in this section should go without saying. It is certainly not to be taken as a general statement that Christians who have no doubt about the rightness of what they do are blessed; for that would be merely an assertion of the blessedness of those Christians who have insensitive consciences.[3]

23. ὁ δὲ διακρινόμενος ἐὰν φάγῃ κατακέκριται follows naturally upon the previous sentence as we have just explained it. The weak Christian, who has not received that particular inner liberty which his strong brother has received and so is doubtful about the rightness of the action he proposes,[4] is here contrasted with the strong Christian who (as described in the previous sentence) is not troubled by such doubts. And this weak Christian stands condemned, if he eats meat.

ὅτι οὐκ ἐκ πίστεως indicates why this is so: it is because he has eaten meat without having received the inner freedom to do so, without having full confidence that his faith (in the basic

[1] Or, according to others, in the sense of having to pass judgment upon himself. So, for example, Michel, p. 350, understands Paul's thought to be that the strong Christian, if he eats knowing that he is thereby causing his weak brother to stumble, must condemn himself for his loveless conduct.

[2] If κρίνων ἑαυτόν has the sense of bringing God's judgment or condemnation upon himself, then ἐν is most naturally taken as instrumental (see Bauer, s.v. ἐν III); but, if κρίνων ἑαυτόν is understood in the sense indicated in the previous foot-note, ἐν may be taken to mean 'in' or 'in the matter of'.

[3] Cf. Chrysostom, col. 640: Οὐχ ἁπλῶς δὲ περὶ πάντων λέγων τοῦτο τέθεικεν. Εἰσὶ γὰρ πολλοὶ μὴ κατακρίνοντες ἑαυτούς, καὶ σφόδρα πλημμελοῦντες· οἱ πάντων εἰσὶν ἀθλιώτεροι· ἀλλὰ τέως τῆς προκειμένης ὑποθέσεως ἔχεται.

[4] On the use of διακρίνεσθαι in the sense 'waver', 'doubt', see on 4.20, the only other place where διακρίνεσθαι is found in the Pauline corpus (the active διακρίνειν occurs five times—all in 1 Corinthians). Whereas διακρίνεσθαι is there used with reference to a radical failure of faith in God, here in 14.23 it has a narrower reference corresponding to the special sense which πίστις has in this verse.

NT sense of the word) allows him to do so. The sense which πίστις has here may be discussed with reference to the second part of the verse (that it has the same sense in both its occurrences in the verse is clear enough).

πᾶν δὲ ὅ οὐκ ἐκ πίστεως ἁμαρτία ἐστίν[1] is a sentence about which there has been much controversy down the centuries and about which interpreters still differ very widely. There are at any rate three questions which need to be decided:

(i) How general is the statement?
(ii) In what sense is πίστις used?
(iii) Exactly what is meant by ἁμαρτία ἐστίν ?

With regard to (i), opinions range from that which regards the statement as general, simply in the sense of being applicable to the various matters at issue between the weak and the strong referred to in this section, to that which regards it as universally applicable, including non-Christians as well as Christians in its scope.

With regard to (ii), the main possibilities to be considered are: (a) that πίστις here denotes faith in its basic Christian sense; (b) that it means something like 'a good conscience'; (c) that it denotes the confidence that one's Christian faith permits one to do a particular thing, an inward liberty with reference to it. It is clear that, if (a) or (b) is accepted, it is possible (though not necessary) to understand the statement as general in the widest sense. Thus Augustine and many others, accepting (a), have understood Paul to be enunciating the doctrine that works done before justification and all works done by pagans can only be sin,[2] while others, accepting (b), have taken him to mean that all actions which are done contrary to the doer's conscience, whether the person is a Christian or not, are sin.[3] If, however, (c) is adopted, the statement will naturally be understood as of limited applicability.

That the right answer to (i) is the one which Chrysostom gave, namely, that the statement refers only to the matters which have been under discussion, the matters at issue between the weak and the strong,[4] is, we think, hardly to be doubted; for it alone really fits the context. A statement of universal

---

[1] On the problems indicated in the textual apparatus to this verse the reader is referred to pp. 5–11.

[2] So, e.g., Augustine, Contra Julianum 4.32.

[3] Reference may be made to the interesting discussion in Aquinas, p. 212f (1140–41); also to the passage cited from the Summa 1.2, qu.19, art. 5, by Sanday and Headlam, p. 394.

[4] col. 640: Ὅταν γὰρ μὴ θαρρῇ, φησί, μηδὲ πιστεύῃ ὅτι καθαρόν, πῶς οὐχ ἥμαρτε; Ταῦτα δὲ πάντα περὶ τῆς προκειμένης ὑποθέσεως εἴρηται τῷ Παύλῳ, οὐ περὶ πάντων.

application would be inapposite here. It would break the continuity between v. 23a and 15.1. And this view with regard to (i) receives confirmation from what must be said about (ii); for of the three possibilities which we mentioned the only one which suits all the other occurrences of πίστις in chapter 14 (that is, vv. 1, 22 and 23a) and also the use of πιστεύειν in v. 2 is (c), and, in view of what may be called the thematic importance of πίστις/πιστεύειν in this section, it would seem to be extremely improbable that πίστις would be used in v. 23b in a different sense from that which it has elsewhere in chapter 14. It may further be said in favour of (c), that it actually combines those elements of truth which both (a) and (b) contain. For, on the one hand, it does justice to the element of truth in (a), which is the fact that basic Christian faith is indeed involved in what is signified by πίστις in this chapter, for, according to (c), πίστις here denotes one's confidence that one's *faith* (in the basic NT sense of the word) allows one to do a particular thing; and, on the other hand, it does justice to the element of truth in (b), which is the fact that something akin to the possession of a good conscience is indeed involved in what is signified by πίστις here, for, according to (c), it means *one's confidence that* one's Christian faith *allows one* to do something.

With regard to (iii) it is important to recognize that Paul is here using ἁμαρτία in a rather different way from that in which he normally uses it. Whereas he usually thinks of ἁμαρτία as a power controlling man (see on 3.9), he is here using the word in a more relative way, to characterize the conduct of the Christian who does a particular action in spite of the fact that he has not received the inner freedom to do it, contrasted with the conduct of the Christian who does possess the inner freedom to do that which he does. It is a usage which is more akin to the use of the plural to denote individual sinful acts than to Paul's normal usage. The implication of the sentence we are at present concerned with would indeed seem to be that the action of the strong Christian, for which he has the necessary inner freedom, is (provided he is not thereby hurting a weak brother) not sin. But it is important to see that this implied 'not sin' belongs to a special and relative usage: according to Paul's more characteristic way of thinking and speaking (cf., especially 7.14ff), none of the actions of Christians in this life, however truly described as ἐκ πίστεως, is altogether free from sin.

1. Ὀφείλομεν δὲ ἡμεῖς οἱ δυνατοὶ τὰ ἀσθενήματα τῶν ἀδυνάτων βαστάζειν. The first three verses of chapter 15 may be said to sum up Paul's exhortation to the strong (the term δυνατός is used for the first time in this connexion in the present verse, and ἀδύνατος is a new term introduced here to denote the person so far referred to as ὁ ἀσθενῶν (τῇ πίστει)); and the natural inference to be drawn from ἡμεῖς οἱ δυνατοί is that he includes himself in their number. Under the gospel the strong, those who, because of the inner freedom which has been given to them, have plenty of room in which to manoeuvre, have an inescapable obligation (ὀφείλομεν)[1] to help to carry[2] the infirmities, disabilities, embarrassments and encumbrances[3] of their brothers who are having to live without that inner freedom which they themselves enjoy. Their response to this obligation will be a test of the reality of their faith (in the sense of basic Christian faith); for what is required of them is utterly opposed to the tendency of our fallen human nature, which—

---

[1] ὀφείλειν here clearly denotes moral obligation—'ought'. See also on 13.8 and 15.27 (the other places in the epistle in which ὀφείλειν occurs), and on 1.14 and 8.12 (the occurrences of ὀφειλέτης), and on 13.7 (ὀφειλάς); also Bauer, s.v. ὀφείλω; and F. Hauck, in *TWNT* 5, pp. 559ff.

[2] *Pace* Barrett, p. 269, it is unlikely that βαστάζειν means 'endure' here. Of the twenty-seven occurrences of the word in the NT, there is only one in which it quite certainly has the sense 'bear with', 'put up with', namely, Rev 2.2 (there are two or three others, where it perhaps has this meaning): in the vast majority of its occurrences the idea of carrying is definitely present, and it is 'carry' which suits the present context. Paul is requiring from the strong something much more positive than that they should tolerate the weaknesses of the weak (mere toleration might well, as Schlatter, p. 379, notes, involve putting a certain pressure upon the weak to do that which he personally cannot do in integrity of faith, and it would not exclude an attitude of superiority and condescension). What is required is that the strong should actually help the weak by taking something of the weight of the burden which they have to carry off their shoulders on to their own. Cf., e.g., Gaugler 2, p. 361f.; Murray 2, p. 197, who aptly refers to Gal 6.2. (In Ignatius, *Polyc.* 1.2 (πάντας βάσταζε, ὡς καὶ σὲ ὁ κύριος) βαστάζειν is more likely (*pace* Bauer, s.v. βαστάζω 2.b.β) to have some such sense as 'help' (K. Lake's rendering in the Loeb edition) than 'bear patiently'; for, if it meant 'bear patiently', the πάντων ἀνέχου in the following sentence would be a repetition out of keeping with the style of the context.) The case for understanding βαστάζειν to mean 'carry', 'help to carry', is further strengthened, if Michel, p. 354, is right in seeing here the influence of Isa 53.4 in a form similar to that in which it appears in Mt 8.17 (αὐτὸς τὰς ἀσθενείας ἡμῶν ἔλαβεν καὶ τὰς νόσους ἐβάστασεν). (In this connexion it is interesting that this Isaiah quotation in its Mt 8.17 form is echoed in Ignatius, *Polyc* 1.3 (πάντων τὰς νόσους βάσταζε ὡς τέλειος ἀθλητής) not with reference to Christ but with reference to Polycarp.)

[3] ἀσθένημα occurs in the Greek Bible only here, but is used by Aristotle (see LSJ and Bauer, s.v.). Paul might perhaps have been influenced by the ἀσθενείας of the version of Isa 53.4 quoted in Mt 8. He may well be using a term already applied by the strong to the peculiarities of the weak. In any case, he has in mind the various distresses under which the weak labour.

so far from being to help those weaker than oneself with their
burdens—is for the strong to seek to compel the weak to
shoulder the burdens of the strong as well as their own. That
Paul is still thinking specially of the problem with which he
has been concerned in chapter 14 may be taken as certain; but
the possibility[1] that already in 15.1 he is beginning to widen
the scope of his exhortation, so as to be no longer exclusively
concerned with the problem faced in chapter 14, should be
reckoned with.

καὶ μὴ ἑαυτοῖς ἀρέσκειν. These words serve to clarify what
has just been said. This helping to carry the burden of the
infirmities which weigh the weak down will involve not pleasing
oneself. That it would be perverse to read into Paul's μὴ ἑαυτοῖς
ἀρέσκειν any notion that everything which is delightful to one
ought to be avoided simply because it is delightful (a notion
which the ill-informed not infrequently ascribe to the Puritans
and their heirs) should be obvious. What is meant here by not
pleasing oneself is not pleasing oneself regardless of the effects
which one's pleasing oneself would have on others. What Paul
is forbidding in particular is that strong Christians should
please themselves by insisting on exercising outwardly and to
the full that inner freedom which they have been given, when
to do so would be to hurt a weak brother's faith.

2. ἕκαστος ἡμῶν[2] τῷ πλησίον[3] ἀρεσκέτω puts the matter
positively. Every strong Christian is to learn to please his

[1] To use more confident language than that of possibility here, as a
number of commentators do, seems to us unwarranted. But it is certainly
true that what is said here may properly be applied more widely, and
the comment on this verse as a whole in chapter 4 of George Eliot's
Adam Bede ('There's a text wants no candle to show 't; 't shines by its
own light') was perceptive.

[2] If ἡμῶν is, read, as it surely should be, rather than the less well-
attested ὑμῶν, it is more natural to understand it as denoting the same
people as are denoted by the first person plural in v. 1 than as including
the Christian community as a whole. While the exhortation could at
this point be generalized without inappropriateness, since it is, of course,
true that the weak in faith, as well as the strong, ought to be considerate
toward his fellows, the need of the strong for this particular exhortation
is much more urgent, both because their very strength constitutes a
special opportunity, and so a special temptation, to be inconsiderate,
and also because the weak are the ones who are specially liable to be
seriously hurt. ἕκαστος emphasizes the fact that no individual strong
Christian has any right to except himself (cf. the πᾶσα ψυχή of 13.1 and
the even more emphatic παντὶ τῷ ὄντι ἐν ὑμῖν of 12.3). No strength of
faith, no spiritual gift, however superlative, can constitute a valid claim
to exemption from this rule.

[3] Käsemann, p. 365, sees in the use of ὁ πλησίον an intentional
reminiscence of the commandment of Lev 19.18, which was quoted in
13.9: cf. Michel, p. 355.

neighbour, instead of pleasing himself regardless of his neighbour's interest. He is to be considerate, to take due account of the position in which his brother is placed. Compare the use of ἀρέσκειν in 1 Cor 10.33. But, since not all pleasing of one's fellow-men is good (cf. Gal 1.10; 1 Th 2.4; also Eph 6.6; Col 3.22), Paul adds the necessary qualification εἰς τὸ ἀγαθὸν πρὸς οἰκοδομήν as a necessary qualification.[1] The latter phrase clarifies the former (cf. Käsemann, p. 365). The neighbour is very likely to be ready to be pleased by flattery and by the condonement of his wrong-doing; but the pleasing of the neighbour which is here commanded is such a pleasing as has regard to his true good, to his salvation,[2] a pleasing which is directed toward his edification,[3] a pleasing of one's neighbour which is no mere man-pleasing but has regard to God.[4]

3. **καὶ γὰρ ὁ Χριστὸς οὐχ ἑαυτῷ ἤρεσεν.** Paul appeals to the example of Christ[5] Himself (cf. 2 Cor 8.9; Phil 2.5ff; also 1 Cor 11.1, which follows on Paul's statement πάντα πᾶσιν ἀρέσκω, μὴ ζητῶν τὸ ἐμαυτοῦ σύμφορον ἀλλὰ τὸ τῶν πολλῶν, ἵνα σωθῶσιν: in the Gospels we may think especially of Mk 10.45 = Mt 20.28). The statement οὐχ ἑαυτῷ ἤρεσεν sums up with eloquent reticence both the meaning of the Incarnation and the character of Christ's earthly life. He most certainly did not seek to please Himself, but sought rather to please His Father and to please men εἰς τὸ ἀγαθὸν πρὸς οἰκοδομήν.

ἀλλὰ καθὼς γέγραπται. It has struck many people as very surprising that at this point Paul should, instead of citing an example or examples from the history of Christ's earthly life,[6] simply quote the OT. But, in view of the great importance for Paul of the recognition that Jesus Christ is the true meaning

---

[1] Cf. the qualifications εἰ δυνατόν and τὸ ἐξ ὑμῶν in 12.18.

[2] See on 8.28 (εἰς ἀγαθόν); 13.4 (σοὶ εἰς τὸ ἀγαθόν).

[3] For the meaning of οἰκοδομή see on 14.19.

[4] Cf. Calvin, p. 303.

[5] For Χριστός preceded by the article cf. 7.4; 8.35; 9.3, 5; 14.18; 15.7, 19; 16.16, and also many examples in the other Pauline epistles. Michel, p. 355, appeals to the presence of the article as support for taking Χριστός here as a title (cf. Käsemann, p. 366). The presence of the article with Χριστός probably gives emphasis to its titular significance, though we think it unlikely that Paul ever used the word (whether with or without the article) as a mere proper name without any consciousness of its titular character. (See on 1.1 (Χριστοῦ Ἰησοῦ).)

[6] On the question of Paul's relationship to the historical Jesus reference may be made to, *inter alia*, W. G. Kümmel, 'Jesus und Paulus', in *NTS* 10 (1963–64), pp. 163–81; G. Bornkamm, *Paul* (Eng. tr. of *Paulus*, Stuttgart, 1969), New York and London, 1971, pp. 228–39; J. W. Fraser, *Jesus and Paul*, Appleford, 1974; F. F. Bruce, *Paul and Jesus*, Grand Rapids, 1974; id., 'Paul and the historical Jesus', in *BJRL* 56 (1974), pp. 317–35.

and substance of the law and the prophets (cf., e.g., 1.2; 3.21; 9.30–10.8) and also of the whole early Church's interest, in particular, in assuring itself that the scandal of the Passion was actually an essential element of God's eternal plan, the appeal to the OT is thoroughly understandable.

οἱ ὀνειδισμοὶ τῶν ὀνειδιζόντων σε ἐπέπεσαν ἐπ᾽ ἐμέ is an exact quotation from LXX Ps 68.10[RV: 69.9].[1] In the psalm it is the righteous sufferer who speaks, and the second person singular pronoun refers to God: the reproaches levelled against God have fallen upon this righteous sufferer. The suggestion that in Paul's use of the words Christ 'is represented as addressing a man. Christ declares that in suffering it was the reproaches or sufferings of others that He bore'[2] is most unlikely. As in the psalm, so in this verse of Romans the σε must refer to God.[3] Christ is addressing God, and saying that the reproaches with which men reproached God have fallen on Him (i.e., on Christ). We may distinguish several different elements in what Christ bore in His passion:

(i) God's hostility toward sinful men—God's wrath (cf. 1.18; Mk 14.36 (cf. Isa 51.17–23); 15.34; Gal 3.13);[4]

(ii) men's hostility toward their fellow-men (this would seem to be the thought behind the reference to Abel in Heb 12.24);

(iii) men's hostility toward God.

It is to (iii) that Paul refers here. The purpose of the reference is to indicate the lengths to which Christ went in His not pleasing Himself rather than specially to encourage the strong Christians in Rome to imitate this particular element of Christ's endurance. If, for our sakes, He was willing to go as far as this in His not pleasing Himself, how ungrateful should we be, if we could not bring ourselves to renounce our self-gratification in so unimportant a matter as the exercising of our freedom with regard to what we eat or whether we observe special days —for the sake of our brothers for whom He suffered so much! To the question, 'Why did Paul choose to refer here to this element in Christ's suffering rather than to that which was surely more essential, His bearing of the wrath of God?', we

---

[1] For quotations and echoes of this psalm in the NT see Mt 27.34, 48; Mk 15.36; Lk 12.50 (perhaps: cf. Ps 69.14–16); 23.36; Jn 2.17; 15.25; 19.29; Acts 1.20; Rom 11.9f; Heb 11.26 (perhaps); Rev 3.5; 13.8; 16.1; 17.8; 20.12, 15; 21.27.

[2] Sanday and Headlam, p. 395.

[3] Cf., e.g., Barth, *Shorter*, p. 172; Murray 2, p. 198f; Käsemann, p. 366; Black, p. 172.

[4] Reference may be made to pp. 106–10, and also 208–18.

might perhaps suggest as a very tentative answer that it may
have been that he felt that in a way this was the most humili-
ating part. To bear the wrath of God against sinners was by far
the most terrible thing (we may think of Mk 15.34); but it was
meaningful suffering—there was nothing irrational in God's
hostility toward sinful men. And even the hatred of man for
man, wicked and hideous though it most certainly was, was
not totally irrational, since the Abels of this world are never
entirely innocent of the role of Cain. But man's enmity against
God was pure evil, pure absurdity, the totally irrational and
inane, and yet, while it was just that, seemed—in the conditions of this world—to be possessed of overwhelming power
and credibility, so that to bear men's hatred of God meant
having to experience to the full the menace of the world's

> 'As for you,
> Say what you can, my false o'erweighs your true'.[1]

So perhaps it is understandable that here, in order to indicate
the lengths to which Christ was willing to go in His not
pleasing Himself, Paul should have singled out specially for
mention this particular element in His suffering.

4. ὅσα γὰρ προεγράφη,[2] εἰς τὴν ἡμετέραν διδασκαλίαν ἐγράφη,[3]
ἵνα διὰ τῆς ὑπομονῆς καὶ διὰ[4] τῆς παρακλήσεως τῶν γραφῶν τὴν ἐλπίδα
ἔχωμεν[5] justifies the use for the purpose of exhortation of the
christologically understood OT passage just quoted.[6] All Scripture has its relevance and applicability to us—though of course
it must be applied intelligently. The noun διδασκαλία denotes
instruction, and in the AV translation 'for our learning' means
not 'for us to learn it' but 'for our instruction'. For the general
thought of the first half of the verse compare 4.23f; 1 Cor 9.10;
10.11. The practical conclusion to be drawn is stated succinctly
in the latter half of the quotation from Bengel's preface to his
edition of the Greek NT of 1734 quoted in Nestle: 'Te totum

---

[1] Shakespeare, *Measure for Measure*, 2.4. 170f.

[2] προεγράφη is surely to be preferred as the more difficult reading
(προγράφειν occurs only three other times in the NT) to the ἐγράφη
attested by B lat Cl. The πάντα inserted before the following εἰς by B P
69 *pc* is doubtless secondary, an attempted improvement.

[3] The variant προεγράφη (A 𝕂 *pl*) is no doubt an assimilation to the
first verb of the verse.

[4] The omission of the second διά by D G P *pm* lat Cl probably reflects
the tendency to take τῆς ὑπομονῆς as well as τῆς παρακλήσεως as dependent
on τῶν γραφῶν.

[5] B Cl insert τῆς παρακλήσεως (it would have to be construed as an
objective genitive depending on ἐλπίδα) after ἔχωμεν: this variant
probably originated in an accidental repetition of the preceding τῆς
παρακλήσεως.

[6] Cf. Käsemann, p. 366.

applica ad textum: rem totam applica ad te'.[1] The second part
of the verse brings out what Paul sees as the aim of this
instruction, and so the (or, at least, one very important)
purpose[2] of all the OT Scriptures—namely, that Christians may
have hope. The words τὴν ἐλπίδα ἔχωμεν have puzzled commentators. Why should Paul specially single out hope as the
one thing to be mentioned just here? At first sight it seems
rather surprising; but, in view of the importance of hope in
Romans (see 4.18; 5.2, 4f; 8.17-30; 12.12; 15.12f: also 13.11-14)
and in the rest of the NT (see, e.g., Acts 26.6f; 28.20; 2 Cor 3.12;
Eph 1.18; 2.12; Col 1.23, 27; 1 Th 4.13; 1 Pet 1.3, 13; 3.15;
1 Jn 3.3), it is not really surprising. To speak of Christians as
holding fast their hope[3] is, in fact, a very appropriate way of
indicating their continuing to live as Christians. With regard
to the words διὰ τῆς ὑπομονῆς καὶ διὰ τῆς παρακλήσεως τῶν
γραφῶν too there are some questions which have to be asked:
(i) Is τῆς ὑπομονῆς as well as τῆς παρακλήσεως to be connected
with τῶν γραφῶν?
(ii) In what sense is the first διά used?
(iii) What is the meaning of παράκλησις here?
As to (i), to take τῆς ὑπομονῆς by itself[4] seems on the whole
preferable to taking τῶν γραφῶν as dependent on it,[5] for the
presence of the second διά according to the best authorities
tells against the latter explanation. As to (ii), Käsemann[6] is
quite probably right in understanding the first διά as an
example of διά of attendant circumstances, though a negative
answer to (i) does not necessitate this. As to (iii), Barrett[7]
prefers 'exhortation' to 'comfort', but his reason for so doing

---

[1] The relevance of the OT to the life of the Christian should be considered in the context of the wider subject of the doctrine of Scripture
as a whole. For a very brief discussion of this (containing some bibliographical suggestions) reference might perhaps be permitted to C. E. B.
Cranfield, 'The preacher and his authority', in *Epworth Review* 2 (1975),
pp. 95-106.

[2] The purpose Paul has in mind is of course the divine purpose, God's
purpose in causing the Scriptures to be written.

[3] The suggestion that ἐλπίς is here to be understood in the sense of
'object of hope', as in 8.24, and ἔχειν in the sense of 'obtain', though it
might seem to give to τὴν ἐλπίδα ἔχωμεν a stronger meaning, is not very
likely; but the reference to ὑπομονή in this verse does suggest that ἔχειν
should be taken to have a continuous sense—'to hold fast' or 'go on
having', rather than just 'to have'.

[4] With, e.g., Michel, p. 356, though his interpretation of τῆς ὑπομονῆς
as referring directly to the endurance of Christ in His passion is hardly
acceptable; Käsemann, p. 367.

[5] With, e.g., Lagrange, p. 343; Schlatter, p. 381f.

[6] p. 367.

[7] p. 270.

(that τῆς παρακλήσεως is followed by a genitive) seems to have no force. In the next verse παράκλησις surely means 'comfort', and this favours taking it to mean 'comfort' here too.[1] To sum up, in this verse, in justification of his appeal to Ps 69.9 as an indication of the lengths to which for our sakes Christ was willing to go in not pleasing Himself but pleasing others and so a challenge to the strong among the Roman Christians to be considerate toward their weak brothers, Paul states that all the Scriptures (of the OT) were written for the instruction of Christians, in order that they might, with patient endurance and strengthened by the comfort and encouragement which the Scriptures give, hold fast the hope which is theirs in Christ.

5f is a prayer-wish: for this form compare vv. 13 and 33; 1 Th 5.23; 2 Th 3.5, 16a; 2 Tim 1.16, 18; Heb 13.20f.[2] To describe this as 'an eloquent way of doing two things at the same time, exhortation to men and prayer to God', noting that 'No form of exhortation is more effective in address to men than this', as Murray does,[3] is scarcely fair; for, though the prayer-wish of the NT epistles is formally a wish and not a prayer (since in it God is not directly addressed, but the church), it is surely more closely akin to prayer than to exhortation. In fact it is really tantamount to a prayer. And the element of implicit exhortation which may be present in it is to be recognized as secondary, comparable, it may be suggested, to the firm intention, which is a necessary accompaniment of all sincere petition and intercession directly addressed to God, to try to do what one can oneself do toward the fulfilment of one's prayer.

ὁ δὲ θεὸς τῆς ὑπομονῆς καὶ τῆς παρακλήσεως. The δέ here marks the fact that the prayer-wish brings the present paragraph to a conclusion (cf. the δέ in, e.g., vv. 13 and 33, and in 2 Th 3.5). For the use of genitives to describe God by reference to His gifts or attributes (a characteristic, as Michel[4] notes, of the style of praise) compare vv. 13 and 33; 16.20; 2 Cor 1.3; 13.11;

---

[1] Cf. Käsemann, p. 367, who compares 1 Macc 12.9 (παράκλησιν ἔχοντες τὰ βιβλία τὰ ἅγια). On παράκλησις see on 12.1 and 8.

[2] In 16.20; Phil 4.19; 1 Pet 5.10, there are variant readings (aorist optative instead of future indicative) which would give additional examples of the prayer-wish. Reference may be made here to R. Jewett, 'The form and function of the homiletic benediction', in *Anglican Theological Review* 51 (Evanston, 1969), pp. 18–34.

[3] 2, p. 200.

[4] p. 357. See also G. Delling, 'Die Bezeichnung "Gott des Friedens" und ähnliche Wendungen in den Paulusbriefen', in E. E. Ellis and E. Grässer (ed.), *Jesus und Paulus:Festschrift für W. G. Kümmel zum 70. Geburtstag*, Göttingen, 1975, pp. 76–84.

1 Th 5.23; 2 Th 3.16a; Heb. 13.20. God is here characterized as the source of patient endurance and of comfort, the two words ὑπομονή and παράκλησις[1] being taken up from the preceding verse.

δώη.[2] The use of the optative is a distinguishing feature of the prayer-wish form. It occurs in all the examples cited at the beginning of the note on these two verses, apart from v. 33, where the verb is not expressed.

With ὑμῖν Paul changes to the second person plural, which he has so far used only twice (in 14.1 and 16) in this section (according to the Nestle text), having preferred to use the first person plural and the second person singular. For the rest of the section he addresses all the Christians of Rome alike and together.

τὸ αὐτὸ φρονεῖν ἐν ἀλλήλοις κατὰ Χριστὸν Ἰησοῦν.[3] For the expression τὸ αὐτὸ φρονεῖν see on 12.16. That in all its Pauline occurrences it means 'be of the same mind', 'agree', may be taken as certain; but it is not easy to decide whether in the present context the agreement referred to must include agreement over those questions about which the weak and the strong are still sincerely disagreeing. At first sight the advantage might seem to lie with the view that it must, and that, in view of 14.14a and the 'we who are strong' of 15.1, Paul's desire must really be—though his sensitiveness prevents him from stating it unambiguously—that the weak may be enabled to be fully convinced of the rightness of the position of the strong. But Paul's whole treatment of his subject throughout this section surely tells strongly against this view. And in this verse his addition of the words κατὰ Χριστὸν Ἰησοῦν suggest that he has not presumed to decide already in his own mind the exact content of the agreement he desires to be given, but is humble enough to leave that decision to Christ the Lord. Such an agreement among the Christians of Rome as is according to the will[4] of Christ Jesus is desired and prayed for; and this may, or may not, include identity of conviction on the matters at issue between the weak and the strong, but must certainly mean a common sincere determination to seek to obey the Lord Jesus

---

[1] For τῆς παρακλήσεως with θεός compare 2 Cor 1.3 (θεὸς πάσης παρακλήσεως).

[2] For δώη, the Hellenistic form of the third person singular aorist optative active of διδόναι (instead of δοίη) see BDF, § 95(2).

[3] ℵ A C 69 al vg sy reverse the order of Χριστόν and Ἰησοῦν; but there seems to be no good ground for preferring this variant.

[4] We agree with W. Michaelis, in TWNT 4, p. 671, n. 18, and Käsemann, p. 367, in thinking that in κατὰ Χριστὸν Ἰησοῦν the thought is of the will of Christ rather than His example.

Christ together with the mutual respect and sympathy befitting brethren.

ἵνα ὁμοθυμαδὸν ἐν ἑνὶ στόματι δοξάζητε τὸν θεὸν καὶ πατέρα τοῦ κυρίου ἡμῶν Ἰησοῦ Χριστοῦ expresses the goal of the desired agreement—that the Roman Christians may glorify God with one heart and one voice. On ὁμοθυμαδὸν[1] ἐν ἑνὶ στόματι we may quote Beet's comment: 'With one accord: else the one mouth is hypocrisy. But it is also needful that inward harmony find suitable outward expression.'[2] Such united praise of God will make impossible the despising and the passing judgment to which 14.3 referred and the heartlessness which can cause a brother to be grieved (14.15) and for a mere food's sake destroy the work of God (14.20). On δοξάζειν see on 1.21. For the words τὸν θεὸν καὶ πατέρα τοῦ κυρίου ἡμῶν Ἰησοῦ Χριστοῦ compare 2 Cor 1.3; 11.31; Eph 1.3; 1 Pet 1.3.[3] Some interpreters[4] have argued for the translation, 'God, even the Father of our Lord Jesus Christ'. In support of this, it has been said that, whereas 'father' is a word which requires some correlative word, 'God' is naturally absolute; and that the expression ὁ θεὸς καὶ πατήρ occurs absolutely (as in 1 Cor 15.24). But Sanday and Headlam are surely right in deciding that 'It is better and simpler to take the words in their natural meaning, "The God and Father of our Lord Jesus Christ"' and comparing, for the reference to the Father as 'the God . . . of Jesus Christ', Mt 27.46 = Mk 15.34; Jn 20.17; Eph 1.17; Heb 1.9.[5] In this connexion a couple of sentences of Calvin's comments on Jn 20.17 may not inappropriately be quoted: 'Now Christ calls Him *his God*, inasmuch as by taking the form of a servant, He humbled Himself. This is therefore proper to His human nature, but it is applied to His whole person in respect of His unity, because the same one is both God and man'.[6] The expression, 'the God and Father . . .', may perhaps be a liturgical formulation. There is a noticeable gradation, as Michel points out,[7] from ὁ Χριστός in v. 3, through Χριστὸν Ἰησοῦν in v. 5, to τοῦ κυρίου ἡμῶν Ἰησοῦ Χριστοῦ in v. 6.

---

[1] The word (on which see H. W. Heidland, in *TWNT* 5, p. 185f) occurs quite often in the LXX, but in the NT, apart from this place, only in Acts (1.14; 2.46; 4.24; 5.12; 7.57; 8.6; 12.20; 15.25; 18.12; 19.29).

[2] p. 345.

[3] In Col 1.3 the reading which omits the καί between θεῷ and πατρί should be accepted, as it is by Nestle.

[4] e.g., Weiss; Gifford; Lipsius.

[5] p. 397.

[6] *The Gospel according to St John 11–21 and the First Epistle of John*, Eng. tr. by T. H. L. Parker, Edinburgh, 1961, p. 201.

[7] p. 358, continuation of n. 3 from previous page.

7. Διό introduces the concluding paragraph of the section. The conclusion which the Christians of Rome must draw from what has been said in 14.1–15.6 is summed up in the following command.

προσλαμβάνεσθε ἀλλήλους. For the meaning of προσλαμβάνεσθαι see on 14.1. Both in 14.1 and here the second person plural is addressed to the church as a whole; but, whereas in 14.1 the church as a whole is contrasted with the individual who is 'weak in faith', here the church as a whole is thought of as composed of the two groups, the strong and the weak. Hence the use of ἀλλήλους. Both groups are to recognize and accept each other.

καθὼς καὶ ὁ Χριστὸς προσελάβετο ἡμᾶς. It is probably better (with Käsemann)[1] to take καθώς in its causal sense[2] and understand the clause as stating the reason why they must accept one another (14.1–15.6 has already made it clear that Christ has accepted both the strong and the weak—cf., e.g., 14.3f, 8f, 15) than to take καθώς in its strictly comparative sense and understand the clause as bringing out the fact that in accepting each other they will be following the example of Christ. Instead of ἡμᾶς we should probably prefer the reading ὑμᾶς (ᵽ K G al lat sy bo), which is more pointed (referring to the fact that Christ has accepted both groups): ἡμᾶς may be explained as reflecting the usage of worship.

εἰς δόξαν τοῦ θεοῦ can be connected either with προσλαμβάνεσθε ἀλλήλους or with the subordinate clause. *Pace* very many commentators (including Sanday and Headlam,[3] Lagrange,[4] Michel,[5] Barrett,[6] Murray,[7] Käsemann[8]), we are inclined to think that the RV was right in connecting the phrase with προσλαμβάνεσθε ἀλλήλους, for the following reasons:
(i) the phrase may be seen as resuming the thought of v. 6 (ἵνα . . . δοξάζητε τὸν θεόν);[9]
(ii) while there is no doubt at all that Paul believed that Christ had done all that He had done to the glory of God, it would seem to be rather more apposite to Paul's purpose of persuading

---

[1] p. 369 (he is following A. E. S. Nababan, *Bekenntnis und Mission in Römer 14 und 15* (Heidelberg thesis, 1963), p. 112).
[2] See on 1.28.
[3] p. 397.
[4] p. 345.
[5] p. 358.
[6] p. 270 (though he goes on to say that 'it is probably not wrong to take' the words 'with both verbs', which is what Calvin, p. 306, favours).
[7] 2, p. 204.
[8] p. 368 (in his translation).
[9] Cf. Denney, p. 709.

the Roman Christians to comply with his imperative to indicate that what they are being bidden to do will be to the glory of God than to remind them that Christ's acceptance of them had been for the sake of God's glory;

(iii) The fact that in v. 9 the subject of δοξάσαι τὸν θεόν is τὰ ἔθνη seems to us to tell in favour of connecting εἰς δόξαν τοῦ θεοῦ with προσλαμβάνεσθε rather than with προσελάβετο.

(iv) though stylistic arguments should not be pressed too much, it certainly seems to us that, if the last four words of the sentence are connected with the main clause, we have a balanced sentence, but that, if they are connected with the subordinate clause, the result is a rather ungainly imbalance between the clauses.

8. λέγω γάρ here introduces a solemn doctrinal declaration.[1] The 'I mean' of NEB is too weak a translation: better something like 'For I declare'. The γάρ is, in our view, better understood as marking the relation between vv. 8–12 and the main sentence of v. 7 than as connecting vv. 8–12 with the subordinate clause of v. 7. For we get a more straightforward and natural connexion of thought (particularly, if the last four words of v. 7 are understood as part of the main clause), if we take vv. 8–12 as intended as additional support for the command of v. 7 (though this additional support for the command does also as a matter of fact help to clarify the subordinate clause of that verse)[2] than we get, if we regard vv. 8–12 as intended simply as support for, or explanation of, the subordinate clause of v. 7.

Χριστὸν διάκονον γεγενῆσθαι περιτομῆς ὑπὲρ ἀληθείας θεοῦ, εἰς τὸ βεβαιῶσαι τὰς ἐπαγγελίας τῶν πατέρων is the first, and less difficult, part of what Paul declares: namely, that Christ has become the servant of the Jews for the sake of God's faithfulness, in order to establish the divine promises made to the fathers. περιτομή is no doubt[3] to be understood here as in 3.30 and in the former of the two occurrences of the word in 4.12, that is, as denoting the Jewish people.[4] And the natural inference to be drawn from this reference (and from the subsequent reference to the Gentiles in the next verse) would seem

---

[1] Cf. Michel, p. 358; Käsemann, p. 369.

[2] In that it clarifies the meaning of ἡμᾶς—both Jews and Gentiles are included.

[3] *Pace* Sanday and Headlam, p. 397f.

[4] For the different meanings which the word can have reference may be made to volume I, p. 171, n. 4. The suggested interpretations of the present verse which take περιτομή to mean circumcision in the sense of the state of having been circumcised (Barrett, p. 271, mentions two of them) must be rejected as decidedly forced.

to be that the division between the weak and the strong with which Paul has been concerned in this section was also, to a large extent at any rate, a division between Jewish and Gentile Christians. Christ has become (the force of the perfect infinitive γεγενῆσθαι[1] is that He not only became but also remains)[2] the servant of the Jewish people. For the word διάκονος see on 11.13 (τὴν διακονίαν μου). It is used here, as the cognate verb διακονεῖν is used in Mk 10.45 = Mt 20.28, with reference to Christ's service of men, and characterizes it as a humble personal service. That behind the use of the word διάκονος here is the thought of Christ, as the 'ebed YHWH, though not certain, would seem to be likely.[3] He is the servant of the Jewish people, inasmuch as, born a Jew, of the seed of David according to the flesh, living almost all His life within the confines of Palestine, limiting His ministry of teaching and healing—apparently with the deliberate intention of obeying God's will (cf. Mt 15.24)— almost exclusively to Jews, He both was in His earthly life and His atoning death, and also still is, as the exalted Lord, the Messiah of Israel. The words ὑπὲρ ἀληθείας θεοῦ, εἰς τὸ βεβαιῶσαι τὰς ἐπαγγελίας τῶν πατέρων indicate the reason why Christ had to become the servant of the Jewish people. It was for the sake of God's faithfulness (that ἀλήθεια has here its sense of 'faithfulness'[4] is made clear by the following expression of purpose, which serves to interpret ὑπὲρ ἀληθείας θεοῦ). It was in order that God's faithfulness to His covenant might be honoured; it was in order that He (Christ) might fulfil[5] the

---

[1] The variant γενέσθαι (B C* D* G pc) may be regarded as the easier reading, to which the perfect could well have been altered.

[2] Cf., e.g., Barrett, p. 271.

[3] Cf. Michel, p. 359. Morna D. Hooker's objection, made with reference to Mk 10.42ff (Jesus and the Servant: the influence of the Servant concept of Deutero-Isaiah in the New Testament, London, 1959, p. 74f), that the Servant in Second Isaiah 'is primarily Yahweh's Servant', need not discourage us, since, while it is true that the word 'ebed is used to indicate the Servant's relation to God, it is clear that the actual content of the Servant's service of God is a service of men (see, e.g., Isa 49.5f; 53.4–6, 11f). And, while it is true that no word of the διακονεῖν group is ever used in the LXX in the Servant Songs, the Greek language contains no single word more appropriate for the purpose of summing up all that is said in them of the service to men which the Servant of the Lord is to render than a word of this group (see further Cranfield, The Gospel according to Saint Mark, Cambridge, ⁶1977, p. 486f).

[4] See on ἀληθής in 3.4 and ἀλήθεια in 3.7; and compare the use of πίστις in 3.3.

[5] For βεβαιοῦν used of proving promises reliable by fulfilling them see Bauer, s.v. βεβαιόω 1: the use is found in Polybius, Diodorus Siculus, and the Priene inscriptions.

promises[1] made by God to the patriarchs.[2] It is to be noted that in this first part of his solemn doctrinal declaration Paul has underlined yet once more the special priority and privileges of the Jews (cf. 1.16; 2.9; 3.1–4; 9.4–5; also 11.13–24), and that there is a special significance in his doing this in the present context, since most, if not all, of the weak will have been Jews, and a good many of the strong will have been Gentiles.[3] It might perhaps be a further encouragement to the strong to show considerateness.

9. τὰ δὲ ἔθνη ὑπὲρ ἐλέους δοξάσαι τὸν θεόν is specially difficult. Various suggested explanations have to be considered:

(i) that it is dependent on εἰς τό and co-ordinate with βεβαιῶσαι τὰς ἐπαγγελίας τῶν πατέρων (the thought being that Christ has become the servant of the Jewish people for the sake of God's faithfulness, in order (a) to fulfil . . . and (b) that the Gentiles may glorify God for His mercy);

(ii) that it is dependent on εἰς τό and co-ordinate with βεβαιῶσαι, κ.τ.λ., but ὑπὲρ ἀληθείας θεοῦ is to be understood as a phrase parallel in meaning to, and anticipatory of, εἰς τό βεβαιῶσαι τὰς ἐπαγγελίας τῶν πατέρων, rather than as a truly integral part of the clause upon which the present clause depends;

(iii) that it is directly dependent on λέγω, δοξάσαι indicating a past action ('I declare that Christ has become . . . but that the Gentiles glorified . . .');

(iv) that it is directly dependent on λέγω, δοξάσαι indicating a present action ('I declare that . . . but that the Gentiles are glorifying . . .');

(v) that it is directly dependent on λέγω, δοξάσαι having the sense 'are to glorify', 'ought to glorify';

(vi) that it does not depend on anything in v. 8, but is the beginning of a new sentence altogether, δοξάσαι being not the aorist infinitive active but the third person singular[4] of the aorist optative active (for the form see on πληρῶσαι in v. 13), so that the words express a wish ('But may the Gentiles glorify. . . .').

In favour of both (i) and (ii) it may be said that, according to them, first, the connexion of v. 9a with Christ's work, which, if any of the other explanations is accepted, is no more than implicit, becomes perfectly clear (this is, indeed, a very big

[1] Cf. 9.4, and see note thereon.
[2] Cf. 9.5, and see note thereon.
[3] Cf. Michel, p. 358.
[4] A plural verb is used with ἔθνη in the quotation in v. 12 (cf. 2.14; Gal 3.8); but in 9.30 a singular verb was used (cf. Eph 4.17).

advantage, since the context leads us to expect a definitely christological content in v. 9a; and, secondly, 'the call of the Gentiles is shown to be (as it certainly was), equally with the fulfilment of the promise to the Jews, dependent on the covenant made with Abraham'.[1] Against (i) alone two objections lie: that, first, it involves weakening the connexion of ὑπὲρ ἀληθείας θεοῦ with εἰς τὸ βεβαιῶσαι τὰς ἐπαγγελίας τῶν πατέρων, which it is extremely difficult to believe was not intended as explicatory of it; and, secondly, it destroys the correspondence between ὑπὲρ ἀληθείας and ὑπὲρ ἐλέους, which certainly look as if they were intended to balance each other. These two objections do not apply to (ii). But (ii) may well seem rather forced, and, anyway, both (i) and (ii) are open to the very strong objection that an εἰς τό clause extending over vv. 8b and 9a and containing an extraordinarily harsh change of subjects (the change of subjects, which the other explanations assume, is much less harsh, if harsh at all)[2] and further complicated by the fact that v. 9b is dependent on it, is a stylistic horror in Greek, however successfully English versions which take δοξάσαι as dependent on εἰς τό may disguise the fact. We think (*pace* very many commentators)[3] that both (i) and (ii) ought to be rejected. (vi) may also, we think, be set aside as thoroughly unlikely: the expression of a wish at this point would be inappropriate. Of (iii), (iv) and (v) there can be little doubt that (iv) is the most acceptable (it may be doubted whether (v) is, grammatically, a possibility, and (iii) gives an inappropriate sense). We conclude that (iv) is the right way of construing the Greek, and the Greek, so construed, is to be explained along the lines suggested by Cornely. In a remarkably perceptive comment, which seems to have been overlooked by recent interpreters, Cornely suggests that Paul meant the conclusion to be drawn from v. 8 by the Jewish Christians that they, above all others, ought to glorify God for His faithfulness especially, but regarded this implication as so clear as not to need to be expressed explicitly; and then in v. 9 Paul has been even more elliptical, passing over in silence the parallel thought to v. 8 (which was actually in his mind), namely, that Christ has called the Gentiles for the sake of God's mercy, in order to manifest His kindness, and simply indicating the conclusion to be drawn by the Gentile Christians from this implied parallel to v. 8, or, rather, the result of

[1] Sanday and Headlam, p. 398, who appropriately refer to 4.11f and 16f.
[2] *pace* Barrett, p. 271.
[3] e.g., Sanday and Headlam, p. 398; Barrett, p. 271f.

that conclusion's being drawn by them—the fact that the Gentile Christians are actually glorifying God for His mercy.[1] On the basis of what is surely, as far as grammatical and stylistic considerations are concerned, the most natural way of construing the Greek of v. 9a, Cornely managed, by his penetrating insight into the elliptical nature of what Paul has said here, to reveal in vv. 8 and 9a a sense which is thoroughly suitable to the context and thoroughly consonant with what Paul has said elsewhere.[2]

καθὼς γέγραπται· διὰ τοῦτο ἐξομολογήσομαί σοι ἐν ἔθνεσιν καὶ τῷ ὀνόματί σου ψαλῶ. The first of a series of four supporting OT quotations follows the text of LXX Ps 17.50[RV: 18.49][3] exactly, apart from the omission of κύριε. It is sometimes assumed that the series of quotations is intended simply to

---

[1] Cornely's comment on vv. 8 and 9a takes up pp. 736–39; but the suggestion summarized above is made on p. 738, the paragraph in question being as follows: 'Ex priore hoc asserto Apostolus, uti iam diximus, colligi vult, Iudaeochristianos prae reliquis ad fidelitatem divinam celebrandam esse obligatos. Iam eodem modo, si voluisset, alterum membrum exprimere potuisset: "dico Christum Iudaeorum ministrum fuisse propter veritatem Dei . . ., gentes autem vocasse *propter misericordiam Dei, ad manifestandam eius benignitatem*" (vel etiam: "ad implenda vaticinia, quae dicunt" etc.), ut Ethnicochristiani inde colligerent, sibi prae reliquis Dei attributis misericordiam esse celebrandam. At pro conciso concitatoque suo dicendi modo, quo in priore iam membro conclusionem, utpote per se claram, silentio praeteriit, accurato membrorum parallelismo neglecto in altero nostro membro solam conclusionem ponere maluit, quia ex priore, quae praemissae sint supplendae, facile cognoscitur. Immo si accurate loqui volumus, eum ne ipsam quidem conclusionem sed eius exsecutionem posuisse dicamus oportet. Etenim quamvis eius verba: λέγω. . . τὰ ἔθνη ὑπὲρ ἐλέους δοξάσαι τὸν Θεόν, si nude spectantur, recte verti possint: "dico gentes propter misericordiam *debere glorificare* Deum", ita ut conclusionem enuntient, . . . haec tamen explicatio nostro loco non congruit, quia verbum λέγω (*dico*), quum ad prius quoque membrum quo factum enuntiatur pertineat, hic praecipiendi notionem annexam non habet. Retinenda igitur est *Vulg.* nostrae versio: *dico gentes propter misericordiam honorare Deum*, quae solum factum enuntiat. Paulus nempe id quod Christus in vocandis gentibus spectavit iam videt impletum. De facto Ethnicochristiani, quotiescumque vocationis suae recordantur, Dei benignitatem iam laudibus exornant; ideo argumentatione relicta ostendere mavult, gentes praesente sua glorificatione iam vaticinia prophetarum implere.'

[2] For the special association of God's faithfulness with the Jews compare especially 3.3f; 11.29: for the special association of God's mercy with the Gentiles compare especially 11.31 (τῷ ὑμετέρῳ ἐλέει). It should, of course, go without saying, that Paul was also well aware of the fact that Jewish Christians, no less than Gentile Christians, stand by the sheer free mercy of God (cf., e.g., 11.32), and, similarly, of the fact that the Gentiles no less than the Jews have an interest in God's faithfulness to His promises (cf., e.g., 4.11f, 16f).

[3] The psalm also occurs as 2 Sam 22.2–51.

support v. 9a;[1] but, in view of the close connexion between
vv. 8 and 9a, and also the connexion (γάρ) between them and
v. 7, it seems intrinsically more likely that the OT quotations
are intended as support, not just for v. 9a but for Paul's
solemn declaration (vv. 8–9a) as a whole. *Pace* Gaugler, who
dismissed as unlikely the view that Paul saw in these quotations a reference to the combination of Jews and Gentiles in the
believing community (and so support for v. 8 as well as for
v. 9a) on the ground that it is only in the second of the four
quotations that such an idea can be detected without undue
subtlety,[2] we are inclined to think that Paul did see such a
reference in this first quotation. Ps 18 is introduced in the OT
(MT Ps 18.1 = the psalm title in RV: cf. 2 Sam 22.1) as a psalm
sung by David 'in the day that the LORD delivered him from
the hand of all his enemies, and from the hand of Saul'.[3] Paul
may, in quoting v. 49, have thought of the words as spoken by
David in his own name and so as linking the Gentiles with the
Jewish king's praise of God; or he may have seen in the
psalmist's words a foreshadowing of his own mission as the
Jewish apostle of the Gentiles[4] (cf. the way in which the OT is
quoted in the latter part of chapter 10 and the beginning of
chapter 11). In either case, the thought of the combination of
Jews and Gentiles in the believing community to the glory of
God would be present for him in the quotation. But perhaps
the most likely view is that he took the words messianically.[5]

---

[1] So, e.g., Barrett, p. 272, sees Paul's intention as being to prove that
the inclusion of the Gentiles is no afterthought, but was foretold in
Scripture, and goes on to say, with regard to the first quotation, 'the
point (as in the quotations that follow) lies in the reference to the
Gentiles, and, secondarily, in the offering of praise for God's faithfulness
and mercy'; and Murray 2, p. 206, states: 'Common to all of these
quotations in the form quoted by the apostle is the reference to the
Gentiles. . . . this is the interest that guided the selection. . . . They are
all adduced to support the proposition that one of the designs in Christ's
being made a minister of the circumcision was the salvation of the
Gentiles . . .'.

[2] 2, p. 369f: cf. Lagrange, p. 347.

[3] According to A. Weiser, *The Psalms: a commentary*, London, 1962,
p. 185f, 'the psalm itself does not contain anything which could exclude
the possibility that it was composed at the time of David. . . . On the
other hand, the psalm exhibits some features which make it impossible
to assign a late date to it'.

[4] Käsemann, p. 370, understands Paul to see his own ministry foreshadowed here.

[5] The fact that the κύριε, which is present in the LXX text, has been
omitted in the quotation is perhaps support for the view that Paul
understood the words as words of Christ (cf. Lagrange, p. 347). (The
presence of κύριε in some witnesses to the text of Romans is no doubt to
be explained as assimilation to the psalm.)

But in that case too it seems natural enough to assume that he saw in them support not just for what he had said in v. 9a but also for what he had said in v. 8; for in the person of the exalted Christ, that is, the exalted Messiah of the Jews, proclaiming the praise of God among the Gentiles by the voices of His evangelists, is surely to be seen both God's fulfilment of His promises to the patriarchs and also His mercy to the Gentiles—and so too the union of Jews and Gentiles to the praise of God.

10. καὶ πάλιν λέγει introduces the second supporting quotation. Compare the Rabbinic use of *weʾ ōmēr*. The subject to be supplied here, in view of the γέγραπται of the preceding verse, is probably ἡ γραφή (cf. 4.3; 9.17; 10.11; 11.2): otherwise it would seem better to supply Μωϋσῆς than ὁ θεός, in view of the αὐτοῦ of the quotation. On the use of πάλιν here and in the two following verses see Bauer, s.v. 3.

εὐφράνθητε, ἔθνη, μετὰ τοῦ λαοῦ αὐτοῦ is an exact quotation of part of LXX Deut 32.43. It is an express summons to the Gentiles to rejoice[1] together with God's own people.[2] So it may clearly be regarded as support for the declaration of vv. 8–9a as a whole, and for the command in v. 7.

11. καὶ πάλιν· αἰνεῖτε, πάντα τὰ ἔθνη, τὸν κύριον, καὶ ἐπαινεσάτωσαν αὐτὸν πάντες οἱ λαοί.[3] The third supporting quotation agrees with LXX Ps 116.1[RV: 117.1], except for the transposition of τὸν κύριον and πάντα τὰ ἔθνη, the addition of καί, and the substitution of ἐπαινεσάτωσαν for ἐπαινέσατε. With its repeated use of πᾶς, it stresses the fact that no people is to be excluded from this common praise of God.

12. καὶ πάλιν Ἡσαΐας λέγει. Only in the case of the last of the four supporting quotations is the book from which it is taken indicated. A quotation from Isaiah completes the OT validation of Paul's declaration in vv. 8–9a. In that fourfold testimony each of the three divisions of the OT Canon is represented (one passage being from the Law, one from the Prophets, and two from the Writings).

ἔσται ἡ ῥίζα τοῦ Ἰεσσαί, καὶ ὁ ἀνιστάμενος ἄρχειν ἐθνῶν· ἐπ' αὐτῷ ἔθνη ἐλπιοῦσιν follows the LXX text of Isa 11.10, except

---

[1] On εὐφραίνειν (it occurs in Romans only here, and in the rest of the Pauline corpus only in 2 Cor 2.2 and Gal 4.27) see R. Bultmann, in *TWNT* 2, pp. 770–73. In the LXX the passive is specially used with reference to rejoicing in God's protection and help, to the exultant joy expressed in cultic worship, and to the joy of the eschatological fulfilment.

[2] The MT has *harnînû gôyīm ʿammô*, but see the apparatus in Kittel, and commentaries.

[3] λαοί in the LXX here represents the plural of the rare word *ʾummāh*, which occurs in the MT only in Gen 25.16; Num 25.15; Ps 117.1 (in all three places in the plural).

for the omission of ἐν τῇ ἡμέρᾳ ἐκείνῃ after ἔσται.[1] Though it is
clear that in the LXX version of Isa 11.1 ῥίζα, like the
Hebrew šōreš which it represents, must have its ordinary sense
'root', it seems likely that in Isa 11.10 both šōreš and ῥίζα mean
rather 'shoot (springing from the root)', 'scion', as is apparently
the case in Isa 53.2.[2] If this view is right, then the first part of
the quotation is a promise of the appearance of the messianic
Son of David.[3] The words καὶ ὁ ἀνιστάμενος ἄρχειν ἐθνῶν will
then be a further description of this same Son of David as the
one who rises[4] to rule the Gentiles. The last sentence quoted
(ἐπ' αὐτῷ ἔθνη ἐλπιοῦσιν) makes a fitting conclusion to the series
of OT passages as a whole. In the quotation of the promise
that Gentiles shall hope in the coming scion of Jesse, the
Messiah of the Jews, a promise now already being fulfilled in
the lives of the Gentile Christians in Rome, there is an implicit
appeal to the δυνατοί (many of them Gentile Christians) to
receive (cf. v. 7), and show considerateness to, those weak
brothers (most, if not all, of them Jewish Christians), according
them special honour for the sake of their Kinsman, the Messiah
of the Jews, who is the Gentiles' only true hope.

13 concludes the section with a prayer-wish (see on v. 5f). It
is not certain whether in Ὁ δὲ θεὸς τῆς ἐλπίδος the genitive
is intended to describe God as the source, or as the proper
object, of hope. The last words of v. 12 might seem to favour
the latter explanation;[5] but it is to be noted that αὐτῷ in that
verse refers to the Messiah rather than to God, and it is rather
more probable that Paul's thought is of God as the Giver of
hope,[6] the genitive being similar to those in v. 5 (see note on

---

[1] The Greek of the LXX is here only a paraphrase of the Hebrew,
which the RV renders: 'And it shall come to pass in that day, that the
root of Jesse, which standeth for an ensign of the peoples, unto him shall
the nations seek; . . .'

[2] Cf. Bauer, s.v. ῥίζα 2, where quite a number of examples of the word's
being used with the meaning 'Wurzelschössling', 'Sprössling' are cited;
also LSJ Suppl., s.v., where the additional meaning 'shoot or scion
growing from the root' is given.

[3] If, however, ῥίζα has its ordinary meaning, then this will be a
promise of the endurance of the root of Jesse, and ὁ ἀνιστάμενος will then
refer to the scion who will spring from it in due time.

[4] ὁ ἀνιστάμενος is to be explained as meaning 'he who rises' in the sort
of sense indicated in Bauer, s.v. ἀνίστημι 2.c (cf., e.g., 1 Macc 14.41, where
the intransitive second aorist active is used). It is hardly likely that
Paul, in quoting, actually had in mind another meaning of the word,
'rise (from the dead)', though there would of course be a theological
appropriateness in connecting Christ's rule with His resurrection.

[5] Cf., e.g., Calvin, p. 309.

[6] Cf. 8.17–30; also 5.2, 4f; 12.12; 15.4, and outside the Pauline corpus,
particularly 1 Pet 1.3.

that verse). πληρῶσαι is the optative required by the prayer-wish form.[1] Paul's desire is that God may fill[2] ὑμᾶς πάσης χαρᾶς καὶ εἰρήνης ἐν τῷ πιστεύειν, εἰς τὸ περισσεύειν ὑμᾶς ἐν τῇ ἐλπίδι ἐν δυνάμει πνεύματος ἁγίου. Its fulfilment would carry with it, as Barth notes,[3] the success of all the exhortation of this section and, indeed, of all his exhortation from 12.1 onward. There is real point in the inclusion of ἐν τῷ πιστεύειν;[4] for it serves to qualify 'joy' and 'peace'.[5] There are sorts of joy and peace which Paul certainly does not desire for the Christians of Rome: what he does desire is all the joy and peace which result from true faith in Christ. The following words indicate the desired goal of their being filled with joy and peace (for a purpose-clause within a prayer-wish compare v. 6: the presence of final clauses in prayers is of course extremely common). περισσεύειν takes up the idea of abundance already suggested by πληρῶσαι; and ἐν τῇ ἐλπίδι picks up the τῆς ἐλπίδος by which God has just been described. The double reference to hope in this verse is specially significant. An essential character-istic of the believer, as this epistle has very clearly shown, hope is perhaps also that characteristic which has at all periods most strikingly distinguished the authentic Christian from his pagan neighbours. The last phrase, ἐν δυνάμει πνεύματος ἁγίου, indi-cates the fact that the existence of this hope in men is no human possibility but the creation of the Spirit of God. Com-pare chapter 8, in which Paul has shown that it is because the life promised for those who are righteous by faith is a life characterized by the indwelling of the Holy Spirit that it is also a life characterized by hope.

---

[1] On the use of the Aeolic ending of the third person singular of the aorist optative active in the NT see BDF, § 85.

[2] The variant πληροφορήσαι . . . ἐν πάσῃ χαρᾷ καὶ εἰρήνῃ in B (and in G with the omission of ἐν) is puzzling. It is certainly the more difficult reading. πληροφορεῖν occurs in the NT only six times and of these only once (2 Tim 4.5) in the active. In none of these occurrences does it have the simple sense 'fill', which seems natural here. 'Satisfy fully with all joy . . .' would perhaps be a conceivable meaning. But it seems wiser to follow the great majority of authorities here. One might wonder whether the use of the word in 14.5 could have suggested it to a copyist here.

[3] *Shorter*, p. 173.

[4] It is omitted by D G *pc* it; but it seems more probable that it was accidentally omitted by haplography than that it was inserted by ditto-graphy on εἰς τὸ περισσεύειν (*pace* BDF, § 404(1)) or is simply a gloss (*pace* Pallis, p. 154). Cf. Käsemann, p. 371.

[5] Used here in the genitive in conjunction with πληρῶσαι ὑμᾶς, εἰρήνη is more naturally taken to mean inward peace of mind than the actual state of having been reconciled with God (contrast 14.17); but it should be recognized that the former is a fruit of the latter.

VIII

CONCLUSION TO THE EPISTLE
(15.14–16.27)

In 15.14–29 Paul takes up again the subject with which he was concerned in 1.8–16a, namely, that of his interest in, and his intention to visit, the Christians in Rome. He emphasizes his confidence in their Christian maturity, so as to prevent possible misinterpretation of the boldness which he is conscious of having shown in part of his letter. His words of explanation in v. 15 lead naturally into some statements in vv. 16–21 about his ministry as apostle of the Gentiles. It is the demands which this ministry as he has understood it have made upon him which have so far hindered him from visiting Rome (v. 22). The unfinished sentence which forms vv. 23 and 24a contains the first mention in the epistle of Spain and of Paul's purpose to go there; and the latter part of v. 24 discloses his hope that on his way thither he may at last visit the Christians who are in Rome and, having enjoyed their fellowship for a while, be assisted by them in the accomplishment of his Spanish plans. But, before he can come to them, he must go to Jerusalem in connexion with the collection which the churches of Macedonia and Achaia have made on behalf of the poor of the church in Jerusalem (vv. 25–29). Verses 30–33 consist of his request for the Roman Christians' earnest prayers for himself and for the success of his visit to Jerusalem and a prayer-wish for the Christians in Rome.[1]

On the question of the relation of chapter 16 to the rest of the epistle the reader may be referred to pp. 5–11.[2]

---

[1] In connexion with 15.14–33 reference may be made to L. Gaugusch, 'Untersuchungen zum Römerbrief: der Epilog (15.14–16.27)', in *BZ* 24 (1938–39), pp. 165–84, 252–66; K. H. Schelkle, 'Der Apostel als Priester', in *Theologische Quartalschrift* 136 (Tübingen, 1956), pp. 257–83; J. Knox, 'Romans 15.14–33 and Paul's conception of his apostolic mission', in *JBL* 83 (1964), pp. 1–11; A. M. Denis, 'La fonction apostolique et la liturgie nouvelle en esprit', in *RSPT* 42 (1958), pp. 401–36, 617–56; H. Schlier, 'Die "Liturgie" des apostolischen Evangeliums (Röm 15.14–21)', in O. Semmelroth (ed.), *Martyria, Leitourgia, Diakonia: Festschrift für H. Volk zum 65. Geburtstag*, Mainz, 1968, pp. 242–59.

[2] Also Käsemann, pp. 390f, 393, 397ff; Schlier, pp. 9–12.

The first two verses of chapter 16 are Paul's commendation of Phoebe, the bearer of his letter. Verses 3–15 are a series of greetings to named individuals and other, unnamed, Christians associated with some of these in church life and also to two other easily identifiable groups of Christians (vv. 10b and 11b). Verse 16 bids the Roman Christians greet one another with a holy kiss, and assures them of the greetings of all the churches of Christ.

In vv. 17–20a we have a piece of pastoral counsel, warning them to be on their guard against plausible false teachers and encouraging them to continue to live up to their good reputation. Verse 20b is Paul's customary *subscriptio*. It is followed by a postscript consisting of greetings from persons who are with Paul, including (v. 22) that of Tertius whose hand it has been which has actually written the letter. Verses 25–27, though unlikely (we think) to be Pauline, form (when correctly construed) a not unfitting doxological appendage to the epistle.

[14]But, as to myself, I too am persuaded, my brothers, concerning you, that you yourselves are full of honesty, being filled with all knowledge, able also to admonish one another. [15]But in part *of my letter* I have written to you rather boldly, as putting you again in remembrance because of the grace given me from God [16]to be a minister of Christ Jesus unto the Gentiles, serving God's message of good news with a holy service, in order that the offering consisting of the Gentiles may be acceptable, having been sanctified by the Holy Spirit. [17]This glorying then I have in Christ Jesus with regard to what pertains to God; [18]for I am not going to dare to speak of anything of the things which Christ has not wrought through me to bring about obedience of the Gentiles, by word and deed, [19]in the power of signs and wonders, in the power of the Spirit, so that from Jerusalem and round even to Illyricum I have fulfilled the message of good news of Christ. [20]But I made it my earnest endeavour so to preach the good news not where Christ had already been named, that I might not build upon another man's foundation, [21]but, as it is written, 'They shall see, to whom it has not been announced concerning him, and those who have not heard shall understand'. [22]Wherefore I have also been hindered these many times from coming to you. [23]But now, no longer having room in these regions and having for enough years desired to come to you [24]whenever I should go to Spain (for I hope to see you on my way and to be set forward by you on my journey thither, having first in some measure had my fill of your company)—[25]but now I am going to Jerusalem to minister to the saints. [26]For Macedonia and Achaia have resolved to make a contribution for the poor among the saints in Jerusalem. [27]They have resolved to do this, and, indeed, they are under an obligation to them; for, if the Gentiles have partaken of their spiritual good things, then they are under an obligation to render them service in the things necessary for their bodily welfare. [28]So, when I have completed this task and sealed for them this fruit,

I shall set out for Spain by way of your city. ²⁹And I know that, when I do come to you, it will be with the fullness of Christ's blessing that I shall come.

³⁰I exhort you [, brethren,] by our Lord Jesus Christ and by the love of the Spirit to join earnestly with me in prayers on my behalf to God, ³¹that I may be delivered from the disobedient in Judaea and that my ministry to Jerusalem may be acceptable to the saints, ³²so that, if it be God's will, my coming to you may be a matter of joy and I may find full refreshment in your fellowship.

³³May the God of peace be with you all. Amen.

¹I commend to you Phoebe, our sister who is [also] a deacon of the church in Cenchreae, ²that you may give her a welcome in the Lord that is worthy of the saints, and assist her in any matter in which she may need your help; for she herself has been a source of assistance to many, myself included.

³Greet Prisca and Aquila, my fellow-workers in Christ Jesus, ⁴who risked their necks to save my life and to whom not only I but all the churches of the Gentiles are grateful, ⁵and the church in their house. Greet my beloved Epaenetus, who is Asia's first-fruits for Christ. ⁶Greet Mary who laboured much for you. ⁷Greet Andronicus and Junia, my kinsfolk and fellow-prisoners, who are outstanding among the apostles and who also were in Christ before me. ⁸Greet Ampliatus, my beloved in the Lord. ⁹Greet Urbanus, our fellow-worker in Christ and my beloved Stachys. ¹⁰Greet Apelles who has been proved in Christ. Greet the *brethren* among the members of the household of Aristobulus. ¹¹Greet Herodion my kinsman. Greet those from the household of Narcissus who are in the Lord. ¹²Greet Tryphaena and Tryphosa who labour in the Lord. Greet Persis the beloved, who has laboured much in the Lord. ¹³Greet Rufus, the elect in the Lord, and his mother who is also a mother to me. ¹⁴Greet Asyncritus, Phlegon, Hermes, Patrobas, Hermas, and the brethren who are with them. ¹⁵Greet Philologus and Julia, Nereus and his sister, and Olympas, and all the saints who are with them. ¹⁶Greet one another with a holy kiss. All the churches of Christ greet you.

¹⁷I exhort you, brethren, to mark those who cause divisions and occasions of stumbling in opposition to the teaching you have learned. Avoid them; ¹⁸for such people serve not our Lord Christ but their own bellies, and deceive the hearts of the simple by their high-sounding plausibility. ¹⁹For your obedience is known to all, and for this I rejoice over you. But I want you to be wise unto that which is good, but kept pure from what is evil. ²⁰And the God of peace shall crush Satan under your feet soon.

The grace of our Lord Jesus Christ be with you.

²¹Timothy, my fellow-worker, greets you, and *so do* Lucius and Jason and Sosipater, my kinsmen. ²²I, Tertius, who have written this letter, greet you in the Lord. ²³Gaius, my host (and, indeed, the whole church's) greets you. Erastus, the city treasurer, and brother Quartus greet you.

²⁵To him who is able to confirm you in accord with my gospel and the proclamation of Jesus Christ, *which is* according to the revelation of the mystery which has been hidden in silence for ages from before creation ²⁶but has now been manifested and in accordance with the command of the eternal God clarified through the prophetic scriptures for the purpose of bringing about obedience of faith among all the Gentiles,—²⁷to the only wise God, through Jesus Christ, to him be glory for ever and ever. Amen.

14. Πέπεισμαι δέ, ἀδελφοί μου, καὶ αὐτὸς ἐγὼ περὶ ὑμῶν, ὅτι καὶ αὐτοὶ μεστοί ἐστε ἀγαθωσύνης, πεπληρωμένοι πάσης τῆς γνώσεως, δυνάμενοι καὶ ἀλλήλους νουθετεῖν. This sentence is often taken to be an instance of *captatio benevolentiae*. But it is difficult to believe that Paul is likely to have thought that the Christians in Rome, if they were not favourably disposed to him after reading or hearing fourteen and a half chapters of his epistle, could be won over at this stage by a flattering sentence. It seems more probable that he felt that, in addressing the particular exhortation of 12.1–15.13 to a church which he had not himself founded and which he had so far never even visited, he had taken a liberty (cf. what is said on the following verse), with reference to which, while, in view of his commission as apostle of the Gentiles, there was no need of any apology, a word of explanation would nevertheless be appropriate. Nothing which he had said in 12.1–15.13 had been intended as a calling in question of the spiritual adulthood of the Christians in Rome. Paul recognized—something which the clergy have too often been apt to forget—that it is courteous to assume that one's fellow-Christians are moderately mature until they have given positive evidence of their immaturity.[1] What we have here is Christian courtesy,[2] not flattery, though there is no doubt an element of hyperbole in the use of the words μεστοί,[3] πεπληρωμένοι and πάσης. For πέπεισμαι see on 8.38. For ἀδελφοί see on 1.13; the addition of μου, which gives special warmth to the vocative, is particularly appropriate here.[4] The words καὶ αὐτὸς ἐγώ as such could have the force, 'I myself too (no less than others)', but here no doubt simply emphasize Paul's personal commitment to the conviction expressed. The corresponding καὶ αὐτοί[5] underlines Paul's

[1] Contrast, e.g., 1 Cor 3.1 and Gal 3.1, which were addressed to people who had already given proof of their immaturity.

[2] That Paul was aware of the truth that such courtesy can serve to encourage one's fellow-Christian to try to be worthy of the confidence placed in him is not unlikely: cf. Ambrosiaster, col. 175 ('per laudem . . . provocat eos ad meliorem et intellectum et vitam. Qui enim videt se laudari, data opera elaborat ut vera sint quae dicuntur') and Pelagius, p. 116 ('Bonus doctor laudando prouocat ad profectum, ut erubescerent tales non esse quales ab apostolo esse credebantur').

[3] For μεστός (the word is attested from the fifth century B.C. onward) cf. 1.29; also Mt 23.28; Jn 19.29 (*bis*); 21.11; Jas 3.8, 17; 2 Pet 2.14.

[4] The omission of μου (𝔓⁴⁶ D* G 1739 it) is readily explicable as due to the fact that the combination of μου with the vocative ἀδελφοί is rare in the Pauline letters (cf. 1 Cor 1.11 (where it is omitted by 𝔓⁴⁶ C* d); 14.39; Phil 3.1: in 1 Cor 15.58 and Phil 4.1 we have ἀδελφοί μου followed by ἀγαπητοί and by ἀγαπητοὶ καὶ ἐπιπόθητοι, respectively).

[5] The variant reading which omits these words (𝔓⁴⁶ D G it) is unlikely to be original.

acknowledgment of the Roman Christians' adulthood as
Christians: they themselves—quite independently of him—
are already believers, and it is therefore both his right and his
duty to expect them to be frank and sincere in their dealings[1]
and to have a firm grasp of the truth of the gospel,[2] and so to
be capable of admonishing[3] one another.[4]

15f. τολμηροτέρως[5] δὲ ἔγραψα ὑμῖν[6] is slightly apologetic. The
comparative adverb may be rendered in some such way as
'somewhat boldly' or 'rather boldly'.

ἀπὸ μέρους is connected with the following words by Barrett
who observes that 'we do not learn the other part of Paul's
intentions';[7] but it is surely much more natural to connect it
with ἔγραψα—in part of his letter (12.1–15.13) he had indeed
taken a certain liberty in that he had addressed quite particular
exhortation to a church which he had not founded nor even
visited.[8]

---

[1] The variant ἀγάπης (G latt) is clearly secondary. For ἀγαθωσύνη see
Bauer, s.v., as well as W. Grundmann, in *TWNT* 1, p. 17. It is better
understood here (cf. Käsemann, p. 374) as denoting the honesty which
expresses itself in frank and sincere dealings with others than as
denoting moral goodness quite generally or as having its narrowest sense
of 'kindness'.

[2] The knowledge referred to (γνώσεως) will be the knowledge of the
gospel. Though Nestle reads τῆς after πάσης (with B ℵ 1739 *al* Cl), one
might possibly be inclined to prefer the widely attested omission
of τῆς (𝔓⁴⁶ A C 𝔎 D G *pm*) and to regard the B ℵ reading as an Alexandrian refinement (for πᾶσα ἡ γνῶσις cf. 1 Cor 13.2); but perhaps, in
view of 1 Cor 1.5, one should rather regard the reading without the
article as the more likely to be secondary. On the uses of πᾶς with, and
without, the article see, in addition to Bauer, s.v. πᾶς, and BDF,
§§ 270 (2), 275, Moule, *Idiom-Book*, pp. 93–95. If the distinction between
πάσης τῆς γνώσεως and πάσης γνώσεως can be pressed, the former should
mean 'with all (i.e. the whole range of) knowledge', the latter 'with every
kind of knowledge'. In either case, we may assume that Paul is thinking
specifically of knowledge directly related to the gospel.

[3] For the use of νουθετεῖν cf. Acts 20.31; 1 Cor 4.14; Col 1.28; 3.16;
1 Th 5.12, 14; 2 Th 3.15; also the occurrences of νουθεσία in 1 Cor 10.11;
Eph 6.4; Tit 3.10. What is denoted is the earnest attempt by words
spoken (or written) to correct what is wrong in another, to encourage
him to do what is right and to refrain from what is evil. See further
J. Behm, in *TWNT* 4, pp. 1013–16.

[4] For the sort of meaning which δυνάμενοι, κ.τ.λ. would have, were the
𝔎 33 *al* sy variant ἄλλους accepted, cf. ἄλλοις κηρύξας in 1 Cor 9.27 and
ἄλλους ἐδιδάξατε in Ignatius, *Rom.* 3.1; but the better-attested ἀλλήλους
fits the thought of v. 14f rather better, and should surely be read.

[5] On this word and the variant τολμηρότερον (𝔓⁴⁶ ℵ C 𝔎 D G *pl*) see
BDF, § 102 (1).

[6] ἀδελφοί is added by 𝔓⁴⁶ 𝔎 D G *pl* lat sy.

[7] p. 275.

[8] The suggestion that ἀπὸ μέρους is to be connected with ὑμῖν (Paul's
thought being that his letter has been too bold for a part of the Christian
community in Rome) seems unlikely.

ὡς ἐπαναμιμνῄσκων ὑμᾶς. The double compound verb ἐπανα-
μιμνῄσκειν is found in the Greek Bible only here;[1] but the
thought that men need to be reminded again and again of
truths they already know is, of course, continually presupposed
and acted upon both in the Bible and outside it, though—not
unnaturally—it is expressed directly only occasionally.[2] Here,
in view of the contents of v. 14, we may assume that Paul is
specially desirous of drawing attention to the fact that he has
been appealing to knowledge already possessed by the
Christians of Rome.

διὰ τὴν χάριν τὴν δοθεῖσάν μοι ἀπὸ[3] τοῦ θεοῦ εἰς[4] τὸ εἶναί με
λειτουργὸν Χριστοῦ Ἰησοῦ εἰς τὰ ἔθνη.[5] The first question to be
asked about these words is whether they are to be connected
with ἐπαναμιμνῄσκων ὑμᾶς or with τολμηροτέρως . . . ἔγραψα ὑμῖν
ἀπὸ μέρους.[6] On the whole it seems rather better to choose the
former alternative. The words are then to be seen as indicating
the basis of Paul's authority to put the Christians in Rome in
remembrance. But it is hardly possible to decide this question
with certainty; and it is not a very important question, since,
in either case, the words διὰ τὴν χάριν, κ.τ.λ. will have an indirect connexion with those words from which the punctuation
adopted divides them. The basis of Paul's authority to put the
Roman Christians in remembrance is the fact that he has
received a commission from God which is altogether God's
gracious gift, something which he has in no way merited. On
the use of χάρις here see on 1.5; 12.3, 6. εἰς τὸ εἶναι, κ.τ.λ. is
better understood as final (cf. the following ἵνα) than as consecutive (as indicating the divine purpose behind the gift just
mentioned rather than the result of the gift)—though in the
case of a divine purpose which is thought of as being in the
process of fulfilment the distinction is not sharp.

The next question to be asked concerns the word λειτουργός.
Something has already been said about this word in connexion

---

[1] It is found in Plato, *Lg.* 688a; Aristotle, *Mem.* 451ᵃ 12; Demosthenes
6.35; Hermas, vis. 4.1.7.

[2] Cf., e.g., the use of ἀναμιμνῄσκειν in 1 Cor 4.17; 2 Tim 1.6; and of
ὑπομιμνῄσκειν in 2 Pet 1.12 (also the noun ὑπόμνησις in the following verse).

[3] The variant ὑπό (𝔓⁴⁶ A C 𝕶 D G *pl*) is strongly supported and could
be original (the ἀπό of B 𝕬 * F could conceivably be explained as assimilation to the salutation formula—cf., e.g., 1.7; 1 Cor 1.3; 2 Cor 1.2); but
ἀπό is perhaps to be preferred as being the less obvious reading.

[4] 𝔓⁴⁶ has διά instead of εἰς—this looks like a slip, perhaps due to the
διά before τὴν χάριν.

[5] It is probably safe to assume that the omission of εἰς τὰ ἔθνη by B
was accidental.

[6] As is presupposed by the comma placed after ὑμᾶς in WH (cf., e.g.,
AV and RV).

with its occurrence in 13.6, where it was used of the civil
authorities. That in the present verse it does have a sacral sense
is strongly suggested by the context (especially by the presence
of ἱερουργοῦντα, προσφορά, εὐπροσδεκτός and ἡγιασμένη). But it
does not follow that the generally accepted view that Paul is
here thinking of himself as exercising a priestly ministry[1] is
necessarily to be upheld. While it is, of course true that
λειτουργεῖν and λειτουργία are in the LXX quite often used with
reference to priests,[2] their use in connexion with the Levites is
specially common (it will be enough to refer to Exod 38.21
[LXX: 37.19]; Num 1.50; 3.6, 31; 4.3, 9, 12, 14, 23f, 26-28, 30,
33, 35, 37, 39, 41, 43; 7.5, 7f; 8.22; 16.9; 18.2, 4, 6, 21, 23;
1 Chr 6.32f[LXX: 17], 48[LXX: 33]; 15.2; 16.4, 37; 23.28;
2 Chr 23.6; Ezek 45.5: cf. the occurrences of λειτούργημα in
Num 4.32 and 7.9).[3] In view of this LXX evidence, the suggestion of Barth that Paul is thinking of himself as fulfilling the
function not of a priest but of a Levite[4] deserves to be taken
very seriously. The fact that λειτουργόν is followed by Χριστοῦ
Ἰησοῦ is surely a very strong argument in favour of this
interpretation; for a genitive (referring to a person) dependent
on λειτουργός used in its special sense of priestly minister would
naturally be understood to denote the one to whom the
λειτουργός offered sacrifice—so, if λειτουργόν here really did
have the sense of priestly minister, one would expect not
Χριστοῦ Ἰησοῦ but τοῦ θεοῦ either expressed or understood. On
the assumption that the thought of ministry intended by
λειτουργόν here is of the Levite's ministry, the dependent
genitive which we have here is fully understandable; for the
idea conveyed is that Paul fulfils a ministry subordinate and
auxiliary to that of Christ the Priest (we may compare with
the genitive used here with the noun λειτουργός the dative used
with λειτουργεῖν in, for example, LXX Num 3.6 and 18.2). This
understanding of λειτουργόν is, we believe, fully compatible
with the remainder of v. 16 following the words εἰς τὰ ἔθνη

---

[1] To be seen, e.g., in Calvin, p. 310f; Michel, p. 364; Barrett, p. 275;
Käsemann, p. 375; Black, p. 175: cf. H. Strathmann, in *TWNT* 4, p. 237.

[2] e.g. Exod 28.35 and 43; 29.30; 30.20; 35.19; 39.1[LXX: 12]; also
LXX 38.27; Deut 17.12; Ezek 40.46.

[3] The noun λειτουργός occurs much less often than λειτουργεῖν or
λειτουργία—less than a dozen times in the canonical books, and then
usually in a non-cultic sense. (2 Ἔσδρ 20.40 (=Neh 10.39) would be an
example of λειτουργός used to denote a Levite, if καί were read with B S
between οἱ ἱερεῖς and οἱ λειτουργοί (but it is not read by Rahlfs).) In the
NT λειτουργός is used in connexion with Christ's High Priesthood in
Heb 8.2.

[4] *Shorter*, p. 177. Cf. Bengel's comment, p. 564: 'Jesus est sacerdos:
Paulus, sacerdotis minister'.

(for these cf. 1.5; 11.13; and see on the latter of these verses).

ἱερουργοῦντα τὸ εὐαγγέλιον τοῦ θεοῦ indicates the activity wherein Paul's λειτουργία consists. The verb ἱερουργεῖν occurs frequently in Philo and Josephus but always in the sense of offering (a sacrifice), sometimes with, and sometimes without, an object expressed. That that sense is impossible here is obvious. The word is also found in Plutarch, Philostratus, and in the third century A.D. historian Herodian; and occurs in an inscription with τὴν κλείνην as its object as an equivalent of the Latin *lectisternium facere*. Specially interesting as a parallel to its use in Romans is its appearance as a variant (ἱερουργοῦντας instead of δημιουργοῦντας)[1] in 4 Macc 7.8 with τὸν νόμον as object.[2] The thought of specifically priestly activity, while it clearly can be, does not seem to be necessarily, present in the use of the verb. So here we may take it to mean 'serve with a holy service'. To preach the gospel is to be engaged with a holy thing and to fulfil a holy ministry.

ἵνα γένηται ἡ προσφορὰ τῶν ἐθνῶν εὐπρόσδεκτος, ἡγιασμένη ἐν πνεύματι ἁγίῳ indicates the purpose behind God's giving His gracious commission to Paul to be Christ's λειτουργός with regard to the Gentiles by his service of the gospel—it was that the sacrifice consisting of the Gentiles[3] might be acceptable to God,[4] sanctified by the Holy Spirit. As the purpose of the due fulfilment by the Levites of their subordinate and auxiliary role in the cultus was that the sacrifices offered by the priests might be acceptable to God, so Paul's preaching of the gospel to the Gentiles is a service subordinate and auxiliary to Christ's priestly service of offering them to God as a sacrifice, and the preaching of the gospel is a necessary service if that sacrifice is to be truly well-pleasing to God, including in itself the willing and intelligent response of their gratitude for all that God has done for them in Christ. ἡγιασμένη ἐν πνεύματι ἁγίῳ fills out the

---

[1] It is read by the Sixtine edition of the LXX, but is not mentioned by Rahlfs.

[2] On ἱερουργεῖν see further LSJ and Bauer s.v. ἱερουργέω; G. Schrenk, in *TWNT* 3, p. 251f; C. Wiéner, '*Hierourgein* (Rom 15.16)', in *Studiorum Paulinorum Congressus Internationalis Catholicus* (1961) 2, Rome, 1963, pp. 399–404.

[3] In the Pauline corpus προσφορά occurs only here and in Eph 5.2, while the cognate verb does not occur at all. προσφορά can denote either the act of offering or the thing offered (cf. the two meanings of θυσία). In the NT it is nearly always used in the latter sense, as it is here. The genitive τῶν ἐθνῶν is a genitive of apposition.

[4] εὐπρόσδεκτος (it is omitted in G, probably by accident) occurs also in v. 31. For its use with reference to sacrifices cf. 1 Pet 2.5. See on εὐάρεστον in 12.1 and 2.

meaning of εὐπρόσδεκτος. The sacrifice offered to God by Christ, which Paul has here in mind, consists of the Gentile Christians who have been sanctified by the gift of the Holy Spirit (Paul is speaking as ἐθνῶν ἀπόστολος—that there is also a προσφορὰ τῶν Ἰουδαίων goes without saying). The verb ἁγιάζειν occurs in the Pauline corpus only here and in 1 Cor 1.2; 6.11; 7.14 (bis); Eph 5.26; 1 Th 5.23; 1 Tim 4.5; 2 Tim 2.21. All these occurrences are in the passive except for those in Ephesians and 1 Thessalonians. It is God who sanctifies (makes ἅγιος). See on ἁγίοις in 1.7, and, for the sanctification of believers, on chapters 6–8. For the association of the Holy Spirit with sanctification compare 8.1–16 (though in these verses neither ἁγιάζειν nor ἁγιασμός (see 6.19, 22) occurs); 1 Cor 6.11; 1 Th 4.7f; 2 Th 2.13; 1 Pet 1.2.

17. ἔχω οὖν τὴν καύχησιν ἐν Χριστῷ Ἰησοῦ[1] τὰ πρὸς τὸν θεόν. If (with 𝔓⁴⁶ ℵ A 𝕶 pm) we omit the article before καύχησιν, the meaning will be 'I have then my glorying in Christ . . .'; but, if (with B D G al) we read it, as we probably should,[2] the sense will be 'This glorying then I have in Christ . . .', the article having here the effect of a demonstrative adjective pointing back to what has been said in v. 16.[3] Paul is asserting that the glorying which he has allowed himself in v. 16 is a legitimate glorying, since it is a glorying in Christ concerned with what truly pertains to God,[4] being a glorying in the results of his mission viewed not as his achievements (so to have understood them would indeed have been to glory in man), but as the works of Christ in obedience to the will of God.

18-19a. οὐ γὰρ τολμήσω τι λαλεῖν ὧν οὐ κατειργάσατο Χριστὸς δι' ἐμοῦ εἰς ὑπακοὴν ἐθνῶν, λόγῳ καὶ ἔργῳ, ἐν δυνάμει σημείων καὶ τεράτων, ἐν δυνάμει πνεύματος explains how it is that the glorying contained in v. 16 is really, as v. 17 has claimed that it is, a glorying ἐν Χριστῷ Ἰησοῦ τὰ πρὸς τὸν θεόν. It is because Paul has no intention[5] of presuming to refer to anything other than

---

[1] The absence of Ἰησοῦ in 𝔓⁴⁶ Ambst is probably to be explained as due to accidental omission.

[2] Pace Sanday and Headlam, p. 405f. The reading with the article should probably be preferred both as the lectio difficilior (the fact that v. 16 is a glorying is not obvious) and also as intrinsically superior (as giving a more meaningful connexion between v. 17 and v. 16). Cf. Cornely, p. 753; Lagrange, p. 351; Käsemann, p. 375f. (Could the omission of the article perhaps have come about through unconscious assimilation to ἔχει καύχημα in 4.2?)

[3] Cf. the article before ἐλπίς in 5.5 (see the translation on p. 256 and n. 1 on p. 262).

[4] On the different possible kinds of glorying see on 2.17 (καυχᾶσαι ἐν θεῷ). For the expression τὰ πρὸς τὸν θεόν cf. Heb 2.17; 5.1.

[5] The present (τολμῶ) is read by B ℵ ³ lat syᵖ (cf. 2 Cor 10.12), but the future should surely be preferred.

what Christ has wrought through him by word and deed, in the power of signs and wonders, in the power of the Spirit, to bring about obedience of the Gentiles. Such seems to be the simplest and most natural way (and the most suitable to the context) of understanding Paul's decidedly clumsy sentence. Paul's meaning (if we have understood it correctly) would have been conveyed more straightforwardly, if, instead of the ὧν οὐ (= ἐκείνων ἃ οὐ), which he has written, he had used one of the possible Greek equivalents of our 'except what'. It looks as if he has substituted the negative formulation ὧν οὐ κατειργάσατο Χριστός for the simpler positive formulation (making use of πλήν or ἐκτός or equivalent expression) with the intention of giving greater emphasis to his rejection of the possibility of referring to something other than what Christ has wrought through him, but, by so doing, has succeeded in making the rest of the sentence follow extremely awkwardly and greatly puzzling his interpreters.[1] What Paul has done as the λειτουργός of Christ Jesus has not only been a subordinate service subsidiary to Christ's own priestly work, it has also been something which Christ has actually Himself effected, working through His minister. For κατεργάζεσθαι see on 1.27. With εἰς ὑπακοὴν[2] ἐθνῶν compare εἰς ὑπακοὴν πίστεως ἐν πᾶσιν τοῖς ἔθνεσιν in 1.5. For the combination of λόγῳ and ἔργῳ compare 2 Cor 10.11; Col 3.17; 2 Th 2.17. It has been suggested that ἐν δυνάμει[3] σημείων[4] καὶ τεράτων, ἐν δυνάμει πνεύματος[5] is meant

---

[1] Cf. Cornely's perceptive comment (p. 753f). Many commentators have asserted that the clumsiness has been caused by Paul's trying to say two things at once; but the fact that there is considerable disagreement as to what the two things are should discourage us from accepting this line of explanation without careful scrutiny. See, e.g., Lietzmann, p. 120 (he sees the two things as being: 'ich kann nichts berichten, was nicht Christi Werk wäre' and 'ich würde nicht wagen, dies zu sagen, wenn es nicht Christi Werk wäre'); Lagrange, p. 352; Barrett, p. 276 (according to him, the two things are: 'I would not dare to speak of this if it were not Christ's work (rather than mine)' and 'I would not dare to speak of this if it were not Christ's work through me (rather than anyone else)'); Käsemann, p. 376.

[2] The B variant ἀκοήν is unlikely to be original: it would appear to be connected with another B variant in this verse, the insertion of λόγων after δι' ἐμοῦ, which was presumably due to a desire for an antecedent to ὧν.

[3] 𝔓⁴⁶ D G it add αὐτοῦ, the reference presumably being to Christ (in view of v. 18). The reading could conceivably be original (for the thought of the exalted Christ's confirming the preaching by σημεῖα καὶ τέρατα cf. Acts 14.3; also Mk 16.20, which mentions only σημεῖα); but should probably be rejected as secondary.

[4] 𝔓⁴⁶ adds τε.

[5] ἁγίου is added by A C D G 1739 al lat sy^hmg aeg, θεοῦ by 𝔓⁴⁶ ℵ K pm sy^p.h; but B should doubtless be followed here, the alternative additions being obvious 'improvements'.

to be taken chiastically with the preceding phrase, the former element explicating ἔργῳ and the latter λόγῳ.[1] This could conceivably be right; but, since ἔργον, though occurring very frequently in the Pauline corpus, is used nowhere else in it of a miraculous work, it is probably better to understand ἔργῳ in v. 18 quite generally ('action' as opposed to 'speech') and to explain λόγῳ καὶ ἔργῳ as describing Paul's ministry by reference to the means by which it is being fulfilled ('word' including words spoken and written, and 'deed' including things done and suffered, conduct generally, the example set by his steadfast endurance, etc.[2]) and the two following phrases as further characterizing his ministry as both powerfully confirmed and attested by[3] accompanying miracles[4] and also accomplished as a whole in the power of the Holy Spirit.[5] While it is undoubtedly true that Paul was very much aware of the fact that some Christians were prone to make bold and boastful claims in their

[1] e.g. Bengel, p. 564; Cornely, p. 754f; Michel, p. 366; Leenhardt, p. 369, n. §; Black, p. 175; also K. H. Rengstorf, in *TWNT* 7, p. 259.

[2] Cf. the words ἐν πάσῃ ὑπομονῇ in their context in 2 Cor 12.12.

[3] The word δύναμις could, of course, itself denote a miracle, a 'mighty work' (as in 2 Cor 12.12); but here it seems to be best understood to refer to the power of Christ (cf. οὐ . . . τι . . . ὧν οὐ κατειργάσατο Χριστός above) manifested in the σημεῖα καὶ τέρατα. To understand it of Paul's ability to work miracles (so, e.g., Lagrange, p. 352) seems less suitable to the context.

[4] σημεῖον has already been used in 4.11, and occurs otherwise in the Pauline letters only in 1 Cor 1.22; 14.22; 2 Cor 12.12 (*bis*); 2 Th 2.9; 3.17: τέρας occurs elsewhere in Paul only in 2 Cor 12.12 and 2 Th 2.9. For accounts of the complexities of the ways in which these two words are used in extra-biblical Greek, in the LXX and in the NT, reference should be made to K. H. Rengstorf, in *TWNT* 7, pp. 199–261, and 8, pp. 113–127. The combination of the two words in the NT (in the NT the latter word is never used except in the company of the former) occasionally refers to deceiving signs and wonders (as in Mk 13.22 and 2 Th 2.9), but here obviously has a good sense, referring to the signs and wonders accompanying the apostolic mission (cf., e.g., Acts 2.22, 43; 4.30; 5.12; 14.3; 15.12; 2 Cor 12.12; Heb 2.4). For the testimony of Acts with reference to Paul, see 14.8–10; 16.16–18, 25–26; 20.9–12; 28.8f. Paul's own claim here in Romans and in 2 Cor 12.12 (see too Gal 3.5) is difficult to brush aside; and Lagrange's comment, 'Il faut beaucoup d'audace pour le taxer d'illusion ou de mensonge' (p. 352), seems to us to be justified.

[5] ἐν δυνάμει πνεύματος is surely best understood neither as saying again in a different way what has just been said in the preceding phrase, nor yet as limited in its reference to Paul's ministry 'by word' (in spite of the very close association between this and πνεῦμα indicated by 1 Cor 2.4), and still less as limited to such special kinds of speaking as prophecy and glossolaly, but as indicating that Paul's ministry as a whole is accomplished by the Spirit's enabling. Two different sorts of relationship are indicated by the genitives dependent on the first and the second δυνάμει.

certainty of being 'spiritual', it does not seem necessary to assume, as Michel does,[1] that he must have had a consciously polemical intention here, to defend himself against the suspicion of having behaved as such a 'spiritual'.

19b. ὥστε με ἀπὸ Ἰερουσαλὴμ κύκλῳ μέχρι τοῦ Ἰλλυρικοῦ πεπληρωκέναι τὸ εὐαγγέλιον τοῦ Χριστοῦ.[2] It is not absolutely clear how far back ὥστε looks. It could conceivably be right back to the latter part of v. 15, the whole context from τὴν χάριν τὴν δοθεῖσάν μοι onwards being included in its reference; but more probably ὥστε looks no further back than v. 18, its purpose being to indicate that the progress of the gospel described in v. 19b is the result of the work of Christ through Paul referred to in vv. 18–19a. ἀπὸ Ἰερουσαλήμ is somewhat puzzling. In view of the evidence of Galatians 1 and 2 (and also, for that matter, of Acts), a reference to a significant preaching mission conducted by Paul in Jerusalem would seem to be ruled out; and, in any case, a preaching in Jerusalem would not naturally be thought of as forming part of the Gentile mission,[3] with which this context is concerned. Conceivably Jerusalem is simply mentioned as one geographical limit and intended (as may also be the case with the reference to Illyricum) exclusively rather than inclusively. That Paul is thinking of his vision in the Temple (Acts 22.17–21) or the interview described in Gal 2.1–10 as marking the beginning of his mission[4] does not seem at all likely.[5] The most probable

---

[1] p. 366. It is very questionable whether the occurrences of τολμᾶν in 2 Cor 10.2, 12; 11.21 are sufficient justification for seeing in its use in v.18 a reference to the boldness of such a 'spiritual's' self-confidence; and the further appeal to the presence of τολμηροτέρως in v. 15 is hardly convincing.

[2] The western variant (D G it), which instead of με . . . πεπληρωκέναι has πεπληρῶσθαι ἀπὸ Ἰερουσαλὴμ μέχρι τοῦ Ἰλλυρικοῦ καὶ κύκλῳ, is not likely to be original. The transposition of καὶ κύκλῳ may perhaps have been due to a desire to do more justice to the breadth of the area covered, while the substitution of the passive for με and the active may be due to a feeling that Jerusalem is outside the scope of Paul's mission to the Gentiles.

[3] It is true that in Acts 9.29 (in the course of a brief passage, vv. 26–29, which tells of a sojourn of Paul in Jerusalem during which he was παρρησιαζόμενος in the name of the Lord and speaking and disputing) there is a variant Ἕλληνας for Ἑλληνιστάς, and that in Foakes-Jackson and Lake, *Beginnings* 4, p. 106, it is argued that the people referred to were Gentiles; but Haenchen, *Apostelgeschichte*, p. 280, n. 3, is surely right in claiming that the last part of the verse would be surprising if these people really were Gentiles.

[4] Bruce, p. 261, mentions these two suggestions as conceivable, but sets them aside as unlikely.

[5] According to Acts 9.19–22, Paul actually began his work as a Christian preacher in Damascus.

explanation would seem to be that Paul refers to Jerusalem as being 'the starting-point and metropolis of the Christian movement as a whole',[1] and in a very real sense his own spiritual base as well as that of the Jewish Christian mission (cf. the way in which he speaks in vv. 25–31—note especially v. 27—and also Gal 1.18; 2.1–10).[2] The following καὶ κύκλῳ has sometimes[3] been taken to mean 'and round about it (i.e. Jerusalem)'. But, since that sense would have been expressed more naturally by καὶ τῆς κύκλῳ χώρας or perhaps καὶ τοῦ κύκλῳ,[4] and since the fact that κύκλῳ is followed directly by μέχρι τοῦ Ἰλλυρικοῦ strongly suggests that it is to be connected with that phrase, and since, moreover, we have no clear evidence of any Pauline mission in the immediate neighbourhood of Jerusalem, this explanation is surely to be set aside as quite unlikely. The probable explanation is that in using κύκλῳ Paul has in mind one, or two, or possibly all three, of the following thoughts: that the area which he has covered in his preaching may be said to form a great arc; that he has not gone from the one to the other point mentioned by the most direct possible, but by a circuitous, route; that between the two limits he has made numerous missionary journeys in various directions from various centres.[5] The exact significance of μέχρι τοῦ Ἰλλυρικοῦ cannot be determined, since we cannot be sure whether μέχρι is used inclusively or exclusively, and there is also room for doubt as to whether τὸ Ἰλλυρικόν here denotes the Roman province of Illyricum (the meaning which naturally comes first to mind and which we are inclined to regard as more probable) or is used of a part of the province of Macedonia inhabited by people of Illyrian race.[6] We are nowhere else informed of Paul's having gone 'as far as Illyricum' in any of the senses the phrase could bear; but it is not at all impossible that he reached the border of the province of Illyricum or that he crossed it (if he followed the Via Egnatia to its western end at Dyrrhachium

---

[1] Bruce, p. 261.

[2] That the author of Acts thought of Paul as having a close connexion with Jerusalem is clear enough. On this see, e.g., A. Ehrhardt, *The Framework of the New Testament Stories*, Manchester, 1964, pp. 94–97.

[3] e.g., Fritzsche; Gifford; Weiss.

[4] Cf. Sanday and Headlam, p. 407.

[5] Cf., e.g., Chrysostom, col. 656 (Διὰ γὰρ τοῦτο εἶπε "καὶ κύκλῳ", ἵνα μὴ τὴν κατευθὺ λεωφόρον ἔλθῃς μόνον, ἀλλὰ καὶ πᾶσαν καὶ τὴν κατὰ νότον Ἀσίαν περιδράμῃς τῇ διανοίᾳ); Sanday and Headlam, p. 407; Lagrange, p. 353; Käsemann, p. 377.

[6] See *OCD*, p. 541f (s.vv. 'Illyricum' and 'Illyrii'); also Josephus, *B.J.* 2.369; Strabo 7.7.4; Appian, *Illyrike*. The view that Paul only used the Roman provincial names for territories cannot be sustained (cf., e.g., Kümmel, *Introduction*, p. 192).

(Durazzo or Durrës), he would have been close enough to the border to be able to say without too great exaggeration that he had gone 'as far as (the province of) Illyricum'; for Lissus (Lesh), which was within it, was only about forty miles away), and to have approached or entered a part of Macedonia that might be referred to as Illyrian he would have had to go less far. The period of time indicated by the last few words of v. 1 and the two participial clauses of v. 2 of Acts 20 may well have been long enough to allow such a journey. That the function of the phrase is to indicate the north-western limit of the area Paul has covered is clear.

Still to be considered are the words με . . . πεπληρωκέναι τὸ εὐαγγέλιον τοῦ Χριστοῦ. It is the only occurrence in Romans of the qualification of εὐαγγέλιον by τοῦ Χριστοῦ (but cf. 1 Cor 9.12; 2 Cor 2.12; 9.13; 10.14; Gal 1.7; Phil 1.27; 1 Th 3.2; 2 Th 1.8): the genitive is of course objective. The suggestion that πληροῦν is here used with reference to the fullness with which Paul has preached the gospel (cf. the thought of Acts 20.20 and 27) may be set aside as altogether unlikely. Also unlikely are the suggestions that the reference is to the fact that Paul has so preached the gospel that it has not been just a recital of past history but has been effective in the lives of the hearers,[1] and that the meaning is that he has 'filled the whole of the Mediterranean East with the Gospel of the Messiah'.[2] There has recently been a good deal of support for the view that Paul's meaning is that he has completed, as far as the area indicated is concerned, all the preaching of the gospel which must be done before the Parousia (cf. Mk 13.10).[3] This explanation fits well, of course, the widespread assumption that it is an 'assured result' of modern NT scholarship that the primitive Church was sure that the End would come within a few years;[4] but it would seem that Paul has himself given in the next two verses a fairly clear clue to his meaning, and, in view of their contents, we understand his claim to have completed the gospel of Christ to be a claim to have completed that trail-blazing, pioneer preaching of it, which he believed it was his own special apostolic mission to accomplish.[5]

[1] So Schlatter, p. 387.
[2] Black, p. 176, asks whether this could be the meaning, but apparently is inclined not to think so himself. Similar language was earlier used by Michel, p. 367, who saw in Paul's claim an appropriateness to what he regarded as Paul's καύχησις in the face of Roman *Pneumatiker*.
[3] e.g. Munck, *Paul*, pp. 48–55, 301; Barrett, p. 276f; also id., 'New Testament Eschatology', in *SJT* 6 (1953), p. 228; Käsemann, p. 377.
[4] See on 13.12, and also on vv. 23 and 24 of the present chapter.
[5] For the use of εὐαγγέλιον in a pregnant way (what Paul has completed

20f. οὕτως δὲ φιλοτιμούμενον[1] εὐαγγελίζεσθαι οὐχ ὅπου ὠνομάσθη Χριστός. The adverb οὕτως is here used with reference, not to what precedes, but to what follows;[2] and in what follows it is to be connected, not with φιλοτιμούμενον, but with εὐαγγελίζεσθαι,[3] its purpose being to anticipate οὐχ ὅπου ὠνομάσθη Χριστός (Paul's point is not that he was so eager to preach the gospel where, etc., but that he was eager so to preach the gospel as to do it where, etc.). The δέ is, we think, best explained as having its proper adversative force, the sentence which it introduces being intended as a qualification of the claim made in v. 19b: Paul's statement that he has completed the gospel in the area mentioned is not to be taken in an absolute sense but in relation to what he understands to be his own particular function in the service of the gospel, namely, that of a pioneer preacher.[4] The decisive ground of his eagerness is surely neither to avoid possible rivalry nor yet (*pace* Barrett, p. 277) to cover as wide an area as possible, but his under-

is, of course, not the gospel itself, but—in some measure—the preaching of it) see p. 54, n. 2. For the expression πληροῦν τὸ εὐαγγέλιον cf. Col 1.25 (πληρῶσαι τὸν λόγον τοῦ θεοῦ).

[1] The rather more difficult φιλοτιμούμενον is surely to be preferred to the φιλοτιμοῦμαι supported by 𝔓⁴⁶ B D* G. Though, from the point of view of a copyist, the less obvious choice, the neuter participle is by virtue of its very indefiniteness intrinsically better suited than the first person singular of the present indicative to indicate a general principle which has in the past governed, in the present governs, and in the future still will govern, Paul's missionary practice. On this verb see LSJ and Bauer, s.v. φιλοτιμέομαι (especially LSJ, s.v. II). *Pace* Cornely, p. 757; Lagrange, p. 354; Michel, p. 367, n. 2; Barrett, p. 273 (translation); Käsemann, p. 377; RSV; NEB; B. Rigaux, *Saint Paul: Les Épîtres aux Thessaloniciens*, Paris, 1956, p. 520, it seems very doubtful whether insistence on the presence here of the thought of honour, ambition or emulation is justified, in view of the only other occurrences of the word in the NT (2 Cor 5.9 and 1 Th 4.11, in which it is perhaps possible, but certainly not necessary, to see the idea of ambition) and such examples as those cited by Sanday and Headlam, p. 408, following F. Field. In Polybius 1.83.3 ἐφιλοτιμεῖτο seems to be used as a synonym of μεγάλην ἐποιεῖτο σπουδήν, and the three other instances given by Sanday and Headlam (Diodorus Siculus 12.46.2; 16.49.8 (here it is διαφιλοτιμεῖσθαι that is used); Plutarch, *Caes.* 54.1) tell the same story. A good many further examples could be cited where some such rendering as 'be eager', 'strive eagerly', 'aspire', would seem to be required.

[2] See Bauer, s.v. 2.

[3] Cf. Michel, p. 367, n. 2. *Contra* Käsemann, p. 377.

[4] *Pace* Lagrange, p. 353; Käsemann, p. 377, who see v. 20f, not as a qualification of v. 19b but as a preparation for the announcement of plans in vv. 23ff (Käsemann actually refers to the plans announced in vv. 22ff; but v. 22 goes more closely with what precedes, and the νυνὶ δέ at the beginning of v. 23 seems to us to weigh against the contention that the primary purpose of v. 20f is to prepare for the announcement of the future plans).

standing of the nature of the particular commission entrusted
to him by God, confirmation of which he sees in the scriptural
words he is about to quote. Barrett's comment with regard to
οὐχ ὅπου ὠνομάσθη Χριστός, that 'the position of the negative
invites the supplement' ἀλλ' ὅπου οὐδέποτε ὠνομάσθη[1] is no
doubt right. It is probably better, with Sanday and Headlam,[2]
Michel,[3] Leenhardt,[4] Murray,[5] Käsemann,[6] and others, to take
the passive of ὀνομάζειν to be used here with some such
solemn sense as 'be named in worship' or 'be acknowledged
and confessed' or 'be proclaimed (as Lord)',[7] than to understand it as signifying merely 'be known'.[8] The aorist is here
equivalent to an English pluperfect.[9]

ἵνα μὴ ἐπ' ἀλλότριον θεμέλιον οἰκοδομῶ. The final clause is
explicatory of the preceding part of the verse. For Paul's
description of his own particular function as that of the one
who lays the foundation, leaving to others the task of ἐποικο-
δομεῖν, compare 1 Cor 3.10a; and see further the whole passage
1 Cor 3.9–17. For the use of the language of building see on
14.19 (τὰ τῆς οἰκοδομῆς τῆς εἰς ἀλλήλους).

Verse 20 has—not unnaturally—seemed to some to be inconsistent with Paul's addressing the Christians of Rome and with
his expressed intention of visiting them. Some have thought
that he was himself conscious of inconsistency between his
stated principle and his purpose of visiting Rome, and have
suggested that the anacoluthon at the end of v. 24 may be the
result of his embarrassment. It has also been suggested that
v. 20 was meant to assure the Christians of Rome that he did
not intend to missionize there, while others have thought to
discern in this verse an indirect reproach for those judaizing
agitators who were in the habit of following him and causing
trouble in the churches which he had established. But it is
quite unnecessary to look for an explanation of v. 20 along the
lines of either of the last two suggestions mentioned, if the
connexion between this verse and v. 19b is as we have argued

---

[1] p. 277. (For a variant order, ὅπου οὐκ, see Merk's apparatus.)
[2] p. 408.
[3] p. 367.
[4] p. 371, n. *.
[5] 2, p. 215. He rightly notes that the thought of the foundation of a
church already laid, present in the last clause of v. 20, suggests that
'named' means more than just known or reported.
[6] p. 377.
[7] Isa 26.13; Jer 20.9; Amos 6.10; 1 Cor 5.11; 2 Tim 2.19 are cited
in support.
[8] As does Bauer, s.v. ὀνομάζω 3. He cites for this meaning Esth 9.4;
1 Macc 3.9; 14.10; Ep. Arist. 124; and the Byzantine reading in 1 Cor 5.1.
[9] See Burton, MT, §§ 48, 52–54.

above: the need to guard against misunderstanding of his use of πεπληρωκέναι τὸ εὐαγγέλιον is a perfectly adequate reason for introducing a statement of his missionary policy at this point. That there is inconsistency between this verse and Paul's visiting Rome is only to be maintained on the assumption that Paul thought of the particular commission which he believed God had entrusted to him in a singularly rigid, unimaginative and legalistic way, quite out of keeping with all we know about him. And v. 20f is anyway not a statement of an absolute rule to be followed irrespectively of all other considerations, but a statement of Paul's own earnest desire and endeavour (φιλοτιμούμενον), grounded in his understanding of God's special assignment to him, to act as a pioneer missionary rather than as one who builds ūpon foundations already laid by another. There is no suggestion here that he felt himself under an absolute obligation to refrain from ever visiting a church which had been founded by someone else; and Rome was after all a very special case.

ἀλλὰ καθὼς γέγραπται· ὄψονται οἷς οὐκ ἀνηγγέλη περὶ αὐτοῦ, καὶ οἳ οὐκ ἀκηκόασιν συνήσουσιν. The quotation follows the LXX version of Isa 52.15b exactly, except that ὄψονται is placed before οἷς instead of after αὐτοῦ.[1] Paul sees the words of the prophet as a promise which is even now being fulfilled by the spreading of the knowledge of Christ, the true Servant of Yahweh, to those who have not yet heard of Him, accomplished by his own mission.[2]

22. διὸ καὶ ἐνεκοπτόμην τὰ πολλὰ τοῦ ἐλθεῖν πρὸς ὑμᾶς. Compare 1.13 (. . . πολλάκις προεθέμην ἐλθεῖν πρὸς ὑμᾶς, καὶ ἐκωλύθην ἄχρι τοῦ δεῦρο . . .). There no indication was given as to what had hindered: here an indication is given. Pace Gaugler,[3] B. Noack,[4]

[1] The strongly supported variant (𝔓⁴⁶ 𝔅 𝔎 D G pl) is no doubt to be rejected as simply an assimilation to the LXX. The MT differs in emphasis (not in substance) from the LXX, in that it focuses attention on the fact that what the persons referred to are going to see and hear is something they have not yet been told about and have not yet heard, whereas the LXX focuses attention on the fact that persons, who have not yet been told about the Servant of Yahweh (the LXX with its περὶ αὐτοῦ is much more definite than the MT) and not yet heard, are going to see and understand. The LXX form suits Paul's purpose more naturally.

[2] The suggestion that Paul is here seeing himself as fulfilling the Servant's role (e.g. J. D. G.ˉDunn, *Jesus and the Spirit*, London, 1975, p. 113, and p. 389, n. 70) is surely to be rejected, as Käsemann, p. 378, rightly maintains (but is not Käsemann wrong in attributing the notion that Paul does do this to Jeremias, in *TWNT* 5, p. 706, and to Gaugler and Leenhardt?).

[3] 2, p. 383.

[4] 'Current and backwater in the Epistle to the Romans', in *ST* 19 (1965), p. 160f.

Käsemann,[1] *et al.*, it seems more natural to take διό to be
referring back to the missionary activity described in v. 19b
(to which v. 20f was, as we understood it, a necessary qualification) than to take it as referring simply to the principle
(stated in v. 20f) of not preaching where Christ has already
been proclaimed. What has hindered Paul from fulfilling his
purpose to visit Rome so far has been the demands of his
missionary labours. ἐνεκοπτόμην (the variant ἐνεκόπην of D G F
is no doubt secondary, an easier reading—cf. the aorist ἐκωλύθην
in 1.13) may be translated by an English perfect.[2] τὰ πολλά[3]
is rather stronger than πολλάκις would have been: perhaps
'these many times'.[4]

23–24a. The sentence which begins with νυνὶ δέ is broken
off, there being no main verb expressing what Paul is about
to do.[5]

μηκέτι τόπον ἔχων ἐν τοῖς κλίμασι τούτοις is no doubt to be
understood in close connexion with v. 19b, and, if we were
right in our interpretation of that half-verse, Paul's meaning
here is simply that his presence is no longer required in the
regions in which he has laboured up till now, since in them the
pioneer work of evangelism which is his special task has already
been accomplished.[6] Those who take πεπληρωκέναι τὸ εὐαγγέλιον
to denote the completion of the preaching which has to be done
before the Parousia are naturally inclined to explain these
words accordingly. But to say, as Barrett does,[7] that 'Since the
eastern end of the Mediterranean had been dealt with and Paul
had "no more scope in these parts" there remained for missionary work the north coast of Africa (from Alexandria to the
province of Africa), Gaul, and Spain', is surely to attribute to
Paul a notion which it is altogether unlikely that he could ever
have entertained. There might be a certain superficial plausibility in maintaining that the early Church thought of only a
token preaching to all nations as having to be accomplished
before the Parousia; but, when once we begin to speak in terms
of lists of countries remaining to be evangelized, the obligation
to ask about the probable extent of Paul's geographical

---

[1] p. 379.
[2] Cf. Burton, *MT*, § 28.
[3] The variant πολλάκις attested by 𝕻⁴⁶ B D G is doubtless secondary—
cf. 1.13.
[4] See LSJ, s.v. πολύς, III.a; Bauer, s.v. πολύς, I.2.b. β. For τοῦ ἐλθεῖν
after ἐνεκοπτόμην see Burton, *MT*, § 401f; BDF, § 400 (4).
[5] 𝕶 *pl* complete the sentence with ἐλεύσομαι πρὸς ὑμᾶς, an obvious
improving addition.
[6] For the use of τόπος cf. 12.19, and see H. Köster, in *TWNT* 8, p. 206.
[7] p. 277.

knowledge can scarcely be evaded. To think of him as oblivious
of the existence of territories figuring prominently in the OT
is surely a nonsense. He himself uses elsewhere the name
'Scythian'. It is hardly conceivable that any intelligent Roman
citizen of Paul's time could be ignorant of the existence of
Parthia ('Parthians', of course, occurs in Acts 2) or of Britain
(the southern part of which had been conquered by Claudius's
troops only a few years before the epistle was written) or of
Germany, where Varus's army had been destroyed in the reign
of Augustus and from which the adopted son of the Emperor
Tiberius had taken his surname of 'Germanicus'. And it is
highly unlikely that someone who had travelled and mixed
with different sorts of people as much as Paul had done would
have been unaware of the existence of India, to which Alexander the Great had penetrated and which is quite frequently
mentioned by Greek and Latin writers, and of other distant
lands. In this connexion the reader's attention may be drawn
to the numerous relevant articles in *OCD*, e.g., those on
'Britannia', 'commerce, Greek and Roman', 'Eratosthenes',
'geography',' Germania',' Germanicus Julius Caesar','Pytheas',
'Seres' (it is interesting that σηρικόν, evidence of the trade with
China, occurs in Rev 18.12), 'silk', 'Strabo', 'Thule', and to
M. P. Charlesworth, *Trade Routes and Commerce of the Roman
Empire*, Cambridge, ²1926, and J. I. Miller, *The Spice Trade of
the Roman Empire*, 29 B.C. to A.D. 641, Oxford, 1969. In
view of the information easily accessible in the sources just
mentioned, it is surely time that NT scholars abandoned the
notion that Paul thought, when he wrote vv. 19b and 23, that
he had already completed all the preaching to the Gentiles
which had to be accomplished before the Parousia, as far as
'the East' was concerned, and now hoped himself 'to deal with
the West'.[1] To say, as Munck does, that Paul 'thinks in nations'[2]
and that, for him, 'The nations stand as a whole before God
and his judgment. They are whole entities. If the word has
come to a people in its last generation, even to only a few of
its members, that means that all are reached, and that the
whole nation is responsible'[3] could help only on the extremely
improbable assumption that Paul both had a very inadequate
conception of the number of nations embraced within the

[1] C. K. Barrett, 'New Testament Eschatology', in *SJT* 6 (1953),
p. 228.
[2] Munck, *Paul*, p. 52, following W. Wrede, *Paul* (Eng. tr. of *Paulus*,
1905), London, 1907, pp. 47ff, *et al.*
[3] Althaus, p. 126, according to the translation given in Munck, *Paul*,
p. 52.

Roman Empire of his time and also regarded the multitude of nations outside its bounds as being beyond God's concern.

ἐπιποθίαν δὲ ἔχων[1] τοῦ ἐλθεῖν πρὸς ὑμᾶς ἀπὸ ἱκανῶν[2] ἐτῶν, ὡς ἂν πορεύωμαι εἰς τὴν Σπανίαν comprises a second causal participial clause (parallel with μηκέτι τόπον, κ.τ.λ.) and a temporal subordinate clause depending on it. Not only is Paul now free to visit the Christians of Rome because he has fulfilled those prior obligations of his mission, which had up to the present made such a visit impossible; he is also moved by a strong desire, which he has had for a number of years, to come to them (cf. 1.9–16a) when[3] he is on his way to Spain. This is the first mention of Paul's intention to go to Spain (he made no mention of it in 1.8–16a) and the only other reference to Spain in the NT is in v. 28, apart from the ἐκεῖ later in v. 24. Whether Paul ever did get to Spain is uncertain (as far as the interpretation of Romans is concerned, the question is not really of any great importance: what is relevant is simply that at the time of writing he was hoping to go there); but 1 Clement 5.7 would seem to be fairly strong evidence in favour of the view that he did get there, since τὸ τέρμα τῆς δύσεως can scarcely[4] refer to anywhere other than Spain in a document written in Rome and it is difficult to believe that firm information about the end of Paul's life was not readily available in the Roman church in the last decade of the first century, when people who had known him must surely still have been alive. (For a bibliography on the question reference may be made to Bauer, s.v. Σπανία.) That Paul should have decided to embark on the evangelization of Spain is in no way surprising. Many centuries before Christ the Phoenicians of Tyre had colonized Cadiz. Later Phocaean colonists had settled in Spain, and they had been followed by colonists from their own colony of Marseilles. Later still (in the third century B.C.) Carthage had conquered large territories in Spain, and New Carthage (Cartagena) had been founded. Towards the end of the third century

---

[1] D G 69 *pc* it support ἔχω, which is no doubt an attempt to get rid of the anacoluthon. The secondariness of this reading is betrayed by the presence of δέ immediately before it, and the participle is anyway very strongly attested.

[2] The use of ἱκανός ('sufficient') to convey such senses as 'considerable', 'great', 'much', 'many'—an example of meiosis—is common in Hellenistic Greek (though not limited to it). The variant πολλῶν may be explained as a stylistic improvement. For the bearing of ἀπὸ ἱκανῶν ἐτῶν on the question of the date of the introduction of Christianity into Rome see p. 16.

[3] On ὡς ἄν with the subjunctive used as equivalent to ὅταν with the subjunctive see BDF, § 455 (2).

[4] *Pace* Sanday and Headlam, p. 414.

B.C. the Carthaginians had been driven out by Scipio Africanus, and Rome had held territory in Spain from that time onward, though it was not till the time of Augustus that the whole Iberian peninsula had been subjugated by the Romans and organized in the three provinces of Baetica (senatorial) and Tarraconensis and Lusitania (imperial). By Paul's time a good deal of Spain was thoroughly romanized, though some parts (particularly the north-west) were much less civilized. It is likely that there were by this time some Jewish settlements,[1] and Paul may well have hoped that these would afford him some openings. (Further information about Roman Spain is easily accessible in the OCD article on 'Spain', which includes a useful bibliography.)

24b. ἐλπίζω γὰρ διαπορευόμενος θεάσασθαι ὑμᾶς καὶ ὑφ' ὑμῶν προπεμφθῆναι ἐκεῖ, ἐὰν ὑμῶν πρῶτον ἀπὸ μέρους ἐμπλησθῶ is explanatory of the substance of the preceding incomplete sentence. Paul hopes to visit[2] the Roman Christians in the course of his journey[3] to Spain and to receive from them active help towards the carrying out of his proposed mission.[4] Exactly how much in this way of help and support for his Spanish mission Paul hoped to receive from the Christians of Rome we cannot tell; but it seems extremely likely that he hoped for considerably more than a mere farewell accompanied with prayers and good wishes. He may well have hoped, for example, that Roman Christians with a knowledge of Spain might be commissioned to accompany him thither, as Käsemann (p. 380) suggests. The last clause indicates his wish to enjoy, before being sent onward on his travels by them (πρῶτον), at any rate some measure of fellowship with them—

[1] Cf. Michel, p. 369, n. 2, where reference is made to E. Schürer, *Geschichte des jüdischen Volkes* 3, Leipzig, 1898, p. 38; CIL 2, 1982; and to the trilingual inscription at Tortosa.

[2] For the use of θεάσασθαι in the sense of 'visit' cf. LXX 2 Chr 22.6; Josephus, *Ant.* 16.6; also perhaps Mt 22.11.

[3] The variant πορευόμενος (𝔓⁴⁶ A *pc*) is perhaps due to the preceding πορεύωμαι. The compound suits the context much better: it is in the course of his journey to Spain by way of Rome that he will visit them, as one in transit.

[4] The variants ἀπό (𝔓⁴⁶ B) and ἀφ' (D G *pc*), while giving a possible sense, are intrinsically less likely than ὑφ', which brings out the thought of the active part to be played by the Roman Christians. προπέμπειν was used to denote the fulfilment of various services which might be required by a departing traveller, such as the provision of rations, money, means of transport, letters of introduction, and escort for some part of the way. It became a regular technical term of the Christian mission. Cf. Herodotus 1.111; 3.50; Xenophon, *An.* 7.2.8; 1 Macc 12.4; Ep. Aristeas 172; Acts 15.3; 20.38; 21.5; 1 Cor 16.6, 11; 2 Cor 1.16; Tit 3.13; 3 Jn 6.

though it cannot be enough to be all the fellowship that he would like to have with them.

25. —νυνὶ δὲ πορεύομαι εἰς Ἰερουσαλὴμ διακονῶν τοῖς ἁγίοις. But there remains one more task which must be accomplished before Paul can direct his course towards Rome—he has still to go to Jerusalem (cf. Acts 19.21; 20.3, 16, etc.) with the collection which the Gentile churches have made on behalf of the poor among the Jerusalem Christians.[1] The present indicative πορεύομαι indicates that he is actually about to go. With regard to the use of διακονεῖν see on 12.7 (comment and bibliography). An earlier collection for the Jerusalem church is mentioned in Acts 11.27–30; 12.25: Gal 2.10b may also be a reference to it (if the visit to Jerusalem related in Gal 2.1ff is to be identified with that referred to in the passages of Acts just cited). For the collection to which the present verse refers compare Acts 24.17; 1 Cor 16.1–4; 2 Cor 8–9, and also Gal 2.10a. That Paul regarded this collection as of great importance is clear from the rest of this chapter and the passages cited above from 1 and 2 Corinthians. No doubt he thought of it as likely to contribute to the cause of unity between the Gentile and Jewish parts of the Church (cf. vv. 27 and 31b) as well as being an appropriate response to human need on the part of Christians in a position to make such a response, an act of love—in this case, of brotherly love. But Barrett's 'politic expedient'[2] is misleading even as an expressly partial description of it. That 'it was intended to play a vital part among the events of the last days'[3] is true in the sense that every action which is truly an act of ἀγάπη fulfils a vital part in the history (as seen by God)[4] of that period which (whether short or long) is determined by the fact that it began with the Incarnation and is to end with the Parousia (cf. on 13.12); but there is no good reason, as far as we can see, for thinking it true, if it was meant to imply that Paul was confidently expecting his collection to be among the events of the last few years before the Parousia.

With regard to the use of the present participle (διακονῶν),

---

[1] Reference may be made to H. W. Bartsch, 'Die Kollekte des Paulus', in *Kirche in der Zeit* 20 (1965), pp. 555ff; D. Georgi, *Die Geschichte der Kollekte des Paulus für Jerusalem*, Hamburg, 1965; L. Keck, 'The poor among the saints in the New Testament', in *ZNW* 56 (1965), pp. 100–29; K. F. Nickle, *The Collection: a study in Paul's strategy*, London, 1966; L. Keck, 'The poor among the saints in Jewish Christianity and Qumran', in *ZNW* 57 (1966), pp. 54–78.

[2] p. 278.

[3] Barrett, ibid.

[4] Cf., e.g., Mt 10.42 = Mk 9.41; Mt 25.40.

as against Michel, who maintains that it signifies duration and is best translated by 'im Dienst',[1] it is perhaps better to understand it as expressing purpose (with J. J. O'Rourke[2]). By τοῖς ἁγίοις[3] the church in Jerusalem is meant, not the churches of Macedonia and Achaia, as Schlatter asserted.[4]

26. ηὐδόκησαν γὰρ Μακεδονία καὶ Ἀχαΐα κοινωνίαν τινὰ ποιήσασθαι εἰς τοὺς πτωχοὺς τῶν ἁγίων τῶν ἐν Ἰερουσαλήμ is explanatory of the preceding verse. ηὐδόκησαν expresses the voluntariness of the offering, the fact that it is the result of a decision freely and responsibly taken by the churches concerned.[5] There is no need to see any inconsistency between this emphasis and the evidence in 1 Cor 16.1–4 and 2 Cor 8–9 of Paul's own eager and energetic promotion of the collection; for a Christian's decision to do what is right is no less his own free personal decision because he has been enabled to recognize, and strengthened to do, his duty by the faithful exhortation of another Christian (though it is, of course, true that there are some forms of psychological and social pressure which Christians are sometimes tempted to exert—and indeed do not seldom exert—against their brethren, which do in fact rob the decision to do what is right of its proper freedom and so of its human dignity—but we have no reason to suppose that Paul had gone beyond the bounds of proper Christian exhortation). And, even if Paul's visit to Jerusalem referred to in Gal 2.1–10 is correctly identified with the Council visit (something which is by no means certain), there is but little justification for regarding the μόνον τῶν πτωχῶν ἵνα μνημονεύωμεν of Gal 2.10 as a reference to the imposition of a levy rather than a request for generous help. Käsemann's assertion that 'Man wird eine retuschierende Tendenz konstatieren dürfen, welche die Kollekte als reine Liebesgabe erscheinen lässt und die Pls

---

[1] p. 370, n. 3.

[2] 'The Participle in Rom 15.25', in *CBQ* 29 (1967), pp. 116–18. O'Rourke compares Mt 20.20; 22.16; Lk 10.25, and other passages. Both the variants διακονῆσαι (𝔓46 D G latt) and διακονήσων (ℵ*) are easier readings giving such a final sense.

[3] It is possible that Paul's use of οἱ ἅγιοι here reflects a special use of it as a designation of the Jerusalem church (see Lietzmann, pp. 121–23); but (*pace* Michel, p. 370, and Käsemann, p. 381) this should not be stated more strongly, since neither here nor in v. 31 is the expression really used absolutely, as in both cases the immediately preceding mention of Jerusalem serves to indicate which saints are intended, and in v. 26 τῶν ἁγίων is explicitly qualified by τῶν ἐν Ἰερουσαλήμ. But see 1 Cor 16.1 (Jerusalem is not mentioned until v. 3); 2 Cor 8.4; 9.1.

[4] p. 390.

[5] On εὐδοκεῖν see G. Schrenk, in *TWNT* 2, pp. 736–40; Bauer, s.v. εὐδοκέω.

offensichtlich drückenden persönlichen Verpflichtungen ver-
schweigt'[1] should not be accepted uncritically.

The use of the names of countries to signify their peoples is
natural enough (cf., e.g., the use of *Ἑλλάς* in Thucydides 1.6
and of ἡ *Ἰουδαία χώρα* in Mk 1.5), and it is a very natural
extension of this usage for a Christian to employ the names of
territories (in this case those of two Roman provinces) to
denote the churches to be found in them (cf. Paul's use of
Ἀχαΐα in 2 Cor 9.2). It is perhaps slightly surprising that Paul
mentions only *Μακεδονία καὶ Ἀχαΐα*, and not also churches of
Asia Minor (the churches of Galatia are mentioned in 1 Cor
16.1); but the fact that Paul does not give a more complete list
is no firm ground for a suspicion that he is deliberately con-
cealing the fact (as some scholars take it to be) that the
collection is a levy on his whole mission field.[2]

The use of the abstract noun *κοινωνία* here to denote the
concrete contribution collected (as it is probably used in 2 Cor
9.13) is significant. The contribution is an expression of
Christian fellowship.[3] That Paul by his choice of the word here
gives special emphasis to the fellowship aspect of the collection
is true and important; but it is highly doubtful whether it is
justifiable to see in his choice of word a deliberate avoidance of
other words which might have been more liable to be understood as referring to a levy,[4] and whether the presence of *τινά*
may properly be regarded as further evidence of Paul's desire
to play down any possible suggestion of a 'festgelegter Betrag'.[5]

The words *τῶν ἁγίων τῶν ἐν Ἰερουσαλήμ* are naturally understood as partitive:[6] the collection is intended for the benefit of
those of the Jerusalem brethren who are particularly poor. To
explain the genitive as epexegetic is surely forced. That the
primitive Jerusalem church may have referred to itself as 'the
poor', thereby taking to itself a self-designation of the Jewish
pious,[7] is possible enough; but it is surely forced exegesis to
find evidence of this here.[8]

---

[1] p. 381.

[2] *Pace* Käsemann, ibid.

[3] See on 12.13, where the verb *κοινωνεῖν* was used.

[4] As Käsemann, p. 381, is inclined to do, following K. Holl, D. Georgi
and L. Keck. Is there really adequate justification for designating
ἁδρότης (used in 2 Cor 8.20), *λογεία* (used in 1 Cor 16.1) and *λειτουργία*
(used in 2 Cor 9.12; Phil 2.30) so confidently as 'die juridischen Termini'
(Käsemann, ibid.)?

[5] As it is by Käsemann, ibid.

[6] So Käsemann, p. 383, rightly.

[7] See E. Bammel, in *TWNT* 6, pp. 888–915.

[8] *Pace* Bammel, op. cit., p. 909. As far as Gal 2.10 is concerned, it is
scarcely clear that *πτωχοί* can be understood only as a title of honour

27. The nature of the decision of the churches of Macedonia and Achaia as a free responsible decision is underlined by the repetition of ηὐδόκησαν γάρ.[1] But now another aspect of the matter has to be made clear. καὶ ὀφειλέται εἰσὶν αὐτῶν insists on the fact that the Gentile churches are under an obligation to these poor ones (as well as to the rest of the Jerusalem church)[2]—they are their debtors. On the use of ὀφειλέτης see on 1.14, though the thought expressed by it in the present verse is different from that which it expresses in 1.14, for here, as the latter half of this verse makes clear, the idea of obligation to someone on account of a benefit received from that person is definitely involved.

εἰ γὰρ τοῖς πνευματικοῖς αὐτῶν ἐκοινώνησαν τὰ ἔθνη, ὀφείλουσιν καὶ ἐν τοῖς σαρκικοῖς λειτουργῆσαι αὐτοῖς. If the Gentile Christians have become partakers in the spiritual good things of these representatives of the Jerusalem Christians, then they owe it to them as a debt that they should in return minister to them in matters pertaining to the flesh. It is to be noted that κοινωνεῖν τινί here signifies 'receive a share in (or 'of') something', whereas in 12.13 it meant 'contribute to the relief of something (e.g. a need, necessity)'; that τὰ πνευματικά does not here have the special sense it has in 1 Cor 14.1, but refers rather to those spiritual good things which have been mediated to the Gentiles through the original Jerusalem church (we should think, in particular, no doubt, of the gospel message itself and of the whole tradition of the works and words of Jesus, but perhaps also of all the spiritual blessings which had come with the mission which had originated in Jerusalem);[3]

(*pace* Käsemann, p. 383). Why should it not there also refer to the poor among the believers, the context making it clear that it is the poor among the believers in Jerusalem in particular who are intended?

[1] That the omission of ηὐδόκησαν γάρ, καί by D and also (with the insertion of γάρ after ὀφειλέται) by 𝔓⁴⁶ G *m* Ambst is secondary is hardly to be doubted.

[2] It seems more natural (even if perhaps it is not absolutely necessary) to take αὐτῶν (and also the second αὐτῶν and the αὐτοῖς in this verse and the αὐτοῖς in v. 28) to refer to τοὺς πτωχούς than to τῶν ἁγίων; but Paul is likely to have thought of these poor saints as being representative of the whole Jerusalem church.

[3] It is perhaps apposite to refer to 1.16 ('Ιουδαίῳ . . . πρῶτον); 9.4–5; 11.11–32, and to observe that the privileges of Israel, neglected and despised for the time being by the vast majority of Jews, might be said to be, in a real sense, specially the spiritual good things of those comparatively few Jews who had believed in Christ. The ingrafted branches had indeed received a share of the sap by which those native branches, which had *not* been broken off, still lived. With regard to the precise significance of πνευματικά here, it is not easy to come to a firm conclusion. Does it include a reference to the work of the Holy Spirit in connexion

and that τὰ σαρκικά here denotes the things pertaining to the flesh in the sense of the material resources necessary for the well-being of the body. For λειτουργεῖν (the verb occurs only two other times in the NT, in Acts 13.2 and Heb 10.11) see on 13.6 and 15.16, in which λειτουργός is used. Though he thought of this service as having an important theological significance, as his use of the word κοινωνία in v. 26 suggests, Paul clearly regarded it as being in no way an equivalent to that which the Jerusalem church had rendered to the Gentiles: material succour, however lovingly and generously supplied, could never repay the debt owed by the Gentile churches.

28. τοῦτο οὖν ἐπιτελέσας, καὶ σφραγισάμενος αὐτοῖς τὸν καρπὸν τοῦτον, ἀπελεύσομαι δι' ὑμῶν εἰς Σπανίαν sums up Paul's statement of his plans. When he has completed[1] his task in connexion with the collection[2] and sealed this fruit to them,[3] he will set out for Spain by way of Rome. That the καρπός referred to is to be identified with the total of the collection is scarcely to be doubted.[4] The use of σφραγίζεσθαι is puzzling, and has been very variously explained as referring: (i) to the formal handing over of the collection; (ii) to its final delivery into safe custody;[5] (iii) to the guaranteeing of its intactness (in support of this suggestion 2 Cor 8.20f and 12.16–18 are some-

---

with the proclamation of the gospel message, the success of the Gentile mission, etc.? Or is the word perhaps used rather generally to denote things which are spiritual as opposed to the material things indicated by τὰ σαρκικά?

[1] While it is clear that Paul did see an important theological significance in the collection, it is doubtful whether his use of ἐπιτελεῖν should be pressed as supporting evidence of this (as it is by Sanday and Headlam, p. 413). While it is true that this verb is often used outside the NT of the fulfilment of religious rites, it probably means here simply 'complete'. Its other occurrences in the NT are in 2 Cor 7.1; 8.6, 11 (bis); Gal 3.3; Phil 1.6; Heb 8.5; 9.6; 1 Pet 5.9.

[2] For the reference of τοῦτο compare v. 25.

[3] The omission of αὐτοῖς (𝔓46 vid B pc c) looks as if it was probably accidental. The people referred to will surely be the same as those to whom the double αὐτῶν and the αὐτοῖς of v. 27 refer (though some, e.g. Michel, p. 371, understand it as referring to the Gentile Christians (cf. Chrysostom, col. 662)).

[4] So Käsemann, p. 383, rightly, as against H. W. Bartsch, 'Die historische Situation des Römerbriefes', in *Studia Evangelica* 4, Berlin, 1968, p. 290f; id., ' "Wenn ich ihnen diese Frucht versiegelt habe" Röm 15.28: Ein Beitrag zum Verständnis der paulinischen Mission', in *ZNW* 63 (1972), pp. 95ff (Bartsch argues that by 'this fruit' Paul means the churches in Macedonia and Achaia which, by his handing over of their collection to the Jerusalem church, he is 'sealing' as true and authentic fruit of the *Urgemeinde*).

[5] Chrysostom, col. 662, comments: τουτέστιν, ὡς εἰς βασιλικὰ ταμιεῖα ἐναποθέμενος, ὡς ἐν ἀσύλῳ καὶ ἀσφαλεῖ χωρίῳ.

times cited as evidence that unpleasant insinuations had been made); (iv) to the confirmation (whether by the act of handing over itself or by words spoken) of the collection's significance whether as the token of the Gentile churches' love and gratitude to the Jerusalem church or as the fruit of the spiritual blessings which had been mediated by the Jerusalem church to the Gentiles or even as a justification of Paul's own mission to the Gentiles; (v) quite simply to the completion of the whole matter. While there is force in Gaugler's support of (v) on the ground that what the context requires is merely an indication of the time when he will be free to start for Rome,[1] the combination of σφραγίζεσθαι and καρπός is perhaps rather too striking for this explanation to be altogether satisfying. Maybe the first or second of the three possibilities mentioned under (iv) above should be regarded as most probable.

29. οἶδα δὲ[2] ὅτι ἐρχόμενος πρὸς ὑμᾶς ἐν πληρώματι[3] εὐλογίας[4] Χριστοῦ ἐλεύσομαι expresses Paul's firm confidence ('And I know'—it is a matter, not just of hoping, but of knowing) that, when at last he does come to the Christians in Rome, he will come with the fullness of Christ's blessing. The thought behind the use of πλήρωμα here is probably that Christ's blessing on his visit will be pure blessing, without any admixture of something other than blessing, a blessing altogether unambiguous and reliable. Something of what Christ's blessing might be expected to bring with it may be learned from v. 24, and still more from 1.11f, 13 (the last clause) and 15.[5]

30. Παρακαλῶ δὲ ὑμᾶς [,ἀδελφοί,][6] is the beginning of a new

---

[1] 2, p. 386f. He argues that the point of the metaphor is simply that the sealing is the last act before the handing over of an article, and that all that Paul wants to say by its use is, 'when I am completely finished with this matter'.

[2] The variant γινώσκω γάρ (G (it syᵖ)) is quite unlikely to be original. The γάρ would seem to be a clumsy attempt at improving on the part of someone who wrongly understood this verse as intended to give Paul's reason for his plan to visit Rome on his way to Spain.

[3] The reading πληροφορίᾳ (D* G) appears to be a misguided 'improvement', introducing the thought of Paul's confidence (expressed adequately by οἶδα) into the ὅτι clause in which it is not really appropriate.

[4] The addition of τοῦ εὐαγγελίου τοῦ after εὐλογίας (𝔎 pl vgᶜˡ sy) is another quite unnecessary attempted improvement.

[5] But there is no need to limit the range of Christ's blessing to the Roman Christians and Paul, as Barrett, p. 279, inclines to do. Paul himself would surely have hoped that the effects of Christ's blessing would reach beyond the Roman Christians both to others in Rome who were not yet Christians and also to the peoples of Spain whom he hoped to visit with some assistance from the Christians of Rome.

[6] 𝔓⁴⁶ B Chr are a strong combination of witnesses for the omission of ἀδελφοί. But the fact that its presence here agrees well with Paul's usage

paragraph, in which Paul expresses his desire for the prayers of the Roman Christians. Whether παρακαλεῖν has its special sense of 'exhort' (see on 12.1) here or its more ordinary sense of 'ask', 'request', is not clear, though perhaps, on the whole, it is rather more naturally understood here as simply meaning 'ask', since the prayers Paul desires, though certainly not without a significance for others, are primarily prayers on behalf of himself. That the request (if 'request' rather than 'exhortation' is the right word) is exceedingly urgent the sequel makes very obvious.

διὰ τοῦ[1] κυρίου ἡμῶν Ἰησοῦ Χριστοῦ καὶ διὰ τῆς ἀγάπης τοῦ πνεύματος indicates the authority invoked and the ground of appeal in Paul's urgent entreaty. For this use of διά see on 12.1. Here it is used first with a personal name, indicating that Paul appeals to Christ's authority in order to drive home his entreaty to his readers' hearts, and then, in the second place, with an abstract noun, indicating what is more naturally regarded as a ground of appeal than as an authority invoked. τοῦ πνεύματος is best understood as a genitive of origin, the whole phrase τῆς ἀγάπης τοῦ πνεύματος meaning 'the love which the Spirit works', that love between Christians which is the effect of the Holy Spirit's indwelling.[2]

συναγωνίσασθαί μοι ἐν ταῖς προσευχαῖς ὑπὲρ ἐμοῦ πρὸς τὸν θεόν. This is the only occurrence of the verb συναγωνίζεσθαι in the Greek Bible; but the simple verb occurs a number of times in the NT; and there is one place (Col 4.12), where, like the compound verb here, it is used in connexion with prayer. It is sometimes assumed that here and in Col 4.12 the thought is of a wrestling with God. So, for example, Black comments: 'For prayer as an "agonizing", "wrestling" with God, cf. Col. 4:12; the image no doubt could go back to Gen. 32.24ff.'[3] But, while there is most certainly deep spiritual truth in such an exposition of Gen 32.22–32 as is to be found in Charles Wesley's

_____

(see on 1.13) should probably tell in favour of retaining it: a copyist is not very likely to have added it for this reason—it would not have been at all an obvious consideration.

[1] The addition of ὀνόματος τοῦ after διά (L *pc*) is an obvious 'improvement'.

[2] *Pace* Chrysostom, col. 662, and Murray 2, p. 221, who take the genitive as subjective (Chrysostom referring to the Spirit's love for the world, Murray to His love for believers).

[3] p. 177. He goes on to indicate that others explain the nature of the struggle envisaged differently; but, while he does not make absolutely clear which view he himself prefers, the natural inference would seem to be that it is the one which is given first.

hymn, 'Come, O Thou Traveller unknown',[1] it is very doubtful
whether Paul had the story of Jacob's wrestling in mind when
he used συναγωνίζεσθαι here or the simple verb in Col 4.12 in
connexion with prayer. It is significant that no word of the
ἀγών word-group occurs in LXX Gen 32.23–33, the verb
παλαίειν being used in vv. 25 and 26 and ἐνισχύειν in v. 29.
Others have suggested that the thought here is rather of
wrestling against opposing powers, temptations, distractions,
which hinder prayer;[2] and others suppose that the use of ἀγών-
language with regard to the prayer is a reflection of the actual
situation of danger facing Paul.[3] But, against all these explanations, it should be noted that there is no mention of any
opponent either in Col 4.12 or in the verse with which we are
concerned (that πρὸς τὸν θεόν is to be connected with προσευχαῖς
and not with the verb hardly needs to be said). In view of this,
and since ἀγωνίζεσθαι can certainly bear, in addition to such
meanings as 'contend for a prize' (in the public games or on
the stage), 'contend in court', the general sense of 'struggle',
'exert oneself' (cf., e.g., Thucydides 4.87.6; Luke 13.24;
1 Clement 35.4, in all of which it is used with an infinitive:
it is used in a general sense without an infinitive in Lysias
20.22[4]), we are inclined to think that Barrett's translation of
συναγωνίσασθαι, κ.τ.λ. by 'to join me in earnest prayers to God
on my behalf'[5] probably gives about the right sense: what Paul
is entreating them to do is simply to pray for him and with
him, not half-heartedly or casually, but with earnestness,
urgency and persistence.

31 is the first of two verses beginning with ἵνα, which continue the sentence begun in v. 30. It indicates two things for
which this earnest prayer is to be made. The first is ἵνα ῥυσθῶ

---

[1] Reference should also be made to Calvin's *Commentaries on the First
Book of Moses, called Genesis* 2, Eng. tr. by J. King, Edinburgh, 1850,
pp. 195–203, and to his *Commentaries on the Twelve Minor Prophets* 1,
Eng. tr. by J. Owen, Edinburgh, 1846, pp. 422–28 (on Hos 12.3b–4).
That in the thinking of minds less firmly controlled by Holy Scripture
than were those of Calvin and Charles Wesley the use of the image of
wrestling with God in connexion with prayer can, of course, very easily
lead to a most serious misunderstanding of the nature of Christian
prayer, needs to be said. To entertain any notion of trying to exert
pressure upon God to compel Him to do that which He Himself does not
will to do or of mobilizing one's fellow-Christians with a view to con-
straining Him by a combination of forces is to lapse into paganism, as
Gaugler 2, p. 389f, rightly stresses.
[2] e.g. Sanday and Headlam, p. 415, and Origen's comment, which
they quote.
[3] e.g. Käsemann, p. 389.
[4] Cf. Plutarch, *Phocion* 37.
[5] p. 274.

ἀπὸ τῶν ἀπειθούντων ἐν τῇ Ἰουδαίᾳ. Paul knows well that he is the object of fierce hostility on the part of the unbelieving Jews (for the designation of them as 'disobedient' cf. 11.31: also 10.16 (οὐ πάντες ὑπήκουσαν τῷ εὐαγγελίῳ); 10.21 (πρὸς λαὸν ἀπειθοῦντα); 11.30 (τῇ τούτων ἀπειθείᾳ)); and a special concentration of this hostility must be expected in Judaea and particularly in Jerusalem itself. For the testimony of Acts to this hostility reference may be made to Acts 9.29; 13.45, 50; 14.19; 17.5–8, 13; 18.12–17; 19.9; 20.3, 23; and (with reference to a time later than the writing of this epistle, when Paul is already on his way to Jerusalem) 21.10–14. The verb ῥύεσθαι, which we have already had in 7.24 and 11.26, occurs quite often in the NT and denotes deliverance from serious danger or evil (so that here the thought that Paul's life may well be in danger is suggested). The second thing to be prayed for is indicated by καὶ[1] ἡ διακονία[2] μου ἡ εἰς[3] Ἰερουσαλὴμ εὐπρόσδεκτος τοῖς ἁγίοις γένηται. Those who still labour in the shadow of the Tübingen school's continuing influence are naturally prone to welcome these words as additional grist for their mill, additional evidence of serious tension between Paul and the Jerusalem church.[4] But to say with regard to them, as Michel does, 'Es zeigt sich, dass auch die jerusalemische Gemeinde in starker Spannung zu Pls lebt',[5] is to read more into them than they actually express. Some tension there undoubtedly was;[6] but any one who has had any considerable experience not just in organizing a church's collection of money for charitable purposes but also in the actual passing on of it to those in need will know full well that its being εὐπρόσδεκτος is no foregone conclusion, and will be more likely to recognize in these words evidence of Paul's spiritual and human sensitivity and freedom from self-centred complacency than to draw from them any confident conclusions about the tension between the Jerusalem church and Paul.[7]

---

[1] 𝔎 pl add ἵνα after καί.

[2] The variant δωροφορία (B D* G) for διακονία would appear to be a 'Western' explanatory variation: see the fuller apparatus in UBS. We have here an example of the presence of a 'Western' element in B.

[3] The substitution of ἐν (B D* G pc) for εἰς is connected with the reading δωροφορία for διακονία.

[4] The tendency to see here evidence of Paul's fear that he might 'be suspected and unwelcome' among the Jerusalem Christians goes back, of course, much farther than the Tübingen school: see, e.g., Calvin, p. 318.

[5] p. 373.

[6] Acts 21.20ff indicates the existence of suspiciousness of Paul on the part of some members of the Jerusalem church.

[7] Having quoted Michel above, I must in fairness indicate that on

32. ἵνα ἐν χαρᾷ ἐλθὼν πρὸς ὑμᾶς διὰ θελήματος θεοῦ συναναπαύσωμαι ὑμῖν[1] is a final clause depending on v. 31, and expresses
the more distant hope which the fulfilment of the twofold
prayer indicated in v. 31 will make possible of realization.
Both deliverance from the dangers threatening him from the
side of the unbelieving Jews and also the peace of mind resulting from the truly brotherly acceptance of the Gentile churches'
gifts by the Jerusalem church are necessary to Paul, if his
coming to Rome is really to be fraught with joy and he is to
find full refreshment there in Christian fellowship. With διὰ
θελήματος θεοῦ compare ἐν τῷ θελήματι τοῦ θεοῦ in 1.10 (also in
connexion with his coming to Rome).

33. ὁ δὲ θεὸς τῆς εἰρήνης μετὰ πάντων ὑμῶν· ἀμήν.[2] The paragraph ends with a prayer-wish (for this form see on v. 5f). The
phrase ὁ θεὸς τῆς εἰρήνης is found in 16.20; 2 Cor 13.11; Phil 4.9;
1 Th 5.23; Heb 13.20; also in Test. Dan 5.2 (ὁ κύριος τῆς εἰρήνης
occurs in 2 Th 3.16): behind it lies an OT and Jewish background—see, for example, Lev 26.6; Num 6.26; Judg 6.24; Ps
29.11; Isa 26.12; Jer 16.5; and compare *Siphre* Num 6.26 § 42
(12b) (with reference to Judg 6.24).[3] On εἰρήνη see p. 72 (on 1.7).

the same page in note 3 he says: 'εὐπρόσδεκτος . . . bezeugt . . . die
apostolische Demut des Pls'—a comment for which Käsemann, p. 389,
unwisely takes him to task.

[1] There is a large amount of textual variation in this verse. The
variation between θεοῦ, κυρίου Ἰησοῦ, Χριστοῦ Ἰησοῦ and Ἰησοῦ Χριστοῦ is
the less complicated element. Elsewhere Paul speaks of God's, rather
than Christ's, will (though τὸ θέλημα τοῦ κυρίου occurs in Eph 5.17, and
the αὐτοῦ in Col 1.9 could perhaps refer to Christ, who has been mentioned in v. 7), and θεοῦ should probably be read here. The cause of most
of the other variations is probably (cf. Sanday and Headlam, p. 415) the
strangeness of the use of συναναπαύεσθαι, a verb which elsewhere is used
in the sense 'sleep with' (Dionysius of Halicarnassus, *Rh.* 9.4; Plutarch,
Mor. 125A; Arrian, *Cyn.* 9.2; Heliodorus (erotic writer of 3rd century
A.D.) 6.8); and in LXX Isa 11.6—its only other occurrence in the Greek
Bible—of the leopard's lying with the kid. The only other occurrence of
it used in the sense, which it has here, namely, 'be refreshed together
with', which is adduced, is in a quotation from Hegesippus in Eusebius,
H.E. 4.22.2. In view of the difficulty of συναναπαύσωμαι, its omission
accompanied with the consequent substitution of ἔλθω for ἐλθών (𝔓⁴⁶ B)
is easily understandable, as is also the substitution of ἀναψύξω (in
G ἀναψύχω) μεθ' ὑμῶν (D G lat) for συναναπαύσωμαι ὑμῖν. The addition
of καί after θεοῦ (or one of its variants), attested by 𝔎 D G *al* lat sy, is
explicable as resulting from the change of ἐλθών to ἔλθω (it appears that
only 𝔓⁴⁶ and B, which have no verb at the end of the sentence, have
ἔλθω without καί).

[2] The ἀμήν is omitted by 𝔓⁴⁶ A G *pc*. On the placing of the doxology
(16.25–27) after this verse in 𝔓⁴⁶ see pp. 5–11.

[3] Reference may be made to G. Delling, 'Die Bezeichnung "Gott des
Friedens" und ähnliche Wendungen in den Paulusbriefen', in E. E. Ellis
and E. Grässer (ed.), *Jesus und Paulus: Festschrift für W. G. Kümmel
zum 70. Geburtstag*, Göttingen, 1975, pp. 76–84.

Here in the present verse it probably signifies the sum of all true blessings including final salvation. By calling God 'the God of peace' Paul is characterizing Him as the Source and Giver of all true blessings, the God who is both willing and able to help and save to the uttermost. The sense is well brought out in P. Doddridge's paraphrase of Heb 13.20f ('Father of peace, and God of love') by the words 'We own Thy power to save'. For the thought of God's being with someone to protect and help him compare, for example, Gen 21.22; 26.3; 31.3, 5; Exod 3.12; Josh 1.5; 1 Chr 11.9; Job 29.5; Ps 23.4; 46.7, 11[MT: 8, 12]; Isa 7.14; 8.10 (in all of which *'im* is used);[1] Lk 1.28; Jn 3.2; 2 Cor 13.11; Phil 4.9: we may also compare references to the exalted Christ's being with someone (as in 2 Th 3.16). That (*pace* Lagrange[2] and Käsemann[3]) this verse is rather to be compared with such prayer-wishes as 15.13 and 1 Th 3.11–13 and the promise in Phil 4.9 than with the concluding greetings of Paul's letters is indicated by the fact that all the concluding greetings of the whole Pauline corpus include the word χάρις.

1–2. Συνίστημι δὲ ὑμῖν Φοίβην begins the commendation of Phoebe which occupies these two verses. The presence of δέ (though omitted by D* G it arm, it should surely be read) tells against the suggestion that we have in chapter 16 a self-contained and independent letter of commendation and in favour of the view that this is simply the beginning of a new section of main division VIII. συνιστάναι is the regular term for bringing persons together as friends or (as here) introducing or recommending one person to another.[4] It is highly probable that Phoebe was to be the bearer of Paul's letter to Rome. That she was a Gentile Christian may be inferred from her name; for a Jewess would scarcely have had a name deriving from pagan mythology.[5] With such a name she may well have been a freedwoman.

τὴν ἀδελφὴν ἡμῶν indicates her membership of the Christian community. The ἡμῶν[6] is probably more naturally understood with reference to the community of believers as a whole than

---

[1] See BDB, s.v. עַם I.a.

[2] p. 361.

[3] pp. 388–90.

[4] See LSJ, s.v. συνίστημι IV.1; Bauer, s.v. συνίστημι 1.b; and s.v. συστατικός. Cf. 2 Cor 3.1.

[5] See OCD, s.v. 'Phoebe'. For the use of the name generally cf., e.g., Suetonius, *Aug.* 65.2; Dittenberger, *Syll.* 805.10 (*c.* A.D. 54); P. Flor. 50.61 (3rd century A.D.). See also M. D. Gibson, 'Phoebe', in *ET* 23 (1911–12), p. 281.

[6] The variant ὑμῶν attested by 𝔓46 A G *pc* d* would seem to be a mistake.

as indicating either a special association with Paul or association with the particular church whose hospitality he was
currently enjoying.

οὖσαν [καὶ] διάκονον τῆς ἐκκλησίας τῆς ἐν Κεγχρεαῖς. Phoebe is
not only a fellow-Christian: she is also[1] a διάκονος of the church
in Cenchreae, the eastern port of Corinth.[2] It is perhaps just
conceivable that the word διάκονος should be understood here
as a quite general reference to her service of the congregation;
but it is very much more natural, particularly in view of the
way in which Paul formulates his thought (οὖσαν . . . διάκονον
τῆς ἐκκλησίας, κ.τ.λ.), to understand it as referring to a
definite office. We regard it as virtually certain that Phoebe is
being described as 'a (or possibly 'the') deacon' of the church
in question, and that this occurrence of διάκονος is to be
classified with its occurrences in Phil 1.1 and 1 Tim 3.8 and 12.
And, while it is true that the functions of a διάκονος are not
expressly indicated in Phil 1.1 or in 1 Tim 3.8ff or in the
present two verses, there is nothing in any of these passages
in any way inconsonant with the inherent probability that a
specialized use of διάκονος in NT times will have corresponded
to the clearly attested specialized use of διακονεῖν and διακονία
with reference to the practical service of the needy, and there
are some features, for example, what is said about Phoebe in
v. 2b, which would seem to afford it some support.[3] That a port
would provide plenty of scope for the practical expression of
Christian compassion and helpfulness is hardly to be doubted.
With regard to the rather surprising fact that the word ἐκκλησία
occurs here for the first time in Romans—and it is here introduced only incidentally—see p. 22.

ἵνα introduces a statement of the twofold purpose of Paul's
commendation of Phoebe.

αὐτὴν προσδέξησθε[4] ἐν κυρίῳ ἀξίως τῶν ἁγίων. In the first place,
Paul wants the Christians in Rome to welcome[5] her 'in the

[1] καί is attested by 𝔓⁴⁶ B C* pc bo, and, in spite of its omission by
ℵ* A 𝕂 D G pl lat sy, should quite probably be read. It makes good
sense as emphasizing an additional consideration in Phoebe's favour.

[2] See Bauer, s.v. Κεγχρεαί; also OCD, s.v. 'Corinth'; R. Scranton, J. W.
Shaw, L. Ibrahim, Kenchreai . . . : results of investigations . . . for the
American School of Classical Studies in Athens 1, Leiden, 1978,

[3] See further on 12.7 (εἴτε διακονίαν, ἐν τῇ διακονίᾳ) and the literature
there cited, and also on 12.8.

[4] B C D G it reverse the order of αὐτήν and προσδέξησθε.

[5] Käsemann's categorical statement (p. 391) that προσδέχεσθαι does
not have the 'religiös vertieften Sinn' which προσλαμβάνειν has in chapters
14 and 15 but bears only a secular sense ('sondern profan . . . meint')
referring merely to the provision of hospitality and such practical
assistance as may be required, does not seem to be justified; for, while it

Lord',[1] that is, as Christians receiving a fellow-Christian, beloved for the Lord's sake. The words ἀξίως τῶν ἁγίων add nothing that goes beyond ἐν κυρίῳ in actual content, but call into play a special motive for the required Christian behaviour, namely, the motive of Christian self-respect, of respect for one's own dignity as that of someone who belongs to Christ.

καὶ παραστῆτε αὐτῇ ἐν ᾧ ἂν ὑμῶν χρῄζῃ πράγματι: 'and assist her in any matter in which she may need your help'. παριστάναι, which (itself or its collateral form παριστάνειν) occurs nearly fifty times in the NT (in Romans it occurs in 6.13 (bis), 16, 19 (bis); 12.1; 14.10), is here used in the sense it has in 2 Tim 4.17,[2] namely, 'stand by (to defend or help)', 'help', 'assist', a sense similar to that expressed in the next sentence by προστάτις (which is, of course, cognate with a different compound of ἱστάναι). In view of the indefinite ἐν ᾧ ἂν ὑμῶν χρῄζῃ, it is unlikely that πρᾶγμα carries here its special sense of 'law-business', 'law-suit'. In widely varying matters Phoebe could stand in need of their help; and in all such matters they are loyally to stand by their fellow-Christian.

καὶ γὰρ αὐτὴ προστάτις πολλῶν ἐγενήθη καὶ ἐμοῦ αὐτοῦ adds a further reason why they ought to be ready to help Phoebe, in addition to the reasons already indicated by τὴν ἀδελφὴν ἡμῶν and οὖσαν [καὶ] διάκονον, κ.τ.λ. and by ἐν κυρίῳ and ἀξίως τῶν ἁγίων: she has herself[3] already been a προστάτις of many, including Paul himself.[4] With regard to the word προστάτις[5] see on 12.8 (ὁ προϊστάμενος). It can hardly have here any technical legal sense such as the masculine form προστάτης could bear; for Paul himself is not likely to have stood in need of such

is true that προσλαμβάνειν has a very special depth of meaning in its occurrences in chapters 14 and 15, the presence of ἐν κυρίῳ is surely an indication that here in 16.2 the προσδέχεσθαι expressing itself in practical assistance is not thought of in any merely secular way.

[1] ἐν κυρίῳ and ἐν Χριστῷ are specially characteristic of this chapter, the former occurring also in vv. 8, 11, 12 (bis), 13 and 22, the latter in vv. 3, 7, 9, and 10.

[2] Cf. Homer, Il. 10.279; 21.231; Herodotus 1.87; Sophocles, Aj. 1384; Xenophon, Cyr. 5.3.19; Josephus, BJ 2.245; Ant. 1.341.

[3] The variant αὕτη (L al) would be practically indistinguishable in meaning from αὐτή in its common unemphatic sense ('she'); but αὐτή in its emphatic sense ('she herself') seems rather more appropriate here, and should surely be accepted.

[4] The words καὶ ἄλλων, which appear before πολλῶν in 𝔓⁴⁶ (D G) and result in the sense 'both of many others and of me myself', are no doubt secondary—a logical improvement, but decidedly stilted. Paul must have meant 'of many, including me myself', but has expressed himself loosely.

[5] The variant παραστάτις (G) is most likely an assimilation to the παραστῆτε in the same verse.

formal legal protection as is sometimes indicated by the use of the masculine form προστάτης, and it is doubtful whether Phoebe, as a woman, would have been able to fulfil the formal legal functions involved. However, while it is possible that the word is here used in its most general sense of 'helper', it seems quite probable that we should be justified in supposing that its choice implies that Phoebe was possessed of some social position, wealth and independence.

3–5a. Ἀσπάσασθε Πρῖσκαν καὶ Ἀκύλαν is the first of a series of greetings which extends without a break to the end of v. 15 (so long a list of greetings, though without a parallel elsewhere in the NT, makes quite good sense in connexion with v. 1f, since it would have served to give Phoebe an immediate introduction to a large number of individuals in the Christian community in Rome). The two are always mentioned together in the NT, in the same order as here in Acts 18.18 and 26 and 2 Tim 4.19, in the reverse order in Acts 18.2 and 1 Cor 16.19, the lady's name being given in its diminutive form of 'Priscilla' in Acts but as 'Prisca' in the epistles.[1] Aquila is described in Acts 18.2 as 'a certain Jew . . ., a man of Pontus by race', and, unless fairly strong grounds can be shown for thinking otherwise, the probability that his wife also was Jewish must be reckoned very high. Apparently the couple had been established in Rome, since their presence in Corinth is explained as due to the edict of Claudius by which Jews had been expelled from Rome. As Aquila was a σκηνοποιός like Paul, as well as being a Christian, Paul made his home with them in Corinth. Then, when, after eighteen months in Corinth, Paul set out for Syria, they accompanied him as far as Ephesus, where (after Paul had left them) they got to know the learned Alexandrian Jew Apollos, who, on his arrival, though 'knowing only the baptism of John', began to teach 'the things concerning Jesus', and received him[2] and instructed him more fully in the truth of the gospel. It was from Ephesus that they sent their greetings and the greetings of the church 'in their house' to the church in Corinth (1 Cor 16.19). That Prisca and Aquila should be back in Rome at the time of the writing of the epistle is in

---

[1] Πρίσκιλλαν and Πρίσκιλλα appear as variant readings in the present verse and in 1 Cor 16.19, respectively.

[2] It is possible that προσελάβοντο αὐτόν in Acts 18.26 has some such sense as 'took him aside' (in order to be able to talk with him privately), as Bauer, s.v. προσλαμβάνω, 2. a., understands it (cf. Mk 8.32), but it seems rather more probable that what is meant is that they received him either into their home as a guest (cf. Acts 28.2) or into their fellowship (cf. Rom 14.1, 3; 15.7).

no way surprising (see p. 18). The noteworthy fact that the wife's name is more often placed before her husband's than after it in the NT is, we would think, much more probably to be explained as due either to her having been converted before him (and perhaps having led her husband to faith in Christ) or to her having played an even more prominent part in the life and work of the Church than Aquila had, than to her having been socially superior to him.[1]

τοὺς συνεργούς μου ἐν Χριστῷ Ἰησοῦ[2] is the first of the things Paul has to say about this couple. Three points may be made with regard to it:

(i) The emphasis on working is a characteristic of this greetings-list (cf. vv. 6, 9, 12a and b). For Paul, being a Christian involves being set to work, an active and responsible partici-

---

[1] Future archaeological researches may perhaps provide additional solid information about Prisca and her husband (and conceivably tell us something definite about one or two of the other persons who are named in this list of greetings); but it must be admitted that the evidence which has so far come to light, while some of it is certainly highly stimulating to the imagination and could very well be the basis of several romances, does not seem to afford anything more solid than possibilities. A connexion between the Church of Saints Aquila and Prisca on the Aventine and the site of the house of Prisca and Aquila cannot be said to have been at all securely established. But the evidence suggesting that the Catacomb of Priscilla was originally a burying-place of the Acilian *gens*, to which the Manius Acilius Glabrio belonged who was consul with Trajan in A.D. 91 and a few years later was executed very probably for being a Christian (though Sanday and Headlam, p. 419f, is misleading in referring to 'the statement of Dio Cassius' that this Acilius Glabrio 'was a Christian and died as such'; for, while this is very probably the correct inference to draw from what is said in Dio Cassius 67.14, it is certainly not said there in so many words), and that Prisca and its diminutive form Priscilla were common female names in the Acilian *gens* seems to indicate that some connexion between the Prisca of the NT and the Acilian *gens* is a real possibility. It could well be that she was a freedwoman, or that both her husband (the name Aquila might perhaps be connected with Acilius, which was sometimes written as 'Aquilius') and she were freedmen, of a distinguished Roman family, and that the presence of Christianity in this family at a later date is to be traced back to their influence. The suggestion that Prisca was actually an aristocratic Roman lady, and that it was for this reason that she was named before her husband, while it can scarcely be ruled out as impossible, seems unlikely. Reference may be made to the long note in Sanday and Headlam, pp. 418–20.

[2] The D* G it variant, which has the first six words of v. 5 immediately after v. 3 instead of after v. 4, is not likely to be original. It could perhaps be due to remembrance of 1 Cor 16.19; and it is possibly significant that the resulting harshness would be a little less obvious in the Latin, since the use of the adjective 'domesticam' made it natural to put 'eorum' after 'ecclesiam' and the relative clauses of v. 4 might therefore perhaps seem to follow fairly smoothly on v. 5a.

pation on the part of the believer in the work of the gospel[1] (that 'work' here has particular reference to missionary activity and those other activities which are directly ancillary to it is, no doubt, true: at the same time it must be said that too rigid a distinction ought not to be drawn between the Christian's missionary work and the rest of his work of obedience, in view of the fact that every part of his obedience contributes to his witness to the gospel).

(ii) The fact that Paul so naturally describes persons who are not apostles but are engaged in the gospel work as his fellow-workers (cf. vv. 9 and 21; 2 Cor 8.23; Phil 2.25; 4.3; Col 4.11; Philem 1, 24) is an indication that he did not regard his apostleship as a professor who takes himself too seriously might regard his professorship (there is here no high and mighty sense of superiority), though he was, of course, ready (as his epistles show clearly) to maintain its full authenticity with vigour when occasion demanded.

(iii) ἐν Χριστῷ Ἰησοῦ clearly serves to indicate that it is in relation to Christ and in the work of the gospel of Christ rather than in any other sphere or matter that they are Paul's fellow-workers; but it seems probable that the deeper meaning of the formula 'in Christ' (see p. 315f together with pp. 298–300) is also present to his mind, and the thought that it is on the basis of God's decision to see them in Christ—to accept what Christ has done as done for them—that Paul and Prisca and Aquila have all alike been claimed as Christ's and set free to work for Him.

οἵτινες ὑπὲρ τῆς ψυχῆς μου τὸν ἑαυτῶν τράχηλον ὑπέθηκαν, οἷς οὐκ ἐγὼ μόνος εὐχαριστῶ ἀλλὰ καὶ πᾶσαι αἱ ἐκκλησίαι τῶν ἐθνῶν. It is possible that it was during the serious disturbance at Ephesus, which is related in Acts 19.23–40, that Prisca and Aquila risked their lives[2] to save Paul's life; but we cannot be certain, and v. 4a could refer to something which took place on an occasion of which we have no record. What is clear is that we have here Paul's own testimony to the fact that they had on some occasion risked their lives for his sake; and the latter half of v. 4 suggests that knowledge about their action was widespread in the churches of the Gentile mission. That

---

[1] Cf. Barth, K.E., p. 223. Barth, Shorter, p. 182 (sentence beginning, 'We cannot read') seems to give a somewhat blurred impression of Barth's meaning.

[2] That this is the meaning of τὸν ἑαυτῶν τράχηλον ὑπέθηκαν in the present context is clear. Cf. Bauer, s.v. τράχηλος, where parallels from the Vita Philonidis (SAB, 1900, p. 951) and from a Herculaneum papyrus (Deissmann, Light, p. 117f) are cited.

these churches should be conscious of their deep indebtedness to persons who had thus acted on behalf of the ἐθνῶν ἀπόστολος (11.13) is—on the assumption that the fact was well known—no more surprising than that Paul himself should feel great gratitude to them. While it can scarcely be doubted that the gratitude spoken of in v. 4b is gratitude for the particular action to which v. 4a refers, it should be said that the way in which Prisca and Aquila are mentioned at the very beginning of this series of greetings, the relative fullness of what is here said about them, and the other references to them in the NT, all combine to suggest that they were a couple for whom Paul and the churches of the Gentiles had also many other reasons for being profoundly thankful.

καὶ τὴν κατ᾽ οἶκον αὐτῶν ἐκκλησίαν. For this formula compare 1 Cor 16.19 (also referring to Prisca and Aquila); Col 4.15; Philem 2. Grammatically the expression ἡ κατ᾽ οἶκον αὐτῶν ἐκκλησία could certainly mean the church consisting simply of the Christian members of their household ('household' denoting not just the family in our sense of the word 'family' but also their slaves, employees, and other dependants); but it is not to be doubted that what is meant is rather the community of Christians regularly meeting in their house, including, in addition to the Christian members of the household or *familia*, other Christians for whom it was convenient to meet for worship in their house. There were of course no buildings specially appropriated to church purposes at this time. (See also p. 22.)[1] Zahn suggested that the church which met in the house of Prisca and Aquila included all the persons mentioned in vv. 5b–13;[2] but it seems more natural to understand the following greetings as fresh greetings rather than as a singling out of individuals already included in the general greeting of v. 5a.

5b. ἀσπάσασθε Ἐπαίνετον τὸν ἀγαπητόν μου, ὅς ἐστιν ἀπαρχὴ τῆς Ἀσίας εἰς Χριστόν. Epaenetus is not mentioned anywhere else in the NT. It may be assumed that he was a Gentile. The name is Greek, and was probably quite common, there being evidence of its occurrence in places as widely scattered as Athens, Corcyra, Ephesus, Sicily, southern Italy, Rome (see Bauer, s.v.; also Sanday and Headlam, p. 421; Lagrange, p. 364). The description of Epaenetus as Paul's 'beloved' is not to be taken to imply that he was more beloved than those who are not so described. Paul seems to have tried to attach some

[1] For references to house-churches at a later date see the passages from Pseudo-Clement, *Recogn.* 10.71, and *Acta Justini Martyris* 2f, quoted in Sanday and Headlam, p. 421.

[2] p. 607.

expression of kindly commendation to all the individuals he mentions. He has managed to keep this up (apart from v. 10b) right to the end of v. 13; but with v. 14 he simply lists names. Epaenetus is also described as being 'Asia's first-fruits unto Christ'. For the word ἀπαρχή[1] see on 8.23 and 11.16, and for its use to denote the first convert (or one of the first converts) in a particular area compare 1 Cor 16.15. That the earliest converts in a particular place often became leaders in the local church is understandable (cf. 1 Clement 42.4). That the correct reading is Ἀσίας is not to be doubted, Ἀχαίας (Χ pl sy) being most likely due to a memory of 1 Cor 16.15. The reading εἰς Χριστόν should also certainly be preferred to ἐν Χριστῷ (D G pc lat) both because it is much more strongly attested and also because it suits the context much better (while an alteration to the familiar ἐν Χριστῷ would be understandable).

6. ἀσπάσασθε Μαρίαν, ἥτις πολλὰ ἐκοπίασεν εἰς ὑμᾶς. In the NT Μαριάμ and Μαρία both occur frequently, and in many places there is variation between them in the textual tradition. The former is, of course, a transliteration of the Hebrew 'Miriam'. In all its other occurrences in the NT the latter is naturally assumed to be the Hellenized form of the Hebrew name;[2] but in the present verse it is possible that it[3] is a Roman name, the feminine form of 'Marius'. Whether the woman referred to was a Jewish Christian or a Gentile is therefore uncertain.[4] On the significance of ἐκοπίασεν see on v. 3 (συνεργούς). That the reading ὑμᾶς is to be preferred to ἡμᾶς is hardly to be doubted: her much labouring was for the good of the Roman Christians, not a service rendered specially to Paul and his companions.

[1] The reading ἀπ' ἀρχῆς (𝔓⁴⁶ D* g) is an obvious error.

[2] According to Nestle, Luke uses Μαριάμ for the nominative in Lk 1.27, 34, 38, 39, 46, 56, but Μαρία in 2.19; Μαριάμ for the vocative in 1.30, for the accusative in 2.16 and 34, and for the dative in 2.5; but Μαρία—so τῆς Μαρίας—for the genitive in 1.41.

[3] That is assuming that we should read Μαρίαν here rather than the Μαριάμ supported by 𝔓⁴⁶ Χ Χ D G pm. Μαριάμ is read by UBS, but Μαρίαν should perhaps on the whole be preferred.

[4] If the name is Roman, the woman will naturally have been a Gentile; but, if Μαριάμ is read or if Μαρίαν is the Hellenization, she will have been Jewish. It has been argued, but with little cogency, both (i) that the woman was probably a Gentile since Paul does not described her as his kinswoman (see vv. 7, 11, 21—but Aquila was a Jew, according to Acts, and Paul does not call him his 'kinsman', and the case of Herodion in v. 11 is different from that of Mary in that nothing else but the fact of his Jewishness occurs to Paul as something to say about him here, whereas in the case of Mary Paul has her much labouring for the good of the Roman Christians to mention); and also (ii) that Paul did not call Mary his kinswoman, though she was a Jewess, because (forgetting

7. ἀσπάσασθε 'Ανδρόνικον καὶ 'Ιουνιᾶν τοὺς συγγενεῖς μου καὶ συναιχμαλώτους μου, οἵτινές εἰσιν ἐπίσημοι ἐν τοῖς ἀποστόλοις οἳ καὶ πρὸ ἐμοῦ γέγοναν ἐν Χριστῷ. 'Ανδρόνικος is a Greek name, found among members of the imperial household. It is borne by a Jew mentioned by Josephus, *Ant.* 13.75 (being non-mythological, it would not be offensive to a Jew). In CIL 6.5325 and 5326 it is the name of a freedman, in 6.11626 the name of a slave. It occurs nowhere else in the NT. 'Ιουνιᾶν[1] is specially interesting, since, if it is accentuated as in Nestle, it must be the accusative of 'Ιουνιᾶς and masculine, but, if it is accentuated 'Ιουνίαν, it will be the accusative of the Greek form of the common Roman female name 'Junia'. 'Junias' might perhaps be a contraction of 'Junianus', and there is possibly just a little weight in the appeal of Sanday and Headlam[2] to the fact that three other names ending in -ᾶς (Patrobas, Hermas and Olympas) occur in this list of greetings; but their statement that 'Junias . . . is less usual as a man's name' is misleading, since the truth seems to be that, apart from the present verse, no evidence of its having existed has so far come to light (cf. Bauer, s.v. 'Ιουνιᾶς). In view of this last fact, it is surely right to assume that the person referred to was a woman (with Chrysostom, col. 670, and Lagrange, p. 366) and to accentuate 'Ιουνίαν (and not as the word is printed in the Nestle text and in the lemma above). The assertion of Lietzmann, p. 125, that the possibility of the name's being a woman's name here is ruled out by the context may be dismissed as mere conventional prejudice. Most probably Andronicus and Junia were husband and wife. By συγγενεῖς 'Paul almost certainly means . . . fellow-countrymen, and not relations':[3] compare vv. 11 and 21; also 9.3, where the meaning is clear. We have no knowledge of a time when Paul and Andronicus and Junia were prisoners

the fact that 'Maria' was also a Roman name?) he thought that her Jewishness was clear enough from her name. The Roman name 'Maria' interestingly occurs in a pagan inscription from Rome combined with the feminine form of 'Ampliatus', another name in Paul's list (see v. 8), 'D.M. Mariae Ampliatae . . .' (CIL 6. 22223).
[1] 𝔓46 seems to be alone among Greek MSS. in reading Ιουλιαν: it is supported by some Old Latin MSS. (see UBS apparatus), bo aeth Ambst. The variant is unlikely to be original, and is probably to be explained by the presence of the name in v. 15.
[2] p. 422f.
[3] Sanday and Headlam, p. 423. The view that Paul means fellow-tribesmen, i.e. fellow-Benjamites, to which Cornely, p. 776, inclines, seems unlikely. Lagrange, p. 366, thinks of relations in an extended sense ('Il s'agit plutôt de la parenté orientale très large, qui peut comprendre des centaines de personnes, dispersées sans perdre le souvenir de leur origine commune, une sorte de clan'); but this is less than convincing.

together, though it is not impossible that there was such an
occasion (Paul had already been ἐν φυλακαῖς more abundantly
than his adversaries, according to 2 Cor 11.23; and 1 Clement
5.6—taking into account no doubt his complete ministry—
speaks of him as ἑπτάκις δεσμὰ φορέσας). It would, however, be
not unnatural for him to call them his fellow-prisoners, if they,
like him, had been prisoners for Christ's sake, though not
actually together with him. The attempts to explain συναιχμαλώτους metaphorically may be dismissed as far-fetched.

ἐπίσημοι ἐν τοῖς ἀποστόλοις has sometimes been understood
as meaning 'outstanding in the eyes of the apostles'[1] (for ἐν
meaning 'in the eyes of', 'according to the judgment of', see
Bauer, s.v. ἐν I.3, and compare 1 Cor 14.11; Sophocles, *Ant.*
925); on this view 'the apostles' could mean the apostles in the
more limited sense of the word. While this must be judged
grammatically possible, it is much more probable—we might
well say, virtually certain—that the words mean 'outstanding
among the apostles', that is, 'outstanding in the group who
may be designated apostles', which is the way in which it was
understood by the patristic commentators (it would seem,
without exception). On this interpretation 'the apostles' must
be given a wider sense as denoting those itinerant missionaries
who were recognized by the churches as constituting a distinct
group among the participants in the work of spreading the
gospel (cf., e.g., Acts 14.4, 14; 1 Cor 12.28; Eph 4.11; 1 Th 2.7;[2]
also *Didache* 11.3–6).[3] That Paul should not only include a
woman (on the view taken above) among the apostles but
actually describe her, together with Andronicus, as outstanding
among them,[4] is highly significant evidence (along with the
importance he accords in this chapter to Phoebe, Prisca, Mary,
Tryphaena, Tryphosa, Persis, the mother of Rufus, Julia and
the sister of Nereus) of the falsity of the widespread and
stubbornly persistent notion that Paul had a low view of
women and something to which the Church as a whole has not
yet paid sufficient attention.

[1] e.g., Cornely, p. 776f; Zahn, p. 609.
[2] It seems probable that Paul here includes Silvanus and Timothy
(cf. 1 Th 1.1), and is not using the plural simply of himself.
[3] Reference may be made to pp. 51–53. A recent valuable discussion
of Paul's use of 'apostle' is R. Schnackenburg, 'Apostles before and
during Paul's time', in *Apostolic History*, pp. 287–303.
[4] Cf. Chrysostom, col. 669f. On col. 670 he says of Junia: Βαβαί, πόση
τῆς γυναικὸς ταύτης ἡ φιλοσοφία, ὡς καὶ τῆς τῶν ἀποστόλων ἀξιωθῆναι
προσηγορίας, and just before this (col. 669f) he remarks: Καίτοι καὶ τὸ
ἀποστόλους εἶναι μέγα, τὸ δὲ καὶ ἐν τούτοις ἐπισήμους εἶναι, ἐννόησον ἡλίκον
ἐγκώμιον.

The last words of the verse[1] indicate that Andronicus and Junia were converted before Paul and are senior to him as Christians.[2] They must then have been converted within a very short time from the earliest beginnings of the Church. Did they perhaps belong to the Greek-speaking Jewish Christian group in Jerusalem of which we hear in Acts 6?

8. ἀσπάσασθε ᾿Αμπλιᾶτον[3] τὸν ἀγαπητόν μου[4] ἐν κυρίῳ. ᾿Ampliatus' is a common slave name, occurring often in central Italy, less often in the provinces. It has been found in Ephesus (CIL 3.436), and is specially common in Rome, where it occurs as a slave name in inscriptions of the imperial household. There is a burial-chamber in the Catacomb of Domitilla containing two inscriptions which may perhaps bear on the present verse. In one (not earlier than the end of the second century A.D. and apparently Christian) an Aurelius Ampliatus is named. It is natural to suppose that he was a descendant of the person commemorated by the other, which consists of the single word AMPLIAT[I]. The tomb which bears this single name, inscribed in bold, well-formed lettering, belongs—to judge from its decoration—to the first, or early second, century A.D. Its character suggests that it is the tomb of someone who was specially esteemed. There seems to be a real possibility—we cannot put it more strongly—that this Ampliatus is the person greeted by Paul, and that it may have been through him—probably a slave—that the gospel first penetrated into the noble household to which Flavia Domitilla, the Emperor Domitian's niece and wife of Flavius Clemens,[5] belonged. (See further Sanday and Headlam, p. 424f; Lagrange, p. 366f.)

9. ἀσπάσασθε Οὐρβανὸν τὸν συνεργὸν ἡμῶν ἐν Χριστῷ καὶ Στάχυν τὸν ἀγαπητόν μου. ᾿Urbanus' is another common Roman slave name, found among members of the imperial household. The

---

[1] Of the variants noticed by Nestle, the former (the reading of 𝔓⁴⁶, which gives the singular ὅς . . . γέγονεν) can only be a mistake. The latter (τοῖς πρὸ ἐμοῦ instead of οἳ καὶ πρὸ ἐμοῦ γέγοναν), which is attested by D G, and which changes the part of the verse which follows ἀποστόλοις from a relative clause naturally taken as referring to Andronicus and Junia into a qualification of ἀποστόλοις, looks as if it may have originated as an attempted improvement by someone who wrongly understood οἵ to refer, not to ᾿Ανδρόνικον καὶ ᾿Ιουνίαν (or ᾿Ιουνιᾶν), but to τοῖς ἀποστόλοις (cf. Gal 1.17: τοὺς πρὸ ἐμοῦ ἀποστόλους).

[2] The Greek perfect tense here conveys the idea that they still are in Christ: the rendering of this by the perfect in English in the RV obscures the sense (cf. Sanday and Headlam, p. 424).

[3] The abbreviated form ᾿Αμπλιᾶν is read by ℵ D pl sy, but the ᾿Αμπλιᾶτον printed in the Nestle text is to be preferred.

[4] 𝔓⁴⁶ B F omit μου: cf. v. 12b.

[5] See OCD, s.v. 'Domitilla, Flavia'; Dio Cassius 67.14. 1–2.

reason for the use of ἡμῶν rather than μου is perhaps that Urbanus had not been a colleague of Paul personally, though, as a worker for Christ, he was a colleague of all gospel-workers generally. 'Stachys' is a rare Greek name, though it too is found as the name of a slave in the imperial household (CIL 6.8607).

10. ἀσπάσασθε Ἀπελλῆν τὸν δόκιμον ἐν Χριστῷ. 'Apelles' is quite a common Greek name (it was borne by a well-known painter of the fourth century B.C.). It was latinized as 'Apella' or 'Apelles', and was sometimes borne by Jews (cf. Horace, *Sat.* 1.5.100f: 'credat Iudaeus Apella, non ego'). It also occurs in the imperial household. This Apelles is described as δόκιμος in Christ, possibly because Paul happened to know that under some particular serious trial he had proved himself a faithful Christian, or perhaps simply because Paul wished to vary his commendatory observations and any true Christian could be so described. On δόκιμος see on 14.18.

ἀσπάσασθε τοὺς ἐκ τῶν Ἀριστοβούλου. Paul greets the Christians among the members of the household of Aristobulus. Aristobulus himself is not greeted. So, if he is alive, the presumption must be that he is not a Christian.[1] Aristobulus is a familiar Greek name, which was much used in the Hasmonean dynasty and in the family of Herod the Great. A quite likely explanation[2] of these words is that the Aristobulus referred to is the grandson of Herod the Great and brother of Agrippa I, who apparently lived in Rome as a private person and was a friend of the Emperor Claudius.[3] He probably died between A.D. 45 and 48.[4] It is probable that after his death his household was united with the imperial household; but, in that case, its members would still have borne his name—as 'Aristobuliani' (cf. 'Maecenatiani' in CIL 6.4016, 4032; 'Amyntiani' in CIL 6.

---

[1] *Pace* B. Reicke, who in *BHH* 1, col. 128, describes the Aristobulus of this verse as 'Haupt einer christl. Hausgemeinde' (cf. Ambrosiaster, col. 179: 'Aristobulus iste congregator fuisse intelligitur fratrum in Christo').

[2] Put forward by J. B. Lightfoot, *Saint Paul's Epistle to the Philippians*, London, 4th ed. 1878, reprinted 1908, p. 174f, it was accepted as probable by Sanday and Headlam, p. 425; Zahn, p. 610; cf., e.g., Lagrange, p. 367f; Michel, p. 380; Black, p. 181. While this explanation (as its supporters have always recognized) cannot be more than a probability, it has not yet been challenged, as far as we know, by any more likely suggestion. What justification S. Sandmel has for calling it 'farfetched' (*IDB* 2, p. 593) or for his assertion that 'modern scholarship uniformly rejects' it (*IDB* 1, p. 222) is not apparent.

[3] See Josephus, *BJ* 2.221–22; *Ant.* 18.273–76; 20.13.

[4] Cf. W. Otto, in A. Pauly, G. Wissowa, *Real-Encyclopädie der klassischen Altertumswissenschaft*, Supplement 2 (1913), on Herod (family tree opposite cols. 15 and 16).

4035), in Greek probably οἱ Ἀριστοβούλου.[1] Among them there would presumably be a good many Jews, a number of whom might well be Christians. That Paul is greeting the Christians among these Aristobuliani seems highly probable. That the Aristobulus referred to is rather this Aristobulus's nephew of the same name, the son of Herod of Chalcis and ruler of Armenia Minor,[2] who may perhaps have left part of his household in Rome, or this second Aristobulus's third son (also called Aristobulus),[3] who, it has been suggested, might perhaps have had charge of such a part of his father's household, would seem to be much less well grounded suggestions.

11. ἀσπάσασθε Ἡρῳδίωνα τὸν συγγενῆ μου. The fact that Paul next mentions someone called Herodion, a name which naturally suggests a connexion (probably a slave or freedman) of the Herod family, may perhaps be some support for the suggestion that the Aristobulus of v. 10 belonged to the family of Herod. For the use of συγγενής see on v. 7.

ἀσπάσασθε τοὺς ἐκ τῶν Ναρκίσσου τοὺς ὄντας ἐν κυρίῳ is similar in form to v. 10b. Narcissus himself is not greeted, and must therefore be either a deceased Christian[4] or more probably[5] a pagan (either still alive or dead). The suggestion, supported by J. B. Lightfoot,[6] that the Narcissus referred to is the notorious freedman of the Emperor Claudius, whose wealth was proverbial (cf. Juvenal, 14.329) and whose influence with Claudius had been practically unlimited, but who had been

---

[1] *Pace* J. B. Lightfoot, op. cit., p. 179, it seems more natural to take οἱ Ἀριστοβούλου rather than οἱ ἐκ τῶν Ἀριστοβούλου as equivalent to the Latin 'Aristobuliani', and to understand Paul to mean by the latter Greek expression the Christians among the Aristobuliani.

[2] See Tacitus, *Ann.* 13.7; 14.26; Josephus, *BJ* 2.252; *Ant.* 18.135, 137; 20.158.

[3] See Josephus, *Ant.* 18.137.

[4] Or just conceivably perhaps a Christian leader whom Paul knew to be at that time absent from Rome (cf. Ambrosiaster, col. 179f: 'Narcissus hic illo tempore presbyter dicitur fuisse, sicut legitur in aliis codicibus. Et quia praesens non erat, videtis qua causa eos in Domino salutet ut sanctos, qui ex ejus erant domo. Hic autem Narcissus presbyter officio peregrini fungebatur, exhortationibus firmans credentes; et quoniam non sciebat Apostolus merita illorum, qui cum illo fuerant, sic dixit . . .').

[5] Were he a deceased Christian, it would seem natural to infer from this greeting that he must have been a prominent member of the Christian community, and in that case one would rather expect some commendatory expression with regard to him to have been included. The same argument would apply with regard to Aristobulus in v. 10.

[6] op. cit., p. 175. Cf., e.g., Calvin, p. 323; Sanday and Headlam, p. 425f; Dodd, p. 16; Barclay, p. 233f. Others repeat the suggestion without indicating definitely that they are inclined to accept it: e.g. Lagrange, p. 368; Black, p. 182.

forced to commit suicide by Agrippina shortly after Nero's accession and only a year or two before Paul was writing, seems to us quite probable. After his death his household most probably passed into the possession of Nero, its members still forming a distinct group within the imperial household, Narcissiani, as they would be called.[1] That Narcissiani should be represented in Greek by οἱ Ναρκίσσου would be natural enough. Here, in contrast with v. 10b, Paul indicates explicitly by the words τοὺς ὄντας ἐν κυρίῳ that those members of the group who are to be greeted are those who are Christians.

12. ἀσπάσασθε Τρύφαιναν καὶ Τρυφῶσαν τὰς κοπιώσας ἐν κυρίῳ. ἀσπάσασθε Περσίδα τὴν ἀγαπητήν, ἥτις πολλὰ ἐκοπίασεν ἐν κυρίῳ. The verse comprises greetings to three women all of whom are commended for their labours in the Lord. The first two names, while certainly not among the commonest Greek female names, are not specially uncommon. They both occur also in Latin. For examples from both Greek and Latin sources (including inscriptions of the imperial household) see Bauer, s.v. Τρύφαινα and s.v. Τρυφῶσα, and Sanday and Headlam, p. 426. Both names are connected with the words τρυφή (according to LSJ, 'softness, delicacy, daintiness') and τρυφᾶν (according to LSJ, 'live softly, luxuriously, fare sumptuously'). Paul may, or may not, have been conscious of the irony of the contrast between the significance of their names and the fact of their toiling, which some commentators have noted. The suggestion—often repeated—that the two women were sisters, maybe twin sisters, seems (*pace* Käsemann, p. 395) likely, though the possibility that there were two Christian women in Rome, quite unrelated, who were associated together because of the similarity of their names, cannot, of course, be ruled out. Πέρσις, meaning 'Persian woman', occurs in Latin in CIL 6. 23959, as the name of a freedwoman. It is a typical Greek slave name. Persis is specially warmly commended. She is beloved and has laboured much in the Lord.[2]

13. ἀσπάσασθε Ροῦφον τὸν ἐκλεκτὸν ἐν κυρίῳ καὶ τὴν μητέρα αὐτοῦ καὶ ἐμοῦ. Lightfoot's considered opinion that, since the fact that Mark alone of the Evangelists describes Simon of Cyrene as 'the father of Alexander and Rufus' (Mk 15.21) implies that someone called Rufus must have held a prominent place among the Christians of Rome, there is, in spite of the

[1] For 'Narcissiani' cf., e.g., CIL 3. 3973; 6. 9035, 15640.
[2] Does the use of the aorist indicative here (cf. v. 6; but in the present verse the close proximity of the present participle seems to make the tense more striking by contrast) suggest that she already has behind her a considerable amount of Christian work which can in some sense at any rate be regarded as something completed?

commonness of the name 'Rufus', 'at least fair ground for identifying the Rufus of St Paul with the Rufus of St Mark'[1] still stands as a balanced scholarly judgment. We should not wish to rank the probability that the Rufus of this verse is the son of Simon of Cyrene more highly than this: at the same time, to rank it less highly seems to us (*pace* Käsemann)[2] unreasonable. There has been a very widespread tendency to explain τὸν ἐκλεκτὸν ἐν κυρίῳ as meaning something like 'that outstanding Christian'[3] on the ground that 'there would be no point' in Paul's using it here in its usual NT sense of 'chosen', 'elect', since that would be applicable to all Christians.[4] But, in spite of the volume of opinion supporting this view, its rightness should not be allowed to go unquestioned; for it is presumably also true that ἀγαπητός, as used in v. 12 (without the limiting μου)[5] would apply to all Christians. We suspect that Paul wanted to attach some commendatory expression to the names he mentioned and found it not easy to avoid repetition. In such a situation there would seem to be nothing very surprising in his specially applying to an individual a commendation equally applicable to all believers. We take it then that ἐκλεκτός probably has here its sense of 'chosen by God', 'elect'.[6] If we had to give an alternative interpretation, we should be inclined to regard that of Ambrosiaster, col. 180 ('electus enim erat, id est, promotus a Domino ad res ejus agendas'),[7] as preferable to the explanation of ἐκλεκτός as meaning 'outstanding', 'eminent' or 'choice'. With regard to the words καὶ ἐμοῦ, we may presume that on some occasion Rufus's mother had befriended Paul in a motherly way, and that this is Paul's graceful acknowledgment and expression of his grateful affection.[8]

[1] op. cit., p. 176.

[2] p. 395.

[3] Barrett, p. 280. Cf., e.g., Bengel, p. 567 (this seems to be the point of his comment); Sanday and Headlam, p. 426f; Lagrange, p. 369; Murray 2, p. 231; Black, p. 182; RSV; NEB; Bauer, s.v. ἐκλεκτός 1.

[4] Barrett, p. 284.

[5] Barrett, p. 280, translates τὴν ἀγαπητήν here 'my beloved', not distinguishing it from τὸν ἀγαπητόν μου in vv. 5, 8 and 9.

[6] Cf. Käsemann, p. 395. I had come to this conclusion before reading Käsemann's comment. Reference should also be made to the interesting discussion in Barth, CD II/2, pp. 428ff (=KD II/2, pp. 473ff), in the course of which Rom 16.13 is mentioned.

[7] It would seem that Ambrosiaster had in mind the way in which σκεῦος ἐκλογῆς is used in Acts 9.15 with reference to God's choice of Paul for a particular ministry. In this connexion too reference may be made to Barth, CD II/2, p. 429f (=KD II/2, p. 476).

[8] Martyr, p. 681, comments: 'Hanc appellat matrem affectu, non natura'.

14. ἀσπάσασθε Ἀσύγκριτον, Φλέγοντα, Ἑρμῆν, Πατροβᾶν, Ἑρμᾶν, καὶ τοὺς σὺν αὐτοῖς ἀδελφούς. All the five men named in this verse are likely—to judge from their names—to have been either slaves or freedmen. For the name Ἀσύγκριτος see Bauer, s.v. Φλέγων is the name of a dog in Xenophon, *Cyn.* 7.5, but occurs later as a slave name. Ἑρμῆς was specially common among slaves. Πατροβᾶς is an abbreviation of Πατρόβιος (see BDF, § 125). Ἑρμᾶς can be either a dialect form of Ἑρμῆς or an abbreviation for several names beginning with Ἑρμ-. The notion of Origen that this Hermas is to be identified with the author of *The Shepherd* may be dismissed, the probable date of that work being the middle of the second century. By τοὺς σὺν αὐτοῖς ἀδελφούς are presumably indicated the other members of the particular house-church, to which the five persons named belonged (cf. v. 15; also v. 5; and see p. 22).

15. ἀσπάσασθε Φιλόλογον καὶ Ἰουλίαν,[1] Νηρέα καὶ τὴν ἀδελφὴν αὐτοῦ, καὶ Ὀλυμπᾶν,[2] καὶ τοὺς σὺν αὐτοῖς πάντας ἁγίους. 'Philologus' is a common slave name. Julia is perhaps Philologus' wife or sister, as she is thus coupled with him. 'Julia', while it is, of course, a common name of free women of the Julian *gens*, is also an exceedingly common slave name, particularly in the imperial household. Nereus and his sister are possibly the children of Philologus and Julia. In the legendary *Acta Nerei et Achillei*[3] a Nereus is a chamberlain of Flavia Domitilla; but the connexion traced between the Nereus of this verse and Flavia Domitilla by Barclay, p. 237, is, as he himself is aware, decidedly fanciful. Ὀλυμπᾶς is another abbreviated name, similar to Patrobas. For καὶ τούς, κ.τ.λ., see on v. 14.

16. ἀσπάσασθε ἀλλήλους ἐν φιλήματι ἁγίῳ. Having completed his greetings to particular individuals and the groups associated with some of them, Paul now makes a general request to the Christians in Rome to greet one another with a holy kiss. The same request is made, in identical form, in 1 Cor 16.20; with φιλήματι and ἁγίῳ in reverse order, in 2 Cor 13.12; with τοὺς ἀδελφοὺς πάντας instead of ἀλλήλους, in 1 Th 5.26; and, with ἀγάπης instead of ἁγίῳ, in 1 Pet 5.14. The earliest clear reference to the kiss as a regular part of the Church's worship

---

[1] C* G have Ἰουνιαν: cf. v. 7. Doubtless Ἰουλιαν should be read here. As in v. 7, it is possible to accentuate either as -ίαν (feminine) or as -ιᾶν (masculine); but to prefer the latter is surely rather perverse (*pace* Barrett, pp. 281, 284).

[2] G has Ὀλυμπιδα, and lat Olympiadem.

[3] It is to be found in Texte und Untersuchungen 11.2 (1893). See also Sanday and Headlam, p. 428; F. L. Cross and E. A. Livingstone (ed.), *The Oxford Dictionary of the Christian Church*, Oxford, ²1974, under 'Nereus and Achilleus, Sts'.

is in Justin, *1 Apol.* 65, according to which it was given between the intercessory prayers and the offertory.[1] Tertullian refers to it as 'the kiss of peace'.[2] Origen, commenting on this verse, says: 'From this injunction and several similar ones the custom has been handed down to the churches, that after the prayers the brethren shall greet one another in turn'.[3] It is not impossible, however, that Paul's injunction itself presupposes the likelihood that the Christians in Rome were already accustomed to exchange a kiss in preparation for their celebration of the Holy Supper (the way the injunction is given suggests that he did not expect it to cause any surprise).[4] It is likely that he expected his letter to be read out when the church was assembled for worship. Ambrosiaster comments on Paul's ἁγίῳ 'that is, in the peace of Christ—not in carnal desire, but in the Holy Spirit; that their kisses may be devout, not carnal'.[5]

ἀσπάζονται ὑμᾶς αἱ ἐκκλησίαι πᾶσαι τοῦ Χριστοῦ[6] might seem to have a special appropriateness, addressed to the Christians of Rome, the imperial capital. For Paul's speaking on behalf of the churches generally compare v. 4, where he speaks for all the Gentile churches. (Compare also the references to 'all the churches' in 1 Cor 7.17; 14.33; 2 Cor 8.18; 11.28.) Paul was, in fact, in constant touch at this time with the churches of Galatia, Asia, Macedonia and Achaia.[7] The expression αἱ ἐκκλησίαι τοῦ Χριστοῦ occurs nowhere else in the NT. Paul's custom is to speak of ἡ ἐκκλησία (or αἱ ἐκκλησίαι) τοῦ θεοῦ, though in Gal

---

[1] The relevant passage is: ἀλλήλους φιλήματι ἀσπαζόμεθα παυσάμενοι τῶν εὐχῶν. ἔπειτα προσφέρεται τῷ προεστῶτι τῶν ἀδελφῶν ἄρτος καὶ ποτήριον ὕδατος καὶ κράματος . . .

[2] *De oratione* 18 [14]: 'osculum pacis'.

[3] col. 1282f ('Ex hoc sermone, aliisque nonnullis similibus, mos ecclesiis traditus est ut post orationes osculo se invicem suscipiant fratres. Hoc autem osculum sanctum appellat Apostolus').

[4] On kissing in the ancient world generally, the OT and Judaism, the NT and early Church, reference may be made to G. Stählin, in *TWNT* 9, pp. 112 (bibliography), 116–26, 136–43. On the eucharistic kiss see also G. Dix, *The Shape of the Liturgy*, Westminster (London), [2]1945, pp. 105–10; F. L. Cross and E. A. Livingstone, op. cit., s.v. 'kiss of peace'. Judas's choice of the kiss as a sign (Mk 14.44f) implies that it was in common use as a greeting between Jesus and His disciples, as it was between other Rabbis and their pupils. Pelagius's comment (p. 124) brings out clearly the significance of the kiss of peace in the Church: 'ideo enim in ecclesia pax primum adnuntiatur, ut ostendat se cum omnibus pacificum esse, qui corpori communicaturus est Christi'.

[5] col. 180 ('Omnes quibus scribit, et quos nominat, jubet salutare se invicem in osculo sancto, id est, in pace Christi, non in desiderio carnis, sed in Spiritu sancto; ut religiosa sint oscula, non carnalia').

[6] D G it omit 16b, but D* G it add καὶ αἱ ἐκκλησίαι πᾶσαι τοῦ Χριστοῦ at the end of v. 21.

[7] Cf. Michel, p. 382.

1.22 he has ταῖς ἐκκλησίαις τῆς Ἰουδαίας ταῖς ἐν Χριστῷ. The
purpose of this sentence is, no doubt, as Calvin noted,[1] to
contribute to the binding together of all Christians by the bond
of love.

17. **Παρακαλῶ δὲ ὑμᾶς, ἀδελφοί, σκοπεῖν τοὺς τὰς διχοστασίας
καὶ τὰ σκάνδαλα παρὰ τὴν διδαχὴν ἣν ὑμεῖς ἐμάθετε[2] ποιοῦντας,
καὶ[3] ἐκκλίνετε ἀπ' αὐτῶν.** The abruptness of the introduction of
vv. 17–20a at this point has, in our judgment, been greatly
exaggerated.[4] (i) It is often stated that these verses interrupt
the series of greetings; but Paul's greetings are complete with
v. 16, and the greetings in vv. 21–23 are a postscript added in
the hand of Tertius after Paul's autograph *subscriptio* (v. 20b),[5]
and are, not Paul's, but his companions' greetings. (ii) There is
alleged to be a sharp contrast between the authoritative and
somewhat severe tone of these verses and the rest of the letter;
but Paul has already used an authoritative παρακαλῶ in 12.1,
has taken considerable liberties with those he is addressing in
the whole division 12.1–15.13, and has evinced as stern a
severity in 3.8b; 14.10–12, 15f, 20, as in 16.17f. (iii) It is said
that there is nothing in the context to explain the introduction
of these verses at this point; but, in answer to this, it may be
said that there are two quite natural connexions of thought
between v. 16 (which itself follows very naturally on vv. 3–15)
and vv. 17–20a: (a) the injunction to greet one another with a
holy kiss, pointing as it does to the need and the obligation to
maintain the peace of the church, contains within itself an
implicit warning against those things which are able to destroy
that peace and against the unholy kisses of those who would
attach themselves to the church's fellowship insincerely, remaining all the time alien from it in doctrine or life;[6] (b) the
mention of all the churches indicates that Paul's mind was not
so concentrated on the situation of the Christians in Rome as

---

[1] p. 323.

[2] The addition of (ἢ 𝔓46) λέγοντας ἢ before ποιοῦντας by 𝔓46 D G m
looks like an unsuccessful attempt at improving the sentence by
someone who felt that Paul's meaning would be more adequately
expressed if a reference to speaking (contrary to the true doctrine) were
included, but failed to notice that the effect of the addition would be to
leave τὰς διχοστασίας καὶ τὰ σκάνδαλα in the air.

[3] καί is omitted by 𝔓46 m.

[4] e.g., by Käsemann, p. 397.

[5] That the secretary should take the pen again and add a postscript, after the sender had authenticated the letter by writing the
subscriptio in his own hand, was quite a normal practice in the composition of ancient Greek letters. See Roller, *Formular*, pp. 191–99.

[6] The validity of (a) is quite independent of acceptance of the liturgical framework assumed by Michel, p. 382.

to exclude all thought of other churches well known to him, and, if he began to think about those other churches, it would be but natural for him to remember the troubles which had afflicted them, and from which the Christian community in Rome was unlikely to be exempt.

For παρακαλῶ[1] see on 12.1, 8; 15.30; and for ἀδελφοί see on 1.13. σκοπεῖν[2] occurs in the NT also in Lk 11.35; 2 Cor 4.18; Gal 6.1; Phil 2.4; 3.17: here it means 'mark (so as to avoid)', whereas in Phil 3.17 it means 'mark (so as to follow)'. The only other NT occurrence of διχοστασία is in Gal 5.20, where (used in the plural as here) it is associated with ἐριθεῖαι and αἱρέσεις. For the word σκάνδαλον see on 9.33; 11.9; 14.13. The διδαχή which the Roman Christians have learned is no special Pauline teaching; for, though some of them have indeed had contact with Paul, the community as a whole is not of his founding. We must assume rather that the reference is to what is common primitive Christian teaching.[3] The question of the identity of the people Paul has in mind in referring to those who, in opposition to the truth of the gospel, cause divisions and occasions of stumbling—so damaging the unity and threatening the faith of the Church—will be more conveniently discussed in connexion with the next verse in the light of the further indications it gives. But it should be noted that the words παρὰ τὴν διδαχὴν ἣν ὑμεῖς ἐμάθετε are of vital importance in this sentence. It is those who cause divisions and occasions of stumbling contrary to the truth of the gospel against whom Paul warns. Sometimes divisions have to be caused for the sake of the truth (see, for example, Gal 1.8f; and Jesus Himself was a cause of division—cf., e.g., Mt 10.34–36) and in certain circumstances the truth itself is a stumbling-block (see, for example, 9.32b–33; Lk 7.23). The words καὶ ἐκκλίνετε ἀπ' αὐτῶν clarify and strengthen σκοπεῖν: the Roman Christians are not only to mark such people in the sense of recognizing them for the danger which they are: they are actually to avoid them, to keep out of their way.[4]

---

[1] The variant ἐρωτῶ is most likely due to the influence of the use of 'rogo' in the Latin here.

[2] D G it attest the stronger ἀσφαλῶς σκοπεῖτε in place of σκοπεῖν.

[3] The noun διδαχή occurs only six times in the Pauline corpus—in 6.17 and here; in 1 Cor 14.6 and 26; in 2 Tim 4.2 and Tit 1.9. But the verb διδάσκειν occurs rather more frequently (see on 12.7).

[4] There are several problems connected with the last three words of this verse. (i) There is a variation in the textual tradition between the present imperative (𝔥 69 pc) and the aorist imperative (𝔓⁴⁶ A 𝔎 D G pl). The latter would rather suggest that a definite breaking off of relations is being required, and so might be taken as suggesting more strongly

18. οἱ γὰρ τοιοῦτοι τῷ κυρίῳ ἡμῶν Χριστῷ οὐ δουλεύουσιν ἀλλὰ τῇ ἑαυτῶν κοιλίᾳ, καὶ διὰ τῆς χρηστολογίας καὶ εὐλογίας ἐξαπατῶσιν τὰς καρδίας τῶν ἀκάκων is clearly intended to explain why it is that the people to whom Paul has just referred constitute so serious a danger. The first half of the verse declares that they are no servants of Christ, who is Paul's and the Roman Christians' Lord, but instead of serving Him serve their own belly. Barrett takes the reference to be to 'their preoccupation with food laws';[1] but, while this interpretation goes back to the early Church[2] and has some modern

that Paul has a particular group or particular groups in mind. The former could be explained as implying that a course of action already being followed is to be continued or as indicating that no definite goal is envisaged—the action is to go on indefinitely. It might be held to fit in rather better with the view that Paul is speaking generally. We should probably prefer ἐκκλίνετε as the more difficult reading (an alteration in the direction of greater definiteness is more likely than one in the opposite direction): its attestation also is strong in quality, if not numerically. (ii) Not unconnected with the question of reading is the further question whether what is intended is a breaking off of relations as a matter of church discipline (comparable with 1 Cor 5.9–13; 2 Th 3.6), as Michel (p. 383) asserts, or simply an avoidance of dangerous society, a keeping out of the way of temptation. Two things would seem to tell against Michel's, and in favour of the second, view: (a) the very great difficulty of envisaging Paul's interference in the church discipline of the Roman church; and (b) the conclusion we have already reached with regard to (i). (iii) The question how such avoidance of dangerous society or the sort of disciplinary action which Michel thinks Paul has in mind here (and which he certainly does have in mind in some other passages) can be consonant with the fulfilment of the obligation to love even the propagators of false teaching is a serious question which cannot be dealt with here; but it may just be pointed out that one can avoid subjecting oneself to a person's evil influence without hardening one's heart against him or refusing him kindly help should he be in distress, though the task of responding to the deeper need which lies behind his false teaching is one which the more immature Christians may well leave to the more mature and informed of their brethren; and that, whenever a church is constrained in loyalty both to God and to men to apply its ultimate sanction of excommunication to someone, it must of course hope for, and actively seek, the repentance and restoration of the offender. (See further C. E. B. Cranfield, *The Service of God*, London, 1965, pp. 19–21 = 'Divine and human action: the biblical concept of worship', in *Interpretation* 12 (1957–58), p. 396f.)

[1] p. 285.

[2] e.g., Gennadius, as given in Cramer, p. 525: . . . οὓς καλῶς οὐχὶ τῷ Χριστῷ δουλεύειν, ἀλλὰ τῇ ἑαυτῶν, ἔφη, κοιλίᾳ. διὰ τὸ μονονουχὶ τὴν εὐσέβειαν αὐτοὺς ἐν τῇ παρατηρήσει τῶν βρωμάτων ὁρίζεσθαι. Ambrosiaster explains ὧν ὁ θεὸς ἡ κοιλία in Phil 3.19 in this way (*PL* 17, col. 417: '. . . Quos cum dolore et lacrymis memorat; quia saluti credentium obsistebant, de cibis edendis, et non edendis quaestiones moventes, quasi salus in esca sit, aut venter Deus, quem juxta legem mundis escis delectari putabant . . .'), but in his comment on this passage in Romans (col. 181), while he

supporters,[1] it does not seem very likely. If κοιλία is really to be taken quite literally, a much more natural explanation, in view of 14.15–21, would surely be that Paul has in mind the selfish insistence of the 'strong' of 14.1–15.13 on eating meat even at the cost of the spiritual ruin of their 'weak' brothers (see, especially, 14.17f, where the strong are reminded that the kingdom of God is not a matter of eating and drinking, and their selfish and frivolous conduct is contrasted with the proper service of Christ (ὁ . . . ἐν τούτῳ δουλεύων τῷ Χριστῷ)). But it seems more probable that the expression 'serve one's own belly' is here used in a less narrowly literal sense. One might perhaps take it to denote a seeking to live sumptuously or, more generally, greed. So Chrysostom, for example, while mentioning gluttony[2] in his comment, goes on, after referring to Phil 3.19, to cite in illustration of Paul's meaning a number of biblical passages, including Mt 23.14 ('ye devour widows' houses'), which suggest that he thinks that Paul has in mind these persons' greed quite generally.[3] Aquinas interprets of the motive of gain: 'Non enim praedicabant propter gloriam Christi, sed propter quaestum, ut suum ventrem implerent'.[4] And there is a good deal of support for the view that what is meant is avarice of the sort referred to in 2 Cor 11.20; Tit 1.10f, the avarice which is ever ready to exploit the simple.[5] There remains a further possibility—that 'serve one's own belly' is used in the sense of serving oneself, of being the willing slave of one's egotism, of that walking according to the flesh and having one's life determined by the flesh, to which 8.4 and 5 refer.[6] On the whole, it is this last possibility which seems to us the most probable interpretation.

The second half of the verse declares that these persons (whoever they are) deceive the hearts of the innocent through their χρηστολογία and εὐλογία. The word ἄκακος sometimes has—this is particularly so in LXX Proverbs (e.g. 21.11)—a some-

---

understands the people to whom reference is being made to be Judaizers (as he does in Phil 3.19), he has nothing to say about τῇ ἑαυτῶν κοιλίᾳ, though he may perhaps have had this explanation of it in mind.

[1] e.g., J. Behm, in TWNT 3, p. 788 (his claim that Theodore of Mopsuestia (PG 66, col. 875) supports this interpretation is not accurate: the Greek in the opposite column (876) has the words: εἰ γε ὑπὲρ τοῦ ἀπατῶντας δύνασθαι τὴν ἑαυτῶν γαστέρα πληροῦν πάντα ποιοῦσιν, the thought being similar to that of Chrysostom, col. 676).

[2] col. 676: . . . οὓς μάλιστα ἀεὶ διαβάλλειν εἴωθεν ὡς γαστριμάργους.

[3] ibid., while on col. 675 he explains that the false teachings come Ἀπὸ τοῦ γαστρὶ δουλεύειν καὶ τοῖς ἄλλοις πάθεσιν.

[4] p. 228f (1218).

[5] e.g., Lagrange, p. 374; Huby, p. 505.

[6] See on 8.4f.

what pejorative sense, just as the English word 'innocent' can do; and it probably bears this sense here—that is, 'innocent' in the sense of 'simple', 'unsuspecting'. Paul was realistic enough to recognize that Christians are very often quite as far from being φρόνιμοι ὡς οἱ ὄφεις as they are from being ἀκέραιοι ὡς αἱ περιστεραί, lacking that true understanding of their fellow-men's and of their own hearts which only a deep engagement with the gospel can give. So he knew they would always be very prone to be taken in by fair-sounding and hypocritical speech.[1]

We must now look back to the question of the identity of the persons referred to in this and the previous verse. Very many interpreters have assumed that they must be Judaizers. Some patristic writers were inclined—and in this they have been faithfully followed by a good many recent scholars—to see Jews or Judaizers 'under every bed'. Others have seen a reference to antinomians. So, for example, Dodd says, 'We know that Paul had trouble, not only with the extreme Jewish party in the Church, but also with people in the Gentile churches who practised and defended immoral licence in the name of Christian liberty . . . The language . . . would suit such tendencies better than the propaganda of extreme Judaism, and they were equally disruptive'.[2] We may think of the selfish among the 'strong' of 14.1–15.13—those who insisted on the outward expression of their (in itself proper) liberty regardless of the effects on their 'weak' brothers. We may wonder whether possibly Paul has in mind people of 'gnosticizing' tendencies; or persons who put great emphasis on their possession of the Spirit and tended to value exciting and showy gifts unduly highly, to the detriment of charity and brotherliness. And the probability that there were in the early Church, as there are in the Church today, people eager to cause divisions and to set stumbling-blocks in the way of their fellows not because of any more or less seriously held theological or practical convictions

---

[1] The suggestion that χρηστολογία is an intentional pun (χρηστός and Χριστός) is rightly rejected by Käsemann, p. 398, as unlikely. The explanation of χρηστολόγος afforded by the fourth-century writer on Pertinax in the *Historia Augusta* (Julius Capitolinus, *Pertinax* 13.5: 'χρηστολόγον eum appellantes, qui bene loqueretur et male faceret'), quoted in Bauer, s.v. χρηστολογία, may be accepted as giving the right clue to the meaning of χρηστολογία here, while the use of εὐλογία in a bad sense to denote false fine-speaking or plausibility is quite well attested in secular Greek (see Bauer, s.v. 2; LSJ, s.v. I.2). The two words may be taken together as an example of hendiadys (cf. Käsemann, p. 398). Both the variant εὐγλωττίας (460) and the omission of καὶ εὐλογίας (D G 33 *pc* it) are explicable as attempts to get rid of a difficulty on the part of people unfamiliar with this non-biblical use of εὐλογία.
[2] p. 244f.

but simply out of a desire to gratify their own self-importance, should certainly not be overlooked. To imagine that one can, on the basis of these two verses or of any other evidence afforded by the epistle, single out one group of trouble-makers, either already present in the church in Rome or as yet only constituting a possible danger from outside, as the people whom Paul has in mind, seems to us quite unrealistic. If Paul had one particular group in mind, we cannot be at all certain which it was. But he may well have had more than one group in mind, or he may have been warning in a quite general way against a danger which he knew would always threaten the churches but could present itself in many different forms.

19. ἡ γὰρ ὑμῶν ὑπακοὴ εἰς πάντας ἀφίκετο supports the exhortation of v. 17f: the Roman Christians have a reputation to live up to. For the meaning of ὑπακοή see on 1.5 (p. 66f). For the general sense of the sentence compare 1.8b and see note thereon.

ἐφ' ὑμῖν οὖν χαίρω[1] may be compared with 1.8a, Paul's rejoicing over them because of the fact which has just been stated in the first sentence of this verse corresponding to his thanking God in 1.8a for the fact which is stated in 1.8b.

θέλω δὲ[2] ὑμᾶς σοφοὺς[3] εἶναι εἰς τὸ ἀγαθόν, ἀκεραίους δὲ εἰς τὸ κακόν. The words are a little reminiscent of Mt 10.16, but the similarity of thought is hardly close enough to warrant a confident assertion that Paul's thought here 'is clearly dominically inspired'[4] (at least in the sense of dependence on the tradition of Jesus' sayings). Paul's meaning seems to be that he desires that they should be wise unto—in the direction of, for the purpose of—that which is good,[5] and therefore constant in

---

[1] 𝔓⁴⁶ D G *pc* have these words in the more ordinary, less interesting, order χαίρω οὖν ἐφ' ὑμῖν, while 𝔎 *al* have the word-order of 𝔓⁴⁶, with the addition of τό before ἐφ'.

[2] D G have καὶ θέλω instead of θέλω δέ, while 𝔓⁴⁶ has καὶ θέλω δέ. The strongly attested θέλω δέ should surely be preferred: it fits the context better, though a not very attentive reader could well think καί more suitable than δέ.

[3] The addition of μέν after σοφούς (𝔥 𝔎 *pm* Cl) is obviously attractive, but is likely to be secondary.

[4] Black, p. 184. Bruce, p. 278, wrongly states that 'in Greek the same two adjectives, *sophos* and *akeraios*, are used in both places' (i.e. in Mt 10.16b and here); but in Mt 10.16 φρόνιμος, not σοφός, is used. 1 Cor 14.20, which Bruce also cites, would seem to be nearer to the thought of Mt 10.16 than the present passage.

[5] One might wonder whether ἀγαθόν should here be understood to refer to their final good, i.e., their salvation (see on 8.28 and 13.4), and whether 2 Tim 3.15 (. . . σε σοφίσαι εἰς σωτηρίαν) might be compared; but probably the sense of the morally good (see on 12.2) should, in view of the contrast with τὸ κακόν, be preferred here.

their ὑπακοή, which has just been mentioned; but preserved in their integrity over against that which is evil,[1] and so proof against the specious approaches of those against whom they have just been warned.

20. ὁ δὲ θεὸς τῆς εἰρήνης συντρίψει τὸν σατανᾶν ὑπὸ τοὺς πόδας ὑμῶν ἐν τάχει. For the phrase ὁ θεὸς τῆς εἰρήνης see on 15.33. In view of what was said in connexion with that verse, the suggestion that Paul used the phrase here with the thought of the removing of 'the discord in the Church' specially in mind[2] seems not very likely. The variant συντρίψαι (A *pc* it vg^cl), which makes this sentence into a prayer-wish, is an understandable attempted improvement (cf. 1 Th 5.23; Heb 13.20f), and is not likely to be original. What we have here is a promise. Paul possibly had the MT of Gen 3.15 in mind (not the LXX which has αὐτός σου τηρήσει κεφαλήν); but there are other passages which should be compared: e.g. Ps 91.13; Lk 10.18–20; Test. Simeon 6.6; Test. Levi 18.12. It is very often assumed both by those who think that the reference is to a deliverance in the ordinary course of history[3] and those who think the reference is to the final eschatological defeat of evil[4] that Paul must have in mind the rout of the people mentioned in v. 17f regarded as the servants of Satan.[5] But this is by no means clear. It seems indeed more probable that v. 19 has completed what Paul wants to say concerning the matter raised in v. 17, and that this last sentence before the *subscriptio* is a promise of much more far-reaching significance. That the promise refers to the eschatological consummation, and not to some special divine deliverance in the course of their lives, seems to us virtually certain. But this does not mean that we should see in ἐν τάχει a proof that Paul was sure that the Parousia would occur within, at the most, a few decades. On this important question see on 13.12, and also on 15.19 and 23.

Ἡ χάρις τοῦ κυρίου ἡμῶν Ἰησοῦ μεθ' ὑμῶν is Paul's *subscriptio*. The omission of these words by D G it (that is, by some of the authorities which include v. 24) is no doubt to be explained

---

[1] On ἀκέραιος see G. Kittel, in *TWNT* 1, p. 209f; Bauer, s.v.

[2] Which seems to be implied by Black, p. 184 (cf. Chrysostom, col. 677).

[3] e.g., Gaugler 2, p. 411f; Leenhardt, p. 386.

[4] e.g., Michel, p. 385.

[5] This is assumed by, for example, G. Bertram, in the article on συντρίβω, in *TWNT* 7, p. 924. On 'Satan' reference may be made to W. Foerster, in *TWNT* 7, pp. 151–64; Barth, *CD* III/3, pp. 289–368, 519–31 (=*KD* III/3, pp. 327–425, 608–23); and to the present writer's *The Gospel according to Saint Mark*, Cambridge, ⁶1977, passages cited in the index s.v. 'Satan'.

as due to their apparent redundancy when once v. 24 had been introduced. That the 'grace' should be read here, and that v. 24 should be omitted (with 𝔓⁴⁶ 𝕳 *pc* vg^codd Or) may be regarded as certain. The addition of v. 24 would be thoroughly natural, if vv. 21–23 were not recognized as a postscript and, as a consequence, v. 20b was not recognized as a subscription.[1] The Χριστοῦ after Ἰησοῦ attested by A C 𝖝 *pl* is no doubt secondary: it is similarly added by many authorities in 1 Cor 16.23.

The ordinary concluding greeting written by the sender of a letter in his own hand as subscription was ἔρρωσο or ἔρρωσθε. Just as Paul did with the epistolary prescript,[2] so he also transformed the subscription into a vehicle of specifically Christian and theological content. The Pauline subscription occurs in varying forms. The closest to that used here are 1 Cor 16.23 (identical except for the omission of ἡμῶν); 1 Th 5.28 (identical except for the addition of Χριστοῦ); 2 Th 3.18 (identical except for the addition of Χριστοῦ and of πάντων before ὑμῶν). In Galatians, Philippians and Philemon μετὰ τοῦ πνεύματος ὑμῶν is used instead of μεθ' ὑμῶν; in 2 Corinthians a fuller (Trinitarian) formula is used, while in Colossians and the Pastorals a shortened form is used. In Ephesians the formula is general and not in the second person (ἡ χάρις μετὰ πάντων τῶν ἀγαπώντων, κ.τ.λ.). In every concluding greeting in the Pauline corpus the word χάρις occurs.[3]

For χάρις see on 1.7, where we have 'grace to you . . . from God our Father and the Lord Jesus Christ'. Paul refers both to the grace of God (so 3.24) and to the grace of Christ (as here), and in 5.15 he refers to both in the same verse. Compare the way in which he speaks both of Christ's love (so 8.35; 2 Cor 5.14) and of God's love (so 5.5; 8.39). For the significance of μεθ' ὑμῶν see on 15.33, where the thought is of God's being with the Roman Christians Himself. But, since the grace of Christ is the undeserved and triumphant love of God acting in and through Christ, by which and in which God gives Himself to men to be their saving God, there is no really substantial difference between a prayer-wish that the grace of God or of Christ should be with someone and a prayer-wish that God or Christ should be with him. But it is very understandable that, while for the person whose understanding has been moulded by the truth of the gospel, there is no substantial difference between 'our Lord Jesus be with you' and 'the grace of our

---

[1] On the textual problem see pp. 5–11, especially p. 6.
[2] See pp. 45–48.
[3] On the Pauline subscription see further Roller, *Formular*, pp. 72ff.

Lord Jesus be with you', the latter is a rather more satisfactory concluding greeting, in that it actually includes an explicit reference to the essential nature of God's dealings with His creatures in 'our Lord Jesus'.

21. Ἀσπάζεται¹ ὑμᾶς Τιμόθεος ὁ συνεργός μου,² καὶ Λούκιος καὶ Ἰάσων καὶ Σωσίπατρος οἱ συγγενεῖς μου³ is the first of three verses conveying greetings from various friends of Paul who are with him. For Timothy see 1 Cor 4.17; 16.10f; 2 Cor 1.1, 19; Phil 1.1; 2.19–24; Col 1.1; 1 Th 1.1; 3.2, 6; 2 Th 1.1; Philem 1; to which should be added Acts 16.1–3; 17.14f; 18.5; 19.22; 20.4f (specially relevant—see p. 12), and, of course, 1 and 2 Timothy. He had certainly earned the description ὁ συνεργός μου.

The only other occurrence in the NT of the name Λούκιος is in Acts 13.1; but a case can scarcely be made for identifying the Lucius of this verse with Lucius of Cyrene.⁴ Some have suggested that this Lucius is to be identified with Luke, the Λουκᾶς of Col 4.14; Philem 24; 2 Tim 4.11.⁵ It is true that Λουκᾶς is a possible equivalent of Λούκιος;⁶ and also that Acts 20.5ff implies that the author of the 'we' passages of Acts was with Paul at the appropriate time. But a definite decision about this seems to be impossible. (The presence of οἱ συγγενεῖς μου need not be any objection—on the widely held but by no means certain assumption that Luke was a Gentile⁷—since it could be taken to refer only to the last two persons mentioned in the sentence.)

A Jason is mentioned in Acts 17.5, 6, 7, 9. He was Paul's host on his first visit to Thessalonica. Though he is not named as a Thessalonian delegate in Acts 20, it would seem quite possible that he is the same person as the Jason mentioned

---

¹ The plural ἀσπάζονται of ℵ 33 al is an understandable grammatical correction, no doubt secondary: the use of the singular here is perfectly natural.

² The omission of μου by B is surely simply accidental. It is intrinsically unlikely that Paul would have omitted it with reference to Timothy.

³ D* G it add καὶ αἱ ἐκκλησίαι πᾶσαι τοῦ Χριστοῦ. See notes on v. 16. There is a certain tidiness in placing the greeting of all the churches here among the greetings from named persons rather than at the end of the series of greetings from Paul himself to named individuals in Rome, and this was possibly the motive for the transposition. That v. 16b is original and the additional words here secondary is not to be doubted.

⁴ *Pace* Sanday and Headlam, p. 432.

⁵ A suggestion noted by Origen, col. 1288, it was taken up in modern times by Deissmann, *Light*, pp. 435–38. For a bibliography of the discussion see Bauer, s.v. Λουκᾶς.

⁶ See BDF, § 125 (2); Bauer, s.v. Λουκᾶς.

⁷ See, e.g., the discussion in E. E. Ellis, *The Gospel of Luke*, London, 1966, p. 52f.

here.¹ The name was common among Jews, being used as a pure Greek substitute for ᾿Ιησοῦς, which was simply a transliteration of Yēšûa'.

Sosipater is very likely to be identified with the 'Sopater of Beroea, *the son* of Pyrrhus', mentioned in Acts 20.4. 'Sopater' would be a quite likely abbreviated form of 'Sosipater'. It is interesting that in at least one other case—if this is one—Paul uses the more formal name, and the writer of Acts the less formal, that is in the case of Prisca ('Prisca' being the proper form of the name, the 'Priscilla' of Acts being a diminutive).

22. ἀσπάζομαι ὑμᾶς ἐγὼ Τέρτιος ὁ γράψας τὴν ἐπιστολὴν ἐν κυρίῳ. For discussion of this verse see pp. 2–5. It remains to refer here to the question whether ἐν κυρίῳ should be taken with ἀσπάζομαι² or with γράψας.³ While there is a considerable attractiveness in the view that ἐν κυρίῳ should be connected with γράψας (one might understand Tertius to be expressing by this ἐν κυρίῳ a certain awareness of the importance of that in which he had played a vital part, or simply indicating that he had done what he had done as a Christian as part of his service of his Lord; and in some at least, if not all, of vv. 3, 7, 8, 9, 10, 11, 12a and b, and 13 we have examples of ἐν Χριστῷ (᾿Ιησοῦ) or ἐν κυρίῳ connected not with the initial ἀσπάσασθε but with what is said about the persons to be greeted),⁴ the balance of probability would seem to lie with the more commonly held view that ἐν κυρίῳ should be taken with ἀσπάζομαι. If this alternative is accepted, then we may understand that Tertius is indicating his solidarity in Christ with the Roman Christians. It could be that he had some connexion with Rome and would be known to some of the Christian community there.

23. ἀσπάζεται ὑμᾶς Γάϊος ὁ ξένος μου καὶ ὅλης τῆς ἐκκλησίας. The name 'Gaius' occurs in a number of other places in the NT (Acts 19.29; 20.4; 1 Cor 1.14; 3 Jn 1). If the Gaius mentioned here is a Corinthian, as seems likely, we may leave out of account not only the Gaius of 3 John but also the persons of that name mentioned in the two Acts verses, since one of them

---

¹ *Pace*, e.g., Bauer, s.v. ᾿Ιάσων 2; Black, p. 184; Käsemann, p. 401.
² So, e.g., Sanday and Headlam, p. 431; Michel, p. 375; Käsemann, p. 399; RSV; NEB; JB.
³ So, e.g., Bengel, p. 568; Barrett, p. 286; Leenhardt, p. 387.
⁴ Bengel's comment is interesting: 'ἐν, *in*) Constr. cum *qui scripsi.* Implicita fidei confessio'. So too is Leenhardt's. Cornely's comment, while his interpretation is probably correct, seems rather unduly hard on the other view: '. . . satis mire autem iuniores quidam eam [i.e. locutionem *in Domino*] ad verbum *scripsi* trahere volunt, acsi Tertius se epistolam "ad gloriam Christi" (Est.) aut "propter Dominum" (Iust.) aut gratis ac sine mercede (Cai.) scripsisse asserat' (p. 789).

is described as a Macedonian and the other as 'of Derbe',[1] but there would seem to be a real possibility that we should identify our Gaius with the one mentioned in 1 Cor 1.14, though the name is, of course, an extremely common Roman praenomen. The suggestion that it is the same person as is referred to in Acts 18.7 as 'Titius Justus'[2] seems possible, though more can hardly be said. (Titius Justus received Paul and—it is probably implied—the Corinthian believers into his house, when they were driven out of the neighbouring synagogue. Since 'Titius' is a Roman nomen (i.e. *gens* name), the person is likely to have had also a praenomen, which might easily have been Gaius.) It is not clear whether ὅλης τῆς ἐκκλησίας is meant to indicate that he afforded hospitality to the whole local church (in the sense that they regularly met in his house) or that he gave hospitality to travelling Christians passing through Corinth (ὅλη ἡ ἐκκλησία denoting the Church as a whole). In either case, the implication would probably be that he was, at least, fairly wealthy. The natural conclusion to draw from ὁ ξένος μου, introduced at this point, is that Paul is actually staying with Gaius at the time of writing (cf. p. 12).

ἀσπάζεται ὑμᾶς Ἔραστος ὁ οἰκονόμος τῆς πόλεως. It has been argued that the Erastus of Acts 19.22 and 2 Tim 4.20 can hardly be the Erastus of this verse, since such an official would hardly be able to leave his city for a long period. The name was common enough; so Bauer's distinction between *Erastus* 1 and 2 may well be right. But a definite conclusion as to whether two different persons are involved does not seem to be possible. (About the Erastus of 2 Tim 4.20 it is anyway said that he ἔμεινεν ἐν Κορίνθῳ.) The Erastus of the present verse has been identified with a civic official bearing this name, who is mentioned in a Latin inscription on a marble paving-block discovered at Corinth, which reads: 'ERASTUS PRO: AED: S: P: STRAVIT' ('Erastus, commissioner for public works, laid this pavement at his own expense'). The inscription belongs to the first century A.D.; but aedile and city treasurer are not the same thing (the Greek equivalent of aedile was ἀγορανόμος), though it would have been possible for the same man to have held both offices at different times. Again, we have to leave the matter

---

[1] In Acts 20.4 there is a variant Δουβ(ε)ριος (D* gig).

[2] Cf. W. M. Ramsay, *Pictures of the Apostolic Church: its life and teaching*, London, 1910, p. 205; E. J. Goodspeed, 'Gaius Titius Justus', in *JBL* 69 (1950), p. 382f; Bruce, p. 280. It would seem that Nestle is right in reading Τιτίου rather than Τίτου or omitting the first of the two names altogether.

open.[1] But it is anyway interesting to find as responsible an official of an important city, as the city treasurer of Corinth was, a member of the Christian community at this time.

καὶ Κούαρτος ὁ ἀδελφός. Nothing is known about Quartus beyond this mention of him. By ὁ ἀδελφός is surely meant 'the fellow-Christian', as we might say 'brother Quartus'. To Bruce's question why, if 'brother' simply means 'fellow-Christian', 'is he singled out to receive a designation which was common to them all',[2] we would reply: (i) that it is quite likely that τὴν ἀγαπητήν in v. 12 and τὸν ἐκλεκτὸν ἐν κυρίῳ in v. 13 are similar cases (see notes on those verses); (ii) that, whereas Paul seems to take considerable pains to find appropriate commendatory descriptions of the people whom he greets, the things which he says about the people with him who are sending greetings are of a more matter-of-fact kind, so that it is not really surprising that the last person should just be called 'brother Quartus'. The suggestions that ὁ ἀδελφός is intended to indicate that Quartus is the brother of Erastus or that he is the brother of Tertius (v. 22)[3] strike us as highly improbable: if the former were meant, αὐτοῦ would surely have been added, and the latter suggestion cannot claim to be more than an exercise of free fancy.

On **[24]** see on v. 20; also pp. 5–11, especially p. 6 (ii). That it is secondary may be regarded as certain.

25–27. With regard to these verses reference should be made to pp. 5–11, especially to p. 6 (i) and (vi) and to p. 8. The extremely complicated evidence we had to consider led us to the conclusion that this doxology, either in its present form or in a somewhat briefer form, was first added to a short form of Romans (ending with 14.23 and due to the heresiarch Marcion), in order to round off what was obviously incomplete, and was subsequently (in its present form) added, because its intrinsic merit commended it, both to the full form of the epistle and also to a form ending with 15.33. If it originated in a Marcionite milieu, then its original form will have been briefer than that which we now have, and Harnack's suggestion that τὸ κήρυγμα Ἰησοῦ Χριστοῦ and διά τε γραφῶν προφητικῶν and γνωρισθέντος were orthodox expansions might be correct. But the clumsiness and overloading, which are certainly noticeable, are probably not—in material of this solemn, liturgical nature—a sufficient

---

[1] See H. J. Cadbury, 'Erastus of Corinth', in *JBL* 50 (1931), pp. 42–58 and further literature cited in Bauer, s.v. Ἔραστος and also s.v. οἰκονόμος 1.b.; cf. also Bruce, p. 280.

[2] p. 281.

[3] See Bruce, ibid.

warrant for assuming that editorial expansion has taken place; and there does not seem to be any good reason for denying that its origin was orthodox. The suggestion that it is a Pauline fragment which had been preserved and was then used for the purpose of providing a conclusion to the truncated form of Romans does not seem very likely. While it would be rash indeed to assert that Paul could not have written it, it strikes us as much more likely to be post-Pauline. That it has a liturgical flavour is, of course, clear. Whether it is an actual piece of liturgy which has been taken over, into which τὸ εὐαγγέλιόν μου and possibly one or two other expressions from Romans have been worked, or a fresh doxology composed for the specific purpose of rounding off a Romans which stopped at 14.23, can scarcely be decided with any certainty (though we are inclined to think the latter alternative more likely). In any case, placed where it now is, it seems to us to form a not unworthy, even if non-Pauline, doxological appendix to Paul's most weighty epistle.[1]

Τῷ δὲ δυναμένῳ. For these words used with reference to God in this position in this sort of context compare Eph 3.20; Jude 24; *Martyrium Polycarpi* 20.2.

ὑμᾶς στηρίξαι. See on 1.11 (εἰς τὸ στηριχθῆναι ὑμᾶς).

The phrase κατὰ τὸ εὐαγγέλιόν μου has already been used in 2.16 (cf. 2 Tim 2.8). The sense of κατά is not easy to determine. In 2.16 it is no doubt 'according to', and it is possible here to understand the point to be that, according to the gospel which Paul preached, God is able to accomplish this work of confirming and strengthening. Some have taken it to mean 'through', indicating the means by which the confirming is to take place (see Bauer, s.v. κατά II.5.a.δ.). But perhaps the best way to understand κατά here is to take it in the sense 'according to', not with δυναμένῳ ('who, according to my gospel, is able . . .'), but to connect it (together with what follows it), not with στηρίξαι ('who is able to confirm you in accord with my gospel', i.e., to confirm you in your belief in, in your obedience to, the gospel).[2] The significance of μου is not that the reference is to

---

[1] Further reference may be made to (in addition to the works cited in the course of pp. 5–11) J. Dupont, 'ΜΟΝΩΙ ΘΕΩΙ (Rom 16.27)', in *Ephemerides Theologicae Lovanienses* 22 (1946), pp. 362–75; G. Delling, 'ΜΟΝΟΣ ΘΕΟΣ', in *TLZ* 77 (1952), cols. 469–76; E. Kamlah, *Traditionsgeschichtliche Untersuchungen zur Schlussdoxologie des Römerbriefes*, Tübingen thesis, 1955; D. Lührmann, *Das Offenbarungsverständnis bei Paulus und in den paulinischen Gemeinden*, Neukirchen, 1965; L.-M. Dewailly, 'Mystère et silence dans Rom 16.25', in *NTS* 14 (1967–68), pp. 111–18.

[2] Cf. Lagrange, p. 377: 'dans les sentiments de'.

a peculiarly Pauline gospel, but that the gospel referred to is
that which Paul (together with other Christian preachers) has
constantly preached. The words καὶ τὸ κήρυγμα Ἰησοῦ Χριστοῦ
are best taken as explicatory of the preceding three words—
'my gospel, that is to say, the proclamation of Jesus Christ'.[1]
Ἰησοῦ Χριστοῦ is here, surely, an objective genitive.[2] The
further explicatory material introduced by the second κατά of
v. 25 and continuing down to the end of v. 26 would seem to be
designed to characterize still more closely the content of the
preaching which is also the content of τὸ εὐαγγέλιόν μου. This
means that it is to be connected not, like κατὰ τὸ εὐαγγέλιον,
κ.τ.λ., with στηρίξαι, but with τὸ κήρυγμα Ἰησοῦ Χριστοῦ. The
apostolic preaching of Jesus Christ is κατὰ ἀποκάλυψιν μυστηρίου
χρόνοις αἰωνίοις σεσιγημένου, φανερωθέντος δὲ νῦν. That is, it is a
matter of God's revelation of His secret which has been hidden
in silence[3] for ages[4] from before the creation of the universe but
has now been manifested. For the thought of God's μυστήριον
foreordained before all ages and now at last made manifest we
may compare 1 Cor 2.6–10 (especially, Σοφίαν δὲ λαλοῦμεν . . .
θεοῦ σοφίαν ἐν μυστηρίῳ, τὴν ἀποκεκρυμμένην, ἣν προώρισεν ὁ
θεὸς πρὸ τῶν αἰώνων . . . ἡμῖν γὰρ ἀπεκάλυψεν ὁ θεὸς διὰ τοῦ
πνεύματος); also Col 1.26f; 2 Tim 1.9f; Tit 1.2f; 1 Pet 1.20; and
several passages in Ephesians 1 and 3. It is only in the present

---

[1] For epexegetic καί see BDF, § 442 (9); and cf. Käsemann, p. 405.

[2] Though (apart from the Shorter Ending of Mk—τὸ . . . κήρυγμα τῆς
αἰωνίου σωτηρίας) there is no other example of κήρυγμα with an objective
genitive in the NT. To explain it as subjective genitive, appealing to the
idea of the exalted Christ's speaking through the preachers (cf. 10.14b
and c, 17), is forced, in view of the NT usage of κηρύσσειν and its cognates.

[3] This is the only occurrence in the NT of σιγᾶν used transitively.
Compare, e.g., Aeschylus, Pr. 106, 441; Ag. 36; Herodotus 5.21;
Theocritus 16.54. It is pedantic to try to make a significant distinction
between a secret which is ἀποκεκρυμμένον and one that is σεσιγημένον, as
Corssen did (in ZNW 10, 1909, pp. 32ff), and as Käsemann, p. 405f,
seems to be inclined to do. σιγᾶν in this connexion is surely no more than
an equivalent of a negative of γνωρίζειν, λαλεῖν, λέγειν, or καταγγέλλειν
(verbs which are used in the NT with μυστήριον as object); and the
distinction between ἀποκεκρυμμένον and σεσιγημένον is really only a
matter of whether the mystery is thought of in terms of seeing or in
terms of hearing. (While the thought of the pre-creation ages is indeed
included in χρόνοις αἰωνίοις, there is no real warrant for seeing here any
special reference to the primal silence of 2 Esdr 6.38f; 7.30; 2 Bar. 3.7, or
any beginnings of a gnostic σιγή-speculation.) And there is no need to see
in σεσιγημένον a flat contradiction of the insight of 1.2; 3.21b (cf., e.g.,
Heb 1.1); for the NT recognition that Christ was foretold, and indeed is
in a sense actually present, in the scriptures of the OT must not be
distorted into a denial of the utterly decisive nature of the event
indicated by the statement ὁ λόγος σὰρξ ἐγένετο.

[4] For the dative see BDF, § 201.

time (νῦν) of the earthly ministry of Jesus Christ and the on-going proclamation of Jesus Christ by the Church that the secret of God has been revealed, manifested. The contrast expressed by the δέ at the beginning of v. 26 is the contrast between the ages before Christ's incarnation and the period which began with it. It was in the gospel events, the life, death, resurrection and ascension of Jesus Christ, that the mystery was manifested decisively,[1] but there is a continuing manifesta-tion (wholly dependent on the manifestation in the gospel events) in the on-going proclamation of that once for all manifestation.[2]

διά τε γραφῶν προφητικῶν[3] κατ' ἐπιταγὴν τοῦ αἰωνίου θεοῦ εἰς ὑπακοὴν πίστεως εἰς πάντα τὰ ἔθνη γνωρισθέντος. The translations of these words given by Barrett[4] and Käsemann[5] presuppose the omission of τε. The resulting connexion of διὰ γραφῶν προφητικῶν with φανερωθέντος δὲ νῦν is exceedingly difficult, since it involves recognizing the vital contrast expressed in the part of the sentence which extends from κατὰ ἀποκάλυψιν down to the end of v. 26 as a contrast between the mystery's past hiddenness and its having been made manifest in the present through the prophetic writings. This is hardly the contrast to be expected. What one naturally expects to find opposed to the past hiddenness is surely the manifestation in the gospel events and the subsequent proclamation of them, not the revelation mediated through the writings of the OT prophets.[6] But the τε, which (according to Merk) is omitted by

---

[1] Cf. Origen, col. 1290: 'nunc vero, hoc est in adventu Christi prae-sentia corporali manifestatum est et apertum . . .'

[2] Cf. what was said on the present tenses in 1.17 and 18 and the perfect tense in 3.21. At the same time it must, of course, be remembered that, while the manifestation which has taken place in the gospel events and takes place in their proclamation is utterly real, decisive and full, there is still a veiledness about it, in the sense that only God-given faith can recognize it for what it is, and the final removal of that element of veiledness is not till the Parousia.

[3] The addition of καὶ τῆς ἐπιφανείας τοῦ κυρίου ἡμῶν Ἰησοῦ Χριστοῦ (plerique codd. apud Hier) Or is reminiscent of 2 Tim 1.10, and is surely secondary. It has the effect of turning τε (if read, as it undoubtedly should be) from τε (='and') into τε (='both') and so connecting at any rate some of the words which follow νῦν with φανερωθέντος rather than with γνωρισθέντος or of making some sort of satisfactory theological sense out of a form of v. 26 which lacked the τε.

[4] p. 286: he does not discuss the textual question at all.

[5] p. 401: he also omits discussion of the textual question, but on p. 406 makes a statement about τε ('Denn dem Schweigen . . . steht nun, durch τε hervorgehoben, die Offenbarung durch prophetische Schriften entgegen') which I cannot understand.

[6] The suggestion that the prophetic writings referred to are Christian, not OT, we regard as a counsel of desperation.

D lat sy and Chrysostom (neither Nestle nor UBS mention this textual variant), is surely to be read.[1] We then have in the words διά τε down to γνωρισθέντος a quite understandable third member of the series begun with χρόνοις αἰωνίοις σεσιγημένου and φανερωθέντος δὲ νῦν: the manifestation, which has taken place in the gospel events and their subsequent proclamation, and is contrasted with the hiddenness of the mystery in the past, is a manifestation which is properly understood in its true significance only in the light of its OT foreshadowing and attestation. It is when the manifestation of the mystery is understood as the fulfilment of God's promises made in the OT (cf. 1.2), as attested, interpreted, clarified, by the OT (cf., e.g., 3.21; 9.33; 10.4–9, 11, 13, 16, 18–21; 11.2, 26f), that it is truly understood as the gospel of God for all mankind. γνωρισθέντος is best taken in this general sense as referring to the attestation and clarification by the OT of the gospel events and their proclamation (εἰς πάντα τὰ ἔθνη is to be connected with εἰς ὑπακοὴν πίστεως, not with γνωρισθέντος).[2] κατ' ἐπιταγὴν τοῦ αἰωνίου θεοῦ[3] indicates that it is in accordance with God's will and appointment that this attestation and clarification have been effected, and εἰς ὑπακοὴν πίστεως εἰς πάντα τὰ ἔθνη indicates the goal of this attestation and clarification—God's purpose in so ordering things was that 'obedience of faith' (for the meaning of this phrase see on 1.5)[4] might be brought about among[5] all the Gentiles.[6]

[1] With regard to the Latin tradition here reference may be made to the note in Lagrange, p. 380.

[2] So Sanday and Headlam, p. 434, correctly (contrast what they say about 'The last phrase' on p. 435, which seems inconsistent with p. 434). If the meaning were 'made known to all the nations', the dative πᾶσιν τοῖς ἔθνεσιν would have been required, as a study of the NT occurrences of γνωρίζειν makes clear.

[3] αἰώνιος is nowhere else in the NT used to qualify θεός; but cf. the use of ἄφθαρτος in 1.23 and in 1 Tim 1.17 (where it is associated with τῶν αἰώνων) and also ἡ . . . ἀΐδιος . . . θειότης in Rom 1.20. Cf. too the use of αἰώνιον with πνεῦμα in Heb 9.14. In the LXX αἰώνιος is used occasionally with θεός (e.g., Gen 21.33; Isa 40.28). More characteristic of Scripture is the designation of the true God as θεὸς ζῶν or ὁ θεὸς ὁ ζῶν.

[4] While it is possible that the author of the doxology, in adopting the Pauline phrase, used it in a different sense from that which it has in 1.5 and intended πίστεως as an objective genitive, there seems to be no cogent reason for assuming this, as does Käsemann, p. 407.

[5] εἰς πάντα τὰ ἔθνη may either be simply equivalent to ἐν πᾶσιν τοῖς ἔθνεσιν (cf. 1.5) or else indicate the extent of this bringing about of obedience of faith (εἰς meaning 'unto', i.e. 'as far as'). See C. E. B. Cranfield, The Gospel according to Saint Mark, Cambridge, ⁶1977, pp. 398f (on Mk 13.10) and 417f (on εἰς ὅλον τὸν κόσμον in Mk 14.9).

[6] On the question whether ἔθνος has its proper sense of 'nation' or its special sense of 'Gentile' see on 1.5.

Thus interpreted, v. 26 yields a reasonably clear and satisfactory sense, as it stands. While we cannot rule out the
possibility that the doxology originated in Marcionite circles
and that διά τε γραφῶν προφητικῶν and γνωρισθέντος are anti-
Marcionite additions to a shorter original text, there seems to
be no justification for pronouncing v. 26 as it stands an obvious
piece of botching.

μόνῳ σοφῷ θεῷ, διὰ Ἰησοῦ Χριστοῦ, continues in the course
already set for the doxology by vv. 25 and 26, a course which
leads us to expect an ascription of glory to God. The following
ᾧ (which, though omitted by B *pc f* syᵖ, should surely be
retained, both as strongly attested and as the more difficult
reading)[1] disturbs the flow of the sentence. Without it, the
doxology would be a clear ascription of glory to God, the words
ἡ δόξα εἰς τοὺς αἰῶνας τῶν αἰώνων·[2] ἀμήν following naturally.
There are at any rate two possible explanations of the puzzling
ᾧ:
(i) that it is a relative pronoun, the antecedent of which is
Ἰησοῦ Χριστοῦ[3], and that the author of the doxology slipped
from an ascription of glory to God into an ascription of glory
to Christ without noticing the grammatical awkwardness he
was producing. If this is the correct explanation, then the final
paragraph of Barrett's commentary (to the effect that the
anacoluthon 'may serve to remind the reader that glory should
be ascribed at once to God the Father . . . and to Jesus Christ
his Son . . .') is a very appropriate comment.
(ii) that it is a relative pronoun, the antecedent of which is
θεῷ, used as an equivalent to an ἐκείνῳ picking up the preceding words (Τῷ . . . δυναμένῳ . . . μόνῳ σοφῷ θεῷ). A not dis-
similar use of the relative pronoun is quite probably to be
recognized in 1 Pet 4.11, and perhaps also in Heb 13.21. This
explanation, though not without difficulty, should probably be
preferred. The difficulty is considerably lessened if we are
prepared to see here the influence of a liturgical use of the

---

[1] *Pace* BDF, § 467.
[2] The omission of τῶν αἰώνων (𝔓⁴⁶ B C L *al*) is almost certainly secondary, an assimilation to the simpler formula, which (either in the singular
or the plural form) is predominant in most of the NT. The longer form
occurs in Gal 1.5; Phil 4.20; 1 Tim 1.17; 2 Tim 4.18; Heb 13.21; 1 Pet 4.11;
perhaps 5.11; and often in Revelation. It occurs in the LXX—so
LXX Ps 83.5; 4 Macc 18.24 (also sometimes in the singular form
εἰς τὸν αἰῶνα τοῦ αἰῶνος, as, e.g., in LXX Ps 110.3).
[3] For δόξα ascribed to Christ in this sort of way (there are, of course,
other passages which refer to Christ's glory) cf. 2 Tim 4.18; 2 Pet 3.18;
Rev 1.6; 5.12, 13.

relative pronoun (with the sense of a demonstrative) to introduce the congregation's response.[1]

It is not certain whether μόνῳ and σοφῷ are intended to be taken independently of each other ('to the only (and) wise God') or together ('to the only wise God', i.e., 'to God who alone is wise').[2] If the former explanation is accepted, we may compare, for the thought of μόνῳ, the first words of 3.30 (see on that verse); Jn 5.44; 17.3; 1 Tim 1.17; Jude 25, and, for the thought of σοφῷ, the passages cited below in connexion with the latter explanation and a good many other passages besides. If the latter explanation is accepted (and it seems rather more probable than the former), we may compare 11.33–35 (see notes *in loc.*); also, for example, 1 Cor 1.20–25; 3.18–20; Ecclus 1.8. For the διὰ Ἰησοῦ Χριστοῦ here we may compare (on the assumption that the relative pronoun refers to God) 1 Pet 4.11 and Jude 25.

ESSAY I

PAUL'S PURPOSE OR PURPOSES IN WRITING ROMANS

We indicated on the first page of this commentary our intention of reserving our discussion of Paul's purpose or purposes in writing Romans till the end of the exegetical notes, and on pp. 22–24 limited ourselves to a listing of just some of the questions relevant to this subject which we thought the reader would do well to bear in mind during his study of the epistle. In our own study of it we have tried to bear them in mind together with a good many other related questions. The time has now come when we must attempt to state some conclusions.[3]

---

[1] Cf. Käsemann, p. 403, following E. Kamlah, op. cit., pp. 72 and 86.

[2] μόνος σοφὸς θεός occurs in the NT only here and in secondary variants in 1 Tim 1.17 and Jude 25. In Philo it is a stereotyped expression (cf. Kamlah, op. cit., p. 83f, *apud* Käsemann). But the idea that only God can really appropriately be described as σοφός is already to be found in Plato, *Phdr.* 278d (Τὸ μὲν σοφόν, ὦ Φαῖδρε, καλεῖν ἔμοιγε μέγα εἶναι δοκεῖ καὶ θεῷ μόνῳ πρέπειν). Cf. Pseudo-Phocylides 54 (εἷς θεός ἐστι σοφός); *Hermetica* 14.3.

[3] Reference may be made here to G. Schrenk, *Studien zu Paulus*, Zurich, 1954, pp. 81–106 ('Der Römerbrief als Missionsdokument'); B. Noack, 'Current and backwater in the Epistle to the Romans', in *ST* 19 (1965), pp. 155–66; M. J. Suggs, ' "The Word is near you": Rom 10.6–10 within the purpose of the letter', in W. R. Farmer, C. F. D. Moule and R. R. Niebuhr (ed.), *Christian History and Interpreta-*

It may be said at once that the words 'purpose or', though they stand in the title of this essay because they were used in the introduction where we wished to leave this matter as open as possible, are really unnecessary; for it is surely quite clear that Paul did not have just one single purpose in mind but rather a complex of purposes and hopes, as he and Tertius set to work.

That, in the circumstances indicated by 1.8–16a and 15.14–16.23 (we here assume the correctness of the position taken on pp. 5–11 with regard to the integrity of the epistle), it was very natural that Paul should decide to write a letter to the Christians in Rome is obvious enough. Since he was intending to visit them in the near future (15.22–25), it was now appropriate to inform them of his intention without delay. So here we have the first and most obvious purpose. A second purpose, also indicated in 15.14ff, is to tell the Roman Christians of his Spanish plans and to secure, or, at least to prepare the way for securing, their interest and active assistance in their accomplishment. In 15.30–32 a third purpose is disclosed—to ask their prayers for himself. Two particular requests which he wants them to make on his behalf are specified: first, that he may be delivered from the dangers he is about to face from the side of the unbelieving Jews in Judaea and, secondly, that the Jerusalem church may accept the Gentile churches' collection with a brotherly responsiveness answering to the spirit in which that collection has been organized (a further final clause expresses a hope, the fulfilment of which hangs on the answer to

tion: studies presented to J. Knox, Cambridge, 1967, pp. 289–312; W. Marxsen, Introduction to the New Testament, Philadelphia and Oxford, 1968, pp. 92–109; G. Klein, Rekonstruktion und Interpretation: gesammelte Aufsätze zum Neuen Testament, Munich, 1969, pp. 129–44 ('Der Abfassungszweck des Römerbriefes'); W. Wiefel, 'Die jüdische Gemeinschaft im antiken Rom und die Anfänge des römischen Christentums: Bemerkungen zu Anlass und Zweck des Römerbriefes', in Judaica 26 (Zurich, 1970), pp. 65–88; Bornkamm, Gesammelte Aufsätze 4, pp. 120–29 ('Der Römerbrief als Testament des Paulus'); J. Jervell, 'Der Brief nach Jerusalem: über Veranlassung und Adresse des Römerbriefes', in ST 25 (1971), pp. 61–73; P. S. Minear, The Obedience of Faith: the purposes of Paul in the Epistle to the Romans, London, 1971; R. J. Karris, 'Rom 14.1–15.13 and the occasion of Romans', in CBQ 25 (1973), pp. 41–48; W. S. Campbell, 'Why did Paul write Romans?', in ET 85 (1973–74), pp. 264–69; K. P. Donfried, 'False presuppositions in the study of Romans', in CBQ 36 (1974), pp. 332–55; R. J. Karris, 'The occasion of Romans: a response to Prof. Donfried', in CBQ 36 (1974), pp. 356–58; W. Wuellner, 'Paul's rhetoric of argumentation in Romans: an alternative to the Donfried-Karris debate over Romans', in CBQ 38 (1976), pp. 330–51; K. P. Donfried (ed.), The Romans Debate, Minneapolis, 1977; A. J. M. Wedderburn, 'Purpose and occasion of Romans again', in ET 90 (1978–79), pp. 137–41.

be given to that twofold prayer, namely, the hope that he may come to the Roman Christians with joy and have a period of deep refreshment in their fellowship).

But, as soon as we begin to try to explain the relation of 1.16b–15.13 to the three purposes listed above, we encounter a series of difficult problems to which a great variety of solutions has been proposed.

The view that the great body of theological and practical teaching extending from about the middle of chapter 1 to not far from the middle of chapter 15 is a kind of parenthetic insertion in the letter proper, something which is easily detachable from its epistolary context and which could just as well have been sent to another church, we reject. It would only be plausible, if it were altogether impossible to suggest any reasonably convincing connexion between this body of theological and practical teaching and the purposes indicated by 1.1–16a and 15.14ff, which, as we shall see, is certainly not the case. It should also be noted that the process of detaching the main bulk of the document from the opening verses is by no means as simple and straightforward an operation as this view presupposes, since what appears to be the statement of the theme to be worked out in the great central body of the epistle (whether this statement is taken to be 1.16b–17, as in the present commentary, or the whole of 1.16 and 17 or 1.17 by itself) is both grammatically and substantially an integral part of Paul's expression of his readiness to visit Rome,[1] and the links between the sentences which make up 1.14–24 and also the way in which the reference to the gospel in 1.15–17 are prepared for by what is said about the gospel in 1.2–4 make it very much more natural to see an integral connexion between the early verses of Romans and the theological teaching which follows than to see some sort of more or less artificial suture. We may also note that 15.14 and 15 would seem to imply that a section (does the formulation rather suggest a substantial section?) of teaching, probably—to judge from the language used—ethical exhortation,[2] has just preceded: the connexion with 12.1–15.13 would seem to be natural.

Over the years the conviction has grown stronger and stronger with us that what we set out below is adequate *at least as a basic explanation* of the relation of 1.16b–15.13 to the three purposes already mentioned (or, to put the matter other-

[1] See p. 87.
[2] Note especially the use of ἀγαθωσύνη and νουθετεῖν. See commentary *in loc.*

wise, of Paul's inclusion of 1.16b–15.13 in his letter to the Christians of Rome):

(i) Paul judged that, since he was known to the great majority of the Christians in Rome only by repute, it would be appropriate to introduce himself to them at the same time as he informed them of his intention to visit them, and told them of, and sought their support for, his proposed mission to Spain, and asked their prayers for himself. It is significant, in this connexion, that the superscription of Romans is much longer than that of any other Pauline epistle.[1]

(ii) He judged that, since he would be coming to them as the apostle of the Gentiles and since he had no raison d'être as an apostle apart from the gospel, the appropriate way to introduce himself would be to set before them a serious and orderly summary of the gospel as he had come to understand it.[2]

(iii) Several considerations may well have combined to encourage him to make this summary one of considerable length and to devote special care to its composition: (a) he had now been preaching the gospel of Christ for about twenty years and it is not unlikely that he was conscious of having reached a certain maturity of experience, reflection and understanding, which made the time ripe for him to attempt, with God's help, such an orderly presentation of the gospel; (b) he may possibly have felt that the weeks before it would be time for him to set out for Jerusalem held some promise of affording him the necessary relative freedom from pressure, in which he might be able to set his thoughts in order; (c) he may well have thought that, in view of the size and importance of the Roman Christian community and its location in the imperial capital to which very many Christians from other places would be likely to come at one time or another, a setting within his letter to the Roman Christians would be a specially good setting, from the point of view of benefiting as many people as possible (both by edifying believers and also by affording guidance for the Church's missionary endeavours), for such a careful presentation of the gospel; (d) he may also have considered that such a summary of the gospel as he had come to understand it might encourage the Roman Christians to give their support—and to give it wholeheartedly and confidently—to his proposed Spanish mission; (e) it is also quite possible, in view of the

---

[1] See p. 47.

[2] This is not, of course, to countenance the suggestion that Paul entertained the notion that every church required the validation of an apostolic foundation such as the Roman Christian community had not yet had—a suggestion which Käsemann, p. 384f, rightly dismisses.

probable connexions between the Jewish Christian part of the Roman Christian community and the church in Jerusalem, that Paul may have hoped that, if his careful and balanced presentation of the gospel were successful in clearing away some misunderstandings and suspicions against himself among the Jewish Christians in Rome, this might have some good results also in his relations with the Jerusalem church.[1]

Closely connected with the conviction which we have just expressed with regard to Paul's inclusion of 1.16b–15.13 in his letter to the Roman Christians is a further conviction, namely, that, once having decided to attempt to compose a summary of the gospel as he had come to understand it, he allowed the inner logic of the gospel as he understood it[2] itself to determine, at any rate for the most part, the structure and contents of what was now going to be the main body of his letter. We have said 'at any rate for the most part' (just as we also qualified what we said on p. 816 by '*at least as a basic explanation*'), because we recognize the possibility, indeed probability, that considerations connected with his missionary plans, with his concern for the unity of the churches, with his hopes for the conversion of the still unbelieving Jews, his knowledge of his own circumstances, of opposition, of misunderstandings encountered, of objections likely to be raised, and what knowledge he had of the composition and condition of the Christian community in Rome and the problems facing it, played *some* part in shaping this main body of the epistle. We can see, for example, in 3.5–8 and 6.1 and 15 signs of the influence of experienced misunderstandings of his teaching on the way he shapes his argument. What we are here concerned to maintain is certainly not the quite unacceptable position that the structure and contents of 1.16b–15.13 were determined simply and solely by the logic of the gospel, but that, while we do well to keep a very sharp look-out for possible traces of the influence of other considerations and clues to other purposes Paul may have had in mind, we must—if as true an understanding of the epistle as is possible is really our aim—beware of the temptation to become so preoccupied with the quest for such traces

---

[1] Cf. Käsemann, p. 387.

[2] We have spoken of 'the logic of the gospel as he understood it'. We recognize that a distinction is to be admitted between the gospel itself as God's gospel and even an apostle's understanding of it (cf. the words from Augustine's first homily on St John's Gospel quoted in Barth, *CD* I/1, p. 128 (=*KD* I/1, p. 117)—though they refer to John's speaking rather than understanding); but we are convinced that Paul understood the gospel very well.

and clues that we have not adequate time and energy to devote to the more demanding task of following with really serious attentiveness the course that Paul has actually taken in 1.16b–15.13. We are convinced that close attention to the course of Paul's argument, the connexions of thought between his sentences (which are usually indicated with care) and the general structure of the whole of 1.16b–15.13, together with, of course, close attention to what he has actually said explicitly in 1.1–16a and 15.14–16.23, is absolutely indispensable, if we are to obtain anything approaching an objective understanding of what Paul was trying to do in his letter to the Romans. No amount of more or less ingenious and imaginative, or even intelligent, reading between the lines can ever make up for failure to keep our eyes on the course which Paul has actually followed and to try with proper seriousness to understand what he has actually said in the order in which he has said it.

Having tried again and again over many years to follow Paul's course in Romans with some application, we can only confess to an overwhelming and ever-increasing sense of the unity of the epistle and especially of 1.16b–15.13. We are impressed again every time we re-read it by the unity of structure of that great central mass of Romans, by its orderliness in detail, and by its sheer intelligibility (by 'its intelligibility' we mean, not of course that it is easy reading—there is much in it we do not expect to have grasped properly this side of death!— but that it makes more and more sense, the longer and harder and the more rigorously one concentrates on what it is saying, and that the teasing difficulties it contains in abundance are not the sort of difficulties which a careless author creates by impreciseness of thought and slovenliness of expression but the sort which are inherent in any serious human discussion of the realities it deals with, God, man, sin, death, forgiveness, sanctification, resurrection—to mention only some). We are more and more convinced that 1.16b–15.13 is a theological whole from which nothing at all substantial can be taken away without some measure of disfigurement or distortion.

We realize, of course, that where we think we see unity, articulation, coherence, some think they see so much confusion and such gross inconsistencies, that they feel constrained to regard much of the epistle as the workmanship of would-be interpreters who have more or less seriously misunderstood Paul's own thought. To all such we can only say, with respect, that they do not seem to us to have read Paul very attentively or patiently. There are a good many other interpreters of Romans who, while they certainly do not share the view we have just referred to, seem to us to offer explanations of what Paul was trying to do in Romans which are unconvincing because they fail to do justice to the unity of 1.16b–15.13. Thus there are those who see the essential core of Romans only in 1.16b–8.39, and regard 9.1–11.36 as a sort of excursus owing its existence to the inner struggles and distress of Paul's own personal Jewish patriotism and 12.1–15.13 as a mere paraenetic appendix, while others would still further diminish the essential core by characterizing 1.18–3.20 as only propaedeutic and to a large extent hypothetical. We hope that the foregoing commentary has gone some way towards making it clear that 9.1–11.36 is an essential element in the structure of Paul's attempted summary of the gospel as he understands it and owes its place not to Paul's personal emotional strains and stresses but to the logic of the gospel itself; that, while the presence of some items in 12.1–15.13 may possibly reflect circumstances either experienced by Paul or known by him to obtain in Rome, an element of concrete particular exhortation of the sort this division of Romans contains is—in Paul's understanding of things—an essential part of any substantial summary of the gospel as it has to be presented to Christians in the conditions of this life; and that 1.18–3.20 is no pre-evangelical propaedeutic but speaks of the judgment which the gospel itself pronounces. Yet another proposed explanation of Paul's intention in Romans which does scant justice to the unity of the central bulk of the epistle is that, according to which the real main stream of the letter continuous with the interests revealed in the first part of chapter 1 and in 15.14ff is to be recognized in chapters 9 to 11, while by comparison 1.16b–8.39 is to be regarded as a 'backwater'.[1]

As an example of the tendency (which has manifested itself again in recent years) to look to what may be known or surmised about the situation of the Roman Christian community for the clues to the understanding of the epistle we may mention P. S. Minear's *The Obedience of Faith*.[2] It is his contention that the epistle 'reflects a primary concern with pastoral problems and therefore presents a continuous argument designed to meet specific situations in Rome'.[3] Starting from chapters 14–16, he concludes that no united church of Rome had as yet been formed, but the Christian community consisted

---

[1] B. Noack, op. cit.

[2] London, 1971. Others who have looked in this direction recently include H. W. Bartsch, W. Marxsen and W. Wiefel.

[3] op. cit., p. ix.

of 'several congregations, separated from each other by sharp mutual suspicions'.[1] He finds evidence of five different factions or theological positions in the Christian community.[2] The first group, the 'weak in faith' group condemned the second, the 'strong in faith' group, who in turn ridiculed and despised the first group. The third group Minear identifies as 'the doubters'. The fourth and fifth groups he sees as composed of 'weak in faith' and 'strong in faith', respectively, but distinguished from the first and second groups by the fact that they did not condemn or despise the others. Minear claims to discern which particular groups are being addressed in the various sections of the epistle, though admitting that in some passages 'All readers' or 'All readers, but with distinctions recognized' are addressed.[3] This claim strikes us as far from convincing. Minear's book is certainly stimulating and contains a good deal that is helpful and illuminating; and some of his contentions are probably correct (for example, that the Christian community in Rome was not organized as a single united church but was made up of a number of churches).[4] But it is marred by over-confidence, over-simplification and some very questionable exegesis.[5] That, in drawing out what Christian obedience must mean in the sort of circumstances envisaged in

---

[1] ibid.

[2] op. cit., pp. 8–15.

[3] See especially op. cit., p. 45, n. 8. However, in fairness it should be said that on p. 57 Minear does say: 'We assume that he always had some concrete purposes in saying what he had to say, albeit the resulting utterance usually embraced a perspective which transcended those motives. . . . Although we believe that each appeal is slanted in the direction of a specific faction in Rome, we also believe that this slant does not exclude the author's concern for all the factions in Rome'.

[4] This is of course no new contention: see p. 22 of this commentary.

[5] We read, for example, on p. 47: 'One can be quite confident, therefore, that in this whole section of the epistle [i.e. 1.18–4.25] the author was speaking directly to the Jewish spokesmen of the weak in faith and that these paragraphs give a polemical portrait of their position'; on p. 54: 'Paul took good care to dissociate Abraham from the weak in faith, using precisely the same phrase in this connection, "he did not become weak in faith" '; on p. 68: 'To those ridiculed because of their weakness in faith, Paul asserted that it was not they who were weak, but that weakness and impotence came from the ways in which the flesh had distorted the Law. (It is noteworthy that in 8.3 two words are used which in 14.1 and 15.1 are the chief identifications of Group One—ἀδύνατος and ἀσθενέω.) . . . This accomplishment had required not the condemnation of men but the condemnation of "sin in the flesh". The whole argument becomes very concrete and relevant when we define this particular "sin in the flesh" as the tendency to condemn fellow-Christians as an act of supposed loyalty to God's Law'.

14.1–15.13,[1] Paul wanted to contribute to the peace and unity of the Christian community in Rome is extremely likely; but to attempt to make the situation in Rome as reflected (according to Minear) in chapters 14 to 16 the basis for the interpretation of the entire epistle is surely asking too much of the reader's credulity.

We refer, finally, to Käsemann's extremely valuable discussion on pp. 372f and 384–87 of his commentary. Käsemann is a commentator on Romans who, even when we disagree most strongly with what he says, leaves us in no doubt whatsoever that he has at least read Romans again and again with thoroughly serious attentiveness and with real personal involvement, and his views on Paul's purposes in writing it are therefore of quite outstanding interest. After an excellent survey of the confusing welter of published opinions on the subject (one cannot help admiring greatly the amazing breadth of his reading of the mass of relevant modern literature and the incisiveness of his comments) he comes on p. 386f to his summing up of his own view of Paul's *Abfassungszweck*; and it is a very carefully balanced and impressive statement indeed, in which a really serious attempt is made to take properly into account both the carefully structured theological nature of the bulk of the epistle and also the evidence provided by the first part of chapter 1 and by 15.14ff.

He is surely absolutely right to start from the fact that Paul really does introduce himself to the Roman Christian community, which is unknown to him personally, by means of a weighty statement of the gospel as he understands it, and to draw attention to the fact that the epistle is distinguished from other Pauline epistles by the extent to which it is characterized by the presence of the results of reflection concerning past experiences. He goes on to consider the evidence of 15.14ff (we may here register our reservations about his reference to Paul's 'apocalyptic self-understanding'), and makes the important statement: 'Das eigentliche Problem des Textes und damit des Abfassungszweckes liegt in der Kombination Rom-Jerusalem-Spanien und, wenn die Wichtigkeit der beiden letzten Faktoren genügend gewürdigt ist, in der Mittlerfunktion der römischen Gemeinde'. We are inclined to think (as indicated above)[2] that he may be right in believing that Paul hoped that, if he could win the support of the Roman Christian community and

---

[1] We suspect that it is rather more difficult than Minear assumes to decide with certainty what exactly the problem is with which Paul is concerned in this section (see our introduction to 14.1–15.13).

[2] p. 817f ((iii) (e)).

especially of its Jewish element or could at least to some extent overcome any mistrust of him which it might be entertaining, this would strengthen his position in Jerusalem. But we question whether the various features of the epistle which Käsemann lists, such as Paul's gentle attitude toward the weak and his emphasizing of the salvation-historical advantage of the Jew,[1] are rightly explained as actually *motivated* by Paul's desire to win Jewish Christian support whether in Rome or in Jerusalem.[2] The impression we get from our study of Romans is rather that the things which Käsemann lists here are to be explained as arising directly and necessarily from Paul's understanding of the gospel itself.[3]

ESSAY II

CONCLUDING REMARKS ON SOME ASPECTS OF THE THEOLOGY OF ROMANS

If any reader, turning to this page before he has worked through the commentary, should be tempted to start here in the hope that this essay might prove (in spite of what was said on p. 1) to be a helpful introduction to what precedes it or even

---

[1] The relevant sentence is: 'Eben deshalb geht er auf die Vorwürfe seiner judenchristlichen Gegner ein, betont er den heilsgeschichtlichen Vorrang und die endliche Annahme ganz Israels, urteilt er über die Konflikte zwischen Starken und Schwachen bis zum Thema der Tagwählerei so ungewöhnlich milde und den Judenchristen entgegenkommend, begründet er sein Evangelium unentwegt aus der Schrift, aus der er sogar seine eigene weltweite Aufgabe ableitet'.

[2] The operative phrase is Käsemann's 'Eben deshalb'. The following sentence with its 'In der Sache gibt er nichts preis', while it denies that Paul surrendered anything essential to the truth of the gospel, does not take back the suggestion of the preceding sentence that the motive behind these features was Paul's purpose to win support or at least diminish mistrust.

[3] The reader might be referred to many pages in the foregoing commentary, but perhaps it is enough to mention, in particular, our discussion of chapters 9–11 and of 14.1–15.13. Of course, the features referred to are all in a sense indirectly connected with the purpose with which Käsemann connects them directly, inasmuch as Paul's whole summary of the gospel in Romans, of which they are features, was, we believe, intended to introduce Paul to a Christian community to which he was unknown, and in introducing himself in this way he no doubt hoped, among other things, to clear away misunderstandings and allay mistrust and win understanding support; but to affirm this is quite a different thing from suggesting that the presence of these particular features is to be directly explained by this motive.

render the toil of reading the commentary itself unnecessary, he is herewith respectfully but with the utmost urgency and seriousness entreated to resist the temptation and to work patiently on from p. 1—or, if he prefers it, from p. 45. No attempt is going to be made in the following pages to present an ordered or in any way complete account of the theology to be found in the epistle. To do so even in the most summary form would necessitate an altogether disproportionately lengthy essay and would also involve a great deal of tiresome repetition of things already said in the commentary. So all that we propose to do here is to try to draw together some of the ends which seem to us to be most loose and to clarify a few of the matters concerning which we feel we may not have made our meaning sufficiently clear. Some of the most important theological matters in the epistle will not be touched on at all in this essay for the simple reason that Paul has treated them in such a way that the relevant discussion in the commentary is compact and readily locatable. From what has just been said it should be obvious that to read the following essay in isolation from the preceding commentary would be quite certain to result in very serious misunderstanding.

I. GOD'S RIGHTEOUSNESS FROM FAITH TO FAITH

We gave to 1.16b–17 the heading, 'The theme of the epistle is stated'; but, while we indicated our acceptance of the view that the Habakkuk quotation in 1.17 is expounded in 1.18–8.39,[1] we did not in the course of the commentary on 1.16b–17 indicate how we understood the second half of the epistle to be related to this verse and a half, nor did we make clear how 1.17 may properly be regarded as an adequate explanation and confirmation of 1.16b (or—to put this in a different way—how 'God's righteousness from faith to faith', that is, 'God's righteousness which is altogether by faith', is a sufficient indication of what is being revealed in the preaching of the gospel). The former of these two omissions we attempted to make good in the introductions to main divisions VI (9.1–11.36) and VII (12.1–15.13). It is now time to try to do something about the latter.

In 1.16b the claim is made that the gospel 'is God's saving power for everyone who believes, both for the Jew first and for the Greek'. The 'For' with which the next verse begins implies

[1] p. 102.

that its statement that in the gospel 'God's righteousness is being revealed from faith to faith, even as it is written: "He who is righteous by faith shall live" ' is an explanation and confirmation of that claim. But is the revelation of the righteous status before God, which is God's gift and altogether by faith, really something which can be appropriately described as God's *power* and God's *saving* power? And is the *fullness* of the gospel really indicated, or even hinted at, with anything like sufficient clarity by simply saying that in it such a righteous status is being revealed?

One approach toward a solution of this problem is, of course, to interpret 'righteousness' of God's *action*; another is to claim that in this verse it denotes at the same time *both* the gift given to man by God *and also* the active power of God. But, even after reading what Käsemann has said about this verse in his commentary, we are still convinced that 'righteousness' in 1.17 is better understood as referring simply to the status bestowed by God. The preached gospel is indeed God's saving power by the very fact that in it God is revealing, and making available, to all men, Jews and Gentiles alike, such a status of righteousness before Himself. It is not necessary, in order to justify the description of the gospel as God's saving power, to take 'righteousness' here to mean anything other than, or more than, this gift; for by revealing, and making available, just this gift, God is indeed acting mightily to save. And taking 'righteousness' in the sense of the righteous status given by God in no way involves a limiting of the gospel to something individualistic; for this gift, though it is certainly not in itself the whole content of the gospel, is that without which there is no good news at all, the utterly undeserved and yet altogether essential gift, which is the basis and the firm assurance of the ultimate fulfilment of all God's promises for the individual, for mankind as a whole, and for the whole of God's creation. (As man's unrighteousness before God, the inevitable consequence of sin, is the cause of the subjection of the sub-human creation itself 'to vanity' (8.20), so the justification of the ungodly carries in itself the promise of the ultimate liberation of the whole creation 'from the bondage of decay into the liberty of the glory of the children of God' (8.21).) So it is surely not surprising that the revelation of a status of righteousness before God for the ungodly should here be mentioned by itself, as being in itself a sufficient indication of the fullness of what God has done, is doing, and will do, for all His creation in Jesus Christ His Son.

The rest of what we want to say here about 'God's righteousness from faith to faith' it will be convenient to include in the next section.[1]

2. THE DEATH AND RESURRECTION OF JESUS CHRIST

As rather more will need to be said in this section about the Cross than about the Resurrection, it is specially important to emphasize at the start that, for Paul, there is no good news in the former apart from the latter, and we may be sure that, wherever he refers to the former without also referring directly and explicitly to the latter, he is always assuming the truth of the latter. It was the Resurrection which put God's seal upon the Cross and made clear its altogether decisive and transcendent significance. Its truth is, for Paul as for the rest of the NT and for all truly Christian theology, the real *articulus stantis et cadentis ecclesiae*. Hence the formulation of 10.9 ('For, if thou dost confess with thy mouth Jesus as Lord and dost believe in thine heart that God has raised him from the dead, thou shalt be saved') with which may be compared the categorical statement of 1 Cor 15.14 (RV: 'if Christ hath not been raised, then is our preaching vain, your faith also is vain'). Compare too the formulation of 8.34 ('. . . It is Christ Jesus who died, and, more than that, who was also raised from the dead, who is at the right hand of God, who also intercedes for us'). Only rarely is the Resurrection mentioned otherwise than in close association with a corresponding explicit reference to the death of Christ. Thus—in addition to 10.9—we have it mentioned by itself in 1.4 as marking the beginning of the time of Christ's being 'Son of God in power' (contrasted in Paul's mind, we assume, with the veiledness of His Sonship during the days of His earthly life), and in 8.11 a reference to it is twice introduced as a means of describing God ('him who raised Jesus from the dead' and 'he who raised from the dead Christ Jesus'): the thought of the raising of Jesus is probably present in the background in 4.17 —though this is not the primary reference of 'who quickens the dead' here. For the rest the Romans references to the Resurrection are in close association with corresponding references to the death of Christ.

Though there is no doubt that recognition of the connexion

[1] With regard to the meaning of 'believe' and 'faith' as used in 1.16b–17 the reader is referred back to pp. 89f and 99f. See also the notes on Romans 4 and, for a discussion of the different senses which πίστις has in Paul's writings see the introduction to 14.1–15.13.

between the divine justification of sinners and the death of Jesus Christ is basic to Paul's thinking throughout Romans, there are, as a matter of fact, only three passages in the epistle in which justification *actually indicated by a word of the δικαιος group* is quite directly connected with Christ's death. They are: (i) the words 'Since, then, we have been justified by his blood' in 5.9 (here the words 'by his blood' correspond to 'through the death of his Son' in the following verse); (ii) 4.25, which is 'who was delivered up for our trespasses and raised for our justification' (where the formulation of the two clauses does not dissociate our justification from Christ's death, but indicates that what was in the first place necessitated by our sins was Christ's atoning death but that, had it not been followed by His resurrection, that death would not have effected our justification); and (iii) 3.21–26, which we have called the 'heart of the whole of Rom 1.16b–15.13'. Of those three passages it will be enough here to take another look at the third only.

In 3.24 Paul speaks of men's being justified 'through the redemption *accomplished* in Christ Jesus', thereby implying, at any rate, that the believer's status of righteousness before God has been brought about by a definite and decisive action on God's own part accomplished in the person and work of the Messiah Jesus. That the death of Christ is an essential element of this divine action is indicated by the reference to His blood in v. 25. But it is v. 26b ('so that he might be righteous even in justifying the man who believes in Jesus') which is the key to the understanding of 3.21–26 as a whole and also to the understanding both of Paul's doctrine of the death of Christ and of his doctrine of justification. It declares the object of God's purposing Christ Jesus 'to be by the shedding of his blood a propitiatory sacrifice' to have been that He might be righteous even in His very action of justifying or—to express the same thought differently—that He might justify sinners righteously, that is, in a way that is altogether worthy of Himself as the truly loving and merciful eternal God.[1] Such a way could only be one which involved no condoning of their sin. For for God to have forgiven their sin lightly would have been to have compromised with the lie that moral evil does not matter and so to have violated His own truth and mocked men with an empty, lying reassurance, which, at their most human, they must have recognized as the squalid falsehood which it would have been. God would have Himself cruelly destroyed men's

---

[1] That such a justifying of the ungodly (cf. 4.5) differs *toto caelo* from the sort of action which Exod 23.7; Prov 17.15; 24.24; Isa 5.23, condemn, should go without saying.

dignity as creatures accountable to Him. Such a cheap forgiveness would have been the death of God's love—or, rather, its exposure as something all along unreal. But Paul sees clearly that God has revealed Himself as the eternally good and loving God that He is by the fact that He has not dealt with sinners in any such way, but instead has, according to His eternal purpose of mercy,[1] directed upon His very Self in the person of His own dear Son the full weight of His wrath[2] against sinners, so delivering them from it at His own cost—righteously and authentically. In the fulfilment of the divine purpose that Christ should be 'by the shedding of his blood a propitiatory sacrifice' the wrath of God against sinners was manifested in its full intensity and seriousness in the very action by which the sinners themselves were delivered from it by God Himself. With the use of 'propitiatory sacrifice' in 3.25 (clarified, as we have seen that it is, by what is said in 3.26b) it is natural to connect the statement in 1.18 that 'God's wrath is being revealed . . . against every kind of ungodliness and unrighteousness of men . . .'; for it is because the wrath of God has been manifested in its terrible seriousness in the sufferings and death of Jesus Christ that there also occurs a revelation of the wrath of God in the on-going preaching of the gospel.

Other points in 3.21–26 which must be noted here are: first, that the 'But now . . . has been manifested' of v. 21 underlines the objective reality of the gospel events as events of history which took place at a particular time in the past, these being the basis of the righteous status bestowed on sinners; secondly, that 'attested by the law and the prophets' in the same verse shows that Paul sees the gift of righteousness which has been made available through these events as foreshadowed, attested and interpreted, by the OT scriptures (see, for example, 10.6–13, and, for the thought of the death and resurrection of Christ, or of one or the other of them, as so foreshadowed, attested and interpreted, see 4.25; 15.3 and very probably 10.5: outside Romans a very obvious passage to compare is 1 Cor 15.3f); and, thirdly,[3] that it is probable that at least in 3.25 the death of Christ is thought of as having a sacrificial significance (some take περὶ ἁμαρτίας in 8.3 to mean 'as an offering for sin', but we have argued against this interpretation in the commentary).

We noticed above the connexion between the revelation of

---

[1] We may refer to what was said about προέθετο on pp. 208–10.

[2] On the meaning of 'God's wrath' see p. 108f.

[3] This third point may, of course, be regarded as covered by the second; but seems to be of such special interest as to deserve separate mention.

God's wrath in the preaching of the gospel (referred to in 1.18) and the prior revelation of God's wrath in the gospel events themselves. But from 1.18–3.20 we learn also that by the preaching of the gospel sin is shown up in its true character; and the conclusion is naturally to be drawn that, for Paul, the Cross is not only the revelation of the divine wrath but also the revelation of the true nature of human sin. The Cross once and for all exposed man's sin as the attack upon the divine majesty and violation of God's just order, the violent but futile attempt to suppress, bury out of sight, and for ever forget, the truth and reality of God, which it is (cf. 1.18: '. . . every kind of ungodliness and unrighteousness of men who try to suppress the truth by their unrighteousness'). In fact it exposed sin as hatred of God. We may compare 'when we were enemies' in 5.10 and 'the mind of the flesh is enmity toward God' in 8.7.[1] The quotation in 15.3 of the words of the righteous sufferer in Ps. 69.9 with reference (according to the most likely interpretation) to Christ's bearing in His passion men's reproaches and revilings against God is witness to the fact that one of the things which He had to endure was men's hostility toward God, which He exposed for what it was—and is—by His enduring it.

In 5.6–8 we learn that it was 'at the appointed time', that is, the time appointed by God, that Christ died; that His death was on behalf of ($ὑπέρ$) the 'ungodly' (who are also described in these verses as 'powerless' and as 'sinners'); and that by Christ's having died for us thus, when we were still sinners without any merit or strength by which to help ourselves, 'God proves his love for us'—that is, both proves the reality of His love for us and reveals its character as altogether undeserved and spontaneous, originating wholly in Himself, and going to the very utmost of self-giving (cf. 8.32: 'who did not spare his own Son, but gave him up for us all'). Connected with the character of God's love, with God's being the sort of loving God that He is, is the further fact (which we learn from 5.10a) that Christ's death is the means of our reconciliation, that is, in the first place, of His giving Himself to us in friendship, becoming our friend instead of being our enemy, and, in the second place, of His overcoming our fierce hostility toward Him; for, God being the loving God He is, His relationship with men is altogether personal, and His justification of sinners involves of necessity therefore the restoration of friendship between Himself and them. Three other points from chapter 5 may be

[1] In 1.30 the expression 'haters of God' would seem to be used with reference to those in whom this general hostility toward God is specially strident.

mentioned here. One is that the 'righteous conduct' of v. 18 and the 'obedience' of v. 19, while certainly not referring exclusively to Christ's death, certainly do include it. His submission to death was the climax of His 'righteous conduct', that is, of His 'obedience' to His Father's will (revealed in the law and in the OT scriptures generally and also in the unique relationship between the Father and the Son). A second point is the reference in v. 20 to the fact that 'where sin increased, grace superabounded', in which Paul no doubt had in mind above all the fact that it was precisely at the point where sin's increasing reached its hideous climax in Israel's rejection of the true Messiah and handing over of Him to the pagans and in the pagan world's response to Israel's challenge by prostituting the reverend institution of civil justice to the requirements of sordid and false expediency and making use of the most hateful method of destroying a human life then known,[1] that God's grace superabounded in the divine self-giving of the Cross. A third point is that vv. 12–21 draw the conclusion from what has been said in the first paragraph of the chapter that what God has accomplished in the death of Jesus Christ does not just concern believers but is as universal in its effects as was the sin of Adam and is the innermost mystery of the life of every human being. The verses are one of the passages which form the NT basis for Shakespeare's triumphant description of Jesus as 'the world's ransom, blessed Mary's Son'.[2]

It will possibly be helpful at this point to sum up what we have so far seen of Paul's doctrine of the death of Christ by setting down in order three statements which have to be distinguished for the purpose of analysis but which we certainly must not think of in isolation from one another if we are to grasp Paul's meaning. They are: (i) The Cross reveals the reality and the nature of human sin; (ii) The Cross reveals the reality and the nature of the wrath of God against sin; (iii) The Cross reveals the reality and the nature of God's love, being the way by which it overcomes evil, justifying sinners worthily of itself.

In the first half of chapter 6 Paul has much to say about the believer in his relation to the death and resurrection of Christ. Verses 2–14, the purpose of which is first to justify (vv. 2–11)

---

[1] See M. Hengel, '*Mors turpissima crucis:* die Kreuzigung in der antiken Welt und die "Torheit" des "Wortes vom Kreuz" ', in J. Friedrich, W. Pöhlmann, P. Stuhlmacher (ed.), *Rechtfertigung: Festschrift für Ernst Käsemann zum 70. Geburtstag*, Tübingen and Göttingen, 1976, pp. 125–84.

[2] *The Tragedy of King Richard the Second* 2.1.56.

his emphatic rejection in v. 1 of the false inference which he knows some people will be inclined to draw from what was said in 5.20b (namely, the false inference that we should continue in sin in order that grace may increase) and then to indicate (vv. 12–14) the conclusion to be drawn from vv. 2–11, are all about the believer's death and resurrection with Christ. In the commentary we argued that Paul's meaning here can be properly understood only when it is recognized that there are different senses in which the Christian's death and resurrection with Christ must be spoken of, and that these must be both carefully distinguished and also at the same time understood in the closest relation to one another. Paul's thought in the course of these verses moves between these different senses. We distinguished four: (i) we died with Christ, when He died on Golgotha, and were raised with Him on the first Easter morning, in that by God's gracious decision what He did was done for us, so that in God's sight we shared in it (cf. 2 Cor 5.14; Col 3.1–4)—the juridical sense; (ii) we died and were raised with Christ, when we were baptized, in that our baptism, as well as being the ratification of our acceptance of God's decision, was also God's bestowal on us of the sign and seal of the fact that His gracious decision concerned us personally and individually—the baptismal sense; both these dyings and risings with Christ are in the past, but there are also senses in which the reference is to the present and the future; (iii) we are called, and have been given the freedom, to die daily and hourly to sin in our actual living and to rise daily and hourly to newness of life, so approximating more and more in our concrete living to that which we already are in God's sight by God's decision of justification—the moral sense; and (iv) we have still to die one day, and our death in the ordinary matter of fact sense will be our final and irreversible death to sin, our final sharing in Christ's death, and we shall also at the last be raised up to the resurrection life with Him—the eschatological sense. In this connexion we saw (on p. 305f, with reference to 6.4) how Paul has preferred in this passage to speak of both the twofold fact of our death and resurrection in God's decision and also the twofold fact of our death and resurrection in baptism in terms of the single fact of death (or burial), and of the twofold fact of our moral dying and being raised in terms simply of resurrection—probably because he wanted particularly to bring out the positive character of the new obedience of Christians.

Three other points concerning the death of Christ as understood by Paul emerge from this passage. First, we may notice the use in v. 10 of a dative of the person affected to express the relation of Christ's death to sin, the sense apparently being that by His death He decisively affected sin, decisively weakened its power (compare what is said below with regard to the pregnant 'condemned' in 8.3). Secondly, this deed decisively affecting sin, which His death was, was a once for all event ('once and for all'—v. 10), never needing to be repeated. Thirdly, the passage brings out emphatically the fact that Christ's death was followed by His being raised from the dead (see vv. 4, 5, 8, 9), which was the beginning of His risen life, which is beyond the reach of death's power (v. 9) and, as a life lived 'to God' (v. 10), is life eternal.

In 7.4 Paul tells the Roman Christians that they 'were made dead to the law through the body of Christ', which we take to mean that God has freed them from His condemnation pronounced through the law by taking it upon Himself in the Person of His Son in that death which He died on the cross for them (that death, which, because it was died for them, was also —in God's gracious decision—their death). We may compare 8.1 ('So then there is now no condemnation for those who are in Christ Jesus'), which sums up 7.1–6 (and also 6.14b). In 8.2 ('For the law of the Spirit of life has in Christ Jesus set thee free from the law of sin and of death'), which confirms the truth of 8.1 by appealing to the fact of a further liberation itself made possible by this liberation from God's condemnation, Paul indicates by 'in Christ Jesus'[1] that it is God's action in Christ Jesus which is the ground of the freedom described in this verse (it is on the basis of what God has done in Christ that the Holy Spirit is given); and the significance of this 'in Christ Jesus' is then clarified by what is said in 8.3. The words 'condemned sin in the flesh', while they may well include a reference to the whole course of Christ's earthly life, refer in particular no doubt to His death as the event in which God in His mercy and faithfulness decisively unmasked the true nature of the sin of all mankind and pronounced its ultimate condemnation, as He took its penalties and shame upon Himself in the human nature of His Son, and wrought in the agony and desolation of the Cross the justification and reconciliation of sinners and the foundations of their sanctification, thus winning the decisive victory over sin which must in the end effect its final and total overthrow.

In 14.9 Paul supports his statement of the previous verse that both in life and in death we belong to Christ by declaring

---

[1] We connected the phrase ἐν Χριστῷ Ἰησοῦ with the verb ἠλευθέρωσεν (see p. 374f).

that it was to this end that He died and lived again, namely, that He might be the Lord of the dead and the living alike. It is to be noted that in this declaration Christ's death and resurrection are thought of as a unity (both His being Lord of the dead and His being Lord of the living depend equally on both His death and His resurrection).

There is, if we are not mistaken, only one direct reference to the death of Christ in Romans which we have not yet mentioned —that in 14.15 (with which 14.20 should be compared, 'God's work' there being probably a reference to Christ's death). What this verse brings out is that Christ's death is the revelation of the true worth of the fellow-Christian and also by implication (since we must take into account the significance of 5.12–21) of the fellow-man as such. In each individual fellow-man we are to recognize one for whom Christ died. This is his inalienable and altogether ungainsayable dignity. To dishonour him is to trample under foot the blood of Christ.

3. 'IN CHRIST'

There are twenty-one occurrences in Romans of ἐν Χριστῷ or an equivalent expression. ἐν Χριστῷ Ἰησοῦ τῷ κυρίῳ ἡμῶν occurs twice (6.23 and 8.39); ἐν Χριστῷ Ἰησοῦ six times (3.24; 6.11; 8.1, 2; 15.17; 16.3); ἐν Χριστῷ five times (9.1; 12.5; 16.7, 9, 10); ἐν κυρίῳ Ἰησοῦ once (14.14); and ἐν κυρίῳ seven times (16.2, 8, 11, 12 (bis), 13, 22 (Tertius, not Paul)). It seems to us clear enough that not all of these can be brought at all naturally within the compass of a single uniform explanation. In 3.24 the ἐν is best explained as instrumental: the redemption referred to is defined as that which has been accomplished in and through the person and work of Christ. In 8.2 ἐν Χριστῷ Ἰησοῦ is, we think, best connected with the verb ἠλευθέρωσεν and understood as indicating that Christ Jesus and what God has accomplished in and through Him is the basis of, is that which has made possible, the liberation wrought by the Holy Spirit's exercised authority. In 8.39 ἐν Χριστῷ Ἰησοῦ τῷ κυρίῳ ἡμῶν expresses the truth that the love of God, from which nothing shall be able to separate us, is that love which has revealed itself, and may be known as it truly is, in Christ. The ἐν Χριστῷ Ἰησοῦ of 15.17 is simply a matter of the use with ἔχω . . . τὴν καύχησιν of the ἔν τινι commonly used with καυχᾶσθαι (see Bauer, s.v. καυχάομαι 1).

But in 6.11 and 8.1 we have something different. In the

former verse Paul calls the Roman Christians to recognize the gospel truth that they are 'alive to God in Christ Jesus', while in the latter he speaks of 'those who are in Christ Jesus'. It is necessary to clarify now what was said on pp. 315f and 373. On p. 316 it was suggested that what had already been said with reference to 6.2 (pp. 298–300) contained the key to a proper understanding of Paul's special use of the 'in Christ' formula; but we did not make it clear that we were suggesting not just that 'in Christ' is to be understood in a sense corresponding to sense (i) of our dying and being raised with Christ (that is, that we are in Christ in that God has decided so to see us), but that four different senses have to be distinguished with reference to the 'in Christ' formula corresponding to the senses (i) to (iv) listed on p. 299f. Thus, (i) we are in Christ in God's sight, in that God has decided to see us in Him; (ii) we are in Christ through baptism, in that in the sacrament we have received God's attestation of His decision to see us in Christ (cf. Paul's use of the imagery of putting on Christ in Gal 3.27: ὅσοι γὰρ εἰς Χριστὸν ἐβαπτίσθητε, Χριστὸν ἐνεδύσασθε); (iii) we are called, we are permitted, to put on Christ again and again, day by day, and hour by hour, in the moral sense (cf. the imperative ἐνδύσασθε τὸν κύριον Ἰησοῦν Χριστόν in 13.14); and (iv) an eschatological sense of 'in Christ' has to be distinguished (it is perhaps here that 6.23 should be mentioned: cf. 1 Cor 15.22b), though it would seem that in this connexion Paul preferred to use σύν (see p. 311f)—perhaps because he sensed a danger that, used in this connexion, ἐν might suggest the thought of the believer's absorption into Christ rather than of his perfect eternal fellowship with Christ.

In 6.11 'in Christ' is used in senses (i) and (ii), the fact of the Roman Christians' being 'in Christ' in those two senses being the basis for the implicit imperative to strive to be 'in Christ' in sense (iii). In 8.1 senses (i) and (ii) are presumably predominant, but sense (iii) is of course not excluded; and the situation with regard to 'in Christ' in 12.5 would seem to be similar.[1] On ἐν κυρίῳ Ἰησοῦ in 14.14 the reader may be referred back to the note in loc. In 9.1 the use of 'in Christ' is an appeal to Christ as the guarantor of the truth of Paul's statement: Paul claims that he is speaking in accordance with the standards which obtain for one who is 'in Christ' (in senses (i), (ii) and (iii)).

---

[1] 12.5 expresses the truth that the believer's being in Christ (in senses (i) and (ii)) necessarily binds him to all others who are also thus in Christ. That an essential part of our being in Christ in sense (iii) is a sincere and strenuous endeavour to realize this bond in our concrete relationships should hardly need to be said.

Of the remaining occurrences of 'in Christ', etc., in the epistle (all of them in chapter 16) six (those in vv. 2, 3, 9, 12 (two) and 22 (whether ἐν κυρίῳ is to be connected with ἀσπάζομαι or with γράψας)) can, we think, be fairly naturally explained as instances of the formula in its moral sense (sense (iii)). The relative clause οἱ καὶ πρὸ ἐμοῦ γέγοναν ἐν Χριστῷ in v. 7 indicates that Andronicus and Junia were converted before Paul—so here we could think either of sense (ii) or of sense (iii) or of both senses together. In v. 11 τοὺς ὄντας ἐν κυρίῳ serves to indicate that it is the Christians among the members of the group of people mentioned who are to be greeted, and, as Christians, they will be 'in Christ' in senses (i), (ii) and (iii). If ἐν κυρίῳ in v. 13 is to be classified among the instances of Paul's special 'in Christ' formula, we should presumably—if our understanding of that formula is on the right lines—have to think of sense (i), while, if ἐν κυρίῳ in v. 8 and ἐν Χριστῷ in v. 10 are to be taken as instances of the special formula, we should presumably have to think of sense (iii); but it is perhaps better to regard these last-mentioned occurrences, and possibly also those in vv. 2, 3, 9, 12 and 22, as falling outside the scope of the special formula use.

4. CHRISTOLOGY

That teaching which we have just been considering in sections 1, 2 and 3 necessarily involves a doctrine of Christ's person. We shall, therefore, at this point take a quick survey of what strike us as the most significant features of Paul's christology as it is to be seen in this epistle.

(i) The *true humanity* of Christ is implied by the references to His death (discussed in 2 above). That Paul thought of it as being absolutely real is obvious: in this connexion we may note both the references to His being raised and also the reference to His burial implicit in 6.4 (with which 1 Cor 15.4 should be compared). In 5.15 ('the one man Jesus Christ') the word ἄνθρωπος is used of Him (it is also to be supplied with reference to Him at least in 5.19); and it is quite clear that in this context the word expresses His true humanity (this is true, whether or not we should recognize in 5.12ff the presence of the 'Son of man' title familiar to us from the Gospels).[1] The reference of ἄνθρωπος in 10.5 is also to Christ, in Paul's mind, if our

---

[1] See Cullmann, *Christology*, pp. 170–74.

exegesis of that verse is correct. We should also note here the uses of κατὰ σάρκα in 1.3 and 9.5: both point to Christ's real humanity, though in both contexts (if we are correct in our understanding of 9.5b) there is also an indication of the fact that, when we have affirmed His real humanity, we have by no means exhausted what has to be said of His person. In 8.3 the difficult 'in the likeness of sinful flesh' (as we understand it) serves both, on the one hand, to indicate that Christ's human nature was indeed the same fallen human nature as ours, though Paul certainly believed that Christ was sinless (see, e.g., 5.18f; 2 Cor 5.21), and also, on the other hand, to safeguard the point which in 1.3 and 9.5 is made clear by the context (cf. the ἐν ὁμοιώματι ἀνθρώπων of Phil 2.7).

(ii) For Paul Jesus is *the Messiah* of Israel. In Romans Ἰησοῦς Χριστός occurs some nineteen times, Χριστὸς Ἰησοῦς some sixteen, Χριστός some twenty-four times, and ὁ Χριστός some eight times.[1] It is sometimes said that Paul normally uses 'Christ' as just a proper name; but this we regard as quite unlikely (cf. p. 51). While it is improbable that he ever used 'Christ' without any awareness that it was a translation of the Hebrew *māšîaḥ* and Aramaic *mᵉšîḥā'*, it seems likely that, where he has put 'Christ' before 'Jesus' and in most, if not all, the places where he has used the article with Χριστός (7.4; 8.35; 9.3, 5; 14.18; 15.3, 19; 16.16), he has done so in order to give the title extra emphasis. A connexion may be discerned, we would suggest, between the importance for Paul of Jesus' Messiahship[2] and the fact that in this, the most systematic of his extant letters, so much attention is given to the interpretation of the OT,[3] to the election of Israel, to the relation of the

---

[1] The reason for the indefiniteness of these figures is that in a number of places there is a variation in the textual tradition.

[2] In Romans, 1.3 is an obvious verse to mention in this connexion, in addition to the actual occurrences of the word 'Christ'. As far as occurrences of the word are concerned, its prominence is, of course, characteristic of the Pauline epistles generally (to take another long epistle for comparison, it occurs almost exactly as many times in 1 Corinthians as it does in Romans). Taylor, *Person of Christ*, p. 41f, is, in our view, a serious underestimation of the importance that the Messiahship of Jesus had for Paul, and the same could be said of various other scholars' discussions of this subject.

[3] A comparison of the amount of bold type per page of text in Romans in Nestle with the amount per page in the other Pauline letters is suggestive—though this is, of course, far from being anything like an accurate way of measuring the relative amounts of OT interpretation, since many verses which contain no bold type are quite definitely OT interpretation (thus, for example, all twenty-five verses of chapter 4, and not just the nine which contain words in bold type, should be recognized as being interpretation of the OT).

Gentile Christians to the people of Israel, and to the position of the still unbelieving Jews. That nothing of those political and military associations, which made 'messiah' during the period of the earthly ministry of Jesus a dangerously misleading term to apply to Him, adheres to 'Christ' as used in Romans, should hardly need to be said; for Paul uses it in the light of the Cross, Resurrection and Ascension, and in close conjunction with complementary christological material.

(iii) It will be convenient to group together at this point several matters of christological interest in the epistle, which, while each of them is important in itself and could well be discussed at length, will in this essay be only briefly mentioned. We have already noticed in passing (under (i) above) the possibility that in 5.12ff the Aramaic expression *bar-nāš(ā')* was present to Paul's mind. That its use by Jesus (that He had used it is, in our judgment, in spite of opinions to the contrary, virtually certain) and something of the background of His use of it were known to Paul is scarcely to be doubted. The evidence of 1 Cor 15.21f, 25–27,[1] 45–49, suggests that Paul was fully conscious of the linguistic equivalence of 'Adam', $\mathring{a}\nu\theta\rho\omega\pi o\varsigma$ and *bar-nāš(ā')* (too literally represented in the Gospels by $\acute{o}$ $\upsilon \acute{i}\grave{o}\varsigma$ $\tau o \hat{\upsilon}$ $\mathring{a}\nu\theta\rho\acute{\omega}\pi o\upsilon$). It is possible, therefore, that, as he composed 5.12ff, the thought was actually present to his mind that 'the one man Jesus Christ' (v. 15), whose 'righteous conduct' triumphed over the evil entail of Adam's sin, was the selfsame One who shall come at the last day from heaven as the Son of man in His manifest glory, or, as 1 Cor 15.45 puts it, $\acute{o}$ $\mathring{e}\sigma\chi a\tau o\varsigma$ $\mathring{}A\delta\acute{a}\mu$, the eschatological Man. But this thought is not explicit in the Romans passage.[2]

In connexion with this same passage we may register our agreement with Käsemann's impatience with the excessive confidence which in recent years has often been placed in the appeal to 'the Hebrew conception of corporate personality'[3] as a key to the understanding of Paul's thought.[4] In our view, on

[1] Note here the combination of Ps 8.6b [MT: 7b], which refers to one who has just been called in v. 4 [MT: 5b] 'the son of man' (*ben-'āḏām*), with Ps 110.1, the application being messianic.

[2] In 1 Cor 15.45ff Paul clearly has a polemical interest, to combat the idea (which is to be seen in Philo) that the heavenly Man is to be identified with the primal man, Adam.

[3] The phrase is the title of H. W. Robinson's essay in a supplement to *ZAW* 66 (1936), which initiated this popularity of the idea of 'corporate personality' in biblical studies.

[4] See Käsemann, pp. 132ff. Reference may also be made here to J. W. Rogerson, 'The Hebrew conception of corporate personality: a re-examination', in *JTS* n.s. 21 (1970), pp. 1–16.

the one hand, the truth of the solidarity of all men in their
sinfulness is readily understandable without our needing to
have recourse to allegedly special semitic ways of thinking;
and, on the other hand, the relationship between Christ and all
men is only satisfactorily explained as a matter of God's utterly
free decision of grace (cf., in addition to pp. 269ff, pp. 299 and
316). The one solidarity is an altogether natural solidarity, the
evidence of which is to be observed on all sides; the other is a
mystery of the unfathomable grace of God.

The clearest evidence in Romans of the influence of the OT
concept of the Servant of the LORD on Paul's thought about
Christ's work (and so also of its having been an element in his
christological thinking) is 4.25 (see p. 251f); but reference
should further be made to 3.25 (see p. 218), 5.19 (cf. Isa 53.11),
8.32 (see p. 436), 8.34 (see p. 439), and also to the quotations of
Isa 53.1 in 10.16 and of Isa 52.15 in 15.21 (though these are
applied to the missionary preaching rather than to the actual
work of Christ).

The idea of Christ as High Priest would seem to be present in
8.34: note both the reference to the exalted Christ's intercession
(cf. Heb 7.25; 9.24)[1] and also the ἐν δεξιᾷ τοῦ θεοῦ which is
reminiscent of Ps 110, the psalm which contains (v. 4) 'Thou art
a priest for ever after the order of Melchizedek'.

(iv) Of special importance is the use of κύριος with reference
to Christ. As this has been discussed fairly fully in the note on
10.9, we shall here only set out some relevant statistics and
give a very brief summary of our main conclusions on the
subject.

In eight, or nine, of the word's occurrences in Romans[2] it
clearly refers to God. In at least twenty-nine it refers to Christ;
but this figure should almost certainly be increased to thirty-
one by the addition of 12.11 and 13.14, since in both cases the
Nestle text should surely be accepted. The two further occurrences in 14.6 are not absolutely clear. In 10.12 a supplementary
second κύριος referring to Christ is probably to be understood;
and the use of the verb κυριεύειν in 14.9 may also be taken into
consideration. In eleven of the twenty-nine occurrences, in
which Christ is clearly referred to, there is a dependent μου or
ἡμῶν or ὑμῶν: in these a sense of personal commitment and
allegiance is specially given expression.

[1] One of the links between the concepts of the High Priest and the
Servant of the LORD is perhaps to be recognized here, since (according
to the MT, though not the LXX) it is said of the Servant in Isa 53.12
that he 'made intercession for the transgressors'.

[2] 4.8; 9.28, 29; 10.16; 11.3, 34; 12.19; 14.11 (with regard to this
occurrence see commentary *in loc.*); 15.11.

That Paul's use of κύριος with reference to Christ indicates an attitude of religious reverence and devotion is undeniable. The suggestion that the usage is to be explained as having originated under the influence of the use of κύριος in Hellenistic religion (a use of which 1 Cor 8.5 shows that Paul was well aware) must, we submit, be rejected as incredible. The presence of the Aramaic formula in 1 Cor 16.22 strongly suggests that the usage did not begin in Greek-speaking Christianity but goes back to the Aramaic-speaking Christian community. But much more decisive, surely, is the particular character of Paul's relationship to the OT. While his letters show him to have been open to influences of various sorts from the Gentile world around him, a Hellenistic religious influence of this particular kind is precisely the sort of thing to which his fundamental commitment to, and unwearying engagement with, the OT must have made him peculiarly unreceptive. That the true background of his use of κύριος is the LXX, in which the word represents YHWH more than six thousand times, is indicated by the astounding fact that he is able to apply to Jesus Christ without any sign of any sense of incongruity LXX passages in which κύριος stands for YHWH (10.13; cf., e.g., 1 Th 5.2),[1] and by the further evidence set out under (v) below. By his use of the title Paul designates the exalted Christ as Him who shares the name, the majesty, the authority, of God, and to whom the worship which belongs only to the one true God may properly be offered.

(v) That Paul, who certainly had not cast away his commitment to the first two of the Ten Commandments (to have done so would surely have seemed to him the final and absolute apostasy), could countenance prayer to Christ (10.12–14; cf. 1 Cor 1.2: for ἐπικαλεῖσθαι as a technical term for invoking in prayer see Bauer, s.v. ἐπικαλέω 2.b: cf. also 1.a) is something which has often not received adequate attention. To grasp its full significance, one needs to consider, in addition to Exod 20.2–6; Deut 5.7–10, such passages as Deut 6.4; 11.16; Isa 42.8; Mt 4.10; Mk 12.29, 32, and, in Romans itself, 3.30.

(vi) In this epistle—and the same could be said of other Pauline letters—Paul again and again and in a rich variety of ways associates Christ with God with an uninhibitedness, which, because it is so familiar, we are apt to pass over without noticing, but which, when once we begin to reflect on the implications of what we are reading, can scarcely fail to strike us as altogether extraordinary and astonishing. It will suffice to

[1] Other probable examples include 1 Cor 10.21, 22, 31; 2 Cor 3.16; 10.17; 2 Th 1.9.

give just a few examples. In 1.7 'the Lord Jesus Christ' and 'God our Father' are mentioned together as the source of grace and peace for the Roman Christians. The 'message of good news . . . concerning . . . Jesus Christ our Lord' (1.1, 3, 4) is, according to 1.16b, 'God's saving power'; and in its being proclaimed God's gift of righteousness and also His wrath are being revealed (1.17 and 18). According to 2.16 God's final judgment is to be 'through Jesus Christ'. In 5.8 we read that 'God proves his love for us by the fact that Christ died for us when we were still sinners'. In 8.35 and 39 'the love of Christ' and 'the love of God which is in Christ Jesus our Lord' are used, respectively, in two closely corresponding contexts. And, with regard to 3.21–26, it seems fair to say that, on the assumption that Paul was convinced that God's own very Self was truly present in Jesus in His passion as well as at the same time reigning 'in heaven', we have here a profound and sublime statement of the mystery of God's costly forgiveness, but on the assumption that Paul believed less than this, we have a morally offensive piece of false theologizing.

(vii) Christ is referred to as 'Son of God' in 1.4, 'his [i.e. God's] Son' in 1.3, 9; 5.10; 8.29, 'his [i.e. God's] own Son' in 8.3 (=τὸν ἑαυτοῦ υἱόν) and 8.32 (=τοῦ ἰδίου υἱοῦ); and God is referred to as 'the God and Father of our Lord Jesus Christ' in 15.6 (compare also 'the Father' in 6.4). It is quite clear that the relationship Paul intends to indicate is nothing less than a relationship involving a real community of nature between Christ and God.

(viii) On 9.5b the reader may be referred to the full discussion in the commentary. That the whole of v. 5b was intended to refer to Christ we regard as virtually certain. In view of what we have seen in (iv), (v), (vi) and (vii) above, there is, as far as we can see, no good ground for denying that Paul here affirms that Christ, who, in so far as His human existence is concerned, is of Jewish race, is also Lord over all things and by nature God blessed for ever.

5. THE HOLY SPIRIT

The main passage for Paul's teaching on the Holy Spirit in Romans is clearly chapter 8, in which the word πνεῦμα occurs twenty-one times (that is much more frequently than in any other single chapter of the NT). In two of its occurrences in this chapter πνεῦμα does not, but certainly in the great majority, and probably in all, of the other occurrences, πνεῦμα does, refer to the Holy Spirit. There are also a number of passages outside this chapter which are relevant, and the word πνεῦμα occurs five times in chapters 1 to 7, and eight times in chapters 9 to 16. The material may be considered under four heads.

(i) *The work of the Holy Spirit*

At first sight the variety of the things which the Spirit is said to do and of the things which are associated with πνεῦμα, in ways which suggest that they are thought of as effects of His activity, is baffling. But, as soon as the association of life with πνεῦμα (8.2, 6, 10, 11, 13b) is seen in the light of the special importance of the Habakkuk quotation in 1.17 ('He who is righteous by faith shall live'), it begins to be possible to discern something of a comprehensible pattern (though one in which there is much overlapping, the same things being repeated in different ways). The Holy Spirit is 'the Spirit of life' (8.2), that is, the life-giving Spirit, the One who, on the basis of God's work in Christ, brings about the fulfilment of the promise, 'He who is righteous by faith shall live', of 1.17. This He does—

(a) *in this present life*: (α) by entering into the sinner, for whom Christ has died and been raised, and, so to speak, opening him from the inside to the gospel message as He enables him to understand the wonder of God's love for him (5.5: 'God's love has been poured out in our hearts through the Holy Spirit who has been given to us'), thus creating the response of faith[1] and bringing into being the man 'who is righteous by faith'; (β) by exerting His authority and constraint over the believer and thereby making him free from the tyrannous authority of sin (8.2: 'the law of the Spirit . . . has . . . set thee free from the law of sin'), free for a beginning of obedience to God's law (8.4: 'so that the righteous requirement of the law might be fulfilled in us'),[2] free to be a son of God (8.15: 'you have received the Spirit of adoption'), to know himself to be such (8.16: 'The Spirit himself assures our spirit that we are children of God') and to begin to behave as such (8.15b: 'by whose enabling we cry, "Abba, Father" '); (γ) by dwelling in him continually (8.9: 'God's Spirit dwells in you'; compare v. 11 and see also the note

---

[1] We may compare the phrase τὸ . . . πνεῦμα τῆς πίστεως in 2 Cor 4.13.

[2] This freedom to begin to obey God's law is described in 8.5 in terms of being κατὰ πνεῦμα, that is, of allowing one's life to be determined by the Spirit, and so being on the side of the Spirit, and in 8.14 in terms of being led by the Spirit.

on 7.18a) and effecting his sanctification (15.16: 'sanctified by the Holy Spirit'; compare 'if by the Spirit you put to death the activities of the body' in 8.13 taken in association with the thought of dying with Christ (in the third sense mentioned on p. 300) in chapter 6 and with the use of ἁγιασμός in 6.19 and 22, and perhaps also πνεῦμα ἁγιωσύνης in 1.4); (δ) by interceding for him and helping his weakness (8.26f); (ε) by His renewing activity (7.6; with which we should probably compare 6.4; 12.2, and also 9.1); (ζ) by His gifts of love (15.30), joy (14.17), hope (8.17ff in association with vv. 14–16; in 8.23 believers are described as possessing τὴν ἀπαρχὴν τοῦ πνεύματος), power (15.13, 19) and peace (8.6).[1]

(b) *in the future*: by playing His vital part in the accomplishment of the believer's final deliverance from the power of death (8.2: 'the law of the Spirit of life has . . . set thee free from the law of . . . death'; 8.6: 'the Spirit's mind is life'; 8.10f: 'But, if Christ is in you, though your body is indeed mortal because of *your* sin, the Spirit is life because of *your* justification. But, if the spirit of him who raised Jesus from the dead dwells in you, he who raised from the dead Christ Jesus shall quicken your mortal bodies also through his Spirit who dwells in you'; compare also 8.13b: 'but if by the Spirit you put to death the activities of the body, you shall live', and, in view of the connexion noted above between 8.13b and features of chapter 6, perhaps 6.5b and 8 should also be mentioned).

(ii) *The Holy Spirit's relation to God*

The Spirit is the Spirit of God (8.9a and 14: πνεῦμα θεοῦ; 8.11: 'his Spirit' and 'the Spirit of him who raised Jesus from the dead'). The same truth is elsewhere indicated by the qualification of πνεῦμα by ἅγιον (5.5; 9.1; 14.17; 15.13; also in 15.19 according to a number of textual witnesses). That, for Paul, the authority of the Spirit is God's own authority is strongly suggested by 5.5 ('for God's love has been poured out in our hearts through the Holy Spirit who has been given to us'), and even more strongly by 8.15f—for none but God Himself has in Himself the right to allow us to address Him with the words, 'Abba, Father', and can with absolute authority assure us that

---

[1] It is to be noted that, while the phrase χάρισμα πνευματικόν occurs in 1.11, where χάρισμα is best understood in a general sense as denoting a blessing which God will bestow on the Roman Christians through Paul's coming to them, there is no explicit reference of any sort to any connexion with the Spirit in the paragraph 12.3–8 which contains (in v. 6) the only occurrence in the epistle of χάρισμα used in its special sense of an endowment bestowed on a particular member of the church to enable him to fulfil a particular ministry.

we are His dear children. The frequent association of the Spirit and life, which was noticed above under (i), is a further pointer in the same direction; for the giving of life, whether by creation out of nothing or by raising the dead, belongs peculiarly to God (compare the notes on 4.17b). But at the same time the Spirit is clearly distinguished from God by 5.5; 8.11, 16, 26f.

(iii) *The Holy Spirit's relation to Christ*

The Spirit is the Spirit of Christ (8.9b: πνεῦμα Χριστοῦ). It is on the basis of what God has accomplished in Christ—and not otherwise—that the law of the Spirit has been brought to bear upon the believer to set him free from the law of sin and of death (8.2: the 'in Christ Jesus' is of vital importance). The fact that immediately after referring in 8.9 to the Spirit's dwelling in the Roman Christians Paul goes on to speak in 8.10 of Christ's being in them and the apparent equivalence of 'in Christ Jesus' in 8.1 and 'in the Spirit' in 8.9 have led some to conclude that he saw no distinction between the Spirit and the exalted Christ (compare ὁ δὲ κύριος τὸ πνεῦμά ἐστιν in 2 Cor 3.17a); but in the same context (8.9) the phrase πνεῦμα Χριστοῦ (compare τὸ πνεῦμα κυρίου in 2 Cor 3.17b) serves to distinguish the Spirit from Christ, as does also 8.11, and it is not to be doubted that the contention that, for Paul, the Spirit and the exalted Christ are simply identical must be rejected.

(iv) *References to the Spirit in contexts which also refer to God (the Father) and to Christ*

The following passages seem to us to constitute adequate grounds for affirming that at any rate the basis of a Trinitarian doctrine of the Spirit is contained in Romans: 1.1–4 ('Paul, slave of Christ Jesus, . . . set apart for *the work of proclaiming* God's message of good news, which he promised beforehand . . ., concerning his Son, . . . who was appointed Son of God in power according to the Spirit of holiness from the resurrection of the dead, even Jesus Christ our Lord'); 5.1–5 ('Having been justified then on the basis of faith, we have peace with God through our Lord Jesus Christ, . . . we exult in hope of the glory of God . . . And this hope does not put us to shame, for God's love has been poured out in our hearts through the Holy Spirit who has been given to us'); 8.11 ('But, if the Spirit of him who raised Jesus from the dead dwells in you, he who raised from the dead Christ Jesus shall quicken your mortal bodies also through his Spirit who dwells in you'); 14.17f ('For the kingdom of God is not eating and drinking, but righteousness and peace and joy in the Holy Spirit; for he who therein serves Christ is well-pleasing to God and deserves men's approval'); 15.16 ('to be a minister of Christ Jesus unto the Gentiles, serving God's message of good news with a holy service, in order that the offering consisting of the Gentiles may be acceptable, having been sanctified by the Holy Spirit'); and 15.30 ('I exhort you [,brothers,] by our Lord Jesus Christ and by the love of the Spirit to join earnestly with me in prayers on my behalf to God').

6. ESCHATOLOGY

In order to avoid unnecessary repetition, we shall here refer the reader back to six passages in the commentary which, taken together and read (we suggest) in the order in which they are cited below, will give, we hope, a reasonably clear and full account of our understanding of the eschatological teaching of the epistle. They are: pp. 679–86 (on 13.11–12); pp. 760–62 (on 15.19b); pp. 766–68 (on 15.23a); pp. 87–89 (on εἰς σωτηρίαν in 1.16b; pp. 142–63 (on 2.2–16) and pp. 403–20 (on 8.17–25). To supplement these passages, reference might also be made to p. 260 (on ἐπ᾽ ἐλπίδι τῆς δόξης τοῦ θεοῦ in 5.2); p. 300 (on the eschatological sense of dying and being raised with Christ); pp. 389–92 (on 8.10f); pp. 561–63, 573–79, and 586–88 (on 11.15, 25–27 and 32, respectively) and pp. 709–11 (on 14.10-12).

7. DEATH UNDERSTOOD AS THE CONSEQUENCE OF SIN

In commenting on 5.12 we indicated (on p. 281) an intention of trying to say something more with regard to the problems raised by Paul's understanding of human death as being the consequence of sin, which is to be seen not only in 5.12–21 but also elsewhere in Romans (e.g., in 6.23; 8.2, 10f). It will be appropriate, in view of the connexions that there are between this matter and sections 2, 5 and 6 of this essay, to attempt to do at this point the very little which we are at present in a position to do toward fulfilling that promise.

With regard to the difficulty of relating Paul's doctrine to modern scientific knowledge, it may be tentatively suggested that, while there would seem to be clear enough evidence that human death as a biological phenomenon is not consequential on sin but natural (in the phraseology used by Aquinas, 'non . . . ex peccato, sed magis ex natura'),[1] it is not necessarily obscurantist to believe that at the point (or, maybe, points) at which man first appeared as recognizably man he was faced with, but rejected, a God-given possibility of, and a God-given summons to, a human life such as did not need to be terminated by the death which we know, that is, a death which is for all men objectively (according to the witness of Scripture) death-as-the-wages-of-sin, whether or not they subjectively know it as such.

Three further points may be made: (i) that it is only in the death of Jesus Christ that we see the full reality and seriousness of human death as the death which we all objectively—but only those, who heed the witness of Scripture, subjectively—know, that is, as death-as-the-wages-of-sin; (ii) that in His human life alone we see a human life which did not in itself merit the death which we know; and (iii) that in His risen and glorified humanity we see the immortality which is the life which, from all eternity, God purposed as the ultimate destiny of those of His creatures-to-be whom He would at last make to be 'conformed to the image of his Son'.

8. THE OT LAW[2]

(i) For Paul, *the law is God's law*. In 7.22, 25; 8.7 it is explicitly called God's law (cf. 1 Cor 7.19; 'the commandments of God'). Being God's law, it is 'spiritual' (7.14), 'holy', 'righteous' and

---

[1] p. 75 (416).

[2] In view of our conviction that there has been widespread misunderstanding of Paul's attitude to the law, which has involved a serious distortion of his theology as a whole and has also bedevilled a good deal of discussion of other matters such as the authorship of Acts and of St Luke's Gospel, we have allowed this section to run to a greater length than any of the other sections of this essay, and have taken into account other Pauline epistles as we have not done in the preceding sections. This section represents a considerable proportion of the substance (in a revised form) of 'St Paul and the Law', which was originally published in *SJT* 17 (1964), pp. 43–68, and re-published in a slightly shortened and revised form in R. Batey (ed.), *New Testament Issues*, New York and London, 1970, pp. 148–72. The author is indebted to the editors and publishers of *SJT* and to Professor Batey and Messrs. Harper and Row for allowing him thus to make further use of already published material. Among recent publications bearing on this subject reference may be made to K. Barth, *God, Grace and Gospel*, Edinburgh, 1959, pp. 3–27 ('Gospel and Law', originally published in German in 1935); W. D. Davies, 'Law in the NT', in *IDB* 3, pp. 95–102; W. Niesel, *Reformed*

'good' (7.12: 'the law is holy, and the commandment holy and righteous and good'). In the translation 'good' is again used of the law in 7.16, but it represents a different Greek word, καλός, whereas in 7.12 ἀγαθός was used. All this the law not only was originally but also continues to be, even when it is misused and dishonoured by men (as is implied by the context of the statements in 7.12 and 14). It is God's word—the phrase 'the oracles of God' in 3.2 certainly includes the law. As the revelation of God's will, the law has for its true and proper purpose 'life' (7.10) for men, whatever other consequences it may have as it is met by human sin. So 'the legislation' is reckoned by Paul among the great and glorious privileges of Israel (9.4). To have been entrusted with the law of God is an altogether real, and in no way illusory, though it is a dangerous, privilege (3.2). And it is consonant with his conviction that the law is God's, that throughout his epistles he treats the OT as a whole with the greatest respect as having divine authority.

(ii) As the revelation of God's will for men, *the law makes sin manifest as sin, as disobedience to God*. According to 5.13f, sin was already in the world and men were already sinners before the law was given. Their thoughts, words and deeds were contrary to the will of God, objectively disobedient, and as a consequence of their sin they died. But they did not disobey a known commandment in the way that Adam did (Gen 2.17) and Israel after the law had been received. In the absence of

Symbolics: A comparison of Catholicism, Orthodoxy, and Protestantism (Eng. tr. of *Das Evangelium und die Kirchen: ein Lehrbuch der Symbolik*, Neukirchen, ²1960), Edinburgh, 1962, pp. 211–24 (an illuminating chapter entitled 'Gospel and Law'); A. J. Bandstra, *The Law and the Elements of this World*, Kampen, 1964; C. F. D. Moule, 'Obligation in the ethic of Paul', in W. R. Farmer, C. F. D. Moule and R. R. Niebuhr (ed.), *Christian History and Interpretation: studies presented to J. Knox*, Cambridge, 1967, pp. 389–406; M. Barth, 'The kerygma of Galatians', in *Interpretation* 21 (1967), pp. 131–46; A. van Dülmen, *Die Theologie des Gesetzes bei Paulus*, Stuttgart, 1968; R. Bring, *Christus und das Gesetz*, Leiden, 1969; F. F. Bruce, 'Paul and the Law of Moses', in *BJRL* 57 (1974–75), pp. 259–79; J. A. Sanders, 'Torah and Christ', in *Interpretation* 29 (1975), pp. 372–90; G. E. Ladd, *A Theology of the New Testament*, Guildford and London, 1975, pp. 495–510; F. Hahn, 'Das Gesetzesverständnis im Römer- und Galaterbrief', in *ZNW* 67 (1976), pp. 29–63; H. Hübner, 'Das Gesetz als elementares Thema einer biblischen Theologie?', in *Kerygma und Dogma* 22 (Göttingen, 1976), pp. 250–76; F. Lang, 'Gesetz und Bund bei Paulus', in J. Friedrich, W. Pöhlmann, P. Stuhlmacher (ed.), *Rechtfertigung: Festschrift für E. Käsemann*, Tübingen and Göttingen, 1976, pp. 305–20; J. A. Sanders, 'Torah and Paul', in J. Jervell and W. A. Meeks (ed.), *God's Christ and His People: studies in honour of Nils Alstrup Dahl*, Oslo, 1978 (copyright 1977), pp. 132–40; H. Hübner, *Das Gesetz bei Paulus: ein Beitrag zum Werden der paulinischen Theologie*, Göttingen, 1978.

the law, sin, though real, was not clearly visible. But, when the law was given, sin became plainly and unmistakably visible, something sharply defined. The law makes its recipients recognize sin as sin, and themselves as sinners (cf. 3.20).

(iii) But this means that *the law actually enhances sin*; for, by showing men that what they are doing is contrary to God's will, it gives to their continuing to do it the character of conscious and wilful disobedience, thereby increasing their sin in the sense that it makes it more sinful. And that it should have this effect was part of the divine intention in giving the law (cf. 5.20a: 'But the law came in as a new feature of the situation in order that the misdeed might increase' and Gal 3.19: τῶν παραβάσεων χάριν—that is, in order that there might be transgressions, the conscious disobeying of definite commandments).

(iv) But *the law* not only increases sin in the sense that it makes it more sinful, it also *increases sin in the sense that it makes men sin more*. As God's explicit prohibition (Gen 2.17) constituted the opportunity which the serpent was able to exploit for the purpose of deceiving and ruining Adam (Gen 3.1ff), so the law serves sin as an ἀφορμή (7.8 and 11); for the law's presence makes it possible to inveigle men into deliberate rebellion against God—so that Paul can actually say (1 Cor 15.56b), ἡ δὲ δύναμις τῆς ἁμαρτίας ὁ νόμος. The opposition which the law offers to men's sinful desires has the effect of stirring them up to greater fury. (See commentary on 7.5, 8, 11.)

(v) *In particular, the law makes men sin more, in that it establishes the possibility of legalism.* For sinful man the very existence of the law is necessarily a temptation to try to use it as a means by which to establish a claim upon God and so to assert a measure of independence over against Him. He imagines that he can so adequately fulfil the law's demands as to be in a position to flaunt as a crown of his merit what is in reality God's indictment.[1] But the legalist's confidence of being 'justified . . . on the ground of having done what the law requires' is utterly vain (3.20), since fallen man can never adequately obey the law of God. When Paul says of himself in Phil 3.6, 'as touching the righteousness which is in the law, found blameless', he is indicating, not how he sees himself now that he is a Christian, but how he seemed to himself and to his fellows before his conversion. That 'righteousness of mine own, *even* that which is of the law', to which he refers (Phil 3.9), is an illusion of the Pharisee's heart (cf. the reply of the rich man to

---

[1] To use the suggestive imagery of Job 31.35f (cf. C. E. B. Cranfield, 'An Interpretation of the Book of Job', in *ET* 54 (1942–43), pp. 295–98, especially p. 297.

Jesus in Mk 10.20: 'Master, all these things have I observed from my youth')—an illusion supported by a constant tampering with the law. Such a tampering with the law of God the Jewish oral law largely was—Jesus bluntly called it 'the tradition of men', according to Mk 7.8; for, instead of recognizing in the demands of the law the absolute demand of God, by which He claims us wholly for Himself and for our neighbour, and with which men cannot live on terms of merit but only on terms of divine forgiveness, it sought to turn them into something manageable and achievable.[1]

(vi) *The law pronounces God's condemnation and curse.* So in 2 Cor 3.9 the giving of the law is referred to as 'the ministration of condemnation'. The condemnation from which Christ has freed us (8.1) is condemnation pronounced by the law. In Gal 3.10 Paul writes: 'For as many as are of the works of the law [i.e., as many as are legalists, refusing to accept the righteous status God has made available in Christ and insisting on thinking that they can earn their own righteous status by their fulfilment of the law's demands] are under a curse: for it is written, Cursed is every one which continueth not in all things that are written in the law, to do them'; and in Gal 3.13: 'Christ redeemed us from the curse of the law, having become a curse for us: for it is written, Cursed is every one that hangeth on a tree'. And the condemnation and curse of the law involve death. So in 2 Cor 3.7 the giving of the law is called 'the ministration of death'. It is not that the law is injurious to us in its own nature, but, as Calvin says, 'because our corruption provokes and draws upon us its curse'.[2] It is because it encounters sin that the law, which was intended 'unto life', actually results in 'death' (7.10).

(vii) But *the ultimate goal and inmost meaning of the law are* not the condemnation of sinners, but *Jesus Christ.* We may refer to the full discussion in the commentary of the meaning of τέλος in 10.4. Of the three possible meanings, we decided in favour of 'goal'. What content, then, can we give, on the basis of Paul's epistles, to the statement that Christ is the goal of the law? The following points may be made here:

(a) The law has Christ for its goal, is aimed at, directed toward, Him, bears witness to Him, by virtue of the promises which it contains. Highly significant in this connexion is 10.6–10; for there Paul discerns the voice of 'the righteousness

[1] Cf. C. E. B. Cranfield, *The Gospel according to Saint Mark*, Cambridge, [6]1977, pp. 243f, 329.
[2] p. 145.

which is of faith' speaking in Deuteronomy, and refers what is spoken to Christ. Compare 3.21, where 'attested by the law', though the direct reference is to 'God's righteousness', refers, in effect, to Christ, in view of the intimate connexion between this righteousness and the person and work of Christ indicated in the next few verses; also 1.1–3 ('. . . God's message of good news, which he promised beforehand through his prophets in the holy scriptures, concerning his Son . . .'), in which the law is hardly to be thought of as excluded, since Moses was regarded as a prophet (cf. Deut 18.15, 18; 34.10); Gal 3.8 ('And the scripture . . . preached the gospel beforehand unto Abraham, *saying*, In thee shall all the nations be blessed'), where the quotation is from Genesis.

(b) The law has Christ for its goal, bears witness to Him, by virtue of its revelation of God's will for man, of God's absolute claim to man's life, man's allegiance, man's obedience. It draws the outline of a perfect obedience, pointing forward to one who will truly do the righteousness which is of the law (cf. 10.5) and Jesus Christ is the goal, the meaning, the substance, of the law, in virtue of the fact that He is the one and only Man who has truly and fully loved God with all His heart and with all His soul and with all His might (Deut 6.5) and has fully and truly loved His neighbour (cf. Lev 19.18), the one and only Man who has been completely and utterly obedient (5.19; cf. Phil 2.8[1]).

(c) The law has Christ for its goal, bears witness to Him, by virtue of its ceremonies, and He is its goal, as being their meaning and substance. So Paul sees the work of Christ in the light of the sacrifices ordained by the law. In 3.25, whatever be the exact significance of the word ἱλαστήριον, the death of Christ is interpreted in terms of sacrifice. It is implied by 1 Cor 5.7f ('Purge out the old leaven, that ye may be a new lump, even as ye are unleavened. For our Passover also hath been sacrificed, *even* Christ: wherefore let us keep the feast, not with old leaven . . .') that Christ is the true and final Paschal lamb, to whom all the Paschal lambs sacrificed according to the law were pointing forward. Reference must also be made to 1 Cor 11.25, in which Paul repeats the words ('This cup is the new covenant in my blood'—compare Exod 24.6–8) by which Jesus

---

[1] *Pace* F. W. Beare, *The Epistle to the Philippians*, London, 1959, p. 84, there seems to be no justification in the context for taking the meaning to be that Christ submitted to the power of the 'Elemental Spirits': the explanation that the reference is to His obedience to God (e.g., J. B. Lightfoot, *Saint Paul's Epistle to the Philippians*, London, reprinted 1908, p. 113) is surely to be preferred.

had stamped a sacrificial significance on His approaching death. A number of other passages might be cited, but these will suffice.

(d) The law has Christ for its goal and meaning, and bears witness to Him, in virtue of its revelation of men's sinfulness and helplessness, and He is the goal of the law, in that He is the one and only remedy of men's desperate condition, which the law brings to light. By making objectively visible—though the legalists fail to see what is before their eyes—the impossibility, for sinful men, of a righteousness earned by works, the law points to the righteousness of faith. We may refer to 3.20; 4.14–15a; 5.20f; Gal 3.22, 24.

(e) The law has Christ for its goal and meaning, and bears witness to Him, in virtue of the fact that it sets the necessary forensic stage on which Christ's saving work is wrought, and He is its goal, in that the justification which He achieves for us is no mere amnesty or indulgence, no caprice or sentimentality on the part of God, but acquittal 'in God's severe and true judgment which searches the hearts and is no respecter of persons'.[1] So far from its being true to claim, as G. W. H. Lampe does, that 'St Paul realized the essential truth that the act of God in Christ had taken the whole question of man's relationship to God out of this area [i.e., of law]',[2] Paul underlines again and again by his language the legal framework of Christ's action. But, be it carefully noted, this legal framework is the framework, not of human law and, of course, not of legalism, but of God's law.[3] Lampe regards it as disastrous that we should suppose 'that God's action takes place within a framework of law';[4] but the fact that our justification is truly acquittal by the just Judge and not mere caprice seems to us to be something which the Epistle to the Romans was designed to emphasize. And in this fact which Paul brings out so clearly is to be recognized God's respect for His creature man, His taking His creature seriously in the dignity of his moral respon-

[1] Barth, *Shorter*, p. 43.

[2] In A. R. Vidler (ed.), *Soundings: essays concerning Christian understanding*, Cambridge, 1963, p. 178.

[3] It is not, of course, intended to suggest that there is no human element in the OT law. In the law, as everywhere else in the Bible, God's word is given to us through the words of men—with all that that involves. The point we wish to make is that there are very significant differences between the OT law and all other bodies of law and that the strong antipathy felt by many theologians toward the OT law is to a large extent due to their failure to recognize the existence and the significance of these differences.

[4] op. cit., p. 183.

sibility, so His mercy which is truly mercy, His love which is truly love—and not a basically unloving sentimentality.[1]

(viii) The epistles reveal *Paul's radical rejection of legalism* (we have already seen in (v) something of what legalism is) *and of* what is so inextricably bound up with legalism that we may treat the two things as one, *an understanding of the law which fails to recognize the fact, or the full implications of the fact, that Christ is its inmost meaning and goal.* Each of these two leads to the other: preoccupation with the quest for a righteous status of one's own earned by one's merits has the effect of blinding one to the righteous status which God has made available in Christ as a free gift, while failure to see that the real substance of the law is Christ opens the way to the legalistic misunderstanding and perversion of the law. With reference to the inextricable mutual involvement of these two things see the commentary on 9.30–33 and 10.3.

For Paul the legalism which prevailed among the Jews of his day meant slavery. So in Gal 4.25 he can say of 'the Jerusalem that now is' that 'she is in bondage with her children'. The covenant 'from mount Sinai', understood legalistically and without regard to Christ, bears 'children unto bondage' (Gal 4.24), and the Galatian Christians are warned against getting themselves 'entangled again in a yoke of bondage' (Gal 5.1b). It is a slavery from which Christ has freed us (Gal 5.1a), and the men who are trying to make the Gentile Christians judaize are 'false brethren . . . who came in privily to spy out our liberty which we have in Christ Jesus, that they might bring us into bondage' (Gal 2.4).

To practise the observances of Judaism while rejecting Christ is to be left with only the letter of the law, without the Spirit (cf. Rom 7.6; 2 Cor 3.6); but the letter of the law in separation from the Spirit is the law—so to speak—denatured, for the law of God is by nature 'spiritual' (7.14). The literal observance of circumcision and other ceremonies of the law was valuable and significant as 'a shadow of the things to come', a pointer forward to Christ; but to regard these things as possessed of an independent value in themselves quite apart from Him is to be left with a mere empty 'shadow' in isolation from the 'the body' which gives it meaning (cf. Col 2.16f).[2]

---

[1] The chapter entitled 'The Gospel as the Divine Justification of those who believe', in Barth, *Shorter*, should be read as a much needed antidote to Lampe's essay in *Soundings*.

[2] It should, however, be noted that in Colossians Paul seems to be dealing not with a simple judaizing but with some sort of amalgam of Christian, Jewish and pagan elements.

While Paul seems to have made no objection to, indeed to have approved of (cf. 1 Cor 9.20; Acts 16.3; 21.26), Jewish Christians' continuing to observe the ceremonies as a mark of their solidarity with their kinsmen according to the flesh, whose salvation he so earnestly desired, and may perhaps have allowed the Gentile Titus to be circumcised (Gal 2.3, where the Greek is ambiguous) on the principle of 'all things to all men, that I may by all means save some' (1 Cor 9.22), he opposed the false teachers, who were troubling the Galatian churches, with uncompromising vehemence; for they were maintaining that circumcision was necessary to salvation, and thereby both propagating the legalistic notion that justification is by works —or at least partly by works—instead of by faith alone, and also calling in question the truth that Christ is the goal of the law (for to know that the goal of the law is Christ is to know that now that He, to whom the ceremonies pointed, has come, their literal observance cannot any longer be obligatory). So he writes about these false teachers, that their version of the gospel is a different gospel altogether, and in fact not a gospel at all (Gal 1.6f), and, with them in mind, he warns the Galatian Christians: 'Behold, I Paul say unto you, that, if ye receive circumcision, Christ will profit you nothing', and 'Ye are severed from Christ, ye who would be justified by the law; ye are fallen away from grace' (Gal 5.2 and 4).[1]

With regard to the legalism of contemporary Judaism he seems even to go so far (however we understand the perplexing 'rudiments of the world') as to put it on the same level as, or, at the least, to suggest that it has much in common with, paganism: this is the implication of Gal 4.3 (cf. 4.9), for the first person plural links together under a common denominator the pasts of both Jewish and Gentile Christians. But this passage, together with a number of other passages which are relevant here, it will be more convenient to treat in the next section.

(ix) *For Paul, the law is not abrogated by Christ.* This thesis is stated in full awareness of the widespread tendency today, observable not only in popular writing but also in serious works of scholarship, to regard it as an assured result that Paul believed that the law had been abrogated by Christ. This

---

[1] For Paul, it would seem, it was one thing for a Gentile Christian to be circumcised simply for the sake of facilitating the evangelization of unbelieving Jews, but quite another thing for a Gentile Christian to submit to circumcision either under the false impression that circumcision was a necessary condition for sharing in the full benefits of the gospel or in order to satisfy legalistic fellow-Christians whether Jewish or Gentile.

'assured result', like so many others, needs to be re-examined.

There are, of course, a number of passages in the epistles which, at first sight, seem to provide support for the view we are opposing, and these we must now consider. In doing so, it will be well to bear in mind the fact (which, so far as we know, had not received attention before it was noted in *SJT* 17, 1964, p. 55) that the Greek language of Paul's day possessed no word-group corresponding to our 'legalism', 'legalist' and 'legalistic'. This means that he lacked a convenient terminology for expressing a vital distinction, and so was surely seriously hampered in the work of clarifying the Christian position with regard to the law. In view of this, we should always, we think, be ready to reckon with the possibility that Pauline statements, which at first sight seem to disparage the law, were really directed not against the law itself but against that misunderstanding and misuse of it for which we now have a convenient terminology. In this very difficult terrain Paul was pioneering. If we make due allowance for these circumstances, we shall not be so easily baffled or misled by a certain impreciseness of statement which we shall sometimes encounter.

As far as 10.4 is concerned, we simply refer back to (vii) and to the relevant notes in the commentary. In 3.21 'apart from the law' might at first sight suggest that Paul regarded the law as having been superseded, brushed aside as out of date by the manifestation of God's righteousness. But the words 'attested by the law' in the same verse and the emphatic statement in v. 31 show the wrongness of such an inference. The simplest explanation of 'apart from the law' is that it is shorthand for 'apart from works of the law' (v. 28): God's gift is not earned by man's fulfilment of His requirements. That in 'you are not under the law' in 6.14, 'you . . . were made dead to the law' in 7.4, and 'now we have been released from the law' in 7.6, 'law' has the limited sense of 'the law as condemning you (us)' is confirmed by 8.1 ('So then there is now no condemnation for those who are in Christ Jesus'), which draws out the significance of 7.1–6 which in its turn takes up and elucidates the statement made in 6.14b. We shall refer to 8.2 below under (x). Suffice it here to say that by 'the law of sin and of death' we understand the power exercised over us by sin and the resulting power over us of death.

We turn now to 2 Corinthians 3, which, as it contains a good deal which has often been taken to disparage the law and to imply that it is done away in Christ, must be looked at in some detail. Verse 3 provides a transition from the subject of the letter of commendation to that of the ministry of the new covenant. The contrast between the old and the new covenants is already in Paul's mind when he speaks of 'tables of stone' (cf. Exod 24.12) and 'tables that are hearts of flesh' (cf. Jer 31.33; Ezek 11.19f; 36.26f). The reference to Jer 31.31ff is picked up in v. 6: Paul is a minister of the 'new covenant'. There is no suggestion in Jer 31.31ff of a new law to replace that given through Moses: the suggestion is rather that the same law of God—'my law' (Jer 31.33)—will be given in a new way. What is looked forward to is not the abolition of the law, but its true and effective establishment. So far there is nothing in what Paul has said in this chapter which needs to be taken as disparagement of the law. But what about v. 6b? The contrast here between 'the letter' and 'the spirit' (better 'the Spirit') we take to be a contrast not between the OT law which is written and a spiritual religion which knows no law, but between the legalistic relation of the Jews of Paul's time to God and to His law and the new relation to God and to His law established by the Holy Spirit and resulting from Christ's work. In the absence of the Spirit the law is misused and comes to be for those who misuse it simply 'letter' (compare what was said under (viii) above on this verse and Rom 7.6b), and this law without the Spirit 'killeth' (v. 6c: cf. Rom 7.10). So in v. 7 the ministry or service performed by Moses[1] at the giving of the law is referred to as 'the ministration of death': it was a service of death, in that the law, at the giving of which Moses served, would indeed kill—though this is very far from being the whole of the story. Paul's point in vv. 7–11 is that, since the service rendered by Moses at the giving of the law, which was actually going to effect 'condemnation' (v. 9) and 'death' (v. 7), was accompanied by glory (the glory on Moses' face—Exod 34.29ff), the service of the Spirit rendered by himself (and other Christian preachers) in the preaching of the gospel must much more be accompanied by glory. Verse 10 is difficult; but the general meaning would seem to be that the glory of the ministry of the gospel is so surpassingly great that, in comparison with it, the glory which, according to Exodus, accompanied the ministry fulfilled by Moses can scarcely be called glory at all. In v. 11 the vital question is: To what does 'that which passeth away' refer? In view of the use of 'pass away' in vv. 7 and 13, we

---

[1] The word which the RV renders in this chapter by 'ministration' is διακονία, which means 'service' or 'ministry' (cf. 2 Cor 4.1, and also, e.g., Rom 11.13; 2 Cor 5.18; Col 4.17). In v. 7 Paul's language is elliptical: he does not mean that Moses' ministry was 'written, and engraven on stones'. We might supply something like 'which was a ministry of that which was' before 'written' in the RV translation, and substitute 'was' for 'came' (RV 'came' renders ἐγενήθη).

might possibly be tempted to try to take it to refer to the glory on Moses' face; but the structure of vv. 7–11 is clearly against this. It is best to take the reference to be, not to the law or 'the whole religious system based on the law',[1] but to the ministry of Moses at the giving of the law; and we may translate with an imperfect as the RV does the same Greek in v. 13—'that which was passing away'. The service which Moses rendered was passing away, and yet it was accompanied by glory. How much more then must the service of the minister of the gospel, a service 'which remaineth', be clothed with glory! The key to the true understanding of this whole passage is to recognize that it is really the two ministries which are being contrasted rather than the two covenants themselves; when this is recognized the connexion between vv. 7–11 and vv. 4–6 and 1–3 becomes clear. And the true explanation of the superiority of the glory of the Christian minister's ministry over that of Moses' ministry is not that the law which was given through Moses has been abolished, but that these two ministries are differently related to the ministry of Jesus Christ. Whereas Moses' ministry belongs wholly to the time of expectation, that of even the lowliest of Christian ministers belongs to the time of fulfilment, the time which is characterized by the fact that the work of Him who is the substance and the meaning of the law has been accomplished. What is said in Mt 11.11b with regard to John the Baptist, who, though he lived to see Jesus, did not live to see the completion of His work, is even more clearly applicable to Moses, who had died many centuries before the Incarnation.

In vv. 12ff Paul's thought is based on the detail of the veil which Moses wore (Exod 34.33). Unlike Moses, the minister of the gospel, since his ministry 'remaineth' (v. 11) with its glory, does not need to veil his face. Barrett maintains that τὸ καταργούμενον ('that which was passing away') in v. 13 is 'the whole religious system based on the law',[2] and appeals to Paul's use of the verb καταργεῖν in this verse and also in v. 11 (he explains τὸ καταργούμενον there in the same way) 'in relation to the law' in support of his statement, 'Paul knows that the law, and the covenant inaugurated on the basis of it, great as they are, are nevertheless in process of being done away'.[3] But Barrett's interpretation here is surely impossible; for the con-

[1] Barrett, *From First Adam to Last*, p. 52, n. 1; and cf. id., *The Second Epistle to the Corinthians*, London, 1973, p. 118.

[2] *From First Adam to Last*, p. 52, n. 1; cf. his 2 Corinthians commentary, p. 119.

[3] *From First Adam to Last*, p. 52.

temporaries of Moses were in no danger of looking on the end of 'the whole religious system based on the law'.[1] What is meant must be the glory on Moses' face (cf. v. 7). In vv. 14–16 another idea, suggested by the reference to Moses' veil, is brought out, namely, that up to the present time, when the law is read in the synagogue, a veil rests on the hearts of the Jews, so that they do not understand its true meaning; but whenever 'their heart' turns to Christ, the veil is taken away (in v. 16 Paul is echoing Exod 34.34). There is here no suggestion that the law is done away, but rather that, when men turn to Christ, they are able to discern the true glory of the law. Calvin's comment is apt: 'The law is in itself full of light but we appreciate its clarity only when Christ appears to us in it.'[2] (The NEB translation of v. 14, '. . . because only in Christ is the old covenant abrogated', is perverse; for it is altogether more natural to take the subject (which is not expressed in the Greek) of καταργεῖται (NEB: 'is abrogated') to be the same thing as is described as μὴ ἀνακαλυπτόμενον (NEB: 'and it is never lifted'), i.e. the veil, than to supply 'the old covenant' as the NEB does. And the interpretation which is the natural way of taking the Greek in v. 14 is surely confirmed beyond all reasonable doubt by v. 16. The translation which the NEB has given in v. 14 would scarcely occur to a translator who was free from preconceptions with regard to Paul's attitude to the law.)

Verse 17 is a notorious *crux interpretum*. It is, we believe, best interpreted thus: But the Lord (i.e. the risen and exalted Christ), of whom it may truly be said that, when Israel's heart turns to Him, the veil which prevents it understanding the law is taken away, is the Spirit to whom reference has been made in vv. 6 and 8, and where the Spirit of the Lord (i.e. of Christ) is present, there is liberty. The fact that the Lord and the Spirit, while they are identified in the first half of the verse, are distinguished in the second half, is an indication that we should not take 'the Lord is the Spirit' to imply that, for Paul, the exalted Christ and the Holy Spirit are identical, but rather that to turn to Christ is to be introduced into the realm of the Spirit.[3] The point of v. 17b we take to be that the law, when it is understood in the light of Christ, when it is established in its

---

[1] This statement would be equally true, if we understood 'end' in the sense of goal rather than termination; but to take τέλος here in the sense of goal is really not feasible.

[2] *The Second Epistle of Paul the Apostle to the Corinthians and the Epistles to Timothy, Titus and Philemon*, tr. by T. A. Smail, Edinburgh, 1964, p. 47.

[3] Cf. E. Schweizer, in *TWNT* 6, p. 416.

true character by the Holy Spirit, so far from being the 'bondage' into which legalism has perverted it, is true freedom (cf. Jas 1.25: 'the perfect law, the law of liberty'). But with this verse, and with v. 18 which we need not discuss here, we have passed into the province of our next section.

We must turn now to Gal 3.15–25, which—perhaps more than any other single passage—has encouraged readers of St Paul to assume that he believed that the law is done away by Christ. We need not linger over vv. 15–18, in which Paul argues that it is unthinkable that the law, which was only given four hundred and thirty years later, should disannul the promise made to Abraham, 'a covenant confirmed beforehand by God'. It is vv. 19 and 20 which contain what G. S. Duncan has called Paul's 'depreciatory account of the Law'.[1] The details may be set out as follows:

(a) 'was added'. Duncan takes this to imply that the law 'is a mere addition to the main stream of God's purpose'.[2]

(b) 'because of transgressions', i.e., to give to men's wrong-doing the character of conscious disobedience.

(c) 'till the seed should come to whom the promise hath been made'. On this Duncan writes: 'its reign, so far from being eternal, is a strictly limited one, ceasing when in the promised "Offspring", viz. Christ, the Promise began to receive its fulfilment', and 'the reign of the Law is essentially temporary'.[3] We may compare Gal 3.25: 'But now that faith is come, we are no longer under a tutor.'

(d) 'ordained through angels'. We may quote Duncan again: 'Paul's view is that they indicated that God was not present in person, and that a law which was merely transmitted by angels lacked the glory of the true life-giving Word. . . . even those [angels] who were not essentially evil might, as on this occasion, exercise an evil influence by intervening between the worshipper and God, and by having their activities erroneously accepted as the activities of God Himself.'[4]

(e) 'by the hand of a mediator. Now a mediator is not *a mediator* of one; but God is one.'

With regard to the details we have just listed the following points must be made:

(1) We must beware of the danger of exaggerating the depreciatory tendency of these verses. With regard to (a), Duncan reads more into 'was added' than there is any firm

---

[1] *The Epistle of Paul to the Galatians*, London, 1934, p. 115.
[2] op. cit., p. 111.
[3] op. cit., p. 112.
[4] op. cit., p. 114f.

warrant for doing: there is no need to see more in it than an indication that the law was, as a matter of fact, given after the promise (cf. v. 17). With regard to (b), Calvin's reminder is sufficient: 'The law has many uses, but Paul [here] confines himself to one which serves his present purpose . . . Therefore this definition of the use of the law is not complete . . .'.[1] With regard to (d), it is not absolutely certain that Paul's mention of the angels has a depreciatory intention at all (in Acts 7.53 Stephen's reference to the angels' part in the giving of the law is meant to emphasize the majesty of the law). The tradition of the presence of the angels at the giving of the law goes back to the LXX version of Deut 33.2. If, however, there is a depreciatory purpose here (and we are inclined to think that there is), it is probably simply to suggest a certain superiority of the promise, as given directly by God, over the law, as given by means of the angels. In detail (e) we probably should recognize a certain depreciatory flavour. The reference is of course to the part played by Moses. The point is probably that in the Sinai covenant two parties, Israel as well as God, were involved (hence the presence of a mediator), whereas the promise was simply God's and altogether independent of Abraham.

(2) In trying to evaluate the true significance of that element of depreciation which is present in these verses, it is of the first importance to bear in mind the polemical nature of Galatians. In this epistle Paul is seeking to undo the damage done by false teachers who have, in effect, exalted the law above the gospel. In arguing against their perverse, excessive exaltation of the law Paul naturally has to attempt to reduce the law's importance, in the eyes of those who have been led astray, to its true magnitude. It is not that Paul desires, absolutely, in any way to disparage the law, but that, in relation to this false exaltation of the law, he is forced in some measure to depreciate it. To fail to make full allowance for the special circumstances which called forth the letter would be to proceed in a quite uncritical and unscientific manner. In view of what has just been said, it should be clear that it would be extremely unwise to take what Paul says in Galatians as one's starting-point in trying to understand Paul's teaching on the law.[2]

---

[1] *The Epistles of Paul the Apostle to the Galatians, Ephesians, Philippians and Colossians*, tr. by T. H. L. Parker, Edinburgh, 1965, p. 61.

[2] We cannot admit the cogency of J. W. Drane's objection (in his *Paul Libertine or Legalist?*, London, 1975, p. 7) that the fact that Galatians was written before Romans invalidates this contention. Paul's more careful and balanced statement may still surely be the better starting-point *for us*, if we really want to be fair to him.

(3) We should recognize a tendency in this passage to regard the law somewhat narrowly. Indications of this can be seen in the fact that Paul here distinguishes the promise from the law (vv. 17 and 21), although the promise in question is contained in the Pentateuch, and in the concentration in v. 19 on just one purpose, 'because of transgressions'. In this connexion it is worth quoting an interesting passage in Calvin's *Institutes*, in which, having just referred to Gal 3.19, he goes on to say: Paul 'was disputing with perverse teachers who pretended that we merit righteousness by the works of the law. Consequently, to refute their error he was sometimes compelled to take the bare law in a narrow sense, even though it was otherwise graced with the covenant of free adoption'.[1] Perhaps we have here a clue to the right understanding of (c) above. This 'bare law' ('nuda lex') understood 'in a narrow sense' ('praecise') is not the law in the fullness and wholeness of its true character, but the law as seen apart from Christ. It is this law-apart-from-Christ, this law that is less than its true self, which is temporary. When once 'the seed' has come, 'to whom the promise hath been made', the One who is the goal, the meaning, the substance, of the law, it is no longer an open possibility for those who believe in Him to regard the law merely in this nakedness (though even in this forbidding nakedness it had served as a tutor to bring men to Christ). Henceforth it is to be recognized in its true character 'graced' or clothed 'with the covenant of free adoption' ('gratuitae adoptionis foedere . . . vestita').

It is sometimes argued, on the strength of the nowadays popular explanation of στοιχεῖα as denoting the spirits thought to rule the heavenly bodies, the 'elemental spirits',[2] that the στοιχεῖα in Gal 4.3 and 9 are to be identified with the angels referred to in Gal 3.19. If this identification were accepted, the implication would be that the giving of the law was the work of elemental spirits which can be described as 'of the world' (Gal 4.3) and 'weak and beggarly' (Gal 4.9), and this would seem to carry with it a disparagement not merely of legalism but of the law itself, and also, in view of Col 2.20, the implication that the law is done with as far as Christians are concerned. But it is to be noted that (a) this explanation of στοιχεῖα, though popular, is far from assured (it has been vigorously challenged

[1] 2.7.2 (quoted according to *Calvin: Institutes of the Christian Religion*, ed. by J. T. McNeill and tr. by F. L. Battles, London, 1961).

[2] See, for example, Duncan, op. cit., pp. 134–36; P. Bonnard, *L'Épître de Saint Paul aux Galates*, Neuchâtel, 1953, p. 84f; and, for a different view, C. F. D. Moule, *The Epistles of Paul the Apostle to the Colossians and to Philemon*, Cambridge, 1957, pp. 90–92.

by G. Delling);[1] (β) even if it is right, the identification of the angels of Gal 3.19 with these 'elemental spirits' is an unwarranted assumption; and (γ) if Paul really thought that the law had been given through the agency of 'weak and beggarly' elemental spirits 'of the world', it is strange that in 9.4f he sets ἡ νομοθεσία among the privileges of Israel in the company of the adoption, the glory, the covenants, the promises, and, finally, Christ Himself. We conclude that in Gal 4.3 and 9 Paul is referring not to the law itself, but to the legalistic misunderstanding and misuse of it.

Col 2.14 should perhaps be mentioned here, since it might possibly be thought that the law is meant by 'the bond written in ordinances', and that Paul is saying that Christ has 'blotted out' the law, and 'taken it out of the way, nailing it to the cross'. But this is not a likely interpretation. The word χειρόγραφον is a technical term for a signed 'IOU', and the explanation given by Moule may be on the right lines: 'The bond in question here is signed by men's consciences: for a Jew, it is his acceptance of the revealed Law of God as an obligation to abide by; for the Gentile, it is a corresponding recognition of obligation to what he knows of the will of God. In either case, it is an "autographed" undertaking: "I owe God obedience to his will. Signed, Mankind." This χειρόγραφον is "against us" because we have manifestly failed to discharge its obligations. . . . '.[2] But, as χειρόγραφον can also be used in a general sense to denote a manuscript note or document, it is perhaps possible that the reference is to the law's condemnation of us: 'that was against us, which was contrary to us' would fit this explanation equally well. Another explanation is that followed by C. Masson, which understands the reference to be to God's books in which men's deeds both good and bad were thought to be recorded (Masson explains the awkward 'written in ordinances' as an addition to what Paul had written by the author of Ephesians, which, according to Masson, is non-Pauline).[3] In any case, it seems altogether unlikely that 'the bond' is actually the law itself.

Eph 2.15, containing as it does the very words, 'having abolished . . . the law', looks at first sight like a clear statement that Christ has abolished the law. But, when one considers the way in which 'the law' is qualified and the context of the verse, this interpretation looks much less convincing. The qualification, 'of commandments *contained* in ordinances', is most probably to be explained as a rather clumsy way of limiting the

[1] *TWNT* 7, pp. 670–87.   [2] op. cit., p. 97.
[3] *L'Épître de Saint Paul aux Colossiens*, Neuchâtel, 1950, pp. 127–9.

meaning of 'the law', of indicating that what is meant is not
the law itself and as a whole; and the context suggests strongly
that the meaning of v. 15a is simply that Christ has by His
death abolished the ceremonial ordinances, in so far as they
have the effect of maintaining the separation of, 'the enmity'
between, Jews and Gentiles, by doing away with the obligation
to fulfil them literally. That the writer (whether Paul or
another) did not mean to assert that Christ had abolished the
law as such is clear enough from 6.2f.

We have now completed our survey of passages which have
been taken to support the view that, for Paul, the law is
abolished by Christ. We submit that our exegesis of 10.4 has
been confirmed, and that, when to our exegesis of these
passages the clear positive evidence of such verses as 3.31; 7.12,
14a; 8.4; 13.8–10,[1] is added, a strong case has been made for
our thesis that, for Paul, the law[2] is not abrogated by Christ.

(x) *For Paul, the giving of the Spirit is the establishment of
the law.* In 8.1–16 he shows that the life promised for the
righteous by faith is a life characterized by the indwelling of
the Holy Spirit and therefore also a life in which God's law is
being established and fulfilled (vv. 4, 12–16). God's law is
being established in the life of the believer, (a) in that the
Holy Spirit is freeing him more and more to give up tampering
with God's commandments in the hope of exploiting them for
his self-justification, to give up his 'glorying' (3.27) and humbly
and frankly to allow the law to discover him to himself as the
sinner that he is; (b) in that the Holy Spirit is setting him free
to allow the law to point him again and again to Christ, its
goal, and to help to keep him in the way of faith in Him (this
the law does no longer as a strict 'tutor' (Gal 3.25), giving
commands which may seem harsh and arbitrary because their
purpose is not understood; for now that Christ Himself has
come the gracious purpose of the law is clearly seen); and (c)
in that the Holy Spirit is setting him free for obedience,
enabling him to begin to call God 'Father' sincerely, soberly,
intelligently, and to go on doing so more and more consistently.

(xi) If the foregoing exposition of Paul's teaching on the law

---

[1] To these we may add 9.30–33, on which see the commentary.

[2] In this we include the ceremonial part. It is not, for Paul (as we
understand him), abrogated by Christ; but, while it has no longer to be
observed in a literal way (cf. p. 713), it remains valid as witness to
Christ, and we ought to honour and observe it by striving to believe in
Him according to the fullness of the Scriptures' attestation of Him. So,
e.g., we honour the rules about sacrifices, not by offering lambs in church,
but by believing ever more and more fully in that 'Lamb of God, which
taketh away the sin of the world'.

is substantially correct, it is clear that his authority cannot justly be claimed for that modern version of Marcionism which regards the law as a disastrous misconception on the part of religious men from which Jesus desired to set us free; nor for the view that the law was an unsuccessful first attempt on God's part at dealing with man's unhappy state, which had to be followed later by a second (more successful) attempt (a view which is theologically grotesque, for the God of the unsuccessful first attempt is hardly a God to be taken seriously); nor yet the view that in law and gospel two different modes of God's action are manifested, the ultimate unity of which, while it may indeed be supposed to exist in God, has not yet been revealed to us men. On the contrary, it is clear that we are true to Paul's teaching, when we say that *God's word in Scripture is one*; that there is but one way of God with men, and that an altogether gracious way; that gospel and law are essentially one, and their unity, so far from being a mystery still hidden from us, has been once and for all revealed to us in that one gracious Word of God, whose name is Jesus Christ, in whom at the same time God gives Himself wholly to man, and claims man wholly for Himself.[1]

9. USE OF THE OT

While there is, of course, a very considerable overlap between this subject and that of the preceding section, it is quite apparent that the discussion contained in the preceding section could not by any stretch of the imagination be said to have covered the ground indicated by the heading of the present section. So at least something must be said here under this head. But, since, on the one hand, a certain amount has already been said in the commentary in connexion with the various quotations which occur, and, on the other hand, a reasonably

---

[1] In this connexion it is most instructive to note that all the initial statements of sections (ii), (iii), (iv), and (vi) with reference to the law can also be made with reference to the gospel. The gospel reveals sin—the Cross shows us our sin; the gospel enhances sin, giving to our continuing sin the character of wilful rejection of God's love; the gospel increases sin—for when God's claim on man is most clear and pressing, it enrages our sinfulness most, our self-centredness recognizing the seriousness with which it is threatened; the gospel declares God's condemnation—it is declared in the Cross even as it is being borne for us. (Incidentally, it would hardly be unfair to say that the arguments advanced by G. B. Caird, *Principalities and Powers: A Study in Pauline Theology*, Oxford 1956, pp. 41–43, to prove that Paul regarded the law as a 'demonic agency' could, for the most part at any rate, equally well be used to prove the demonic character of the gospel!)

full treatment (for which it would anyway be unsatisfactory to confine our attention to Romans) would require an altogether disproportionate amount of space, we shall limit ourselves to making just a few observations.[1]

Explicit OT quotations, that is, quotations which are clearly identified as such by the presence of one or another formula of quotation, occur in 1.17 (καθὼς γέγραπται); 2.24 (καθὼς γέγραπται following); 3.4b (καθάπερ γέγραπται), 10–18 (καθὼς γέγραπται ὅτι); 4.3 (τί γὰρ ἡ γραφὴ λέγει;), 7–8 (καθάπερ καὶ Δαυὶδ λέγει),

[1] There is a considerable body of relevant literature from among which we may refer to the following: A. F. Kautzsch, *De Veteris Testamenti locis a Paulo allegatis*, Leipzig, 1869; H. Monnet, *Les citations de l'Ancien Testament dans les épîtres de St Paul*, Lausanne, 1874; H. Vollmer, *Die alttestamentlichen Zitate bei Paulus*, Freiburg, 1896; O. Michel, *Paulus und seine Bibel*, Gütersloh, 1929 (new imp. with 9 pp. supplement, Darmstadt, 1972); J. Bonsirven, *Exégèse rabbinique et exégèse paulinienne*, Paris, 1939; L. Goppelt, *Typos: die typologische Deutung des Alten Testaments im Neuen*, Gütersloh, 1939 (reprinted Darmstadt, 1966); R. Bultmann, 'Ursprung und Sinn der Typologie als hermeneutische Methode', in *TLZ* 75 (1950), cols. 205–12; B. M. Metzger, 'The formulas introducing quotations of Scripture in the New Testament and the Mishna', in *JBL* 70 (1951), pp. 297–307; C. H. Dodd, *According to the Scriptures: the sub-structure of New Testament Theology*, London, 1952; P. Bläser, 'Schriftverwertung und Schrifterklärung in Rabbinentum und bei Paulus', in *Theologische Quartalschrift* 132 (Tübingen, 1952), pp. 152–69; F. Baumgärtel, *Verheissung: zur Frage des evangelischen Verständnisses des Alten Testaments*, Gütersloh, 1952; E. E. Ellis, *Paul's Use of the Old Testament*, Edinburgh, 1957; J. Schmid, 'Die alttestamentlichen Zitate bei Paulus und die Theorie vom sensus plenior', in *BZ* 3 (1959), pp. 161–73; S. Amsler, L'Ancien Testament dans l'Église, Neuchâtel, 1960; J. A. Fitzmyer, 'The use of explicit Old Testament quotations in Qumran literature and in the New Testament', in *NTS* 7 (1960–61), pp. 297–333; B. Lindars, *New Testament Apologetic*, London, 1961; R. Le Déaut, 'Traditions targumiques dans le corpus paulinien', in *Biblica* 42 (1961), pp. 28–48; C. Dietzfelbinger, *Paulus und das Alte Testament*, Munich, 1961; J. Coppens, 'Les arguments scriptuaires et leur portée dans les lettres pauliniennes', in *Analecta Biblica* 18 (Rome, 1963); H. Ulonska, *Paulus und das Alte Testament*, Münster, 1964; L. Goppelt, 'Apokalyptik und Typologie bei Paulus', in *TLZ* 89 (1964), cols. 322–43; U. Luz, *Das Geschichtsverständnis des Paulus*, Munich, 1968; S. Jellicoe, *The Septuagint and Modern Study*, Oxford, 1968; E. E. Ellis, 'Midrash, Targum and New Testament quotations', in *Neotestamentica et Patristica*, pp. 61–69; P. Vielhauer, 'Paulus und das Alte Testament', in L. Abramowski and J. F. G. Goeters (ed.), *Studien zur Geschichte und Theologie der Reformation: Festschrift für Ernst Bizer*, Neukirchen-Vluyn, 1969, pp. 33–62; C. K. Barrett, 'The interpretation of the Old Testament in the New', in P. R. Ackroyd and C. F. Evans (ed.), *The Cambridge History of the Bible* 1, Cambridge, 1970, pp. 377–411; M. Black, 'The Christological use of the Old Testament in the New Testament', in *NTS* 18 (1971–72), pp. 1–14; A. T. Hanson, *Studies in Paul's Technique and Theology*, London, 1974; J. Blank, 'Erwägungen zum Schriftverständnis des Paulus', in J. Friedrich, W. Pöhlmann, P. Stuhlmacher (ed.), op. cit., pp. 37–56.

17 (καθὼς γέγραπται ὅτι), 18 (κατὰ τὸ εἰρημένον); 7.7 (ὁ νόμος ἔλεγεν); 8.36 (καθὼς γέγραπται ὅτι); 9.9 (ὁ λόγος οὗτος), 12 (ἐρρέθη αὐτῇ ὅτι), 13 (καθάπερ γέγραπται), 15 (τῷ Μωϋσεῖ γὰρ λέγει), 17 (λέγει γὰρ ἡ γραφὴ τῷ Φαραώ), 25f (ὡς καὶ ἐν τῷ Ὡσηὲ λέγει), 27f ('Ησαΐας δὲ κράζει ὑπὲρ τοῦ 'Ισραήλ), 29 (καθὼς προείρηκεν 'Ησαΐας), 33 (καθὼς γέγραπται); 10.5 (Μωϋσῆς γὰρ γράφει ὅτι), 6–8 (ἡ δὲ ἐκ πίστεως δικαιοσύνη οὕτως λέγει and ἀλλὰ τί λέγει;), 11 (λέγει γὰρ ἡ γραφή), 15 (καθάπερ γέγραπται), 16 ('Ησαΐας γὰρ λέγει), 19 (πρῶτος Μωϋσῆς λέγει), 20 ('Ησαΐας δὲ ἀποτολμᾷ καὶ λέγει), 21 (πρὸς δὲ τὸν 'Ισραὴλ λέγει); 11.3 (in v. 2 ἢ οὐκ οἴδατε ἐν 'Ηλίᾳ τί λέγει ἡ γραφή;), 4 (ἀλλὰ τί λέγει αὐτῷ ὁ χρηματισμός;), 8 (καθάπερ γέγραπται), 9f (καὶ Δαυὶδ λέγει), 26f (καθὼς γέγραπται); 12.19 (γέγραπται γάρ); 13.9 (τὸ γάρ and καὶ εἴ τις ἑτέρα ἐντολή, ἐν τῷ λόγῳ τούτῳ ἀνακεφαλαιοῦται, [ἐν τῷ]); 14.11 (γέγραπται γάρ); 15.3 (ἀλλὰ καθὼς γέγραπται), 9–12 (καθὼς γέγραπται and καὶ πάλιν λέγει and καὶ πάλιν and καὶ πάλιν 'Ησαΐας λέγει), 21 (ἀλλὰ καθὼς γέγραπται). We might perhaps also count among the explicit quotations those in 9.7 (introduced by ἀλλ'); 10.13 (introduced by γάρ), 18 (introduced by μενοῦν γε), and 12.20 (introduced by ἀλλά after the explicit quotation of the preceding verse); but these are not so clear.

Further, there are quotations, which are not identified as such by any formula but may be assumed to be (at any rate in most cases) conscious quotations, to be seen in 2.6; 3.4a, 20; 8.33f; 11.1f, 34f; 12.16f; and echoes or allusions, some of which are almost certainly, others probably, intentional, while others may perhaps be quite unconscious, in 1.23; 2.9, 11, 15; 4.11, 25; 5.5, 12; 7.8–11; 8.32; 9.18, 20–22; 11.11; and 14.13.

As a number of the quotations in Romans are composite (that in 3.10–18 is actually a catena constructed out of at least half a dozen passages), the total of OT passages quoted, alluded to, or echoed, is considerably larger than the total of Romans passages listed in the preceding two paragraphs. The great importance of the OT in the making of the letter is evident. OT books from which there are explicit quotations in Romans are Genesis, Exodus, Leviticus, Deuteronomy, 1 Kings, Job, Psalms, Isaiah, Hosea, Habakkuk and Malachi, to which, if we include the quotations listed in the last sentence of the last paragraph but one, we must add Proverbs and Joel. When we take into account quotations not identified as such and also allusions and echoes, we have to add at any rate 1 Samuel, 2 Chronicles and Jeremiah. (If the other Pauline epistles were included in our inquiry, the list would be still further enlarged.) There would seem to be no good reason for doubting that Paul recognized as authoritative scripture either all, or almost all, the books which are contained in the Hebrew canon as we know it.[1]

That Paul knew other Jewish writings which were current in his time may be taken as certain; but Romans affords no evidence at all that he regarded any of them as authoritative scripture.[2] With respect to Wisdom, the book of the OT Apocrypha which is probably most frequently in the thoughts of the student of the epistle (see, especially, on Rom 1.20ff; 2.1–3.20; 9.20–22), it seems clear that Paul, while quite often expressing thoughts which are reminiscent of it, felt no inhibition at all about flatly contradicting some of its assumptions.[3]

In the Romans passages listed in the second paragraph of the present section there are (according to our reckoning)[4] fifty-eight OT passages quoted. These may be divided into two groups: (a) passages where the LXX and MT agree, and (b) passages where the LXX and MT differ. Under (a) we reckon twenty-five OT passages. In thirteen of these Paul agrees with the LXX exactly and in seven he only slightly differs from it, while in the case of the remaining five (Ps 14[LXX: 13].1c–3 (in 3.10–12); Hos 2.23 [MT and LXX: 25] (in 9.25); 1 Kgs 19.14 (in 11.3); Isa 29.10 and Deut 29.4[MT and LXX: 3] (in 11.8)) it would seem that the LXX was probably the basis upon which he was working. Under (b) we reckon thirty-three OT passages. In nine of these Paul agrees with the LXX against the MT, and in a further eighteen he either only differs slightly from the LXX or else at least seems nearer to it than to the MT. But in 11.35 we have a quotation which agrees with the MT against the LXX (MT Job 41.3: the LXX is here quite different); in 9.33 the words introduced from Isa 8.14 are closer to the MT and to Aquila and Theodotion than to the LXX; in 10.15 the quotation from Isa 52.7 is nearer to the MT than to the LXX; in 9.17 Paul's knowledge of the MT may well have played some part in his quotation of Exod 9.16, which differs considerably

[1] Cf. Ellis, *Paul's Use of the Old Testament*, p. 33f. See further G. W. Anderson, 'Canonical and non-canonical', in Ackroyd and Evans, op. cit., pp. 113–59.

[2] Elsewhere in the Pauline corpus there are a few seeming quotations introduced in ways normally used in quoting Scripture which do not seem to have come from the OT—at any rate, directly. But they afford no evidence of Paul's having regarded any book of the Apocrypha or the pseudepigrapha as possessing canonical status. (See further Ellis, op. cit., pp. 34–37.)

[3] See on 2.1ff.

[4] A variety of totals is possible according to the decisions one takes on such questions as whether to count the words in 9.9 taken from Gen 18.10 and 14 as two quotations (as we have done) or as one.

from the LXX; in 11.4 the quotation of 1 Kgs 19.18 is closer
to the MT and the Targum and the Lucianic text of the LXX
than to the A or B text of the LXX; and in 12.19 Deut 32.35 is
quoted in a form nearer to the Targum than to either the LXX
or the MT.

The brief survey given in the preceding paragraph, rough
and seriously over-simplified though it is, will at least have
served to show that in his use of the OT in the composition of
Romans it was on the LXX that Paul mainly relied. It was
with it that he lived. But a good knowledge of the Hebrew text
will have been stored in his memory from close study of it in
his youth and early manhood, and he must have listened quite
often to Hebrew lections in later life. And possible traces of his
knowledge of the Hebrew may be recognized in the epistle.
But there are many complicating factors which need to be
borne in mind in considering Paul's OT quotations, such as the
existence of targums and the possibility that Paul sometimes
made use of them, uncertainties with regard to the history of
the LXX to which recent study has directed attention,[1] and
the possibility that variations of the LXX from the MT may
quite often represent variants of the Hebrew text—to mention
only some of them.

That throughout the Epistle to the Romans the divine
authority of the OT is assumed does not need to be proved
here. Already in 1.2 it is referred to as 'the holy scriptures', and
again and again it is appealed to as the altogether trustworthy
source of information about God, His character, His purposes,
His works and ways in the past, in the present and in the
future. There is no doubt that it was as authoritative for the
author of Romans as it was for the Rabbis—and for Jesus. It
was because he recognized so wholeheartedly its divine
authority that, in what is clearly the most comprehensive and
systematic writing which we have from him, he was so largely
concerned with its interpretation, setting forth the gospel as he
understood it in a framework of OT exegesis.

The most important thing to be said about the author's
engagement with the OT scriptures is, of course, that, while
from his early youth he had lived with them and accepted their
authority, he had, since he had been convinced that Jesus of
Nazareth was God's Messiah, become possessed of what he saw
to be the key to their interpretation. The one and only key to
their proper interpretation was the recognition that Jesus, who
had been rejected by the leaders of Israel, who had died a

[1] Reference may be made to the useful supplement in the 1972 reprint
of Michel's *Paulus und seine Bibel*, pp. 213–23.

˛felon's death at the hands of the Gentiles, who had been raised
from the dead by the power of God, who was now exalted as
the living and reigning Lord, and who was yet to come again
in glory, was the One to whom they bore witness, the One in
whom the hopes of Israel and of all men were destined to find
their true fulfilment. Jesus the Messiah made sense of the OT.
He unlocked its meaning. Understood as pointing to Him, the
whole OT came to life and was seen in its true unity. We may
refer, by way of examples, to 1.2; 3.21; 9.30–10.13. But this
worked in both directions. It was a two-way clarification. Belief
in Jesus as the Messiah opened the way to the understanding of
the OT, and at the same time the OT interpreted Jesus. Once
He was recognized as being the substance of the scriptures, the
One to whom they were pointing, the significance of those
scriptures as a whole and of very many particular passages
began to stand out clearly; and at the same time the scriptures
clarified Jesus, attesting Him as the One whom they had in
manifold ways foreshadowed, attesting Him as the One whom
God had long ago promised, attesting Him as the Servant of
God delivered up for men's transgressions and raised up for
their justification, the exalted Lord sitting at the right hand of
God, the High Priest interceding for His brethren, the true
King of Israel who would be a stone of stumbling and a rock of
offence for many of His own people and yet also the source of
salvation for all who should believe on Him, the scion of Jesse
in whom Gentiles would come to put their hope. Because he
kept his eyes so steadily fixed on Jesus, the author of Romans
was able to hear and to comprehend the message proclaimed
by the OT; and, because in his total commitment to Jesus as
Saviour and Lord he never ceased to be seriously engaged with
the OT scriptures, he perceived with amazing clarity of vision
vast and splendid reaches of the truth of Christ which lie
beyond the ken of all Marcionites and semi-, crypto-, and
unwitting, Marcionites. Because he saw Christ steadily in the
light of the OT—not abandoning the real Christ, who is the
Christ of Israel, for any imaginary Christ more flattering to
human self-importance—he did not refuse to grapple with the
mystery of God's gracious election or fail to hold firmly to the
truth of God's faithfulness—His faithfulness (which does not
exclude, but includes, severity) to the Jewish people, all human
unbelief and disobedience notwithstanding, His faithfulness to
all mankind (Paul saw the Gentile mission foretold in the OT)
and His faithfulness as the Creator of heaven and earth to His
whole creation.

Something must now be said very briefly about the exegetical methods used by Paul. In Romans, at any rate,[1] there is no example of the sort of Hellenistic allegorical interpretation which one finds in Philo, the origins of which may be traced back by way of the Stoics to the allegorizing of Homer by earlier philosophers. In fact, Paul's interest in the historical reality of the OT figures to whom he refers stands out in strong contrast to Philo's treatment of OT personages as embodiments of the philosophical concepts and ideals which tend to be his real concern. For Paul the movement of history is important, and Abraham, Sarah, Isaac, Ishmael, Rebecca, Jacob, Esau, Moses, Pharaoh, all belong to an on-going history—even though he sometimes in using a personal name may actually have in mind the nation descended from the person and that nation's historical role more than the individual person himself. Typology is a different matter, and does occur in the epistle, an obvious reference being 5.14, where Adam is described as 'the type ($\tau \acute{u} \pi o s$) of him who was to come'. Typological interpretation differs from allegorical, in that, while the latter is destructive of real interest in what is being interpreted, in and for itself, and rests on imagination, the former, presupposing as it does a purpose which is being worked out in the course of history, takes the reality of the type seriously as well as that of the antitype. Some similarities to Qumràn exegesis are to be seen in Romans. We may refer in particular, in this connexion, to the notes on 10.6–10, though there are quite a number of places in the epistle where one may sense an element of similarity to the OT exegesis of the Qumran texts. That Rabbinic methods should be in evidence in the epistle is, of course, only to be expected. Paul certainly did not unlearn, when he became a Christian, everything which he had learned from his Rabbinic teachers—nor was there any good reason why he should have tried to do so. The use of the verb 'to be' in the present indicative in Acts 23.6 should not be seized on as a proof that Acts could not have been written by a companion and friend of Paul; for the Epistle to the Romans is powerful evidence that the Christian Paul—and, indeed, the mature Christian Paul—had by no means rejected root and branch everything of his Pharisaic upbringing and his Rabbinic training.[2] Suffice it here just to mention the presence in Romans of instances of *ḳal wāḥômer*, of *gᵉzērāh šāwāh*, of the combination of texts taken from the Law, Prophets and

---

[1] With regard to the other Pauline epistles reference should be made to Ellis, op. cit., pp. 51–54; Hanson, op. cit., pp. 159–66.

[2] We surely ought to resist the temptation to understand Phil 3.7f in such a sense.

Writings, and the evidences of knowledge of midrash and targum.

It is more difficult to draw out correctly, and to do justice to, what is distinctive about Paul's OT exegesis in Romans. But we hope that at least something of its special character may already have become clear in the course of the commentary, and that it may suffice now to add just a very few sentences.

What we have described above as the most important thing about Paul's engagement with the OT, namely, his recognition, on the one hand, that Jesus is the key to its proper understanding and, on the other hand, that it is only in its light that He can be properly understood, is, of course, something which Paul had in common with others; but it is, we submit, the steadiness and consistency and the sheer intellectual power with which this twofold primitive Christian insight has been followed through in Romans which give the epistle's OT exegesis its distinctiveness.

That this OT exegesis is sometimes characterized by considerable freedom is apparent. In this connexion the question must be raised whether the freedom with which Paul has treated the OT text in a number of passages (reference may be made, for example, to 2.24; 9.25f; 10.18, and indeed also to 1.17) should be recognized as a masterful use of the text, a readiness to force it to render service to the interpreter's own purposes, in other words, a freedom of arbitrariness, more or less, or as—something altogether different—a freedom which has not been arrogated to himself by Paul but has been given to him, a legitimate freedom of the δοῦλος and κλητὸς ἀπόστολος of Jesus Christ, the σκοπός of the OT, from time to time to take a certain liberty with a particular passage, in order thereby to bring out the more faithfully and clearly the overall sense of the OT's witness. In indicating our personal conviction that an answer should be given along the lines of the latter alternative, we draw attention at the same time to the need to reckon with (i) the possibility that some of the passages where Paul seems to have taken a liberty are not instances of deliberate liberty-taking but the result of quotation from memory (Paul will scarcely have been in a position to check every quotation and reminiscence even in Gaius's hospitable home); (ii) the possibility that in some cases we may have to do with a purely literary use of OT language (without any intention of appealing to the passage in question as an authority) simply as a convenient medium for the expression of his own thought—something which would be readily understandable in someone who lived constantly with the OT; and (iii) the probability that in several of the cases which have to be considered the liberty taken may be defended as substantially justifiable and therefore in fact not really an instance of liberty-taking at all.

It is noteworthy that Paul, while he does on occasion appeal to grammatical points, is generally much less concerned than the Rabbis with the minutiae of the text, and also much more concerned than they with contexts, and is indeed concerned to interpret particular passages in relation to what he sees as the significance of the scriptures as a whole. But this must not be taken to mean that he in any way disparages the written words as such. Paul's use of the word γράμμα in a way which sets it in contrast to πνεῦμα is wrongly understood, when he is taken to be referring to the OT in its character of writtenness (as though he wished to suggest that the significance of Scripture can somehow be separated from the text which expresses it and valued and retained in isolation from the text, while the text is simply discarded) or, as is quite often assumed to be the case, to one element of the OT, particularly the legal element, as opposed to some other element, particularly the grace or promise element, or maybe the prophetic. What Paul denotes by γράμμα (when contrasted with πνεῦμα) is rather that mere letter, which is what one is left with in the OT as a whole or in any part of it, when one insists on interpreting it independently of the illumination of the Holy Spirit and so without reference to Him to whom the OT bears witness, Jesus Christ.

INDEX I

PASSAGES CITED

A. OLD TESTAMENT

B. NEW TESTAMENT

19.5	672	20.12f	146	21.6	206
19.7	249	20.12	733	21.15	615
19.8	289	20.15	733	21.27	733
19.16	654	21	578	22.12	146
20.1	525	21.1	305	22.16	58
20.3	525	21.2	497	22.17	206
20.4	288	21.5	305	22.20	528, 683

C. APOCRYPHA AND PSEUDEPIGRAPHA OF THE OLD TESTAMENT

2 ESDRAS		6.5	570	1.10	424
3.7	280	7.26	115	2.15f	424
3.8	280	11–15	138, 141, 144	4.5	646
3.21	280	11.6f	106	5.2	122
4.30	280	11.9f	141	5.4	144
6.38f	810	11.10	570	7.30	424
7.30	810	11.15f	106	7.34	642
7.[72]	280	11.15	120, 132	9.9	333
7.[75]	415	11.23	145	10.21	562
7.[92]	280	12.9	570	13.22	646
7.48	280	12.10	145	15.7	132
7.49	280	12.12	490, 491	18.11	144, 263
16.53	650	12.19	145	19.17	646
		12.22	141	21.18	132
TOBIT		12.23	106	22.13	132
4.11	603	12.24	120	22.15	132
13.2	244	13.1–9	124	23.2	211
		13.8	116	23.14	119
JUDITH		13.10	120	24.9	418
8.18	169	13.14	120	25.24	280
9.4	514	14.12	122	26.8	126
16.19(A)	457	14.25f	129	27.5	491
		14.26	127	28.1–7	647
THE REST OF ESTHER		15.1	144	30.13	126
16.1	386	15.2	141, 144	33.13	491
16.6	130	15.7–17	491	34.7	472
		15.7	491f	34.16	424
THE WISDOM OF SOLOMON		16.13	244	35.1f	603
		17.11	700	35.9	627
1.5	132	18.4f	106	37.11	633
2.23	115, 275	18.4	166	38.12	646
2.24	274	18.9	115	38.29–30	491
3.13	477	18.14–16	88	39.24–27	429
3.16	477	18.15	570	43.27	591
5.8	131	18.16	630	44.8	250
5.18	630	18.22	462	44.10	250
5.20	570			44.11	462
6.3	663	**ECCLESIASTICUS**		44.14f	250
6.4	665	1.8	814	44.18	462

D. QUMRAN TEXTS

E. RABBINIC LITERATURE

INDEX II

GREEK WORDS AND PHRASES

INDEX III

SUBJECTS

INDEX IV

AUTHORS AND WORKS